THE PAPERS OF ALEXANDER HAMILTON

Alexander Hamilton, 1792. Oil portrait by John Trumbull

National Gallery of Art, Washington

THE PAPERS OF

Alexander Hamilton

VOLUME XII

JULY 1792–OCTOBER 1792

HAROLD C. SYRETT, EDITOR

JACOB E. COOKE, ASSOCIATE EDITOR

Assistant Editors

JEAN G. COOKE   CARA-LOUISE MILLER

DOROTHY TWOHIG   PATRICIA SYRETT

 COLUMBIA UNIVERSITY PRESS

NEW YORK AND LONDON, 1967

FROM THE PUBLISHER

The preparation of this edition of the papers of
Alexander Hamilton has been made possible by the
support received for the work of the editorial and
research staff from the generous grants of the
Rockefeller Foundation, Time Inc., and the Ford
Foundation, and by the far-sighted cooperation of
the National Historical Publications Commission. To
these organizations, the publisher expresses gratitude
on behalf of all who are concerned about making
available the record of the founding of the United
States.

The Bank of New York, through a special gift,
has enabled the Press to publish this volume.

ACKNOWLEDGMENTS

Since the publication in 1966 of Volumes X and XI of *The Papers of Alexander Hamilton*, the editors have incurred new obligations which they wish to take this opportunity to acknowledge. Of the many individuals who generously shared their specialized information or provided assistance, the editors are especially indebted to

Dr. Evan R. Collins, President, State University of New York at Albany

Mrs. Matthew Cullen, Plainfield, Massachusetts

Dr. Webb S. Fiser, Vice President for Academic Affairs, State University of New York at Albany

Miss Alice T. Hastings, Director of Libraries, State University of New York at Albany

Mrs. Mildred Ledden, Senior Librarian, Rare Books, New York State Library, Albany

Mr. Warren B. Scott, Assistant to the Vice President for Academic Affairs, State University of New York at Albany

Miss Eleanor Streun, Head Reference Librarian, State University of New York at Albany

Mr. Mason Tolman, Acting Director, New York State Library, Albany

Miss Juliet Wolohan, Head, Manuscripts and History Section, New York State Library, Albany

PREFACE

THIS EDITION of Alexander Hamilton's papers contains letters and other documents written by Hamilton, letters to Hamilton, and some documents (commissions, certificates, etc.) that directly concern Hamilton but were written neither by him nor to him. All letters and other documents have been printed in chronological order. Hamilton's legal papers are being published under the editorial direction of Julius Goebel, Jr., George Welwood Murray Professor Emeritus of Legal History of the School of Law, Columbia University. The first volume of this distinguished work, which is entitled *The Law Practice of Alexander Hamilton*, was published by the Columbia University Press in 1964.

Many letters and documents have been calendared. Such calendared items include routine letters and documents by Hamilton, routine letters to Hamilton, some of the letters or documents written by Hamilton for someone else, letters or documents which have not been found but which are known to have existed, letters or documents which have been erroneously attributed to Hamilton, and letters to or by Hamilton that deal exclusively with his legal practice.

Certain routine documents which Hamilton wrote and received as Secretary of the Treasury have not been printed. The documents that fall within this category are warrants or interest certificates; letters written by Hamilton acknowledging receipts from banks, endorsing margins of certificate of registry, and enclosing sea letters; letters to Hamilton transmitting weekly, monthly, and quarterly accounts, or enclosing certificates of registry and other routine Treasury forms; and drafts by Hamilton on the treasurer. Statements of facts from the judges of the District Courts on cases concerning violations of the customs laws and warrants of remission of forfeiture issued by Hamilton have generally been omitted unless they pertain to cases discussed in Hamilton's correspondence.

The notes in these volumes are designed to provide information concerning the nature and location of each document, to identify Hamilton's correspondents and the individuals mentioned in the text, to explain events or ideas referred to in the text, and to point out textual variations or mistakes. Occasional departures from these standards can be attributed to a variety of reasons. In many cases the desired information has been supplied in an earlier note and can be found through the use of the index. Notes have not been added when in the opinion of the editors the material in the text was either self-explanatory or common knowledge. The editors, moreover, have not thought it desirable or necessary to provide full annotation for Hamilton's legal correspondence. Perhaps at this point it should also be stated that arithmetical errors in Hamilton's reports to Congress have not been corrected or noted. Finally, the editors on some occasions have been unable to find the desired information, and on other occasions the editors have been remiss.

GUIDE TO EDITORIAL APPARATUS

I. SYMBOLS USED TO DESCRIBE MANUSCRIPTS

AD	Autograph Document
ADS	Autograph Document Signed
ADf	Autograph Draft
ADfS	Autograph Draft Signed
AL	Autograph Letter
ALS	Autograph Letter Signed
D	Document
DS	Document Signed
Df	Draft
DfS	Draft Signed
LS	Letter Signed
LC	Letter Book Copy
[S]	[S] is used with other symbols (AD[S], ADf[S], AL[S], D[S], Df[S], L[S]) to indicate that the signature on the document has been cropped or clipped.

II. MONETARY SYMBOLS AND ABBREVIATIONS

bf	Banco florin
V	Ecu
f	Florin
₶	Livre Tournois
medes	Maravedis (also md and mde)
d.	Penny or denier
ps	Piece of eight

£	Pound sterling or livre
Ry	Real
rs vn	Reals de vellon
rdr	Rix daller
s	Shilling, sou or sol (also expressed as /)
sti	Stiver

III. SHORT TITLES AND ABBREVIATIONS

Annals of Congress, I, II, III — *The Debates and Proceedings in the Congress of the United States; with an Appendix, Containing Important State Papers and Public Documents, and All the Laws of a Public Nature* (Washington, 1834–1849).

Arch. des Aff. Etr., Corr. Pol., Etats-Unis — Transcripts or photostats from the French Foreign Office deposited in the Library of Congress.

Archives Parlementaires — *Archives Parlementaires de 1787 à 1860* (Paris, 1868–).

ASP — *American State Papers, Documents, Legislative and Executive, of the Congress of the United States* (Washington, 1832–1861).

Bayley, *National Loans* — Rafael A. Bayley, *The National Loans of the United States from July 4, 1776, to June 30, 1880* (Washington, 1882).

Boyd, *Papers of Thomas Jefferson* — Julian P. Boyd, ed., *The Papers of Thomas Jefferson* (Princeton, 1950–).

Davis, *Essays* — Joseph Stancliffe Davis, *Essays in the Earlier History of American Corporations* ("Harvard Economic Studies," XVI [Cambridge, 1917]).

Executive Journal, I — *Journal of the Executive Proceedings of the Senate* (Washington, 1828), I.

Ford, *Writings of Jefferson*
Paul Leicester Ford, *The Writings of Thomas Jefferson* (New York, 1892–1899).

Freeman, *Washington*
Douglas Southall Freeman, *George Washington* (New York, 1948–1957). Volume VII of this series was written by John Alexander Carroll and Mary Wells Ashworth.

GW
John C. Fitzpatrick, ed., *The Writings of George Washington* (Washington, 1931–1944).

Hamilton, *History*
John C. Hamilton, *Life of Alexander Hamilton, a History of the Republic of the United States of America* (Boston, 1879).

Hamilton, *Intimate Life*
Allan McLane Hamilton, *The Intimate Life of Alexander Hamilton* (New York, 1910).

Hamilton, *Life*
John C. Hamilton, *The Life of Alexander Hamilton* (New York, 1840).

HCLW
Henry Cabot Lodge, ed., *The Works of Alexander Hamilton* (New York, 1904).

Hogan, *Pennsylvania State Trials*
[Edmund Hogan], *The Pennsylvania State Trials: Containing the Impeachment, Trial, and Acquittal of Francis Hopkinson, and John Nicholson, Esquires* . . . (Philadelphia, 1794).

Hunt and Scott, *Debates*
Gaillard Hunt and James Brown Scott, eds., *The Debates in the Federal Convention of 1787 Which Framed the Constitution of the United States of America. Reported by James Madison* (New York, 1920).

JCC
Journals of the Continental Congress, 1774–1789 (Washington, 1904–1937).

JCH Transcripts
John C. Hamilton Transcripts. These transcripts are owned by Mr. William H. Swan, Hampton

Bays, New York, and have been placed on loan in the Columbia University Libraries.

JCHW
John C. Hamilton, ed., *The Works of Alexander Hamilton* (New York, 1851–1856).

Journal of the House, I
Journal of the House of Representatives of the United States (Washington, 1826), I.

Knopf, *Wayne*
Richard C. Knopf, ed., *Anthony Wayne: A Name in Arms; Soldier, Diplomat, Defender of Expansion Westward of a Nation; the Wayne-Knox-Pickering-McHenry Correspondence* (Pittsburgh, 1960).

Laws of the State of New York, III
Laws on the State of New York Passed at the Sessions of the Legislature Held in the Years 1789, 1790, 1791, 1792, 1793, 1794, 1795 and 1796, inclusive, Being the Twelfth, Thirteenth, Fourteenth, Fifteenth, Sixteenth, Seventeenth, Eighteenth and Nineteenth Sessions (Albany, 1887), III.

Miller, *Treaties*, II
Hunter Miller, ed., *Treaties and Other International Acts of the United States of America* (Washington, 1931), II.

"Minutes of the S.U.M."
MS minutes of the Society for Establishing Useful Manufactures, City of Paterson, New Jersey, Plant Management Commission, Successors to the Society for Establishing Useful Manufactures.

Mitchell, *Hamilton*
Broadus Mitchell, *Alexander Hamilton* (New York, 1957–1962).

Morris, *Diary of the French Revolution*
Gouverneur Morris, *A Diary of the French Revolution,* ed. by Beatrix Cary Davenport (Boston, 1939).

Nussbaum, *Commercial Policy in the French Revolution* — Frederick L. Nussbaum, *Commercial Policy in the French Revolution* (Washington, 1923).

Pennsylvania Archives, 2nd ser., IV — *Pennsylvania Archives*, 2nd ser., IV (n.p., 1876).

Pennsylvania Archives, 9th ser., I — *Pennsylvania Archives*, 9th ser., I (n.p., 1931).

Pennsylvania Statutes — James T. Mitchell and Henry Flanders, eds., *The Statutes at Large of Pennsylvania from 1682 to 1801* (Harrisburg, 1896–1908).

PRO: F.O., or PRO: C.O. — Transcripts or photostats from the Public Record Office of Great Britain deposited in the Library of Congress.

PRO: F.O., or PRO: C.O. (Great Britain) — Public Record Office of Great Britain.

Records of Rhode Island — John Russell Bartlett, ed., *Records of the State of Rhode Island and Providence Plantations in New England* (Providence, 1856–1865).

"Reynolds Pamphlet" — Alexander Hamilton, *Observations on Certain Documents Contained in No. V and VI of "The History of the United States for the Year 1796," in which the Charge of Speculation against Alexander Hamilton, Late Secretary of the Treasury, is Fully Refuted. Written by Himself* (Philadelphia: Printed for John Fenno, by John Bioren, 1797).

1 *Stat.* — *The Public Statutes at Large of the United States of America* (Boston, 1845).

6 *Stat.* — *The Public Statutes at Large of the United States of America* [Private Statutes] (Boston, 1856).

IV. INDECIPHERABLE WORDS

Words or parts of words which could not be deciphered because of the illegibility of the writing or the mutilation of the manuscript have been indicated as follows:

1. ⟨– – – – –⟩ indicates illegible words with the number of dashes indicating the estimated number of illegible words.
2. Words or letters in broken brackets indicate a guess as to what the words or letters in question may be. If the source of the words or letters within the broken brackets is known, it has been given a note.

V. CROSSED-OUT MATERIAL IN MANUSCRIPTS

Words or sentences crossed out by a writer in a manuscript have been handled in one of the three following ways:

1. They have been ignored, and the document or letter has been printed in its final version.
2. Crossed-out words and insertions for the crossed-out words have been described in the notes.
3. When the significance of a manuscript seems to warrant it, the crossed-out words have been retained, and the document has been printed as it was written.

VI. TEXTUAL CHANGES AND INSERTIONS

The following changes or insertions have been made in the letters and documents printed in these volumes:

1. Words or letters written above the line of print (for example, 9th) have been made even with the line of print (9th).
2. Punctuation and capitalization have been changed in those instances where it seemed necessary to make clear the sense of the writer. A special effort has been made to eliminate the dash, which was such a popular eighteenth-century device.
3. When the place or date, or both, of a letter or document does not appear at the head of that letter or document, it has been

inserted in the text in brackets. If either the place or date at the head of a letter or document is incomplete, the necessary additional material has been added in the text in brackets. For all but the best known localities or places, the name of the colony, state, or territory has been added in brackets at the head of a document or letter.

4. In calendared documents, place and date have been uniformly written out in full without the use of brackets. Thus "N. York, Octr. 8, '99" becomes "New York, October 8, 1799." If, however, substantive material is added to the place or date in a calendared document, such material is placed in brackets. Thus "Oxford, Jan. 6" becomes "Oxford [Massachusetts] January 6 [1788]."

5. When a writer made an unintentional slip comparable to a typographical error, one of the four following devices has been used:

   a. It has been allowed to stand as written.

   b. It has been corrected by inserting either one or more letters in brackets.

   c. It has been corrected without indicating the change.

   d. It has been explained in a note.

6. Because the symbol for the thorn was archaic even in Hamilton's day, the editors have used the letter "y" to represent it. In doing this they are conforming to eighteenth-century manuscript usage.

THE PAPERS OF ALEXANDER HAMILTON

1792

Conversation with George Hammond [1]

[Philadelphia, July 1–2, 1792]

In one of my recent conversations with Mr Hamilton, I took occasion from the accidental mention of some circumstances relative to the Mississippi, to enquire of him the actual state of the negociation with the Court of Spain on the subject of the navigation of that river.[2] Mr. Hamilton informed me that the negociation was indeed pretty far advanced, but that the conditions, by which the object of it was to be attained, did not at present appear to be so extensively beneficial as might have been desired, since the Spanish government still pertinaciously resisted any cession to the United States of a Sea-port communicating with the Mississippi.[3] He added that an acquisition of this nature was essential to the security and improvement of all the other advantages derivable from the internal navigation of the river, and he presumed that if it could not be effected by negociation, the necessity of obtaining it by any means must at some period ultimately lead to a rupture between this Country and Spain.

This language afforded me a fair opportunity of repeating to Mr Hamilton my expectation that, whatever might be the event of the negociation this Country would not enter into any engagements with Spain, which might be injurious to the rights secured by treaty to Great Britain.[4] Mr Hamilton assured me that all the members of this government were *unanimous* in opinion that the participation of Great Britain in the free navigation of that river was to the United States an object of advantage and not of jealousy. To this I answered that, if such were the real dispositions of the Gentlemen composing this administration I trusted that, whenever the subject came into discussion, I should find these inclined to such a regulation of the boundaries as would afford to his Majesty's subjects an effectual communication with the Mississippi.[5] Mr Hamilton in reply said he conceived it would well deserve the attention of the United States to consent to as liberal a measure of accommodation in that respect as would not be detrimental to their own interests.[6]

As the information I have received from Mr Hamilton does not seem exactly to co-incide with the account communicated by Mr Carmichael to Lord St. Helens,[7] I must own that I am disposed to ascribe the difference to an alteration of system in the Spanish Court rather than to any deception on the part of Mr Hamilton: As in my communications with him I have never yet at any time had reason to suspect him of artifice or imposition.

D, PRO: F.O., Series 4, Vol. 16, Part I.

1. Hammond was appointed British Minister Plenipotentiary to the United States in 1791.

This conversation has been taken from Hammond to Lord Grenville, July 3, 1792, Dispatch No. 27.

2. See "Notes on Thomas Jefferson's Report of Instructions for the Commissioners to Spain," March 1-4, 1792, and "Conversation with George Hammond," March 31, 1792, note 3.

3. How H acquired this information is not known. Although William Short and William Carmichael had been appointed on January 24, 1793, commissioners to settle differences between the United States and Spain, Short did not arrive in Spain until February, 1793, and no letter from Carmichael containing such information has been found. The only known progress which had been made was the extension of the negotiation to include commerce. This was approved by the Senate on March 16, 1792.

4. Article VIII of the treaty of peace between the United States and Great Britain guaranteed Britain free navigation of the Mississippi River (Miller, Treaties, II, 155).

5. The treaty of peace between Great Britain and the United States had run the northwestern boundary between the United States and British America west from the Lake of the Woods to the Mississippi (Miller, Treaties, II, 153). Hammond, having learned that a line due west from the Lake of the Woods might not touch the Mississippi, argued that, conformable to the treaty, territory should be given Great Britain to make the Mississippi accessible.

6. According to an entry by Jefferson in the "Anas," Hamilton brought up the question of British entry to the Mississippi at a cabinet meeting on October 31, 1792. At that time H suggested that, in view of deteriorating relations between Spain and the United States, the opening of the Mississippi to the British might be used to entice Great Britain into an Anglo-American combination against Spain. Among other inducements to Britain, according to Jefferson, H favored "admission to some navigable part of the Mississippi, by some line drawn from the lake of the woods to such navigable part. He had not, he said, examined the map to see how such a line might be run so as not to make too great a sacrifice. The navign of the Missis being a joint possn we might then take measures in concert for the joint security of it. He was therefore for immediately sounding them on this subject thro' our Minister at London. . . ." Although Henry Knox concurred in H's views, Thomas Jefferson, Edmund Randolph, and George Washington displayed no enthusiasm for

the proposal. The President observed that "the remedy would be worse than the disease" (Ford, *Writings of Jefferson*, I, 207).

7. Lord St. Helens was British Ambassador to Spain from 1790 to 1794. Carmichael's communication to St. Helens was reported by the British ambassador to Lord Grenville in a letter of November 25, 1791. Grenville, in turn, sent a copy of St. Helens's letter to Hammond on January 5, 1792. See "Conversation with George Hammond," March 31, 1792, note 3.

To George Bush [1]

Treasury Department, July 2, 1792. ". . . I wish to be informed, what will be the expense of providing and maintaining for one year such a boat as is contemplated by you for Port Penn, and of another for the Port of New castle."

LC, RG 56, Letters to Collectors at Small Ports, "Set G," National Archives.
1. Bush was collector of customs at Wilmington, Delaware.

To Tench Coxe [1]

Treasury Department, July 2, 1792. "It appears to be requisite that the sum of one thousand Dollars, which was advanced by the Collector of New York [2] to the late Supervisor,[3] should be refunded by the present Supervisor,[4] in order that it may be carried into the proper account. . . ."

LS, from a typescript furnished by Mr. Herman K. Crofoot, Moravia, New York.
1. Coxe was commissioner of the revenue.
2. John Lamb.
3. William S. Smith, the son-in-law of John Adams, had resigned as supervisor of the revenue for the District of New York on March 1, 1792.
4. Richard Morris, a former chief justice of New York, was appointed supervisor of the revenue for the District of New York on March 8, 1792. On May 24, 1792, Coxe had written to Morris that the one thousand dollars on account of revenue collection expenses was legally payable out of receipts of the collection and should be paid to the collector of customs (LC, RG 58, Letters of Commissioner of Revenue, 1792–1793, National Archives).

For similar loans made by the collectors of customs to supervisors of the revenue in other states, see H to Otho H. Williams, December 5, 1791; H to Jeremiah Olney, February 4, 1792. See also Coxe to George Gale, July 26, 1792 (LC, RG 58, Letters of Commissioner of Revenue, 1792–1793, National Archives); Coxe to George Clymer, July 5, 1792 (LC, RG 58, Letters of Commissioner of Revenue, 1792–1793, National Archives).

To Sharp Delany [1]

Treasury Department, July 2, 1792. "I have this day decided upon the case of Hollingsworth, Shallcross, Lovering and Le Maigre.[2] There being no appearance of fraud or wilful negligence in the transaction, the interest of all parties in the forfeiture is remitted to the Petitioners, upon their paying costs and charges. . . ."

LS, Bureau of Customs, Philadelphia; LC, RG 56, Letters to the Collector at Philadelphia, National Archives; copy, RG 56, Letters to Collectors at Small Ports, "Set G," National Archives.
  1. Delany was collector of customs at Philadelphia.
  2. John Hollingsworth, John Shallcross, and Peter Le Maigre were Philadelphia merchants. S. Lovering was a ship captain and merchant.

To William Ellery [1]

[*Philadelphia, July 2, 1792.* On July 16, 1792, Ellery wrote to Hamilton: "I have recd. your . . . letter of the 2nd. of July last." *Letter not found.*]

  1. Ellery was collector of customs at Newport, Rhode Island.

To George Washington

[Philadelphia, July 2, 1792]

Mr. Hamilton presents his respects to the President & has the honor to enclose the sketch of a letter to be written by Mr. Lear to Mr. Langdon.[1]

2d July 1792.

LC, George Washington Papers, Library of Congress.
  1. Woodbury Langdon, the brother of Senator John Langdon of New Hampshire, was a New Hampshire merchant and politician. In June, 1790, after he had served five years on the state superior court, he was impeached for neglect of duty by the lower house of the state legislature. The trial, however, was not held until January, 1791, and Langdon was allowed to resign. On December 24, 1790, he was appointed one of the commissioners for settling the accounts between the states and the United States.
  On July 2, 1792, Tobias Lear, who was Washington's secretary, wrote to

Langdon stating the need for a final settlement of the accounts between the states and the United States and requesting that Langdon either resign or return to Philadelphia so that the settlement could "be pursued with diligence and perseverence" (LC, George Washington Papers, Library of Congress).

From Benjamin Lincoln [1]

Boston July 3 1792

Sir

Notwithstanding our wishes to the contrary, we are too often impelled to call your attention from the more important duties of your Office to circumstances trivial indeed compared therewith. However painful the measure we cannot avoid it & preserve that uniformity in the different Offices so much to be desired, as thereby the general interest is promoted & the minds of the People kept in a state of quiet.

By the Act entitled "an act to provide more effectually for the collection of the Duties imposed by Law on Goods Wares & Merchandise imported into the United States, & on the Tonnage of Ships or Vessels" [2] it is enacted in the 41st. section, that where the duties Shall exceed fifty Dollars they Shall be Secured by bond with condition for the payment thereof if accruing upon articles of the produce of the West Indies in four months; if accruing upon Madeira wine, twelve months; if accruing upon any other Goods Wares & Merchandize other than Teas imported from China Six months.

By the 42 Section of the same Law, it is enacted that all Teas imported from China may &c—the whole Section Seems to refer wholly to Teas imported from China, so that the Duties on all Teas other than such were to be Secured as other merchandise by bonds payable in six months.

The "Act making farther provision for the Collection of the Duties by Law imposed on Teas, & to prolong the term for the payment of Duties on Wines" [3] is so drafted as to lead us to construe it more generally.

The preamble which often serves as a key to the whole stands very general. "Whereas it is conceived the following regulations concerning Teas may be conducive both to the accommodation of Importers thereof, & to the security of the Revenue"—In the first Section of this Law it is enacted, that in addition to the provisions contained in the fortieth and forty first section of an act entitled an Act to provide more effectually for the Collection of the Duties &c, "as they regard the payment or Securing the payment of the Duties on Teas, it Shall be lawful for *every* Importer of Teas if he or she Shall elect, So to do, to give his or her bond to the Collector of the District in which any of the said Teas Shall be landed in double the amount of the Duties thereupon with condition for the payment of the Duties in two years &c." In the first Act, whenever the Duties on Teas were mentioned as they refered to the Duties on teas from China they were always So expressed. When we attended to the last Law which passed 3d. March 1791 and found that the Legislature directed *additional provisions* to those mentioned in the 41 and 42 sections of the Same Law, & that *every* Importer of Teas at his or her option Should give bond for two years, &c we thought the words *every* Importer of Teas to be full, & that they could not have a limited operation when compared with the Sections to which there was to be an additional provision.

In those Sections care was taken to designate fully the Teas intended when we came therefore to find that in the new Law all distinction of Teas were thrown down, & instead of Saying therein as before all Teas imported from China, a new Stile was adopted— the comprehensive one,—*it Shall be lawfull for every Importer of Teas*, &c—from a view of the whole matter, it was the opinion in this Office that *every* Importer of Teas was intitled to equal benefits. On that we Should have practiced without troubling you on the Subject had we not found that in New York one mode was adopted in Philadelphia a different one, & that from our construction of the Law, the practice here would be different from both. Will you be so good as to say what is right?

Secy of the Treasury

LC, Massachusetts Historical Society, Boston; LC, RG 36, Collector of Customs at Boston, Letter Book, 1790–1792, National Archives; copy, RG 56, Letters from the Collector at Boston, National Archives.
  1. Lincoln was collector of customs at Boston.
  2. 1 *Stat.* 145–78 (August 4, 1790).
  3. 1 *Stat.* 219–21 (March 3, 1791).

To Charles Lee [1]

Treasury Department
July 4 1792.

Sir

I have to request that the Boat mentioned in your letter of the 11th of April last [2] may be delivered to the Collector of Cedar Point.[3]

In your letter, under date the 21st of September last, was enclosed a copy of an order of the District Court for compensating Charles Page, who was called as a Witness in the suit against William Simpson, which, agreeably to my Circular letter of the 8th Ultimo, can now be settled.

I am, Sir, with consideration,   Your Obedt Servant. A Hamilton

Charles Lee Esqr.
Alexandria

LS, RG 56, Letters to and from the Collector at Alexandria, National Archives; LC, Letters to Collectors at Small Ports, "Set G," National Archives.
    1. Lee was collector of customs at Alexandria, Virginia.
    2. Letter not found.
    3. John Coats Jones was appointed collector of customs at Cedar Point, Virginia, on August 10, 1790.

To Henry E. Lutterloh [1]

[*Philadelphia, July 4, 1792.* On September 9, 1792, Lutterloh wrote to Hamilton: "Your favor of the 4th July . . . I had the honour to receive." *Letter not found.*]

    1. Lutterloh came to America from Germany during the American Revolution and served as a deputy quartermaster general of the Continental Army with the rank of colonel. He subsequently settled in Fayetteville, North Carolina.

From Charles Lee

Collectors Office, Alexandria [Virginia]
5th. July 1792

Sir!

Your Circular of the 25th. June last, has been received in which among other things is explained how the additional 10 per Cent on the duties upon Goods, imported in Vessels not of the United States is to be computed; I shall conform to your instruction though I own had I not received it, the computation would have been made on the total Duties without distinguishing the old from the new duties,[1] the last Act having substituted other duties in lieu of the old and not expressing the distinction taken by you.

Permit me to suggest the doubts which occur in the construction of the 8th. Section of the Act for raising a further sum of money for the protection of the frontiers &c.[2]

1st. Whether the duties payable one half in six, one quarter in nine and one quarter in 12 months, ought not to be bonded in separate bonds; I have supposed they ought to be, in order that the mode already prescribed for stating the Bonded Duties in the books, may be continued and so a consistency and uniformity will be preserved in this respect, and because in some instances it would be inconvenient to the revenue by occasioning a delay of payment of the dividends last coming due.

For instance if one Bond be taken for the payment of the Duties by instalments, if default be made in paying the first instalment and a suit be commenced the Bond must be transmitted to Richmond to the Clerks Office to obtain a Judgment, and when the 2nd. Instalment shall be payable, it will not be paid, because the Bond cannot be seen, and a receipt cannot thereon be endorsed in presence of the Merchant, the Bond not being in the Office of the Collector, but of the Clerk of the Court.

3rd. Whether the Duties arising on Salt and all other goods, except on the produce of the West Indies, may be Bonded though the amount be less than 50 Dollars, payable by each Importer. I understand the Law to require immediate payment of the duties on the produce of the West Indies if the amount be under 50 Dollars and not in the other cases. This seems to be warranted by the order as well as by the words of the sentence, which will not admit of any other grammatical interpretation.

I am Sir! respectfully Your most Obedient Servant

Charles Lee, Collector
at Alexandria

Copy, RG 56, Letters to and from the Collector at Alexandria, National Archives.

1. The "old" duties were established by "An Act making further provision for the payment of the debts of the United States" (1 *Stat.* 180–82 [August 10, 1790]). These duties were changed by "An Act for raising a farther sum of money for the protection of the frontiers, and for other purposes therein mentioned" (1 *Stat.* 259–63 [May 2, 1792]).

2. Section 8 provided: "That the term of credit for the payment of duties on salt shall be nine months, and on all articles, the produce of the West Indies, salt excepted, where the amount of the duty to be paid by one person or co-partnership shall exceed fifty dollars, shall be four months, and that the duties on all other articles, except wines and teas, which shall be imported after the last day of June next, shall be payable, one half in six, one quarter in nine, and the other quarter in twelve calendar months from the time of each respective importation" (1 *Stat.* 260–61).

From Jeremiah Olney [1]

Providence, July 5, 1792. "On Monday Morning, the 2nd. Instant, the Master of the Ship Hope from Surinam, the Cargo of which was discharged the preceding Saturday afternoon, informed me that from a hint given by one of his Sailors, he had discovered a bag and one keg of brown Sugar, weighing 109 lb, concealed within the Sealing of the Cabin, but by whom he could not learn: a design to defraud the Revenue being evident in this transaction, I seized the Sugar, and requested the District Attorney [2] to file a Libel against it. . . ."

ADfS, Rhode Island Historical Society, Providence.

1. Olney was collector of customs at Providence.

2. William Channing was the United States attorney for the District of Rhode Island.

Draft of a Resolution for
the Society for Establishing Useful Manufactures [1]

[Newark, New Jersey, July 5, 1792]

That a Committee of three be appointed to receive proposals and conclude contracts for conveying the requisite water from the River to the seat of the Mills on the following plans severally

First to convey the Water across the Gully from   [2] to by troughs or trunks [supported] [3] by a wall

Secon[d] to convey the Water from the last mentioned point to the seat of the Mill so as to have at the Mill a head of   feet.

Thirdly to convey the Water from   to No. 14 in the Road by means of a dam across the Gully of sufficient height to deliver the Water at No. 14.

Fourthly to convey the Water from thence to the seat of the Mill with a head of   feet.

5th to convey the Water from   to No. 14 by means of a canal & a dam equal in height to the Bank of the canal at the point from which it issues into the Gully.

6 to convey the Water from thence to the Mill with a head of   feet.

ADf, The Passaic County Historical Society, Lambert Castle, Paterson, New Jersey.
  1. The directors of the Society for Establishing Useful Manufactures met at Newark, New Jersey, from July 3 to July 7, 1792. H was present at all the meetings except the one held on July 3. A committee, which had been "appointed for the purpose of fixing upon a proper place on the Waters of the Passaick for the Seat of the Factory, for fixing the Town of Paterson and making the necessary purchases of Land," reported on July 4 ("Minutes of the S.U.M.," 42). On the following day, the directors of the society passed a number of resolutions carrying out the suggestions of the committee.
  No evidence has been found that this resolution by H was ever acted upon by the directors of the Society for Establishing Useful Manufactures. On July 5, 1792, however, it was "Resolved that this Board do immediately take measures to bring the Water from above the Great Falls across the Gap to Station No. 14" ("Minutes of the S.U.M.," 44).
  2. This space and subsequent spaces left blank in MS.
  3. In MS, "supposed."

Draft of Resolutions for
the Society for Establishing Useful Manufactures

[Newark, New Jersey, July 5, 1792]

Resolved—[That the Water of the Passaick be conveyed across the adjacent Gully passing near a point or place distinguished as No. 16 upon the summit of a Wall to be erected for that purpose and preserving the head thereof] [1]

Resolved That the sd. Water be conveyed from a station or stake marked No. 1 to a place at or near another stake marked No. 2, from thence to a place at or near another station or cedar shrub at the brink of the Rock marked No. 3, from thence across the adjacent gully to a place at or near another station marked No. 4— from thence to a place at or near another station marked No. 5— from thence to a place at or near another station marked No. 6— from thence to a place at or near another station marked No. 7— from thence to a place at or near another station marked No. 8, from thence to a place at or near another station marked No. 9, and from thence to a place at or near another station marked No. 10. And That it be conveyed across the said gully upon the summit of a wall to be raised on a level with the bed of the said River—And that a sum not exceeding twenty thousand dollars be appropriated for that purpose.

Resolved that a Cotton Mill [of eight Drums] be erected and That for the Building of the Same [& providing the requisite Machinery] the sum of fifteen Thousand Dollars be appropriated—which Cotton mill shall be of the following description viz as pr. M A.[2]

Resolved that a Printing Shop & Calander House be erected & That for the Building of the Same [and providing the requisite Machinery for the Printing business,] the sum of twelve Thousand Dollars be appropriated and that ye description thereof be as follows. vist. as pr. ⊗ A.[3]

Resolved that a Carding & Ropeing house be erected & That for the Building of the same [& providing] Machinery [for spinning weft and weaving] The sum of six Thousand Dollars be appropriated and that the description &c.

Df, partly in the handwriting of H, The Passaic County Historical Society, Lambert Castle, Paterson, New Jersey.

1. The parts of these resolutions which are in H's handwriting are enclosed in brackets.

The preceding resolution in the society's minutes reads as follows: "Resolved that this Board do immediately cause the following works to be erected, namely, first, a Building and Machinery for carrying on the business of the Cotton Mill, secondly the Building and Machinery for carrying on the Printing business. Thirdly, the Building and Machinery for carrying on the Business of Spinning, Weft, and Weaving, fourthly that a Number of Houses be erected for the accomodation of the Workmen to be employed by this Society" ("Minutes of the S.U.M.," 45).

2. The paper marked "M A" has not been found among the drafts of the "Minutes of the S.U.M." A description of the building, however, is included in the society's minutes ("Minutes of the S.U.M.," 46).

3. The paper marked "⊗ A" has not been found among the drafts of the society's minutes, but specifications for the printing shop and calendar house are included in the minutes ("Minutes of the S.U.M.," 46).

From Jeremiah Olney [1]

Providence, Custom House, 6th. July 1792.

Sir.

I have received your several Letters of the 26, 27th. & 28th of June. The circular Letter, dated the 6th of February last, to which you refer has never come to hand; I am therefore under the necessity of postponing the notification of Mr. Arnold's [2] delinquincy until I do receive it.

I have the honor to be &c.   Jereh. Olney Collr.

Alexr. Hamilton Esqr.
Secy. of the Treasury.

ADfS, Rhode Island Historical Society, Providence.
1. For background to this letter, see Olney to H, May 19, 1792, and H to Olney, June 26, 1792.
2. Welcome Arnold was a Providence merchant.

Draft of a Resolution for
the Society for Establishing Useful Manufactures

[Newark, New Jersey, July 6, 1792]

[Resolved that 50 Houses be built for the accommodation of the Workmen to be employed in the service of the Society] [1] and of other Mechanics who may choose to settle at the Town of Patterson [and that the materials thereof be Stone & Clay & *Pointed*] unless [the expence of such materials] shall [exceed] by [Thirty per Cent the expence of a House of the same Dimensions of Wood] in which case they shall be of wood and that the dimensions of each of the said houses shall be in length 24 feet in width 18 feet in height from the lower floor to the Plate 12 feet each house having a Cellar & a Garret [& that a Sum not exceeding 8500 Dollars be appropriated for defraying the expence] thereof.

That the foregoing houses stand each of a lot of ¼ of an acre and that the house and lot be valued at Two hundred & fifty Dollars —that any Mechanic being of good character & a married man may be accommodated with a house and lot either upon a lease for one or more years not exceeding 20 years at an annual rent of Twelve & a half Dollars payable quarter yearly or with a right to become the proprietor thereof at the said value of 250 Dollars paying for the same at any time and in any proportions he shall think fit upon condition that he pay in the mean time at the rate of 5 ₱ Ct. ₱ annum on the whole or so much of the said principal sum as shall remain unpaid until the whole be discharged.

That any Mechanic who may incline to build for himself may have a lot of the above dimensions at the sum of 80 Dollars upon the like terms of payment as above specified so as the whole term of payment shall not exceed twenty years.

That William Hall Joseph Mort [Thomas] Marshall & William Pearce may each have a lot not exceeding half an acre of ground at the rate of 175 Dollars ₱ Lot, and that there be advanced to William Hall & Joseph Mort each a sum not exceeding 1000 Dollars upon condition that the same be applied to the erecting of a dwelling house upon the Lot to him appertaining. The value of the said Lot and the sum advanced to be payable in four equal installments the first at the end of 5 years the second at the end of five years next suceeding the third at the end of 5 years next succeeding & the 4 at the end of 5 years then next succeeding with interest at the rate of [five] ₱ Centum ₱. annum.

ADf, The Passaic County Historical Society, Lambert Castle, Paterson, New Jersey.
1. Words within brackets in this document are in an unidentified handwriting.

To Benjamin Walker [1]

[Newark, New Jersey, July 6, 1792]

Dr. Walker

It is indispensable that an Ordinance should pass for the next election in October and it appears clearly that this cannot be done without the presence of Seven Directors. As five only are here, it is essential that two should come from New York. I beg you to do it without fail, so as to reach New Ark if possible by Eight tomorrow Morning. Without this another Meeting of the Directors for this single purpose will be unavoidable. You may be assured you will not be detained—Every thing will be prepared. I again entreat you not to fail. Bring Lewis [2] with you. He is equally essential. [3]

Yrs. sincerely   A Hamilton

New Ark July 6. 1792
Benjamin Walker Esq

ALS, Harvard College Library.
    1. Walker, a New York financier, was a director of the Society for Establishing Useful Manufactures.
    2. George Lewis, a New York broker, was a director of the society.
    3. On July 7 the directors of the society, including Lewis and Walker, met and adopted the following ordinance: "Be it Ordained by the Deputy Governor and Directors of the Society for establishing useful Manufactures, That the Election of Directors of the said Society on the first Monday in October next agreeably to Law of Incorporation, shall be held at the Court House in New Ark in the County of Essex, which Election Shall begin between the hours of twelve and two in the afternoon of the same day and may be continued by adjournment from day to day for three days counting the first day as one. . . . Be it Ordained by the authority aforesaid That the said Election shall be by ballot . . ." ("Minutes of the S.U.M.," 52–53).

To George Washington

Treasury Department, July 8, 1792. Submits "the inclosed Contract between the Superintendant of the Delaware Lighthouse [1] &c. and Benjamin Rice, for the making of two mooring chains for the use of the Beacon boats on the River Delaware."

LC, George Washington Papers, Library of Congress.
1. William Allibone was superintendent of lighthouses, beacons, buoys, and public piers for Philadelphia, Cape Henlopen, and Delaware.

From Tench Coxe[1]

Treasury Department
Revenue Office July 9th: 1792.

Sir,

Among the papers which I had the honor to present to You, several suggestions in regard to the compensations to the Inspectors of the Revenue for ports will be observed. When the directions of the Legislature in regard to foreign distilled Spirits, wines and teas[2] are considered it will be perceived, that the duties of the port Inspectors of the Revenue, and those of the Inspectors of the customs deputed by them are extended, and that their responsibilities are encreased.[3] In regard to Teas some of the most responsible services originally performed by the Collectors are transferred to them. The influence of these Circumstances, increased no doubt by his own interest, has occasioned one of the Supervisors to suggest the Idea of the duty on foreign Spirits being paid ultimately into their Hands. Altho' this cannot be done as the laws now stand,[4] even

LC, RG 58, Letters of the Commissioner of Revenue, 1792–1793, National Archives.
1. Coxe was preparing a supplementary arrangement of revenue offices and compensation to revenue officers. On May 11, 1792, Coxe had requested that the supervisors of the revenue send him statements of the probable charges and proceeds of the excise together with any information which would facilitate the arrangements for compensation which H would suggest to the President (LC, RG 58, Letters of Commissioner of Revenue, 1792–1793, National Archives).

The arrangement which Coxe sent to H on July 25, 1792, was approved by the President on August 4, 1792. See Coxe to H, July 25, 1792.

2. Coxe is referring to two acts: "An Act repealing, after the last day of June next, the duties heretofore laid upon Distilled Spirits imported from abroad, and laying others in their stead; and also upon Spirits distilled within the United States, and for appropriating the same" (1 Stat. 199–214 [March 3, 1791]) and "An Act making farther provision for the collection of the duties by law imposed on Teas, and to prolong the term for the payment of the Duties on Wines" (1 Stat. 219–21 [March 3, 1791]).

3. For a discussion of the duties of inspectors of the customs, see "Treasury Department Circular to the Collectors of the Customs," May 26, 1791; H to Otho H. Williams, June 18, 1792; Williams to H, June 28, 1792.

4. Coxe is referring to Section 53 of "An Act to provide more effectually for the collection of the duties imposed by law on goods, wares and mer-

should it appear equitable and expedient, yet a question arises in regard to the three Articles which are within the Care of the Revenue officers, whether the attention required of them does not entitle them to a share of the Commission accruing on those high duties in a greater degree than the Collectors of the Customs whose services in relation to these Articles are so much less troublesome. The certificate business [5] is very important, as it regards imported articles, the whole burden of it falls on the officers of the Revenue. As it respects teas, very little being imported except at Salem, Boston, Providence, New York and Philadelphia, Inspectors of other ports need not be compensated but in a small degree. The importation of wines is more diffusive in regard to the places of entry, and that of Spirits is general. Tho' the present arrangement contemplates only distilled Spirits, it may not be improper perhaps informing it to take all the Services of the Revenue Officers (viz: those relative to Wines and Teas) into view, and the Case of the persons (who are not inspectors of the customs) who have been deputed by the Inspectors of ports or appointed by the Supervisors as in New York &c. require consideration. In making the contemplated Arrangement the actual Emoluments of the Inspectors of ports (in their quality of Surveyors or Collectors) should be taken into the Calculation. Should any thing be granted to the port Officers, a retrospect will probably be found just. The propriety of withholding it from those who have refused to perform the service so as to dishonor Goverment, impede its operations and incommode the Merchants, is respectfully suggested for Consideration. It is probable that the retrospective Compensations to the Revenue officers would be satisfactory tho less than what may be requisite in future. There are some argument[s] for some compensation to in-

---

chandise imported into the United States, and on the tonnage of ships or vessels," which specified that payments be made to inspectors as follows: "To each inspector there shall be allowed for every day he shall be actually employed in aid of the customs, a sum not exceeding one dollar and twenty-five cents" (1 *Stat.* 172 [August 4, 1790]).

5. Section 10 of "An Act repaling, after the last day of June next, the duties heretofore laid upon Distilled Spirits imported from abroad, and laying others in their stead; and also upon Spirits distilled within the United States, and for appropriating the same" provided that certificates were to be issued for spirits imported from abroad but intended for a port in the United States other than the vessel's first port of call (1 *Stat.* 201–02).

spectors for ports, which seem to be almost conclusive. An expence of Clerk hire and in some degree of a Deputy is incurred also of Office Rent, lights and fuel. The inspection of the Exportation of Spirits distilled in the United States, is a duty irrelative to the original Nature of their offices and to the Customs or impost.

The Supervisors appear to have aimed at placing the secondary and particularly the subordinate offices of Inspection in the hands of very respectable persons. This was a good view, as the law was unpopular in some places, but required bounds. It has not perhaps been duly limited, nor has it proved in every instance that a respectable and influential *man* has made an active and efficient Collector. A Consequence has followed also, which is inconvenient—the expectation of a compensation rather proportioned to the personal Character of the Officer than the Nature of the service or the Amount of the Revenue collected within his sphere.

There appear in some Districts to be too many collectors. In Virginia there are 58, which I suppose to be one for each County. Three Counties of Pennsylvania have only one, viz. Philadelphia, Bucks and Montgomery.

I do not believe the postages are included in the returns of charges—they are not mentioned in any.

A regular guager at a Salary as proposed at New York, would be an expensive Officer. The Revenue in that district has not been collected on 300 puncheons of domestic Spirits. It is probable guagers would execute that quantity of Business for Merchants in the six principal ports for a compensation of ten Cents pr. Cask. The Idea of trying the proof at the same time and of making a return is a very valuable one. Unless an account of the proof as well as the Quantity of Spirit be taken the Revenue must suffer, and practices destructive of candid dealing with the United States, on the part of the distillers will be introduced.

It [is] thought by the Comptroller [6] that the simplicity which will be given to the accounts and the consequent facility of adjusting them, strongly recommend the grant of a Commission on the gross Amount of duties to the Supervisors and Inspectors of Surveys.

The Supervisor of Massachusetts [7] seems to be of opinion that his

6. Oliver Wolcott, Jr., was comptroller of the Treasury.
7. Nathaniel Gorham.

Collectors can be satisfied without a restrospective compensation, if some charges which he specifies can be defrayed by the United States.

It is observable in the District of New York that Mr. Geary who is a confidential Guager is a distiller.[8] The continuance of this precedent appears so dangerous, as to be inadmissible—also that there is in the estimate a charge for two office rooms for the Supervisor, who has only one Clerk, and for fuel for the two offices. The question whether an office keeper, messenger & Stamper of certificates should be regularly employed occurs also in that district. The Supervisors Estimate of 81,000 Dollars for the duties on foreign Spirits imported [into] New York must be very far short of the true Amount.

It is uncertain how far the practice has been observed in the several ports of performing the revenue services relative to foreign Spirits, wines and teas by deputing the Inspectors of the Customs. A circular letter [9] has been prepared on that subject for all the Districts, but those of New York, Pennsylvania and Maryland, in regard to which the facts are known and variant.

In Rhode Island a small charge of fuel for the Collectors, Inspectors and Supervisors office is made.

It merrits particular attention that the conversion of the Molasses distilleries every where into grain and fruit distilleries which appears certain, will enhance the Commissions of the officers in those Scenes.

The charges of marking and certifying old Stock are not entitled to a place among the ordinary expences of collecting this Revenue —nor are any of the Charges accruing in the offices of the port Inspectors.

The cases of some at least of the Supervisors who are also inspectors of Surveys appear to merit consideration.

8. A New York directory for 1792 lists James Geary as an "inspector of the revenue and superintendent of distilleries" (*The New-York Directory, and Register for the year 1792 . . . by William Duncan* [New York: Printed for the Editor, by T. and J. Swords, No. 27, William-Street, 1792]). On August 2, 1792, Coxe wrote to Richard Morris, supervisor of the revenue for New York, concerning the possibility and propriety of using Geary's services (LC, RG 58, Letters of Commissioner of Revenue, 1792–1793, National Archives).

9. The circular is dated July 9, 1792 (LC, RG 58, Letters of Commissioner of Revenue, 1792–1793, National Archives).

The Supervisor of Maryland [10] thinks the compensations of the Inspector of the small Survey No. 2 [11] of four Counties is too small. His Judgment may be influenced by the recollection that there is a much larger survey under his own Inspection. The Supervisor of Virginia,[12] thinks that the inspectors of his seven surveys who have 9 to 10 Counties each on a Medium under their charge, are and ought to be satisfied with their Compensations, which are precisely the same as to Salary and rate of Commission.

You will perceive, sir, objections are strongly urged by the Supervisor of Virginia and supported by one of his Inspectors (General Stevens) [13] against marking and certifying Spirits distilled in the Country, and the Supervisor adds that he did not include that service in his estimate of Compensations.

I have the honor to be, with the most respectful Attachment, sir,   Your most obedt. Servant   Tench Coxe,
                                                                     Commissr. of the Revenue

The honble.
The Secretary of the Treasury.

10. George Gale.
11. Philip Thomas.
12. Edward Carrington.
13. Edward Stevens was inspector of the revenue for Survey No. 2 in Virginia. During the American Revolution Stevens had been a brigadier general in the Virginia militia.

To William Ellery

[*Philadelphia, July 9, 1792.* On July 30, 1792, Ellery wrote to Hamilton: "I have received your letter of the 9th of this month." *Letter not found.*]

From Sharp Delany

[*Philadelphia, July 10, 1792.* On July 12, 1792, Hamilton wrote to Delany and referred to "your letter of the 10th instant." *Letter not found.*]

From William Ellery

[Newport, Rhode Island]
Collector's Office July 10th 1792

Sir

I recd. a letter from the Collr. for Providence last saturday in which he observes that he had received a letter from you [1] referring him to a *circular* one dated the 6th. of February last, relative to notifying to other Collrs when a bond for duties is put in suit, and desires me to furnish him with a copy as soon as possible if I had received such an one, as he had not. I have not received any such letter; but should be happy to be favoured with one, and if it should be convenient would wish to receive an answer to my letter of the 25th of last month.

I have recd. your letters of the 7th 22nd. and 28th of the last month,[2] and will attend to their contents.

I am Sir Yr. most obedt. servt.   Wm Ellery Colle

A Hamilton Esqr
Secry Treasy.

LC, Newport Historical Society, Newport, Rhode Island.
  1. See H to Jeremiah Olney, June 26, 1792, and Olney to H, July 6, 1792.
  2. None of these letters have been found.

From Rufus King [1]

[New York] Tuesday 10 July [1792]

You will see by our papers to what we are tending [2]—hitherto I have been quite aside, and have not engaged in the controversy. The addresses from albany and other northern Towns, together with Mr. Jays answers [3] leave no room to doubt that the question will be brought to a decision in some way or other—if it can be done under any authority of Law I shall rejoice, because I consider the Determination to be a precedent dangerous to free Elections. Still however I do not clearly see the prudence of an appeal to the People—yet others have no doubts on that subject, and there is reason to conclude that Mr. Jay deems the occasion such as will justify the step should it be found that the powers of government are insufficient to afford a Remedy. He has an idea of a convention for the sole purpose of canvassing the canvassers and their Decision.

But Mr. Clinton is in fact Governor, and though he may not be free from anxieties & Doubts, he will not willingly relinquish the Office—the majority, and a very great one are now against him— should he persist, and the sword be drawn, he must go to the wall —but this my dear Sir, is a dreadful alternative, and what & whom it may affect is altogether uncertain. If this case will justify a recurrence to first Principles, what are we not to expect from the disputes, which must & will arise in the Succession of the Presidency? and how are we able to place confidence in the security of our Government?

Tuesday Evening

Mr. Jay has arrived. Notice was given in the morning papers that he would be in Town this Evening, and "the friends of Liberty" were invited to go forth to meet him. I took Benson [4] with me in my carriage. The concourse was immense, & Mr. Jay has been recd. with the ringing of Bells, firing of cannon, huzzaings & clapping of hands. The shout was for "Jay & Liberty." [5]

Yr's &c.

R King

ALS, Hamilton Papers, Library of Congress.

1. King was a Federalist Senator from New York.

2. King is referring to the disputed gubernatorial election in New York. See Philip Schuyler to H, May 9, 1792, note 4; H to John Adams, June 25, 1792, note 2; H to King, June 28, 1792.

3. In reply to the address of a committee of citizens of Lansingburgh John Jay said: "The citizens of the state know the value of their Rights; and it is to be expected, as well as sincerely to be wished, that their efforts to assert and maintain them, will on every occasion, be marked by temper and moderation, as well as by constancy and zeal." At Albany he said: "When sentiments and opinions, relative to public measures, are capable of being ascribed to private and personal considerations, prudence dictates a great degree of delicacy and reserve—But there are no considerations which ought to restrain me from expressing my ardent wishes, that the important question you mention, may be brought to a decision, with all that mature reflection, as well as manly constancy, which its connection with the rights of freemen demands . . ." (The [New York] Daily Advertiser, July 7, 10, 1792).

4. Presumably Egbert Benson, member of the House of Representatives from New York.

5. A notice for those who intended to meet Jay near Harlem Heights was placed in The Daily Advertiser on July 10, 1792. The next issue carried a description of Jay's arrival in the city.

From Tobias Lear

[*Philadelphia*] *July 10, 1792.* Returns "with the President's approbation thereunto subjoined, a Contract between the Superintendant
of the Delaware Lighthouse &c. and Benjamin Rice, for making two
mooring chains for the use of the Beacon boats in the River Delaware."[1]

LC, George Washington Papers, Library of Congress.
   1. See H to George Washington, July 8, 1792.

Receipt from Andrew Mayer

[Philadelphia, July 10, 1792]

Received Philadelphia July 10th 1792 of Alexander Hamilton
Seventy four Dollars & sixty seven Cents on account of William
Pearce.[1]   Andrew Mayer

D, in the handwriting of H and signed by Mayer, Hamilton Papers, Library
of Congress.
   1. For information concerning William Pearce, see "Receipt from William
Pearce," August 20, 1791.

From George Washington

United States 10th. July 1792

   The Secretary of the Treasury will cause to be paid to the Director of the Mint, Ten thousand Dollars for the purposes above specified.[1]   G: Washington

LC, George Washington Papers, Library of Congress.
   1. This is a reference to an estimate by David Rittenhouse, director of the
Mint. The estimate reads as follows:
         "Estimate of immediate Expenditures for the Mint.

	Dollars.
Price of the House & Lot, to be paid on executing the Conveyance	4266 2/3
15 Tons of Copper, suppose 10 Cents ⅌ lb.	4800.
Repairs of the Buildings, workmen's wages &c.	933.1/3
Dollars	10,000.

10th. July 1792" (LC, George Washington Papers, Library of Congress).

From Edward Carrington

[*Richmond, July 11, 1792*. On July 25, 1792, Hamilton wrote to Carrington: "I have received . . . your two letters of the 11 instant." *Letters not found.*]

To Tench Coxe

Treasury Department, July 11, 1792. Returns "Contract between the Superintendant of the Delaware Lighthouse and Benjamin Rice . . . which the President has approved." [1]

LS, RG 26, Lighthouse Letters Received, "Segregated" Lighthouse Records, Hamilton, National Archives.
  1. See H to George Washington, July 8, 1792, and Tobias Lear to H, July 10, 1792.

To Samuel Gerry [1]

Treasury Department, July 11, 1792. Cites case of the Schooner *Dolphin*, which was "admeasured" at both Baltimore and Marblehead. Asks why results of the "admeasurement" at Marblehead were different from those at Baltimore and asks "to be particularly informed of the usal process which prevails at your port for the admeasuring of vessels."

LC, Essex Institute, Salem, Massachusetts.
  1. Gerry was collector of customs at Marblehead, Massachusetts.

Proposals to Contract for the Construction of the Manufacturing Plant of the Society for Establishing Useful Manufactures [1]

[Philadelphia, July 11, 1792] [2]

Proposals to contract for the following purposes will be received at New York by N Lowe at New Ark by Elisha Boudinot at New Brunswick by John Bayard and at Philadelphia by   [3] Vizt.

1 To cut a Canal from the River Passaick beginning at a point near a Station where stands a Stake marked No. 1 & continuing thence to the brink of a Precipice at or near a rock marked No. 3. This canal must be thirty feet wide and must be sunk to a level with the Surface of the water in the driest season.

II To erect flood gates in the said Canal near the brink of the Precipice.

3. To erect a Dam on the River Passaick above the Great Falls and below the Place of the Canal. The Dam to be four feet above the level of the Surface of the Water at the driest season.

4 To erect a dry Wall across a Gully adjacent to the above-mentioned precipice, in a direction from the said Station No. 3 to another Station being a stake marked No. 6 on or near the summit of a hill extending from the one to the other and to make a wooden trough upon the said Wall sixteen feet wide by seven feet deep.

5 To extend a trough of the same dimensions from the said Station No. 6 to another Station being a Tree marked No. 7 with a dry wall on one side, the whole length thereof, of the thickness of six feet.

6 To erect at the Town of Patterson near the Falls of the Passaick a stone building 55 feet long by 32 feet wide four Stories high exclusive of a cellar the whole length thereof.

7 To erect another stone building at the said Town of Patterson 78 feet long by 31 feet wide three Stories high exclusive of a Cellar the whole length thereof.

8 To erect another stone building, at the said Town of Patterson 38 feet long by 27 feet wide two stories high exclusive of a Cellar the whole length thereof.[4]

9 To erect another Stone building 68 feet long by 36 feet wide two stories high exclusive of a cellar the whole length thereof.

10 To erect fifty houses of Stone or Wood as may be afterwards determined each 24 feet long by 18 feet wide, in height from the lower floor to the Plate 12 feet, with a cellar and a Garret. Two houses to be under one roof with a party wall. The proposals will specify severally the rates at which these buildings will be undertaken in stone and wood.

Descriptive plans of the several objects above specified number 2. 3. 4. 5. 7. 8. 10 may be seen in the possession of Nicholas Low at New York Elisha Boudinot at New Ark John Bayard at New

Brunswick   [5] at Philadelphia & William Hall at the Town of
Paterson at the Great Falls of the Passaick. The said Wm. Hall will
give such explanation as may be necessary.

A descriptive plan of the building above specified No. 6 may be
seen in the possession of the four first above mentioned persons &
of Thomas Marshall at the Town of P[aterson] who will give &c [6]

A descriptive plan of the building above specified No. 9 may be
seen &c.   Wm. Pearce [7]

All materials are to be found brought to the spot & erected by the
Contractors, to whom liberty will be granted under proper regulations to use any stones or Timber which may be on the lands of
the Society.

The proposals may comprehend either the whole or any one or
more of the foregoing objects. The proposers may accompany their
proposals by the suggestion of any other methods which shall occur
to them for constructing a competent Wall across the Gully from
Station No. 3 to station No. 6 and for conveying the Water from
thence to Station No. 7 and the terms upon which they may be
disposed to contract according to those methods.

All the works for conveying the water must be warranted for
seven years.

Proposals must be in writing & under seal addressed to the Society for establishing useful Manufactures. [8]

ADf, The Passaic County Historical Society, Lambert Castle, Paterson, New
Jersey.
    1. At a meeting of the directors of the Society for Establishing Useful
Manufactures held at Newark, New Jersey, from July 3 to July 7 and at-
tended by H after the first session, a committee consisting of Nicholas Low,
John Bayard, and Elisha Boudinot was appointed to carry out the resolutions
of the society for the erection of its manufacturing plant at Paterson, New
Jersey ("Minutes of the S.U.M.," 49–50). H apparently served as an adviser
to the committee. See "Draft Minutes of a Meeting of a Committee of the
Society for Establishing Useful Manufactures," August 1, 1792.
    Low, a New York City merchant and land speculator, was a director of the
Bank of New York and of the New York branch of the Bank of the United
States. Boudinot, a prominent lawyer and businessman in Newark, New Jersey,
was a brother of Elias Boudinot, a member of the House of Representatives
from New Jersey. Bayard, a former resident of Philadelphia, was a prominent
businessman and Federalist in New Brunswick, New Jersey.
    This document was prepared for publication in the newspapers. It appeared,
for example, in The New-York Journal & Patriotic Register, July 18, 1792.
    2. H did not date this document. The date assigned is that which was given
to the "Proposals" published in The New-York Journal.
    3. Space left blank in MS. In The New-York Journal the name of Charles

Pettit was inserted. Pettit, who had been an assistant quartermaster general during the American Revolution, became a prominent Philadelphia merchant after the war. He served successively as a member of the state legislature, delegate to the Continental Congress, and state agent to present Pennsylvania's claims before the commissioners to settle the accounts between the states and the United States.

4. In the margin opposite this paragraph, H wrote "materials."

5. Space left blank in MS. In *The New-York Journal* the name of Charles Pettit was inserted.

6. In *The New-York Journal* this sentence was completed by the addition of the words "such explanations as may be necessary."

7. In *The New-York Journal* this paragraph was completed to read as follows: "A descriptive plan of the building above specified No. 9, may be seen in the possession of the four first, abovementioned persons, and of William Pearce, at the town of Paterson, who will give such explanations as may be necessary."

8. In *The New-York Journal* the following material was added to the last sentence: "and delivered to one of the said persons first mentioned, on or before the twenty sixth of July instant."

To Benjamin Walker

Philadelphia July 11. 1792

Dr. Sir

The bearer of this Mr. Douthat [1] is lately from Europe. His views are towards the Woolen Manufacture, which he professes to understand in all its branches—and he is steering his course to Hartford in Connecticut.

As he is a stranger & I presume stands in need of œconomy, I will thank you to put him in the way of the cheapest conveyance to his destination. Will not this be by Water?

Yrs. sincerely   A Hamilton

B Walker Esqr.

ALS, Mr. Joseph M. Levine, New York City.

1. Francis Douthat subsequently settled in Staunton, Virginia, where he made an unsuccessful attempt to establish a textile business.

To Elisha Boudinot

Philidelphia, July 12th, 1792.

Dear Sir:

I wrote to you, a day or two since, on the subject of the advertisement.[1]

You recollect there is a power to borrow to be given to the Committee, under the seal of the Corporation.[2] No time ought to be lost in preparing and executing the power, and making application for the loan. Not more than 30,000 dollars, in addition to the 10,000 already borrowed, need at first be asked for. I shall write to Mr. Seton [3] by to-morrow's post.

Pray, my friend, let nothing slumber.

Yours,   A. Hamilton

JCHW, V, 514.

  1. Letter not found. H is referring to "Proposals to Contract for the Construction of the Manufacturing Plant of the Society for Establishing Useful Manufactures," July 11, 1792.

  2. On July 6, 1792, the directors of the Society for Establishing Useful Manufactures gave the committee "authority . . . to borrow on account of the Society a sum not exceeding seventy Thousand Dollars and to Pledge as a Security, The Stock of the Society in the funds of the United States. And that the Deputy Governor execute under the Seal of the Corporation a Competent power to the said Committee to make the said loan and pledge the said Stock . . ." ("Minutes of the S.U.M.," 49).

  3. William Seton was cashier of the Bank of New York.

To Sharp Delany

Treasury Department
July 12. 1792.

Sir

The practice of demanding Tonnage of a licensed vessel, when clearing out on a foreign voyage, and delivering up her license, as mentioned in your letter of the 10th instant,[1] is conceived not to be conformable with law.[2] A vessel cannot be liable to the Tonnage Duty whilst trading under a legal license. The practice must therefore be discontinued, and the Tonnage, charged in such cases, ought to be refunded to the parties.

It might happen, as you state, that a vessel would pay Tonnage but twice in three years, as a *licensed vessel*; if, in the last month of the year, she should clear for Europe, and, after a voyage of six months, was to renew her license, paying Tonnage for one year— then, at the expiration of the year, should again clear for a foreign port, and return in six months. But such vessel would, in the mean time, pay the *Tonnage Duty upon each entry from her foreign voyage,* and would fully have complied with what the laws require in those cases.

I am, Sir,   Your Obedt Servt.   Alexander Hamilton

Sharp Delany Esqr.

LS, Harvard College Library.
  1. Letter not found.
  2. "An Act imposing duties on the tonnage of ships or vessels" provided that tonnage duties would be paid "upon all ships or vessels which . . . shall be entered in the United States from any foreign port or place . . . also . . . upon every ship or vessel of the United States which . . . shall be entered in a district in one state from a district in another state. . . ." The act also provided that these duties "shall not be paid on any ship or vessel having a license to trade between the different districts of the United States . . . more than once a year" (1 *Stat.* 135–36 [July 20, 1790]).

From Thomas Jefferson

Philadelphia July 12. [1792]

Sir

By an act of Congress passed on the last day of their session it was made the duty of the Secretary of state to have seals prepared for the courts of the two Western governments,[1] but nothing particular was said as to the resource for making payment for them. I have therefore to ask the favor of information from you whether there are any funds which you should think it justifiable to apply to the payment of these objects. I assume they will amount to several hundred dollars. I have the honor to be with great respect Sir

Your most obedt. and most humble servt   Th: Jefferson

The Secretary of the Treasury

ALS, letterpress copy, Thomas Jefferson Papers, Library of Congress; LC, Papers of the Continental Congress, National Archives.
  1. "An Act respecting the government of the territories of the United States northwest and south of the river Ohio" (1 *Stat.* 285–86 [May 8, 1792]).

From John Lowell [1]

Roxbury [Massachusetts] July 12th: 1792.

Sir

I recd. your Letter of the 30th: of June last [2] by the Post of Saturday: I recd. the Papers you refer to & returned a new Statement of the Cases, on which I conversed with you when I was in Phila. last Winter. You then seemed to think that Norton might be entituled to a Remission [3] but that Lincoln & others should be pardoned. Soon after my Return I recd. a Letter from you [4] in which you say that you must make further Enquiry as to Norton's Case at Martha's Vine Yard. Mr. Gore [5] informs me that you have forwarded to him a Pardon for Lincoln & others. I presume from these Circumstances that by some Means these Transactions have escaped your Recollection. The Papers when I last saw them you took out of a File in your own Room in the Office. If however they are mislaid I will get them made out again & send them on, for If I can relieve a Moments Attention of a Mind perhaps almost overplied with public Energies believe me Sir I not only think it the Duty of a Friend to his Country but I shall receive Pleasure from doing it. I am with Sentiments of the most perfect Esteem & Respect

Your most obedt. Servt   J Lowell

ALS, Hamilton Papers, Library of Congress
  1. Lowell was United States judge for the District of Massachusetts.
  2. Letter not found.
  3. At the September, 1790, term of the District Court of Massachusetts Elijah Norton had submitted a petition for remission of forfeiture of "sundry goods" which had been seized for infractions of the revenue laws by John Pease, collector of customs at Edgartown, Massachusetts. The case was continued on the court dockets until it was dismissed during the March, 1795, term for failure of the claimant to appear (Massachusetts Circuit Court Records, Federal Records Center, Boston).
  4. Letter not found.
  5. Christopher Gore was United States attorney for the District of Massachusetts.

From Jeremiah Olney

Providence, July 12, 1792. Transmits "Accounts and Returns for the last Quarter" and "a Receipt of the Cashier of the Providence

Bank for 1,000 Dollars, which I have charged to the United States."
States: "your circular Letter of the 25th of June, I have recd., and
will attend to the contents. . . ."

ADfS, Rhode Island Historical Society, Providence.

From Benjamin Walker

New York July 12. 1792

Dear Sir

You will oblige me in giving the necessary directions for permit-
ting me to transfer on the Power of Atty from Colonel Smith.[1]

I will thank you also for your advice what steps are best to
pursue to save something out of the 50,000 dollars of the Manufacty
Society committed to Dehurst.[2] He remitted Macombs [3] bills to his
Correspondent Mr. Hill.[4] Mr. Hill pledged these bills for money
taken up in London. The bills are not accepted but they lay over
and eventually there is every prospect that they will be paid. Mr.
King [5] to whom the Pilot boat was sent acquainted Phyn & Ellice [6]
on whom the bills are drawn, that they belonged to the Society
and desired them not to pay them. Such is their situation at present
and I think something may be done—the money borrowed on the
bills by Hill is not perhaps half the Amount. Payment of the bills
can be refused in honour. They then will come back and have
Claim on Macombs Estate—or Smith may compound for them
there by paying the money borrowed on them. You had better see
Dewhurst who is in Philadelphia [7]—he can tell more exactly the
state of the Affair. No time should be lost in doing something.

Notwithstanding you told us at Newark that the Coasting fees
were to be taken on the first Construction [8]—& that we were intitled to pay for the three bonds under the New Law [9]—the Collector [10] will not comply till he receives a Letter from you on the
subject. It is no object to him who receives so much—but to my
small pittance every little addition is of Consequence.

I am Dr. Sir   Very sincerely your most Obed Servt Ben Walker

Willett & Wilcocks fired a Shot yesterday Evening without execution.[11]

A. Hamilton Esqr.

ALS, Hamilton Papers, Library of Congress.

1. William S. Smith, the son-in-law of John Adams, had left New York in the spring of 1792 and arrived in England at the end of April. During his absence Walker had assumed responsibility for Smith's financial affairs in the United States.

2. For information on the fifty thousand dollars which the Society for Establishing Useful Manufactures had entrusted to John Dewhurst, see Nicholas Low to H, April 10, 1792.

3. Alexander Macomb, a New York speculator and a director of the Society for Establishing Useful Manufactures, was imprisoned for debt in April, 1792.

4. See Nicholas Low to H, April 10, 1792.

5. Joseph King was the Liverpool agent for the Society for Establishing Useful Manufactures.

6. James Phyn, Alexander Ellice, and John Inglis were partners of the London firm of Phyn, Ellice, and Inglis in 1792. Before the American Revolution, as Phyn and Ellice, the firm had worked with William Duer and Alexander Macomb in connection with projects for provisioning the western posts and prosecuting the fur trade; after the Revolution William Constable had taken over the firm's New York business.

7. Dewhurst had moved to Philadelphia in order to take advantage of the Pennsylvania bankruptcy law. On June 7, 1792, a commission of bankrupt was issued against him in Philadelphia.

8. Walker is referring to the controversy regarding the "construction" of various sections of "An Act for Registering and Clearing Vessels, Regulating the Coasting Trade, and for other purposes" (1 *Stat.* 55–65 [September 1, 1789]). See "Treasury Department Circular to the Collectors of the Customs," July 22, 1792.

9. Section 8 of "An Act for raising a farther sum of money for the protection of the frontiers and for other purposes therein mentioned" provided that the term of credit for the payment of duties on all articles except wines, teas, and produce of the West Indies imported after June 30, 1792, should be payable "one half in six, one quarter in nine, and the other quarter in twelve calendar months from the time of each respective importation" (1 *Stat.* 260–61 [May 2, 1792]).

"An Act to provide more effectually for the collection of the duties imposed by law on goods, wares and merchandise imported into the United States, and on the tonnage of ships or vessels," which had made earlier provision for the collection of duties, stipulated that duties on such imports should be paid in full within six months (1 *Stat.* 168 [August 4, 1790]).

10. John Lamb was collector of customs at New York City.

11. Following an argument in a tavern about the disputed New York gubernatorial election of 1792, Marinus Willett, a Clinton supporter, challenged William Willcocks, a Jay supporter, to a duel.

From Oliver Wolcott, Junior

T. D.

C. Off July 12. 1792

Sir,

It is my opinion that compensations for the services of the Clerks of the Circuit Courts in making records & issuing Certificates for the pensions of Invalids are fully provided for, by the third section of the Act intittled "an Act for regulating processes in the Courts of the United States and providing compensations for the Officers of the said Courts & for Jurors & Witness" [1] and that Certificates from the Courts of the sums which shall be adjudged to be due for such services, will authorize the admission thereof at the Treasury.

It is also my opinion that Mr. Ellery [2] may be authorized to procure a press for the seals of the Circuit & District Courts, and that his account for the expence thereof, may be paid out of the fund appropriated for defraying the Contingent Expences of Government, pursuant to the resolution of Congress passed on the 2nd. of August 1790. [3]

I have the honor to be &c

The honble
Alex Hamilton Esqr

ADf, Connecticut Historical Society, Hartford.
    1. Section 3 of this act reads in part as follows: "*And be it further enacted,* That from and after the passing this act, the fees and compensations to the several officers and other persons hereafter mentioned, shall be as follows; . . . To the clerk of the supreme court of the United States, ten dollars per day for his attendance in court, and for his other services in discharging the duties of his office, double the fees of the clerk of the supreme court of that state in which the supreme court of the United States shall be holden. To the clerk of the district and circuit courts such fees in each state respectively as are allowed in the supreme courts of the same; and five dollars per day for his attendance on any circuit or district court, and at the rate of ten cents per mile for his expenses and time in traveling from the place of his abode to either of the said courts. And in case any clerk of a court of the United States shall in discharging the duties of his office perform any kind of service which is not performed by the clerks of the courts of the state, and for which the laws of the state make no allowance, the court in which service shall be rendered may allow a reasonable compensation therefor . . ." (1 *Stat.* 276–77 [May 8, 1792]).
    2. Edmund T. Ellery was clerk of the district court of Rhode Island.
    3. This resolution reads as follows: "Resolved *by the Senate and House of Representatives of the United States of America in Congress assembled,* That the expense of procuring seals for the supreme, circuit, and district courts of the United States, shall be defrayed out of the money appropriated, by an act of the present session, for defraying the contingent charges of government" (1 *Stat.* 187).

From Sharp Delany

[*Philadelphia, July 13, 1792*. On July 26, 1792, Hamilton wrote to Delany: "I have considered the case represented in your letter of the 13. instant." *Letter not found.*]

To Sharp Delany

Treasury Department, July 13, 1792. "I have desired eleven Hydrometers to be sent to Your Office, which I request you will please to forward by water to the Collectors of the several ports. . . ."

LS, from the original in the New York State Library, Albany.

To William Gardner [1]

[Philadelphia, July 13, 1792]

I duly received your letter of the 24th ult.[2] and it gives me pleasure to learn that your determination is in favor of a continuance in office.

[New York] *Argus*, July 31, 1798.
 1. Gardner was commissioner of loans for New Hampshire. For background to this letter, see H to Gardner, June 14, 1792.
 2. Letter not found.

From Thomas Jefferson

Philadelphia, July 13, 1792. "Permit me to request the favor of you to cause a warrant to be issued on the Treasurer of the United States payable to George Taylor Junior[1] to the amount of five hundred and twenty dollars for defraying the contingent expences of the Department of State."

Letterpress copy, Thomas Jefferson Papers, Library of Congress; LC, Papers of the Continental Congress, National Archives.
 1. Taylor was chief clerk of the Department of State.

Meeting of the Commissioners of the Sinking Fund

[Philadelphia, July 13, 1792]

At a meeting of the trustees of the sinking fund, July 13, 1792.

Present: The Secretary of State, the Secretary of the Treasury, and the Attorney General.

The Secretary of the Treasury having informed the Board, that there were, at the disposal of the Board, pursuant to the 7th section of the act, entitled "An act supplementary to the act making provision for the debt of the United States"[1] forty thousand four hundred and fifty-one dollars fifty-one cents and four mills, arising from dividends of interest on the public debt, heretofore purchased, under the authority of the Board:

Resolved, That the interest on so much of the debt of the United States as has been purchased, or redeemed for or by the United States, and as may have been paid into the Treasury thereof, in satisfaction of any debt or demand, and the surplus of any sum or sums appropriated for the payment of interest upon the said debt, which may have remained after paying such interest, be applied, within the time limited for that purpose, to the purchase of the several kinds of stock, at the lowest prices for which they can be obtained, if not exceeding the respective rates authorized by a resolution of the Board, of the ———— day of last ————.[2]

That Samuel Meredith, Treasurer, be the agent for making the said purchases.

That they be made by receiving sealed proposals for any sums which parties offering shall incline to sell, preferring the lowest offers, with regard, as far as may be, to the purchasing of equal proportions of the several kinds of stock; and that the said agent, forthwith, advertise to receive such proposals until the 28th day of July, instant, inclusively.[3]

ASP, Finance, I, 237.

1. Section 7 of this act reads as follows: "And whereas it is expedient to establish a fund for the gradual reduction of the public debt: *Be it further enacted,* That the interest on so much of the debt of the United States, as has been or shall be purchased or redeemed for or by the United States, or as shall be paid into the treasury thereof in satisfaction of any debt or demand,

and the surplus of any sum or sums appropriated for the payment of the interest upon the said debt, which shall remain after paying such interest, shall be, and hereby are appropriated and pledged firmly and inviolably for and to the purchase and redemption of the said debt, to be applied under the direction of the President of the Senate, the Chief Justice, the Secretary of State, the Secretary of the Treasury and the Attorney General for the time being, or any three of them, with the approbation of the President of the United States, for the time being, in manner following, that is to say: First, to the purchase of the several species of stock constituting the debt of the United States, at their respective market prices, not exceeding the par or true value thereof, and as nearly as may be, in equal proportions, until the annual amount of the said funds, together with any other provisions which may be made by law, shall be equal to two per centum of the whole amount of the outstanding funded stock bearing a present interest of six per centum. Thenceforth, secondly, to the redemption of the said last mentioned stock, according to the right for that purpose reserved to the United States, until the whole amount thereof shall have been redeemed. And lastly, after such redemption, to the purchase, at its market price, of any other stock consisting of the debt of the United States, which may then remain unredeemed: and such purchase, as far as the fund shall at any time extend, shall be made within thirty days next after each day, on which a quarterly payment of interest on the debt of the United States shall become due, and shall be made by a known agent, to be named by the said commissioners" (1 *Stat.* 283 [May 8, 1792]).

2. Dashes in this sentence indicate places left blank in the original.

3. Section 8 of the act provided: "That all future purchases of public debt on account of the United States, shall be made at the lowest price, at which the same can be obtained by open purchase, or by receiving sealed proposals, to be opened in the presence of the commissioners, or persons authorized by them to make purchases, and the persons making such proposals" (1 *Stat.* 283).

To Thomas Jefferson

Philadelphia July 14th. 1792

Sir,

There are two funds out of which the expense you mention [1] may be defrayed, one a sum originally of 10,000 Dollars, placed under the disposition of the President to defray the Contingent charges of government [2]—another a sum of 5,000 Dollars appropriated at the last Session to satisfy demands liquidated and admitted at the Treasury for which there was no special appropriation.[3] In this Case the accounts for the seals must be presented to the Treasury for settlement. Some arrangement in one way or other can and will be made, if you procure the seals.

I have the honor to be &c.   A. Hamilton

The Secretary of State

Copy, RG 217, Miscellaneous Treasury Accounts, 1790–1894, Account No. 3299, National Archives.

1. See Jefferson to H, July 12, 1792.

2. Section 3 of "An Act making appropriations for the support of government for the year one thousand seven hundred and ninety" reads as follows: "*And be it further enacted,* That the President of the United States be authorized to draw from the treasury a sum not exceeding ten thousand dollars, for the purpose of defraying the contingent charges of government, to be paid out of the monies arising as aforesaid from the duties on imports and tonnage; and that he cause a regular statement and account of such expenditures to be laid before Congress at the end of the year" (1 *Stat.* 105 [March 26, 1790]).

3. Section 1 of "An Act making certain appropriations therein specified" provided in part as follows: "That there be granted and appropriated . . . For the discharge of such demands against the United States, not otherwise provided for, as shall have been ascertained and admitted, in due course of settlement at the treasury, and which are of a nature, according to the usage thereof, to require payment in specie, five thousand dollars" (1 *Stat.* 284–85 [May 8, 1792]).

From Giuseppe Ceracchi [1]

Amsterdam 16 juliet, 1792

Je l'honneur de vous parteciper mon heureux arrivee en Europe en parfaitte Sante. De tout cotè on me fait des recherches empresseè sur le Monument National. On ne peù pas ce persuader du succes si peu favorable, car on L'envisage comme un objet qui doivent interesser une Nationne Trionfante de satisfaire la juste embition pour Celebrer l'Epoque de sa Gloire.

Quant a moi pour me consoler en partie de la mauvaise Campagne je me rendrois a Rome le plus tot, ou J'aurois la satisfaction d'enfoncer mon Ciseau dans le marbre pour en developper quelque Hero de l'Amerique, c'est pour cela mon cher Monsieur, qu'il me retarde de recevoir la *terre* que jeu la satisfaction de former d'aprez votre spirituelle et significante Fisionomie; [2] je ne dirois pas d'avantage, crainte d offancer la delicatesse de là Personne que j'estime le plus et qui pourra m anoncer lè chaimin pour franchir la marche de la glorieuse posteriteè.

Je rapell que en quittent Philadephie Vous etiez d'avis Monsieur que je devois vous envoyer un plan des depances qu exigeroit là Monument en question ainsi que le voici.

Pour ce donner une idee de la grandeur de L'objet, il faut s'immaginer un gruppe en Sculpture de *60* pieds dèlevation dont lè

subbasement en occupent *700* de circonference. Que cet Gruppe
est composee de *11* Statues Colossals de la proportion de *15* pied,
6. Statues de demi caracter, une Aigle un Lup et plusieurs autres
ornements, lè tout en marbre Statuair, onsuitte la Statue Equestre
de L'Héro en bronce, erigeè sur un vaste piedistall; qui couronnent
lè gruppe, et un subbasement en marbre coloreè qui donnerà soli-
dite et accorde au total.

Le Bloc de marbre pour chacque Statue de *15.* quil faut le con-
siderer de 16-6 puces avec la plante; mesure 300 pieds cubes, ainsi
que pour le *11.* Statues, avec le *6.* de demi caracter il ne faudrà pas
moin que *3.300* pieds cubes de marbre Statuaire, valuè pour le moin
deu. Ginee por pied a cause de la grandeur de mafis somme.

Le depances de la main deuvre deu fois autent	7600
pour lè vaste subbasement de marbre coulor.	15200
radier et autres ornement	3000
Pour les etudes Monter et quaisser &&	3000
Pour le modelle de la statue Equestre, un jet de Cire; un	
Autre en Bronce, operation tres serieuse	21200
Ginee	50000

Pour cette somme je m'obligerois de L'execution et depances pour
cet ovrage payable en *10.* portionnes annuelles comme jai projettè
au commancement.

Au reste Monsieur conoissent Votre Ame elèveé, et liberal fait
pour consevoir la Magnificence du Projet, je me repromet de pouvoir fixer por votre moyen une reputation distinguee c'est le seul
profit que je me reserve et que j'enbitionne.

Monsieur J'ai l'honneur d'etre Vtr trs Humb Serv J Ceracchi

ALS, Hamilton Papers, Library of Congress.
    1. Ceracchi was a Roman sculptor. For background to this letter, see H to
Richard Harison, March 7, 1792.
    2. Although Congress on May 7, 1792, had rejected Ceracchi's plans for a
monument, Ceracchi had already executed busts of George Washington,
Thomas Jefferson, H, and several other prominent Americans. These busts,
designed with the understanding that they were for the artist's own use, were
actually sent to the respective subjects together with bills for the sculptor's
work. A note in H's "Cash Book" for the seventeen-nineties states that six
hundred and twenty dollars was paid on March 3, 1796, and reads as follows:
"for this sum through *delicacy* paid upon cherachi's draft for making my
bust on his own importunity & as a favour to him" (AD, Hamilton Papers,
Library of Congress).

From William Ellery

[*Newport, Rhode Island*] *July 16, 1792.* "I have recd. your letter
of the 25 of June last,[1] advising me that my accounts as Superintendant of the Light house on James Town Island from the 13th.
of Sept. to 31st. of Decr. 1791 have been adjusted at the Treasy. and
that there is stated to be due from the United States to me the Sum
of Seven hundred and thirty seven dollars & fifty three and one half
cents. . . . On inspecting my accounts of Expenditures as Super-
intendt. of the Light house I find that I had in the time abovementioned expended Seven hundred and forty seven dollars and
four and one half Cents. to which sum a common~ of one per
centum, and a common~ on the amount of the one per centum
being added the result is Seven hundred and fifty four dolls. and
fifty eight and one half cents. . . . This appearing to be the case
I cannot with propriety acknowledge a debt adjusted as my due
the 31st of Decr. 1791. by giving a receipt therefor, when I conceive it to be short of what was then due to me. I have therefore
transmitted two receipts of the same tenour and date, one of them
to your Office, and the other to the Treasurer[2] for the Sum of
Seven hundred fifty four dollars and fifty eight one half cents. . . .
If I am right please to pass this sum to my credit in the settlement
to the 31st of Decr. last. If wrong I wish to be put right. . . ."

LC, Newport Historical Society, Newport, Rhode Island.
  1. Letter not found.
  2. Samuel Meredith.

From William Ellery

[*Newport, Rhode Island*] *July 16, 1792.* "I have recd. your Circular of the 25th. of June and another letter of the 2nd. of July
last,[1] to which a due regard will be paid. . . ."

LC, Newport Historical Society, Newport, Rhode Island.
  1. Letter not found.

To Charles Lee

Treasury Department
July 16 1792

Sir

I have this day decided upon the case of Thomas Triplett.[1] I could not consider the excuse which was alleged as a sufficient cause to induce a total remission. The interest of the United States is remitted to him, and he is to pay fifty Dollars for the benefit of persons, other than the United States. [That is to say there is a total remission on paying fifty Dollars & reasonable Costs & charges to be assessed by the Judge.] [2] A duplicate of my decision is sent to the Clerk of the District Court, at Richmond.[3]

A decision on the case of William Wilson and Company [4] will be made directly I receive some additional information from the District Judge, to whom I have applied for this purpose.

I am, Sir, with consideration,   Your Obedt Servant   A Hamilton

Charles Lee Esqr.
Alexandria

LS, RG 56, Letters to and from the Collector at Alexandria, National Archives; LC, Letters to Collectors at Small Ports, "Set G," National Archives.

1. Triplett, master of the brig *Betsey*, had petitioned for a remission of forfeiture on the ground that command of the *Betsey* was the first he had obtained in some time and that he was therefore ignorant of regulations concerning the importation of foreign goods (Records of the District Court of Virginia, Archives Division, Virginia State Library, Richmond).

2. Cyrus Griffin was judge of the District Court of Virginia. The sentence within brackets, which was inserted at the bottom of the page, is in the handwriting of H.

3. William Marshall was clerk of the District Court.

4. William Wilson and Company, an Alexandria mercantile firm, was part owner of goods brought into the District of Alexandria in the sloop *Rainbow*. In a petition for remission of forfeiture the firm stated that, although duties had been paid at Philadelphia, Isaac Mackie, the master, had failed to put the certificate with the goods. H remitted the forfeiture on Wilson's brandy and claret on September 24, 1792 (Records of the District Court of Virginia, Archives Division, Virginia State Library, Richmond).

From Jeremiah Olney

Custom House
District of Providence 16 July 1792.

Sir

Messrs Clarke and Nightingale are about Exporting a Quantity of Brandy to Cape Francois—imported into this district in the Ship Lark in May last from Bourdeaux—and have applyed to me for information. Wheather said Brandy may not on Return of the Vessel be relanded here, (in case it cannot be Sold to advantage in the Cape) Free of duty and the Exportation Bond Cancelled without a Breach of Law, no fraud being intended; or, if they shall be Subject to pay the duties on relanding it, whether they will not be entitled to receive the Draw Back of the first duties when it becomes due, and on Producing a Certificate that said Brandy had been actually landed and delivered at the Cape their Bond shall not be cancelled? But as the 62 Section of the Collection law[1] & 55 Section of the Excise Act[2] seems so pointed against relanding any Goods Wares or Merchandize, intended for Exportation, with intent to draw back the duties, or to obtain any allowance given by law on the Exportation thereof, I have thought it my duty to decline giving them a Definitive answer, untill I should be favoured with your opinnion Relative to the Case.

I enclose my genl. Return of Exports for the last Quarter, amounting to 95,844 Dolls. and 3 Cents.

I have the Honor to be &c.   Jereh. Olney Collr.

Alexr. Hamilton Esqr.
Secretary of the Treasury.

ADfS, Rhode Island Historical Society, Providence.
1. For a similar problem which Olney had encountered with the Providence merchant and trading firm of John Clark and Joseph Nightingale under Section 60 of "An Act to provide more effectually for the collection of the duties imposed by law on goods, wares and merchandise imported into the United States, and on the tonnage of ships or vessels" (1 Stat. 145–78 [August 4, 1790]), see Olney to H, December 29, 1791, and H to Olney, January 8, 1792. Olney is mistaken; he is actually referring to Section 60 of this act.
2. Section 55 of "An Act repealing, after the last day of June next, the

duties heretofore laid upon Distilled Spirits imported from abroad, and laying others in their stead; and also upon Spirits distilled within the United States, and for appropriating the same" provided that spirits shipped for exportation would be subject to forfeiture if relanded, except under necessity, distress, or a change of course while still within four leagues of the coast of the United States (1 *Stat.* 212 [March 3, 1791]).

To George Washington

Philadelphia July 16. 1792.

Sir,

I have the honor to enclose a Resolution of the Commissioners of the Sinking Fund of the 16th. inst:,[1] for your consideration and approbation.

My absence from Town[2] and hurry after my return, prevented the making of the arrangement before you left this place.[3] I shall hope to receive your determination previous to the day which limits the receiving of proposals, as the purchases must be made within the month. Nothing else new has occurred since your departure.

With perfect respect & the truest attachment, I have the honor to be &c. A. Hamilton

LC, George Washington Papers, Library of Congress.

1. See "Meeting of the Commissioners of the Sinking Fund," July 13, 1792. The proceedings were transmitted to Washington in the following form:

"The Secretary of the Treasury having informed the Board that there are, at their disposal, certain sums of money, arising from the funds assigned by law:

"*Resolved,* That the said sums of money be applied within the time limited by law, to the purchase of the several kinds of stock, at the lowest prices, pursuant to the directions of the law, and according to the rates prescribed in the last resolution of this Board, concerning such purchases.

"*Resolved,* That Samuel Meredith, Treasurer of the United States, be the agent for the foregoing purpose; that he receive sealed proposals to any amount; that he prefer the lowest offers; that he have regard, as far as may be, to the purchasing of equal proportions of the several kinds of stock; and that he advertise to receive proposals until the 28th of July, instant, inclusively." (*ASP, Finance,* I, 237.)

2. H had attended a meeting of the directors of the Society for Establishing Useful Manufactures in Newark, New Jersey, from July 4 to July 7, 1792.

3. Washington had left Philadelphia for Mount Vernon on July 11, 1792.

To Wilhem and Jan Willink, Nicholaas and Jacob Van Staphorst, and Nicholas Hubbard [1]

Treasury Department
July 16th. 1792.

Gentlemen,

I have directed the Treasurer of the United States to draw Bills upon you, for five hundred thousand Guilders, at ten days sight, in favor of John Kean Esquire, Cashier of the Bank of the United States, which drafts, I request, may be duly honored, when presented.

I am &c.   Alexander Hamilton

Messrs. Willink, Van Staphorst
& Hubbard.
Amsterdam.

Copy, RG 233, Reports of the Treasury Department, 1792–1793, Vol. III, National Archives. This letter was enclosed in H's "Report on Foreign Loans," February 13, 1793.
1. Willink, Van Staphorst, and Hubbard were the bankers for the United States at Amsterdam.

From John Daves [1]

New Bern [North Carolina] July 17, 1792. "I received yours dated June 21st and in obedience thereto have made inquiry for proper Persons to fill the second & third Mates birth of the Revenue Cutter of this State. For the second mates birth I beg leave to recommend James Sandy of this Town, being a sober man a good seamen a good Pilot. . . . Capt: Cooke [2] of the Cutter begs leave to recommend his son William Harrison Cooke, for the third Mates birth. . . ."

Copy, RG 56, Letters from the Collector at New Bern, National Archives.
1. Daves was collector of customs at New Bern.
2. William Cooke.

To William Seton [1]

Philadelphia
July 17. 1792

My Dear Sr

I find on examination that I have drawn out of the Bank of New York more money than I intended. It was my intention to keep there about 100 000 Dollars but I will contrive ere long to replace; and in the mean time I wish you to understand [2] that if any ballance in favour of the Branch should at any time *press you unduly* I will upon notice come to your aid as far as my deposits there will permit. I do not however believe that this will be necessary as I have full evidence that a good disposition towards you will continue to be cultivated.

A Mr. Greene of your City [3] has solicited my interposition to prevent if possible a suit being brought against him, which it seems is committed to the agency of Mr. Pollock,[4] and which if brought will as he represents be ruinous to him. I answered him at first that any interference of mine would be very delicate that I was not intimate enough with Mr. Pollock to take such a liberty with him, and that I should imagine it would be fruitless if I did, as he would probably be bound down by instructions. The distress with which he was menaced made him urgent and my good nature at length gave way so far as to induce me to promise that I would write on the subject to some friend of mine who was an acquaintance of Mr. Pollock. In compliance with this promise I shall now trouble you with a few words on the subject of Mr Greene.

This Gentleman some time since imported from the British East Indies to Rhode Island a large quantity of goods, for which he regularly paid the duties at the place of Exportation and which he afterwards shipped to Ostend where they were sold to certain persons whose names I have forgotten. These persons having afterwards gone to England, Mr. Greene brought a suit against them there and was non suited upon the strength of a British Statute— which annuls the contracts of all British subjects who trade to

India without license from the East India Company.[5] The sum in question was upwards of 40 000 Sterling.

Such is the representation of Mr. Greene and if true his case is certainly unfortunate.[6]

This representation has been made to the Government here & has been committed to our Minister to the Court of Great Britain to examine fully into it and to endeavour to obtain redress for Mr. Greene.[7]

The actual toleration of the Trade by the local Government would amount in good faith to a license from the Company and ought, *as it now appears,* to have secured Mr. Greene from the penalties of the Act.

In this situation he thinks it hard to be pursued by British Creditors in this Country.

The little knowlege I have of Mr. Greene makes me uncertain what degree of credit is due to his representation. Not admitting it to be literally accurate could I wish to say or do any thing which if it were in my power might divert Mr. Pollock from any measures which the security of his friends or propriety of conduct as an Agent may dictate. I wish him only through you to be apprised of the state of things as it regards the interposition of this Government, with this observation that Mr. Greens presence in England will probably be of consequence to the prosecution of his affair, by enabling him to furnish all the requisite evidence in the progress of the discussion. How far this may make it the interest of Mr. Pollock's principal, that a suit, which would detain him here, should not be commenced, he will best judge.

You can be at no loss My Dear Sir to appreciate my situation in this affair and you will have the goodness to move in it in such a manner as will commit me & embarrass others as little as possible.

You see I do not scruple to burthen you even with the consequences of my weaknesses. I rely on your friendship & obliging disposition.

Truly Yrs   A Hamilton

Wm. Seton Esqr

ALS, Bank of New York, New York City.
    1. Seton was cashier of the Bank of New York.

2. In MS, "unsterdand."

3. In May, 1786, the Rhode Island General Assembly passed an act for naturalizing William Green (Greene), a "native of Great Britain, and a subject of his Brittannic Majesty" (*Records of Rhode Island*, X, 197). Green, who had come to the United States in 1784, was a merchant who traded with the Far East. Some time after his arrival in the United States he moved to New York City.

4. George Pollock, a New York merchant.

5. H is presumably referring to 21 Geo. III, C. 65 (1781). In the margin opposite this sentence H wrote: "Mr. Greene became a Citizen of the UStates since the Revolution."

6. In a letter to George Hammond on May 29, 1792, Thomas Jefferson wrote: "A judge of the King's bench lately declared, in the case of Greene, an American citizen, *v.* Buchanan and Charnock, British subjects, that a citizen of the United States, who had delivered 43,000*l* sterling worth of East India goods to a British subject at Ostend, receiving only 18,000*l* in part payment, is not entitled to maintain an action for the balance in a court of Great Britain, though his debtor is found there, is in custody of the court, and acknowledges the fact" (*ASP, Foreign Relations*, I, 212). John Buchanan and Company and Robert Charnock and Company were Ostend mercantile firms.

7. On June 11, 1792, Jefferson wrote to Thomas Pinckney, United States Minister to Great Britain: "Mr. Green of Rhode Island will deliver you his papers, and I am to desire that you may patronize his claims so far as shall be just and right, leaving to himself and his agent to follow up the minute details of solicitation, and coming forward yourself only when there shall be proper occasion for you to do so in the name of your Nation" (LC, RG 59, Diplomatic and Consular Instructions of the Department of State, 1791–1801, National Archives). Six months later Jefferson wrote to Pinckney that Green "purposes to go to England to conduct his claim himself" (LC, RG 59, Diplomatic and Consular Instructions of the Department of State, 1791–1801, National Archives).

Receipt from William Pearce

[Philadelphia, July 18, 1792]

Received Philadelphia July 18. 1792 of Alexander Hamilton Two hundred & fifty Dollars on account of the Society for establishing useful manufactures.   Wm Pearce

D, in the handwriting of H and signed by Pearce, Hamilton Papers, Library of Congress.

To Wilhem and Jan Willink, Nicholaas and Jacob Van Staphorst, and Nicholas Hubbard

[*Philadelphia, July 18, 1792.* A "List of papers received from the files of the Office of the House of Representatives, for the use of the Committee appointed to enquire into the State of the Treasury department"[1] dated April 8, 1794, refers to "Copy of letters from the Secretary of the Treasury, to Wilhem, Willink &c. relating to the application of the monies arising from the loans—of the respective dates following to wit . . . July 18th," 1792. *Letter not found.*]

1. Copy, RG 233, Papers of the Select Committee Appointed to Examine the Treasury Department, Third Congress, National Archives.

To Jeremiah Olney

[*Philadelphia, July 19, 1792.* On July 27, 1792, Olney wrote to Hamilton: "I have recd. your Letter of the 19th Inst." *Letter not found.*]

To Otho H. Williams [1]

Treasury department, 19 July 1792

Sir

It was with real reluctance and regret that I found myself, as I conceived, in a situation, not only to be justified but constrained to use a stile of expostulation in my letter of the 28th. of last month.[2] It is my earnest wish that the public business committed to my superintendance may proceed with harmony and cordiallity between myself & those united with me in the execution of it. And I may truely add that my impression of you have always been of a nature to give force to that sentiment in a case, in which you were concerned. But I thought and still think, that the affair, which is the subject of this correspondence warranted dissatisfaction on my part. And as far as there may have been an expression of it, I do not fear that it can be a matter of surprize, to any one whose sensibility is not too much alarmed to leave the judgment impartial.

Let the circumstances be reviewed.

Copy, Maryland Historical Society, Baltimore.
  1. Williams was collector of customs at Baltimore.
  2. This is a mistake. H meant to refer to his letter of June 18, 1792, to which Williams had replied on June 28.

The Legislature pass an Act introducting a new branch of the Revenue, involving among other things the appointment of a new sett of Officers.[3] They are aware that the new provision will have to encounter objections and obstacles; and that among other topics of objection the multiplication of Officers and the expence of Collection are likely to be urged. Towards obviating both, they indicate their sense, that it may be expedient to call in the aid of the Officers of the customs, in the execution of the law.

The expence of executing this new system being untried is unknown. Difficulties are found to attend a previous legislative speculation of the proper compensations and allowances. It is therefore made the duty of the executive to regulate that detail, under a limitation as to the totality of the expence to be incured.[4]

The executive, in concerting the necessary arrangements for carrying the law into effect, finds itself urged to avail itself of the aid contemplated by the legislature, not only by the same considerations which influenced them, and by respect for the intimation in the law on that head, but by a conviction, upon examination, that the restriction as to expence rendered such an expedient indispensable, from the impossibility of compensating a sufficient number of *distinct* officers.

The President therefore, in his general arrangement concludes to appoint—the Collectors of the Customs, at ports where there are no Surveyors, and the Surveyors at Ports where those Officers are established—*Inspectors of the Revenue* for the respective ports; charging them with the performance of services which though originating under the new system are *immediately connected with the revenue of the Customs*, which were before entrusted to their care and management.

The Secretary of the Treasury, in the details, connected with and resulting from the general plan, designates another description of Officers of the Customs, namely the Inspectors, as assistance to those who had previously been appointed by the President.

And relying on the efficacy of this resource, no other is pointed

3. This is a reference to "An Act repealing, after the last day of June next, the duties heretofore laid upon Distilled Spirits imported from abroad, and laying others in their stead; and also upon Spirits distilled within the United States, and for appropriating the same" (1 *Stat.* 199–214 [March 3, 1791]).
4. See H to Williams, June 18, 1792, note 6.

out, by which the Inspectors of the Revenue for ports can procure the requisite assistance for fulfilling the law. The instructions[5] respecting the whole matter are transmitted to all the Collectors of the Customs, and their co-operation is desired.

I mentioned in my former letter,[6] as a motive to this arrangement, that there was no danger of an interferance of duties. In this you differ from me. Let facts decide.

The duties of a Surveyor of the Customs by the 6th. Section of the Collection law[7] are "to *superintend* and *direct* the *Inspectors,* measurers, and guagers within his district, to visit and inspect the ships and vessels which arrive within his district, with power to put on board *one* or *more inspectors,* to ascertain the proof of distilled Spirits, to examine whether goods imported in any ship or vessel and the deliveries thereof are conformable to the *entries* of such goods and the permits for landing the same" and he is placed under the Controul of the Collector.

The duties of the Inspector of the Revenue for a port under the Act in question[8] and the inspections concerning it are—1st to receive the reports of Masters of vessels having on board distilled spirits brought from foreign ports, 2d. to receive from owners, importers and consignees, entries of such Spirits after they have been previously certified by the Collector of the Customs and to inspect record and indorse the permits granted by them. 3rdly to *superintend the landing of Spirits, cause the Casks and vessels containing them to be marked* and to *Issue the requisite certificates to accompany them* 4—to certify the quantities and particulars of distilled Spirits entered and landed at one port in cases in which a part of those imported in a vessel are intended to be delivered at another port. 5th—to superintend the shipment of distilled spirits intended to be exported in order to their being entitled to the benefit of drawbacks.

On comparing the particulars of the duties of these two offices it

5. H is referring to instructions enclosed in "Treasury Department Circular to the Collectors of the Customs," May 26, 1791.

6. H to Williams, June 18, 1792.

7. "An Act to provide more effectually for the collection of the duties imposed by law on goods, wares and merchandise imported into the United States, and on the tonnage of ships or vessels" (1 *Stat.* 145–78 [August 4, 1790]).

8. These duties are given in several sections of the act of March 3, 1791.

will be seen, that they are either substantially the same or closely allied to each other, and that they would be more naturally performed by the same than by different persons.

If the law had in the first instance annexed the duties of an Inspector of the Revenue for a Port to those of the Surveyor of a Port (which perhaps would have been a desirable course) no doubt could have been entertained of their perfect congruity. Their being united by an executive arrangement cannot, in this respect, vary the effect.

Responsibility to different superiors,[9] is the only circumstance which can give colour to suppose the possibility of collusion. But the duties in the two Cases are so much *parts* of a *whole* that it would be no easy matter to make them clash, even by design; and if so improper a design could appear, there are not wanting means of repressing it.

The union therefore of the Offices of Surveyor and Inspector of the revenue, for a part, clearly does not naturally involve any interference of duties.

It remains to see if that of Inspector of the Customs and deputy inspector of the Revenue for a port is chargeable with any greater degree of incompatibility.[10]

As Inspector of the Customs, the person who bears that Office, is by the Collection law put under the *immediate* direction of the *Surveyor*. As deputy Inspector of the Revenue he is under the immediate direction of *the same person* in the capacity of *Inspector of the Revenue*. Here the responsibility to the same superior, in both capacities is found to second the analogy of duties.

As Inspector of the Customs his duties are not specifically defined by law—he is to be employed generally *in aid of the Customs*, and by the day, upon a compensation not exceeding a dollar and a quarter ℔ day. But from certain intimations in the law, and from

---

9. When a surveyor also held the office of inspector of the revenue, he was, in his capacity as surveyor, responsible to the collector of the customs and, as inspector, to the supervisor of the revenue.

10. The act of March 3, 1791, imposing duties on distilled spirits and prescribing regulations for their collection, authorized the President to designate officers of the customs as inspectors of the revenue. Inspectors of the customs in Baltimore had accordingly been made deputy inspectors of the revenue. Williams had objected to this arrangement in his letter to H of June 28, 1792.

practice, the prominent features of his duty consists in aiding the
Surveyor in the *inspection of vessels* and in *overseeing the landing
of goods.* I say in aiding the Surveyor, because it is expressly declared, that the Surveyor shall *superintend* and *direct* him and shall
have power to put on board of each Vessel one or more *Inspectors.*

As deputy Inspector of the Revenue, under the arrangement
which has been adopted, he is to assist the same Surveyor in the
capacity of Inspector of the Revenue, in *overseeing the landing of
certain goods,* with the additional circumstance of marking the
Casks and packages containing them, when landed, and of *delivering*
descriptive certificates to accompany them.

This additional circumstance may be regarded as a natural appendage of the principal service to be performed, and in most cases
may be executed without difficulty by the same person.

If on particular occasion, through any extraordinary press of
business, some embarrassment might be experienced, the remedy as
I mentioned in my former letter would be a special and temporary
appointment of additional Inspectors, an expedient in the discretion
and power of the Collector, and the use of which in certain cases
is contemplated by the collection law itself, which expressly authorizes the Surveyor to put on board a vessel, *one* or *more* inspectors.

To this you made two objections. First, that men selected for
their integrity and abilities might be diverted from the business of
the Customs, by a department over which you had no controul, to
execute that of the revenue, leaving you to supply their places by
unworthy or ignorant persons picked up in a hurry. Secondly—
That it might expose those whom you had selected to perform
certain duties to less compensation, in performing others, than they
would be entitled to for performing those to which they had been
appointed, or perhaps to no compensation at all.

The answer to the first objection is plainly this. The officers in
question in the capacity of deputy Inspectors of the Revenue have
no services to perform, but such as are in *substance,* however they
may be in form, *exclusively relative to the Customs;* They have no
concern with any but imported articles, the duties upon which are
paid to and received by the Collector of the Customs only; and the
direct object of the services they are to perform is the *security* of

that branch of the revenue. They have nothing to do with the in-land duties. They are therefore in fact, though not in Name, auxiliary officers of the Customs. The criterian, upon this occasion, must be that the services to be performed are relative to duties on *imported articles*, which duties are *payable* to officers of the Customs. And it has been shewn that the services to be performed in both cases are either the same or coincident. Nothing therefore like a neglect of the service of the Customs was involved in the arrangement, on the contrary it tended to second and promote that service.

It may be further answered that you would alway have a right to say to the Inspector of the Revenue, who as Surveyor is under your controul "The established Inspectors being at this time too much occupied otherwise to perform the additional services of marking &c, you are for the present to employ for these purposes *occasional* Inspectors, whom I will appoint to assist you." It would become his duty in such case to Conform and the inconvenience to which you allude might be avoided.

To the second objection it may be answered—That the compensation from the course prescribed, would rest with yourself, within the limit of a dollar and a quarter per day since the persons employed would be to be compensated as Inspectors of the Customs.

What you remark by anticipation in opposition to this is I conceive easily obviated. If a particular form from the Treasury, from an imperfect view of the law in the first instance, confined the compensation of Inspectors to cases of attendance on board of vessels, the error was by your own shewing rectified on further consideration, and the sense of the law was admitted to be that compensation would follow any services rendered by the Inspectors *in aid of the Customs*.

But you observe that it was "impossible for you to conceive the propriety, *even if it might be admitted at the Treasury*, of charging the *Customs* with expences incidental to the *Revenue*."

But when it is observed, as is truely the case, that these expences are incidental to the *Customs* and not to the *Revenue* as distinguished from them, in other words "the inland duties" it cannot be very difficult to conceive the propriety of the charge, which likewise, it was to have been presumed from the arrangement adopted by the head of the department would have been admitted at the

Treasury. And it surely would have been perfectly safe and intirely in order, to have left the responsibility for a wrong construction in such a case where the law has placed it, namely with the Treasury. I might perhaps have contented myself on this point of the interferance of duties with refering to your own words in your letter of the 3d. of May last to the Surveyor [11]—in which you admit that the duties of the two offices though distinct are "practicable by the same persons."

From the question of interference, I return to the review of the cause of the transaction, which is the subject in discussion.

The arrangement adopted and notified from the Department of the Treasury, is carried into general execution, without objection or complaint, though in some instances representations are prefered of the considerable addition, which is made to the duties of the Officers of the Customs, and of the reasonableness of some further compensation; which are of necessity refered to future consideration, when greater latitude in the article of expence should be allowed by the Legislature; an event which took place last session of Congress,[12] and the effects of which have been heretofore suspended, only by the requisite preliminary inquiries and investigations.

A question arises in your district, as to the obligation of the Inspectors of the Customs to perform the additional services required of them. Not a syllable of this is communicated to the Treasury. No opportunity is offered of reconsidering the arrangement—none of providing, by a new instruction to the Officers of the Revenue, a substitute for the expected co-operation of the Inspectors of the Customs in cases of refusal, if such refusal were justifiable.

On an application from those Officers to you—you write to the Surveyor enjoining him to avoid as much as possible demanding of the Inspectors of the Customs services which may interfere with their particular duties as such, and especially *such as they are unwilling to undertake*—declaring your opinion that they are not

11. Robert Ballard. See H to Williams, June 18, 1792.
12. This is a reference to Section 16 of "An Act concerning the Duties on Spirits distilled within the United States" (1 *Stat.* 267–71 [May 8, 1792]). For this section, see Ballard to H, May 31, 1792.

bound to officiate in the capacities of deputy Inspectors and that their services must be *voluntary*.

You state, that in fact you gave no answer at all to the representation of the Inspectors. The Surveyor however States, that the opinion given to him, in the above mentioned letter *was also given* to the Inspectors, and that in *consequence* of it, they refused to mark. It would be improper for me now to decide which of these two apparently contradictory statements is the most accurate—but with one only before it was natural I should suppose it correct, especially when I adverted to the Result.

The Surveyor further states, that your deputy "*took pains* to induce the Inspectors not to mark."

From a disposition the reverse of unconciliating, I was disposed to suppress these unpleasant particulars. But the turn which your letter has given to the thing appears to me to render it necessary they should now be brought to view.

The issue of the whole affair is, as stated by the Surveyor—that the Inspectors refuse to mark—that he in consequence is compelled to have the Spirits, which are landed Stored, without it, 'till from courtesy and a disposition to oblige him, he is able to prevail upon two or three Inspectors to perform the services at their leisure— that the *Merchants complain,* and talk of protesting against the officers—that some of the Inspectors go so far as not only to refuse to mark, but to declare that they "will not examine to see if spirits when landed are accompanied with the proper certificates."

I appeal to your own candour and good sense. Was all this as it ought to have been? Was not the public service embarrassed? Were not the wheels of administration so far clogged? Was no example of disorder given? Had I no causes to feel dissatisfied or pained at such a scene? Could I consistently with what was due to my official situation, or the public service, forbear to expostulate?

I proceed to take notice of some particulars in your letter.

You express your surprize that what has occured shd. have been represented to me "as a controversy between the officers respecting the limits of duty." In your letter of the 3d. of May to the Surveyor you state that it has been intimated to you that "*a misunderstanding* subsisted *between* the *Surveyor* and the *Inspectors of the Customs* for the port of Baltimore respecting the duty of the latter, when

deputed by the Inspector of the Revenue to aid the execution of
the duties of the latter office." I regard this misunderstanding as a
controversy between the officers concerned respecting the limits of
duty—and this was all that was meant by the observation

You ask whether you could have apprehended that the business
of the *Customs* was to have been retarded by that of the *Revenue;*
or that if additional aid was necessary it was material to the Government by which department it was procured? and you add, that
there were *officers enough* in one department and it never occured
to you that it was your duty to create more, in order to supply
the other, in which the power of creation is by law made adequate
to its occasions.

The first of these questions have been already answered. The
service to be performed was in every substanial sense, the business
of the Customs, and there were means in your power to forward
all the parts of it without suffering any part to be retarded by
another. But could you imagine, if additional aid was necessary, it
was material, by which department it was procured? The instructions, which had been given on the subject, were imparted to you,
and the only agents, which these contemplated for the services in
question, were the Inspectors of the Customs. No pecuniary provision was made to enable the Officers of Inspection to procure
additional aid by exercising their power of creation. It was natural
therefore to suppose, that if necessary it was to be procured through
the same means from which the aid in ordinary cases was to be
derived. Oeconomy recommended the main expedient; uniformity
the auxiliry one.

I am satisfied, from your assertion, that the expedient did not
occur to you; but if the difficulty, which appeared to you in the
case, had been suggested to me, an explanation would have obviated
the necessity of embarrasment. I wish this had been done.

If there were existing *officers enough* in the Revenue department,
to answer the purposes, it is unknown to me.

You say that you feel not a little from my suggestion that the
Inspectors' not performing the duties required of them whether
legally obligatory on them or not would be a good reason to substitute others.

I can see no cause to retract that opinion—nor am I unwilling to submit to the severest examination the idea, that there are causes in which a non compliance with official requisitions of superior authority, reasonable in themselves, forming a part of a general arrangement, dictated by particular circumstances, and productive of material convenience to the public service, though not strictly within the compass of the duties legally annexed to an office—would betray a disposition so unaccommodating and improper as to justify the substituting of persons better disposed.

I meet without hesitation the allusion you make to the case of the Surveyor. If he had refused to accept and execute the Office of Inspector of the Revenue, I have no doubt that the chief Magistrate would have been justifiable in seeking and substituting some other person, who would have been willing (in conformity to a general arrangement deemed by him eligible for the public service and even intimated as expedient by the Legislature) to act in the double capacity of Surveyor and Supervisor of the Revenue. Nor do I perceive how it can be doubted, as long as it is admitted that the public good ought to be the guide in the exercise of legal discretion; and that there is a discretion in the chief Magistrate to substitute a person willing to fulfil the legal and reasonable intentions of Government, to one who is not so disposed.

This doctrine too is such an one, as I do not feel myself degraded by supposing equally applicable to the Secretary of the Treasury with any other officer in the department; and I shall flatter myself, that I have competent ideas of my Official and personal dignity.

But while I adhere to the principle, I am sensible, that, like every other, it is capable of being abused, but the right or the ill use of it must in this, as in every other case, depend on the circumstances.

You remark on the respectability of the Charactors, who at present fill the offices of Inspectors. I had too much confidence in your care and judgment to doubt that so respectable a trust would be confided to respectable men. But I acknowledge that I can see nothing derogatory in the services, which are expected from them, as deputy Inspectors of the Revenue. If they have been made so, by the manner of executing them, it ought to be corrected, and I shall readily co-operate in any manner for that end, which upon a knowledge of facts shall appear to be requisite.

Upon the concluding passages of your letter, I shall make no other remark, than that you seem to have made there, as in one or two other instances, a more personal application, than was intended by me, of some observations merely general and argumentative.

In thus fully develloping the view I have taken of the subject I have been influenced by a wish at least to prevent a final difference of opinion between us. If this wish does not succeed, I shall regret it—but having acted upon mature reflection, according to the best light of my judgment and with no feelings whatever, of which I am conscious, to misguide it, it will be a matter of course, on my part to persevere in the expectations I have signified, as far as the complete execution of the arrangement which has been made, may require.

With consideration and esteem I remain, Sir Your obedient Servant

From Timothy Pickering [1]

Boston July 20. 1792.

Sir,

I have just read a passage in your circular letter of June 25th to the Collectors of the Customs, putting on the 12th section of the Post-Office-Law [2] a construction which I conceive to be erroneous & which will materially injure the revenue of the department. I recollect your dropping the same idea transiently when I last saw you. I then searched for but overlooked the clause which showed that *coasting* vessels as well as those *from abroad* were obliged to deliver their letters at the Post-Office. That clause is in the 10th section. 'Tis the last half of the section, in which "every letter or packet brought into the U. States, *or carried from one port therein to another by sea,* in any private ship or vessel" is charged with "four cents" of which (by the 13th section) two are to be paid to the master. The charge for such letters being thus prescribed, the 12th section provides the means of *compelling* their delivery at the post offices, by forbidding the Custom House Officers to admit such vessels "to report, make entry or break bulk," till the master or commander shall have delivered his letter to the postmaster. The only doubt on my mind respected the meaning of the phrase "by sea." Some gentlemen at Providence thought that letters going in the packets between that place and Newport, were not within meaning of the act. I asked them what they would call the water between those two places: They answered "only an arm of the sea." Then, I remarked it is *a part of the sea*, & within the meaning of the act. Letters passing by the packets between Providence or Newport and New York are in the same predicament; & it must be quite immaterial whether those packets sail on the south or north side of Long Island.

Your not seeing the clause I have now pointed out in the 10th section respecting letters brought by coasting vessels, has led to the construction which so evidently appears erroneous and which therefore I beg you as early as possible to correct.

ADf, Massachusetts Historical Society, Boston.
1. Pickering was appointed Postmaster General in August, 1791.
2. Pickering is referring to "An Act to establish the Post-Office and Post Roads within the United States" (1 *Stat.* 232–39 [February 20, 1792]). For Section 12, see "Treasury Department Circular to the Collectors of the Customs," June 25, 1792, note 4.

Treasury Department Circular to the Collectors of the Customs

Treasury Department,
July 20, 1792.

Sir,

It is with great satisfaction I have it in my power to acknowledge the zeal and good disposition, with which the Officers of the Customs generally have executed the instructions which have, from time to time, proceeded from the Treasury Department. I am happy to be able to say, that the instances of exception are few, and I ascribe such as have happened rather to an inaccurate view of the subject than to improper intention.

LS, Rhode Island Historical Society, Providence; LS, RG 36, Collector of Customs at Boston, Letters from the Treasury, 1789–1807, Vol. 4, National Archives; LS, MS Division, New York Public Library; LS, Office of the Secretary, United States Treasury Department; LC, Essex Institute, Salem, Massachusetts; copy, United States Finance Miscellany, Treasury Circulars, Library of Congress; copy, Circulars of the Office of the Secretary, "Set T," National Archives.

But as a few instances exist of deliberate deviations from instructions, and as explanations, in one or two cases, disclose opinions which in practice would be subversive of uniformity in the execution of the laws, it becomes advisable to state the ideas, which are entertained at the Treasury respecting the nature of the power of the head of the department "to superintend the Collection of the Revenue," and the obligation incident to it on the part of the Officers immediately charged with that Collection.

This will be done, to obviate, as far as possible, misconceptions, which may not only disturb the course of public business, but may lead to disagreeable discussions, and even, perhaps, to painful altercations.

It is my earnest wish to cultivate harmonious and cordial co-operation; and it is essential to this, that correct opinions should be mutually entertained. If those I shall express are liable to objections, I shall be glad they may be freely made, and I promise maturely and candidly to consider the force of them.

The Act constituting the Treasury Department,[1] expressly makes it the duty of the head of the Department "to superintend the Collection of the Revenue."

The power of *superintending* the Collection of the Revenue, as incident to the duty of doing it, comprises, in my opinion, among a variety of particulars, not necessary to be specified, the right of *settling*, for the Government of the Officers employed in the Collection of the several branches of the Revenue, the *construction* of the laws relating to the Revenue, in all cases of doubt.

This right is fairly implied in the force of the terms, "to superintend," and is essential to uniformity and system in the execution of the laws.

It is evident that without it the most incongruous practices upon the same laws might obtain in different districts of the United States —according to the different portions of intelligence and attention of different Officers, and according to the different mediums through which objects are often seen, even with equal degrees of intelligence and attention.

Merchants might have to pay higher duties at one port, than at

1. H is referring to Section 2 of "An Act to establish the Treasury Department" (1 *Stat.* 65–66 [September 2, 1789]).

another, upon the same articles; higher fees at one port than at another for the same services; and might otherwise be subjected to very dissimilar burthens and requisitions. Such a state of things would undoubtedly be a state of disorder; inconsistent with every idea of a well regulated government, and would have a natural tendency to produce discontent and disgust among individuals, and to bring upon the laws contempt and odium.

It is true that a remedy, in a large proportion of the cases, might be obtained from the Courts of Justice; but the vexatious course of tedious law suits to decide whether the practice of one Officer, or of another, was the most legal, would be a mode of redress very unsatisfactory to suffering parties—and very ill suited, as an ordinary expedient, to the exigencies and convenience of Trade.

A reference has been made to the Oath of Office, prescribed by the first Collection law [2] for the Officers of the Customs.

They are by that law severally required to swear or affirm, that they will execute and perform all the duties of their respective Offices *according to law;* whence it seems to have been inferred, that they are bound each to pursue *his own opinion of the meaning of the law.*

But it is conceived that an Officer of the Customs executes his duty, according to law, when, in the cases mentioned, he conforms his conduct to the construction, which is given to the law, by that Officer, who, by law, is constituted the general Superintendant of the Collection of the Revenue. The power to superintend must imply a right to judge and direct, of course an obligation to observe the directions which are given, on the part of those, to whom they are addressed. The observance of them therefore cannot be contrary to the engagement of an Officer to execute the duties of his Office according to law; because, as a general principle, it is a part of his duty, enjoined by the law, to pursue those directions; and because of course the responsibility for a wrong construction rests with the head of the department, when it proceeds from him.

It is not possible to conceive how an Officer can *superintend* the

---

2. This is a reference to "An Act to regulate the Collection of the Duties imposed by law on the tonnage of ships or vessels, and on goods, wares and merchandises imported into the United States" (1 *Stat.* 29–49 [July 31, 1789]). The oath is prescribed in Section 8.

execution of a law, for the collection of a tax or duty, or for any other purpose, unless he is competent to the interpretation of the law, or in other words, has a right to judge of its meaning. If then that competency and right are attached to the head of the Treasury Department, as general Superintendant of the Collection of the Revenue, it must follow that his judgments are directory to those, who are merely Superintendants within *particular spheres,* as the Collectors of the Customs, within their respective districts. For it is an universal principle of jurisprudence, and a clear dictate of reason, that authorities within *particular spheres,* are subordinate to a general authority relating to the same subject, and pervading *the whole of them.*

I am aware of the reasonable limitations to which the general principle is subject; as restrictions, in the nature of things, upon abuses of authority, applying as well to the operation of laws as of instructions relating to their execution. But the admission of exceptions in extraordinary cases, does not militate against the general rule.

With regard to the oath,* which is prescribed to the Officers of the Customs, it is to be observed that it is equally prescribed to all of them, from the Collector down to the Inspector of the Customs. It is easy to discern the confusion which would result from the principle, that each of these Officers is bound, by his Oath, to pursue his own construction of the law, though contrary to that of his official Superior.

Two instances shall be mentioned, for the sake of illustration, in which the binding force of instructions from this department has been either questioned, or, in practice, denied.

One relates to the duty on Spikes. The Acts of the first and second session, which impose duties on imported articles,[4] lay a duty

---

* In the new Collection law,[3] the words "according to law" are omitted, which is barely mentioned to shew that the Legislature laid no stress upon them.

3. This is a reference to "An Act to provide more effectually for the collection of the duties imposed by law on goods, wares and merchandise imported into the United States, and on the tonnage of ships or vessels" (1 *Stat.* 145–78 [August 4, 1790]).

4. "An Act for laying a Duty on Goods, Wares, and Merchandises imported into the United States" (1 *Stat.* 24–27 [July 4, 1789]) and "An Act making further provision for the payment of the debts of the United States" (1 *Stat.* 180–82 [August 10, 1790]).

of one cent per pound on "*nails* and *spikes*," expressly naming each, and thereby implying that the one was not included in the other. In the Act of the last Session, "for raising a further sum of money for the protection of the frontiers, and for other purposes therein mentioned," [5] Nails are rated at two cents per pound, and nothing is said about Spikes.

The construction upon this at the Treasury, and which has been signified by the Comptroller,[6] is, that the duty on spikes remains as before, and that the duty on nails only is varied; the reasons of which construction are, that the Legislature named spikes, in one instance, and did not name them in the other, and though there is a duty of ten per centum ad valorem on manufactures of iron generally; yet it is with the exception of those *otherwise particularly enumerated;* which expressions not being confined to the Act, in which they are used, by the usual word *herein*, or any word of similar import, naturally extend to enumerations in any prior Act, as well as to those in that in which they are used. Consequently spikes being among the enumerated articles, in the previously existing law, were considered as excepted, and as continuing under the same duty as before. The last Act does not alter the duties generally, but merely on such articles as are therein enumerated and described.

A doubt has nevertheless been communicated, not only as to the justness of this construction, but whether an Officer who doubts is, in such a case, at liberty, from the tenor of his Oath, to comply with it.

The other case alluded to, relates to the question of fees under the Coasting Act.[7] The instructions which were given on this head,[8] though punctually observed in most of the districts, have been materially departed from in some of them.

The first being a case, relating merely to the *quantum* of revenue, is certainly one in which the opinion of the Officer at the head of the finances of the United States ought to be conclusive.

5. 1 *Stat.* 259–63 (May 2, 1792).
6. Oliver Wolcott, Jr.
7. "An Act for Registering and Clearing Vessels, Regulating the Coasting Trade, and for other purposes" (1 *Stat.* 55–65 [September 1, 1789]). For a discussion of this question, see "Treasury Department Circular to the Collectors of the Customs," July 22, 1792.
8. See "Treasury Department Circular to the Collectors of the Customs," November 30, 1789.

The second being a question between the pecuniary rights of the Officers, and the pecuniary obligations of the Citizens, in a point in which their contentment or dissatisfaction with the laws, and the interest and convenience of a most precious branch of Commerce, the Coasting Trade, were materially concerned—it is conceived that the opinion of the Officer who, by law, is charged with the general superintendance of the Collection of the Revenue, ought to have prevailed.

These examples are mentioned to shew to those Officers, whose practice has been undeviatingly conformable to the general principle which has been inculcated—that the assertion of it has been called for by instances of departure from it: And the foregoing observations are addressed circularly, rather than to the individual Officers, whose practice in those instances has rendered them necessary, for three reasons—1. That as misconceptions have taken place in some instances, it is possible that similar misconceptions may happen in others, and it is wished to anticipate and prevent them, from an ardent desire to avoid sources of misunderstanding as well as occasions of interruption to the due course of the public business —2. From the possibility that deviations may have happened in more instances than are known at the Treasury—and 3. From a wish to pursue the most delicate mode of animadversion. But while I am desirous, on public principles, of establishing what I suppose to be correct views of the just and necessary authority of this Department, I trust that nothing I have said will tend to discourage freedom of observation on any instruction which may issue from it. I shall constantly think myself indebted to any Officer who shall give me an opportunity of revising an opinion, with the aid of his remarks, which may appear to him not consonant with law, with his own rights, or with the good of the service. To every communication of this sort I have always paid, and shall always pay careful attention. And as often as I can be convinced of an error, I shall, with chearfulness, acknowledge and retract it.

With great consideration, I am, Sir, your obedient Servant,

A Hamilton

To Benjamin Walker [1]

Philadelphia July 20th. 1792

My Dear Walker

The power being legally competent to the purposes desired, I have instructed the Comptroller [2] to give the needful direction to The Commissioner of Loans. [3]

But in friendship to you, I cannot suppress some jealousies which are afloat and which have run before your application as if to prevent a compliance with it. You know the late events with regard to Duer Macombe [4] &c have awakened much suspicion and you will not be surprised, if some portion of it should have lighted upon you.

It is insinuated that there is danger the latitude desired by you upon the strength of your power may be made use of to change the present state of the security of the Creditors of Duer & Macombe.

To this I have answered—1 that if Col Walker should turn out to be a man not strictly and delicately honest I should begin to suspect myself 2 That as your power was legally competent I should run more risk of censure in obstructing its operation, should any ill consequences attend the obstruction than I should do, by giving it a free course, though not agreeable to official forms prescribed for inferior officers in ordinary cases.

But you see my friend; from all this, that unusual circumspection is necessary on your part; and that you must be cautious not to make a change of property under circumstances that can even be tortured into an imputation on your Integrity.

I do not perceive what in the present state of things can be done with Dewhurst. [5] I have myself conversed with him and I understand him as promising to do every thing in his power to indemnify the Society for any loss they may sustain in consequence of a diversion of their funds to the benefit of his English Creditors.

But what says Mr. McComb? If the bills return (the others being paid) ought his other Creditors to derive an accidental benefit to the prejudice of the Society by a dividend of a fund specif[ic]ally pledged to secure the ultimate payment of those bills? According to my present opinion this will be a thing to be contested. Yrs. truly

A Hamilton

B Walker Esquire

ALS, Columbia University Libraries.
1. For background to this letter, see Walker to H, July 12, 1792.
2. Oliver Wolcott, Jr.
3. John Cochran was commissioner of loans for New York.
4. William Duer and Alexander Macomb were the most notorious New York City speculators to fail during the panic of 1792.
5. John Dewhurst. See Walker to H, July 12, 1792.

To William Ellery

[*Philadelphia, July 21, 1792.* On August 6, 1792, Ellery wrote to Hamilton: "I have recd. your . . . letters of the 21. 25. & 26 of the last month." *Letter of July 21 not found.*]

From William Lewis [1]

July 21st 1792

Sir,

The Answers given by me to the several Questions [2] proposed for my opinion relative to the late Election of Governor of the State of New York were as follow:

1   "That RS [3] was on the last Tuesday of April 1792 and at the time he Sealed and Signed the Box Sheriff of the County of Otsego."

2   "That if he was not Sheriff, yet the Canvassers can, According to the terms of the Law & their Oath canvass the votes sent by him" on its being made appear that they are those that were given in at the Election, nor do I perceive the least ground for supposing that the validity of the Election at all depends on the question of his being Sheriff or not.

3   "That the receipt of the votes by the Secretary is not conclusive as to their being returned by the proper officer."

4   "That RS neglecting to put the votes of the Town of Cherry Vally into the Box containing the other ballots & rendering

them in a paper Bundle as is above Set forth will not prevent the Exa⟨mination of the⟩ votes of the sd. County." [4]

5th   "That RS neglecting as Stated to put the votes of the Town of Cherry Vally into the Box &c can *at most* only destroy those votes;" and if no fraud appears, and it can be Satisfactorily proved that the paper Bundle contains the votes as they were actually given in with out addition or diminution I can perceive no good reason agt. their being received & Canvassed.

I have not a Copy of the Case which was sent to me but so much of the Answers as are within inverted Comma's, are (with the addition of an affirmative or negative) in the very words of the Question proposed.

My opinion in Answer to the first question was principally founded on the following Cases—4th Bac: ab. 434 & 444.5.[5] 16th. Vin ⟨ab.⟩ 114.[6] 19 Vin ab: 451.[7] Moore reps. 186. 364.[8] Dyer 355.[9] 2 Com: Dig: 581.[10] 3 B. Par Cases 167.[11] 1 Stra 625.[12] 10 Mod 147.[13] To form a Judgt. of the applicability of such of these Cases as relate to Sheriffs the Stats. of 14th Edw. 3d. Stat. 1 C 7 and 23rd Hen 6th Cap 7th. must be Compared with the Constitution & Laws of New york—also vide Dougl 382.[14]

On the third Question there seems to be no room for Doubt, but that Mr. Clintons friends were right.

My opinion on the 2nd 4th. & 5th. Questions was founded on this Principle, that the important right of Suffrage being Secured to the People by the Laws and Constitution, and not depending on the Conduct of others, they cannot be deprived of it but by their own fault. That the manner of taking, & more especially of transmitting the votes, *being merely directory*, an Error or wilful neglect or disobedience in the officer in either of these particulars, will Subject him to punishment for a misdemeanor in office, but will not affect the Election or destroy the rights of the people, where no fraud or unfairness appears in the Conducting of the Election, and it is made Satisfactorily appear that the votes are the same that were given in witht. alteration Diminution or addition. That this principle applies with great force, where (as in the present Case) the Sheriff was not an Election Officer, nor a Person having anything to do with holding the Election, and where the Election itself is the Substance and the transmitting of the votes is only form. If this were not the Case any Sheriff might at pleasure deprive a whole County of the right of Suffrage! I know of no Case expressly in point, but there are many in the books the Principles of which I think are fully applicable. I am obliged to set off to Court but if you wish to have a note of them I can very soon furnish you with it. A resignation by Mr. Smith without an acceptance thereof & notice being given, or the appointm't of a nothing being made known, I consider as amounting to nothing, *since he had once accepted & a resignation did not therefore depend on himself alone.* If the Law or Constitution of New york disqualifies a Sheriff from holding any other office, its operation is to create an ineligibility to such other office, but not ⟨—⟩ that of Sheriff.

I am My dear Sir   very truly yours   W. Lewis

Ps   when I return from Court I will send you the answers by the Judges. of the Sup: Court of Penna. to some Questions sent to them by the Legislature touching a Contested Election.[15]

Hon'ble Mr. Hamilton

ALS, Hamilton Papers, Library of Congress.

1. On July 21, 1791, Lewis, a Pennsylvania attorney, was appointed judge of the Federal District Court for the Eastern District of Pennsylvania. In April, 1792, he resigned as judge to return to private practice.

For background to this letter, see Philip Schuyler to H, May 9, 1792, note 4; H to John Adams, June 25, 1792, note 2; H to Rufus King, June 28, 1792; King to H, July 10, 1792.

2. Lewis is recapitulating the opinion which he had submitted to the committee of canvassers on May 25, 1792, regarding the legality of canvassing the votes of Otsego, Clinton, and Tioga counties in the disputed 1792 New York gubernatorial election. Lewis is answering only those questions concerning Otsego County, which were similar to those submitted to Rufus King and Aaron Burr. For these questions, see H to King, June 28, 1792, note 2. The committee's decision was made public on June 12, 1792. Other legal opinions both supporting and criticizing the committee's decision continued to be collected and published during the summer and fall of 1792. The questions submitted to Lewis and Lewis's opinion were printed in a pamphlet published in the late fall of 1792 (*An Appendix to the Impartial Statement of the Controversy Respecting the Decision of the Late Committee of Canvassers* [New-York: Printed by Childs and Swaine, 1792]).

3. Richard R. Smith, sheriff of Otsego County. See H to King, June 28, 1792, note 2.

4. Dissatisfied with the officers elected to conduct the registration of voters, a minority of the voters of Cherry Valley prepared a second registration list and handed their votes to the sheriff of Otsego County after the earlier votes had been received. The sheriff sent the second package of votes in a separate

package "to the end that the canvasser or other persons might determine whether they were ballots legally taken or not" (*The* [New York] *Daily Advertiser*, June 2, 18, 1792).

5. *A New Abridgment of the Law. By Matthew Bacon, Of the Middle Temple, Esq; The Fifth Edition, Corrected; with Many Additional Notes and References of and to Modern Determinations* (Dublin, 1786), IV, 434, 444–45.

6. *A General Abridgment of Law and Equity Alphabetically digested under proper Titles with Notes and References to the Whole. By Charles Viner, Esq.* (London, 1742), XVI, 114.

7. *A General Abridgment of Law and Equity, Alphabetically digested under proper Titles; with Notes and References to the Whole. By Charles Viner, Esq.* (London, 1744), REP-STE [Vol. 19], 451.

8. *Cases Collect & Report Per Sir Fra. Moore Chevalier, Serjeant del ley. Imprimé & Publié per l'Original jadis remenant en les maines de Sir Gefrey Palmer Chevalier & Bar. Attoney-Général à son Très-Excellent Majesty le Roy Charles Le Second. Le Second Edition* (London, 1688), 186, 364.

9. *Cy ensuont ascun nouel Cases, Collectes per le iades tresreuerend Iudge, Mounsieur Iasques Dyer, chiefe Iustice del Common Banke. Ore nouelment publies & imprimies* (London, 1601), 354.

10. *A Digest of the Laws of England. By the Right Honourable Sir John Comyns, Knight; Late Lord Chief Baron of His Majesty's Court of Exchequer. Continued down to the present Time, By a Gentleman of the Inner Temple* (London, 1780), II, 581

11. *Reports of Cases upon Appeals and Writs of Error, in the High Court of Parliament; From the Year 1701, to the Year 1779. With Tables, Notes, and References, By Josiah Brown, Esq. Barrister at Law* (Dublin, 1784), III, 167.

12. *Reports of Adjudged Cases in the Courts of Chancery, King's Bench, Common Pleas and Exchequer, From Trinity Term in the Second Year of King George I. To Trinity Term in the Twenty-first Year of King George II. Taken and Collected by the Right Honourable Sir John Strange, Knt. Late Master of the Rolls. in Two Volumes. Published by his Son John Strange, of the Middle Temple, Esq.* (London, 1781), I, 625.

13. *Modern Reports: or, Cases in Law and Equity, Chiefly During the Time the late Earl of Macclesfield presided in the Courts of King's Bench and Chancery, viz. from the Eighth of Queen Anne, to the Eleventh of King George the First inclusive. By Robert Lucas of the Inner Temple, Esq.* (London, 1769), X, 147.

14. *Reports of Cases Argued and Determined in the Court of King's Bench; in the Nineteenth, Twentieth, and Twenty-first Years of the Reign of George III. By Sylvester Douglas, Esq. of Lincoln's Inn* (London, 1783), 382.

15. Lewis is referring to the 1781 election in Philadelphia County of John Bayard to the supreme executive council of the Pennsylvania legislature. Like the New York gubernatorial election of 1792, this election was contested on a technicality. The council requested the opinion of the Pennsylvania Supreme Court, and on March 12, 1782, Justices Thomas McKean and George Bryan, on grounds similar to those held by Lewis in 1792, contended that, while the law stated the hour the polls were to open, it was "only directory. . . . An officer may be punishable for a neglect of duty. The people are not to be deprived of Representatives on account of this omission. . . .

"The election ought not to be declared void because some of the Inspectors left their stations before the election was ended. They indeed were offenders, and may be punished for not performing their duty, unless they quit their stations through indisposition or some other good cause.

"If elections were to be set aside for irregularities which do not effect, obviously and materially, the truth of the poll, the craft of the Judges or Inspectors might lead them to contrive such departure from duty, or to commit some irregularity, in order to overturn an election, in case they should dislike the event of it. The rights of the people do not depend upon so precarious a foundation. . . .

"Upon the whole, fraud, force, or undue influence, may in some instances be sufficient reasons for declaring an election void, but no irregularity, excepting such an one as would render it uncertain whether the candidate returned had a majority of the votes of qualified electors, (that being the substantial point,) ought in our opinion, to affect the rights of the representative or represented, especially where they had no share in it; but in such case, the person committing the offence should be duly punished, according to the nature of it. The true distinction is between the public and private wrong, the generality and particularity of the injury." ("Minutes of the Supreme Executive Council of Pennsylvania," *Pennsylvania Colonial Records* [Harrisburg, 1853], XIII, 229–31.)

To Benjamin Lincoln

Philadelphia July 21st 1792

My dear Sir

In the District of Edgartown there is a Harbour called Holmes hole,[1] where the Collector[2] has appointed an Inspector (Ebenr Smith). It is represented to me, that many vessels come to anchor in that harbour, which are destined for other ports, and it is thought expedient to keep a boat there, for the purpose of boarding vessels, receiving manifests, and to transmit them to the ports, to which they are respectively bound. This Kind of Service it is said has been performed by the Inspector.

If you have any Knowledge of the situation of the Place, so as to form a judgement, to what extent the harbour is frequented, I should be glad of your opinion, how far the expence & maintenance of a boat would be compensated by the advantage that could be derived from the nature of the Service;[3] and what kind of boat would suffice.

If you are acquainted with Mr Smith I could also wish to be informed, whether he is a fit character to have the charge of such a Boat.

I am Dear Sir

Benj. Lincoln Esqr

L[S], RG 36, Collector of Customs at Boston, Letters from the Treasury, 1789–1807, Vol. 4, National Archives; LC, RG 56, Letters to Collectors at

Small Ports, "Set G," National Archives; copy, RG 56, Letters to the Collector at Boston, National Archives.

1. Holmes Hole is a harbor in the northeast part of the town of Tisbury on the north side of Martha's Vineyard.

2. John Pease was collector of customs at Edgartown, Massachusetts.

3. The remainder of this sentence is in H's handwriting.

From Jedediah Huntington [1]

[*New London, Connecticut, July 22, 1792.* On July 25, 1792, Hamilton wrote to Huntington: "Your letter of the 22d instant has been received." *Letter not found.*]

1. Huntington was collector of customs at New London, Connecticut.

Treasury Department Circular to the Collectors of the Customs

Treasury Department,
July 22, 1792.

Sir,

When an appeal was made to me, by certain Officers of the Customs, respecting the fees to which they were entitled under the Coasting Act,[1] I took the only method then in my power, to aid my own judgment to a right decision. The Attorney General not being at the seat of Government, I applied to two of the most able Counsel in the city of New-York, (one of whom is the Attorney of the United States for the District) for their opinions.[2] I carefully examined the law, myself; and, agreeing with those Gentlemen in

LS, RG 36, Collector of Customs at Boston, Letters from the Treasury, 1789–1818, Vol. 5, National Archives; LS, Office of the Secretary, United States Treasury Department; LS, MS Division, New York Public Library; LC, Essex Institute, Salem, Massachusetts; LC, RG 56, Circulars of the Office of the Secretary, "Set T," National Archives; LC, United States Finance Miscellany, Treasury Circulars, Library of Congress.

1. "An Act for Registering and Clearing Vessels, Regulating the Coasting Trade, and for other purposes" (1 *Stat.* 55–65 [September 1, 1789]). For the relevant portions of the act, see Edmund Randolph to H, June 21, 1792, notes 4–8.

2. See H to Richard Harison, November 9, 1789, and Harison and Samuel Jones to H, November 18, 1789.

the construction of it, I signified the result in a Circular communication.[3]

It, however, has since appeared that the construction, then adopted, has been deemed by some of the Officers of the Customs so clearly unfounded as, in their opinion, to warrant a departure from the instruction given.[4] And it has also appeared that respectable law opinions were opposed to those of the Gentlemen whom I had consulted.[5]

Had I not been in continual expectation, that a new law would have obviated the difficulty, I should have taken much earlier measures to settle the question in some definitive, and, if possible, satisfactory mode. But session after session having passed, and further delay being still possible (though I confidently reckon on a new Coasting law in the course of the next session) I have thought it incumbent upon me to bring the affair to an issue.

Circumstanced as it was, amidst a diversity of legal opinions, it seemed to be the proper course to consult the Attorney General, who, by law, is the adviser of heads of departments, as to questions of law.

This has been done, and the event is, that his opinion differs from that which was originally adopted, and communicated by me. A copy of his answer to the questions put to him is herewith transmitted.[6]

In this state of a matter, which so directly concerns the interests of the Officers, I think it proper to rescind the instruction heretofore given; though my own view of the subject remains unchanged. Each Officer will then pursue that course, which appears to him conformable to law, to his own interest and safety, and to the good of the service.

Having said that my view of the subject remains unchanged, I think fit to specify more particularly, than I have yet done, the reasons which govern it.

3. See "Treasury Department Circular to the Collectors of the Customs," November 30, 1789.
4. See "Treasury Department Circular to the Collectors of the Customs," August 5, 1791; Otho H. Williams to H, December 12, 1791; and Benjamin Walker to H, July 12, 1792.
5. See William Heth to H, November 20, 1791.
6. H's letter to Randolph of June 2, 1792, has not been found. For Randolph's reply, see Randolph to H, June 21, 1792.

1. It is conceived to be an important general rule (where no principle of public policy calls for a free interpretation) that the subject shall not be taxed or burthened by construction. This rule, I think, will be violated, if the sixty cents is made a *several* compensation for *several* services; because the coupling of the two objects, which are supposed to be distinct services, by the word "and," and the naming of the compensation but once, at the end of the sentence, does, according to the most obvious, literal and grammatical construction, connect the two objects into one service, entitled to one compensation. The particle "for" does not, in my opinion, weaken this conclusion, as it is in such cases a mere expletive, used, or not, according to the ear of the writer. The rule which has been mentioned is particularly necessary to be attended to, in regard to fees of Office, since the experience of all countries has shewn, that latitude, in this particular, is liable to much abuse, to the great vexation and oppression of the citizen.

2. Though it is true that the words "and" and "or" are sometimes considered as synonimous in legal constructions; yet it is generally to answer some purpose, which the law favours, as the giving effect to some general maxim of law, some general rule of property, some general principle of public policy, &c. The constructive extension of fees of Office is presumed not to be of this nature. The very act upon which the present question arises appears anxious to guard against the danger of abuse from this quarter, by annexing penalties to the demanding of any other or greater fees than are allowed. If there had been no case in which the two items concurred as *parts* of one *entire service*, it would have been a good reason for considering them as distinct, though with some violence to literal construction; but as they do so unite in certain cases, it is a strong argument against the separation contended for.

3. It appears to have been the intention of the Legislature to make a separate enumeration of the same or exactly similar services, annexing to each a separate compensation; and avoiding the conjunction of *dissimilar* services, though attended with *equal* compensations, as in the instances of *permits* to land goods of foreign growth or manufacture and *bonds;* for each of which services twenty cents are allowed. The idea of greater affinity between the services in question, as a reason for their union, is not founded. In

the cases, in which they are really distinct, they are as dissimilar as any two operations can be. The circumstance alluded to is said to be a slight one. Alone, it is confessed, it would have no very decisive weight, though it would not be to be disregarded; yet it is of a nature to fortify other considerations.

4. An *Entry* and the *receiving of* and *qualifying* to a Manifest, in all cases under the 27th section, are essentially *one* and the *same act;* to construe them as several in these cases, would be to multiply one act and one service into two acts and two services; and yet it is not perceived, if a several compensation is understood to be annexed to them, as several services, how it should not apply, when they are performed by one person, as well as when they are performed by two persons.

5. The *association* of an entry with the *receiving of* and *qualifying* to manifests in cases arising under the 27th section is a natural one; the two things being coupled, or rather the one thing constituting the other; but the association of the latter, in cases arising under the 25th and 26th sections where outward bound vessels are contemplated, with the entries of inward bound vessels, would be unnatural and incongruous. The entry being the primary and leading idea, the receiving of and qualifying to the manifest, as incidents to it, are naturally mentioned in the same clause; but not so, if they refer to a substantive and independent service, having a different object, and preceding the entry in the order of the transaction.

It has been objected that it would have been tautology to have mentioned the *receiving of* and *qualifying* to manifests, if they did not mean something distinct from the entry under the 27th section, of which they form a part. But there are other entries, those under the 28th section, with which they do not coincide; and the supposition is, that they were meant to describe the entries under the 27th section, and that a compensation for those under the 28th has been, through mistake, omitted.

6. The construction, which makes the services and the compensations several, will operate in many instances oppressively to the citizens engaged in the business. If a vessel takes on board foreign goods of no greater value than 200 dollars, or 400 gallons of ardent spirits, in one district, and delivers them in another, *even* in an adjoining one, she will have to pay—

Cents.

For receiving and qualifying to her manifest in the District from which she departs,   60

For a permit to proceed to the place of destination,   25

For receiving her entry at the port of delivery,   60

For a permit to land,   20

Making altogether   165

Again, if a vessel takes on board a single barrel of flour in one district to be delivered in another, even an adjoining one, where there is a Collector or Surveyor, she will have to pay

For receiving her entry at the port of
   delivery,   60

For receiving and qualifying to her manifest at the
   same port,   60

Making together,   120

In both cases considerably more than the freight of the articles may amount to—and more than, it is conceived, would be a due compensation for the services rendered, and a reasonable burthen on the trade.

An idea, indeed, has been entertained, that though the service be several and entitled to a distinct compensation, it is not so in regard to cases of the last mentioned kind, because the receiving of and qualifying to manifests is there involved in the entry. But this, it is conceived, would be a departure from consistency of construction. If a particular compensation is annexed to a particular service, as *such,* and in the *abstract,* it follows the service, and attaches itself to it, whether performed by the same or by different persons, whether separately or in connection with another service—especially, if the law designates the latter service as contradistinguished from the former. It is to be remembered too, that the entry always carries with it the *receiving* of a Manifest, though not always the *qualifying* to it.

It has been said, that whether the compensation would be excessive or not, is a question merely for the Legislature. But certainly a presumption of the intention of the Legislature, not to burthen the trade, is a circumstance, which ought to serve as a guide in the construction of provisions, which, it must be confessed, are not free from ambiguity. And this presumption in the present case is suggested by the general policy of the Coasting Act, which evidently aims at privileging and protecting the Coasting Trade.

I shall now take notice of some of the arguments which have been used for a construction opposite to that which I adopt, and which have not been already adverted to.

1. It has been observed that it is customary for the fees of entry and clearance to be equal—that this is so by the Collection Law [7] of the United States, and that it is probable the Legislature intended to preserve the same equality in the Coasting Act.

But this equality would not attend the construction, for which it is made an argument.

The true *Clearance* in the Coasting Act is the permit to depart; and for that the fee is expressly twenty five cents. The entry-fee would be in every case sixty cents in cases under the 27th section, if uniformity of principle be preserved, it would be 120 cents. If the receiving and qualifying to the Manifest are taken in connection with the Clearance, then the expence of a Clearance would be 85 cents, that of an entry in some instance 60, in others 120—for by no mode of reasoning can the fee for the permit to depart, which is the real clearance, be excluded from the comparison.

2. It is objected to my construction, that greater services relating to foreign goods are less compensated, than lesser services relating to domestic commodities; which cannot reasonably be presumed to have been the intention of the Legislature.

This is true, and it constitutes an objection of weight, but not a conclusive one. It is not a very uncommon case for the law to be defective in provisions, necessary to fulfil the intentions of the framers of it; and where the main design of the law would not be fulfilled without supplying, by construction, the deficiency of provision, great latitude ought to be taken. But this is not so as to mere collateral points—no way essential to the principal objects of the law. There, omissions may easily be supposed and admitted, and they ought not to be supplied either by any violence to the literal expression, or at the price of more important inconveniences. Where the question is between individual advantage and public mis-

7. "An Act to provide more effectually for the collection of the duties imposed by law on goods, wares and merchandise imported into the United States, and on the tonnage of ships or vessels" (1 *Stat.* 145–78 [August 4, 1790]).

chief; as by forming a precedent liable to abuse, or by throwing an undue burthen on a branch of industry;—no latitude of construction ought to be indulged to attain the former.

It is certain that the Act in question is very inaccurately drawn, and, in many particulars, unprovisional, which is the reason for admitting it to be so in the particular under consideration.

'Tis not the only instance in which entire classes of services are omitted to be compensated. In this predicament are licenses for vessels under twenty tons—the endorsing upon Registers, &c.—memorandums of changes of Masters and giving notice of them—the administering of oaths, generally, and even where they constitute distinct services, as where the Collector of one District takes the oath of an Owner, in order to the registering of a vessel in another District, which is also attended with the additional service of a transmission to the last mentioned Collector—Permits to land goods not of foreign growth and manufacture.

Hence the idea of finding a compensation for each service is a delusive ground of argument, and that of a proportional compensation is not less so. It belongs indeed to neither construction. It has been already seen that an entry, attended with the only additional circumstance of *swearing* the Master of a vessel to his Manifest, would carry double the compensation of an entry without that circumstance.

3. It has been remarked, as repelling the inference to be drawn from omissions in other cases, that in this the service has been mentioned by the Legislature, and as of equal respectability with an entry—and that, therefore, it ought not to be denied a compensation.

In what light it may be conceived to have been mentioned has been stated; as incidents to the entry in certain cases descriptive of it. But it will not follow that when circumstances, which are incidents in particular cases, are mentioned, in immediate connection with the main object, that the specification is intended to extend to other cases, in which they are incidents to a different service, namely, the *certifying* of the duplicate manifest and the *permit to depart*, or the clearance.

Three circumstances operate, in this view of the subject, against the supposition, that the receiving of and qualifying to manifests were intended to be renumerated as *independent* services.

1. They are in no case *such*. They are either pre-requisites to the *certificate* and *permit* directed by the 25 and 26th sections, which are the principal services there, or concomitants of the entry directed by the 27th section.

2. If the specification was intended to refer specially to cases under the 25 and 26th sections, as has been alleged, the expression would naturally have been "for receiving, qualifying to and certifying every manifest."

3. The receiving and qualifying to manifests are constantly incidents to entries and clearances under the Collection Law; and yet they have no distinct renumeration as such. The *qualifying* to any document is, in none of the Revenue laws, a subject of particular compensation, and yet as the *certificate* is not mentioned, and as the *permit to depart* has a distinct fee, there seems to be no other *act* left, to which the fee of 60 cents is to attach itself. Is it probable that the Legislature intended so considerable a recompence for a service in this case, which in every other they have omitted to reward? Certainly, at least, the argument which asserts that those services would not be intended to be performed for nothing, fails. If they are rewarded under the Collection law, in the fee for a Clearance; so may they equally be conceived to be rewarded under the Coasting Act, in the fee for the *permit to depart*, which is there the Clearance also. This fee cannot even be said to be inadequate to the *whole service*, in that case to be performed; the parts of which are the administering an oath, the certifying upon the manifest, which is supposed to be produced by the party "that it had been sworn (or affirmed) to, and delivered according to law," and the granting permit to depart. Some stress has been laid upon the word *every*.[8] I take this to be, as here used, merely calculated to denote the singular number; and to operate distributively only, as to the plural word "vessels" which follows.

I shall barely add, for greater caution, that the instruction which is meant to be rescinded is merely that which relates to the meaning of the following clause: "For every entry of inward Cargo directed to be made in conformity with this Act, and for receiving of and qualifying to every manifest of vessels licensed to trade as aforesaid."

8. See note 1.

With much consideration,   I am, Sir, your obedient Servant,

A Hamilton

P.S. I should think it a better and more equitable construction of the Act than that which considers the two things as several, to reject, as mere surplussage, the words "and for receiving of and qualifying to every manifest of vessels licensed to Trade," [9] annexing no fee to it, in *any case;* but leaving the entry in *every case,* as well on the 28 and 27th sections, to be entitled to a fee of sixty cents.

9. See note 1.

To George Washington

Private   Philadelphia July 22 1792

Sir

I wrote to you on Monday last, transmitting a resolution of the Commissioners of the Sinking fund.[1] Nothing in the way of public business requiring your attention has since occurred.

There is a matter I beg leave to mention to you confidentially in which your interposition, if you deem it adviseable, may have a good effect.

I have long had it at heart that some good system of regulations for the forwarding supplies to the army, issuing them there and accounting for them to the department of wa⟨r should⟩[2] be established. On conversing ⟨with the⟩ Secretary at War, I do not ⟨find⟩ that any such now exists; nor have the intimations I have taken the liberty to give on the subject, though perfectly well received, hitherto produced the desired effect. The utility of the thing does not seem to be as strongly impressed on the mind of the Secy at War as it is on mine.

It has occurred to me that if you should think fit to call by letter upon the Secretary of the Treasury and the Secretary at War to report to you, the *system and regulations under which the procuring issuing and accounting for supplies to the army is conducted,* it would produce what appears to be now wanting. I submit the idea accordingly.

With the most perfect respect & truest attachment I have the honor to be Sir Your most Obed & hum serv   A Hamilton

⟨Presi⟩dent of the U States

ALS, George Washington Papers, Library of Congress; copy, Hamilton Papers, Library of Congress.
1. H to Washington, July 16, 1792.
2. The material within broken brackets has been taken from the copy in the Hamilton Papers, Library of Congress.

Account with John Nixon [1]

Alexander Hamilton Esqr   Philada. July 23rd. 1792

To John Nixon Dr For Rent of 2 Stores (occupied by Mr Pierce) [2] from Sepr. 8th 1791 to this Day, is 10 Months & 15 Days @ 70/ ℔ Month . . . . £ 36..15..0
For Rent of 2 other Stores (also occupied by
him) from Octr 22 1791 to this day, 9 Months
@ 70 / ℔ Month . . . . 31..10..0

£ 68.. 5 0 [3]

D, Hamilton Papers, Library of Congress.
1. Nixon, a Philadelphia merchant, was president of the Bank of North America.
2. William Pearce, an Englishman whom H had employed to work for the Society for Establishing Useful Manufactures, had set up the machines which he had constructed for the society at Philadelphia. His "Manufactory" was inspected by Philadelphia weavers and by George Washington and Thomas Jefferson. Pearce left Philadelphia in July, 1792, with his machines to go to Paterson, New Jersey, the site of the Society for Establishing Useful Manufactures.
3. A receipt in H's handwriting and signed by Samuel R. Franklin is on the back of this document. The receipt reads as follows:
"Received Philadelphia July 25. 1792 of Alexander Hamilton One hundred & fifty Dollars on account of the within. For John Nixon
Saml. R Franklin"

From Sharp Delany

[*Philadelphia, July 23, 1792.* On July 26, 1792, Hamilton wrote to Delany: "I approve of the arrangement proposed in your letter of the 23rd, instant." *Letter not found.*]

From William Seton

New York 23d. July 1792

My Dear sir

I would not give an earlier reply to your favour of the 17th. till I should have seen the Partys you mention. I have had an interview with Mr. Greene & Mr. Pollock, and the latter I think has with great readiness & propriety met your wishes on the subject. (I say wishes because I offered neither interferance or even recommendation on your part). He has consented to stay suit against Mr. Greene for Twelve Months, he giving satisfactory security that if the accounts between them are not adjusted in the meanwhile, he will then be forthcoming to submit to a judiciary process. This has been complied with on the part of Mr. Greene & the business now rests on that footing—which considering everything is a much as could be expected from Mr. Pollock & I hope will meet your approbation, on my part.

With respect to ourselves & the Branch we go on in perfect Harmony, & there does not appear any disposition on their part to do otherwise. They have called upon us this day for 50,000 Dollars in Gold, which Mr. Burrall [1] tells me is to go to Philadelphia, they had 26,000 Dollars in Silver the other day for their own use. We receive & pay their Notes indiscriminately with our own, & I believe they do the same—we make large interchanges now & then. I feel very grateful for the strength of your expressions on this head, & should any Circumstance occur that augurs hostilities, I shall adress my self freely to you—but I trust there will not.

I am with the greatest sincerity   My dear sir   Your Obliged Obdt. Serv   Wm Seton

Alexr. Hamilton Esqr.

ALS, Hamilton Papers, Library of Congress.
1. Jonathan Burrall was cashier of the New York branch of the Bank of the United States.

Treasury Department Circular
to the Collectors of the Customs [1]

Treasury Department,
July 23, 1792.

Sir,

On a revision of the Act concerning the Post Office,[2] I find the construction communicated in my Circular of the 25th ultimo to be erroneous, the 10th section of that Act expressly imposing specific rates of postage, according to circumstances, for every letter or packet carried from *one port* to *another*, in the United States, by sea, not only in packet boats or vessels, the property of, or provided by the United States, but also "in every *private ship or vessel.*" This provision had escaped attention.

A question arises, whether this will require an entry, in any case, in which a vessel was not antecedently bound by law to make entry. I am of opinion that it will not, as there is nothing affirmatively enjoining an entry, in such cases, and it would be too considerable an innovation in the general policy of the laws, to be required by implication.

Yet the Master of every vessel arriving from one port to another, where a Post Office is established, ought, before he "breaks bulk" to deliver the letters, which are directed to be delivered there, in conformity to the 12th section; and so doing, would be entitled to the compensations prescribed by the 13th section. And it is not clear, but that an omission would be punishable by indictment, where the vessel is not subject to an entry. This, however, is a point most fit for the consideration of the Post Masters.

I am, Sir,   Your obedient Servant,   A Hamilton

LS, Rhode Island Historical Society, Providence; LS, Bureau of Customs, Philadelphia; LS, Mr. Albert C. Wilkerson, Richmond; LS, Office of the Secretary, United States Treasury Department; L[S], RG 36, Collector of Customs at Boston, Letters from the Treasury, 1789–1807, Vol. 4, National Archives; LC, Circulars of the Office of the Secretary, "Set T," National Archives; copy, United States Finance Miscellany, Treasury Circulars, Library of Congress.

1. For background to this letter, see Timothy Pickering to H, July 20, 1792.

2. "An Act to establish the Post-Office and Post Roads within the United States" (1 *Stat.* 232–29 [February 20, 1792]).

To Benjamin Walker

Philadelphia July 23
1792

Dr. Walker

Since my last to you [1] it has occurred to me that the concerns of the Society for establishing useful Manufactures, in England, are not in such hands as might be wished, that is such of which there is sufficient knowlege. Would it not be adviseable that some known and responsible character should be written to and requested to take up the affair in concert if you please with King? [2] The endeavour ought to be not to let the bills return protested. It would be far better to agree to pay off the sums for which they are pledged.

I have received a letter from George Parkinson [3] stating that his family is in great distress at New York; or rather stating as you will see in his letter which is enclosed. He is engaged in the service of the Society by articles, the counterpart of which I have mislaid—but I think he is to have £ 80 Stg ⅌ annum. He is a very ingenious mechanic withal.

I wish you to advance for him 100 Dollars. If it cannot be done out of the funds of the Society for want of authority, I will replace it on your signifying to me that such is the case. It will have a bad effect to let the persons employed suffer.

Yrs   A Hamilton

B Walker Esq

ALS, The Huntington Library, San Marino, California.
  1. H to Walker, July 20, 1792.
  2. Joseph King was the Liverpool agent of the Society for Establishing Useful Manufactures.
  3. On December 7, 1791, H had written to the president and directors of the Society for Establishing Useful Manufactures and recommended that Parkinson be hired as "Foreman or Master of a room in the Cotton Mill." Parkinson's letter to H has not been found. See also "Receipt from George Parkinson," May 2, 1792, and H to Walker, May 7, 1792.

From John Wendell [1]

[*Portsmouth, New Hampshire, July 23, 1792.* On August 30, 1792, Hamilton wrote to Wendell: "I have to acknowledge your favor of the 23d of July." *Letter not found.*]

1. Wendell was a Portsmouth merchant.

From William Green [1]

New York.
the 24th July 1792

Sir

I do myself the honor to enclose to you an Abstract of the Acts of the British Parliament respecting their East India Trade to the Year 1760 Inclusive.[2]

Arrangements are under consideration, but not decided on, for my case; with the result of which, I shall make you early acquainted: but by this post; I am desirous only to convey this Abstract with a line that I may not appear negligent. But I think I shall be able to be particular in my communications of tomorrow or thursday. In the interim I beg you to be persuaded of the perfect respect & consideration of

Sir   Your most Obedt. humble Servant   William Green

Alexr. Hamilton Esqr.
&c &c &c

ALS, Hamilton Papers, Library of Congress.
 1. For information on Green, see H to William Seton, July 17, 1792, and Seton to H, July 23, 1792.
 2. The abstract is entitled "East India Company. The laws of England in regard thereto" (D, Hamilton Papers, Library of Congress).

To John Nicholson [1]

[*Philadelphia, July 24, 1792.* On July 26, 1792, Nicholson wrote to Hamilton: "I sit down to answer your letter of the 24th Instant." *Letter not found.*]

1. Nicholson was comptroller general of Pennsylvania.

From Jeremiah Olney

Providence, July 24, 1792. ". . . Frequent Instances occur of the necessity of granting new Licences before the old ones expire, such as in transfers of Property; and alterations in the size of Vessels, the property remaining the same, and they continuing in the Coasting Business. There is another Instance which sometimes occurs: where a Coasting Vessel is out of employ sometime after the expiration of the Licence, either from want of Business, or during any Repairs which may be made upon her. In these Three Cases I am at a loss to determine, whether the new Licence ought to commence, in the two first, with the commencement of those delivered up, and no Tonnage Duty be demanded until the Year expires; and in the latter, whether it should commence at the expiration of the Old Licence. I beg the favor Sir, of your Opinion on these several Cases, as soon as you can conveniently transmit it. . . ."

ADfS, Rhode Island Historical Society, Providence.

Receipt from William Pearce

[Philadelphia, July 24, 1792]

Received July 24. 1792 of Alexander Hamilton seventy five Dollars on account of the Manufacturing Society.[1]   Wm Pearce

D, in the handwriting of H and signed by Pearce, Hamilton Papers, Library of Congress.
1. The Society for Establishing Useful Manufactures.

To Edward Carrington

Philadelphia July 25. 1792

My Dear Sir

I have received and thank you for your two letters of the 11 instant.[1]

When I asked your opinion concerning the most fit position for a branch of the Bank, I had no idea, that the question would have been decided with so much precipitation, as has happened.[2] After some loose conversations with individual directors, in which the comparitive merits of different places were slightly discussed, & left as I understood for further information—I was surprised with an intimation, that the place had been decided upon—that Richmond was that place—and that some day in August had been assigned for choosing Directors.[3] A predominating motive, though an insufficient one, appears to have been that most of the Bank Stock held in Virginia is held by persons in and about Richmond.

The reasons assigned in your letter in favour of another place are prodigiously weighty. Without committing you, they shall be made known before the thing is finally finished. But I suspect it has gone too far.

Your observations concerning the temper of the people of your state are, as far as they go, consoling. Reflections, according with them, had arisen in my mind; though I could not be sure, that I might not overrate circumstances. I shall wait with expectation, for the further communication, which you are so obliging as to promise.

What you remark concerning the non execution of the Excise Law [4] in N Carolina is very interesting. The probable effect of a continuance of the affair in the same posture is obvious. It has been the wish to win the object from time and reflection. But this can no longer be relied upon. The thing must be brought to an issue; and will be, as soon as the new arrangement respecting compensations is completed. If process should be violently resisted in the parts of N Carolina bordering on your state, how much could be hoped from the aid of the Militia of your State?

Truly Yours   A Hamilton

Ed Carrington Esqr

ALS, MS Division, New York Public Library.

1. Letters not found.

2. As early as November, 1791, H's aid has been requested in establishing a branch of the Bank of the United States in Alexandria, Virginia. See John Fitzgerald to H, November 21, 1791. See also William Heth to H, June 28, 1792.

On July 10, 1792, the president and directors of the Bank of the United States resolved "that an Office of Discount and Deposit, be established in the City of Richmond, State of Virginia" and that the election of directors should take place at Richmond on September 11, 1792 ([Philadelphia] Gazette of the United States, August 1, 1792).

3. In the fall of 1792 the Virginia Assembly considered the possibility of

establishing a bank as a device to prevent the opening of a branch bank. There was opposition in Virginia, however, not only to the presumed Federal influence which might be exerted by a branch of the Bank of the United States, but also to the establishment of any specie banks. In a letter to James Madison on October 1, 1792, Thomas Jefferson expressed this view when he wrote:

". . . I have reflected on Govr. [Henry] Lee's plan of opposing the Federal bank by setting up a state one, and find it not only inadequate, but objectionable highly, & unworthy of the Virginia assembly. I think they should not adopt such a milk & water measure, which rather recognises than prevents the planting among them a source of poison & corruption to sap their catholicism, and to annihilate that power, which is now one, by dividing it into two which shall counterbalance each other. The assembly should reason thus. The power of erecting banks & corporations was not given to the general government it remains then with the state itself. For any person to recognise a foreign legislature in a case belonging to the state itself, is an act of *treason* against the state, and whosoever shall do any act under colour of the authority of a foreign legislature—whether by signing notes, issuing or passing them, acting as director, cashier or in any other office relating to it shall be adjudged guilty of high treason & suffer death accordingly, by the judgment of the state courts. This is the only opposition worthy of our state, and the only kind which can be effectual. If N. Carolina could be brought into a like measure, it would bring the General government to respect the counter-rights of the states. The example would probably be followed by some other states. I really wish that this or nothing should be done. A bank of opposition, while it is a recognition of the one opposed, will absolutely fail in Virginia." (AL, James Madison Papers, Library of Congress.)

Although the Virginia legislature granted two charters in the fall of 1792 for state banks at Alexandria and Richmond, it did not authorize a Virginia branch of the Bank of the United States until 1795. This branch did not open until 1799, and it was located in Norfolk rather than in Richmond.

4. The excise had been established by "An Act repealing, after the last day of June next, the duties heretofore laid upon Distilled Spirits imported from abroad, and laying others in their stead; and also upon Spirits distilled within the United States, and for appropriating the same" (1 *Stat.* 199–214 [March 3, 1791]).

From Tench Coxe

Treasury Department
Revenue Office, July 25th. 1792.

Sir,

Agreeably to your desire I have the honor to inclose to you a draught of a supplementary arrangement of the Business of the Revenue,[1] and of the compensations to the Officers employed in the supervision, inspection and collection thereof, grounded upon the plan delineated in the act of the President of the 15th. day of March

LC, RG 58, Letters of Commissioner of Revenue, 1792–1793, National Archives.
1. See enclosure to this letter.

1791.[2] In transmitting this draught for your modification and for submission to the President, I take the liberty to recapitulate [3] the reasons in support of these supplementary regulations, which occured in the several Conferences, which I had the honor to hold with you upon the Subject.

You will remember Sir, that the 16th. Section of the Act of the 8th of May last "concerning the duties on Spirits distilled in the United States" [4] prescribes two limitations to the aggregate amount of the allowance for compensations to the officers and for the expences of collecting the revenue: first that it shall not exceed seven and one half pr. Centum of the total product of the duties on distilled Spirits, that is as well imported as distilled in the United States, and Secondly that it shall not exceed the Annual Amount of seventy thousand dollars. In regard to the first limitation the allowances (by reason of the second) cannot be extended so far as it would permit, so that, it would be unnecessary to advert to the first, were it not necessary to give perfect satisfaction to the President, that it does not fall short of the second. The paper (A) [5] exhibits the sum to which the duties on foreign distilled Spirits, actually imported in 1791, would have amounted had the duties been as high as they were the year following June 1791. In offering this document for the acceptance of the President, I have no difficulty in *assuring* you Sir, that the quantity of foreign distilled Spirits imported in the year following the 30th: of June 1791 has exceeded that imported in the whole year 1791, but the returns for the last quarter, not being received from the Collectors of the Customs it is not possible to exhibit a regular document to prove the fact. The paper B. exhibits the present state of the returns, and information by letter, concerning the duties on Stills and on Spirits distilled in the United States. The amount of these two documents is 1,124,856 Dollars & 74 Cents, seven & one half pr. Centum on which is 84,363 Dollars & 40½ Cents. For the more perfect satisfaction of the President on this point, the estimate in paper C, for the

---

2. See George Washington to H, March 15, 1791.

3. For one of Coxe's earlier communications concerning this matter, see Coxe to H, July 9, 1792.

4. 1 *Stat.* 270–71. For this section, see Robert Ballard to H, May 31, 1792.

5. Of the enclosures mentioned in this letter only the one marked "E" has been found.

current year has been prepared in conformity with your Judgment on the information from the Supervisors, which I had the honor to lay before you: also the paper D, which shews that the quantity of distilled spirits imported in a year nearly preceeding 1791 was greater than that in paper A, the basis of the Calculation.

Proceeding upon the Idea that the limitation of seventy thousand Dollars in the proviso to the 16th. Section is that, which is to operate: I beg leave to call your attention to Estimate (E) [6] which is conformed to that sum. This paper will be found to comprize the substance of the arrangement which the President was pleased to establish on the 15th of March 1791. The remainder of its contents are the supplementary ideas, which were suggested by yourself, or which occured in the course of the several Conferences upon the subject.

After reminding you of these preliminary circumstances, I will proceed with the draught which for the sake of perspicuity is subdivided under numerical Heads, as is the sequel of this letter.

1st. The detached situation of the Eastern Shore of Maryland in regard to the Residence of the Supervisor,[7] the difficulty of communicating with him in Winter, the number and wealth of the inhabitants, the disinclination to the Revenue on distilled Spirits, which has been expressed by some of the distillers in its three Southern Counties, the extent of the Supervisors Survey, which will contain seven Counties, if the President should deem it expedient to erect a third survey, and the number of ports in the district which are twenty five are the considerations, which occur in favor of creating another survey. The postponement of the appointment with the provision for the temporary execution of the duties by the Supervisor, has arisen from a doubt whether the Power of appointment to any district or survey which may be now erected, did not expire at the end of the last session of the legislature. The power to fill offices during the recess of the senate appears to be applicable, only to such as are established by law, or the constitution.[8]

6. "Estimate E," dated July 25, 1792, and signed by Coxe, is printed in *ASP, Finance*, I, 173–75.

7. George Gale was supervisor of the revenue for the District of Maryland.

8. The concluding proviso of Section 4 of "An Act repealing, after the last day of June next, the duties heretofore laid upon Distilled Spirits imported from abroad, and laying others in their stead; and also upon Spirits distilled

2. The simplicity and consequent facility of settlement, which it will give to the revenue accounts induce a desire that one of the means of increasing the Supervisors emoluments, if any Increase shall appear to the President to be necessary, should be a permission to charge their Commission on the gross revenue collected within their respective spheres of duty. It is probable that great perplexity will arise from confining it to an allowance on the monies received. The limitation of this addition to the beginning of the current (revenue) year has arisen from a presumption, that a retrospective arrangement less expensive to the United States might satisfy the publick policy and equity. This draught will be found to proceed upon that Idea. An additional act of the President will be necessary for the antecedent year, if it shall be deemed proper to exercise the retrospective power. The expediency of granting the allowance, which is the object of this head (No. 2) will be more easily decided upon when the allowances to the Supervisors, as exhibited in the estimate (E) shall have been represented in detail for the collective consideration of the President.

3. In submitting a proposition for an Increase of the Emoluments of the Supervisors, it occured, that it was more easy to excite their attention and Vigilance and to animate their exertions by an addition to their Commissions (at least in part) than to their salaries. On the Necessity for the increase itself, no remark is offered here, because it will rest upon the reasons which apply to the entire compensation of each Supervisor. It will be observed that no addition to the Commissions of the Supervisor in Massachusetts, Rhode Island and Virginia [9] is proposed, because their Salaries appearing comparatively low they seemed to be cases admitting of an addition to that part of the compensation. An addition to the Commissions of the Supervisors of Massachusetts and Rhode Island, where a great deal of Revenue is and will be collected in a small compass (five Counties

---

within the United States, and for appropriating the same" reads as follows: "That if the appointment of the inspectors of surveys, or any part of them, shall not be made during the present session of Congress, the President may, and he is hereby empowered to make such appointments during the recess of the Senate, by granting commissions which shall expire at the end of their next session" (1 *Stat.* 200 [March 3, 1791]).

9. The supervisors of the revenue for Massachusetts, Rhode Island, and Virginia were Nathaniel Gorham, John S. Dexter, and Edward Carrington.

of the two districts) did not appear necessary, and it occured further that a very small addition to the rate of duty (even a quarter pr. Centum) would occasion an increase of Compensation beyond what the services performed appeared to require.

4th. The reasons have already been submitted for prefering to increase the Salaries of the Supervisors of Massachusetts, Rhode Island & Virginia, rather than their Commissions. The reasons for any increase in these Cases remain to be particularized. The great Number of ports in Massachusetts, and the quantity of Revenue collected there, which is estimated to be double that of any State communibus annis and which indeed is greater than that of any two districts seemed to recommend the advancement of the Supervisor's Salary, and it appeared the more worthy of the President's consideration, because of the objections stated to an Increase of his Commissions. The same remarks apply in a proportionate degree in the Case of Rhode Island: as also in the Case of Virginia except that in regard to the quantity of Revenue, which however is and promises to be very considerable, and is collected often in small Sums, in the most extensive of all the districts. It is also worthy of Remark that Richmond, whither his zeal for the public service has induced the Supervisor to remove, is a place of greater expence, than Boston, Providence or probably, Philadelphia in a permanent view.

The Moderation of the comparitive compensations to the Supervisors of New York, Maryland and South Carolina,[10] the extent and population of those districts considered relatively with the most of the others, and the expence of living in the Metropolis of each where their respective Supervisors reside, particularly of the latter district, were [11] the reasons, which occured for suggesting a small addition in the form [of] salary over and above the addition submitted in the shape of Commission.

5th: The Number of Counties in the proposed Survey (No. 3) in the district of Maryland being twice as great, as that in the second Survey, no reason occured against an equality of compensation. The greater Number of ports would appear to recommend more, but as the Revenue will be less, and as all the Inspectors of Virginia and

10. The supervisors of the revenue for New York, Maryland, and South Carolina were Richard Morris, George Gale, and Daniel Stevens.
11. In MS, "where."

Pennsylvania have the same compensations and there is no appearance of dissatisfaction among them, it is to be presumed, that the person on whom the President may confer the appointment to the third Survey will also be contented.

6. The suggestion in regard to the Inspector of the second survey of South Carolina [12] proceeded as you will remember, sir, from a representation of the Supervisor that discontentment had arisen in the mind of the Inspector on account of the distinction made between him and his colleague.[13] This is the only instance of a difference in the compensations to the Inspectors of surveys in the same or even in adjacent districts, excepting the Case of the three Inspectors on the Seacoast Surveys of North Carolina,[14] which I conceive to have been merely experimental should a new arrangement of that district on the receipt of more perfect information, be made by the President, which appears to merit consideration, the case of the Inspector of survey No. 2 in South Carolina will stand alone: It may be further observed that, if that district should distill in proportion to its ability the United States may gain from the Commutation of the Commission (one pr Cent in lieu of two) a part of what may be added to the Salary.

7. The suggestion of the addition of the duty *on stills employed in Cities, Towns and Villages* to the class of duties to be collected at *four* pr. Centum arises from an alteration in the original system made by the last Act of the legislature.[15] Stills under 400 gallons, in Cities, Towns and Villages are now subject only to the duty on their capacity, which not being more difficult to collect than the duty on spirits from domestic materials no reasons of weight in regard to them occur for the advance of commissions which appears to be necessary in regard to country stills. The idea of an increase of the duty upon stills not in Cities, Towns and Villages, and country Stills to five pr. Cent arises in part from the opinions of the

12. Benjamin Cudworth was inspector of Survey No. 2 in South Carolina.

13. Sylvanus Walker was inspector of Survey No. 3 in South Carolina.

14. The inspectors of Surveys No. 1, 2, and 3 in North Carolina were James Read, John Daves, and Thomas Benbury. Coxe is referring to the 1791 arrangement under which these three inspectors received a higher commission than was allowed to the inspectors of the two remaining surveys in North Carolina. No salary was paid to the inspectors of the first three surveys, however, since they also served as officers of the customs. See H to the Senate and the House of Representatives, October 31, 1791.

15. "An Act concerning the Duties on Spirits distilled within the United States" (1 *Stat.* 267–71 [May 8, 1792]).

Supervisors, that it is necessary to increase the compensation for that service, from a comparison of the service and compensation with those of a Collector of state taxes on property, from a consideration of the value of labor and industry of other kinds in the United States, and of the expences of living.

8. It appeared to be sound policy to connect as far as possible the Compensation for each service with the act of performing it. The suggestion under the 8th. head was therefore adopted. It will serve as a mean of defraying little expences for which a precise provision would be Difficult to devise, and it will accrue principally in those places for which the two lowest rates of Commissions have been suggested.

9th: The compensation for gauging liquors is by "the Collection law" eight cents ℔ Cask.[16] This it is believed is more, than it will be at this time necessary to allow in the Business of the Revenue on spirits distilled in the United States, even in cases where a gauger (not being an officer of Inspection) shall be employed. It is presumed that a compensation of six Cents will be sufficient to procure qualified persons. In cases wherein the Collector shall also gauge, a compensation, which with that for marking will make up the sum of five cents is expected to be a desirable object to those officers. The safety of the revenue will be exceedingly promoted by the employment of Collectors, who can guage, and this additional Compensation for that operation will probably induce those employed to acquire the Knowledge, which is easily attainable by a person otherwise qualified for the office.

10. The allowance for measuring stills appears to be recommended by the reason first mentioned under the eig[h]th head. It will be very inconsiderable in Cities, Towns and Villages wherein no collector will probably obtain from it more than five or six dollars pr. Annum. The benefits of it will accrue principally to the Collectors in the Country, who will derive little advantage from the compensation for marking and certifying, and to whom some mean of defraying travelling expences appears necessary. The operation of ascertaining the capacity of a still by measuring the Water with

16. This is stipulated in Section 53 of "An Act to provide more effectually for the collection of the duties imposed by law on goods, wares and merchandise imported into the United States, and on the tonnage of ships or vessels" (1 *Stat.* 171–72 [August 4, 1790]).

which it must be previously filled and of marking both the head and body will be work attended with some labor, and appears to merit compensation.

11. In the present State of the law and of the Business an authority in the Supervisors (duly limited) to reward active, firm and vigilant collectors, and to induce an acceptance of the office by men of respectability and worth where the revenue is small or uncertain, and expences unavoidable, is a measure which appeared to merit the Presidents consideration. In a scene so various and extensive as the United States it seems very difficult to devise a complete arrangement to meet a system so new in this country, and for the first time made general, without a deposit of some discretionary power. In the apportionment of the Number of these compensations, which is suggested, it will be perceived that the extent of Country in each district over which the distillation is diffused, was the consideration that principally influenced.

12. The second Section of the act[17] requires that there should be at least one office of Inspection in every County. Circumstances may hereafter evince that more will be necessary in some places to enable the distillers to make the requisite entries and obtain licences with reasonable convenience. It has appeared from experiment that the business of Collection does not require in some places more than one Collector to *two* and others to *three* Counties. The Collectors house will serve for an office of inspection in the county wherein he may reside, but auxiliary offices of Inspection (under such Collector) will be necessary in the other one or two in which he does not reside. Where little Revenue accrues the sum of twenty dollars will probably be a compensation sufficient to induce an acceptance by some fit person: and where much revenue accrues an addition for his own Emoluments may be made by the Collector. The Number of Counties in each district and the Number of Collectors appointed (so far as is Known) principally governed the appointment of the auxiliary officers suggested in the draught.

The preceeding observations relate to the Business of the Revenue on stills employed and Spirits distilled in the United States. Under Head

17. Section 2 of "An Act concerning the Duties on Spirits distilled within the United States" (1 *Stat.* 268).

13. Will be found some ideas relative to the compensation of the Inspectors of the Revenue for ports, and the persons deputed by them, whose duties comprehend not only foreign distilled spirits, but the several species of wines and teas. The legislature has deemed it expedient to apply to those articles, which are charged with some of the highest duties, the precautionary measures of marking and certifying, and to pass them under the care of the officers of the Revenue: Considerable trouble and expence of clerkship, stationary and office rent, having arisen out of this new duty on the port officers, some compensation was conceived to be due to them on the score as well of policy as equity. It appears to be a recommendation of this suggestion that it connects the compensation in every instance with the service performed.

In addition to the ideas detailed in the foregoing pages it was deemed necessary as you will re[me]mber, Sir, to examine into the result of the compensations that no officer, by the accumulation of particular compensations apparently reasonable, might receive emoluments disproportionate to his services: and altho' this supplementary arrangement appears likely to induce the acceptance of the appointments by eligible persons, it is not apprehended that the compensations will prove extravagant in case of a novelty, considerable responsibility and of a nature requiring in a peculiar degree officers of worth and conduct.

It has been already mentioned, that the services of the year prior to the first instant, do not appear to require precisely the same Compensations, as those from and subsequent to that day. When your Engagements permit, that part of the business will be taken up in detail, after which it will be prepared for submission to the President.[18] It appeared necessary to give a preference in point of preparation to this draught of a supplementary arrangement. For

18. On September 12, 1792, Coxe forwarded to H the draft of an arrangement for one year's retroactive compensation to officers of the revenue (Coxe to H, September 12, 1792). The arrangement was signed by the President on October 1, 1792 (Washington to H, October 1, 1792), dated October 29, 1792 (Coxe to H, October 20, 1792, note 2), and included in a report to Congress submitted by the President on November 22, 1792 (*ASP, Finance*, I, 171–75). In this report the President included his arrangement of August 4, 1792, for the current year, as well as the retroactive arrangement for the year which had ended June 30, 1792. "Statement E," enclosed in the letter printed above, and "Statement A," enclosed in Coxe to H, September 12, 1792, were also included in this report of November 22, 1792.

as it is expected that it will continue (in whatever form it shall be established) to operate during the pleasure of the President untill acted upon by the legislature. The Supervisors in several of the districts appear disposed to postpone the completion of the appointments of Collectors, untill the determination of the President shall be communicated to them.

I have the Honor to be, with the most respectful Attachment, Sir, Your most Obedt. Servt.   Tench Coxe,
                                            Commissr. of the Revenue.

The honorable,
the Secretary of the Treasury.

[E N C L O S U R E] [19]

In pursuance of the powers and authorities vested in me by the Acts of Congress (of the 3d. of March 1791.[20] and the Eighth of May 1792.) [21] relative to the duties on distilled spirits and to the collection thereof, the following alterations and additions to the arrangement of Officers and distribution of compensations made on the 15. day of March 1791. are hereby adopted and established.

1st. The District of Maryland shall be divided into three Surveys. The first consisting of all the Counties on the western side of the Chesapeak Bay (except Montgomery, Frederick, Washington and Alleghaney) namely Harford, Baltimore, Ann Arundel, Prince George's, Calvert, Charles and St. Mary's. The duties of the Inspector of this survey shall be performed by the supervisor. The second survey is to consist as at present, of the counties of Montgomery, Frederick, Washington and Alleghaney. The duties of this Survey will continue to be performed by the Inspector thereto appointed. The third Survey is to consist of all the counties on the Eastern Shore of Chesapeak bay, namely Cecil, Kent, Queen Anne's, Talbot, Dorset, Worcester, Somerset, and Caroline; for which an

19. LC, George Washington Papers, Library of Congress.
20. "An Act repealing, after the last day of June next, the duties heretofore laid upon Distilled Spirits imported from abroad, and laying others in their stead; and also upon Spirits distilled within the United States, and for appropriating the same" (1 *Stat.* 199–214).
21. See note 15.

Inspector will be appointed. The duties of this survey are to be performed by the Supervisor, until that appointment shall be made.
2. The Commissions to be allowed to the Supervisors and Inspectors of surveys shall be upon the whole amount of the duties collected within their respective districts and Surveys upon Stills, and spirits distilled in the United States, and which have or shall accrue after the last day of June 1792.
3. The Supervisors of New Hampshire, Connecticut, New York, Vermont, New-Jersey and Pennsylvania shall each receive a commission on the said amount of the revenue in their respective districts (excepting what accrued prior to the first day of July 1792) of one per centum, in lieu of the commission of one half per centum before allowed.

The Supervisor of Delaware shall receive a commission in manner aforesaid of two per centum in lieu of one per centum.

The Supervisors of Maryland, North Carolina, & South Carolina shall each receive a Commission in manner aforesaid of one and an half per centum in lieu of one per centum.

The Supervisor of Georgia shall receive a commission, in manner, aforesaid, of two per centum, in lieu of one per centum.
4. To the salaries of the following Supervisors there shall be additions as set against the names of their offices to commence on the first day of July 1792.
The Supervisor of Massachusetts an addition of 200 Drs. per annum.

The Supervisor of Rhode Island	100.	"
The Supervisor of New York	100.	"
The Supervisor of Maryland	100.	"
The Supervisor of Virginia	200.	"
The Supervisor of South Carolina	100.	"

5. The compensation to the Inspector of the third survey of the District of Maryland, when appointed, shall be a salary of four hundred & fifty dollars ℔ annum & a commission of one per centum.
6. The compensation to the Inspector of the second survey of the District of South Carolina shall be a salary of Four hundred & fifty Dollars ℔ annum, and a commission of one per centum in lieu of his former compensation.
7. The Collectors of the Revenue shall be entitled to receive the following commissions upon the Revenue on Stills and distilled

spirits by them collected; that is to say, upon the revenue upon spirits distilled from foreign materials two per centum; upon the revenue upon Spirits distilled from domestic materials and upon Stills employed on the said materials in Cities, towns or Villages, four per centum; and upon the revenue upon Stills not in Cities Towns or Villages, five per centum.

8. There shall be allowed to the officers of Inspection who shall legally sign Certificates to accompany each Cask of distilled spirits, and to the officers or other persons, who shall be authorised to mark the same, the sum of five Cents for each & every Cask of Spirits distilled in the United States, so marked and certified, to be divided between the officer or person who shall mark, and the officer who shall sign the Certificates for the same, if those duties shall be performed by different persons.

9. There may also be allowed to persons employed to guage Spirits distilled in the United States, the sum of two Cents and one half for each Cask so guaged, if the person thus employed shall be an Officer of Inspection authorised to mark the Casks containing the said spirits, or to sign Certificates to accompany the same. But if the person employed to guage such distilled Spirits be not an officer of Inspection authorised to mark or issue Certificates for the same, he may be allowed a sum not exceeding six cents for the service of guaging each Cask.

10. There shall likewise be allowed to the Collectors of the revenue for measuring the capacity of each Still, and marking the still & head, according to Law, the sum of Fifty Cents.

11. The Supervisors of the several Districts shall be at liberty to allow to such of the Collectors of the revenue, as, for the execution of the public service, it shall appear to them really necessary, so to compensate, a yearly sum over & above their other emoluments, not exceeding in a district the number of Collectors, nor the average or medium sum to each, or to the whole number, which are set against the same below. That is to say—

In New Hampshire the Supervisor may allow to 2 Collectors 50 Drs. each.

In Massachusetts to 10 do. 400 Dollars to be divided at discretion among them.

In Rhode Island	to 1.
In Vermont	2.
In Connecticut	4.
In New York	2.
In New Jersey	5.
In Pennsylvania	14.
In Delaware	3.
In Maryland	9.
In Virginia	24.
In North Carolina	14.
In South Carolina	8.
In Georgia	3.

that is to 89. Collectors 60 Dollars each, at an average or medium, to be divided within each District at the discretion of the Supervisors.

12. There may be allowed to Eighty auxiliary officers of Inspection, to be appointed by the Supervisors in Counties wherein no Collector of the revenue resides, a sum not exceeding twenty Dollars each for keeping an office to receive entries, issue Licences, and to perform such other services in aid of the Collectors as may be legally authorised and as they may be willing to execute for that compensation. Of these there may be,

in Rhode Island	1.
in New Hampshire	2.
in Massachusetts	10.
in Vermont	4.
in New York	10.
in Pennsylvania	5.
in Maryland	2.
in Virginia	20.
in North Carolina	11.
in South Carolina	10.
in Georgia	5.

13. There shall be allowed to the officers of Inspection & the persons employed to mark foreign distilled spirits, Wines and Teas, the sum of Five Cents for every Cask or package of the Merchandize above mentioned, which shall be legally marked and certified, to be

equally divided between the officer signing the Certificate & the officer or person marking the Cask or package, if those duties shall be performed by different persons.

From Tench Coxe

Treasury Department, Revenue Office, July 25, 1792. Transmits and explains "a contract made by the Collector of Portsmouth in New Hampshire [1] with Titus Salter for keeping and supplying the light house on New Castle Island at the Mouth of Piscataqua River." [2]

LC, RG 58, Letters of Commissioner of Revenue, 1792–1793, National Archives.
  1. Joseph Whipple.
  2. A copy of this contract may be found in RG 26, Lighthouse Letters Received, Lighthouse Deeds and Contracts, National Archives.

To William Ellery

[*Philadelphia, July 25, 1792.* On August 6, 1792, Ellery wrote to Hamilton: "I have recd. your . . . letters of the 21. 25. & 26 of the last month." *Letter of July 25 not found.*]

From Isaac Gregory [1]

[*Plankbridge, North Carolina, July 25, 1792.* On August 20, 1792, Hamilton wrote to Gregory: "Your letter of the 25th. ultimo . . . has been received." *Letter not found.*]

  1. Gregory was collector of customs and inspector of the revenue for the port of Plankbridge, North Carolina.

To Jedediah Huntington

Treasury Department, July 25, 1792. "Your letter of the 22d instant has been received.[1] My Circular of the 23d will have satisfied you on the point of enquiry."

LS, Yale University Library.
1. Letter not found.

To Rufus King [1]

Philadelphia July
25. 1792

My Dear Sir

I received lately a letter from you [2] in which you express sentiments according with my own on the present complexion of your party politics; as, if a letter of mine to you did not miscarry, you will have seen.[3] I wished that Clinton & his party should be placed in a just light before the people,[4] and that a spirit of dissatisfaction within proper bounds should be kept alive; and this for National purposes, as well as from a detestation of their principles and conduct.

But a resort to first principles in any shape is decidedly against my judgment. I don't think the occasion will in any sense warrant it. It is not for the friends of good government to employ extraordinary expedients which ought only to be resorted to in cases of great magnitude and urgent necessity. I reject as well the idea of a Convention as of force.

To rejudge the decision of the Canvassers by a Convention has to me too much the appearance of reversing the sentence of a Court by a Legislative decree. The Canvassers had a final authority in all the forms of the Constitution and laws. A question arose in the execution of their office not absolutely free from difficulty which they have decided (I am persuaded wrongly) but within the power vested in them. I do not feel it right or expedient to attempt to reverse the decision by any means not known to the Constitution or Laws.

The precedent may suit us to day; but tomorrow we may rue its abuse.

I am not even sure that it will suit us at all. I see already publications aiming at a revision of the constitution with a view to alterations which would spoil it.[5] It would not be astonishing, if a Convention should be called, if it should produce more than is intended. Such weapons are not to be played with. Even the friends of good government in their present mood may fancy alterations desireable which would be the reverse.

Mens minds are too much unsettled every where at the present juncture. Let us endeavour to settle them & not to set them more afloat.

I find that strong minded men here view the matter in the same light with me; and that even Mr Jays character is likely in a degree to suffer by the idea that he fans the flame a little more than is quite prudent. I wish this idea to be conveyed to him with proper *management*. I have thoughts of writing to him.

You see, out of the reach of the contagion, I am very cool and reasonable; if I were with you I should probably not escape the infection

Farewell   A Hamilton

Francis Childs is a very cunning fellow. In Philadelphia in the person of his proxy Freneau, he is a good Antifœderalist & Clintonian; in New York he is a good Fœderalist and Jayite [6]—Beckley [7] & Jefferson pay him for the first & the Fœderal Citizens of New York for the last. Observe a paragraph in his Dayly Advertiser of the 18th instant.[8] These things ought, in a proper way, to be brought into view.

Rufus King Esq.

ALS, Hamilton Papers, Library of Congress.
    1. For background to this letter, see Philip Schuyler to H, May 8, 1792, note 4; H to John Adams, June 25, 1792, note 2; H to King, June 28, 1792; King to H, July 10, 1792; William Lewis to H, July 21, 1792.
    2. King to H, July 10, 1792.   3. H to King, June 28, 1792.
    4. During June and July, 1792, Governor George Clinton's policies were repeatedly criticized in the New York press. In addition to attacking the decision of the state's canvassers giving the gubernatorial election to Clinton, writers in various papers criticized the governor's appointments and his handling of the state's land office.
    5. On July 20, 1792, "An Observer of the Times" proposed several changes in the constitution of New York which in effect amounted to a plan for an entirely new constitution. The writer proposed, among other things, that "All freemen paying taxes and rent to a certain amount, ought to be entitled to vote at every public election," that all electors should be eligible for office, and that all offices should be elective. "An Observer of the Times" concluded: "If a new constitution should take place, there will be an election for all the elective officers of government; this in a great measure will rectify many disagreeable circumstances; and add new vigor and peace to the state" (*The* [New York] *Daily Advertiser*, July 20, 1792).
    6. Childs and John Swaine were the publishers of *The* [New York] *Daily*

Advertiser. Douglas Southall Freeman has described Philip Freneau's position with the [Philadelphia] *National Gazette* as follows: ". . . Jefferson on February 28, 1791, transmitted to . . . [Freneau] the offer of a language clerk's position in the Department of State at the annual wage of 250 dollars. The salary was small, the Secretary admitted, but the position 'gives so little to do as not to interfere with any other calling the person may choose'. . . . Not until late July . . . did Freneau make the decision to transfer to Philadelphia. . . . Francis Childs, his employer on the *Daily Advertiser*, agreed to underwrite the entire venture, and Freneau's 'national' paper would be printed in the shop of Childs's partner, John Swaine, who had set up in Philadelphia to do contract work for the government. Out of this Freneau would share as a third partner with no capital investment at all. On August 16 Jefferson signed Freneau's commission as 'clerk for foreign languages' despite full knowledge that his man was equipped only for French. . . . On October 31, 1791, the first issue of the semi-weekly *National Gazette* appeared in Philadelphia" (Freeman, *Washington*, IV, 403–04).

By the summer of 1792 the *National Gazette* had become the leading Republican paper, while *The Daily Advertiser* was an equally important Federalist paper.

7. John Beckley, clerk of the House of Representatives, was a close friend and political associate of Thomas Jefferson.

8. H is perhaps referring to a paragraph in *The* [New York] *Daily Advertiser* of that date, which was reprinted from the [Philadelphia] *National Gazette* and which reads as follows: "We observe, says a correspondent, with great satisfaction, a resurrection of the *justice* of our country in every part of the United States. The universal cry is now against the Congress of 1788 and 89, which funded the public debt into the hands of D—— and Co. The infamous practices, by which this infamous business was effected, begin at least to be developed, and a stain has been discovered, by the enquiry, upon our national honor, that no time will wipe away" (*The* [New York] *Daily Advertiser*, July 18, 1792).

To Jeremiah Olney

Treasury Department
July 25th 1792.

Sir

I have before me your letter of the 16th instant, concerning certain Brandy, intended to be exported by Messrs Clark and Nightingale.

There can be no doubt that the Brandy, being a foreign article, will be liable, as the law stands, to duty on its return. The drawback cannot be allowed, unless the proof required, of its having been actually landed at a foreign port, is produced.[1]

I am, Sir,   Your Obedt Servant.   Alexander Hamilton

Jeremiah Olney Esqr.
Collr Providence.

LS, Rhode Island Historical Society, Providence.
  1. On August 13, 1792, H wrote to Olney clarifying the first sentence in this paragraph and stating that he had been mistaken in the second.

To William Seton

Philadelphia July 25
1792

My Dear Sir

I received your obliging letter by the Post of day [1] and thank you for the first instance of your friendly attention, which it announces. Mr. Pollock certainly has done the utmost that Mr. Greene could have asked and as much as his situation can require, if it is remediable at all.[2]

I have directed the Collector of New York [3] to divide his deposits between your institution & the Branch until he places with you a sum which with what you already have will amount to 100 000 Dollars on account of the U States; a sum it is my intention as far as circumstances will permit to keep continually in your hands. This intention however need not go beyond ourselves.

Truly & most Cordially Yrs   A Hamilton

William Seton Esq

ALS, Bank of New York, New York City.
  1. Seton to H, July 23, 1793.   2. See H to Seton, July 17, 1792.
  3. H's letter to John Lamb has not been found.

To William Short

Treasury Department
July 25th. 1792

Sir

Your letters of the 25th of April and 14th of May have duly reached me; since the receipt of that of the 22nd of April which was acknowleged in mine of the 30th of June.

LS, William Short Papers, Library of Congress; LS, marked "Duplicate," William Short Papers, Library of Congress. A copy of this letter was enclosed in H's "Report on Foreign Loans," February 13, 1793.

In consequence of your letter of the 14th of May I have directed drafts on the Commissioners [1] for five hundred thousand Guilders, and as soon as these are sold, I shall cause further drafts to be made to the extent of [five hundred thousand] [2] Guilders in addition to the above mentioned five hundred thousand. The residue of the monies heretofore announced [to have been borrowed,] will be left subject to your disposition towards payment of interest on the Dutch and Antwerp loans, during the present year, and of the Debt to France, with the surplus.

In speaking of the Interest on the Dutch and Antwerp loans, I wish to be understood that I rely for the payment of this interest during the present year on the funds which are or shall be in the hands of the Commissioners, arising from loans that have been or may be made. Whether you will leave unemployed in their hands, monies equivalent to the interest for the intire year, or will rely upon a further loan to be made, applying a greater proportion of the monies already obtained in payment to France, ought to be regulated upon the degree of certainty of effecting such further loan on admissible terms. This therefore is left to your discretion.

The statements A & B [3] herewith transmitted will shew you the view which I have of the monies that would remain in the hands of the Commissioners on the loans heretofore known to have been effected, after paying all the bills heretofore drawn and deducting the interest on the Dutch and Antwerp loans to the end of the present year—namely [2120477 Guilders and 15 stivers]. From this sum you will only have to deduct, to satisfy any further disposition on my part the sum of [Five hundred Thousand Guilders,] still intended to be drawn for.

This statement however ought not to be acted upon by you as definitively accurate. It will be proper that you ascertain with the Commissioners with greater certainty what will remain at your disposal.

Mr. Morris must have misapprehended the tenor of the Secretary of State's letter, from which he inferred, that it was the intention of [this] Government to transfer to France the loss by depreciation

1. See H to Willink, Van Staphorst, and Hubbard, July 16, 1792.
2. All bracketed material in this letter is in the handwriting of H.
3. See enclosures.

[on] the Assignats.[4] It has been determined by the President that the United States will not take advantage of the depreciation, but will make an equitable adjustment of the affair.

You observe "that the *rate of exchange* and the *current differences* between specie and paper being known here (that is at Paris) furnish the basis for regulating the business." [5] I remark that much will depend on the manner of applying these data. They may be so applied as to create a positive loss to the United States; as if the rate of exchange below par should be less than the rate of depreciation, and the former should be added, the latter deducted.

For example. By a French paper of the 20th of April, if I understand it aright, exchange between Paris and Amsterdam was about 36 ⅌ Cent against Paris, the depreciation of the Assignats about 60 ⅌ Cent.

If then the computation were made by adding the rate of exchange and deducting the rate of depreciation there would be a loss upon [every] hundred Guilders in Amsterdam paid in Paris of 45 Guilders and $^{60}/_{100}$ of a Guilder.

Thus, add to 100 Guilders 36 ⅌ Cent for the rate of exchange
the product is   136   Guilders
Deduct for depreciation 60 ⅌ Cent or   81.   60
            There would remain   54.   40
as the equivalent for 100 Guilders in Amsterdam, which would involve a loss of 45. $^{60}/_{100}$ Guilders per hundred.

I take it for granted that this method of applying the data cannot have been contemplated, as it would throw upon the United States a heavy real loss in consequence of the disorders which exist in the affairs of France. Though the United States are not disposed to take any undue advantage, they cannot be supposed to be willing to suffer a loss.

You will have perceived from my letter of the 4th of June last,[6] that it was the Presidents pleasure, that your Agency in the whole of the pecuniary affairs, originally committed to you, as well respecting [the] debt to France as otherwise, should continue; and that Mr Morris as representative of the United States, at the Court

---

4. See Short to H, May 14, 1792. Gouverneur Morris had arrived in Paris in May, 1792, to assume his duties as United States Minister Plenipotentiary.

5. See Short to H, May 14, 1792.

6. The date is incorrect. H is referring to his letter to Short of June 14, 1792.

of France, would be instructed to co operate. I understand the Secretary of State that this instruction has been forwarded; though I feel full confidence that the requisite co operation will have been afforded independently of any instruction.

With very great consideration and Esteem, I have the honor to be Sir Your obedt Servant   Alexander Hamilton

PS. A Copy of the report of the 23d of January last is here enclosed.[7]

[William Short Esquire
&ca. &ca]

[E N C L O S U R E] [8]

[Philadelphia, July 25, 1792]

A

A Statement of the payments to be made by Messrs Willink, van Staphorst & Hubbard, and of the monies in their hands, on the 1st of February 1792.—
The account current of the said date States
a balance due to the united States of .   .   .   .   .   . 2,500,220.
    On the last 3/m loan they received

1791 Decr 31 509,000		
1792 Jany 31 . . . . 701.000		
remained to be received . .	1,790.000	1,790,000
	3,000,000	

  In the hands of the commissioners   4,290,220.

       Payments to be made
     Draughts remaining unpaid for
     List B.   175,044.15
Jany 27 Draught No 541 favour Thos
    Jefferson   95,947.10

7. "Report on the Public Debt and Loans," January 23, 1792. H had sent his other report dated January 23, 1792, the "Report on Estimates of Receipts and Expenditures for 1791–1792," to Short on January 28, 1792.
8. D, William Short Papers, Library of Congress.

April 17 Draughts No 542 a 628 John
          Kean   500,000.
June 30   Draughts No 630   Thos
          Jefferson   123.750
July   Draughts No 631 a 715 [9] &ca
          John Kean   500,000
                                        _____
                                        1,394.742. 5

                  Interest to be paid

March 1st on 2½ million . . at 5 pCt 125,000.
June 1st on 7 million . . . . . . do   350.000
Septr 1st on 6 million . . . . . . do   300.000   2,169,742. 5—
                                                  _____
          Leaving the Sum not disposed of   2,120,477.15

                    Treasury Department July 25th 1792
                    John Meyer
                    Pe Clk

                    [ENCLOSURE] [10]

                         [Philadelphia, July 25, 1792]

                              B

A Statement of the Treasury draughts on the Commissioners in
Amsterdam which remained unpaid on the 1st of February 1792.

1791   Guilders
October 31 No 361 10,000
Novr   2   No 386 a 391 6 draughts a 4000 each   24,000
 "   No 410 a 411 2 ditto   a 3000   6,000
 "   5   No 425 & 426 2 ditto 3,044.15
 "   8   No 439 . . . .   918.14. 8
 "   10   No 442 a 450 9 ditto   a 1000   . . . . . .   9,000.
            No 454 a 459 6 ditto   a 1000   . . . . . .   6,000.
            No 460 a 467 8 ditto   a 2000   . . . . . . 16,000.
            No 469 a 480 12 ditto   a 2000   . . . . . . 24,000.
            N 481 a 492 12 ditto   a 3000   36,000

9. A footnote at this point in the handwriting of John Meyer, a clerk in the
Treasury Department, reads: "Some of these drafts remain yet to be drawn."
10. D, William Short Papers, Library of Congress.

N	500	. . . .	3,000
N	514	. . . .	1,000
N	516	. . . .	1,081. 5. 8
N	519 a 522 4 ditto a 5000	. . . . . .	20,000.
No	523	. . . .	2,000
N	526	. . . .	4,000
N	527	. . . .	5,000
N	537	. . . .	4,000

175,044.15

Treasury Department
July 25th 1792
John Meyer
Pe Clk

T. L. No. I [1]

[Philadelphia, July 25, 1792]

For the GAZETTE *of the* UNITED STATES.

Mr. Fenno,[2]

The Editor of the "National Gazette" [3] receives a salary from government.

Quere—Whether this salary is paid him for *translations;* or for *publications,* the design of which is to vilify those to whom the voice of the people has committed the administration of our public affairs—to oppose the measures of government, and, by false insinuations, to disturb the public peace?

In common life it is thought ungrateful for a man to bite the hand that puts bread in his mouth; but if the man is hired to do it, the case is altered.   T. L.

[Philadelphia] *Gazette of the United States,* July 25, 1792.
    1. This letter is the first of a series. The other "T. L." letters are dated July 28 and August 11, 1792.
    2. John Fenno, editor of the *Gazette of the United States.*
    3. Philip Freneau, editor of the [Philadelphia] *National Gazette.* See H to Edward Carrington, May 26, 1792, note 8, and H to Rufus King, July 25, 1792, note 6.

To Otho H. Williams

Treasury Department
July 25, 1792.

Sir

After the receipt of this you will divide your deposits between the Bank of Maryland and the Branch of the Bank of the United States, until the first of October ensuing, and thenceforth deposit the public money wholly in the said Branch. The same vouchers, as heretofore, must be taken and forwarded from each.

I am, Sir,   Your Obed Servant.   A Hamilton

P.S. It is at your discretion either to divide between the two Banks the sum each week to be deposited ⟨or⟩ deposit alternately one week with ⟨on⟩e the other with the other.[1]

Otho H. Williams Esqr.
Collr Baltimore.

LS, Columbia University Libraries.
    1. The postscript is in H's handwriting.

To Sharp Delany

Treasury Department
July 26. 1792

Sir

I have considered the case represented in your letter of the 13. instant [1] respecting the duty on certain Whalebone imported by Mr. Joy.

I do not under such circumstances conceive the article to be exempted from the duty; because the evidence of goods of the growth, produce or manufacture of the United States, which are to be exempted, when brought from a foreign port, is prescribed by the 24th Section of the Collection Law; [2] and one of the requisites is, proof upon Oath, that they were previously exported from the

United States, which proof it appears, could not be given in the present case.

I approve of the arrangement proposed in your letter of the 23rd, instant,[3] and you have my consent to employ a couple more hands in the Boat towards the execution of it.

I am   Sir   Your Obedt. Servant   A Hamilton

Sharp Delany Esqr.
Collector, Philadelphia

LS, Bureau of Customs, Philadelphia; LC, RG 56, Letters to the Collector at Philadelphia, National Archives; LC, RG 56, Letters to Collectors at Small Ports, "Set G," National Archives.
  1. Letter not found.
  2. "An Act to provide more effectually for the collection of the duties imposed by law on goods, wares and merchandise imported into the United States, and on the tonnage of ships or vessels" (1 *Stat.* 145–78 [August 4, 1790]). For the provision made by Section 24, see H to Jeremiah Olney, January 8, 1792.
  3. Letter not found.

To William Ellery

[*Philadelphia, July 26, 1792.* On August 6, 1792, Ellery wrote to Hamilton: "I have recd. your . . . letters of the 21. 25. & 26 of the last month." *Letter of July 26 not found.*]

From William Green [1]

New York.
July the 26: 1792.

Sir

I will endeavour as briefly as possible to give you the outline of the transactions which have taken place with Mr. Pollock since my return to this City on the 19. Instt.

My first proposition was that the nature and extent of his demand should be left to an Arbitration here, and that without reference to the National basis, on which so much of my property or right to it rests, as well as the very property in question. I would engage to pay the amount and to give Security for the payments at 6. 12. & 18 Months.

Mr P. negatived the proposition.

I proposed next that a similar arbitration should take place in London & that the Principals of Mr P. should be appointed by me Co.-Agents with my friends there to sollicit redress from the British Govt. and that the first fruits of that sollicitation should go to discharge the amount of the Award.

Mr. P. also negatived this second proposition.

My motive for demanding an Arbitration on the case, is, that the Goods for which the payment of the Bond is claimed were much overrated in their value, of which I have proofs. Three fifths of their nominal or fictitious value was paid at the time of Shipment. Perhaps I shall surprize you when I say, that fraudulent overcharges on India Goods to the amount of 40 or 50 per Cent are very common, and yet they are nevertheless true: and at this moment all the Superior Officers in the Mercantile Service, of the English East India Company in India, are under prosecution in England for charges of this Sort, which have been proved to have been committed by them for several years past.

It was next proposed to this Gentleman to suspend all operation under his power at Law for twelve Months, on condition of receiving his obligation to be here to meet a process to be then issued if necessary against me. To which he answered as an Ultimatum that I must in that case in addition to my own responsibility give one or more Sureties for its due performance, in a penalty of Eight Thousand pounds Sterling.

There are certain circumstances in a Man's affairs in such a crisis, as the present is to mine, when the giving Sureties to this amount makes alienation indispensable, that operate to his destruction. The truth of this observation is I trust palpable. Great Britian sequesterd from me with one hand upwards of Two hundred and fifty thousand dollars, in Europe and her foreign possessions; and with the other she strikes alone in America; *at my home* and strips me of Forty thousand dollars more at the moment when I am compell'd to relinquish my business, my affairs, and my family; and, to lay myself at her feet in Europe to sollicit under the auspices of our Minister [2] a tardy redress.

These facts have been urged to both the Gentlemen to whom the affairs related by recommendation, and by Attorneyship; but without much effect; for there is a Class of Men in this Country who with respect to England, would a Century ago have fought for the Divine right of its Kings; at present they only contend for the Divine right of that Nation—particularly referring to its Supremacy over the ci-devant Colonies. I could not persuade any mind of this complexion: that it is in the highest degree wrong and impolitic in that Government, to continue to harass and distress the Citizens of the United States; and that it cannot much longer be permitted with impunity. And Neither of these Gentlemen can discern Sureties to be less necessary now, than when I went to Europe with my family in the year (90) to collect the proofs that have been since submitted to the Government in order, that at my return, I might be justified in demanding its protection, and exhorting it to endeavour to obtain Justice for me from the British Government.

However, I have in my turn, ultimately informed these Gentlemen, that as I consider my person and Interests in custody of the Executive, and as it has already issued certain Instructions to Mr Pinckney on the subject I cannot think myself warrantable in honor & Justice in signing any paper that may amount to a compromise or committment without first submitting it to your consideration. I shall therefore beg leave to submit it to you so soon as it is ready and I have pledg'd my honor not to make any movement towards quitting the Country for the space of Thirty days.

I have the honor to be, with great respect   Sir   Your most Obedient   Humble Servant   William Green

ALS, Hamilton Papers, Library of Congress.
   1. For background to this letter, which concerns a dispute between Green and George Pollock, see H to William Seton, July 17, 25, 1792; Seton to H, July 23, 1792; Green to H, July 24, 1792.
   2. Thomas Pinckney was United States Minister to Great Britain.

From Benjamin Lincoln

[*Boston*] *July 26, 1792.* "A few days since the Brig Sally arrived here from Amsterdam with a quantity of Ginn on board part of which was in Keggs or Anchors as they are called. This was such an open violation of the Law,[1] after full time had passed for the interested to have know their duty & interest if proper attention had been paid to them, that I could not persuade my self that I should be justified if I let the matter pass with impunity. Bonds have been given for the Vessel. A petition is going on for a remission of the Forfeiture. . . . One of our vessels which sailed for the Northwest Coast of America carried out a quantity of Merchandize imported here from a foreign port. As the duty thereon has been paid the exporter wishes to Avail himself of the drawback prior to the Ships return which probably will not be for two years to come. Untill Her return I cannot receive that evidence of the landing the Goods in a foreign port which the Law requires.[2] What can be done?"

LC, Massachusetts Historical Society, Boston; LC, RG 36, Collector of Customs at Boston, Letter Book, 1790–1797, National Archives; copy, RG 56, Letters from the Collector at Boston, National Archives.

1. Section 33 of "An Act repealing, after the last day of June next, the duties heretofore laid upon Distilled Spirits imported from abroad, and laying others in their stead; and also upon Spirits distilled within the United States, and for appropriating the same" reads in part as follows: "That after the last day of June next, no spirituous liquors except gin or cordials in cases, jugs or bottles, shall be brought from any foreign port or place, in casks of less capacity than fifty gallons at the least, on pain of forfeiting of the said spirits, and of the ship or vessel in which they shall be brought" (1 Stat. 207 [March 3, 1791]).

2. Section 58 of "An Act to provide more effectually for the collection of the duties imposed by law on goods, wares and merchandise imported into the United States, and on the tonnage of ships or vessels" provides in part as follows: "That the said drawbacks or allowances shall not be paid until at least six months after the exportation of the said goods, and until the said exporter or exporters shall produce to the collector with whom such outward entry is made, a certificate in writing of two reputable merchants at the foreign port or place in which the same were landed, together with the oath of the master and mate of the vessel in which they were exported, certifying the delivery thereof" (1 Stat. 174 [August 4, 1790]).

From John Nicholson [1]

Comptroller Genl. Office [Philadelphia]
July 26th 1792

sir

I sit down to answer your letter of the 24th Instant [2] which was received by me on my return home last night.

LC, Division of Public Records, Pennsylvania Historical and Museum Commission, Harrisburg.

1. In this letter Nicholson in his capacity as comptroller general of Pennsyl-

1st Your Office hath been furnished from time to time from me
with the actual state of the New Loan Certificates out, that is those
issued for Continental Certificates—And more especially about the
period to which you refer when the sum thereof outstanding was

---

vania discusses a series of complex arrangements involving the financial relations of certain citizens of Pennsylvania with the Federal Government. During
the Confederation period several states assumed the Continental debts owed
their citizens. In 1786 the Pennsylvania legislature offered to receive Continental certificates held by its citizens in exchange for "new loan" certificates issued
by the state (*Pennsylvania Statutes*, XII, 158–64 [March 1, 1786]). In 1789 the
state reversed its policy, for when it appeared that the new Federal Government would make some provision for the Continental debt, the state legislature
encouraged holders of "new loan" certificates to exchange them for the Continental certificates for which the "new loans" had been issued, or other
Continental certificates of the same value (*Pennsylvania Statutes*, XIII, 263–67
[March 27, 1789]).

"An Act making provision for the (payment of the) Debt of the United
States" (1 *Stat*. 138–44 [August 4, 1790]) defined the terms under which the
Federal Government would liquidate the Revolutionary War debts incurred
under the authority of both the Continental Congress and the state governments. Sections 17 and 18 of this act provided in part as follows: "But as
certain states have respectively issued their own certificates, in exchange for
those of the United States, whereby it might happen that interest might be
twice payable on the same sums: . . . *Be it further enacted*, That the payment
of interest whether to states or to individuals, in respect to the debt of any
state, by which such exchange shall have been made, shall be suspended,
until it shall appear to the satisfaction of the secretary of the treasury, that
certificates issued for that purpose by such state, have been re-exchanged or
redeemed, or until those which shall not have been re-exchanged or redeemed,
shall be surrendered to the United States" (1 *Stat*. 144). After this act had
gone into effect, H wrote a circular letter to the governors of the states calling to their attention the provisions of sections 17 and 18 of the act ("Treasury
Department Circular to the Governors of the States," June 27, 1791). Correspondence and conferences between H and officers of the Pennsylvania government followed. After subscriptions to the Federal loan were closed, Thomas
Smith, commissioner of loans for Pennsylvania, assured the Treasury Department that in Pennsylvania no "new loan" certificates had been subscribed to
the Federal loan for the assumption of state debts. Therefore, the terms of
Section 18 were irrelevant, and interest was accordingly paid on that state's
assumed debt.

On April 10, 1792, Governor Thomas Mifflin of Pennsylvania approved "An
Act to Provide for Paying and Redeeming Certain Public Debts and for Defraying the Expenses of Government" (*Pennsylvania Statutes*, XIV, 305–12),
and on May 8 a Federal statute entitled "An Act supplementary to the act
making provision for the Debt of the United States" was enacted providing
for the reopening of the Federal loan (1 *Stat*. 281–83 [May 8, 1792]). The
1792 Pennsylvania law stipulated that state creditors would be reimbursed at
the state treasury for the nominal value of state debts subscribed to the re-
opened Federal loan if the Federal certificates were transferred to the state
treasurer. See Mifflin to H, June 23, 1792.

According to the returns supplied by Thomas Smith, Nicholson owned
more than ninety percent of Pennsylvania's "new loan" certificates which had

stated to be between forty and fifty thousand pounds,[3] and this hath since been reduced near one half by subsequent Exchanges.

2d. The provision made by Pennsa. for the redemption of this paper with the Continental Certificates to such as so chose, was co-extensive with them all, as represented, this representation was agreeable to the Act of the Legislature which accompanied it.[4]

3d The point of inquiry at the conference I had the honor to hold with you on the subject of our negociation at the close of 1791 and beginning of 1792 [5] (the period refered to) was whether any of these New Loan Certificates had been subscribed to the Loan of Congress which had closed the last of September preceding. I stated there were none, if you find it otherwise I will pay you treble their amount. On this and on the subsequent reports of the Commissioner [6] concerning the sums the restriction on transfers from one Office to another was removed.

---

been presented as payment for the Federal securities offered under the re-opened loan (Smith to Oliver Wolcott, Jr., LC, RG 53, Pennsylvania State Loan Office, Letter Book, 1790–1794, Vol. "615-P," National Archives). Nicholson, who had obtained from Smith a receipt indicating that his "new loan" certificates had been offered to the Federal Government, presented this receipt to Christian Febiger, the state treasurer of Pennsylvania. Febiger then paid to Nicholson cash amounting to the nominal value of the "new loan" certificates held by Nicholson. Despite the fact that he had paid Nicholson, Febiger was "fully convinced . . . that it never was the intention of the Legislature to embrace within the redemption the so called New-Loan certificates, which in fact never were a state debt" (Hogan, *Pennsylvania State Trials*, 67–68). The state treasurer discussed this question with Alexander Dallas, secretary of the Commonwealth, and on June 23, 1792, Dallas at Mifflin's request referred the matter to Jared Ingersoll, the attorney general of Pennsylvania. Dallas also warned Nicholson and John Donnaldson, register general of Pennsylvania, not to sanction the view that the "new loan" certificates were assumable by the Federal Government (Hogan, *Pennsylvania State Trials*, 98, 99, 301).

The question whether "new loan" certificates were redeemable under the Pennsylvania act of April 10, 1792 (and as a consequence part of the state's assumable debt under the provisions of the Federal loan) was a major point at issue in an attempt to impeach Nicholson during 1793 and 1794.

2. Letter not found.

3. See Mifflin to H, December 27, 1791, note 1.

4. Nicholson is referring to "An Act to Repeal So Much of Any Act or Acts of Assembly of This Commonwealth as Directs the Payment of the New Loan Debt or the Interest Thereof Beyond the First Day of April Next, and for Other Purposes Therein Mentioned" (*Pennsylvania Statutes*, XIII, 263–67 [March 27, 1789]).

5. See Mifflin to H, December 27, 1791; Nicholson to H, December 29, 1791, January 16, 17, 18, 1792; H to Nicholson, January 16, 1792.

6. See Nicholson to H, January 18, 1792.

4th   That these Certificates might have been subscribed to the said Loan had the possessors chose,[7] was evident not only from the Act of Congress [8] but these enquiries after the fact made by you in pursuance of that law, to prevent the Union from paying interest twice on the same debt, and considering the different terms between the loan of the *State* and *Continental* debt, the short arrears of interest on State debt and the year's interest for 1791 paid in the one case and not in the other, The United States would have been advantaged by such subscription, but from these or some other causes, existing until the Loan closed as before mentioned none were subscribed.

5th.   A Loan is afterwards opened upon the same terms under another Act of Congress,[9] in which last Loan an additional provision for Subscribers thereto, is made, different from the former and such as to make it the interest of the holders of such debt to subscribe to it—and they accordingly do so.

Under this view of the subject I think you will see nothing incompatible with what passed between us for

1st   I did and only could speak with a reference to the Loan then closed.

2d.   I did not then know that a further or future Loan would ever have been opened.

3d   Or if it had whether the terms would have been similar or otherwise—which is the case as it respects the State and the Creditor though not as it respects the United states. The Creditors by a late Act of the State until the 1st of August next have a motive which (in the circumstances of public credit at the time the former loan was opened) did not before exist to subscribe this species of State Certificates [10]—otherwise at the former enquiry on the closure of the Loan you would have found some of this debt subscribed there also.

4th   If I could have foreknown all the events which have happened as to the State of public Credit, the opening the Loan by subsequent Act of Congress, the terms thereof and the encouragement of the Legislature of Pennsa. to subscribe thereto, It would

7. See note 1.   8. 1 *Stat.* 138-44 (August 4, 1790).
9. 1 *Stat.* 281-83 (May 8, 1792).   10. See Mifflin to H, June 23, 1792.

not have been compatible with common sense in me to have stipulated with you that the holders of these Certificates so far as they were not exchanged having two offers, would not embrace the most advantageous. The encouragement proposed by the Legislature of this State as aforesaid I thought unwise at the time they deliberated thereon, and mentioned the effect it would have on this Species of our debt as well as on the unfunded depreciation debt, neither of which they seemed to intend directly to redeem, but what I said was not attended to.[11]

After what I have written if any part of what I have said should still seem to militate, I should be glad it would be specified, that I may have an opportunity of shewing you that the character of uncandid or inconsistent (which I heartily despise) are not applicable to sir

　　Your Most Obt serv　　　　　　　　　　　　　　　　　　　　J N

Alexr. Hamilton Esqr
Secty Treasy U states

PS　As I informed you on the closure of the former Loan so now on this, I am of opinion that if any New Loans were subscribed the

11. Nicholson is presumably referring to "A plan for modifying the present debt of Pennsylvania," March 15, 1792 (Hogan, *Pennsylvania State Trials*, 279–86). This plan for a state funding law was offered as an alternative to the act of April 10, 1792, which was under consideration at the time (*Pennsylvania Statutes*, XIV, 305–12).

The impeachment proceedings against Nicholson indicate that he had shown his plan to the governor and several members of the Pennsylvania legislature. In a footnote to this plan Nicholson commented on the inclusion of "new loan" certificates as follows: "It is proposed that these certificates should be received with the arrears of their interest on the same term as the other preceding debts of the state. The holders nevertheless to be continued in the privilege of exchanging them as at present. But it would seem proper that after due notice so as not to extend to the period of the limitation of the next loan by Congress, a limitation should by law be put to such power of exchanging, that thereafter the Continental certificates should be subscribed for the use of the state, and that the state having provided for the redemption of such as might remain unexchanged, unsubscribed to the loan herein proposed or unsubscribed to the assumption of the state debts by the United States, should declare that interest should thenceforth cease thereon unless payment were demanded.

"No sum is extended in this case as the Continental certificates will be in possession of the state to be opposed to this debt as far as the same may be subscribed as herein proposed." (Hogan, *Pennsylvania State Trials*, 284–85.)

present Laws of Pennsa. would enable me to give for them an equal Sum of principal and interest respectively in the unsubscribed debt of the United States as required by Act of Congress.

Yours as before

July 26th 1792
J N

To George Washington

Treasury Departmt. July 26. 1792.

Sir,

Samuel Hobart, third Mate of the Cutter on the New Hampshire Station, has tendered his resignation and sent forward his Commission which I retain 'till your return not to encumber you with it at Mount Vernon. This occasions two vacancies, as to that Cutter, of first & third Mate. The Collector of Portsmouth recommends the second Mate, John Adams, for first Mate, and a Benjamin Gunnison, who has been a Master of a Vessel, as second Mate.[1] From a conversation which I had with Mr. Langdon,[2] while here, I believe the recommendation of the Collector well founded.

The Captain of the Cutter, on the New York Station, informs that Mr. Morris[3] the first Mate has accepted an advantageous offer on board of an India-Ship. This leaves the Cutter without any other Officer than the Master,[4] who, and the Collector of New York[5] recommend Capt: Ashur Cook as first Mate, and one John Fenley as second Mate. Captn. Dennis also mentions a son of the present Surveyor of New York[6] for third Mate.

The keeping up in the Cutters their due complement of Officers and Men is now become interesting to the public service. As it will not be easy to obtain better lights, I am induced to submit as they stand the recommendations respecting the first and second Mates of each Cutter. As to the third Mate for the New York Cutter some further enquiry is necessary.

Should you approve, and be without blank Commissions, it is still desireable that I should be able as early as convenient to notify your determination. The persons will enter into service upon that notification and their Commissions can be antedated.

With the most perfect respect and truest attachment,   I have the honor to be &c.   Alexander Hamilton

PS.

May I be permitted to remind you of the vacancies in the Maryland Cutter, about which you intended to enquire on your way?

LC, George Washington Papers, Library of Congress.
  1. See Joseph Whipple to H, October 7, 1791, June 30, 1792.
  2. Presumably Senator John Langdon of New Hampshire.
  3. David Morris.   4. Patrick Dennis.   5. John Lamb.
  6. John Lasher was surveyor of the port of New York.

To Wilhem and Jan Willink, Nicholaas and Jacob Van Staphorst, and Nicholas Hubbard

Treasury Department
July 26th. 1792.

Gentlemen,

You will herewith receive triplicates of my letters of the 7th. of May [1] and 20th. ultimo,[2] also a duplicate of mine of the 16th. instant.

In the latter, I informed you, that I had directed the Treasurer to draw bills upon you, for 500.000 Guilders, and I have now to add, for your information, that, as soon as these bills are sold, I shall cause further drafts to be made, to the extent of 500.000 Guilders, in addition to the sum above mentioned.

I am &c.   Alexander Hamilton.

Messrs. Willink, Van Staphorst
and Hubbard,
Amsterdam.

Copy, RG 233, Reports of the Treasury Department, 1792–1793, Vol. III, National Archives. This letter was enclosed in H's "Report on Foreign Loans," February 13, 1793.
  1. Letter not found.   2. Letter not found.

To Rufus King

[Philadelphia] July 27. 92

Desirous of examining accurately the question decided by the Canvassers [1]—I will thank you for a minute of all the authorities which were consulted by you when you gave your opinion.[2]

Yrs. truly   AH

I shall be glad to have them as soon as may be.

R King Esqr

ALS, New-York Historical Society, New York City.
  1. This is a reference to the decision of the board of canvassers of New York State in the disputed gubernatorial election of 1792. For this election, see Philip Schuyler to H, May 8, 1792, note 4; H to John Adams, June 25, 1792, note 2; H to King, June 28, July 25, 1792; King to H, July 10, 1792; and William Lewis to H, July 21, 1792.
  2. King and Aaron Burr, United States Senators from New York, had been asked to give opinions on the legal aspects of the disputed election. See H to King, June 28, 1792, note 2.

From Jeremiah Olney

Providence, July 27, 1792. "I have recd. your Letter of the 19th Inst.[1] and have charged to the United States the 2,105.12 paid the Marshall of Rhode-Island District. . . ."

ADfS, Rhode Island Historical Society, Providence.
  1. Letter not found. See, however, Olney to H, April 9, 1792, in which William Peck's account with Olney is stated.

From Otho H. Williams [1]

Ceresville [Maryland] July 27, 1792. "I this day received your letter of the 19 Instant. That my disposition has ever been correspondent to your Wish, for the maintanance of harmony and cordiality, in the department over which you superintend, the whole tenor of my conduct will uniformly evince. I do not even except the instance which has occasioned you the trouble of expostulating; for, notwithstanding the perversion of the purport of my letter, of the 3d. of May to the surveyor,[2] a liberlal construction of it will shew that my intention was to prevent disorder by intimating to him the propriety of exercising with discretion that power which is undeniably reposed in the Executive department but which cannot be carried into compleat effect without being delegated, in a degree, to subordinate officers. In your arguments in support of the doctrine of discretionary Executive power, under certain limitations, you seem to contemplate it only in the hands of Superiors, and even there you admit that it may be abused; but you perhaps did not reflect that it was most liable to abuse in its remotest application. The Inspectors, some of them, and I then understood the complaint to be general, complained of harsh and illiberal treatment, and it was intimated to me that apprehensions were entertained of an intention in the Surveyor to involve one of them at least in a premunire, on account of a former misunderstanding. Reflecting on the probable consequences, and the *possibility*, which I still contend for, as it actually occurred, of an interference of duties, I was induced to write to the Surveyor requesting him, *as much as possible* to avoid demanding of the Inspectors of the Customs services which *might* interfere with their particular duties as such: and added also my opinion that their services *ought* to be *voluntary*. My justification is that I had never conceived the idea of compulsory means. That the law requires as specific a qualification to Offi[ce]s in the department of the revenue as in any other, and until persons had been so qualified there could exist I concluded no *legal* obligation on them to act. *Consistency—Expediency*, and the expectations which had been formed might have been suggested as motives for their compliance; I could not have doubted the success of the Arguments and relied too confidently perhaps on the discretion of the Surveyor to make the experiment Being unconscious of and expectations from me in a department with which I was unconnected. When an unconciliatory temper— a proud and a Captious Spirit, aggravated the reluctance of *some* of the Inspectors into a refusal to act, was I instantly to retract the advice and opinion which I had delivered to the *Surveyor* and to insist that if the Inspectors would not undertake an office, novel and unexpected to them, and obey the directions of the *Inspector of the Revenue* however despotic, or illegal, that I would remove them from offices which they had before filled with satisfaction to the public? Whether they were despotic depends on the manner of enforcing them. They were illegal because services were required and performed without the requisite qualification and contrary to an express injunction in the law. I was soon informed of the displacement and threatened with a representation to the secretary: But as one person who had been recommended by the Surveyor, and I think one other who served him as Clerk were there employed as occasional Inspectors of the Customs, and as no idea of the expediency of any addition to the number of Inspectors then employed was ever suggested to me, I concluded that like other fraca's which had happened between them it would soon subside, and the business go on as usual. I could reasonably credit the complaints of the Inspectors because complaints from them had been reiterated before the revenue law came into operation. One of them had been prosecuted by him on a great number of charges, which upon a strict and impartial investigation I concluded to be without foundation. To that decision, for I know of no other cause, I ascribe the designed perversion of the intention of my letter; for if it naturally had the mischievous effects attributed to it the representation to the treasury department ought not to have been delayed for so many Weeks after they were known, and until Ill health and a sickly Season had obliged me to retire from my Office in Town. Whether the complexion of this disagreeable affair recd any unfavorable Shades from the medium through which it passed to the Treasury or not I am warranted in the suspicion that circumstances as well as facts have been misrepresented, otherwise you would not be possessed of 'unpleasant particulars' which you reluctantly impart. You think it now proper to inform me that 'The Surveyor further states that my Deputy *took pains* to induce the Inspectors not to mark.' Whatever credit this assertion may claim, *I must* doubt it. Inclosed is Mr. Deloziers[3] letter to me on the subject; He will support the contradiction by testimony if you think proper to call for it. He is a young Gentleman who has been several years in public service under my particular notice, and from a fortunate experience of his talents I can declare that, he not only possesses a good understanding and an excellent capacity for business, but that he enjoys an amiable disposition and has invariable manifested an integrity which entitles him to my entire confidence. This character will be coroborated by many. The Surveyor personally dislikes him. I will not enter into his motives; but it will be hard for him to make it appear that he has done any thing to embarrass the public service, or to excite prejudices against a government to which he aspires (and I think with well founded hopes) at becoming conspicuously useful. . . . Having no controul over the officers of the revenue and the authority of the Collector over the Inspectors of the Customs becoming questionable whether I shall ever submit to be the mere instrument of rigorous measures respecting them is a consideration humiliating in the extreme. In such an exigency your own feelings would dictate by determination."

ADfS, Maryland Historical Society, Baltimore.
   1. For background to this letter, see H to Williams, June 18, 1792, and Williams to H, June 28, 1792.
   2. Robert Ballard.
   3. Daniel Delozier was deputy collector of customs at Baltimore.

To Thomas Willing [1]

[Philadelphia, July 27, 1792]

Mr. Hamilton presents his Compliments to Mr Willing and sends him a letter [2] which came to hand by yesterday's post for his information. Tis probable, as is not uncommon, when men are in a confessing mood, that more has been confessed, than is true; yet the communication deserves particular attention, as it is certain that the Gang mentioned are the most ingenious set of forgers that perhaps ever infested a Country.

July 27. 1792

AL, Independence National Historical Park Collection, Old Custom House, Philadelphia.
   1. Willing was president of the Bank of the United States.
   2. Letter not found.

To Sharp Delany

Treasury Department, July 28, 1792. "I have this day decided upon the case of Asa Gilbert. There being no appearance of fraud in the transaction, the interest of all parties in the forfeiture is remitted to him, upon his paying the legal Duties and all reasonable costs and charges. . . ."

LS, Bureau of Customs, Philadelphia.

[Detector No. I] ¹

[Philadelphia, July 28, 1792]

[Philadelphia] *Gazette of the United States,* July 28, 1792.
    1. Philip Marsh has written: "After Hamilton's insinuations signed 'T. L.' on July 25th, in the next issue of Fenno's *Gazette* appeared what seems to be a deliberate part of the planned attack on Jefferson and Freneau by Hamilton, in a letter by 'Detector,' who attacked the *National Gazette* as the tool of the Republican 'faction' " ("Hamilton's Neglected Essays, 1791–1793," *The New-York Historical Society Quarterly,* XXXII [October, 1948], 291). No other evidence, however, has been found that H was the author of this letter.
    The second "Detector" letter is dated August 23, 1792.

From Samuel Gerry

[*Marblehead, Massachusetts, July 28, 1792.* On August 18, 1792, Hamilton wrote to Gerry: "Your letter of the 28 Ultimo was duly received." *Letter not found.*]

T. L. No. II ¹

[Philadelphia, July 28, 1792]

FOR THE GAZETTE OF THE UNITED STATES.

Mr. Fenno,²
    In your Gazette of last Wednesday, after observing that the Editor of the National Gazette receives a salary from government,

I enquired "whether this salary is paid him for *translations;* or for *publications,* the design of which is to vilify those to whom the voice of the people has committed the administration of our public affairs." In his paper of this day, he intimates that he "receives a small stipend for services rendered as French Translator to the Department of State, and, *as Editor of a free newspaper.*" [3] This excites my curiosity still farther, and I shall hold myself obliged to any of your correspondents, or to the Editor of this really *National Gazette* (as it now appears to be) if either of them will inform me what inducement our rulers can have to hire a man to abuse them, and whether they do not hereby unnecessarily squander the public money. I have often heard that authors in England, or their booksellers for them, when they find their books do not sell according to their wishes, hire some garretteer to write against them—then publish a reply to his own lucubrations—and so go on, objecting and replying, until the attention of the public is drawn towards the book, and thus it is brought into demand. If there were as many pieces in the National Gazette in favor of government and public characters, as there are against them, I should be apt to conclude that Congress and their officers were playing us the same trick, in hopes of keeping their seats and places for life; but when all the publications are against them, and none in their favor—when this "free newspaper" is always

Free to defame, but never free to praise,

it does not appear easy to account for this branch of national expence. If none of your readers can do it, we must wait with patience 'till the treasury accounts are published, as the Constitution of the United States requires, and then, perhaps, the mystery will be explained.

July 28.   T.L.

[Philadelphia] *Gazette of the United States,* August 1, 1792.
  1. The other "T. L." letters are dated July 25 and August 11, 1792.
  2. John Fenno, editor of the *Gazette of the United States.*
  3. After quoting H's "T. L." letter of July 25, 1792, in full, Philip Freneau, editor of the [Philadelphia] *National Gazette,* wrote: "The above is beneath a reply. It might be queried, however, whether a man who receives a small stipend for services rendered as French translator to the department of state, and, as editor of a free newspaper, admits into his publication impartial strictures on the proceedings of government, is not more likely to act an honest

and disinterested part towards the public, than a vile sycophant, who obtaining emoluments from government, far more lucrative than the salary alluded to (by undermining another who was in possession of the employ) finds his interest in attempting to poison the minds of the people by propagating and disseminating principles and sentiments utterly subversive of the true republican interests of this country, and by flattering and recommending *every* and *any* measure of government, however pernicious and destructive its tendency might be, to the great body of the people. The world is left to decide the motives of each" ([Philadelphia] *National Gazette,* July 28, 1792).

Fenno's reply to Freneau, which is dated July 30, 1792, and which appeared in the following issue of the *National Gazette,* reads as follows:

"It is insinuated in the 'National Gazette' of last Saturday, that 'by undermining another who was in possession of the employ,' the subscriber obtained the work which he has executed for the government. This can refer only to printing the Journals of the Senate of the United States. With some persons it may be sufficient for me to say, the charge is wholly unfounded. Those who wish for further satisfaction, by calling on me, may be convinced that the insinuation is something more than a simple *untruth.*

"With respect to the principles and sentiments propagated by the Gazette of the United States, the Editor of that paper is willing to abide by the general opinion of the public—That public, whose essential *republican* interest he has sedulously attempted to promote for twenty years past—and to which he is now under additional and more forceable obligations of attachment; having as much at stake, as an individual, as the average of his fellow citizens, the freedom and happiness of a numerous family of children." (*National Gazette,* August 1, 1792.)

From Rufus King

[New York] Sunday 29 July 1792

Mr. Jay will be with you this week [1]—you will therefore have an opportunity to converse with him respecting our very unpleasant situation.[2] All the measures which have been pursued have been calculated to induce the Legislature to call a convention to revise the decision of the canvassers. So far as I am able to form an Opinion, a majority of the Assembly are Clintonians, and if so, will not agree to call a convention—should this be the case, the business will then terminate.

I have only a few loose notes concerning the questions decided by the Canvassers.[3] By turning up Bacon [4] or Comins,[5] you will find under the word Sheriff, the english cases referred to, which respect the appointment & discharge of that Office. The Lya[bi]lity of holding the Office beyound the Term for which sheriffs, constables, & other annual Officers are appointed must have arisen from the inconvenience to which the administration of Justice would have been exposed by vacancies in any of those Offices. The Law on that point cannot be doubted—the practice is common in this country as well as in England, and property to a great amount in both Countries is held under decisions of Juries returned by Sheriffs exercising their Office beyound their year.

Old sheriff to continue until another is appointed &c   2. Lill. 633 [6]

Moore— 333 [7]

1 Hales. P.C. 499 [8]

Annually appointed   Str. $\overline{625}$ [9]

de facto Officers their acts valid. Lut. 508 [10]—1 Hales p.C. 499 [11]

10. Mod. 288 [12]—Cro. Eliz. 699 [13]

Andrew. 163 [14]

2. Barnard. B.R. 193

Same   264 [15]

12. Mod   25⟨3⟩ [16]

Sheriffs who begin, shall end, an Exon ~ [17] 11. Mod. 35 [18]—6 Mod. 290 [19]—Ld. Raym. 1072 [20] 1 Salk. 322 [21]—Dyer &c &c [22]
Officer at Pleasure, is at the Kings pleasure—Salk. 466. [23]
Incompatibility of Office—the constitution declares the sheriffs incapable of holding any other Office.
Tioga votes rejected because they were transmitted by a Deputy's Deputy.

a Deputy may appoint a Deputy to do a particular act—

1 Salk. 95 [24]

Clinton votes rejected because the Deputy was appointed by Parol only—

Deputy may be without Deed   9. Rep. 51.b [25]

Cro Eliz. 67 [26]

10. Co. 192 [27]

3. Mod. 150 [28]

Deputy may be by Parol   Jenk. 110. pl. 14 [29]

Yr's sincerely   Rufus King

A Hamilton Esqr.

ALS, Hamilton Papers, Library of Congress.
    1. John Jay was going to Philadelphia to preside over the Supreme Court session which was to begin on August 6, 1792.
    2. King is referring to recent developments in the disputed gubernatorial

election in New York, in which Governor George Clinton had defeated Jay. For background to this election, see Philip Schuyler to H, May 9, 1792, note 4; H to John Adams, June 25, 1792, note 2; H to King, June 28, July 25, 27, 1792; King to H, July 10, 1792; William Lewis to H, July 21, 1792.

3. For the canvassers' questions and King's reply to them, see H to King, June 28, 1792, note 2.

4. *A New Abridgment of the Law. By Matthew Bacon, Of the Middle Temple, Esq; The Fifth Edition, Corrected; with Many Additional Notes and References of and to Modern Determinations* (Dublin, 1786).

5. *A Digest of the Laws of England. By the Right Honourable Sir John Comyns, Knight; Late Lord Chief Baron of His Majesty's Court of Exchequer. Continued down to the present Time, By a Gentleman of the Inner Temple* (London, 1785).

6. *The Practical Register: or, A General Abridgment of the Law, As it is now practiced in the several Courts of Chancery, King's Bench, Common Pleas and Exchequer, digested by way of Common-Place, under Alphabetical Heads, with great Variety of Cases extracted from the Reports. Together with All the Rules of the said Courts brought down to the Year 1719. Collected by the Author, John Lilly, Gent. In Two Volumes. The Second Edition* (London, 1735), 633.

7. Case 333, page 186. See Lewis to H, July 21, 1792, note 8.

8. *Historia Placitorum Coronæ. The History of the Pleas of the Crown By Sir Matthew Hale, Lord Chief Justice of the Court of King's Bench. Published from the Original Manuscripts By Sollom Emlyn, of Lincoln's-Inn, Esq. A New Edition: Carefully Revised and Corrected; with Additional Notes and References to Modern Cases Concerning the Pleas of the Crown. Together with an Abridgment of the Statutes Concerning Felonies Which Have Been Enacted since the First Publication of this Work. By George Wilson, Serjeant at Law. In Two Volumes* (London, 1778), I, 499.

9. See Lewis to H, July 21, 1792, note 12.

10. *The Reports and Entries of Sir Edward Lutwyche, Kt. Serjeant at Law, and late one of the Judges of the Court of Common Pleas. The several Cases therein are truly stated upon the respective Pleadings and Entries, in English. Also, Every Citation in the Report is carefully examin'd by the Law-Books to which they refer, and where they agree, and where they differ from the Point in Question made appear; and those ranged in that Order as in many Places to form an Argument where there was none before; with large Observations. Likewise Many obsolete Words and difficult Sentences are explain'd; which are printed in a different Character. Composed in a plain and easy Method, and made very useful for Students and Practicers of the Common Law. W. Nelson of the Middle Temple, Esq.* (London, 1718), 508.

11. See note 8.

12. See Lewis to H, July 21, 1792, note 13. King is referring to case 149, which appears on page 288.

13. *Reports of Sir George Croke, Knight, Formerly One of the Justices of the Courts of King's-Bench and Common-Pleas, of Such Select Cases As Were Adjudged in the Said Courts During the Reign of Queen Elizabeth. Collected and Written in French By Himself; Revised and Published in English, By Sir Harbottle Grimston, Baronet, Master of the Rolls. the Fifth Edition, Corrected, with Marginal Notes and References to the Later Reports, and Other Books of Authority, By Thomas Leach, Esq. of the Middle Temple, Barrister at Law* (London, 1791), 699.

14. *Reports of Cases Argued and Adjudged in the Court of King's Bench, in the Eleventh and Twelfth Years of the Reign of King George the Second. By George Andrews, Esq. of the Middle Temple. The Second Edition. With*

Notes and References down to Michaelmas Term, 31 Geo. 3. and an Appendix containing some additional Cases not before Published. By George William Vernon, Esq. Barrister at Law (London, 1792), 170

15. *Reports of Cases Determined in the Court of King's Bench, together with some other Cases; from Trin. 12 Geo. I. to Trin. 7 Geo. II. In Two Volumes* (London, 1744), 193.

16. *Modern Reports: or Cases Adjudged in the Court of King's Bench, from the Second Year of King William III. to the End of his Reign. . . . By a Late Barrister of the Middle-Temple* (London, 1769), XII, 253.

17. *Exoneretur* is Latin meaning "let him be relieved or discharged."

18. *Modern Reports: or, A Report of Cases Argued and Adjudged in the Court of King's Bench, in the Time of Queen Anne, viz. From the Fourth to the Eighth Years of her Reign: During which the late Lord Chief Justice Holt presided in that Court. With Tables of the Principal Matters, &c. The Second Edition* (London, 1769), XI, 35–36.

19. *Modern Cases, Argued and Adjudged in the Court of Queen's Bench, at Westminster, in the Second and Third Years of Queen Anne, in the Time when Sir John Holt sat Chief Justice there. With Two Tables: The First, Of the Names of the Cases: And the Other, Of the special Matter therein contained. Vol. VI. The Fourth Edition. Reviewed and Corrected, and many Thousand New and Proper References added, never before Printed from all the Books of Reports, down to the Year 1757. By Danby Pickering, of Gray's Inn, Esq; And Reader of the Law-Lecture to that Honourable Society* (London, 1757), VI, 290–300.

20. *Reports of Cases Argued and Adjudged in the Courts of King's Bench and Common Pleas, In the Reigns of The late King William, Queen Anne, King George the First, and King George the Second. Taken and collected By the Right Honourable Robert Lord Raymond, late Lord Chief Justice of the Court of King's Bench. Vol. II. The Fourth Edition, Corrected; with Additional References to former and later Reports; By John Bayley* (London, 1790), 1072–76.

21. *Reports of Cases Adjudged in the Court of King's Bench: with Some Special Cases in the Courts of Chancery, Common Pleas, and Exchequer, Alphabetically digested under proper Heads: From the First Year of K. William and Q. Mary to the Tenth Year of Q. Anne. By William Salkeld, late Serjeant at Law. With Two Tables; one of the Names of the Cases, the other of the Principal Matters therein contained . . .* (Dublin, 1791) I, 322.

22. See Lewis to H, July 21, 1792, note 12.

23. Salkeld, *Reports*, II, 466. See note 21.

24. Salkeld, *Reports*, I, 95. See note 21.

25. *The Reports of Sir Edward Coke, Kt. In English, In Thirteen Parts Complete; With References to all the Ancient and Modern Books of the Law. Exactly Translated, and Compared with the First and Last Edition in French, and printed Page for Page with the same. To Which are Now Added, The Respective Pleadings, In English: The Whole newly Revised, and carefully Corrected and Translated, with many additional Notes and References, By George Wilson, Serjeant at Law* (London, 1777), Part IX, 51 (b).

26. *Reports of Sir George Croke*, 67. See note 13.

27. This reference has not been found.

28. *Modern Reports: Being a Collection Of Several Special Cases In The Court of King's Bench, In the Last Years of the Reign of King Charles II. In the Reign of King James II. And in the Two First Years of King William and Queen Mary. Together With the Resolutions and Judgements thereupon. The Fourth Edition. Reviewed and Corrected, and many Thousand New and Proper References added, never before Printed, from all the Books of Reports,*

down to the Year 1757. By Danby Pickering, of Gray's Inn, Esq; And Reader of the Law-Lecture to that Honourable Society (London, 1757), III, 150.

29. Eight Centuries of Reports: or Eight Hundred Cases Solemnly Adjudged in the Exchequer-Chamber, or Upon Writs of Error. Published Originally in French and Latin, by Judge Jenkins. Carefully Translated By Theodore Barlow of the Middle-Temple, Esq; With a large Table of the Principal Matters. The Third Edition (London, 1777), 110, Case 14.

From George Washington

Mount Vernon July 29th. 1792.

My dear Sir,   (Private & confidential)

I have not yet received the new regulation of allowances to the Surveyors, or Collectors of the duties on Spirituous liquors;[1] but this by the bye. My present purpose is to write you a letter on a more interesting and important subject. I shall do it in strict confidence, & with frankness & freedom.

On my way home, and since my arrival here, I have endeavoured to learn from sensible & moderate men—known friends to the Government—the sentiments which are entertained of public measures. These all agree that the Country is prosperous & happy; but they seem to be alarmed at that system of policy, and those interpretations of the Constitution which have taken place in[2] Congress.

Others, less friendly perhaps to the Government, and more disposed to arraign the conduct of its Officers (among whom may be classed my neighbour, & quandom friend Colo M)[3] go further, &

ALS, Hamilton Papers, Library of Congress; ADfS, George Washington Papers, Library of Congress; LC, George Washington Papers, Library of Congress.

1. For a discussion of the "new regulation of allowances," see Tench Coxe to H, July 25, 1792.

2. At this point in the draft Washington wrote and crossed out: "the Legislature, and which, they say, the friends to the adoption of it when the enemies were opposing it in the several Conventions averred never could be admitted, or so tortured in that manner. The plea of expediency or a war necessity they say, ought never to be admitted but in the greatest and most pressing emergency and then, acts of indemnity & ratification ought immediately to follow."

3. George Mason, who had been a member of the Constitutional Convention in 1787, was a leader of the opposition to ratification in the Virginia Ratifying Convention the following year. In a conversation with Thomas Jefferson on September 30, 1792, Mason outlined the financial policies which he would have preferred and said "he considered Hamilton as having done us more injury than Gr. Britain & all her fleets & armies" (Ford, *Writings of Jefferson*, I, 202).

enumerate a variety of matters, wch. as well as I can recollect, may be adduced under the following heads. Viz.[4]

First   That the public debt is greater than we can possibly pay before other causes of adding new debt to it will occur; and that this has been artificially created by adding together the whole amount of the debtor & creditor sides of the accounts, instead of taking only their balances; which could have been paid off in a short time.

2d.   That this accumulation of debt has taken for ever out of our power those easy sources of revenue, which, applied to the ordinary necessities and exigencies of Government, would have answered them habitually, and covered us from habitual murmerings against taxes & tax gatherers; reserving extraordinary calls, for extraordinary occasions, would animate the People to meet them.

3d.   That the calls for money have been no greater than we must generally expect, for the same or equivalent exigencies; yet we are already obliged to strain the *impost*[5] till it produces clamour, and will produce evasion, and war on our citizens to collect it, and even to resort to an *Excise* law,[6] of odious character with the people; partial in its operation; unproductive unless enforced by arbitrary & vexatious means; and committing the authority of the Government in parts where resistance is most probable, & coercion least practicable.

4. On May 23, 1792, Jefferson had written to Washington summarizing the expressions of discontent with the administration of the Government currently appearing in the newspapers. Washington in the letter to H printed above repeats Jefferson's summary almost verbatim (Ford, *Writings of Jefferson,* VI, 1–6). On July 10 Washington discussed the contents of Jefferson's letter with Jefferson and indicated that "he did not believe the discontents extended far from the seat of govmt. He had seen & spoken with many people in Maryld & Virginia in his late journey. He found the people contented & happy." Jefferson amplified some of the topics contained in his letter of May 23, 1792, and as Washington appeared to support H's financial policies, Jefferson "avoided entering into argument with him on those points" (Ford, *Writings of Jefferson,* I, 198–201).

5. Washington is referring to "An Act for raising a farther sum of money for the protection of the frontiers, and for other purposes therein mentioned" (1 *Stat.* 259–63 [May 2, 1792])

6. Washington is referring to "An Act repealing, after the last day of June next, the duties heretofore laid upon Distilled Spirits imported from abroad, and laying others in their stead; and also upon Spirits distilled within the United States, and for appropriating the same" (1 *Stat.* 199–214 [March 3, 1791]) and "An Act concerning the Duties on Spirits distilled within the United States" (1 *Stat.* 267–71 [May 8, 1792]).

4th   They cite propositions in Congress, and suspect other projects on foot, still to encrease the mass of the debt.

5th.   They say that by borrowing at ⅔ of the interest, we might have paid of[f] the principal in ⅔ of the time; but that from this we are precluded by its being made irredeemable but in small portions, & long terms.

6th.   That this irredeemable quality was given it for the avowed purpose of inviting its transfer to foreign Countries.

7th.   They predict that this transfer of the principal, when compleated, will occasion an exportation of 3 Millions of dollars annually for the interest; a drain of Coin, of which as there has been no example, no calculation can be made of its consequences.

8th.   That the banishment of our Coin will be compleated by the creation of 10 millions of paper money, in the form of Bank-bills now issuing into circulation.

9th.   They think the 10 or 12 pr Ct. annual profit, paid to the lenders of this paper medium, are taken out of the pockets of the people, who would have had without interest the coin it is banishing.

10th.   That all the Capitol employed in paper speculation is barren & useless, producing, like that on a gaming table, no accession to itself, and is withdrawn from Commerce and Agriculture where it would have produced addition to the common mass.

11th   That it nourishes in our citizens vice & idleness instead of industry & morality.

12th.   That it has furnished effectual means of corrupting such a portion of the legislature, as turns the balance between the honest Voters which ever way it is directed.

13th.   That this corrupt squadron, deciding the voice of the legislature, have manifested their dispositions to get rid of the limitations imposed by the Constitution on the general legislature; limitations, on the faith of which, the States acceded to that instrument.

14th   That the ultimate object of all this is to prepare the way for a change, from the present republican form of Government, to that of a monarchy; of which the British Constitution is to be the model.

15th.   That this was contemplated in the Convention, they say is no secret, because its partisans have made none of it—to effect it then was impracticable; but they are still eager after their object, and are predisposing every thing for its ultimate attainment.

16th. So many of them have got into the legislature, that, aided by the corrupt squadron of paper dealers, who are at their devotion, they make a majority in both houses.

17th   The republican party who wish to preserve the Government in its present form, are fewer even when joined by the two, three, or half a dozen antifederalists, who, tho' they dare not avow it, are still opposed to any general Government: but being less so to a republican than a Monarchical one, they naturally join those whom they think pursuing the lesser evil.

18th. Of all the mischiefs objected to the system of measures beforementioned, none they add is so afflicting, & fatal to every honest hope, as the corruption of the legislature. As it was the earliest of these measures it became the instrument for producing the rest, and will be the instrument for producing in future a King, Lords & Commons; or whatever else those who direct it may chuse. Withdrawn such a distance from the eye of their Constituents, and these so dispersed as to be inaccessible to public information, and particularly to that of the conduct of their own Representatives, they will form the worst Government upon earth, if the means of their corruption be not prevented.

19th. The only hope of safety they say, hangs now on the numerous representation which is to come forward the ensuing year; [7] but should the majority of the new members be still in the same principles with the present—shew so much deriliction to republican government, and such a disposition to encroach upon, or explain away the limited powers of the constitution in order to change it, it is not easy to conjecture what would be the result, nor what means would be resorted to for correction of the evil. True wisdom they acknowledge should direct temperate & peaceable measures; but add, the division of sentiment & interest happens unfortunately, to be so geographical, that no mortal can say that what is most wise & temperate, would prevail against what is more

7. The Congress which met in the fall of 1792 comprised sixty-nine members. In accordance with the 1790 census figures, thirty-four members were added under "An Act for apportioning Representatives among the several States, according to the first enumeration" (1 *Stat.* 253 [April 14, 1792]). The new Congress did not convene, however, until December 2, 1793.

easy & obvious; they declare, they can contemplate no evil more incalculable than the breaking of the Union into two, or more parts; yet, when they view the mass which opposed the original coalescence, when they consider that it lay chiefly in the Southern quarter—that the legislature have availed themselves of no occasion of allaying it, but on the contrary whenever Northern & Southern prejudices have come into conflict, the latter have been sacraficed and the former soothed.

20th. That the owers of the debt are in the Southern and the holders of it in the Northern division.

21st. That the antifederal champions are now strengthened in argument by the fulfilment of their predictions, which has been brought about by the Monarchical federalists themselves; who, having been for the new government merely as a stepping stone to Monarchy, have themselves adopted the very construction, of which, when advocating its acceptance before the tribunal of the people, they declared it insuceptable; whilst the republican federalists, who espoused the same government for its intrinsic merits, are disarmed of their weapons, that which they denied as prophecy being now become true history. Who, therefore, can be sure they ask, that these things may not proselyte the small number which was wanting to place the majority on the other side—and this they add is the event at which they tremble.

These, as well as my memory serves me, are the sentiments which, directly and indirectly, have been disclosed to me.

To obtain light, and to pursue truth, being my sole aim; and wishing to have before me *explanations* of as well as the *complaints* on measures in which the public interest, harmony and peace is so deeply concerned, and my public conduct so much involved; it is my request, and you would oblige me in furnishing me, with your ideas upon the discontents here enumerated—and for this purpose I have thrown them into heads or sections, and numbered them that those ideas may apply to the corrispondent numbers. Although I do not mean to hurry you in giving your thoughts on the occasion of this letter, yet, as soon as you can make it convenient to yourself it would—for more reasons than one—be agreeable, & very satisfactory to me.

The enclosure in your letter of the 16th. was sent back the Post after I received it, with my approving signature; and in a few days I will write to the purpose mentioned in your letter of the 22d. both to the Secretary of War & yourself. At present all my business —public & private—is on my own shoulders, the two young Gentlemen who came home with me,[8] being on visits to their friends—and my Nephew, the Major,[9] too much indisposed to afford me any aid, in copying or in other matters.

With affectionate regard   I am always—Yours   Go: Washington

Alexr. Hamilton Esqr.

8. Bartholomew Dandridge, Martha Washington's nephew, and Howell Lewis, Washington's nephew.
9. George Augustine Washington.

To Elisha Boudinot

[Philadelphia] 30th July, 1792.

Dear Sir:

I expected to have set out to-day to join the Committee to-morrow at Newark, but it is not possible.[1] To-morrow morning I shall embark in the Early Stage, and hope to reach you in the afternoon; but I pray that no business may be deferred on my account.

Truly yours,   Alexr. Hamilton.

JCHW, V, 517.
    1. H attended the meeting of the committee of the board of directors of the Society for Establishing Useful Manufactures which met on August 1, 1792, at Paterson, New Jersey, rather than at Newark ("Minutes of the S.U.M.," 56). See also "Proposals to Contract for the Construction of the Manufacturing Plant of the Society for Establishing Useful Manufactures," July 11, 1792, and H to Boudinot, July 12, 1792.

From William Ellery

Colles Office
Port of Newport [Rhode Island] July 30th 1792

Sir,

I have received your letter of the 9th of this month [1] on the twentieth. The monies I had collected approached so nearly to the sum wanted to discharge the drawbacks due on distilled Spirits exported, that I thought it more adviseable to advance the deficiency, than to apply for it to the Bank of Providence. It has been advanced by the office, the drawback due on the 26th. of June last is paid, and I hope that the like difficulties will not again occur.[2]

By the 8th. Sec. of the Act for raising a further sum of money for the protection of the Frontiers and for other purposes therein mentioned, it is enacted, That the term of credit for the payment of duties on salt shall be nine months, and on all articles, the produce of the West Indies, salt excepted, where the amount of the duty to be paid by one person or copartnership shall exceed fifty dollars, shall be four months."[3] A cargo consisting of Sugar Coffee and salt is imported from the West Indies, the duties to be paid by one person or copartnership, the aggregate amount of which exceeds fifty dollars but the duty upon the salt separately considered doth not exceed that sum; is the duty on the salt in such case to be paid down, or is it to be paid in nine months, or combined with the duties on the other articles is it to be paid in four months?

The Thermomr. designed for the Surveyor of Pawcatuck[4] has been sent to him and arrived safe.

I am, Sir, Yr. most Obedt servt.   Wm Ellery Collr.

A Hamilton Esqr

LC, Newport Historical Society, Newport, Rhode Island.
  1. Letter not found.   2. See Ellery to H, June 25, 1792.
  3. 1 *Stat.* 260–61 (May 2, 1792). For a similar question concerning this section, see Charles Lee to H, July 5, 1792.
  4. George Stillman. See Ellery to H, February 13, March 5, 19, April 9, May 7, 21, June 11, 1792.

To Benjamin Walker

Philadelphia July 30. 1792

Dear Walker

This will be delivered to you by Mr. Pearce.[1] A Vessel has gone round to New York with the Machinery &c. prepared for the Society;[2] the freight will be to be paid and the passages of some workmen Eight or ten, who were with him & who will be immediately necessary in the further construction of Machines &c. Their passage money also will be to be paid. The freight by agreement is 6d. per foot square—the passage money a dollar ⅌ head. Inclosed is a bill of Lading.

Yrs   A Hamilton

Benjamin Walker Esq

ALS, Historical Society of Pennsylvania, Philadelphia.
    1. William Pearce, an employee of the Society for Establishing Useful Manufactures. See "Account with John Nixon," July 23, 1792.
    2. These payments were to be made by Walker under a resolution of July 6, 1792, of the Society for Establishing Useful Manufactures. This resolution reads as follows: "Resolved, That such temporary Sheds as may be necessary be immediately erected and the Machinery and other property of the Society be transported to the Seat of the Factory, and that for effecting the said purpose a sum not exceeding one Thousand Dollars be appropriated" ("Minutes of the S.U.M.," 48). Walker endorsed this letter as follows: "Fred Bird Acco & Rect. 69.33 Manug Society."

To George Washington

Treasury Department July 30. 1792.

Sir,
    I have the honor to transmit herewith sundry papers relative to an arrangement, which has been concerted between the Commissioner of the Revenue and myself, on the subject of compensation to the Officers of Inspection,[1] in consequence of additional latitude given to The President of the United States by the Act of the last Session entitled, An Act concerning the duties on spirits distilled within the United States.[2] This arrangement, founded on the best lights hitherto in the possession of the Department, is respectfully submitted to your consideration & disposal.
    More adequate compensations than those heretofore allowed (and which from necessity were restricted within narrower limits than were originally deemed proper) are essential to the effectual execution of the law. Many Officers wait the issue of a new arrangement to decide their continuance or non-continuance in Office.
    The additions now proposed will, it is not doubted, leave the aggregate expence within the limits prescribed by law; the contingent items having been estimated largely for greater caution.

Intimations have been received that the non-execution of the Law in certain scenes begins to produce discontent in neighbouring ones,[3] in which a perfect acquiescence had taken place. This is natural, and implies a danger of a serious nature, if not timely obviated. The inadequateness of compensation, by preventing the acceptance of Offices, where the Law is least popular, is one of the causes of that non-execution. It is interesting that this cause be removed as a preliminary to the vigorous enforcing of the law in the delinquent scenes; which makes it desireable that a more competent arrangement of compensations should be adopted as speedily as shall consist with due consideration and your convenience.

With the highest respect and the truest attachment, I have the honor to be &c. Alexander Hamilton

LC, George Washington Papers, Library of Congress.
1. See Tench Coxe to H, July 25, 1792.
2. 1 *Stat.* 267–71 (May 8, 1792).
3. See H to Edward Carrington, July 25, 1792, and Daniel Huger to H, June 22–25, 1792.

To George Washington

Philadelphia July 30th [–August 3] 1792

Sir

I received the most sincere pleasure at finding in our last conversation, that there was some relaxation in the disposition you had before discovered to decline a reelection. Since your departure, I have lost no opportunity of sounding the opinions of persons, whose opinions were worth knowing, on these two points—1st the effect of your declining upon the public affairs, and upon your own reputation—2dly. the effect of your continuing, in reference to the declarations you have made of your disinclination to public life— And I can truly say, that I have not found the least difference of sentiment, on either point. The impression is uniform—that your declining would be to be deplored as the greatest evil, that could befall the country at the present juncture, and as critically hazardous to your own reputation—that your continuance will be justified in the mind of every friend to his country by the evident necessity for it. Tis clear, says every one, with whom I have conversed, that the affairs of the national government are not yet firmly established —that its enemies, generally speaking, are as inveterate as ever— that their enmity has been sharpened by its success and by all the resentments which flow from disappointed predictions and mortified vanity—that a general and strenuous effort is making in every state to place the administration of it in the hands of its enemies, as if they were its safest guardians—that the period of the next house of representatives is likely to prove the crisis of its permanent character—that if you continue in office nothing materially mischievous is to be apprehended—if you quit much is to be dreaded—that the same motives which induced you to accept originally ought to decide you to continue till matters have assumed a more determinate aspect—that indeed it would have been better, as it regards your own character, that you had never consented to come forward, than now to leave the business unfinished and in danger of being undone—that in the event of storms arising there would be an imputation either of want of foresight or want of firmness—and, in fine, that on public and personal accounts, on patriotic and prudential considerations, the clear path to be pursued by you will be again to obey the voice of your country; which it is not doubted will be as earnest and as unanimous as ever.

On this last point, I have some suspicion that it will be insinuated to you, and perhaps (God forgive me, if I judge hardly) with design to place before you a motive of declining—that there is danger of a division among the electors and of less unanimity in their suffrages than heretofore. My view of this matter is as follows:

While your first election was depending I had no doubt, that there would be characters among the electors, who if they durst follow their inclinations, would have voted against you; but that in all probability they would be restrained by an apprehension of public resentment—that nevertheless it was possible a few straggling votes might be found in opposition, from some headstrong and fanatical individuals—that a circumstance of this kind would be in fact, and ought to be estimated by you, as of no importance—since their would be sufficient unanimity to witness the general confidence and attachment towards you.

My view of the future accords exactly with what was my view of the past.[1] I believe the same motives will operate to produce the same result. The dread of public indignation will be likely to restrain the indisposed few. If they can calculate at all, they will naturally reflect that they could not give a severer blow to their cause than by giving a proof of hostility to you. But if a solitary vote or two should appear wanting to perfect unanimity, of what moment can it be? Will not the fewness of the exceptions be a confirmation of the devotion of the community to a character, which has so generally united its suffrages, after an administration of four years at the head of a new government, opposed in its first establishment by a large proportion of its citizens and obliged to run counter to many prejudices in devising the arduous arrangements, requisite to public Credit and public Order? Will not those, who may be the authors of any such exceptions, manifest more their own perverseness and malevolence than any diminution of the affection and confidence of the Nation? I am persuaded, that both these questions ought to be answered in the affirmative; and that there is nothing to be looked for, on the score of diversity of sentiment which ought to weigh for a moment.

I trust, Sir, and I pray God that you will determine to make a further sacrifice of your tranquillity and happiness to the public good. I trust that it need not continue above a year or two more— And I think that it will be more eligibible to retire from office before the expiration of the term of an election, than to decline a reelection.

The sentiments I have delivered upon this occasion, I can truly say, proceed exclusively from an anxious concern for the public welfare and an affectionate personal attachment. These dispositions must continue to govern in every vicissitude one who has the honor to be very truly and respectfully

Sir   Your most Obedt. & hum serv   A Hamilton

August 3d. Since writing the foregoing I am favoured with your interesting letter of the 29th of July. An answer to the points raised is not difficult & shall as soon as possible be forwarded.

The President of the U States

ALS, George Washington Papers, Library of Congress.
    1. For H's opinion on Washington's decision to stand for election in 1789, see H to Washington, August 13, September, November 18, 1788.

To William Ellery

[*Philadelphia, July 31, 1792.* On August 20, 1792, Ellery wrote to Hamilton: "I have recd. your letter of the 31st. of the last month." *Letter not found.*]

To Jeremiah Olney

Treasury Department, July 31, 1792. "The Collector of Barnstable [1] has informed me [2] of a seizure made by him of one Hogshead of Rum, three Hogsheads of Molasses, one barrel of Sugar and two hundred and forty bushels of Salt, said to have been fraudulently landed out of the Sloop Polly of Sandwich. It is stated that the Vessel had left the District of Barnstable before the Collector had any knowledge of the fraud; and as it is to be inferred that a forfeiture of the said Sloop has also been incurred, I have to request that you will cause her to be seized, if she should be found in your District. . . ."

LS, Rhode Island Historical Society, Providence; copy, RG 56, Letters to Collectors at Small Ports, "Set G," National Archives; copy, RG 56, Letters to the Collector at Providence, National Archives.
    1. Joseph Otis.   2. Letter not found.

Draft Minutes of a Meeting of a Committee of the Directors of the Society for Establishing Useful Manufactures [1]

[Paterson, New Jersey, August 1, 1792]

At a meeting of the Committee of the Directors for establishing usefull manufactures held at the Town of Paterson on the 1st. day of August 1792.
    Present
    Nicholas Low.
    John Bayard
    Elisha Boudinot [2]

Col. Hamilton attended the meeting at the request of the Committee.

The committee examined the propositions which were received relative to erecting several of the works described in the publick advertisements[3] for that purpose—and finding the proposals but partial and those at a rate which far exceed any Idea that had been formed of the expence attending the same, and after the most mature consideration; Resolved unanimously, that it will be for the interest of the Society to erect the works themselves under the inspection and direction of Agents appointed for that purpose.

Resolved that Major L'Enfant[4] be the Agent for superintending the erection of the works [and buildings][5] ordered by the Directors [conforming as to such as shall regard their respective departments to the plans which shall be furnished to him by Wm. Hall Thomas Marshall & Wm. Pearce within the limitations prescribed by the said Directors]—and that he be [requested to prepare] such a plan for bringing the Water from the River above the falls to [the respective works] as in his opinion will be the best calculated to answer the intention of the Society; and lay the same before the Directors at their next meeting—[and that he be further requested to prepare a plan for laying out the said Town of Paterson.]

Resolved, that John N. Cumming[6] be the Agent, for procuring such workmen and materials [and at such periods] as the said M. L Enfant shall require from time to time for the purposes aforesaid —to pay the expences accruing thereon [keeping regular accounts of the same.] That it [be also his duty to procure such materials for machinery as shall be required in their respective branches by William Hall Thomas Marshall & William Pearce and to pay the workmen whom they shall employ in constructing the said Machinery. That the Chairman of the Committee be authorised to furnish to the said J N Cumming such monies as shall from time to time be necessary for the said purposes upon estimates & statements to be furnished by the said J N Comming.

Resolved—That the compensation of the said Major L'Enfant for his said services be 1500 Dollars provided that he be not required to continue them beyond the term of one year.

That the compensation of the said J N Cumming be a salary at the rate of 600 Dollars ℔ annum.

That if upon experiment it shall appear that the expence of building in stone the houses ordered to be built by the Directors for the use of mechanics who shall settle within the Town of Patterson exceeds the rate of] Sixty five Pounds [⅌ House, the same shall be made of Wood.

That the Machinery for spinning of Weft & for weaving shall be *completed* to four Carding Machines, four roving billies, four slubbing machines if deemed necessary by Mr. Pearce, Twenty five spinning Jennies and Sixty single looms with a proportion of lesser auxiliary machinery and no more shall be prepared until the further order of the Committee.]

Df, partly in the handwriting of H, The Passaic County Historical Society, Lambert Castle, Paterson, New Jersey.

1. A report of the transactions of this meeting taken from the minutes of the Society for Establishing Useful Manufactures was presented to the directors of the society on August 20, 1792 ("Minutes of the S.U.M.," 56–58). See also H to Elisha Boudinot, July 12, 30, 1792.

2. See "Proposals to Contract for the Construction of the Manufacturing Plant of the Society for Establishing Useful Manufactures," July 11, 1792, note 1.

3. The advertisement was drafted by H. See "Proposals to Contract for the Construction of the Manufacturing Plant of the Society for Establishing Useful Manufactures," July 11, 1792.

4. Pierre Charles L'Énfant, a Frenchman who had served with the American forces during the American Revolution, was one of the best-known engineers of his time. His most important commission, which had terminated at the end of February, 1792, was to plan the new Federal city on the Potomac River.

5. The bracketed words in this and the following paragraphs are in the handwriting of H.

6. Cumming, a resident of Newark who was in the stagecoach business, was a stockholder in the Society for Establishing Useful Manufactures. In 1793 he became one of the society's directors.

From Thomas Smith

Loan Office [Philadelphia] Penna Augt 1, 1792

Sir

I have received a letter from Mr. A. J. Dallas secretary to the Commonwealth with enclosures which I now forward for your inspection.[1]

LC, RG 53, Pennsylvania State Loan Office, Letter Book, 1790–1794, Vol. "615-P," National Archives.

1. According to the executive minutes of Pennsylvania, a copy of ". . . the opinion of the Attorney General [Jared Ingersoll] which was received on the twenty-eighth instant, respecting the question whether the New Loan certificates of Pennsylvania are subscribable to the loan proposed by Congress to

The whole of the subscriptions since the 1st June last in Certificates of the Assumed Debt of this State, amo. to £ 46,985. equal to 125,293 30/ which with 674,675 Dollars received before the 30th sepr. 1791 makes in the whole 799,968 30/.

Mr. Donnaldson Regr [2] & Mr Nicholson Compr.[3] are of opinion that there are very few of the Certificates of the State Debt now outstanding.

I have had but one small Certificate of the sort called the New Loan Issued by David Rittenhouse Treasr & John Nicholson Compr. under the funding law of this State [4] since my conference with you which I offered to receive but informed the Person that nothing further could be done in it untill I received further Instructions on which it was withdrawn.

I have the honor &c.

Honble. Alex. Hamilton secy Treasy U S.

[E N C L O S U R E]

Jared Ingersoll to Alexander Dallas [5]

Philadelphia July 28th 1792

Dear Sir.

Engagements at Court have prevented me from returning an earlier answer to your favor of the 23d instant.

I am of opinion that after the passing the act of Assembly of the twenty seventh of March 1789,[6] and the other acts on the subject,

---

the State creditors, . . . was . . . enclosed to Thomas Smith Esquire Commissioner of Loans for this State, in a letter from the Secretary of the Commonwealth" (*Pennsylvania Archives*, 9th ser., I, 433). See enclosure.

2. John Donnaldson was register general of Pennsylvania.

3. John Nicholson was comptroller general of Pennsylvania. See Thomas Mifflin to H, December 27, 1791, note 1.

4. Rittenhouse was treasurer of Pennsylvania from 1776 to 1789.
"New loan" certificates were issued under "An Act for the Further Relief of the Public Creditors who are Citizens of This State by Receiving on Loan Certain Debts of the United States of America . . ." (*Pennsylvania Statutes*, XII, 158–64 [March 1, 1786]).

5. *Pennsylvania Archives*, 9th ser., I, 431–33.

6. Ingersoll is referring to "An Act to Repeal So Much of Any Act or Acts of Assembly of This Commonwealth as Directs the Payment of the New Loan Debt or the Interest Thereof Beyond the First Day of April Next, and for Other Purposes Therein Mentioned" (*Pennsylvania Statutes*, XIII, 263–67).

the New Loan certificates ceased to be a State debt within the view of the Legislature, and could not consistently with those laws be recognized by the officers of the Federal or State government for any other purpose than re-exchanging them for Continental Certificates.

I am also clearly and decidedly of opinion that after the passing the above act, the New Loan certificates cannot be included within the description of the State debts directed to be redeemed and paid by the act of the tenth day of April 1792.[7]

The amount of Continental debt assumed by the State of Pennsylvania and for which New Loan certificates were given was about five millions of Dollars.

Part of this was redeemed by payments made at the Land office and other payments into the State Treasury in these New Loan certificates.

But the sum remaining of this class of certificates was much more than the amount of the sum 2,200,000 Dollars which the United States agreed to assume of State Debt for Pennsylvania.[8]

The State debt, what was originally and properly so called, and which the Legislature could only have had in contemplation when they made provision for such deficiency, as they considered to be left unprovided for the continental rule of assumption was about One Million or say 1,200,000 Dollars.

Suppose this sum to be, interest included, 1,200,000—the United States would give certificates as follows Vizt

At 3 pCent per annum.	400,000
Deferred Debt.	266,666—67
At 6 prCent per annum.	533,333—33
Dr	1,200,000—

So far as 6 per cents extend the State considered this as a full provision in satisfaction of the debt. But for the 400,000 Dollars three pr cent stock, the State considered it as only payment of one half, they therefore issued other three per cent stock payable by

7. "An Act to Provide for Paying and Redeeming Certain Public Debts, and for Defraying the Expenses of Government" (*Pennsylvania Statutes*, XIV, 305–12).

8. "An Act making provision for the (payment of the) Debt of the United States" (1 *Stat.* 138–44 [August 4, 1790]). See also Thomas Mifflin to H, December 27, 1791, note 1.

the State to an equal amount. And for deferred stock on which the United States pay no interest till the year 1801, the State agrees to pay interest annually at six per Cent per annum till that time.[9]

By the act of April last the State agree to redeem these assumptions from the holders of the debt, by paying ten shillings in the pound for the three per Cents, and thirty nine pounds per cent for the deferred part, being the estimated value of the annuity of six per cent per annum for the time limited.

This recapitulation of facts appears to me to suggest the solution of your second question.

If the New Loan certificates are brought in assumable by the United States, the sum may exceed the whole that Congress have agreed to assume, and our Assembly will have encouraged Measures for the exclusion of the whole of our State Debt from being assumed.[10]

Two motives may be supposed to have actuated our Legislature— First, To free the State from debt that in case of necessity they might anticipate their resources by Credit.

Secondly—Selling the three per Cent stock of the United States at twelve shillings and paying off their three per cent stock at ten shillings afords an obvious advantage in the deferred, no loss was suffered and therefore the balance in their favour remained.

On the New Loan certificates they were paying no interest, the Continental certificates furnished the means of redemption at any moment without expence, the reason of the law determines its extent, neither of these motives apply to the New Loan certificates, it is impossible that the State could have intended that they should be

9. Ingersoll is referring to the provision made by "An Act Granting Relief to Certain Creditors of the State and for Repealing Part of an Act, Entitled 'An Act for Furnishing the Quota of This State Toward Paying the Annual Interest of the Debts of the United States, and for Funding and Paying the Interest of the Public Debts of This State'" (*Pennsylvania Statutes*, XIV, 76–79 [April 9, 1791]).

10. Section 14 of "An Act making provision for the (payment of the) Debt of the United States" reads in part as follows: "That if the total amount of the sums which shall be subscribed to the said loan in the debt of any state, within the time limited for receiving subscriptions thereto, shall exceed the sum by this act allowed to be subscribed within such state, the certificates and credits granted to the respective subscribers, shall bear such proportion to the sums by them respectively subscribed, as the total amount of the said sums shall bear to the whole sum so allowed to be subscribed in the debt of such state" (1 *Stat.* 143).

assumed by the United States or that they were in contemplation in the provision made by the act of April last.

To the third question [11] I am not ready at present to give an answer—it requires some information which I do not possess but will endeavor to obtain.

I am Dr Sir &c   J. Ingersoll

A. J. Dallas Esqr.

11. The third question which Dallas had asked at Mifflin's request reads as follows: "Whether the New Loan Certificates being issued after the War and as the preamble of the Act of the first of March 1786, states for the relief of the patriotic Citizens of Pennsylvania, are excluded from the Loan proposed by Congress, by the words or spirit of the proviso, annexed to the 13th Section of the act of Congress of the 4th of August 1790?" (*Pennsylvania Archives*, 9th ser., I, 429.) Section 13 of the act reads in part as follows: "*And provided,* That no such certificate shall be received, which from the tenor thereof, or from any public record, act, or document, shall appear or can be ascertained to have been issued for any purpose, other than compensations and expenditures for services or supplies towards the prosecution of the late war, and the defence of the United States, or of some part thereof during the same" (1 *Stat.* 143).

From George Washington

Mount Vernon, August 1st. 1792

Sir,

I learn with pleasure from the War Office, by the Secretary's last dispatches,[1] that our Northwestern frontier is in a state of tranquility: it may be construed into an indication that *some* of the messages which have been sent by Government have reached the hostile Tribes,[2] and have occasioned them to deliberate thereon. Devoutly is it to be wished that the result may be favorable, both for themselves and the Ud. States.

No expectation of this, however, ought to suspend, or in the smallest degree relax the preparations for War; but as War under any circumstances is expensive, and with such a long & rugged land transportation as the one by which we have to convey the supplies for the Army must, for the quantum of them, be extremely so. It behoves us to be as precise in all our arrangements—as œconomical in our provisions—as strict in our issues, and as correct in accounting for them to the War or Treasury Departments (as the case may happen to be) as possible.³ That I may know under what regulations these matters are, I have, by this days post, written to the Secretary of War desiring him to report to me the mode which is pursued by his direction from thence, for providing, transporting, issueing & accounting for them.⁴ If the Treasury Department has an agency in any of these matters, I require a similar report from thence also.

Mr. Kean by a Letter which I have received from him, accepts his renewed Commission for settling the Accounts between the United States, & the individual States; ⁵ which, please to say to him, gives me pleasure—and add, that any efforts he can make to bring this business to a speedy & happy issue, I shall consider as rendering an important service to the Union; because I view the closing of these Accots. *speedily* as extremely essential to it's interest & tranquility. Let me know if Mr. Langdon (the Commissioner) ⁶ is returned to his duty? and, in that case, when?

I am &c.   G: Washington

LC, George Washington Papers, Library of Congress.

1. Washington wrote to Henry Knox as well as to H on this date and acknowledged receipt of Knox's letters of July 14 and 21, 1792. Knox's letter to Washington of July 14 begins as follows: "The last post which left Pittsburgh on the 6th instant, brings information of entire tranquility on the frontiers" (LS, George Washington Papers, Library of Congress). Knox's letter to Washington of July 21 reads in part as follows: "I have the honor to inform you that General [Anthony] Wayne in his letter of the 13th instant from Pittsburg says. 'There are no traces of hostile Indians to be discovered upon the boarders of the frontiers—all is quiet—and the farmers are assiduously employed in harvesting their hay and grain which I hope they will effect in safety'" (LS, George Washington Papers, Library of Congress). In his letter of July 21 Knox also enclosed an extract of a letter which Brigadier General James Wilkinson had written to him on June 12, 1792. Wilkinson's letter reads in part as follows: "The savages have committed no act of hostilities since my last, other than pursuing . . . a scout. . . . I have not heard one word of or from my messengers first dispatched . . . with public overtures, although they have been out more than seventy days, . . . and I remain in the same state of ignorance with respect to ye issue of Colo. [John] Hardin & Major [Alexander] Truemans mission. My anxiety impresses my mind with apprehension for their safety, and tho' the event be doubtless equivocal, yet all my reasoning upon the subject justifies the conclusion, that the enemy have actually been in deliberation upon the propositions for peace" (copy, George Washington Papers, Library of Congress)

2. The messages concerned an invitation to the northwestern Indian tribes to form a council in order to make peace. On September 27, 1792, Brigadier General Rufus Putnam was able to conclude a treaty with the Wabash and Illinois tribes at Post Vincennes (*ASP, Indian Affairs,* I, 231, 242, 338-40).

3. See H to Washington, July 22, 1792, and Washington to H, July 29, 1792.

4. In his letter to Knox on August 1, 1792, Washington expressed satisfaction with the tranquillity on the northwestern frontiers, and at the same time directed Knox: "Proceed as if war was inevitable; but do it, I entreat you, with all the œconomy which can result from system and good regulations. Our finances call for it, and if these did not, our reputation does. . . . I desire you would report to me the regulations which you have adopted for providing, forwarding, and issuing of them, and the mode of having them accounted for to the departt. of War" (*GW*, XXXII, 104).

5. In a letter to Washington on July 7, 1792, John Kean accepted his renewed commission, noting that, although his position as cashier of the Bank of the United States was demanding, he would give all the time which he could to the settlement of the accounts between the states and the Federal Government (ALS, RG 59, Miscellaneous Letters, 1790–1799, National Archives).

6. Woodbury Langdon. See H to Washington, July 2, 1792.

From Tench Coxe and Richard Harrison [1]

Treasury Department
August 2nd. 1792.

Sir,

In addition to the Circumstances relative to the Case of the Secretary at War, transmitted from the Comptrollers office for our determination we have the honor to state to you the following facts for the purpose of obtaining the Attorney generals opinion after a knowledge of them.

We find that the first appearance of the claim in question, in any form, is in an account current dated at the "War Office, December 30th: 1786" and signed "HKnox" against the ballance of which, being 610 $^{31}/_{90}$ Dollars, the following words are written. "To Cash retained in my hands to defray my travelling expences for various Journeys on public service during the years 1785 and 1786 equal to   [2] Dollars. An application will be made to Congress for an allowance on this Head, which when granted the necessary vouchers will be produced" carried out in the columns 610..31 and cast with the preceeding part of the Account as will be seen on examination of it, for which purpose we have the honor to inclose it. In the report upon this account made by the Auditors examining Clerks to the Auditor,[3] which was confirmed, no notice is taken of this item. In this state the matter appears to have remained untill it was presented to the late Auditor (Mr. Wolcott) [4] after the commencement of the present general Government, when the precise amount was included in an account current and was rejected by the Auditor and Comptroller [5] under the Circumstances stated in the first letter. It is necessary to remark that the communications between the Secretary at War and the late Comptroller were prior to the decision of the Comptroller by three months and that if those communications were to be deemed to contain the appeal the Comptroller three months after acted upon it—If they are not the Appeal then is to be sought elsewhere. The paper dated on the 31st. December 1790, is not addressed to the Comptroller, wherefore it should seem not to have been intended as an appeal to him and being of a date more than six months after the Auditor's settlement it would appear necessary to throw off the restraint imposed by a limitation of the legislature [6] to receive it as such had it been addressed to the Comptroller. It appears further on enquiry that this paper was not presented to the Treasury, as a seperate claim for the objects specified in it, but that it must have continued in the War Office, untill June 1791, when it was first presented at the Auditors Office as an accompanyment of an ordinary account current between the United States and the War Department, dated in that month and commencing with a credit to the United States for the exact sum as ballance, which the settlement of 11th. and 19th. June 1790 (by the Auditor and Comptroller) established. It appears to us that this paper therefore was not intended as an appeal from the Auditor to the Comptroller, that it was presented twelve months after the expiration of the time limited, by the express provisions of the legislature, that it was truly, a *reclaim* in the mass of a new account of certain items previously rejected by the officer of accounts, which rejection had acquired the ordinary legal force by the lapse of twelve months.

We do not conceive that the opinion stated in the account from the War Department of December 30th: 1786 that an application to Congress was necessary, invalidates any legal right to the monies in question, which were before in the Secretary, but we have stated it to shew that the Case was a long while within the knowledge of the officers of the Treasury. No testimony or information is brought up on the application of June 1791, which was not offered in March

1790. Under all the circumstances stated we ask the favor of you, Sir, to obtain the Attorney General's opinions upon these three Questions.

1st. Has the Secretary at War ever appealed to the Comptroller of the Treasury from the settlement of the Auditor of the Treasury in regard to the account in Question.

2dly. If he has appealed is that appeal availing considering the lapse suggested.

3dly. If there has not been an appeal *or* if there has been an appeal and it is not availing on account of the lapse suggested, can the officers named, in the 7th. Section of the act making alterations in the Treasury and War Departments [7] take up and adjust this claim of the Secretary at War.

It is worthy of consideration that the third Question may be thought to involve a similar right in every other person on whose accounts Mr. Wolcott as Auditor has ever determined which we presume was not intended by the legislature—*and* that it may be deemed to establish as a consequence the re-examination of any settlement at the Treasury whenever new officers shall form a Judgment different from their predecessors on the same facts and information.

We have the honor to be with perfect respect, Sir, your most Obt. Servts.

The honble.
The Secretary of the Treasury.

LC, RG 58, Letters of Commissioner of Revenue, 1792–1793, National Archives.

1. For background to this letter, see Coxe to H, June 27, 1792.
2. Space left blank in MS. According to the auditor's Report No. 1756, $674.13 was credited to Knox "By amt: of Sundry expences attending Several Journies of the Secretary at War in the Years 1785. 1786. 1787 & 1788 for the purpose of Inspecting & arrangeing the Stores in the arsenals and magazines of the United States as admitted on the 17th: of Sept. 1792 by Tench Coxe Esqr. Comr. of the revenue and Richard Harrison Esqr. Auditor of the Treasury pursuant to the act of Congress of 8th: May 1792 makeing alterations in the Treasury and War Departments. . . . The Certificate of addmission being anected to the report of the auditor of The Treasury No. 437 dated the 11th: June 1790" (D, Massachusetts Historical Society, Boston).
3. John D. Mercier was auditor under the Board of Treasury from January 28, 1782, until that office was abolished as of November 1, 1787 (*JCC,* XXII, 60; XXXIII, 510).

4. Oliver Wolcott, Jr., had been auditor of the Treasury from September 12, 1789, until his appointment as comptroller was confirmed on October 31, 1791.

5. Nicholas Eveleigh had been comptroller of the Treasury from September 11, 1789, until his death in 1791.

6. This is a reference to a proviso contained in Section 5 of "An Act to establish the Treasury Department" which reads as follows: "That if any person whose account shall be so audited be dissatisfied therewith, he may within six months appeal to the Comptroller against such settlement" (1 *Stat.* 66–67 [September 2, 1789]).

7. "An Act making alterations on the Treasury and War Departments" (1 *Stat.* 279–81 [May 8, 1792]). See Coxe to H, June 27, 1792, note 2.

To William Ellery

[*Philadelphia, August 2, 1792.* On August 20, 1792, Ellery wrote to Hamilton: "I have received your letter of the 2nd of this month." *Letter not found.*]

To Benjamin Lincoln

Treasury Department, August 2, 1792. "I have directed a packet to be sent to you by water, containing two Thermometers which I request you will forward by a safe conveyance; the one to the Collector of Barnstable,[1] and the other to the Collector of Frenchman's bay."[2]

L[S], RG 36, Collector of Customs at Boston, Letters from the Treasury, 1789–1807, Vol. 4, National Archives; copy, RG 56, Letters to the Collector at Boston, National Archives; copy, RG 56, Letters to Collectors at Small Ports, "Set G," National Archives.

1. Joseph Otis.   2. Meletiah Jordan.

From Tench Coxe and Richard Harrison

Treasury Department,
August 3rd: 1792.

Sir,

We have the Honor to inclose to you, a contract made and executed on the 11th. day of January 1776, between the late Silas

Deane,[1] and Barnabas Deane [2] with the following statement for the purpose of obtaining an opinion of the Attorney General on this Question. To whom is the balance due from the United States, on the account arising out of the agency, under that Contract due and payable.

Shortly after Messrs. Silas Deane and Barnabas Deane made the contract, the former went to Europe as we are informed, and it is represented to us that the latter executed the Business. Barnabas Deane received the whole money, and as there is no allegation of a debt due from Silas to Barnabas, the share of Silas in the commissions accruing under the Contract, appear to have remained in the Hands of Barnabas. A small balance was due from the United States, but in Consenquence of a decision upon a litigated demand for freight paid by Barnabas (admitted to be ultimately payable by the United States) the balance is considerably increased, but is less than the whole Amount of the Commissions. Silas and Barnabas were not general copartners in trade, nor is any connexion suggested, but that which arises out of the Contract inclosed. Silas is dead, and his son Silas (now in Connecticut) is his administrator. The Question arises to whom are the United States indebted? Is it to Silas, son and Administrator of Silas the elder deceased, and Barnabas or to Barnabas solely.

We have the Honor to be, with perfect respect, Sir   Your most Obt. Servt:

The honble.
The Secretary of the Treasury.

LC, RG 58, Letters of Commissioner of Revenue, 1792–1793, National Archives.
1. Silas Deane, a prominent Connecticut merchant and lawyer, had been a member of the Continental Congress from 1774 to January, 1776. In March, 1776, he had been ordered to France as a secret agent of the United States, and in September he had been commissioned ambassador with Benjamin Franklin and Arthur Lee.
2. Barnabas Deane, Silas Deane's brother, was a leading Connecticut merchant who in 1776 took over his brother's business. During the American Revolution Barnabas Deane was associated with Jeremiah Wadsworth in the business of supplying the Continental Army.
The contract presumably related to the Continental frigate *Trumbull*, which was built at Chatham, Connecticut, in 1776 under the supervision of Barnabas Deane (Robert A. East, *Business Enterprise in the American Revolutionary Era* [New York, 1938], 87). See also Coxe to Barnabas Deane, August 25, 1792 (LC, RG 58, Letters of Commissioner of Revenue, 1792–1793, National Ar-

chives), and Margaret Elizabeth Martin, *Merchants and Trade of the Connecticut River Valley* ("Smith College Studies in History," XXIV, Nos. 1–4 [Northampton, October, 1938–July, 1939], 76).

To Richard Harrison

[*Treasury Department, August 3, 1792.* Letter listed in dealer's catalogue. *Letter not found.*]

ALS, sold at Parke-Bernet Galleries, Inc., February 19, 1945, Lot 239.

To Charles Lee

Treasury Department
August 3. 1792.

Sir

I have to reply to your letter of the 5th of July.

The instruction respecting the mode of computing the additional ten ₱ Cent on the new Duties [1] is founded on the following reasoning.

The words of the Section which relate to that addition are "The *addition* of 10 ₱ Cent *made by the Second Section* of the 'Act making further provision for the debts of the United States' [2] to *the rates of Duties* on goods, wares and merchandize, imported in Ships or Vessels not of the United States, shall *continue* in full force and operation in relation to the *articles* hereinbefore enumerated and described." [3]

The addition here contemplated is not an *addition* of 10 ₱ Cent generally, but specifically *the* addition, *made by* the *second Section* of the Act quoted, to the *rates of duties* thereby laid; for these words must of necessity be supplied, since the addition *made by that Act* was expressly applied to the rates *mentioned in it.* And this addition, thus precisely defined, is to *continue* in force in relation to the *articles* enumerated and described by the last Act—not to *extend* or *apply* to the *rates* prescribed by that Act.

The construction therefore which has been adopted is clearly the *precise literal* construction of the clause, and it may be also presumed to be agreeable to the intention of the Legislature; because a more simple, as well as a more clear mode of expression could easily have been found to convey the other meaning, if it had been designed, and there was a precedent for it in the antecedent laws. In the first impost Act,[4] an addition of 10 ₱ Cent in the cases in question, is made to the rates therein specified. When new rates are substituted by the Act making further provision for the payment of the debts of the United States, and it is meant to extend that addition to these rates, the mode of expression used is, "that *an* addition of 10 ₱ Centum shall be made to the *several rates* of duties *above specified and imposed &a*,"[5] making thereby a special reference to the rates which had been previously designated in the same Act. A departure from this very proper mode of expression, as relating to the then manifest intent of the Legislature, is a strong argument of a different intention in the last instance.

The presumption is that the increase of duty, in respect to foreign bottoms, resulting from the addition of 10 ₱ Cent to the *former rates* was deemed by the Legislature sufficient encouragement in this particular to Vessels of the United States; and that they were not disposed to increase the encouragement, in prejudice of the Citizens of those States, which are less concerned in navigation. Considering the fact, with regard to the operation of the provision, as corresponding with that presumption, I feel no motive of public policy, to induce a constructive extension of the duty, beyond the letter of the provision. And I adhere to the general rule of avoiding to burthen the Citizen by construction.

Separate bonds are to be taken for the duties in the cases mentioned by you. The Comptroller has it in charge to make a Circular communication on this point.

The question, with regard to Credit, in certain cases, where the amount of the Duty does not exceed 50 Dollars, is before the Attorney General.[6]

I am, with consideration,   Sir, Your Obed Servant.   A Hamilton

Charles Lee Esqr.
Collr Alexandria.

LS, RG 36, Collector of Customs at Alexandria, Letters Received from the Secretary, National Archives.

1. See "Treasury Department Circular to the Collectors of the Customs," June 25, 1792.

2. This is a reference to Section 2 of "An Act making further provision for

the payment of the debts of the United States" (1 *Stat.* 181 [August 10, 1790]).

3. This is a quotation from Section 5 of "An Act for raising a farther sum of money for the protection of the frontiers, and for other purposes therein mentioned" (1 *Stat.* 260 [May 2, 1792]).

4. For the "first impost Act," see "An Act for laying a Duty on Goods, Wares and Merchandises imported into the United States" (1 *Stat.* 24–27 [July 4, 1789]).

5. See note 2.

6. See "Treasury Department Circular to the Collectors of the Customs," August 6, 1792.

From Benjamin Lincoln

[*Boston, August 3, 1792.* On August 14, 1792, Hamilton wrote to Lincoln and acknowledged receipt "of your letter of the 3rd instant." *Letter not found.*]

From Jeremiah Olney

Custom-House,
Providence 3rd. August 1792.

Sir.

I have received your favor of the 25th of July, relative to a quantity of Brandy exported by Messrs. Clark & Nightingale,[1] the Drawback on which, you say, cannot be allowed unless the proof required, of its having been actually landed at a foreign Port, is produced: The Excise Act, generally so called, passed in March 1791, clearly, I think, authorizes the payment of Drawbacks on all Spirits, imported since the last Day of June, in *Six Months* after exportation; and allows One and Two Years for the production of the proof of its being landed at a foreign Port, to cancel the exportation Bond.[2] If there is any other Act which requires this proof before the Drawback on Spirits can be paid, you will much oblige me, Sir, by pointing it out, as I do not recollect any.

I have the Honor to be &c.   Jereh. Olney Collr.

Alexr. Hamilton Esquire
Secretary of the Treasury.

ADfS, Rhode Island Historical Society, Providence.

1. See Olney to H, July 16, 1792.

2. The provisions concerning drawbacks to which Olney is referring are

contained in Sections 51, 54, and 57 of "An Act repealing, after the last day of June next, the duties heretofore laid upon Distilled Spirits imported from abroad, and laying others in their stead; and also upon Spirits distilled within the United States, and for appropriating the same" (1 *Stat.* 210–13).

From William Seton

Bank of New York
3rd. Augt. 1792.

Sir

I am honoured with a letter from your Department of the 1st, inst. respecting the payments that have been made thro' this Institution by your desire to Messrs. Beach & Canfield [1]—the only sums paid to them were 4350 Dollars on the 29th May & 3630 $^{92}/_{100}$ on the 29th. June

Agreeably to your desire no further payments shall be made to them till I receive your special Direction.[2]

I have the honour to be with the greatest respect   sir   Your obedt. humble servt.

Alex Hamilton Esqr.
Secretary of the Treasury of the United states

LC, Bank of New York, New York City.
1. Nathaniel Beach and Abiel Canfield of Newark, New Jersey, had contracted to supply the Army with shoes. See William Seton to H, May 28, June 3, 1792.
2. On August 8, 1792, an explanatory note from the comptroller's office was sent to Joseph Nourse, register of the Treasury, which reads as follows:
"The within balance as stated by the Auditor *Admitted* with the following alteration that instead of the debit for monies received of the Bank of New York which is rejected the within named *Nathaniel Beach & Abiel Canfield* be debited with a warrant on the Treasurer in their favour dated August 8th 1792 for the sum of seven thousand nine hundred and eighty dollars and ninety two cents leaving the same balance as is within stated by the Auditor of the Treasury" (LS, RG 217, Miscellaneous Treasury Accounts, 1790–1814, Account No. 2835, National Archives).

To George Washington

Treasury Departmt. 3d. Augt. 1792

Sir,

I have the honor to enclose a letter from the Commissioner of the Revenue of the 25th. of July,[1] on the subject of a provisional Contract for the supply of the Lighthouse in New Hampshire; together with the Contract for your consideration & decision. I agree in the opinion expressed by the Commissioner of the Revenue.

With the most perfect respect and truest attachment, I have the honor to be &c.   Alexander Hamilton.

P.S. Inclosed you will be pleased to receive the copy of a letter of 31st May, just received from our Commissioners at Amsterdam.[2] It announces a further Loan of 3,000,000 of florins at 4 ₱ Cent.[3]

LC, George Washington Papers, Library of Congress.
1. See the second letter which Tench Coxe wrote to H on July 25, 1792.
2. Letter not found. The American commissioners at Amsterdam were Wilhem and Jan Willink, Nicholaas and Jacob Van Staphorst, and Nicholas Hubbard.
3. For a description of the Holland loan of 1792, see H to William Short, June 28, 1792, note 18.

From John Adams

[*Quincy, Massachusetts, August 4, 1792*. On August 16, 1792, Hamilton wrote to Adams: "I have been duly favoured with your letter of the 4th Instant." *Letter not found.*]

An American No. I[1]

[Philadelphia, August 4, 1792]

For the Gazette of the United States

Mr. Fenno[2]

It was easy to foresee, when the hint appeared in your Gazette of

ADf, Connecticut Historical Society, Hartford; two copies, Hamilton Papers, Library of Congress; [Philadelphia] *Gazette of the United States*, August 4, 1792.
1. This is the first of three articles by "An American." The other two are dated August 11, 18, 1792.
2. John Fenno, editor of the [Philadelphia] *Gazette of the United States*.

[25th July] [3] that the Editor of the National Gazette [4] received a salary from the General Government, advantage would be taken of its *want* of explicitness and particularity to make the circumstance matter of merit in Mr. Freneau and an argument of his independent disinterestedness. Such a turn of the thing cannot be permitted to succeed. It is now necessary that the whole truth should be told, and that the real state of the affair should be well understood.

Mr. Freneau before he came to this City to conduct the National Gazette was employed by Childs & Swaine [5] Printers of the Dayly Advertiser in the City of New York in capacity of [editor or superintendant].[6] A paper more devoted to the views of a certain party of which Mr. Jefferson is the head than any to be found in this City was wanted. Mr. Freneau was thought a fit instrument. His talents for invective and abuse had before been tried as Conductor of the Freemans Journal in this City.[7] A negotiation was opened with him, which ended in the establishment of the National Gazette under his direction. There is good ground to believe that Mr. Madison while in New York in the summer of   [8] was the medium of that Negotiation.

Mr. Freneau came here at once Editor of the National Gazette

3. Space left blank in MS. The date within brackets has been taken from the printed version of this letter in the *Gazette of the United States*. See "T. L. No. 1," July 25, 1792.

4. Philip Freneau, editor of the [Philadelphia] *National Gazette*. See H to Edward Carrington, May 26, 1792, note 8, and H to Rufus King, July 25, 1792, note 6.

5. Francis Childs and John Swaine.

6. Space left blank in MS. Material within brackets has been taken from the *Gazette of the United States*, August 4, 1792.

7. This sentence was omitted in the version of this letter printed in the *Gazette of the United States*.

The first issue of *The* [Philadelphia] *Freeman's Journal: or the North-American Intelligencer*, established by Francis Bailey, appeared on April 25, 1781. By the end of June, 1781, Freneau had become the editor of the newspaper, and he continued as editor until he became a clerk in the Postmaster General's department in the fall of 1782. *The Freeman's Journal* supported the Constitutionalist party in Pennsylvania, and, according to Lewis Leary, neither of the opposition newspapers "which attempted to maintain a judicious attitude in defense of the Dickinsonian group, were any match for the slander and abuse with which contributors to the *Freeman's Journal* attacked them" (Lewis Leary, *That Rascal Freneau* [New York, 1924], 110).

8. This space left blank in MS. The sentence was not used in the version in the *Gazette of the United States*. H is referring to the trip which Thomas Jefferson and James Madison made through New York and New England in the summer of 1791. See Robert Troup to H, June 15, 1791.

and Clerk for foreign languages in the department of Mr. Jefferson, Secretary of State; an experiment somewhat new in the history of political manœuvres in this Country; a news paper instituted by a public officer, and the Editor of it regularly pensioned with the public money, in the disposal of that officer; an example savouring not a little of that spirit, which in the enumeration of European abuses is the continual theme of declamatory censure with the party whose leader is the author of it; an example which could not have been set by any other head of a department without having long since rung throughout the UStates.

Mr. Freneau is not then, as he would have supposed, the Independent Editor of a News Paper, who though receiving a salary from Government has firmness enough to expose its maladministration. He is the faithful and devoted servant of the head of a party, from whose hand he receives the boon. The whole complexion of his paper is an exact copy of the politics of his employer foreign and domestic, and exhibits a decisive internal evidence of the influence of that patronage under which he acts.

Whether the services rendered by him are an equivalent for the compensation he receives is best known to his employer and himself. There is however some room for doubt. Tis well known that his employer is himself well acquainted with the French language; the only one of which he is the translator; and it may be a question how often his aid is necessary.

It is somewhat singular too that a man acquainted with but one foreign language engaged in a particular trade, which it may be presumed occupies his whole time and attention, the Editor of a News Paper, should be the person selected as the Clerk for foreign languages, in the department of the United States for foreign affairs. Could no person have been found acquainted with more than one foreign language, and who, in so confidential a trust, could have been regularly attached to, in the constant employ of the department and immediately under the eye of the head of it?

But it may be asked—Is it possible that Mr. Jefferson, the head of a principal department of the Government can be the Patron of a Paper, the evident object of which is to decry the Government and its measures? If he disapproves of the Government itself and thinks it deserving of opposition, could he reconcile to his own personal dignity and the principles of probity to hold an office under it and employ the means of official influence in that opposition? If he disapproves of the leading measures, which have been adopted in the course of its administration, could he reconcile it with the principles of delicacy and propriety to continue to hold a place in that administration, and at the same time to be instrumental in vilifying measures which have been adopted by majorities of both branches of the Legislature and *sanctionned by the Chief Magistrate of the Union?*

These questions would certainly be natural. An answer to them might be left to the facts which establish the relation between the Secretary of State and the Editor of the National Gazette, as the text, and to the general tenor of that paper as the Commentary. Let any intelligent man read the paper, from the commencement of it, and let him determine for himself, whether it be not a paper virulently hostile both to the Government and to its measures. Let him then ask himself, whether considering the connection which has subsisted between the Secretary of State and the Editor of that Paper, cœval with its first establishment, it be probable that the complexion of the paper is contrary to the views of that officer.

If he wishes a confirmation of the inference, which he cannot fail to draw, as a probable one, let him be informed in addition—

1   That while the Constitution of the United States was depending before the People of this Country, for their consideration and decision, Mr. Jefferson, being in France, was opposed to it, in some of its most important feautures, and wrote his objections to some of his friends in Virginia. That he, at first, went so far as to discountenance its adoption; though he afterwards recommended it, on the ground of expediency, in certain contingencies.[9]

2   That he is the declared opponent of almost all the important measures which have been devised by the Government; more especially the provision which has been made for the public Debt, the institution of the Bank of the United States, and such other measures as relate to the Public Credit and the Finances of the UStates.

It is proper that these facts should be known. If the People of the UStates believe, that their happiness and their safety are con-

9. For an extended discussion of this charge, see "Catullus No. II," September 19, 1792, and "Catullus No. IV," October 17, 1792.

nected with the existence and maintenance of an efficient National or Fœderal Government—if they continue to think that, which they have created and established, worthy of their confidence, if they are willing, that the powers they have granted to it should be exercised with sufficient latitude to attain the ends they had in view in granting them and to do the essential business of the Nation— If they feel an honest pride in seeing the Credit of their country, so lately prostrate, elevated to an equal station with that of any Nation upon earth—if they are conscious that their own importance is increased by the increased respectability of their Country, which from an abject and degraded state, owing to the want of government, has, by the establishment of a wise constitution and by the measures which have been pursued under it, become a theme for the praise and admiration of mankind—if they experience that their own situation is improved and improving—that commerce and navigation have advanced—that manufactures are progressing—that agrigulcure is thriving—that property is more secure than it was— industry more certain of real not nominal reward, personal liberty perfectly protected—that notwithstanding the unavoidable demands upon them to satisfy the justice retrieve the reputation and answer the exigencies of the Country they are either less burthened than they were or more equal to the burthen which they have to sustain —if these are their opinions and their experience, let them know and understand, that the sentiments of the officer who has been mentioned, both as to the principles and the practice of the Constitution, which was framed by them and has been administered by their representatives, freely chosen, are essentially different from theirs.

If on the contrary—The People of the United States are of opinion that they erred in adopting their present constitution—that it contains pernicious principles and dangerous powers—that is has been administered injudiciously and wickedly—that men whose abilities and patriotism were tried in the worst of times have entered into a league to betray and oppress them—that they are really oppressed and ruined or in imminent danger of being so—If they think the preservation of National Union a matter of no or small consequence—if they are willing to return to the situation, from which they have just escaped, and to strip the government of some of the most necessary powers with which they have cloathed it—if they are desirous that those which are permitted to remain should be frittered away by a narrow timid and feeble exercise of them—If they are disposed to see the National Government transformed into the skeleton of Power—and the separate omnipotence of the state Governments exalted upon its ruins—If they are persuaded that Nations are under no ties of moral obligation that public Credit is useless or something worse—that public debts may be paid or cancelled at pleasure; that when a provision is not likely to be made for them, the discontents to be expected from the omission may honestly be transferred from a Government able to vindicate its rights to the breasts of Individuals who may first be encouraged to become the Substitutes to the Original Creditor, and afterwards defrauded without danger.* If to National Union, national respect-

* Such was the advice given by Mr. Jefferson, when Minister Plenipotentiary to the Court of France, to Congress, respecting the debt due to France. The precise terms are not recollected but the substance may be depended upon. The poor Hollanders were to be the victims.[10]

10. This charge is discussed at length in "Catullus No. V," November 24, 1792, and "Catullus No. VI," December 22, 1792.

In 1786 Etienne Clavière, on behalf of a group of Amsterdam bankers, made an offer to Charles-Alexandre de Colonne, the Comptroller General of France, to purchase the debt owed by the United States to France. Jefferson wrote to John Jay concerning the offer on September 26, 1786. The paragraph in Jefferson's letter concerning the French debt was copied and referred by Congress to the Board of Treasury on February 2, 1787. The Board of Treasury's report of February 19, 1787, reads as follows:

"The Board of Treasury to whom was referred an extract of a Letter from the honorable Mr. Jefferson Minister plenipotentiary to the Court of France, having reported,

"That the said Minister states, 'That a proposition has been made to Monsieur de Calonne, Minister of the Finances of France, by a company of Dutch Merchants to purchase the debt due from the United States to the Crown of France; giving for the said debt, amounting to Twenty four million of Livres, the sum of Twenty million of Livres. That information of this proposition has been given to him by the Agent of the said Company, with the view of ascertaining whether the proposed Negotiation should be agreeable to Congress.'

"That the said Minister suggests 'That if there is a danger of the public payments not being punctual, whether it might not be better that the discontents which would then arise should be transferred [from] a Court, of whose good will we have so much need, to the breasts of a private Company.'

"'That the credit of the United States is sound in Holland; and that it would probably not be difficult to borrow in that Country, the whole sum of money due to the Court of France; and to discharge that debt without any deduction, thereby doing what would be grateful to the Court, and establishing with them confidence in our honor.

"On a mature consideration of the circumstances above mentioned, the Board beg leave to observe,

ability Public Order and public Credit they are willing to substitute
National disunion, National insignificance, Public disorder and discredit—then let them unite their acclamations and plaudits in favour
of Mr. Jefferson: Let him be the toast of every political club, and
the theme of every popular huzza. For to those points, without
examining his motives do assuredly tend the political tenets, real
or pretended, of that Gentleman.

These strictures are made from a Conviction, that it is important
to the People to know the characters intrusted with their public
affairs.

As Mr. Jefferson is emulous of being the head of a party, whose

---

"That at the time the debt due from the United States to the Crown of
France was contracted, it could not have been foreseen, that the different
Members of the Union, would have hesitated to make effectual provision for
the discharge of the same; since it had been contracted for the security of the
Lives, Liberties and property of their several citizens, who had solemnly
pledged themselves for its redemption; and that therefore the honor of the
United States cannot be impeached for having authorized their Minister at the
Court of France to enter into a formal Convention acknowledging the amount
of the said debt, and stipulating for the reimbursement of the principal and
interest due thereon.

"That should the United States at this period, give any sanction to the
transfer of this debt, or attempt to make a Loan in Holland for the discharge
of the same, the persons interested in the transfer or loan would have reason
to presume that the United States in Congress would make effectual provision
for the punctual payment of the principal and interest.

"That the prospect of such provision being made within a short period, is
by no means flattering; and though the credit of the United States is still
sound in Holland, from the exertions which have been made to discharge the
interest due to the Subscribers to the Loans in that Country; yet in the opinion of this Board it would be unjust, as well as impolitic, to give any public
sanction to the proposed negociation. Unjust, because the Nation would contract an engagement, without any well grounded expectation of discharging it
with proper punctuality. Impolitic, because a failure in the payment of interest accruing from this negociation (which would inevitably happen) would
justly blast all hopes of credit with the Citizens of the United Netherlands,
when the exigencies of the Union might render new Loans indispensably necessary.

"The Board beg leave further to observe, that although a grateful sense of
the services rendered by the Court of France would undoubtedly induce the
United States in Congress to make every possible exertion for the reimbursement of the Monies advanced by his Most Christian Majesty; yet that they
cannot presume, that it would tend to establish in the mind of the French
Court, an idea of the National honor of this Country, to involve Individuals
in a heavy Loan at a time when Congress were fully sensible, that their resources were altogether inadequate to discharge even the interest of the same;
much less the installments of the principal which would from time to time
become due. How far the idea of transferring the discontents which may prevail in the French Court, for want of the punctual payment of interest to the

politics have constantly aimed at elevating State-power, upon the ruins of National Authority—Let him enjoy all the glory and all the advantage of it. But Let it at the same time be understood by those, who are persuaded that the real and permanent welfare of the Country is to be promoted by other means that such are the views by which he is actuated.   *An American*

---

breasts of the private Citizens of Holland would be consistent with sound policy, the Board forbear to enlarge on.

"It may be proper however to observe that, the public integrity of a Nation, is the best shield of defence, against any calamities, to which in the course of human events, she may find herself exposed.

"This principle so far as it respects the conduct of the United States in contracting the Loans with France cannot be called in question. The reverse would be the case, should the sanction of the United States be given, either to the transfer of the French debt, or to the Negociation of a Loan in Holland for the purpose of discharging it.

"If it be further considered, that the consequences of a failure in the punctual payment of interest on the Monies borrowed by the United States, can by no means be so distressing to a Nation (and one powerful in resources) as it would be to Individuals, whose dependence for support is frequently on the interest of the Monies loaned, the Board presume that the proposed negociation cannot be considered at the present juncture in any point of view, either as eligible or proper. Under these circumstances they submit it as their Opinion,

"That it would be proper without delay to instruct the Minister of the United States at the Court of France not to give any sanction to any negociation which may be proposed for transferring the debt due from the United States, to any State or company of Individuals who may be disposed to purchase the same." (*JCC,* XXXIII, 589–93.) A copy of this report may be found in the Oliver Wolcott Papers, Connecticut Historical Society, Hartford.

The full text of Jefferson's letter to John Jay may be found in Boyd, *Papers of Thomas Jefferson,* X, 405–06. For a defense of Jefferson and a charge that H unfairly and unscrupulously quoted Jefferson out of context, see Dumas Malone, *Jefferson and the Rights of Man* (Boston, 1951), 188–89, 470–71. For a defense of H's charge, see Mitchell, *Hamilton,* II, 212–13.

From Thomas Newton, Junior [1]

Norfolk [*Virginia*] *August 4, 1792.* Describes progress of construction of lighthouse at Cape Henry. Asks Hamilton to instruct John McComb, Jr., the contractor, "To have a pavement without the Light house as the sand drifts very much."

ALS, RG 26, Lighthouse Letters Received, Vol. "A," Pennsylvania and Southern States, National Archives.

1. Newton was inspector of the revenue for Survey No. 4 in Virginia.

To William Short

Treasury Department
August 4. 1792.

Sir

Since my last to you of the 25th Ultimo, I have received a letter from our Commissioners at Amsterdam,[1] informing me of their having recently instituted another loan for the United States, of three millions, at four per Cent interest, to be dated the first of June last.[2]

I have concluded to destine the money arising from this loan towards payment of the debt due to France, and you will accordingly apply it to that object.

With great consideration, I have the honor to be, Sir, Your Obedt Servant.   Alexander Hamilton

William Short Esqr.
Minister Resident of
the United States at the Hague.

LS, William Short Papers, Library of Congress; LS marked "Duplicate," William Short Papers, Library of Congress.
   1. Letter from Willink, Van Staphorst, and Hubbard not found. The letter was dated May 31, 1792. See H to Washington, August 3, 1792.
   2. For a description of the Holland loan of 1792, see Short to H, June 28, 1792, note 17.

From Otho H. Williams

Elizabeth Town [Maryland] August 4, 1792. "The inclosed papers will inform you that a considerable difference is discovered between the instruments used at Philada. and those used at Baltimore, for the ascertaining the quality, or proof, of distilled Spirits. . . ."

ALS, Maryland Historical Society, Baltimore; ADf, Columbia University Libraries.

To Otho H. Williams

Treasury Department, August 4, 1792. "I am informed that there is a vessel in Your Port for Amsterdam; which will sail about the 10th instant. I enclose You a letter for Messrs Willink & van Staphorst,[1] which I request may be forwarded by that vessel. . . ."

LS, Columbia University Libraries.
   1. This is presumably a reference to H to Wilhem and Jan Willink, Nicholaas and Jacob Van Staphorst, and Nicholas Hubbard, July 26, 1792.

From George Washington

Mount Vernon, Augt. 5. 1792.

Sir,

Since the date of my last dispatch to you of the 1st: instant, I have received your Letters of the 26. & 30 ulto., and have affixed my signature to the arrangement of Compensations to the Officers of Inspection[1] in consequence of additional latitude given to the President of the United States by the Act of the last Session, intitled "An Act concerning the duties on spirits distilled within the United States."[2]

I have done this in full conviction that the best information the nature of the case would admit, has been obtained at the Treasury to keep the aggregate within the limitations of the Law, & to proportion the Compensations to the services of the respective Officers, presuming also that it appeared essential (from a full view of circumstances, and the benefits likely to be derived from the measure, to the public) that an increase of the Officers of Revenue was really necessary; for I should be unwilling to add to the former establishment, unless the propriety of it was apparent. Unless the Attorney General should be of opinion that The President of the United States has power under the Act of March 1791.[3] or the subsequent one of last Session,[4] to appoint (in the recess of the Senate) an Inspector of the Survey newly constituted in Maryland, it must remain, as is proposed, under the immediate direction of the Supervisor.

If, after these regulations are in operation, opposition to the due exercise of the collection is still experienced, & peaceable proceedure is no longer effectual, the public interest & my duty will make it necessary to enforce the Laws respecting this matter; & however disagreeable this would be to me, it must nevertheless take place.[5]

The Collector [6] was not at Baltimore when I passed through that place; but from the Naval Officer [7] I learnt that the service wou'd sustain no loss by the resignation of the Master of the Maryland Revenue Cutter [8]—that the first Mate [9] was a more competent character, and that the general expectation was that he would be appointed to command it. That I might know how far the sentiments of others accorded with those of the Naval Officer, I requested the Supervisor (Mr. Gale) [10] to make enquiry & to inform me of the result; but not having heard from him since, the first Mate (his name I do not recollect) may be notified by you, of my intention to commission him Master, so soon as I am provided with Commissions for that purpose—at present I have none. The same may be given to John Adams as first & Benjamin Gunnison as second Mate of the Revenue Cutter in New Hampshire: [11] and to Ashur Cook first and John Fenley second Mate of the New York Cutter.[12] The third Mate for the latter may remain for further enquiry & consideration.

If your information with respect to the proposed characters for the Cutter in New Hampshire is not such as you can entirely rely upon, Mr. Lear [13] who is on the spot might afford you some aid in the investigation of them, or others.

I am Sir &c. G: Washington

PS. As I have neither time nor inclination to copy the enclosed, I would thank you for having a transcript of it made & sent to me.

LC, George Washington Papers, Library of Congress.
1. See the first letter which Tench Coxe wrote to H on July 25, 1792.
2. Washington is referring to Section 16 of this act (1 *Stat.* 270–71 [May 8, 1792]). For this section, see Robert Ballard to H, May 31, 1792, note 2.
3. Washington is referring to the proviso contained in Section 4 of "An Act repealing, after the last day of June next, the duties heretofore laid upon Distilled Spirits imported from abroad, and laying others in their stead; and also upon Spirits distilled within the United States, and for appropriating the same" (1 *Stat.* 200). See Coxe to H, July 25, 1792, note 8.
On August 20, 1792, Coxe wrote to George Gale, supervisor of the revenue

for the District of Maryland: "The appointment of an Inspector for the third survey is defered only because the special power to appoint the Revenue Officers, vested in the President by the Act of March 3d 1791 has expired, and this being a new office created by the President it is conceived that he cannot fill it by his ordinary power of appointment, which is applicable only to vacancies in preexistent offices created by law occasioned by the Death &c in the Recess of the Senate" (LC, RG 58, Letters of Commissioner of Revenue, 1792–1793, National Archives).

Edmund Randolph's opinion on a similar case may be found in Randolph to Thomas Jefferson, July 7, 1792 (LS, Thomas Jefferson Papers, Library of Congress).

4. Section 17 of "An Act concerning the Duties on Spirits distilled within the United States" provided for the continuation of all parts of the act of March 3, 1791, "as if every regulation, restriction, penalty, provision, clause, matter, and thing therein contained were inserted in and re-enacted by this present act, subject only to the alterations hereby made" (1 *Stat.* 170).

5. See H to Washington, July 30, 1792.

6. Otho H. Williams was collector of customs at Baltimore.

7. Robert Purviance.   8. Simon Gross.

9. David Porter was first mate on the Maryland revenue cutter

10. George Gale.   11. See H to Washington, July 26, 1792.

12. See H to Washington, July 26, 1792.

13. Tobias Lear, Washington's secretary, at this time was visiting in Portsmouth, New Hampshire, where his father and his wife's family lived.

From William Ellery

[*Newport, Rhode Island*] *August 6, 1792.* "I have recd. your Circular Letter of the 6th of February last,[1] and three other letters of the 21. 25. & 26 of the last month. . . ."[2]

LC, Newport Historical Society, Newport, Rhode Island.

1. See Ellery to H, July 10, 1792.

2. None of these letters have been found.

To Henry Knox

[*Treasury Department, August 6, 1792.* "All advances for supplies in the quartermaster's department will be made after the first of next month to the quartermaster [1] by warrants in his favor from the treasury, and he will have to account immediately to the treasury for the disbursement of the moneys committed to him. It will, of course, be necessary for the quartermaster to have an attorney or deputy at this place. No provision for compensation of a deputy having been made it is of necessity that he should depute some person who is otherwise in the employ of the government." ² *Letter not found.*]

Extract, Mary Carson Darlington, ed., *Fort Pitt and Letters from the Frontier* (Pittsburgh, 1892), 248.

1. On April 19, 1792, the Senate had approved the President's appointment of James O'Hara as quartermaster general.

2. On August 7, 1792, Knox wrote to O'Hara at Pittsburgh and enclosed this extract of a letter from H. On August 17, 1792, O'Hara sent to Samuel Hodgdon a power of attorney enabling Hodgdon to receive the money issued by the Treasury Department for the quartermaster's department (Darlington, *Fort Pitt*, 248–49).

To Benjamin Lincoln

Treasury Department
August 6. 1792.

Sir

You were perfectly right in making the seizure, announced in your letter of the 26th Ultimo.

I do not see that any thing can be done in respect to the Drawback you mention. No payment on that account can be made until the requisite evidence is produced; and there might be circumstances which would altogether preclude the possibility of producing that evidence.

Benjamin Lincoln Esqr.
Collector Boston.

L[S], RG 36, Collector of Customs at Boston, Letters from the Treasury, 1789–1818 (vol. unnumbered), National Archives; copy, RG 56, Letters to the Collector at Boston, National Archives; copy, RG 56, Letters to the Collectors at Small Ports, "Set G," National Archives.

From William Seton

New York 6 Augt. 1792.

My dear sir

Shortly after I received your kind Letter of the 25th: I found by a Letter from your department you was gone to make a tour in

Jersey[1] therefore delayed answering it. You will observe by the annexed Return that the Collector[2] has begun to comply with your kind orders[3]—& it will be a very pleasant Circumstance that he continues to do so—for the Branch is certainly now getting on very fast, & I think (*in confidence*) their Direction rather wish to take every advantage in Draining us of our Specie—they make pretty frequent & heavy drafts, & rather I think unnecessarily so—because whenever the interchange of Notes leave a balance in their favour, a dft for Specie soon follows.[4] I would not wish to complain just now, but if I find they persist in the draining us, I must implore the aid of your all powerfull hand to convince them we are not destitute of aid in the hour of need.

I have been My dear sir I am sorry to say a very improvident Steward with your Bank Stock.[5] I waited till it got up to 30 ⅌ Cent, and then sold,—but behold it has since risen four or five ⅌ Cent more very unexpectedly—however I did for the best & really thought I had done well but such is the unaccountable change of the value of such property, a breath blowing them up or down, that it is impossible to judge whether we go too fast or too slow. I will thank you to send me the original receipts you had from the Bank, as it is necessary they should be cancelled.

Mr. Green & Mr. Pollock have not quite yet adjusted their business[6] & I fear will not without a further reference to you, but this I will avert if possible.[7]

Believe me with unalterable respect & esteem   My dear sir   Your obliged Obed Hue Servt   Wm Seton

Alexr. Hamilton Esqr.

ALS, Hamilton Papers, Library of Congress.
1. H had gone to Paterson, New Jersey, to attend a meeting of a committee of the directors of the Society for Establishing Useful Manufactures.
2. John Lamb, collector of customs at New York.
3. See H to Seton, July 25, 1792.
4. For an amplification of Seton's complaints about the activities of the New York branch of the Bank of the United States, see Seton to H, July 22, 23, 1792.
5. For information on H's sale of his stock in the Bank of New York, see Seton to H, May 28, June 25, 1792.
6. For background concerning the dispute between William Green and George Pollock, see H to Seton, July 17, 25, 1792; Seton to H, July 23, 1792; Green to H, July 24, 26, 1792.
7. H endorsed this letter "No answer."

From William Short

The Hague Aug. 6. 1792

Sir

I have had the honor of recieving your letter of May the 7th. enclosing the Presidents confirmation of the contract made for the loan at Antwerp, which has been delivered to M. de Wolf.[1]

I informed you in my last[2] that I expected him here in order to speak of a new loan at 4. p. cent; in consequence of his having suppressed a part of the last at 4½. p. cent. I have formerly mentioned[3] to you my having promised to him if he would stop issuing the bonds of that loan, that he should be supplied with at least as many at 4. p. cent interest & that the commission should if necessary be augmented. He in consequence thereof found means to suppress 950. of those bonds viz. deliver only 2050. So that although the loan is nominally of three millions, it is in fact only of two millions & fifty thousand florins—the 950. bonds which were numbered, but have not been signed either by me or the banker were left with M. Morris. In the hurry of my departure I did not take a reciept for them, but have written to him to send me one that I may forward it to you, in order that it may appear that they have not been made use of.[4]

I now have the honor of inclosing you sir, the account of the reciepts & expenditures of these 2050 obligations as furnished me by M. de Wolf. Duplicates of the rects. were regularly forwarded me, which I have put into M Morris's hands in order that he might regulate finally with France the payments made on acct. of this loan.

My former letters explained to you how it happens that these payments were begun by remittances from Antwerp & afterwards

ALS, letterpress copy, William Short Papers, Library of Congress.
1. Charles John Michael de Wolf. See Short to H, December 1, 1791. For a description of the Antwerp loan of 1791, see Short to H, November 8, 1791, note 4, and November 12, 1791.
2. See Short to H, June 28, 1792.
3. Short to H, March 24, 1792.
4. Short to Gouverneur Morris, July 17, 1792 (ALS, Columbia University Libraries).

made in cash there, to the agent employed by France for that purpose.[5] The then situation of affairs added to the intention of the U.S.
to make up the depreciation to France left no hesitation as to the
choice.

I then contemplated the U.S. making a very honorable & advantageous arrangement as to these payments—honorable because they
made up the depreciation on the assignats—& advantageous because
this depreciation if measured by the rise of the price of commodities
in France (which would have been just)—or even by the rise of
the price of gold & silver (wch. for many reasons of locality—such
as want of freedom in their being bought & sold on the market—
acts of violence—& even decrees of the assembly, not imputable to
the U.S, were higher & a less just measure)—this depreciation I say,
would have been much less than the fall of exchange & of course
have left a considerable profit to the U.S.

It was impossible for me at that time to have foreseen that the final
settlement of this depreciation would have been thus delayed, much
less that it wd. have been postponed so as not to have been settled
even by the government which created the assignats (of which
there seems now real risk) & of course with one which will have
much less scruple in arguing that the depreciation was greater than
it really was. As I fear the U.S. will suffer from this delay, I must
beg you to bear in mind the causes of it as related to you in my
several letters. It will be otherwise so natural for you to attribute
this delay & the injury arising from it (if there should be any) to the
person whom you charged with this business, that I hope you will
excuse my anxiety on the subject, & my importunity in here briefly
stating the stages of the delay.

On recieving your letter announcing the intention of the U.S. as
to the depreciation on the assignats [6] I informed the Minister &
commissaries of the treasury of it (confining the promise made to
future payments notwithstanding your letter would have embraced
the former ones also) [7] & desired them to fix on some basis for
ascertaining the real depreciation of assignats. I was obliged to go to
Holland before this was done. I returned to Paris on the 15th of

5. Short to H, January 26, March 24, May 14, June 28, 1792.
6. H to Short, September 2, 1791.
7. See Short to H, November 22, 1791; May 14, 1792.

January. At that time I had been long without hearing from government, but being convinced that the appointment of the minister to Paris could not be postponed & would be made during the then session of Congress, it seemed probable that every day might bring intelligence of the person, & indeed the person himself, even if he should have been in America. Considering therefore that this appointment would be the latest declaration of the will of the President—that the person appointed would necessarily be the one who enjoyed the greatest degree of the confidence of government, & of course most apt to fulfill their expectations & most capable of promoting their interests in every kind of business I thought it my duty, in one of this delicate kind particularly to postpone it, until it should be known to whom the interests of the U. S. in France were to be permanently confided & the more so as it was impossible that any inconvenience could arise from a short delay, the rate of exchange—the price of gold & silver & of the principal articles of consumption in France during that period being known. Let what will be the event I am persuaded sir, you cannot disapprove this disposition in a public servant.

I had not long remained in this situation before I learned from M Morris in London that the President had nominated him for that place, & although he did not arrive in Paris until the month of May, yet it would certainly have been improper in me to have taken any arrangements in any business which would have admitted of delay, before his arrival; & particularly as I had every reason to suppose that he would immediately receive his credentials & come on to Paris.

On his arrival I put him in possession without delay of whatever occurred to me relative to the interests of the U.S. at that place, & particularly pressed on him the necessity of regulating with the present government the depreciation promised them on the payments made at Antwerp. I had the honor of mentioning to you in my letter of June 28 the two causes which occasioned some delay with M Morris, at the time of my leaving Paris. Since my arrival here I have never ceased pressing & importuning him on the subject. I inclosed him also the extract of your letter of April the 2d. relative thereto.[8] The changeable situation of ministry necessarily threw

8. Short to Morris, June 28, 1792 (ALS, Columbia University Libraries).

impediments in the way of business, but this was of peculiar kind &
if connected only with that of making further payments, they
would necessarily have removed all causes of delay. I therefore advised M Morris not to connect it with any other business as I apprehended from his letters he had done, but to reduce it to this simple
proposition "*We have paid* you money at Antwerp on which we
have promised to make compensation for depreciation—we have
now more money ready for you at Amsterdam—fix the depreciation existing at the time of the payments made at Antwerp—say
what it is now & we will immediately order you the payments of
the cash at our disposition *at Amsterdam*." [9] I should have supposed
from their present wants of money abroad their answer would not
have been delayed twenty-four hours & that they would have been
thus placed on the soliciting side of the question, whilst M Morris
would have had the finest opportunity of using all the arguments
which must occur to every body, for shewing what the real difference was between the depreciation of the assignats & the fall of
exchange, wch difference constituted the gain of the U.S. I have
begged him also in my letters to bear in mind the advantage of
settling this depreciation with the government which created the
assignats rather than one that should succeed to them & be built on
their ruin.[10] In fine I have done everything that depended on me to
accelerate this business & do not doubt that M Morris has done the
same. Still it is not settled—& from the present state of things in
France I fear it will not be with the present government.

This leads me also to mention to you another subject which has
given me much uneasiness, namely the suspension of our payments
to France & consequent accumulation of monies in the hands of our
bankers at Amsterdam on which the U. S. pay a dead interest. You
were informed by me from Amsterdam & successively since, of the
cause of this suspension viz. the hope of applying these payments
towards succours to the French islands—of course having them invested in the productions of the U. S.[11] This would have been so
advantageous an operation that I could not hesitate delaying the

9. Short to Morris, July 23, 1792 (ALS, Columbia University Libraries).
10. Short to Morris, August 4, 1792 (ALS, Columbia University Libraries).
11. Short to H, December 28, 1791; April 22, 25, May 14, June 28, 1792.

payments a short time after finding that the minister of the marine [12] had brought forward this proposition to the assembly & the more so as at that time the sums on hand dispensable were small; not knowing then that you had determined not to draw for the whole which you had previously announced to me.

After my return to Paris in Jany there was a constant expectation of the Minister's proposition then referred to the colonial committee, being reported & decided on. Whilst in this expectation I learned that the confidence of government as to their affairs in France was transferred to M. Morris & expecting his arrival without delay in Paris the motives mentioned above could not but have their influence in inducing me to desire the procrastination of this business also; not knowing but, & indeed supposing, that M. Morris from his knowledge in commercial concerns, might chuse some mode unknown to me, for carrying this operation into effect. Still knowing that the operation in itself was highly advantageous I determined to act in it if it became necessary previous to M Morris's arrival. Accordingly being pressed by the Minister I stipulated you should hold 800,000 dollars at his orders for supplies to the islands— & that the rate at which the dollars should be credited should be fixed between the two countries as stated to you in my letter of April 22. Those of April 25 & May 14 will have informed you, how this business came to be again delayed & of its passage into M Morris's hands after his arrival at Paris the 7th of that month.

Thus sir you will see by what means it came to pass that no part of a loan opened in Decr was paid to France at the period of my departure from Paris, although in the mean time the sums in hand had been augmenting & promised to be still more so, by the seizing the opportunity of opening a second loan at 4. p. cent, of which I gave you notice by a few lines written for that purpose only, on the 26th of May.[13]

As to any delay which may have taken place since that time, I can only say that thinking it proper to concert this business with

12. Antoine François, Marquis de Bertrand de Moleville, who had introduced the proposition in December, 1791, was replaced by Jean de Lacoste in March, 1792. Lacoste was in turn replaced by François Joseph Gratet Dubouchage in July, 1792.
13. Letter not found.

the representative of the U. S. at Paris I have not ceased since my arrival here writing & pressing I may add, importuning him to fix with the French government the rate at which they would recieve the florins at Amsterdam or some other mode of paying them the sums on hand. I preferred the former as being more expeditious & more sure in these times of uncertainty—& more advantageous also if the U. S. are to make up depreciation. I pressed him particularly to detach this subject & the settlement of the Antwerp payments from all others, & as the ministry were fluctuating to get over formalities & to apply directly to the commissaries of the Treasury who were a permanent body & to whom the minister would necessarily refer him as had always been done to me by the ministers of my time.[14] Finding that the delay was not removed & seeing no reason to suppose it would be, with the present government, I at length wrote to M Morris, that unless he could immediately fix on some better mode of payments I should think myself obliged to direct our bankers to commence their remittances to France; fearing that I should not be able to justify myself to you for holding so long so large sums at a dead interest to the U. S., when it was expected that they had been applied towards extinguishing their debt to France.[15] The last letter from him in answer there to was dated the 30th. of July & recd. here the 4th inst.[16] In it he informed me that he had the day before recd the acct from the commissaries of the treasury & had written to them that morning to know whether they chose to recieve money in Amsterdam or Paris & that if there was the least difficulty he should direct Grands house [17] to draw on our commissioners at Amsterdam [18] & pay to the treasury. He observes some what less will be gained than by remittances, but that the state of things there is such that remittances are by no means sure. I answered this letter the instant of recieving it to inform him that I had formerly had an application from M Grand to be made use of in this business which judging improper I had referred to you, & that you had approved my not employing an useless intermediary [19]

14. Short to Morris, July 23, 1792 (ALS, Columbia University Libraries).
15. Short to Morris, July 23, 1792 (ALS, Columbia University Libraries).
16. ALS, William Short Papers, Library of Congress.
17. The French banking house of Ferdinand Le Grand.
18. Willink, Van Staphorst, and Hubbard.
19. See Short to H, March 11, 1791; H to Short, June 25, 1791.

—that my own opinion therefore was against his doing it now. I advised his treating immediately with the commissaries of the treasury who might purchase his draughts on the bankers at Amsterdam at the exchange which he might fix with them—& in doing which he might regulate also the depreciation to be allowed. I mentioned that you had formerly suggested my thus selling my bills to them for specie which I had not done, because I thought a more advantageous mode of ascertaining the real depreciation might be adopted.[20] If he thought otherwise he might now make use of the plan suggested by you.[21] I hope this will prevent his employing M Grand, as his treating immediately with the commissaries will not only be a more economical, but also a more unexceptionable mode in other respects.

Mr Morris adds also in this letter that the commissaries state their losses on the Antwerp payments by depreciation (as they have given credit for them in their acct at the current rate of exchange) at 1,368,939 livres & that he shall tell them that these losses & the compensation if any, will form a subject for the consideration of our government "whose order I shall ask." This is in fact nothing more than leaving it unsettled with the present government who created the assignats & levied on them, to be settled by a future one who will be raised perhaps on their destruction & interested in depreciating them [in] the mode which I have always desired so much to avoid. It is possible however M Morris may see some advantages in it which do not occur to me & he will no doubt do whatever shall most advance the public interests.

I have been desirous to explain these several circumstances minutely to you because many of the advantages which I formerly contemplated as possible to obtain for the U.S. both in the payments made & to be made & also in a general conversion of their debt to France, may perhaps be lessened from a delay, which might be attributed in some degree to me, if I did not recall to you sir the motives wch induced me to postpone as much as possible taking definitive arrangements until the will of the U.S. should be more fully represented, & which I cannot doubt would be approved by every government & particularly ours, being at so great a distance.

20. See H to Short, September 2, 1791; Short to H, November 22, 1791.
21. Short to Morris, August 4, 1792 (ALS, Columbia University Libraries).

I shall set out tomorrow for Amsterdam in order to sign the contract & bonds of the second 4. p cent loan.[22] I have already informed you that 2½ millions of florins exclusive of the ½ million you announced to me as having been drawn for in your letter of April 2d. would be held to answer your draughts, & that I meant to comprehend therein the 800,000 dollars mentioned to you from Paris [23] so that except these three millions I considered all other sums arising or on hand of the late loans, (making the proper reservations for your standing orders at Amsterdam) as to be applied towards the French debt unless directed otherwise by some of your future letters—accordingly it was my wish that the payments to France should be immediately made counting on future entries to answer your draughts in proportion as they should arrive.

I observe from your letter of May the 7th that you thought it possible I should be absent from this country. To my great astonishment I have recd. no further orders respecting this absence, than simply a notification of my being designated for that purpose [24]—& that I should find here the instructions relative thereto. From letters which others have recieved here I fear much & cannot doubt indeed that those intended for me have miscarried.

I was inadvertently drawn off from the business at Antwerp, with which I began this letter, before completing what I intended to say to you respecting it. M. de Wolf has been here, & on my objecting to some part of his acct. which from the Cr. side wd seem to indicate that he had disposed of the first 1500 bonds, much sooner than the Dr. side would authorize from the dates of the rects of M. de Broeta.[25] He acknowleged the justice of the observation & attempted to account for it, by my having directed him towards the end of Dec. to suspend his remittances—on which he had told the lenders that not chusing to have so large sums on hand he wished

---

22. The second four percent loan made at Amsterdam commenced on June 1, 1792. For a description of this loan, see Short to H, June 28, 1792, note 17.
23. See Short to H, June 28, 1792.
24. On January 24, 1792, Short and William Carmichael had been appointed "Commissioners for negotiating and concluding, with any person or persons, who shall be duly authorized by his Catholic Majesty, a convention, or treaty, concerning the navigation of the river Mississippi" (*Executive Journal*, I, 99). See also "Notes on Thomas Jefferson's Report of Instructions for the Commissioners to Spain," March 1–4, 1792.
25. Joseph de Broeta.

them not to make the payments until required. On the 6th of Jany I removed the suspension & directed him to make these payments to M. de Broeta. He had then to advertise the several lenders dispersed through the Netherlands to bring on that money wch. occasioned some delay. Yet as they had tendered their money they had a right to take date from that period with the usual term of grace, which de Wolf now tells me he had agreed should be a month as at Amsterdam, although he in the beginning had told me it should be less. Yet as all powers give great facilities in these cases I did not think it would be proper to be too difficult in this instance & after making him consent to the justice of these objections to the statement of his acct. I promised him I would send it to you in its present form with the observations I have made, & particularly as he had made a sacrifice in suppressing the bonds at 4½. p. cent

He had built his hopes on having a loan of 3. millions at 4. p. cent, although I had never promised more than a sum equal to that suppressed of the 4½. p. cent loan & which was as mentioned 950,000 florins. He had written to M. Morris to get him to prevail on me to extend it to three millions, although he was obliged to confess that the Antwerp market was incompetent to so large sums monthly as he had formerly promised—& even that he could not engage for more than ƒ250,000 a month—so that the loan would have been twelve months on the market. There are so many reasons against such a step that I had no difficulty in rejecting it on its own ground, without recurring to your preference to Amsterdam, & the advice of holding out to the bankers the hopes of confining to that place future loans if they can keep the interest at 4. p. cent. Opening a loan elsewhere for 3. millions would totally defeat that idea—but one of a smaller sum at Antwerp might be represented to them, as it really is a continuation & unavoidable consequence of the former loan. Consequently notwithstanding M. Morris's letter I determined to confine the loan at Antwerp to the sum suppressed of the former loan or if I went beyond it, to make de Wolf consider it absolutely as a favor to him & of course pay the sacrifice. When I proposed to him to suppress the bonds at 4½. p. cent in order to substitute to them others at 4. p. cent I held out as an inducement the augmentation of the commission. On his now pressing for this loan being extended beyond the bonds suppressed I told him I would consent to extend it to 1½ million, to be completed in six months at 250,000 florins a month provided he would give up the augmentation of commission, promised on the bonds suppressed—& undertake the whole at a commission of four per cent. To this he consented. I exacted of him however that there should be no kind of uncertainty in this business—that he should have written contracts with the undertakers who should be bound to furnish the sums agreed for. Otherwise he might keep as it were a kind of open shop for the bonds of the U.S.—dispose of as many as he could & keep them until they were all disposed of which though a saving for him, would be an uncertain & dishonorable mode for the U.S. Notwithstanding he made great protestation to the contrary yet I am convinced now he had it in view when he pressed for extending the loan to three millions. For although he would have had no scruple in undertaking for that sum as he proposed—yet on my explaining to him my ideas with respect to his having real & bona fide contracts with the undertakers so that the U.S. might know fully & certainly what to count on, he returned to Antwerp in order to consult with these undertakers & told me he should come here in a short time to conclude the contract. He has written to me from thence that Sweden having opened a loan at 5.p.ct interest & the Emperor also one at 4.p.cent with an high commission—& most of the undertakers being engaged therein—& others being now absent—& himself obliged on account of his health to absent himself also to go to a watering place, he had found it best to postpone the loan until the end of the next month [26] viz this his letter being dated July when he was morally sure of effecting it. Thus that matter now stands. Should it be effected it will be obtaining money at 4.p.cent instead of 4½. which was the rate of the suppressed bonds. Should it not be then effected Antwerp may be still held out *in terrerem* to our bankers at Amsterdam who know nothing of what has passed with respect to the loan there.

I hope in future that my letters to you will be less prolix & tedious. Asking your pardon for the minute details which I have sometimes thought myself obliged to enter into hitherto, I have the honor to add assurance of the sentiments of attachment & respect with which I am

26. Wolf to Short, July 26, 1792 (ALS, William Short Papers, Library of Congress).

sir   your most obedient & most humble servant   W Short

The Honble.
Alexander Hamilton   Secretary of the Treasury   Philadelphia

Treasury Department Circular
to the Collectors of the Customs

Treasury Department,
August 6, 1792.

Sir,
It is the opinion of the Attorney General, that by force of the 8th section of the "Act for raising a further sum of money for the protection of the Frontiers, and for other purposes therein mentioned," the regulation, requiring the immediate payment of the duties on imported articles, when the amount should not exceed fifty dollars, is repealed in all cases, except those relating to Salt, West India produce, Wines and Teas.[1] The words *"the term* of credit" used in respect to Salt, he considers as referring to something preceding, and as comprising only those cases, in which credit was before allowed. It is my desire that this construction be practiced upon at the several custom houses.

A question has been made as to the method of calculating the duty ad valorem upon wines laid by the Act above referred to.[2] I answer, that in that, and every other case of ad valorem rates, under the same act, the rule prescribed by the thirty-eighth section of the Collection Law is to be observed.[3]

It has been signified to me, that the practice at different custom houses respecting brass in plates or sheets has been dissimilar. At some, it has been charged with a duty, at others exempted. The thing is not free from doubt; but considering the spirit of the exemption, which looks to the encouragement of internal manufactures of the article, and that the term Brass, which is singly used, literally applies to the material, in plates or sheets, as well as in pigs.—I adopt the construction which exempts from duty brass in the former as well as in the latter shape. I adopt it the rather, because there is a process in use, by which brass in its primitive state is produced in sheets or plates.

It has also been stated to me, that a difference of practice has obtained upon that part of the Act, entitled, "An Act making further provision for the collection of the duties by law imposed on Teas, and to prolong the term for the payment of the duties on Wines," [4] which relates to Teas; that at some ports all teas whencesoever imported, are understood to be included in the provisions of that Act; while at other ports they are considered as confined to Teas imported from China.

The first of these two constructions is unquestionably the true one. The preamble professes to establish regulations "concerning TEAS" generally. The enacting clause embraces "*every* importer of TEAS" as generally. It also prescribes the new regulation in *addition* to the provisions contained, as well in the 40th section of the Collection Law,[5] which comprises all teas, except those imported from China, as in the 41st section of that law, which applies only to Teas from China; contemplating consequently teas not brought from China equally with those brought from China. It is to be observed that in the volumes of the laws, printed by authority by Childs and Swaine,[6] the Sections of the Collection Law are wrongly enumerated, No. 23 being twice repeated—whence it happens that the sections referred to in the last Act as 40 and 41, are truly 41 and 42. The subject is itself a proof of the Sections really intended.

With great consideration, I am, Sir, Your obedient Servant,

A Hamilton

LS, to Jeremiah Olney, Rhode Island Historical Society, Providence; LS, Bureau of Customs, Philadelphia; LS, Office of the Secretary, United States Treasury Department; LC, Essex Institute, Salem, Massachusetts; copy, United States Finance Miscellany, Treasury Circulars, Library of Congress; copy, RG 56, Circulars of the Office of the Secretary, "Set T," National Archives.

1. On July 5, 1792, Charles Lee had raised this question in a letter he wrote to H. For the text of Section 8 of this act, see Lee to H, July 5, 1792, note 2. See also William Ellery to H, July 30, 1792.

2. Section 1 of "An Act for raising a farther sum of money for the protection of the frontiers, and for other purposes therein mentioned" levied specific duties on designated wines and provided that all other wines should be taxed at "forty per centum ad valorem, provided that the amount of the duty thereupon shall, in no case, exceed thirty cents per gallon" (1 *Stat.* 259 [May 2, 1792]).

3. H is referring to Section 39 of "An Act to provide more effectually for the collection of the duties imposed by law on goods, wares and merchandise imported into the United States, and on the tonnage of ships or vessels," which reads as follows: "*And be it further enacted*, That the ad valorem rates of duty upon goods, wares and merchandise at the place of importation, shall be estimated by adding twenty per cent. to the actual cost thereof, if imported from the Cape of Good Hope, or from any place beyond the same;

and ten per cent. on the actual cost thereof if imported from any other place or country, exclusive of charges" (1 *Stat.* 167 [August 4, 1790]).

4. 1 *Stat.* 219–21 (March 3, 1791). See Benjamin Lincoln to H, July 3, 1792.

5. "An Act to provide more effectually for the collection of the duties imposed by law on goods, wares and merchandise imported into the United States, and on the tonnage of ships or vessels" (1 *Stat.* 145–78).

6. Francis Childs and John Swaine.

To _____

Treasury Department
Aug 7. 1792

Sir

In adjusting the accounts of the contractors for supplying the army with shoes [1] a charge will occur for boxes in which they were packed.[2] This charge in its principle is deemed a reasonable one. It will of course remain to judge of the reasonableness of the quantum and who are the parties intitled; in other words, whether the contractors have paid the money or are authorised to include it in their accounts.

I am with great consideration   Sir   Your obedt servt. A Hamilton

ALS, Boston University.

1. The firm of Nathaniel Beach and Abiel Canfield of Newark, New Jersey, had contracted to supply the Army with shoes. See William Seton to H, May 28, June 3, August 3, 1792.

2. In July, 1792, Jonathan Andress submitted a bill for making shoe boxes to the Treasury Department, and at the same time Stephen Hays submitted a bill for packing 18,376 pairs of shoes. The charges are not included in the statement of Beach and Canfield's account, dated August 8, 1792, but Canfield was directed to accept the payments due both to Hays and to Andress (D, RG 217, Miscellaneous Treasury Accounts, 1790–1894, Accounts No. 2833, 2834, 2835, National Archives).

To Benjamin Lincoln

Treasury Department, August 7, 1792. "I have directed a Thermometer to be sent to You, which I request You will please to forward to the Collector of Machias. . . ." [1]

L[S], RG 36, Collector of Customs at Boston, Letters from the Treasury, 1789–1807, Vol. 4, National Archives; copy, RG 56, Letters to the Collector at Boston, National Archives; copy, RG 56, Letters to Collectors at Small Ports, "Set G," National Archives.

1. Stephen Smith.

From Alexander Dallas

Philadelphia, August 9, 1792. Transmits "a copy of the Laws of Pennsylvania, passed to the last Session of the General Assembly."

LC, Division of Public Records, Pennsylvania Historical and Museum Commission, Harrisburg; copy, Division of Public Records, Pennsylvania Historical and Museum Commission.

To Clement Biddle [1]

Philadelphia August 10, 1792

Dear Sir

I had concluded to offer you the Agency for providing all such supplies for the War Department as are not objects of direct contract with the Treasury. The compensation about 800 Dollars a year. But it occurred to me, that you were engaged in the business of broker; and hence an apprehension has been excited, lest a connection of the kind contemplated with this department should be misinterpreted and misrepresented by those, who are too much disposed to malign and calumniate. I have not however made any other appointment willing to apprise you of my intention before I did it—as I could not know your future plans of business. I trust you will be persuaded in every event of the friendship & esteem with which I am Dr. Sir

Your Obedient servt. A Hamilton

Clement Biddle Esq

ALS, Independence National Historical Park Collection, Old Custom House, Philadelphia.

1. Biddle, a Philadelphia merchant and United States marshal for the District of Pennsylvania, was also a notary public and broker. Biddle had had extensive experience in supplying the Army, for he had served as commissary general of forage under General Nathanael Greene from July, 1777, to June, 1780, and in September, 1781, he had been appointed commissary general of

the Pennsylvania state militia. During 1792 he was the contractor for rations issued to recruits at Philadelphia, as well as for rations issued by the state of Pennsylvania to militia raised for the protection of the frontier.

To James McHenry [1]

[*Philadelphia, August 10, 1792.* On October 20, 1792, McHenry wrote to Hamilton: "I have just recd your letter of the 10th Ulto." *Letter not found.*]

1. At this time McHenry was a member of the Maryland Senate.

To George Washington

Treasury Departmt. Augt. 10th. 1792.

Sir,

I have been duly honored with your Letters of the 1st and 5th instant. A copy of the latter is enclosed according to your desire.

You may depend upon it, Sir, that nothing shall be wanting in this Department to furnish all requisite supplies for the Army with efficiency & œconomy, and to bring to exact account all persons concerned in them as far as shall consist with the powers of the Department. Hitherto monies have been furnished to the War department, as they have been called for, for procuring all those articles which had not been objects of direct Contract with the Treasury. And I learn from the Secretary of War that every thing is in great maturity.

Under the former system, provisions and clothing were the only Articles which the Treasury had the charge of procuring; the receiving, issuing, & inspecting their quality belonged to the Department of War by usage.

The Act of the last Session, entitled "An Act making alterations in the Treasury and War Departments" prescribes that all purchases and Contracts for all supplies for the use of the Department of War, be made *by* or *under the direction* of the Treasury Department.[1]

As much progress had been made in preparations for the Campaign,[2] prior to the passing of this Act, by the Secretary at War, I thought it best to continue the business under his immediate care for some time—'till in fact all the arrangements begun should be compleated. It is now, however, determined that on the first of September the business of procuring all supplies will be begun under the immediate direction of the Treasury, upon Estimates and Requisitions from time to time furnished and made by the Department of War.

The arrangement which is contemplated for this purpose is the following—provisions and Clothing will be provided as heretofore by Contracts made by the Secretary of the Treasury, pursuant to previous Advertisements. Articles in the Quarter Master's Department will be to be procured by him or his Agents or Deputies; for which purpose advances of money will be made to him directly, to be accounted for to the Treasury by him. Ordnance stores, Indian Goods and all contingent supplies will be procured by an Agent who will be constituted for the purpose with an allowance of Eight hundred Dollars a year in lieu of Commission. Accounts for his purchases in every case in which it can conveniently be done (which will comprehend the greatest number of cases) will be settled immediately with the Treasury and the money paid directly to the individuals. In other cases, advances on Account will be made to the Agent, to be accounted for directly to the Treasury.

A leading object of this arrangement is to exempt the Officers, both of the War and Treasury Departments, from the ill-natured suspicions which are incident to the actual handling and disbursement of Public Money. None of the interior officers of either department, except the Treasurer, will have any concern with it.

The supplies of every kind will be delivered to the order of the Department of War. The issuing of them & the accounting for the issues (except as to provisions which are directly issued by the Contractors to the Troops & which are proved to the Treasury upon vouchers prescribed for the purpose) appertain to the Department of War. The Regulations, which have been adopted for the purpose, will no doubt be early reported to you by the Secretary at War; as well as those which have been concerted with the Treasury respecting the paying & accounting for the pay of the Troops.[3]

I beg leave to assure you that in the application of the general arrangement which you have adopted respecting the execution of the Act concerning distilled Spirits,[4] the greatest attention will be paid to œconomy as far as the precautions of the Treasury can ensure it.

I presume it to have been your intention that the opinion of the Attorney General should be taken as to the Power of the President to appoint the supplementary Officers contemplated during the recess of the Senate; which shall accordingly be done.[5]

It affords me much satisfaction to observe that your mind has anticipated the decision to enforce the Law, in case a refractory spirit should continue to render the ordinary & more desirable means ineffectual.[6] My most deliberate reflections have led me to conclude, that the time for acting with decision is at hand, and it is with pleasure, I can add, that an encreasing acquiescence is likely to render this course the less difficult in the cases in which an uncomplying temper may finally prevail.

I shall without delay execute your directions respecting the Officers of Cutters.[7]

With the highest respect and the truest attachment I have the honor to be &c. Alexander Hamilton

LC, George Washington Papers, Library of Congress.

1. H is referring to Section 5 of this act (1 *Stat.* 280 [May 8, 1792]).

2. This is a reference to the proposed campaign against the Indians in the Northwest. See Washington to H, August 1, 1792.

3. The regulations which were adopted at this time may be found in letters which Oliver Wolcott, Jr., sent to Joseph Howell, accountant of the War Department, and to Caleb Swan, paymaster of the troops. See Wolcott to Howell, August 13, 1792 (ADf, Connecticut Historical Society, Hartford), and Wolcott to Swan, July 26, 1792 (Df, partly in the handwriting of Wolcott, Connecticut Historical Society, Hartford). "Regulations for receiving distributing and accounting for all public property designed for the Army of the United States," August 3, 1792, and "Regulations for furnishing the supplies of Forage Stationary and wood for the troops of the United States," August 2, 1792, may be found in RG 94, Instructions to David Henley, 1793–1800, National Archives. See also H to Henry Knox, August 6, 1792.

4. "An Act concerning the Duties on Spirits distilled within the United States" (1 *Stat.* 267–71 [May 8, 1792]). On August 5, 1792, Washington had approved an arrangement for compensation of revenue officers. See the first letter which Tench Coxe wrote to H on July 25, 1792.

5. See the first letter which Coxe wrote to H on July 25, 1792, note 8, and Washington to H, August 5, 1792.

6. See Washington to H, August 5, 1792.

7. See Washington to H, August 5, 1792.

An American No. II [1]

[Philadelphia, August 11, 1792]

For the Gazette of the United States

Facts, Mr. Fenno,[2] speak louder than words, and, under certain circumstances, louder even than oaths. The Editor of the *National Gazette* must not think to *swear away* their efficacy.[3] If he be, truly,

ADf, Connecticut Historical Society, Hartford; two copies, Hamilton Papers, Library of Congress; [Philadelphia] *Gazette of the United States,* August 11, 1792.

1. The other articles by "An American" are dated August 4, 18, 1792.
2. John Fenno, editor of the *Gazette of the United States.*
3. Philip Freneau's reply to the charges made in "An American No. I," August 4, 1792, began with the following affidavit and reads in its entirety as follows:

"*Personally appeared before me,* Matthew Clarkson, *Mayor of the City of Philadelphia*—Philip Freneau, *of the City of Philadelphia, who being duly sworn, doth depose and say, That no negociation was ever opened with him by* Thomas Jefferson, *Secretary of State, for the establishment or institution of the* National Gazette; *that the deponent's coming to the City of Philadelphia, as the publisher of a Newspaper, was at no time urged, advised, or influenced by the above officer, but that it was his own voluntary act; and that the said Gazette, nor the Editor thereof, was ever either directed, controuled, or attempted to be influenced, in any manner, either by the Secretary of State, or any of his friends; nor was a line ever, directly or indirectly, written, dictated, or composed for it by that officer, but that the Editor has consulted his own judgement alone in the conducting of it—free—unfettered—and uninfluenced.*

PHILIP FRENEAU.

"Sworn the 6th August, 1792, before
    "MATTHEW CLARKSON, Mayor.
"The foregoing was thought necessary to justify the Secretary of State from false imputations respecting a supposed patronizing or influencing the *National Gazette.* As to what more particularly concerns myself, I shall just mention briefly, that the clerkship of foreign languages is not a new establishment in the department of State, but has always been occupied by some person in another fixed line of business—as, for instance, Mr. *John Pintard,* of New-York, who held it for years; the salary (two hundred and fifty dollars per annum) being of itself inadequate to the maintenance of any man, that is capable of performing the duties of the office, and who should make his sole dependance thereupon.
"But, I would ask, why is the Editor of a Newspaper disqualified in a greater degree than a person in any other line of business, from holding the above place under the department of State—or, what possible reason can be given why the Secretary of State should be laid under the necessity of translating, any more than the Secretary of the Treasury should be obliged to perform any laborious duty in his own office? The absurdity is too great to bear examination.

as they announce, the pensioned tool of the public character, who has been named, no violation of truth, in any shape, ought to astonish. Equivocations and mental reservations are the too common refuge of minds, struggling to escape from disgraceful imputations.

It may be very true, in a literal sense, that no negotiation was ever opened with Mr. Freneau by Thomas Jefferson Secretary of State, and yet it may be very certain, that a negotiation was opened with him directly or circuitously, by a *particular friend* of that Officer, & expectations given of his patronage and encouragement. It may be very true, in the same sense, that Mr. Freneau's coming to the City of Philadelphia, as publisher of a News Paper, was at no time urged advised or influenced by the same officer; and yet it may be equally a fact that it was urged advised & influenced by *a friend of* his, in concert with him, and to answer his views, and with authority to engage his assistance and support. It may be in the strictest sense true; that Mr. Freneau's coming to Philadelphia was his *own voluntary act;* and yet that he came from interested motives to do the work of a party: for a man acts not the less *voluntarily* because he yields to considerations of Interest. It may even be true, that the Editor of the National Gazette was never either directed controuled or attempted to be influenced, in any manner, either by the Secretary of State, or any of his friends; and yet it may be in the strongest sense true, that under the influence of the emoluments received from that officer, he has acted in precise conformity to his *known* principles and views.

As to the assertion, that not a single line in the National Gazette was ever, *directly* or *indirectly*, written dictated or composed for it by the Secretary of State—it is a shocking instance of rashness and levity. Unless Mr. Freneau be himself the author of every line,

---

"An artful design to mislead, could only have suggested that the political complexion of the *National Gazette* is at all influenced by the trifling salary in question—or could have held up an idea, that if the salary did not exist, the principles of the Gazette would be in any respect different from what they are.

"The 'AMERICAN,' in the performance alluded to, sets out with an affected seriousness of assertion, 'that it was necessary the whole *truth* should be told.' It is now left to the public to determine whether the whole is not A LIE?

PHILIP FRENEAU,
Editor of the National Gazette."

([Philadelphia] *Gazette of the United States,* August 8, 1792.)

which has been contained in every one of his papers (a thing not to be believed) it is impossible that he can know, that none has ever been *directly* or *indirectly* written dictated or composed by the Officer in Question. And if he had been as scrupulous about an oath, as he ought to have been, he never could have sworn, so positively as he has done, to a thing which it was impossible for him to know. Temerity like this would invalidate his testimony, in a Court of Justice, if he were even, as he is not in the present case, a disinterested Witness.

No Mr. Freneau, this is not the way to exculpate yourself before a judicious public, from the conclusions which are to be drawn from the most convincing facts. Nor can it be believed from any thing, that you have either sworn or said, that the whole of what has been alleged is "a lie."

The material facts, which have been alleged, and may be added in confirmation, are either acknowleged or dare not be denied by you; and they prove decisively your *improper* connection with the Secretary of State, and the influence of that connection upon your press.

It is a fact, which you have acknowleged that you receive a regular salary from the Secretary of State, as a Clerk in his department for *foreign languages;* while you pretend not to act in any other capacity than that of Translator of *one foreign language.*

It is a fact, which you tacitly concede, that you came from NY, where you were, in capacity of [an Editor or director of a Newspaper] [4] to become in this City Editor of the N Gazette.

It is a fact, which you dare not deny, that your appointment as Clerk for foreign languages was *cotemporary* with or rather antecedent to the *commencement* of your paper. The first number of your paper is dated the 26th of October 1791. Your appointment is announced in the Dayly Advertiser of the same date (a news paper printed at New York) in the following terms "We hear from Philadelphia, that the Hon T. J Esquire Secretary of State for the U S has appointed Capt P—— F—— Interpreter of the F L for the department of State" *

note * It is believed that Mr. Freneau could throw light upon this question, by naming the day when his salary commenced.

4. Space left blank in MS. Material within brackets has been taken from the *Gazette of the United States*, August 11, 1792.

It is a fact, which the debates in the Virginia Convention will testify, that Mr. Jefferson was in the Origin opposed to the present constitution of the UStates.[5]

It is a fact, known to every man who approaches that officer (for he takes no pains to conceal it and will not thank you to deny it) that he arraigns, the principal measures of the Government; and it may be added with *indiscreet* if not *indecent* warmth.

It is a fact, which results from the whole complexion of your paper, that it is a paper intemperately devoted to the abuse of the government and all the conspicuous actors in it; except the Secretary of State & his coadjutors, who are the constant theme of your panygeric. Even the illustrious patriot who presides at the head of the Government has not escaped your envenomned shafts.

And from these facts the inferences *which have been drawn are* irresistible.

The circumstance of your having come from *another state* to set up and conduct a *new* paper; the circumstance of the *Editor* of that *new paper* being appointed a Clerk in the department of state; the *coincidence* in point of time of that appointment with the *commencement* of your paper or to speak more correctly its precedency —the conformity between the complexion of your paper and the known politics of the head of the department who employs you— these circumstances collectively leave no doubt of your true situation. The conviction arising from them is too strong to be weakened by any of those bold or even solemn declarations, which are among the hackneyed tricks, employed by the *purists* in politics, of every country and age, to cheat the people into a belief of their superior sanctity, integrity and virtue.

If you had been previously the conductor of a News paper, in this City—if your appointment had been any considerable time subsequent to the institutution of your paper—there might have been some room for subterfuge; but as matters stand you have no possible escape.

The fact of the preliminary negotiation which brought you to this City is not material, where so many other facts, presupposing it, concur. But even this, if the scruples of family connection, or the

5. H discusses this charge at length in "Catullus No. II," September 19, 1792, and "Catullus No. IV," October 17, 1792.

dread of party-resentment does not prevent the evidence being brought forward will be proved incontestibly; not indeed a negotiation in which Thomas Jefferson Secretary of State was the immediate Agent, but one carried on by a very *powerful, influential* and *confidential* friend and associate of that Gentleman.[6]

That Officer has had too considerable a part of his political Education amidst the intrigues of an European Court to hazard a direct personal commitment in such case. He knows how to put a man in a situation calculated to produce all the effects he desires, without the gross and awkward formality of telling him—"Sir I mean to *hire* you for the purpose".

It is impossible for a correct mind not to pronounce, that, in the abstract, a connection like that which is acknowleged to subsist between you and Mr. Jefferson; between the *Editor of a News Paper* and the *head* of a department of the Government; is *indelicate* and *unfit;* and consequently of a nature to justify suspicion. A connection of that sort in a free country, is a pernicious precedent, inconsistent with those pretensions to extraordinary republican purity, of which so suspicious a parade is upon every occasion exhibited.

The apology you attempt for it is ill founded and inadmissible. There is no law which annexes a particular salary to the Clerkship in question. The appointment is under the general authority given to the head of the department to appoint Clerks with salaries not exceeding *aggregately* 500 Dollars to each. There is therefore no restriction to the sum you mention, to induce, as matter of necessity, the employment of a person engaged in other occupations—and not ordinarily and regularly attached to the department. Five hundred Dollars, or even more, might be legally given for a Clerk competent to the duty, and if it was not sufficient wholly to employ him his surplus-time might be dedicated to other business of the department. Nor could there have been any mighty difficulty in finding a Clerk so qualified.

But, if there had been such difficulty, some other character should undoubtedly have been found. The precedent of such a species of

6. James Madison. See "An American No. I," August 4, 1792.

influence erected over the Press ought to have been avoided. This is so obvious, that the not having avoided it, is a proof of sinister design.

The employment of Mr. Pintard by the Secretary of State was a natural consequence of particular situation.[7] Mr. Pintard, if I am rightly informed, had been employed in the same capacity under the old government—and it was natural enough to continue him in the occupation & emolument. But Mr. Pintard was not the *Printer of a Gazette*.

These strictures, though involving Mr. Freneau, it shall be confessed, have been drawn forth principally with a view to a character of greater importance in the community. They aim at explaining a public Officer, who has too little scrupled to embarrass and disparage the government, of which he is a member, and who has been the prompter open or secret of unwarrantable aspersions on men, who as long as actions not merely professions shall be the true test of patriotism and integrity need never decline a comparison with him of their titles to the public esteem.

An American

7. John M. Pintard had been the clerk in the State Department who translated foreign languages until the Federal Government moved from New York to Philadelphia.

T. L. No. III [1]

[Philadelphia, August 11, 1792]

For the GAZETTE of the UNITED STATES.

Mr. Fenno,[2]

Please to thank your correspondent X.Y. for setting me right; and assure him that I really understood the Editor of the National Gazette,[3] to mean that he received a stipend both as translator and editor, until he convinced me of the contrary.[4]

I think this tribute due to candor, and do not hesitate to pay it; for although I consider the National Gazette as having a most pernicious tendency, and being eminently calculated to disturb the public peace, and corrupt the morals of the people, I have not a wish to do injustice either to the Gazette itself or to its editor. At the same time allow me to remark, that however I may have mistaken Mr. Freneau's meaning, the information given by "An American,"[5] strongly countenances a belief of the fact, that he receives pay in both characters; to which I will add, that a singularity attending the National Gazette, seems to corroborate the American's assertions—it is said to be "By P. Freneau," and "Printed by Childs and Swaine."[6] It will hardly be thought unfair to infer from this, that Mr. Freneau is at least the editor; can it be supposed that HE devotes his time to this laborious undertaking gratis? I apprehend not: sufficient reasons might be urged to the contrary. Who then pays him? If any body does, then he receives a stipend both as French translator to the department of state, and as editor (or compiler, I don't care which) of a newspaper. If he is in the pay of Messrs. Childs and Swaine, he is at least guilty of ingratitude to the government which has retained him as translator to the department of state; for, as editor or compiler, his attacks upon that government are both frequent and licentious: If on the other hand, he is in the pay of the government, his conduct forcibly reminds us of the Fable of the Viper which stung to death the Countryman, the genial warmth of whose bosom had reanimated its frozen carcase.   T. L.

[Philadelphia] *Gazette of the United States,* August 11, 1792.

1. The other "T. L." letters are dated July 25, 28, 1792.
2. John Fenno, editor of the *Gazette of the United States.*
3. Philip Freneau.
4. See "T. L. No. II," July 28, 1792.

In a letter dated August 2, 1792, and addressed to "The Gazette of the United States," "X. Y." wrote: "Your correspondent T. L. . . . should have quoted fairly and ingenuously. . . . Instead of your correspondent's quotation, which stands thus, 'Receives a small stipend for services rendered as French Translator to the department of State, and *as Editor* of a *free newspaper'*—he should fairly have quoted the words as follow, in the National Gazette of July 28—'Receives a small stipend for services rendered as French Translator to the department of State, and, as Editor of a free newspaper, admits into his publication impartial strictures on the proceedings of government, &c.' . . ." (*Gazette of the United States,* August 4, 1792).

5. See "An American No. I," August 4, 1792.
6. Each issue of the [Philadelphia] *National Gazette* carried the following statement: "Printed by Childs and Swaine, at their office, No. 239 High-Street, near Sixth-Street, Philadelphia."

To George Washington

[*Philadelphia, August 11, 1792.* On August 22, 1792, Washington wrote to Hamilton: "This will merely inform you that your letter of the 10th . . . and that of the 11th. Inst: have been duly received." *Letter of August 11 not found.*]

To Otho H. Williams

Treasury Department, August 11, 1792. "I enclose you an Advertizement, concerning proposals for the supply of rations for the Western Posts, which I request you will have inserted in the paper of your City, stiled 'the Maryland Journal & Baltimore Advertizer' [1] to continue untill the 29th of Septr next. . . ."

LS, Columbia University Libraries.
  1. This advertisement reads as follows:
"Notice is hereby given, that Proposals will be received at the Office of the Secretary of the Treasury, until the Twenty-ninth Day of September next, inclusive, for the Supply of all RATIONS, which may be required for the Use of the United States, from the first Day of *January*, to the Thirty-first Day of *December*, 1793, both Days inclusive, at the Places and within the Districts hereafter-mentioned. . . .
  "Should any Rations be required at any Places, or within other Districts, not specified in these Proposals, the Price of the same to be hereafter agreed on, betwixt the Public and the Contractor.
  "The Rations to be supplied are to consist of the following Articles, viz.
    "One Pound of Bread or Flour,
    One Pound of Beef, or ¾ of a Pound of Pork,
    Half a Jill of Rum, Brandy, or Whisky,
    One Quart of Salt,
    Two Quarts of Vinegar,   ⎱
    Two Pounds of Soap,   ⎰ per 100 Rations.
    One Pound of Candles,
  "The Rations are to be furnished in such Quantities as that there shall, at all Times, during the said Term, be sufficient for the Consumption of the Troops at each of the said Posts, for the Space of at least *Three* Months in advance, in good and wholesome Provisions, *if the same shall be required.*
  "It is to be understood in each Case, that all Losses sustained by the Depredations of the Enemy, or by Means of the Troops of the United States, shall be paid for the Prices of the Articles captured or destroyed, on the Depositions of Two or more creditable Characters, and the Certificate of a commissioned Officer, ascertaining the Circumstances of the Loss, and the Amount of the Articles for which Compensation is claimed.

"The Contract for the above Supplies, will be made either for One Year, or for Two Years, as may appear eligible. Persons disposed to contract will, therefore, confine their Offers to One Year; or they may make their Propositions so as to admit an Election of the Term of Two Years.

"The Offers may comprise all the Places which have been specified, or a Part of them only." (*The* [Baltimore] *Maryland Journal and Baltimore Advertiser*, August 21, 1792.)

To Jonathan Dayton [1]

Philadelphia Aug 13. 1792

My Dear Sir

Some skirmishing having begun in the Gazette of the U States respecting Mr. Freneau's receiving a salary from Government [2]— I mentioned in conversation with a Friend all that I knew of the matter, and among other things, but without naming you, the information you had given me concerning Mr. Madison's negotiation with Freneau. Upon this he founded a very pointed attack upon Mr Freneau & Mr. Jefferson which I dare say you have seen as also Mr. Freneau's affidavit denying all negotiation with "Thomas Jefferson Esquire Secretary of State" &c. &c. The Gentleman has since applied to me to obtain if possible an authentication of the fact of the Negotiation.

If I recollect right you told me that this if necessary could be done. And if practicable, it is of real importance that it should be done. It will confound and put down a man who is continually machinating against the public happiness.

You will oblige me in the most particular manner by obtaining and forwarding to me without delay the particulars of all the steps taken by Mr. Madison the when & where and with liberty to use the name of the Informant. His affidavit to the facts if obtainable would be of infinite value. Care ought to be taken that nothing be affected which is not unquestionable.

Truly & Affectionately Yrs   A Hamilton

P.S. I need not observe that this is perfectly confidential & that my name is to be kept out of sight.

E Dayton Jun Esqr

ALS, Harvard College Library.
1. Dayton was a member of the House of Representatives from New Jersey. *JCHW* (V, 518–19) suggests that the recipient of this letter was Elisha Boudinot, while *HCLW* (X, 14–15) gives the recipient as Elias Boudinot. The evidence indicates that H wrote the same or a similar letter to Elisha Boudinot on the same date that he wrote to Dayton.
2. See "An American No. I" and "An American No. II," August 4, 11, 1792; "T. L. No. I," "T. L. No. II," and "T. L. No. III," July 25, 28, August 11, 1792. See also H to Edward Carrington, May 26, 1792, note 8.

From William Ellery

Newport [*Rhode Island*] *August 13, 1792.* "I have received your Circular letters of the 20th of the 22nd. (inclosg. a copy of a letter to you from the Atty. General of the 21st. of June) and of the 23d. of the last month. With regard to the last, I am happy to find that I had construed the Post office Act [1] rightly. . . ."

LC, Newport Historical Society, Newport, Rhode Island.
1. "An Act to establish the Post-Office and Post Roads within the United States" (1 *Stat.* 232–39 [February 20, 1792]).

From Jeremiah Olney

Providence, August 13, 1792. "The Collector of Barnstable acquainted me, at the Time, with the Transaction [1] communicated in your Letter of the 31st of July, which came to hand yesterday. . . . I caused enquiries to be made, relative to Samuel Bourn and his Vessel, of one Benja: Bourn, who was here with a Sloop of the same Name, from Wareham, and who said, he was informed that the said Samuel Bourn was gone with his Sloop to Georgia. This is all the knowledge I have of him or the Vessel; she never having been licenced at this Office. . . ."

ADfS, Rhode Island Historical Society, Providence.
1. Joseph Otis had written to Olney on June 22, 1792. See Olney to H, August 18, 1792.

To Jeremiah Olney

Treasury Department
August 13th. 1792.

Sir

That part of my letter of the 25th. Ultimo,[1] which says that "the drawback cannot be allowed, unless the proof required of its having been actually landed at a foreign port is produced" is a mistake, arising from my not having at the moment adverted to the difference of the regulations concerning drawbacks, as applied to distilled Spirits, from those relating to other articles.

The drawback may be paid at the end of six months, and the exportation-bond of the exporters will be cancelled on their producing the proper Certificate that the brandy has been actually landed & delivered at a foreign port or place.

It is to be observed that the penalties upon the relanding of goods, apply to their *being relanded,* before they have been at some foreign port.

I am Sir   Your Obed. servant   A Hamilton

Jeremiah Olney Esqr.
Collector, Providence.

LS, Rhode Island Historical Society, Providence; copy, RG 56, Letters to the Collector at Providence, National Archives; copy, RG 56, Letters to Collectors at Small Ports, "Set G," National Archives.
  1. See also Olney to H, August 3, 1792.

To Benjamin Rush [1]

[*Treasury Department, August 13, 1792.* The dealer's catalogue description of this letter reads: "Respecting proposed method for obtaining fresh water from salt water." *Letter not found.*]

ALS, sold at Parke-Bernet Galleries, Inc., May 24, 1943, Lot 117.
  1. Rush, who had been a member of the Pennsylvania Ratifying Convention, was a prominent Philadelphia physician and philanthropist. He was professor of the institutes of medicine and clinical practice at the University of Pennsylvania and physician of the port of Philadelphia.

From George Washington [1]

Mount Vernon Augt. 13. 1792.

Dr Sir,

Under a blank cover, I returned signed the provisional Contract for the supply of the Lighthouse in New Hampshire.

It is pleasing to find by the Letter from our Commissioners at Amsterdam, that the credit of the United States remains upon so respectable a footing in the United Netherlands.

I am Dr. Sir, &c.   G: Washington

LC, George Washington Papers, Library of Congress.

1. For background to this letter, see the second letter Tench Coxe wrote to H, July 25, 1792, and H to Washington, August 3, 1792.

To Otho H. Williams

Treasury Department, August 13, 1792. "The President having signified to me his intention to appoint David Porter, the present first mate in the cutter Active, master of the said Cutter, in the room of Simon Gross, who has resigned; I have to request, that you will notify the intended appointment to Mr Porter. . . ." [1]

LS, Columbia University Libraries.

1. See George Washington to H, August 5, 1792.

From Tench Coxe

Flemington New Jersey [1]
Augt. 14. 1792

Dear Sir

Before I left Philada. I had notice of a cause to be tried on the 10th. instt. at this place, of the Business of wch. I had some knowlege.[2] It has lasted till this day & the council think my staying may become very important to the just decision of the Case. It is with great pain that I remain because I doubt not the Arrangemt. of the

Compensations [3] now requires to be acted upon.[4] I shall hasten to Philada. in five Minutes, after I am dismissed.

There has been a most respectable assemblage of persons from various parts of this State attending the Courts of nisi prius & oyer & terminer, and I have felt infinite satisfaction in manifestations from every description of them, that they equally love the general & state governments, and that they think the great objects of public happiness committed to the former have been faithfully and most beneficially managed. They are full of a firm and generous confidence in the future intentions of the general Government.

I have the Honor to be with the most respectful Attachment, dear Sir,   Your most obedt. Servt.   Tench Coxe

ALS, Hamilton Papers, Library of Congress.
    1. When this letter was written, Coxe was visiting his wife and children, who were staying with his father-in-law, Charles Coxe, at Sidney, New Jersey, a few miles from Flemington, the county seat of Hunterdon County (Coxe to John Adams, September 5, 1792 [ALS, Adams Family Papers, deposited in the Massachusetts Historical Society, Boston]).
    2. The case to which Coxe is referring was presumably an action concerning title to land brought by his father-in-law in the Hunterdon County Court of Nisi Prius (Richard S. Coxe, *Reports of Cases Argued and Determined in the Supreme Court of New-Jersey. From April Term 1790, To November Term 1795, both inclusive,* I [Burlington, 1816], 255–56).
    3. This is a reference to the compensation for officers entrusted with the collection of the duties laid on distilled spirits. See the first letter Coxe wrote to H on July 25, 1792.
    4. Coxe is referring to the necessity of notifying the revenue officers of the August 5, 1792, arrangement for their compensation. See George Washington to H, August 5, 1792. After returning to Philadelphia, Coxe addressed a circular letter, dated August 17, 1792, to the supervisors of the revenue (LC, RG 58, Letters of Commissioner of Revenue, 1792–1793, National Archives).

From Charles Lee [1]

Alexandria [Virginia] 14th. August 1792

Sir!

Your two letters of the 20th and 22d July last have been received, the latter accompanied with the opinion of the Attorney General upon the subject of fees under the Coasting Law; and as his opinion differs from your own, and each Collector is left to act according to Law at his peril, I have been embarrassed whether the practice of this Office, ought to be conformed to the opinion of the Attorney General or not: Were the fees to be my own property, I should not alter, but would wait until the next session of Congress, when it is expected the Coasting Law will be amended, but when I consider that one half of the Coasting fees are to be paid to the Surveyor, it seems necessary for my safety against his claims, to receive the fees, which the opinion of the Attorney General has stated to be legal.

I never entertained any doubt concerning the Obligation upon a Collector of the Customs, to act in all matters of Revenue in obedience to the directions and explanations of the Secretary of the Treasury Department, and by this rule I have endeavoured to transact the business of my Office, The Oath to execute the Office according to Law, I have never supposed to be a justification for deviating from his orders in cases which concerned the public and individuals. But the fees of Office as they concern individuals only, that is to say, the Citizen who pays and the Officer who receives are to be considered as private property, and if a dispute on this subject arises, like other matters of a private nature, it seems to me, to be properly determinable in a Court of Justice. With regard to Coasting fees, which by Law are distributable among the Collector and Naval Officer and Surveyor (and in my humble opinion very unreasonably so far as the Surveyor is concerned, in as much as he performs no service, and is not at any expense) it was incumbent on the Collector to receive all which the Law authorized, for if a suit should be brought against him by the Naval Officer or Surveyor for fees which he ought to have received and did not, I am inclined to think Judgement would be rendered against him in a Court of Justice, though it should appear that he acted agreably to the opinion of the Secretary of the Treasury. I am free to declare that this consideration weighed most with me in departing from the opinion of Jones and Harrison which was grounded as it appeared to me, upon reasons too abstruse and a construction of words too nice to be right.

I am respectfully Sir!   Your most Obedt. H'ble Servant

Charles Lee,
Collector

Copy, RG 56, Letters to and from the Collector at Alexandria, National Archives.

1. For background to this letter, see "Treasury Department Circular to the Collectors of the Customs," July 22, 1792.

To Benjamin Lincoln

Treasury Department, August 14, 1792. "It had been intimated to me, previous to the receipt of your letter of the 3rd instant,[1] that a dissimilar construction was given in the Custom Houses to the laws which relate to the importation of Teas &ca. . . . The mode adopted at your office appears to be comformable to the sense of the law."

L[S], RG 36, Collector of Customs at Boston, Letters from the Treasury, 1789–1807, Vol. 4, National Archives; copy, RG 56, Letters to the Collector at Boston, National Archives; copy, RG 56, Letters to Collectors at Small Ports, "Set G," National Archives.

1. No letter from Lincoln to H of August 3, 1792, has been found. See, however, Lincoln to H, July 3, 1792, and "Treasury Department Circular to the Collectors of the Customs," August 6, 1792.

From Jeremiah Olney

Custom-House,
Providence 14th August 1792.

Sir

The seventh Section of the Act, passed the last Session of Congress, "concerning the Duties on Spirits distilled within the United States,"[1] allows "an abatement for leakage at the rate of Two ₰ Cent, in every case in which the duty shall be payable by the gallon of the spirits distilled:" this abatement, it appears to me, was intended to be made, on securing the Duties at the end of the quarter, from the whole quantity distilled during the preceding Three Months: The Supervisor of Rhode-Island District[2] differs from me in Opinion, and thinks that no abatement ought to be allowed except in cases of actual loss by leakage, to be ascertained at the expiration of the quarter.[3] As it is necessary that the practice upon this part of the Law, of the Collectors of the Revenue in securing the Duties, and of myself on exportation of the Spirits, should be the same, so that the Drawbacks shall be *equal* to the Duties secured, I ask, Sir, the favor of your Opinion on the Matter.

The form of the Account annexed to the Inspector of the Revenue's [4] Certificate of domestic Spirits, laden under his inspection for exportation, (transmitted before the said Act passed) not contemplating the deduction of the Two ℔ Cent, I presume a variation will be necessary, should that abatement be allowed to the Distillers?

I also wish for your directions what steps are to be taken in cases where the quantities or proof of foreign or domestic Spirits, noticed for exportation, disagree with the Certificates given to accompany each Cask?

I have the honor to be &c.   Jereh. Olney Collr.

Alexr. Hamilton Esqr.
Secy. of the Treasury.

ADfS, Rhode Island Historical Society, Providence.
1. 1 *Stat.* 267–71 (May 8, 1792).   2. John S. Dexter.
3. Olney is referring to Section 17 of "An Act repealing, after the last day of June next, the duties heretofore laid upon Distilled Spirits imported from abroad, and laying others in their stead; and also upon Spirits distilled within the United States, and for appropriating the same," which reads as follows: "That the said duties on spirits distilled within the United States, shall be paid or secured previous to the removal thereof from the distilleries at which they are respectively made. And it shall be at the option of the proprietor or proprietors of each distillery, or of his, her or their agent having the superintendence thereof, either to pay the said duties previous to such removal, with an abatement at the rate of two cents for every ten gallons, or to secure the payment of the same, by giving bond quarter-yearly, with one or more sureties, to the satisfaction of the chief officer of inspection within whose survey such distillery shall be, and in such sum as the said officer shall direct, with condition for the payment of the duties upon all such of the said spirits as shall be removed from such distillery within three months next ensuing the date of the bond, at the expiration of nine months from the said date" (1 *Stat.* 203 [March 3, 1791]).
4. William Barton.

To Otho H. Williams

Treasury Department
August 14 1792

Sir

I duly received your Communication of the 4th instant, concerning the difference which has been discovered between the instruments, used for ascertaining the proof of distilled spirits.

The circumstance is very much to be regretted but I do not at present see that it admits of remedy as to the past. The impossibility of ascertaining what is right, is a great objection to restitution, even if I had power to direct it, which I doubt. Almost any rule that could reasonably be adopted would do more than justice in some cases; less than justice in others.

If, as may have been the case at other ports, the inaccuracy of the instrument had been in favour of the importer, it is certain that the difference would never have been demanded or paid, and there appears indeed to be no other safe rule in such cases than to leave the adjustments which have been made untouched and provide remedies for the future.[1]

I am Sir   Your Obedt. Servant   A Hamilton

Otho H. Williams Esqr.
Collector, Baltimore.

LS, Columbia University Libraries; copy, Maryland Historical Society, Baltimore.
    1. Daniel Delozier, deputy collector of customs at Baltimore, had written to Williams on August 1, 1792, stating that more accurate instruments would be used in the future (*Calendar of the General Otho Holland Williams Papers in the Maryland Historical Society* [Baltimore, 1940], 270–71).

To Otho H. Williams [1]

Treasury Department
August 14 1792.

Sir
    I am glad to learn from the letter of Mr Delozier [2] of the 25th of July inclosed in yours of the 27th

"That the difference between the Inspector of the Revenue and the Inspectors of the Customs had subsided, and that the latter were perfectly disposed to perform the services required of them, by the Secretary of the Treasury, whenever they may be directed by the Inspector of the Revenue."

Instructions have been directed to be transmitted to supply what have been deemed omissions, in regard to the qualifications of those Officers, as Deputy Inspectors of the Revenue. As a regular compensation will hereafter be allowed for their services in that capacity, it is presumable that they will have less objection to rendering them.

A disposition to discard a subject which has been not a little distressing to me will render what I have further to say as concise as possible.

When I spoke of the Inspectors of the Customs as Aids to the Surveyor,[3] I had no idea of drawing into question the authority of a superior Officer over them. It does not follow, because the Surveyor, who is himself an aid to the Collector, has power to put on board vessels one or more Inspectors, and to superintend and direct them when there—that his authority in these particulars is exclusive of that of the Collector; especially as he himself is *"in all cases* subject to the controul of the Collector".[4]

The means of restraining any arbitrary or improper conduct of the Surveyor are always at hand. If the powers vested in you for the purpose should at any time fail of their due effect, nothing will be wanting on my part to give energy to the representations which you shall make. In waving at this time a more particular enquiry, I yield to a supposition that you would not wish a turn of this kind to be given to suggestions merely incidental. If I mistake your meaning, you will doubtless explain.

I trust you will believe that it is very far from my disposition to countenance or tolerate arbitrary or oppressive conduct towards any Officer, however subordinate his station, who may be connected with the Department—or to place any Officer in a situation to be the instrument of rigorous measures auxiliary to such arbitrary or oppressive conduct. There are however on all such occasions different paths to be pursued. And the desirable course must be that which will unite the execution of the public service with the protection of the Officer.

With undiminished consideration and esteem, I remain, Sir, Your Obedt Servant   A Hamilton

Otho H Williams Esqr.
Baltimore.

LS, Columbia University Libraries; copy, Maryland Historical Society, Baltimore.

1. For background to this letter, see H to Williams, June 18, July 19, 1792; Williams to H, June 28, July 27, 1792.

2. Daniel Delozier, deputy collector of customs at Baltimore.

3. See H to Williams, July 19, 1792.

4. His quoting from Section 6 of "An Act to provide more effectually for the collection of the duties imposed by law on goods, wares and merchandise imported into the United States, and on the tonnage of ships or vessels" (1 *Stat.* 154 [August 4, 1790]).

To Nathaniel Pendleton [1]

Treasury Department, August 15, 1792. "I have had the statement relative to the petition of John Moore, Master of the sloop Uxbridge Packet, and others under consideration. It does not at present appear to my satisfaction that there was neither intention of fraud nor wilful negligence on the part of the Petitioners. Indeed the case stands ill in my mind . . . , and I could wish a re-examination . . . , for which purpose the papers will be herewith returned. . . . My first impression was to decide against remission of mitigation; but on further reflection I have concluded to give the parties an opportunity of explaining and putting matters in a more satisfactory light, if they can. This motive, on my part, will, I doubt not, excuse to you the additional trouble which I give you. And I persuade myself that in the further examination, you will have a strict eye to the security of the Revenue, and will endeavour to explore any equivocations or subterfuges which may be employed. The Packets are a Channel through which evasions of the Revenue may be expected early to make their way; and they therefore require vigilant observation. You will please to bear in mind that I consider the Act of the Master as that of the Parties and that his Owners and He are to be responsible for any damage, which may have accrued, from his neglect to innocent Individuals. It will be proper to cause the Attorney of the District [2] to be notified of the time and place of the further enquiry, and the Parties must be required to notify the Attorney of the District for South Carolina [3] of the re-examinations which will be necessary there; to whom I have accordingly written." [4]

LS, University of Georgia.

1. Pendleton was United States judge for the District of Georgia.

This letter concerns petitions which were sent to H and which requested the remission or mitigation of fines for alleged violations of customs regulations at Savannah, Georgia.
2. Matthew McAllister was United States attorney for the District of Georgia.
3. John J. Pringle was United States attorney for the District of South Carolina.
4. Letter not found.

To William Skinner

Treasury Department
August 15th. 1792.

Sir

As the blank draughts already in your possession, are much more than sufficient to discharge the interest which will become due the 30th. of September next on the several species of Stock standing on your books; it will supersede the necessity of making you any further remittance at this time.

I have therefore to request, that upon the receipt of this letter, you will immediately proceed to dispose of as many of the bills in question, on the Collectors of Edenton [1] Newbern [2] or Wilmington [3] as will amount to two thousand five hundred dollars, to be applied to the payment of the interest aforesaid.

All the draughts remaining in your hands after this operation are then to be cancelled, by cutting holes through the signatures and forwarded to this Office by the first conveyance.

I am Sir &c

William Skinner Esquire
Commissioner of Loans
North-Carolina

Copy, North Carolina Department of Archives and History, Raleigh. A copy of this letter was enclosed in H's "Report to the Governor of North Carolina," July 31, 1794.
   1. Thomas Benbury.   2. John Daves.   3. James Read.

From Otho H. Williams

Baltimore, August 15, 1792. States "There not being a vessel at this port bound for Amsterdam, I have this day forwarded your letter . . . ⅌ the Brigantine Batavia for Bremen" for forwarding "by the first safe convenance." [1]

Copy, Columbia University Libraries.
1. See H to Williams, August 4, 1792.

To John Adams

Philadelphia Augt 16 1792

Dear Sir

I have been duly favoured with your letter of the 4th Instant.[1] A warrant for 1000 dollars in your favour has issued.[2] If any authorisation from you had been sent to your son [3] or any one else, your signature on the warrant would have been unnecessary. But as it is, it will be indispensable. Perhaps however the Treasurer may pay in expectation of it.

The Question when the Vice President entered upon the duties of his office, is open at the Treasury; though an opinion has obtained that the taking of the Oath was the Criterion. This has been founded on two considerations—analogy to the case of the President. The Constitution requires that he shall take an oath, *before* he enters upon the *execution* of his Office. He cannot enter upon the duties of it, without entering upon the execution of it, and he can't legally do the latter till he has taken the oath prescribed. The same injunction however is not laid upon the Vice President, and therefore except by analogy, resort must be had to the second consideration, namely that the taking of the Oath of Office is the legal act of aceptance, and may be supposed to date the commencment of service.

But this reasoning it must be confessed is not conclusive, and therefore the opinion of the Attorney General will be taken, both as to the President & Vice President—and I presume will guide in the Adjustment.

Twenty thousand dollars have been appropriated[4] and the advances by anticipation may reach that limit.

You forgot that Mr Clinton could feast upon what would starve another.[5] He will not however have an opportunity of making the experiment. And I hope the starvation policy will not long continue fashionable.

Your confirmation of the good disposition of New England is a source of satisfaction. I have a letter from a well informed friend in Virginia who says, all the persons I converse with, acknowlege that the people are prosperous & happy, and yet most of them, including even the friends of the Govt. appear to be much alarmed at a supposed system of policy, tending to subvert the Republican Govt of the Country.[6] Were ever Men more ingenious to torment themselves with phantoms?

Adieu my dear Sir, & believe me always very respectfully & Affectionately   Yr Obed sevt   A H

The Vice President

Copy, Hamilton Papers, Library of Congress.
    1. Letter not found.
    2. Warrant No. 2012 for a payment of one thousand dollars of Adams's salary was dated August 15, 1792. See "Report on an Account of the Receipts and Expenditures of the United States for the Year 1792," December 18, 1793.
    3. Thomas Boylston Adams, John Adams's youngest son, remained in Philadelphia during the summer and fall of 1792. In a letter to his father on August 16 he referred to the problem of obtaining the payment of Adams's salary: "The Secretary of the Treasury has so arranged matters, that you will be at liberty to draw for a thou⟨san⟩d Dollars when you think fit. I presume the warrant may ⟨be received⟩ by Attorney. The Secretary however will probably acquaint you with ⟨the⟩ most practicable method" (ALS, Adams Family Papers, deposited in the Massachusetts Historical Society, Boston). On September 10, 1792, in a letter to his father he again referred to this matter: "I called this day upon Mr. Hamilton concerning the Warrant for 1000 Dollars which at my request was prepared for presentment at the Treasury for Payt. and only wanted a single line under your hand, in order to its being paid. . . . I have been expecting this authority for some time past, but as it has not arrived, feel somewhat anxious lest the circumstance should have slipped your memory" (ALS, Adams Family Papers, deposited in the Massachusetts Historical Society, Boston).
    4. Section 1 of "An Act for allowing a Compensation to the President and Vice President of the United States" reads as follows: "*Be it enacted by the Senate and House of Representatives of the United States in Congress assembled*, That there shall be allowed to the President of the United States, at the rate of twenty-five thousand dollars, with the use of the furniture and other effects now in his possession, belonging to the United States; and to

the Vice President, at the rate of five thousand dollars per annum, in full compensation for their respective services, to commence with the time of their entering on the duties of their offices respectively, and to continue so long as they shall remain in office, and to be paid quarterly out of the treasury of the United States" (1 *Stat.* 72 [September 24, 1789]).

5. This is a reference to the vice presidential candidacy of Governor George Clinton of New York.

6. See George Washington to H, July 29, 1792.

To Nathaniel Appleton [1]

Treasury Department, August 16, 1792. "I have directed the Treasurer [2] to furnish you with draughts on the Office of Discount and Deposit at Boston for seventy six thousand Dollars, to be applied by you towards paying the interest which will become due the 30th of next month on the several species of Stock standing on your books. You will also receive from the Treasurer a further sum of seven Thousand Dollars in a Draught on the Office of Discount and Deposit aforesaid for the purpose of enabling you to discharge the pensions which will become due, to the Invalids of the United States on the 4th of September next ensuing the date hereof. . . ."

LS, The Andre deCoppet Collection, Princeton University Library.

1. Appleton was commissioner of loans for Massachusetts.
2. Samuel Meredith.

From Elisha Boudinot

New-York, August 16th, 1792.

Dear Sir:

I had just returned from the Circuit when I received your letter [1] by yesterday's post, and had not then read the pieces you alluded to. Judge Bradford [2] was with me, and relating the affair—especially the affidavit—he said he was very much mistaken, if he had not the relation from Freneau's [3] own mouth. "This I know," says he, "that at the time I was in New-York, and was informed of Mr. J.'s [4] writing him a letter, which he took in dudgeon, as striking at his independence, &c., and wrote a very insulting answer, which he showed to Mr. Childs, [5] who prevented his sending it, &c; and in fact related the whole story as I had it. I have no doubt, if you fall in company with him, and bring on the conversation with him, as soon as he returns, he will give you satisfaction on the subject. Converse with him as if you had received no information on the head.

Soon after I had the first conversation with you on that subject, I saw the gentleman I referred to, but I found him more attached to F. than I supposed—and he refused allowing me to say any thing from him. I am still in hopes, through another channel, to ascertain the facts, which I will endeavor to do in the course of the week, if possible, though I doubt not Judge Bradford will, on reflection, be able to mention the authority from which he had the story; and if he had it immediately from F. himself, it will be the best evidence that can be procured, and he appears to have no reserve on the subject.

Have you received my letter inclosing Hall and Mort's proposals; [6] if so, will you write your sentiments on the subject? May we expect to see you on the 20th instant? [7] I see by the papers a Mr. Nesbit has arrived from Scotland, and is with General Schuyler.[8] Would it be worth while to wait to have his opinion?

Your letter [9] inclosing the money I have received and forwarded. I am, with esteem, dear Sir,   Yours sincerely,   Elisha Boudinot.

JCHW, V, 519–20.

1. Letter not found, but see H to Jonathan Dayton, August 13, 1792. For the meeting of the circuit court, see Tench Coxe to H, August 14, 1792.

2. William Bradford, judge of the Supreme Court of Pennsylvania, was the husband of Boudinot's niece.

3. For background concerning Philip Freneau and the establishment of the [Philadelphia] *National Gazette*, see H to Edward Carrington, May 26, 1792, note 8; "T. L. No. I," "T. L. No. II," "T. L. No. III," July 25, 28, August 11, 1792; "An American No. I," "An American No. II," August 4, 11, 1792.

4. Thomas Jefferson.

5. Francis Childs was editor of *The* [New York] *Daily Advertiser* and publisher of the [Philadelphia] *National Gazette*.

6. On August 4, 1792, William Hall wrote to Boudinot concerning an alternative plan for providing water power for the Society for Establishing Useful Manufactures (ALS, Hamilton Papers, Library of Congress). The estimate enclosed is signed by Hall and Joseph Mort (DS, Hamilton Papers, Library of Congress).

7. Boudinot is referring to a meeting of the directors of the Society for Establishing Useful Manufactures to be held at Newark, New Jersey, on August 20, 1792. H did not attend this meeting. See H to the Governor and Directors of the Society for Establishing Useful Manufactures, August 16, 1792.

8. On August 4, 1792, *The* [New York] *Daily Advertiser* reprinted from

The Albany Gazette of July 30 an account of proceedings of the board of directors of the Northern Inland Lock Navigation Company. In part the account describes Archibald Nesbit's arrival and his projected tour of proposed navigation improvements with Philip Schuyler, president of the company, and several directors. The credentials with which Nesbit arrived described him "as a master of the science of canaling, from several years experience both in Holland and in Scotland" (*The Daily Advertiser*, August 4, 1792).
9. Letter not found.

To Alexander Dallas

[*Philadelphia, August 16, 1792.* The catalogue description of this letter reads: "Thanking him for copy of laws." [1] *Letter not found.*]

LS, sold at Anderson Galleries, May 4, 1927, Lot 95.
1. See Dallas to H, August 9, 1792.

From James McHenry

[Baltimore] 16 Augt. 1792

My dear Hamilton.

I mentioned Mr. Carroll [1] as proper to be brought forward to oppose a man whom I expect the antifederal interest will unite in supporting in case of an opportunity. I calculate that Mr. Carrol will not succeed; but it may produce more votes in this State for some man who ought. I mean also that it should operate to detach Mr. C.l. from Mr. Jeff. whose politics have in some instances infected him. In all this however you will understand should it be an eligible line of politics, that I do not mean to be an actor. The interest you feel in it more than any other consideration would induce me to take a little trouble.

I still think Mercer [2] will carry his election. I have been with Bishop Carrol [3] whose friendship and intimacy I enjoy. He has much greater controul over the minds of the Roman Catholics than Charles and I believe that description of men will vote for Campbell.[4]

Col. Smith [5] has entered for this district. Mr. Ridgley [6] you know also stands. Ridgley I am told is a friend to a further assumption. Saml. Smith is not. He is however a good federalist. As a merchant he will dislike any increase of duties on dry goods. He is however concerned in shipping, in a sugar house and distillery, and supplies Williams & co.[7] contractors with dry goods for the Indian trade. Besides it would give him great pleasure to get Col. Hall [8] into office, Mr. Robt. Smith [9] his Brother a judge, and Robert's father in law, Wm Smith [10] an office of £1500 a year. On the other hand Ridgley is largely in the iron works a man of great wealth, without skill in public affairs and from habits closely connected with Chase [11]— whom he would wish to see noticed. I inclose you a letter from Mr Perry [12] which you will be pleased to return.[13]

The Printer of the within paper is an ignorant young man and I am led to suspect him directed by some one unfriendly to government. His first paper contained a piece as you have seen from the national gazette.[14] Mr. Geo. Salmon [15] is a relation of his and will endeavour to discover the influence that directs him. Mr. Robinson [16] a young lawyer of promising talent appears the answerer of the pieces he here extracted from the National Gazette.

Jeff. I suspect will say in reply to his having been against the constitution in France that you were for monarchy in the convention; and will take some of the features of your systems which correspond the nearest with the fiscal systems of England as a commentary upon your principles. The exposition which has been given was wanted.

Good bless and preserve you. Yours affectionately

James McHenry

I desire this letter may be disposed of as the former.[17]

ALS, Hamilton Papers, Library of Congress.

1. Charles Carroll of Carrollton, a member of the United States Senate from Maryland.

2. John Francis Mercer was a native of Virginia who had been a delegate from that state to the Continental Congress. He moved to Maryland and was a member of that state's House of Delegates from 1788 to 1792. On February 6, 1792, he became a member of the House of Representatives, filling the vacancy occasioned by the resignation of William Pinckney.

3. John Carroll, the cousin of Charles Carroll, was the first Roman Catholic bishop in the United States and the first archbishop of Baltimore.

4. William Campbell of Annapolis resigned in 1792 as associate justice of the Anne Arundel County Court and later withdrew as a candidate for the House of Representatives.

5. Samuel Smith, who had received a vote of thanks from Congress for his part as a lieutenant colonel in the defense of Fort Mifflin during the American Revolution, was a member of the Maryland House of Delegates and a Baltimore merchant. He was elected to the House of Representatives in 1792.

6. Because of changes during the campaign in the list of those who stood

for various offices, it is difficult to determine which Charles Ridgely is the one to whom McHenry is referring. Two candidates named Charles Ridgely were elected to thé Maryland House of Delegates from the Baltimore district.

7. Robert Elliot and Élie Williams had held various contracts for supplies in the West under the Continental Congress and the Federal Government.

8. During the American Revolution Josias Carvel Hall, a son-in-law of William Smith, had been a colonel in the Second Maryland Battalion of the Flying Camp.

9. Robert Smith, Samuel Smith's brother, was a Baltimore lawyer who specialized in admiralty cases. He subsequently became a member of the Maryland Senate and House of Delegates, a member of the Baltimore city council, and in 1801 Secretary of the Navy.

10. William Smith, whose daughter Margaret married Robert Smith, was a Baltimore merchant. He was a member of the House of Representatives from 1789 to 1791.

11. Samuel Chase, a signer of the Declaration of Independence and delegate from Maryland to the Continental Congress from 1774 to 1778 and from 1784 to 1785, was appointed judge of the General Court of Maryland in 1791.

12. William Perry was a wealthy resident of the Eastern Shore of Maryland and a member of the Maryland Senate.

13. Perry's letter, which concerns the approaching Maryland congressional election in the fall of 1792, contains his belief that Maryland Antifederalists planned to use the campaign as an excuse to attack the Federal Government through H's financial policies. Perry observed that "I have my suspicions that a Gentleman on your Shore (Colo. M[ercer]) is at the Bottom of this Activity and Anxiety" (ALS, Hamilton Papers, Library of Congress). For a description of the extended controversy between H and Mercer arising out of this election, see the introductory note to H to Mercer, September 26, 1792.

14. This is a reference to Philip Edwards, publisher of *The Baltimore Evening Post*. The first issue of the paper appeared on July 13, 1792.

15. In a letter to H on September 30, 1792, McHenry described Salmon as "a respected judge in our criminal and orphan's court."

16. Presumably Archibald Robinson.

17. McHenry's "former" letter has not been found.

To William Short

Treasury Department
August 16. 1792.

Sir

You will herewith receive a Triplicate of my letter to you of the 25th Ultimo and a duplicate of one of the 4th instant.

If the destination of the monies arising from the last loan, as mentioned in my former letter of the said 4th instant, has not already put it out of your power, it would be my wish that you reserve a sufficient sum for the purpose of discharging the debt due to foreign Officers. The sum due, including arrears of interest down to the 31st of December 1791, was 220,646 $^{81}\!/_{100}$ Dollars, to which will be to be added the further interest to the time of payment.[1]

I shall shortly suggest to you the particular mode to be pursued in paying this debt.

With respectful consideration, I have the honor to be, Sir, Your Obedt Servt.   A Hamilton

William Short Esqr
&c. &c

LS, William Short Papers, Library of Congress.

1. For a description of this debt, see Short to H, August 3, 1790, note 5. On May 8, 1792, Congress had passed "An Act supplementary to the act making provision for the Debt of the United States" (1 *Stat.* 281–83 [May 8, 1792]). Section 5 of this act authorized the President "to cause to be discharged the principal and interest of the said debt, out of any of the monies, which have been or shall be obtained on loan."

To the Governor and Directors of the Society for Establishing Useful Manufactures [1]

Philadelphia Aug 16. 1792

Gentlemen

The bearer of this Mr. Trenet is a person whom Col Duer entered into a speculation with for the establishment of a manufacture of brass and iron Wire.[2] He is just returned from France, from which place he has brought tools and one or two hands. And he now with Mr Duers consent offers himself to the Society.

There is no doubt that the manufacture of iron & brass Wire would be an extremely useful one, having an extensive consumption & being applicable to a great variety of purposes. The first is particularly recommended by its connection with the great Iron-branch.

Mr. Trenet will produce all his certificates & papers to shew what are his pretensions and his engagements with Mr. Duer and I presume he will also produce a statement of the Capital necessary & the various objects to be provided.

It will then remain with the Board to determine whether they will engage in this enterprise. It will require to be first satisfied that Mr.

Trenet is in every respect a *competent* and *proper* character—in the second that the object is likely to be profitable and in the third that there are adequate funds. This last will depend on the success of the late payments.

In general a multiplication of the objects of the Society will be inexpedient. But there may be circumstances of sufficient force to induce in special cases a departure.

With great consideration & esteem   I have the honor to be Gentlemen   Yr. Obed serv   A Hamilton

The Governor & Directors of the Manuf Society

ALS, Historical Society of Pennsylvania, Philadelphia.
　　1. On the last page of his letter H named the addressee of this letter as "The Governor & Directors of the Manuf Society." The envelope, however, was addressed to "Archibald Mercer, Deputy Governor of The Society for establishing useful Manufactures New Ark."
　　2. Jerome Trenet had been authorized by William Duer to obtain artisans for the Society for Establishing Useful Manufactures. As early as February 27, 1791, Trenet complained to Duer that he had been unable to obtain funds from Benjamin Walker at Paris which were necessary to enable him to go to Lyons and fulfill his part of the agreement. No record of any action taken by the society appears in "Minutes of the S.U.M.," and on September 11, 1792, Trenet complained to Duer of the "despair in which you have put me by your fall" (ALS, New-York Historical Society, New York City).
　　By October 17, 1792, however, according to Robert Morris's accounts, Trenet had been hired to work at the "Delaware Works," Morris's manufacturing establishment at the falls of the Delaware opposite Trenton, New Jersey. Trenet remained there for several years (D, partly in the handwriting of Robert Morris, Wastebook, 1792–1796, Historical Society of Pennsylvania, Philadelphia).

To the Governor and Directors of the Society for Establishing Useful Manufactures

Philadelphia Aug 16. 1792

Gentlemen

More from the interest I take in the institution than from any supposition of the usefulness of my presence, it would have given me great pleasure to have been able to meet you on Monday next at

New Ark. But very particular circumstances will I fear render it impracticable.

As Major L'Enfant may not be well known to all the Directors, I cannot omit the opportunity of saying that from much experience and observation of him, I have a high opinion of the solidity of his talents, and believe him to be in every respect intitled to the confidence of the Direction.[1]

The interesting problem is yet to be solved—How shall the water be conveyed to the works? On this point I beg leave to say that nothing ought to be risked. Efficacy and solidity ought to outweigh considerations of expence if within any reasonable bounds. I feel persuaded beforehand that those attributes will belong to whatever plan Major L'Enfant may propose; and I doubt not it will meet with the attention it shall merit.

Inclosed is an Agreement which was entered into with Mr. Pearce previous to his leaving this City.[2] The terms of it had been long before settled between us pursuant to the request of the Society but nothing was reduced to form till the date of the inclosed Articles. It will be perceived that enough is left in the power of the Society.

Inclosed also is a paper received from Mr. Pearce which specifies among other things the rates at which different kinds of machinery can be made. He informed me at the same time that there is a person who would contract to make the necessary number at those rates. I feel well convinced that it is the interest of the Society to contract at those rates rather than undertake themselves to have them made.

Inclosed is also an account delivered me by George Parkinson.[3] He is a person who has been engaged to assist Mr. Marshall [4] in the Cotton Mill as well in the construction of the Machinery as in conducting as Master of a room some important part of the business. Mr. Parkinson, if I mistake not is a very sober discreet man and an intelligent ingenious mechanic and will be found among the most useful acquisitions the Society has made. Mr. Marshall however can now speak experimentally of him.

I recollect that the terms promised him were 60 £ Sterling per annum. But no agreement has ever been reduced to form. As to the time prior to the commencement of this salary I do not distinctly recollect what terms were promised to Mr Parkinson; but when Mr. Coxe who is now absent, returns to Town it will be in my power to ascertain it.[5]

By an account *stated* with Mr Pearce up to the   [6] the Society through me were in advance for him   .[7] I believe I made him a subsequent advance but I cannot ascertain this without consulting my papers at the Office.

I mention this as a guide in future advances. And I ought to add that circumspection will probably be necessary to guard against some propensity to extravagance. Mr. Pearce ought to furnish a complete inventory of all the property of the Society which he brought with him. It is somewhat considerable.

I have the honor to be   With great consideration   Gentlemen Your Obed servant   Alex Hamilton

The Governor & Directors of the
Society for establishing useful Manufactures

ALS, Historical Society of Pennsylvania, Philadelphia.
    1. Pierre Charles L'Enfant had been recommended by a committee of the directors of the Society for Establishing Useful Manufactures to superintend "that erection of the works and buildings ordered by the Directors." See "Draft Minutes of a Meeting of a Committee of the Directors of the Society for Establishing Useful Manufactures," August 1, 1792.
    2. William Pearce had been selected by H to prepare machinery for the cotton manufactures of the Society for Establishing Useful Manufactures. See H to the Directors of the Society for Establishing Useful Manufactures, December 7, 1791.
    3. See "Receipt from George Parkinson," July 30, 1791; May 2, 1792.
    4. Thomas Marshall was to be superintendent of the cotton mill which the society proposed to erect.
    5. See Tench Coxe to H, August 14, 1792.   6. Space left blank in MS.
    7. Space left blank in MS.

From Benjamin Lincoln

Boston August 17th. 1792

Sir

At the request of Mr. Foster [1] a merchant in this town I inclose his letter to me stating his situation relative to the draw back of some duties due on a quantity of Coffe exported. His confidence that you will direct the payment on the evidence offered makes it necessary that I should lay the matter before you for your decision thereon.

I am &c

Secy of the
Treasury

LC, Massachusetts Historical Society, Boston; LC, RG 36, Collector of Customs at Boston, Letter Book, 1790–1797, National Archives; two copies, RG 56, Letters from the Collector at Boston, National Archives.
    1. *The Boston Directory* for 1789 and for 1796 lists both Joseph Foster and William Foster as merchants (*A Report of the Record Commissioners of the City of Boston, Containing Miscellaneous Papers* [Boston, 1886], 183–84, 245).

To Archibald Mercer

Philadelphia Aug 17. 1792

Dr. Sir

The bearer of this Mr. Douthat [1] brought some letters, in general terms, from Col Humphreys [2] our Resident at Portugal. I dare say he understands the business about which he means to apply to the Society.[3] He means to submit different alternatives either for carrying it on upon the Account of the Society or upon his own account. The state of the funds of the Society &c. &c. must decide the expediency of seconding his project. The idea of a loan appears to have some recommendations. It would lead to greater œconomy & exertion. With much consideration & esteem I have the honor to be

Sir   Your obed ser   A Hamilton

Archibald Mercer Esq

ALS, Newport Historical Society, Newport, Rhode Island.
    1. The endorsement on this letter reads in part: "Introducing Francis Douthat for manufacturing Cloath." See Benjamin Walker to H, July 11, 1792.
    2. David Humphreys's appointment as United States Minister resident at Lisbon was confirmed by the Senate on February 21, 1791.
    3. H is referring to the Society for Establishing Useful Manufactures.

From Gouverneur Morris

Paris 17. August 1792.

Dear Sir

Mr. Short just before he left this City left with me a memoire in Dutch respecting the Mint. I was to get it translated for you, but not having been able to find a Person acquainted with the Dutch and English languages, I have now determin'd to send you the Original which you will find here enclosed. I hope it may prove useful, and answer the end you had in view.[1] I have transmitted to Mr. Jefferson Copies of my Correspondence with the Commissioners of the Treasury here respecting our Debt.[2] You seem to have suppos'd that the Instalments due had been paid, and this may turn out to be the case when the Account shall have been strictly examin'd, which I shall take care of. Mr. Short left (as I presume he inform'd you) this Business unfinish'd, supposing that my powers would be competent to it, which they are not;[3] and indeed I should be glad to avoid all Interference in pecuniary Affairs if possible. Not on account of the Labor, for you may lay as much of that on me as you please, but I would avoid all Occasions of Slanderous Imputation.

Apropos of these Accounts, I recollect having seen either the original or the Copy of a note, given by the french Ministry to Doctor Franklin, of the Appropriation of the ten Millions arising from the Dutch Loan, whereof only five Millions were paid to our Bankers.[4] This ought to be among the papers of the office of Foreign Affairs, or else among those of the Office of Finance. I rather think the latter. I do not know whether a Copy thereof may be necessary for me, but it certainly can do no harm, and may be useful. I should be glad also to have your Statement of this french Account for my Government, and also such transcript or Extract of the Accounts adjusted by Mr. Barcklay[5] as may apply to that Object.

I formerly recommended to Mr. Short the opening of a Loan at Antwerp, and it was attended with the best Effects;[6] for the Capitalists of Amsterdam, who had shortly before induc'd our Commissioners[7] to beleive that money could not be obtain'd there under five per Cent, soon after let us have it at four.[8] This I was sure would happen for I had been in Holland, had studied the Character of the Money lending people, and made myself acquainted with the manner of transacting Business. I am still of opinion that it is wise to multiply the Scenes on which to display our Credit. Those who have lent money to a Nation naturally incline to speak well of that Nation, first to justify the Confidence they have plac'd, and next to encrease the Value of the Stock they possess. It may at the first Blush seem more eligible, because more convenient, to perform all our pecuniary Operations at one place, and those who are interested in establishing that Doctrine will find many plausible Arguments in Support of their favorite Theory: just as Somebody (I beleive it was Silas Deane) endeavoured to prove that we had better buy Teas and nankins in London than in China. I remember the thing made Impression on me at the Time, as the India Company were then buying at Dunkirk some Teas which had been shipt from America. To return from the Digression I apprehend that confining this Business to one Spot may in the End have a very unfavorable Influence both on our Commerce and Exchange, because the necessity of Remittances being known, and the Periods also, Capitalists can take their measures before hand to give you the law. And if, which God forbid, Public Events should compel us to make Loans, our Creditors knowing our absolute dependence *on them alone*, will impose whatever Terms they please. I do not dwell on these Topics because a Word is sufficient to you.

LC, Gouverneur Morris Papers, Library of Congress.
  1. See H to William Short, April 13, 1791; Short to H, June 3, September 23, December 30, 1791, January 26, 1792.
  2. Morris to Thomas Jefferson, August 16, 1792 (ALS, RG 59, Despatches from United States Ministers to France, 1789–1869, June 17, 1792–March 7, 1794, National Archives). Extracts of this letter and its enclosures were sent to H by Jefferson on October 31, 1792, and are printed as enclosures to that letter.
  3. See H to Short, June 14, July 25, 1792; Short to H, August 6, 1792.
  4. This is a reference to the ten million livres loan of 1782, which France had borrowed in Holland for the United States. For a description of this loan, see Willink, Van Staphorst, and Hubbard to H, January 25, 1790, note 3. According to Rafael Bayley, "It appears that when the money was received from Holland 5,000,000 livres was paid into the French treasury for supplies furnished, amounting to 5,134,065 livres, 7 sols, 6 deniers, leaving a balance due France for supplies amounting to 134,065 livres, 7 sols, 6 deniers" (Bayley, *National Loans*, 14).
  5. Thomas Barclay was appointed by Congress in November, 1782, to settle its accounts in Europe.

6. See Short to H, February 17, April 9, June 3, July 8, 19, 24–25, 1791. For a description of the Antwerp loan of 1791, see Short to H, November 8, 1791, note 4, and November 12, 1791.

7. Willink, Van Staphorst, and Hubbard.

8. This is a reference to the Holland loan of December, 1791, the first four percent loan. See Short to H, December 23, 28, 1791.

From Joseph Nourse

Treasury Department, Register's Office, August 17, 1792. States that William Banks, a clerk in the register's office, "has suggested the following particulars for the notice of the Secretary: 1st. That the Records of Tonage would be kept more compleat, if the collectors were directed to transmit the cancell'd Registers and Emolements Monthly instead of Quarterly. 2d. That there is a defect in the act for registering of Ships and coasting vessels,[1] from there being no penalty annexed in default of taking out Licences for Vessels under 20 Tons. . . . 3d. That if the alphabet of the Articles of Commerce could be revised so as to be forwarded to the Collectors for their government in the 4th Quarter of 1792 it would be a desirable Object." Recommends that Banks "be deemed on a footing with others who receive 700 Dollars." Discusses Banks's possible occupancy of "the Room over the Transfer Office."

LC, RG 53, Register of the Treasury, Estimates and Statements for 1792, Vol. "134-T," National Archives.

1. "An Act for Registering and Clearing Vessels, Regulating the Coasting Trade, and for other purposes" (1 *Stat.* 55–65 [September 1, 1789]).

To William Seton

[Philadelphia] August 17th, 1792.

My Dear Sir:

Your letter,[1] mentioning certain particulars respecting the two banks, has been received, and will be duly attended to. I trust, however, that certain appearances have in no degree proceeded from any unkind disposition. The solution, I believe, is to be found in the necessity of sending here a considerable sum in specie. Large payments into the Bank of North America on account of the State of

Pennsylvania, subscriptions to canals, &c., and large calls upon the Bank of the United States for the service of government, joined to liberal discounts, had produced a considerable balance in favor of the Bank of North America, which rendered it expedient to draw a sum of specie from New-York, not to leave the National Bank in any degree in the power of the Bank of North America, which once manifested a very mischievous disposition, that was afterwards repaid by acts of kindness and generosity. The tide is now changing, and must speedily reverse the balance, and I mention it in confidence, because I wish, by explaining, to cherish confidence between the two institutions at New-York, so necessary to their mutual interest.

Inclosed, my dear sir, is a letter to Mr. Donald [2] of St. Vincents, which I beg your most particular care in forwarding. I presume he is a merchant there; but a gentleman lately mentioned to me, that he thought the name of the governor of St. Vincents was Donald. If so, he is probably the person intended. I received a letter from him,[3] giving me some information of my father.[4] The letter to Mr. Donald covers one to my father,[5] who, from a series of misfortunes, was reduced to great distress. You will perceive from this, that I must be anxious for the safe conveyance of my letter. If there is any person of whom you can make previous inquiry concerning Mr. Donald, you will oblige me by doing it, as a guide in forwarding the letter. I mean to send a duplicate from this place.

Affectionately, and with sincere esteem, Yours, A. Hamilton.

JCHW, V, 520–21.
1. Seton to H, August 6, 1792.
2. Letter not found. H appears to be mistaken. On June 12, 1793, James Hamilton, H's father, wrote to H concerning his friend "Mr. Donald of Virginia." Presumably this is a reference to Alexander Donald of Virginia.
3. Letter not found.
4. H corresponded with his father and urged him to come to the United States to live with H and his family. But when James Hamilton's affairs were finally in order, poor health and the war between England and France forced him to postpone indefinitely his trip to the United States. He died in St. Vincent in 1799. For a summary of H's relations with his father, see Mitchell, *Hamilton*, I, 13–14.
5. H's letter to his father has not been found.

An American No. III [1]

[Philadelphia, August 18, 1792]

FOR THE GAZETTE OF THE UNITED STATES.

The charges which have been brought against "the EDITOR of the NATIONAL GAZETTE," [2] as he himself states them to be, are no otherwise personal charges, than as they designate the *persons*, against whom they are made.[3]

In their application to Mr. Freneau, they affect him solely in his capacity of Editor of a public paper (which may justly be considered as a public capacity) and in relation to matters of public or national concern. It is therefore a meer subterfuge to call them *personal* charges, and then to say, that they shall not be answered, unless the author of them will come forward to support them. It was easily anticipated that he might have good reasons for not discovering himself, at least at the call of Mr. Freneau—and it was necessary for him to find a shelter. What else could he do? The charges brought against him are substantiated by facts, some of them acknowledged by himself, others proved by a reference to public documents, and to his own paper; others of general notoriety.

The inferences from these facts are the only things, which remain for discussion; and these so naturally flow from the premises, that they defy the arts of sophistry to obscure them. The expedient however which has been adopted, comes rather late; considering that Mr. Freneau began to answer even under the solemnities of an oath.   AN AMERICAN.

[Philadelphia] *Gazette of the United States,* August 18, 1792.
    1. The other two articles by "An American" are dated August 4, 11, 1792.
    2. Philip Freneau.
    3. On August 15, 1792, the following letter in reply to "An American" was published in the *Gazette of the United States:*
"If the writer in the Gazette of the United States, under the signature of '*An American,*' will come forward, and support the charges he has made against the Editor of the National Gazette, he shall be answered. Personal charges from an anonymous writer deserve no answer, and shall have none—from   *The Editor of the National Gazette.*
August 14."

[*Candor*] [1]

[Philadelphia, August 18, 1792]

[Philadelphia] *Gazette of the United States,* August 18, 1792.
1. Philip Marsh has written: "On August 18th, answering a charge by 'G.'
in the *National Gazette* for the 15th, 'Candor' demolished the idea that Fenno
had a monopoly of Treasury printing. By the undeniable tone of authority
and the unmistakable style, 'Candor' with little doubt is Hamilton again"
("Hamilton's Neglected Essays, 1791–1793," *The New-York Historical Society Quarterly,* XXXII [October, 1948], 292). No conclusive evidence, however, has been found that H wrote the article signed "Candor."

From *Tench Coxe*

Treasury Department, Revenue Office, August 18, 1792. ". . . The
Attorney of Wm. Allibone, Superintendent of the establishments
on the River and bay of Delaware has made application for the sum
of four hundred Dollars to make the first payment to Thomas Davis
& Thomas Connaroe, Junr. on account of their Contract for re-
building a pier near Mud Island. . . ." [1]

LC, RG 58, Letters of Commissioner of Revenue, 1792–1793, National Archives.
1. See Coxe to H, June 20, 1792; H to George Washington, June 26, 1792;
Tobias Lear to H, June 28, 1792; H to Coxe, June 29, 1792.

To *Samuel Gerry*

Treasury Department
August 18th 1792

Sir,
Your Letter of the 28 Ultimo [1] was duly received. If it should
appear to you that the former admeasurements of Vessels have been
materially inaccurate, readmeasurements may be made. This, however, will not affect any thing past.
A Thermometer was sent to you in March 1791. Inquiry will be

made by what opportunity it was transmitted. In the mean time I should be glad to be informed whether none has come to hand.

I am, Sir,   Your obedt. Servt.   Alex. Hamilton

Samuel R. Gerry Esqr

LC, Essex Institute, Salem, Massachusetts.
   1. Letter not found. See, however, H to Gerry, July 11, 1792.

From Jeremiah Olney

Providence, August 18, 1792. "The Sloop Bacon, Arnold Rhodes Master, Entered here from Washington in North Carolina, on the Eleventh Instant, having on board Seven Puncheons of foreign Spirits, unaccompanied with any other Certificates than a general One. . . . As in this Transaction, there is a deviation from Law,[1] tho' there appears no design to defraud the Revenue, yet I have thought proper to take the Rum into possession, and shall wait your directions how to proceed."

ADfS, Rhode Island Historical Society, Providence.
   1. Section 10 of "An Act repealing, after the last day of June next, the duties heretofore laid upon Distilled Spirits imported from abroad, and laying others in their stead; and also upon Spirits distilled within the United States, and for appropriating the same" reads as follows: "That whenever it shall be intended that any ship or vessel shall proceed with the whole or any part of the spirits which shall have been brought in such ship or vessel from any foreign port or place, from one port in the United States to another port in the said United States, whether in the same or in different districts, the master or person having the command or charge of such ship or vessel, shall previous to her departure, apply to the officer of inspection, to whom report was made, for the port from which she is about to depart, for a certificate of the quantity and particulars of such of the said spirits as shall have been certified or reported to him to have been entered as imported in such ship or vessel, and of so much thereof as shall appear to him to have been landed out of her at such port; which certificate the said officer shall forthwith grant. And the master or person having the command or charge of such ship or vessel, shall within twenty-four hours after her arrival at the port to which she shall be bound, deliver the said certificate to the proper officer of inspection of such last mentioned port. And if such ship or vessel shall proceed from one port to another within the United States, with the whole or any part of the spirits brought in her as aforesaid, without having first obtained such certificate; or if within twenty-four hours after her arrival at such other port, the said certificate shall not be delivered to the proper officer of inspection there, the master or person having the command or charge of said ship or vessel, shall in either case forfeit the sum of five hundred dollars; and the spirits on board of her at her said arrival, shall be forfeited, and may be seized by any officer of inspection" (1 *Stat.* 201–02 [March 3, 1792]).

From Jeremiah Olney [1]

Custom House,
Providence 18th August 1792.

Sir.

Upon re-inspecting my Licence Bonds, I have this Day found that the Sloop Polly of Sandwich, Saml. Bourn Master, was Licenced at this Office on the 20th of June last, to commence, as therein expressed, the 24th of May preceding, when the old Licence, granted by the Collector at Newport,[2] expired. The Licence Bond was filed Samuel *Brown*, which occasioned the oversight, on receipt of your Letter of the 31st. of July; the arrival of the Vessel also was unaccountably omitted in the Inspector's weekly Return; and she departed without clearing out. Mr. Otis'[3] Letter to me was dated the 22nd. of June, and it came to hand the 29th or 30th. He does not mention when the Transaction took place, I therefore cannot say whether it was during the former, or present Licence.

I have the Honor to be &c.   Jereh. Olney Collr.

P.S. I find upon enquiry, that the said Sloop Polly, brot. and landed here a load of Pine Wood.

Alexr. Hamilton Esqr.
Secy. of the Treasury.

ADfS, Rhode Island Historical Society, Providence.
1. For background to this letter, see H to Olney, July 31, 1792; Olney to H, August 13, 1792.
2. William Ellery.
3. Joseph Otis was collector of customs at Barnstable, Massachusetts.

To Jeremiah Olney

Treasury Department
August 18 1792.

Sir.

The Collector of Salem [1] has communicated to me that a small quantity of goods were imported there from France by Mr. Cutts of Portsmouth [2] in April last, upon which the Duties were paid agreeably to the original Invoice, said to have been made out according to the depreciated state of Assignats.

A like importation is said to have been made at the same time into Providence by the same Gentleman, and it is alleged that the invoice produced there having specified the difference between Assignats and specie, the Duties were calculated on the specie amount.

I should be glad to be informed of the precise time when the said importation was made [& of the circumstances attending it.] [3]

I am, Sir,   Your Obed Servant   A Hamilton

Jere. Olney Esqr
Providence

LS, Rhode Island Historical Society, Providence; copy, RG 56, Letters to the Collector at Providence, National Archives; copy, RG 56, Letters to Collectors at Small Ports, "Set G," National Archives.
    1. Joseph Hiller.   2. Samuel Cutts was a Portsmouth merchant.
    3. Words within brackets are in H's handwriting.

To George Washington [1]

Philadelphia Aug 18. 1792

Sir

I am happy to be able, at length, to send you, answers to the objections, which were communicated in your letter of the 29th of July.

They have unavoidably been drawn in haste, too much so, to do perfect justice to the subject, and have been copied just as they flowed from my heart and pen, without revision or correction. You will observe, that here and there some severity [2] appears. I have not

ALS, George Washington Papers, Library of Congress; ADf, Hamilton Papers, Library of Congress; copy, Hamilton Papers, Library of Congress.
    1. H made several additions and deletions in both this letter and its enclosure. When such changes altered either the emphasis or the substance of H's remarks, they have been indicated in footnotes. On the other hand, changes which were designed to make the style more felicitous have not been noted.
    2. In the draft at this point H wrote and crossed out "has been deserved indulged."

fortitude enough always to hear with calmness, calumnies, which necessarily include me, as a principal Agent in the measures censured, of the falsehood of which, I have the most unqualified consciousness. I trust that I shall always be able to [3] bear, as I ought, imputations of error of Judgment; but I acknowlege that I cannot be intirely patient under charges, which impeach the [4] integrity of my public motives or conduct. I feel, that I merit them *in no degree;* and expressions of indignation sometimes escape me, in spite of every effort to suppress them. I rely on your goodness for the proper allowances.

With high respect and the most affectionate attachment, I have the honor to be, Sir Your most Obedient & humble servant

Alexander Hamilton

The President of The United States

[E N C L O S U R E] [5]

Objections and Answers respecting the Administration
of the Government

1 Object. The public Debt is greater than we can possibly pay before other causes of adding to it will occur; and this has been artificially created by adding together the *whole amount* of the Debtor and Creditor sides of the Account.

Answer. The public Debt was produced by the late war. It is not the fault of the present government that it exists; unless it can be proved, that public morality and policy do not require of a Government an honest provision for its debts. Whether it is greater than can be paid before new causes of adding to it will occur is a problem incapable of being solved, but by experience; and this would be the case if it were not one fourth as much as it is. If the policy of the Country be prudent, cautious and *neutral* towards foreign nations,

3. In the draft at this point H wrote and crossed out "submit properly to."
4. In the draft at this point H wrote and crossed out "purity."
5. ADf, Hamilton Papers, Library of Congress.
In his letter to H of July 29, 1792, Washington numbered the "objections" to the Federalist administration of the Government from one to twenty-one. The exact "objection" to which H is replying at any particular point in this enclosure can therefore be ascertained by referring to Washington's letter.

there is a rational probability, that war may be avoided long enough to wipe off the debt. The Dutch in a situation, not near so favourable for it as that of the UStates have enjoyed intervals of peace, longer than with proper exertions would suffice for the purpose. The Debt of the UStates compared with its present and growing abilities is really a very light one. It is little more than 15.000000 of pounds Sterling, about the annual expenditure of Great Britain.

But whether the public Debt shall be extinguished or not within a moderate period depends on the temper of the people. If they are rendered dissatisfied by misrepresentations of the measures of the government, the Government will be deprived of an efficient command of the resources of the community towards extinguishing the Debt. And thus, those who clamour are likely to be [6] the principal causes of protracting the existence of the debt.

As to having been artificially increased, this is denied; perhaps indeed the true reproach of the system, which has been adopted, is that it has artificially diminished the debt as will be explained by and by.

The assertion, that the Debt has been increased, by adding together the whole amount of the Debtor and Creditor sides of the account, not being very easy to be understood is not easy to be answered.

But an answer shall be attempted.

The thirteen States in their *joint* capacity owed a *certain* sum. The same states, in their separate capacities, owed *another sum*. These two sums constituted the *aggregate* of the *public Debt*. The PUBLIC, in a political sense, compounded of the Governments of the Union and of the several states, was the DEBTOR. The individuals who held the various evidences of debt were the CREDITORS. It would be non-sense to say, that the [7] combining of *the two parts* of the public Debt is adding together the Debtor and Creditor sides of the account. So great an absurdity cannot be supposed to be intended by the objection. Another meaning must therefore be sought for.[8]

6. At this point H wrote and crossed out "authors of the only impediment which alone can preclude."
7. At this point H wrote and crossed out "adding of."
8. At this point H wrote and then crossed out the following paragraphs:
"No other than the following occurs.
"Some states, on a settlement of accounts according to some equitable ratio

It may possibly exist in the following misconception. The states individually, when they liquidated the accounts of Individuals for services and supplies towards the common defence during the late war, and gave certificates for the sums due would naturally charge them to the UStates as contributions to the common cause. The UStates in assuming to pay those certificates charge themselves with them. And it may be supposed that here is a double charge for the same thing.

But as the amount of the sum assumed for each state is by the system adopted to be charged to such state, it of course goes in extinguishment of so much of the first charge as is equal to the sum assumed, and leaves the UStates chargeable only once, as ought to be the case.

Or perhaps the meaning of the objection may be found in the following mode of reasoning. Some states, from having disproportionately contributed during the war, would probably on a settlement of accounts be found debtors, independently of the Assumption. The assuming of the debts of such states increases the ballances against them, and as these ballances will ultimately be remitted from the impracticability of enforcing their payment, the sums assumed will be an extra charge upon the U States increasing the mass of the debt.

This objection takes it for granted that the ballances of the Debtor States will not be exacted; which by the way is no part of the system and if it should eventually not prove true, the foundation of the reasoning would fail. For it is evident if the ballances are to be collected (unless there be some undiscovered error in the principle by which the accounts are to be adjusted) that one side of the account will counterpoise the other. And every thing as to the quantum of debt will remain *in statu quo.*

But it shall be taken for granted that the ballances will be re-

---

of contribution to the expences of the late war, would have been found in debt, not having contributed their proportion. Assuming the debts of such states, it may be supposed, was increasing the amount of their debits, and adding so much to the ballances of the Creditor States, which without the assumption, would have been alone to be provided for.

"This proposition admits of several answers.

"1. If the ballances of the Debtor States are ultimately to be paid (and there is no act of the government hitherto which implies the contrary) there can be no increase of the amount of Debt to be provided for."

mitted; and still the consequence alleged does not result. The reverse of it may even take place. In reasoning upon this point, it must be remembered that impracticability would be alike an obstacle to the collection of ballances without as with the Assumption.

This being the case, whether the ballances to be remitted will be increased or diminished must depend on the relative proportions of outstanding debts. If a former *debtor* State owes to individuals a smaller sum in proportion to its contributive faculty, than a former *Creditor* state, the assumption of [9] the debts of both to be provided for out of a *common fund* raised upon them proportionally must necessarily, on the idea of a remission of ballances, tend to restore equality between them, and lessen the ballance of the debtor state to be remitted.

How the thing may work upon the whole, cannot be pronounced without a knowlege of the situation of the account of each State, but all circumstances that are known render it probable that the ultimate effect will be favourable to justice between the states and that there will be inconsiderable ballances either on one side or on the other.

It was observed that perhaps the true reproach of the system which has been adopted is that it has artificially decreased the Debt. This is explained thus—

In the case of the debt of the UStates interest upon two thirds of the principal only at 6 ⅌ Cent is immediately paid—interest upon the remaining third was deferred for ten years—and only three ⅌ Cent has been allowed upon the arrears of interest, making one third of the whole debt.

In the case of the separate debts of the States interest upon $\frac{4}{9}$ only of the intire sum is immediately paid; interest upon $\frac{2}{9}$ was deferred for 10 years and only three per Cent allowed on $\frac{3}{9}$.

The Market rate of interest at the time of adopting the funding system was 6 ⅌ Cent. Computing according to this rate of interest —the then present value of 100 Dollars of debt upon an average, principal and interest, was about 73 Dollars.

And The present *actual* value, in the Market, of 100 Dollars, as the several kinds of Stock are sold, is no more than 83 Dollars & 61 Cents. This computation is not made on equal sums of the several

9. At this point H wrote and crossed out "these two sums."

kinds of Stock according to which the average value of 100 Dollars would be only 78.75 but it is made on the proportions which constitute the Mass of the debt.

At 73 to 100 The diminution on 60 000 000 is 16.200 000 Dollars; at 83.61 to 100 it is 9.834 000 Dollars.

But as the UStates having a right to redeem in certain proportions need never give more than par for the 6 ℀ Cent, the diminution to them as purchasers at the present market prices is 12.168 000 Dollars.

If it be said that the UStates are engaged to pay the whole sum at the Nominal value, the answer is that they are always at liberty if they have the means to purchase at the market prices and in all those purchases they gain the difference between the nominal sums and the lesser market rates.

If the whole debt had been provided for at 6 ℀ Cent the market rate of Interest when the funding system passed the market value throughout would undoubtedly have been 100 for 100. The Debt may then rather be said to have been artificially decreased by the Nature of the provision.

The conclusion from the whole, is that assuming it as a principle that the public debts of the different descriptions were honestly to be provided for and paid—it is the reverse of true that there has been an artificial increase of them. To argue on a different principle is to presuppose dishonesty, and make it an objection to doing right.

Objection II   This accumulation of debt has taken for ever out of our power those easy sources of revenue which applied &c.

Answer. There having been no accumulation of debt, if what is here pretended to have been the consequence were true, it would only be to be regretted as the unavoidable consequence of an unfortunate state of things. But the supposed consequence does by *no means* exist. The only sources of taxation which have been touched are imported articles and the single internal object of distilled spirits. Lands, houses, the great mass of personal as well as the whole of real property remain [10] essentially free. In short, the chief sources of taxation are free for extraordinary conjunctures; and it is one of the distinguishing merits of the system which has been adopted, that it has rendered this far more the case than it

10. At this point H wrote and crossed out "untouched."

was before. It is only to look into the different states to be convinced of it. In most of them real estate is wholly exempted. In some very small burthens rest upon it for the purpose of the internal Governments. In all the burthens of the people have been lightened. It is a mockery of truth to represent the U States as a community burthened and exhausted by taxes.

Objection 3

Answer. This is a mere painting and exaggeration. With the Exception of a very few articles, the duties on imports are still moderate, lower than in any Country of whose regulations we have knowlege, except perhaps Holland, where having few productions or commodities of their own, their export trade depends on the reexportation of foreign articles.

It is true the Merchants have complained, but so they did of the first impost law [11] for a time and so men always will do at an augmentation of taxes which touch the business they carry on, especially in a country where no or scarcely any *such* taxes before existed. The Collection, it is not doubted will be essentially secure. Evasions have existed in a degree and will continue to exist. Perhaps they may be somewhat increased; to what extent can only be determined by experience, but there are no symptoms to induce an opinion that they will materially increase. As to the idea of a war upon the citizens to collect the impost duties, it can only be regarded as a figure of rhetoric.

The Excise law [12] no doubt is a good topic of declamation. But can it be doubted that it is an excellent and a very fit mean of revenue?

As to the partiality of its operation, it is no more so than any other tax on a consumeable commodity; adjusting itself upon exactly the same principles.[13] The consumer in the main pays the tax—and

11. "An Act for laying a Duty on Goods, Wares, and Merchandises imported into the United States" (1 *Stat.* 24–27 [July 4, 1789]).

12. "An Act repealing, after the last day of June next, the duties heretofore laid upon Distilled Spirits imported from abroad, and also upon Spirits distilled within the United States, and for appropriating the same" (1 *Stat.* 199–214 [March 3, 1791]). The original Excise Law had been amended by "An Act concerning the Duties on Spirits distilled within the United States" (1 *Stat.* 267–71 [May 8, 1792]).

13. Following this sentence H wrote and crossed out "It will appear from official documents."

if some parts of the U States consume more domestic spirits, others consume more foreign—and both are taxed. There is perhaps, upon the whole, no article of more *general* and *equal consumption* than distilled spirits.

As to its *unproductiveness*, unless inforced by *arbitrary* and *vexatious* means, facts testify the contrary. Already, under all the obstacles arising from its novelty and the prejudices against it in some states, it has been considerably productive. And it is not inforced by any arbitrary or vexatious means; at least the precautions in the existing laws for the collection of the tax will not appear in that light but to men who regard all taxes and all the means of enforcing them as arbitrary and vexatious. Here however there is abundant room for fancy to operate. The standard is in the mind, and different minds will have different standards.

The observation relating to the commitment of the authority of the Government, in parts where resistance is most probable and coertion least practicable has more weight than any other part of this objection. It must be confessed that a hazard of this nature has been run but if there were motives sufficiently cogent for it, it was wisely run. It does not follow that a measure is bad because it is attended with a degree of danger.

The general inducements to a provision for the public Debt are—I To preserve the public faith and integrity by fulfilling as far as was practicable the public engagements. II To manifest a due respect for property by satisfying the public obligations in the hands of the public Creditors and which were as much their property as their houses or their lands their hats or their coats. III To revive and establish public Credit; the palladium of public safety. IV To preserve the Government itself by shewing it worthy of the confidence which was placed in it, to procure to the community the blessings which in innumerable ways attend confidence in the Government and to avoid the evils which in as many ways attend the want of confidence in it.

The particular inducements to an assumption of the state Debts were I To consolidate the finances of the country and give an assurance of permanent order in them; avoiding the collisions of thirteen different and independent systems of finance under concurrent and coequal authorities and the scramblings for revenue

which would have been incident to so many different systems.[14]
II   To secure to the Government of the Union, by avoiding those
entanglements, an effectual command of the resources of the Union
for present and future exigencies. III   To *equalize the condition* of
the *citizens* of the several states in the important article of taxation;
rescuing a part of them from being oppressed with burthens, beyond their strength, on account of extraordinary exertions in the
war and through the want of certain adventitious resources, which
it was the good fortune of others to possess.

A mind naturally attached to order and system and capable of
appreciating their immense value, unless misled by particular feelings, is struck at once with the prodigious advantages which in the
course of time must attend such a simplification of the financial
affairs of the Country as results from placing all the parts of the
public debt upon one footing—under one direction—regulated by
one provision. The want of this sound policy has been a continual
source of disorder and embarrassment in the affairs of the United
Netherlands.

The true justice of the case of the public Debt consists in that
equalization of the condition of the Citizens of all the states which
must arise from a consolidation of the debt and common contributions towards its extinguishment. Little inequalities, as to the past,
can bear no comparison with the more lasting inequalities, which,
without the assumption, would have characterised the future condition of the people of the UStates; leaving upon those who had
done most or suffered most a great additional weight of burthen.

If the foregoing inducements to a provision for the public Debt
(including an assumption of the state debts) were sufficiently cogent
—then the justification of the Excise law [15] lies within a narrow
compass. Some further source of revenue, besides the duties on
imports, was indispensable, and none equally productive, would have
been so little exceptionable to the Mass of the People.

Other reasons cooperated in the minds of some able men to render
an excise at an early period desireable. They thought it well to lay

14. At this point H wrote and crossed out "In the system of the U Netherlands the reverse of this sound policy has been a perpetual and fruitful source
of disorder and."
15. At this point H wrote and crossed out "is not difficult."

hold of so valuable a resource of revenue before it was generally preoccupied by the State Governments. They supposed it not amiss that the authority of the National Government should be visible in some branch of internal Revenue; lest a total non-exercise of it should beget an impression that it was never to be exercised & next that it ought not to be exercised. It was supposed too that a thing of the kind could not be introduced with a greater prospect of easy success than at a period when the Government enjoyed the advantage of first impressions—when state-factions to resist its authority were not yet matured—when so much aid was to be derived from the popularity and firmness of the actual chief Magistrate.

Facts hitherto do not indicate the measure to have been rash or ill advised. The law is in operation with perfect acquiescence in all the states North of New York, though they contribute most largely. In New York and New Jersey it is in full operation with some very partial complainings fast wearing away. In the greatest part of Pensylvania it is in operation and with increasing good humour towards it. The four Western Counties continue exceptions. In Delaware it has had some struggle, which by the last accounts was surmounted. In Maryland and Virginia, it is in operation and without material conflict. In South Carolina it is now in pretty full operation, though in the interior parts it has had some serious opposition to overcome. In Georgia no material difficulty has been experienced. North Carolina Kentucke & the four Western Counties of Pensylvania present the only remaining impediments of any consequence to the full execution of the law. The latest advices from NC & Kentuke were more favourable than the former.[16]

It may be added as a well established fact that the effect of the law has been to encourage new enterprises in most of the states in the business of domestic distillation. A proof [17] that it is perceived to operate favourably to the manufacture, and that the measure cannot long remain unpopular any where.

Objection IV Propositions have been made in Congress & projects are on foot still to increase the Mass of the Debt.

Ans. Propositions have been made, and no doubt will be renewed

16. For a discussion of the excise situation in the various states, see Tench Coxe to H, October 19, 1792.
17. For this word H originally wrote and then crossed out "symptom."

by the States interested to complete the assumption of the State Debts.[18] This would add in the first instance to the mass of the *Debt of the UStates* between three and four Millions of Dollars but it would not increase the mass of the *public Debt* at all. It would only transfer from particular States to the Union debts which already [19] exist and which if the states indebted are honest must be provided for. It happens that Massachusettes and South Carolina would be chiefly benefitted. And there is a moral certainty that Massachusettes will have a ballance in her favour more than equal to her remaining debt and a probability that South Carolina will have a ballance sufficient to cover hers—so that there is not likely to be an eventual increase even of the *debt of the United States* by the further assumption.[20] The immense exertions of Massachusettes during the late war and particularly in the latter periods of it when too many of the States failed in their fœderal Duty are known to every well informed man. It would not be too strong to say, that they were in a great degree the pivot of the revolution. The exertions sufferings sacrifices and losses of South Carolina need not be insisted upon. The other States have comparitively none or inconsiderable Debts. Can that policy be condemned which aims at putting the burthened states upon an equal footing with the rest? Can that policy be very liberal which resists so equitable an arrangement? It has been said that if they had exerted themselves since the peace their situation would have been different. But Massachusettes threw her Citizens into Rebellion by heavier taxes than were paid in any other State and South Carolina has done as much since the peace as could have been expected considering the exhausted state in which the War left her.

The only proposition during the last session or at any antecedent one which would truly have swelled the debt artificially was one which Mr Maddison made in the first session & which was renewed in the last and generally voted for by those who oppose the system that has prevailed.[21] The object of this proposition was *that all the*

18. See "Report on the Public Debt and Loans," January 23, 1792.
19. For this word H originally wrote and then crossed out "at present."
20. At this point H wrote and crossed out "Nobody knows better than the President."
21. James Madison's speech of April 22, 1790, advocated the assumption of certificates of state debts held in the state treasuries as well as those in the

parts of the State debts which have been *paid* or other*wise ab-sorbed*[22] *by them* should be assumed for the benefit of the States, and funded by the UStates. This measure if it had succeeded would truly have produced an immense artificial increase of the debt; but it has twice failed & there is no probability that it will ever succeed.

Objection 5. By borrowing at ⅔ &c.

Answer. First—All the foreign loans which were made by the UStates prior to the present Government taking into the calculation charges & premiums cost them more than 6 ℔ Cent. Since the establishment of the present Government they borrowed first at about 5¼ including charges & since at about 4¼ including charges. And it is questionable in the present state of Europe whether they can obtain any further loans at so low a rate.

The System which is reprobated is the very cause that we have been able to borrow monies on so good terms. If one, that would have inspired less confidence, certainly if the substitutes which have been proposed, from a certain quarter, had obtained, we could not have procured loans even at six per Cent. The Dutch were largely adventurers in our domestic debt before the present Government. They did not embark far till they had made inquiries of influential public characters, as to the light in which the Debt was & would be considered in the hands of alienees—and had received assurances that Assignees would be regarded in the same light as original holders. What would have been the state of our Credit with them, if they had been disappointed, or indeed if our conduct had been in any respect inconsistent with the notions entertained in Europe concerning the maxims of public Credit?

The inference is that our being able to borrow on low terms is a consequence of the system which is the object of censure and that the thing itself, which is made the basis of another system, would not have existed under it.

Secondly. It will not be pretended that we could have borrowed

---

hands of individuals (*Annals of Congress*, II, 1587–88). On April 3, 1792, Madison amended and supported the motion of Upton Sheredine of Maryland on the ground that debts of the states which had been paid were as much debts against the Union as those in the hands of individuals ([Philadelphia] *Gazette of the United States*, June 6, 1792).

22. H originally wrote and then crossed out "cancelled" in place of this word.

at the proposed low rate of interest in the UStates; and all our exertions to borrow in Europe which have been unremitted, as occasions presented, have not hitherto produced above   of Dollars in space of   ;[23] not even a sufficient sum to change the form of our foreign debt.

Thirdly   If it were possible to borrow the whole sum abroad within a short period, to pay off our debt, it is not easy to imagine a more pernicious operation than this would have been. It would first have transferred to foreigners by a violent expedient[24] the whole amount of our debt; and creating a money plethora in the Country a momentary scene of extravagance would have followed & the excess would quickly have flowed back: The evils of which situation need not be enlarged upon. If it be said that the operation might have been gradual, then the end proposed would not have been attained.[25]

Lastly   The plan which has been adopted secures in the first instance the *identical advantage,* which in the other plan would have been *eventual* and *contingent.* It puts one third of the whole Debt at an interest of 3 ⅌Ct. only—and by deferring the payment of interest on a third of the remainder effectually reduces the interest on that part. It is evident that a *suspension* of interest is in fact a *reduction* of interest. The money which would go towards paying interest in the interval of suspension is an accumulating fund to be applied towards payment of it when it becomes due, proportionably reducing the provision then to be made.

In reality, on the principles of the funding system, the United States reduced the interest on their whole Debt upon *an average* to about 4½ ⅌Cent, nearly the lowest rate they have any chance to borrow at, and lower than they could possibly have borrowed at, in an attempt to reduce the interest on the whole Capital by borrowing and paying; probably by one ⅌Cent. A demand for large loans by forcing the market would unavoidably have raised their price upon the borrower. The above average of 4½ ⅌Ct. is found by calculation, computing the then present value of the deferred

23. Spaces left blank in MS.
24. For this word H originally wrote and then crossed out "operation."
25. After this sentence H wrote and crossed out "The high interest would have run on and procrastinated the final redemption."

Stock at the time of passing the funding Act[26] and of course 3 ⅌Cent on the three per Cent Stock.

The funding system, then, secured in the very outset the *precise advantage* which it is alleged would have accrued from leaving the whole debt redeemable at pleasure. But this is not all. It did more. It left the Government still in a condition to enjoy upon ⅚ of the intire debt the advantage of extinguishing it, by loans at a low rate of interest, if they are obtainable. The 3 ⅌Cents which are one third of the whole may always be purchased in the market below par, till the market rate of interest falls to 3 ⅌Ct. The deferred will be purchaseable below par till near the period of the actual payment of interest. And this further advantage will result; in all these purchases the public will enjoy not only the advantage of a reduction of interest on the sums borrowed but the additional advantage of purchasing the debt under par, that is for less than 20/ in the pound.

If it be said that the like advantage might[27] have been enjoyed under another system, the assertion would be without foundation. Unless some equivalent had been given for the reduction of interest in the irredeemable quality annexed to the Debt, nothing was left consistently with the principles of public Credit but to provide for the whole debt at 6 ⅌Cent. This evidently would have kept the whole at par, and no advantage could have been derived by purchases under the nominal value. The reduction of interest by borrowing at a lower rate is all that would have been practicable and this advantage has been secured by the funding system in the very outset and without any second process.

If no provision for the interest had been made, not only public Credit would have been sacrificed; but by means of it the borrowing at a low rate of interest or at any rate would have been impracticable.

There is no reproach which has been thrown upon the funding system so unmerited as that which charges it with being a bad bargain for the public or with a tendency to prolong the extinguishment of the Debt. The bargain has if any thing been too good

---

26. H is referring to "An Act making provision for the (payment of the) Debt of the United States" (1 *Stat.* 138–44 [August 4, 1790]).
27. For this word H originally wrote and then crossed out "must."

on the side of the public; and it is impossible for the debt to be in a more convenient form than it is for a rapid extinguishment.

Some Gentlemen seem to forget that the faculties of every Country are limited. They talk as if the Government could extend its revenue *ad libitum* to pay off the debt. Whereas every rational calculation of the abilities of the Country will prove that the power of redemption which has been reserved over the debt is quite equal to those abilities, and that a greater power would be useless. If happily the abilities of the Country should exceed this estimate, there is nothing to hinder the surplus being employed in purchases. As long as the three ⅌Cents & deferred exist those purchases will be under par. If for the Stock bearing an immediate interest of six ⅌Cent more than par is given—the Government can afford it from the saving made in the first instance.

Upon the whole then it is the merit of the funding System to have conciliated these three important points—the restoration of public Credit—a reduction of the rate of interest—and an organisation of the Debt convenient for speedy extinguishment.

Object 6 The irredeemeable quality was given to the debt for the *avowed* purpose of inviting its transfer to foreign countries.

This assertion is a palpable misrepresentation. The *avowed purpose* of that quality of the Debt, as explained in the report of the Secretary of the Treasury,[28] and in the arguments in Congress was to give an *equivalent* for the reduction of Interest, that is for deferring the payment of interest on ⅓ of the principal for three years and for allowing only 3 ⅌ Cent on the arrears of Interest.

It was indeed argued, in confirmation of the reality of the equivalent, that foreigners would be willing to give more, where a high rate of Interest was *fixed*, than where it was liable to fluctuate with the market. And this has been verified by the fact—for the 6 ⅌ Cents could not have risen for a moment above par, if the rate could have been lowered by redeeming the Debt at pleasure. But the inviting of the transfer to foreigners was never assigned as a motive to the arrangement.

And what is more, that transfer will be probably slower with the portion of irredeemability which is attached to the Debt than

28. "Report Relative to a Provision for the Support of Public Credit," January 9, 1790.

without it because a larger capital would be requisite to purchase 100 Dollars in the former than in the latter case. And the Capital of foreigners is limited as well as our own.

It appears to be taken for granted that if the Debt had not been funded in its present shape foreigners would not have purchased it as they now do; than which nothing can be more ill founded or more contrary to experience. Under the old Confederation when there was no provision at all foreigners had purchased five or six millions of the Debt. If any provision had been made, capable of producing confidence, their purchases would have gone on just as they now do; and the only material difference would have been that what they got from us then would have cost them less than what they now get from us does cost them. Whether it is to the disadvantage of the Country that they pay more is submitted.

Even a provision which should not have inspired full confidence would not have prevented foreign purchases. The commodity would have been cheap in proportion to the risks to be run. And fullhanded Dutchmen would not have scrupled to amass large sums, for trifling considerations, in the hope, that time & experience would introduce juster notions into the public councils.

Our Debt would still have gone from us & with it our reputation & Credit.

Objection 7

Answer. The same glooming forebodings were heared in England in the early periods of its funding system. But they have never been realized. The money invested by foreigners in the purchase of its Debt being employed in its commerce agriculture and manufactures increased the wealth and Capital of the Nation, more than in proportion to the annual drain for the payment of interest and created the ability to bear it.

The objection seems to forget that the Debt is not transferred for Nothing—that the Capital paid for the Debt is always an equivalent for the interest to be paid to the purchasers. If that Capital is well employed in a young country, like this, it must be considerably increased so as to yield a greater revenue than the interest of the money. The Country therefore will be a gainer by it and will be able to pay the interest without inconvenience.

But the objectors suppose that all the money which come in goes out again in an increased consumption of foreign luxuries. This however is taking for granted what never happened in any industrious country & what appearances among us do not warrant. The expense of living generally speaking is not sensibly increased. Large investments are every day making in ship building, house building, manufactures & other improvements public & private.

The transfer too of the whole debt is a very improbable supposition. A large part of it will continue to be holden by our own citizens.[29] And the interest of that part which is owned by foreigners will not be annually exported as is supposed. A considerable part will be invested in new speculations, in lands canals roads manufactures commerce. Facts warrant this supposition. The Agents of the Dutch have actually made large investments in a variety of such speculations. A young Country like this is peculiarly attractive. New objects will be continually opening and the money of foreigners will be made instrumental to their advancement.

8.th Object

Ans   This is a mere hypothesis in which theorists differ. There are no decisive facts on which to rest the question.

The supposed tendency of bank paper to banish specie is from its capacity of serving as a substitute for it in circulation.[30] But as the quantity circulated is proportioned to the demand for it, in circulation, the presumption is that a greater quantity of industry is put in motion by it, so as to call for a proportionably greater quantity of *circulating medium* and prevent the banishment of the specie.

But however this may be it is agreed among sound theroists that Banks more than compensate for the loss of the specie in other ways. SMITH who was witness to their effects in Scotland; where too a very adverse fortune attended some of them bears his testimony to their beneficial effects in these strong Terms (Wealth of Nations Vol. I Book II. Ch. II. Page 441. to 444). [31]

29. At this point H wrote and crossed out "especially in the North."
30. In MS this word is "circulated."
31. The page references to Adam Smith's *Wealth of Nations* which H noted do not coincide with any edition of that work which has been found.
Smith wrote: "An operation of this kind has, within these five-and-twenty or thirty years, been performed in Scotland, by the erection of new banking companies in almost every considerable town, and even in some country vil-

9 Objection

The 10 or 12 ℔ Ct &c.

Answer   1 The profits of the Bank have not hitherto exceeded the rate of 8 ℔ Ct. per annum & perhaps never may. It is questionable whether they can legally make more than *10 ℔ Ct.*[32]

2   These profits can in no just sense be said to be taken out of the pockets of the people. They are compounded of two things— 1   the interest paid by the Government on that part of the public Debt which is incorporated in the stock of the Bank—2   the interest paid by those *Individuals who borrow* money of the Bank on the *sums they borrow.*

As to the first, it is no *new grant* to the bank. It is the old interest on a part of the old Debt of the Country, subscribed by the proprietors of that Debt towards constituting the Stock of the Bank. It would have been equally payable if the Bank had never existed. It is therefore nothing new taken out of the pockets of the people.

As to the second, it may with equal propriety be said, when one individual borrows money of another, that the interest, which the borrower pays to the lender, is taken out of the *pockets of the people.* The case here is not only parallel but the same. It is a case of one or more individuals borrowing money of a company of

---

lages. The effects of it have been precisely those above described. . . . But though the conduct of all those different companies has not been unexceptionable, and has accordingly required an act of parliament to regulate it; the country, notwithstanding, has evidently derived great benefit from their trade. . . .

"The commerce of Scotland, which at present is not very great, was still more inconsiderable when the two first banking companies were established; and those companies would have had but little trade, had they confined their business to the discounting of bills of exchange. They invented, therefore, another method of issuing their promissory notes; by granting, what they called, cash accounts. . . .

"By means of those cash accounts every merchant can, without imprudence, carry on a greater trade than he otherwise could do. If there are two merchants, one in London, and the other in Edinburgh, who employ equal stocks in the same branch of trade, the Edinburgh merchant can, without imprudence, carry on a greater trade, and give employment to a greater number of people than the London merchant. . . . Hence the great benefit which the country has derived from this trade." (Adam Smith, *An Inquiry into the Nature and Causes of the Wealth of Nations*, The Fourth Edition, with Additions in Two Volumes [Dublin, Printed for W. Colles, R. Moncrieffe, G. Burnet, W. Wilson, C. Jenkin, L. White, H. Whitestone, P. Byrne, J. Cash, W. McKenzie, 1785], 293–97.)

32. In the margin opposite this paragraph H wrote "Quaere."

individuals associated to lend. None but the actual borrowers pay in either case. The rest of the community have nothing to do with it.

If a man receives a bank bill for the ox or the bushel of wheat which he sells he pays no more interest upon it than upon the same sum in gold or silver; that is he pays none at all.[33]

So that whether the paper banishes specie or not it is the same thing to every individual through [34] whose hands it circulates, as to the point of Interest. Specie no more than Bank paper can be borrowed without paying interest for it, and when either is not borrowed no interest is paid. As far as the Government is a sharer in the profits of the Bank which is in the proportion of ⅕ the contrary of what is supposed happens. *Money is put into the pockets of the People.*

All this is so plain and so palpable that the assertion which is made betrays extreme ignorance or extreme disingenuousness. It is destitute even of colour.

10 Objection

This is a copious subject which has been fully discussed in the report of the Secretary of the Treasury on the subject of Manufactures from Page   to   .[35] It is true that the Capital, that is the *specie*, which is employed in paper speculation, while so employed, is barren and useless, but the paper itself constitutes a *new* [36] *Capital*, which being saleable and transferrable at any moment, enables the proprietor to undertake any piece of business as well as an equal sum in Coin. And as the amount of the Debt circulated is much greater than the amount of the *specie* which circulates it, the new Capital put in motion by it considerably exceeds the old one which is *suspended.* And there is more capital to carry on the productive labour of the Society. Every thing that has value is Capital—an acre of ground a horse or a cow or a public or a private obligation; which may with different degrees of con-

---

33. Following this sentence H wrote and crossed out "He either sends the bill to the Bank and gets gold and silver or he passes it away."
34. In MS, "though."   35. Spaces left blank in MS.
In the edition of H's "Report on the Subject of Manufactures," December 5, 1791, printed in 1791 by Francis Childs and John Swaine, H's view of the relation between a funded debt and capital appears on pages 22 through 25.
36. At this point H wrote and crossed out "and a greater."

venience be applied to industrious enterprise. That which, like public Stock, can at any instant be turned into money is of equal utility with money as Capital.

Let it be examined whether at those places where there is most debt afloat and most money employed in its circulation, there is not at the same time a greater plenty of money for every other purpose. It will be found that there is.

But it is in fact quite immaterial to the Government, as far as regards the propriety of its measures.

The Debt existed. It was to be provided for. In whatever shape the provision was made the object of speculation and the speculation would have existed. Nothing but abolishing the Debt could have obviated it. It is therefore the fault of the Revolution not of the Government that paper speculation exists.

An unsound or precarious provision would have increased this species of speculation in its most odious forms. The defects & casualties of the system would have been as much subjects of speculation as the Debt itself.

The difference is that under a bad system the public Stock would have been too uncertain an article to be a substitute for money & all the money employed in it would have been diverted from useful employment without any thing to compensate for it. Under a good system the Stock becomes more than a substitute for the money employed in negotiating it.

Objection 11   Paper Speculation nourishes in our Citizens &c.

Answer   This proposition within certain limits is true. Jobbing in the funds has some bad effects among those engaged in it. It fosters a spirit of gambling, and diverts a [37] certain number of individuals from other pursuits. But if the proposition be true, that Stock operates as Capital, the effect upon the Citizens at large is different. It promotes among them industry by furnishing a larger field of employment. Though this effect of a funded debt has been called in question in England by some theorists yet most theorists & all practical men allow its existence. And there is no doubt, as already intimated, that if we look into those scenes among ourselves where the largest portions of the Debt are accumulated we shall

37. At this point H wrote and crossed out the word "few."

perceive that a new spring has been given to Industry in various branches.

But be all this as it may, the observation made under the last head applies here. The Debt was the creature of the Revolution. It was to be provided for. Being so, in whatever form, it must have become an object of speculation and jobbing.[38]

Objection 12

The funding of the Debt has furnished effectual means of corrupting &c.

Answer   This is one of those assertions which can only be denied and pronounced to be malignant and false. No facts exist to support it, and being a mere matter of fact, no *argument* can be brought to repel it.

The Assertors beg the question. They assume to themselves and to those who think with them infallibility. Take their words for it, they are the only honest men in the community. But compare the tenor of mens lives and *at least* as large a proportion of virtuous and independent characters will be found among those whom they malign as among themselves.

A member of a majority of the Legislature would say to these Defamers—

"In your vocabulary, Gentlemen, *creditor* and *enemy* appear to be [39] synonimous terms—the *support of public credit* and *corruption* of similar import—an *enlarged* and *liberal* construction of the constitution for the public good and for the maintenance of the due energy of the national authority of the same meaning with usurpation and a conspiracy to overturn the republican government of the Country—every man of a different opinion from your own an ambitious despot or a corrupt knave. You bring every thing to the standard of your narrow and depraved ideas, and you condemn without mercy or even decency whatever does not accord with it. Every man who is either too long or two short for your political couch must be stretched or lopped to suit it. But your pretensions must be rejected. Your insinuations despised. Your Politics originate

38. Following this paragraph H wrote and then crossed out the following sentence: "Land-jobbing has at least as many bad sides as stock-jobbing and yet it has been a great cause of accelerating."

39. In place of the words "appear to be" H originally wrote and then crossed out the word "are."

in immorality, in a disregard of the maxims of good faith and the rights of property, and if they could prevail must end in national disgrace and confusion. Your rules of construction for the [40] authorities vested in the Government of the Union would arrest all its essential movements and bring it back in practice to the same state of imbecility which rendered the old confederation contemptible. Your principles of liberty are principles of licentiousness incompatible with all government. You sacrifice every thing that is venerable and substantial in society to the vain reveries of a false and new fangled philosophy. As to the motives by which I have been influenced, I leave my general conduct in private and public life to speak for them. Go and learn among my *fellow citizens* whether I have not uniformly maintained the character of an honest man. As to the love of liberty and Country you have given no stronger proofs of being actuated by it than I have done. Cease then to arrogate to yourself and to your party all the patriotism and virtue of the Country. Renounce if you can the intolerant spirit by which you are governed—and begin to reform yourself instead of reprobating others, by beginning to doubt of your own infallibility."

Such is the answer which would naturally be [41] given by a member of the Majority in the Legislature to such an Objector. And it is the only one that could be given; until some evidence of the supposed corruption should be produced.

As far as I know, there is not a member of the Legislature who can properly be called a Stock-jobber or a paper Dealer. There are several of them who were proprietors of public debt in various ways. Some for money lent & property furnished for the use of the public during the War others for sums received in payment of Debts —and it is supposeable enough that some of them had been purchaser[s] of the public Debt, with intention to hold it, as a valuable & convenient property; considering an honorable provision for it as matter of course.

It is a strange perversion of ideas, and as novel as it is extraordinary, that men should be deemed corrupt & criminal for becoming proprietors in the funds of their Country. Yet I believe the number

40. At this point H wrote and crossed out "constitution of a Government national."
41. In MS this word is "be."

of members of Congress is very small who have ever been considerably proprietors in the funds.

And as to improper speculations on measures depending before Congress, I believe never was any *body* of men freer from them.

There are indeed several members of Congress, who have become proprietors in the Bank of the United States, and a *few* of them to a pretty large amount say 50 or 60 shares; but all operations of this kind were necessarily subsequent to the determination upon the measure. The subscriptions were of course subsequent & purchases still more so. Can there be any thing really blameable in this? Can it be culpable to invest property in an institution which has been established for the most important national purposes? Can that property be supposed to corrupt the holder? It would indeed tend to render him friendly to the preservation of the Bank; but in this there would be no collision between duty & interest and it could give him no improper byass in other questions.

To uphold public credit and to be friendly to the Bank must be presupposed to be *corrupt things* before the being a proprietor in the funds or of bank Stock can be supposed to have a *corrupting influence*. The being a proprietor in either case is a very different thing from being, in a proper sense of the term, a Stock jobber. On this point of the corruption of the Legislature one more observation of great weight remains. Those who oppose a *funded* debt and mean any provision for it contemplate an *annual* one. Now, it is impossible to conceive a more fruitful source of legislative corruption than this. All the members of it who should incline to speculate would have an annual opportunity of speculating upon their influence in the legislature to promote or retard or put off a provision. Every session the question whether the annual provision should be continued would be an occasion of pernicious caballing and corrupt bargaining. In this very view when the subject was in deliberation, it was impossible not to wish it declared upon once for all & out of the way.

Objection the 13   The Corrupt Squadron &c

Here again the objectors beg the question. They take it for granted that their constructions of the constitution are right and that the opposite ones are wrong, and with great good nature and candor ascribe the effect of a difference of opinion to a disposition to get rid of the limitations on the Government.

Those who have advocated the constructions which have obtained have met their opponents on the ground of fair argument and they think have refuted them. How shall it be determined which side is right?

There are some things which the General Government has clearly a right to do—there are others which it has clearly no right to meddle with, and there is a good deal of middle ground, about which honest & well disposed men may differ. The most that can be said is that some of this middle ground may have been occupied by the National Legislature; and this surely is no evidence of a disposition to get rid of the limitations in the constitution; nor can it be viewed in that light by men of candor.

The truth is one description of men is disposed to do the essential business of the Nation by a liberal construction of the powers of the Government; another from disaffection would fritter away those powers—a third from an overweening [42] jealousy would do the same thing—a fourth from party & personal opposition are torturing the constitution into objections to every thing they do not like.

The Bank is one of the measures which is deemed by some the greatest stretch of power; and yet its constitutionality has been established in the most satisfactory manner.[43]

And the most incorrigible theorist among its opponents would in one months experience as head of the Department of the Treasury be compelled to acknowlege that it is an absolutely indispensable engine in the management of the Finances and would quickly become a convert to its perfect constitutionality.

Objection XIV [44]   The ultimate object of all

To this there is no other answer than a flat denial—except this that the project from its absurdity refutes itself.

The idea of introducing a monarchy or aristocracy into this Country, by employing the influence and force of a Government continually changing hands, towards it, is one of those visionary things, that none but madmen could meditate and that no wise men will believe.

If it could be done at all, which is utterly incredible, it would require a long series of time, certainly beyond the life of any individual to effect it. Who then would enter into such plot? For what purpose of interest or ambition?

42. In MS this word is "overweeing."
43. See "Opinion on the Constitutionality of an Act to Establish a Bank," February 23, 1791.
44. In MS H wrote this as "IV."

To hope that the people may be cajoled into giving their sanctions to such institutions is still more chimerical. A people so enlightened and so diversified [45] as the people of this Country can surely never be brought to it, but from convulsions and disorders,[46] in consequence of the acts of popular demagogues.

The truth unquestionably is, that the only path to a subversion of the republican system of the Country is, by flattering the prejudices of the people, and exciting their jealousies and apprehensions, to throw affairs into confusion, and bring on civil commotion. Tired at length of anarchy, or want of government, they may take shelter in the arms of monarchy for repose and security.

Those then, who resist a confirmation of public order, are the true Artificers of monarchy—not that this is the intention of the generality [47] of them. Yet it would not be difficult to lay the finger upon some of their party who may justly be suspected. When a man unprincipled in private life desperate in his fortune, bold in his temper, possessed of considerable talents, having the advantage of military habits—despotic in his ordinary demeanour—known to have scoffed in private at the principles of liberty—when such a man is seen to mount the hobby horse of popularity—to join in the cry of danger to liberty—to take every opportunity of embarrassing the General Government & bringing it under suspicion—to flatter and fall in with all the non sense of the zealots of the day—It may justly be suspected that his object is to throw things into confusion that he may "ride the storm and direct the whirlwind."

It has aptly been observed that *Cato* was the Tory—*Cæsar* the whig of his day. The former frequently resisted—the latter always flattered the follies of the people. Yet the former perished with the Republic the latter destroyed it.

No popular Government was ever without its Catalines & its Cæsars. These are its true enemies.

As far as I am informed the anxiety of those who are calumniated is to keep the Government in the state in which it is, which they fear will be no easy task, from a natural tendency in the state of things to exalt the local on the ruins of the National Government.

45. In MS, "diversied."
46. At this point H wrote and crossed out "under a republican system."
47. In MS, "generalality."

Some of them appear to wish, in a constitutional way, a change in the judiciary department of the Government, from an apprehension that an orderly and effectual administration of Justice cannot be obtained without a more intimate connection between the state and national Tribunals. But even this is not an object of any set of men as a party. There is a difference of opinion about it on various grounds among those who have generally acted together. As to any other change of consequence, I believe nobody dreams of it.

Tis curious to observe the anticipations of the different parties. One side appears to believe that there is a serious plot to overturn the state Governments and substitute monarchy to the present republican system. The other side firmly believes that there is a serious plot to overturn the General Government & elevate the separate power of the states upon its ruins. Both sides may be equally wrong & their mutual jealousies may be materially causes of the appearances which mutually disturb them, and sharpen them against each other.

Objection the 15   This change was contemplated &c

This is a palpable misrepresentation. No man, that I know of, contemplated the introducing into this country of a monarchy. A very small number (not more than three or four) manifested theoretical opinions favourable in the abstract to a constitution like that of Great Britain, but every one agreed that such a constitution except as to the general distribution of departments and powers was out of the Question in reference to this Country. The Member who was most explicit on this point (a Member from New York) declared in strong terms that the republican theory ought to be adhered to in this Country as long as there was any chance of its success—that the idea of a perfect equality of political rights among the citizens, exclusive of all permanent or hereditary distinctions, was of a nature to engage the good wishes of every good man, whatever might be his theoretic doubts—that it merited his best efforts to give success to it in practice—that hitherto from an incompetent structure of the Government it had not had a fair trial, and that the endeavour ought then to be to secure to it a better chance of success by a government more capable of energy and order.[48]

48. H presumably is referring to his own remarks at the Constitutional Convention. See "Constitutional Convention. Speech on a Plan of Government," June 18, 1787; "Constitutional Convention. Remarks on the Term of Office for Members of the Second Branch of the Legislature," June 26, 1787.

There is not a man at present in either branch of the Legislature who, that I recollect, had held language in the Convention favourable to Monarchy.

The basis therefore of this suggestion fails.

16 So many of them &c.

This has been answered above. Neither description of character is to be found in the Legislature. In the Senate there are 9 or ten who were members of the Convention; in the house of Representatives not more than six or seven.[49] Of those who are in the lastmentioned house—none can be considered as influential but Mr. Madison and Mr. Gerry.[50] Are they monarchy men?

As to the 17. 18th and 19th heads—They are rather inferences from and comments upon what is before suggested than specific objections. The answer to them must therefore be derived from what is said under other heads.

It is certainly much to be regretted that [51] party discriminations are so far Geographical as they have been; and that ideas of a severance of the Union are creeping in both North and South. In the South it is supposed that more government than is expedient is desired by the North. In the North, it is believed, that the prejudices of the South are incompatible with the necessary degree of Government and with the attainment of the essential ends of National Union. In both quarters there are respectable men who talk of separation, as a thing dictated by the different geniusses and different prejudices of the parts. But happily their number is not considerable —& the prevailing sentiment of the people is in favour of their true interest, UNION. And it is to be hoped that the Efforts of wise men will be able to prevent a scism, which would be injurious in different degrees to different portions of the Union; but would seriously wound the prosperity of all.

As to the sacrifice of Southern to Northern prejudices—if the conflict has been between *prejudices* and *prejudices*, it is certainly to be wished for mutual gratification that there had been mutual concession; but if the conflict has been between *great* and *substantial*

---

49. In the margin opposite this sentence H wrote "This computation from memory."

50. James Madison and Elbridge Gerry.

51. At this point H wrote and crossed out "differences of opinion on."

national objects on the one hand, and theoretical prejudices on the other, it is difficult to desire that the former should in any instance have yielded.

Objection 20   The Owers of the Debt are in the Southern and the holders of it in the Northern Division.

Answer. If this were literally true, it would be no argument for or against any thing. It would be still politically and morally right for the Debtors to pay their Creditors.

But it is in *no sense* true. The OWERS of the Debt are the people of *every* State, South Middle North. The holders are the Individual Creditors—citizens of the United Netherlands, Great Britain, France & of these States, North, Middle, South. Though some men, who constantly substitute hypothesis to fact, imagination to evidence, assert and reassert that the inhabitants of the South contribute *more* than those of the North; yet there is no pretence that they contribute *all;* and even the assertion of greater contribution is unsupported by documents facts, or, it may be added, probab[il]ities. Though the inhabitants of the South manufacture less than those of the North, which is the great argument, yet it does not follow that they consume more of taxable articles. It is a solid answer to this, that *whites* live better, wear more and better cloaths, and consume more luxuries, than blacks who constitute so considerable a part of the population of the South—that the Inhabitants of Cities and Towns, which abound so much more in the North than in the South, consume more of foreign articles, than the inhabitants of the Country—that it is a general rule that communities consume & contribute in proportion to their active or circulating wealth and that the Northern Regions have more active or circulating wealth than the Southern.

If official documents are consulted, though for obvious reasons they are not decisive, they contradict rather than confirm the hypothesis of greater proportional contribution in the Southern Division.

But to make the allegation in the objection true, it is necessary not merely that the Inhabitants of the South should contribute more, but that they should contribute *all.*

It must be confessed that a much larger proportion of the Debt is *owned* by inhabitants of the States from Pensylvania to New Hampshire inclusively than in the States South of Pensylvania.

But as to the [52] primitive Debt of the United States, that was the case in its original concoction. This arose from two causes. I, from the war having more constantly been carried on in the Northern Quarter, which led to obtaining more men and greater supplies in that quarter, and credit having been, for a considerable time, the main instrument of the Government, a consequent accumulation of debt in that quarter took place. II from the greater ability of the Northern and middle States to furnish men money and other supplies; and from the greater quantity of men money and other supplies which they did furnish. The loan office Debt; the army debt, the debt of the five great departments was *contracted* in a much larger proportion in the Northern and middle, than in the Southern States.

It must be confessed too that by the attractions of a superior monied Capital the disparity has increased, but it was great in the beginning.

As to the assumed debt the proportion in the South was at the first somewhat larger than in the North; and it must be acknowleged that this has since, from the same superiority of monied Capital in the North, ceased to be the case.

But if the Northern people who were originally greater Creditors than the Southern have become still more so, as purchasers, is it any reason that an honorable provision should not be made for their Debt? Or is the Government to blame for having made it? Did the Northern people take their property by violence from the Southern, or did they purchase and pay for it?

It may be answered that they obtained a considerable part of it by speculation, taking advantage of superior opportunities of information.

But admitting this to be true in all the latitude in which it is commonly stated—Is a government to bend the general maxims of policy and to mould its measures according to the accidental course of private speculations? Is it to do this or omit that in cases of great national importance, because one set of Individuals may gain, another lose, from unequal opportunities of information, from unequal degrees of resource, craft confidence or enterprise?

More over—There is much exaggeration in stating the manner of

52. At this point H wrote and crossed out "Debt proper."

the alienation of the Debt. The principal speculations in state debt, whatever may be pretended certainly began, after the promulgation of the plan for assuming by the Report of the Secy of the Treasury [53] to the House of Representatives. The resources of Individuals in this Country are too limited to have admitted of much progress in purchases before the knowlege of that plan was diffused throughout the Country. After that, purchasers and sellers were upon equal ground. If the purchasers speculated upon the sellers, in many instances, the sellers speculated upon the purchasers. Each made his calculation of chances, and founded upon it an exchange of money for certificates. It has turned out generally that the buyer had the best of the bargain; but the seller [54] got the value of his commodity according to his estimate of it, and probably in a great number of instances more. This shall be explained:

It happened that Mr. Maddison and some other distinguished characters of the South started in opposition to the Assumption. The high opinion entertained of them made it be taken for granted in that quarter, that the opposition would be successful. The securities quickly rose by means of purchases beyond their former prices. It was imagined that they would soon return to their old station by a rejection of the proposition for assuming. And the certificate holders were eager to part with them at their current prices; calculating on a loss to the Purchasers from their future fall. The representation is not conjectural; it is founded in information from respectable and intelligent Southern characters—And may be ascertained by Inquiry.

Hence it happened, that the inhabitants of the Southern states sustained a considerable loss,[55] by the opposition to the assumption, from Southern Gentlemen, and their too great confidence in the efficacy of that opposition.

Further—A great part of the Debt which has been purchased by Northern of Southern Citizens has been at high prices; in numerous instances beyond the true value. In the late delirium of speculation large sums were purchased at 25 ⅌Cent above par and upwards.[56]

53. "Report Relative to a Provision for the Support of Public Credit," January 9, 1790.
54. At this point H wrote and crossed out "it must be presumed."
55. At this point H wrote and crossed out "by Mr. Maddison's."
56. During January and early February, 1792, prices quoted for six percents had exceeded twenty-five shillings (Davis, *Essays*, I, 210). See also H to William Seton, January 18, 24, 1792; Seton to H, January 22, 1792.

The Southern people upon the whole have not parted with their property for nothing. They parted with it voluntarily—in most cases, upon fair terms, without surprize or deception, in many cases for more than its value. Tis their own fault, if the purchase money has not been beneficial to them—and the presumption is that it has been so in a material degree.

Let then any candid and upright mind, weighing all the circumstances, pronounce whether there be any real hardship in the inhabitants of the South being required to contribute their proportion to a provision for the Debt as it now exists—whether, if at liberty, they could honestly dispute the doing of it, or whether they can even in candor and good faith complain of being obliged to do it.

If they can, it is time to unlearn all the ancient notions of justice and morality, and to adopt a new system of Ethics.

Observation 21   The Antifœderal Champions &c

Answer   All that can be [57] said in answer to this has been already said.

It is much to be wished, that the true state of the case may not have been, that the Antifœderal Champions have been encouraged in their activity, by the countenance which has been given to their principles, by certain fœderalists, who in an envious and ambitious struggle for power influence and preeminence have imbraced as auxiliaries the numerous [58] party originally disaffected to the Government in the hope that these united with the factious and feeble minded fœderalists whom they can detach will give them the prœdominancy. This would be nothing more than the old story of personal and party emulation.

The Antifœderal Champions alluded to may be taught to abate their exultation by being told that the great body of the fœderalists, or rather the great body of the people are of opinion that none of their predictions have been fulfilled—That the beneficial effects of the Government have exceeded expectation and are witnessed by the general prosperity of the Nation.[59]

Speculative prices received a large share of their impetus from purchases made by the William Duer and Alexander Macomb organization "on time contracts, due in March and April, for prices above 25s., 14s.6d . . ." (Davis, *Essays*, I, 288).

57. In MS, "been."
58. For this word H originally wrote and then crossed out "powerful."
59. For this word H originally wrote and then crossed out "people."

Anti-Defamer

[Philadelphia, August 19, 1792][1]

For the Fœderal Gazette[2]

Russel[3] under an affected moderation veils the most insidious and malignant designs & slily propagates the basest slanders. This is evident from the following passage of his second paper. After stating a visionary and impracticable scheme for avoiding a war with the Indians[4]—he proceeds thus—"But then, how many offices had been wanting, *how many lucrative contracts would have been lost, and how great a waste of money would have been prevented from flowing into the coffers of those concerned in this business?*"

The plain inference from this is, that the public officer who has an agency in making those contracts *shares in the profit of them,* and that a part of the money which is expended *flows into his coffers.* If this is not his meaning then Russel owes it to himself and to justice to disavow the inference. If it is his meaning then he owes it to the Public to answer the following questions—

Does he know by what public Officer the contracts for supplying the army are made? Has he any ground to believe that that officer ever advised a single step which has led to the present Indian War? Does he know what his official conduct has been with regard to it? Does he know what his private character has been as to pecuniary affairs? Is he acquainted with a single *fact,* or even *circumstance,* which can justify a suspicion that he has ever been directly or indirectly interested in any contract in which he has had an agency?

Let him answer these questions or otherwise assign the ground of his insinuation or let him be despised as a wanton calumniator!

Anti Defamer.

ADf, Hamilton Papers, Library of Congress.

1. Since this essay was prepared in reply to a letter by "Russell" which appeared in *The* [Philadelphia] *Federal Gazette and Philadelphia Daily Advertiser* on August 18, 1792, it has arbitrarily been dated August 19, the day following the publication of the "Russell" letter.

2. Although this article was prepared for *The Federal Gazette,* it was not printed in that paper.

3. The "Russell" letters, attacking almost every aspect of the financial arrangements of the Federal Government, appeared in *The Federal Gazette* on August 16, 18, 23, 25, 28, 31, September 5, 8, 1792.

4. Russell's "scheme" was as follows: "To have formed an effectual barrier on our borders, and limited our territorial possessions within their just bounds, would at once have kept both the settlers and Indians in awe, and would have ascertained the hitherto unknown limits of our pursuits; war might thus have been avoided, and the country have been left to pursue the pacifick system, by which alone its public credit can be supported, and its debts be honorably extinguished . . ." (*The Federal Gazette*, August 18, 1792).

From William Ellery

Colles. Off: Port of Newport [Rhode Island]
Augt 20th 1792

Sir,

I have recd. your letter of the 31st. of the last month respecting the Sloop Polly of Sandwich.[1] On the 30th. of last June I received a letter from the Collector of Barnstable,[2] informg. me of the seizure he had made, and of the departure of said Sloop for Providence with some articles of foreign produce, as he supposed concealed under a deck load of pine wood. I immediately directed the Inspectors of this Port to make cautious and diligent inquiry for said Sloop, and wrote to every Surveyor in this District requesting that they would do the same, but as yet we have not found her, nor heard whether she is gone. On the twenty fourth day of May 1791 the said Sloop Samuel Bourn master was licensed here, and on the 20th. of June last was licensed anew at Providence, as appears by an endorsmt. on the returned Licence issued at this port, made by the Collector of the District of Providence.[3] It was under the License issued at this Port that the fraud was committed by Saml. Bourn, who was part owner as well as master of said Sloop when she was licensed, and he gave bond according to Law but as he was a stranger and could not get a surety here a Paul Gifford of Sandwich in the State of Massachusetts was admitted to be surety to the bond, which with the License issued at this Port are in my possession.

A diligent look out will be still continued in this District for said Sloop, and if she can be found herein, She will be seized. The bond and License will remain with me until I shall have received your direction respecting them. In the mean time if Samuel Bourn, and his Surety, or either of them should appear in this State, the bond shall be put in suit, against him or them.

The Inspector of the Revenue for the Port of Bristol [4] has certified that 92082 galls of distilled Spirits first proof exported in the Snow fair Eliza are entitled to a drawback of 11 cents per gallon, and that 7257¾ gallons of distilled Spirits first proof exported as aforesaid are entitled to 10 cents per Gallon. Certificates of the Collectors produced to me for 6968½ gallons of these distilled Spirits are dated prior to the first day of last July, and are by Law entitled to a drawback of eleven cents per gallon, and Certificates of Collectors for 9497¾ gallons of these Spirits are dated since the last day of last June and are I conceive entitled to a drawback of ten cents per gallon.[5] It doth not appear by any of the Certificates of the Collectors when the Spirits were distilled. The question I would raise on this Statement is, whether I am to be governed with respect to the drawback by the Certificates of the Inspector of the Revenue, or by the Certificates of the Collectors? Please to favour me with your directions on this subject as early as may be convenient.

I have received your letter of the 2nd of this month [6] with my Receipt and wait for the directions of the Comptroller [7] respecting it.

I am, Sir, Yr. most obedt. servant　　　　　Wm Ellery Colle

A Hamilton Esqre
Secry Treasy

LC, Newport Historical Society, Newport, Rhode Island.
　1. Letter not found. See H to Jeremiah Olney, July 31, 1792.
　2. Joseph Otis.　　　3. Jeremiah Olney.　　　4. Samuel Bosworth.
　5. Drawbacks on distilled spirits were regulated by three laws: "An Act repealing, after the last day of June next, the duties heretofore laid upon Distilled Spirits imported from abroad, and laying others in their stead; and also upon Spirits distilled within the United States, and for appropriating the same" (1 *Stat.* 199–214 [March 3, 1791]); "An Act for raising a farther sum of money for the protection of the frontiers, and for other purposes therein mentioned" (1 *Stat.* 259–63 [May 2, 1792]); "An Act concerning the Duties on Spirits distilled within the United States" (1 *Stat.* 267–71 [May 8, 1792]).
　6. Letter not found. See Ellery to H, July 16, 1792.
　7. Oliver Wolcott, Jr.

To Isaac Gregory

Treasury Department, August 20, 1792. "Your letter of the 25th. ultimo,[1] concerning a certain seizure made by you, has been received. If the Sloop Polly passed 24 hours within any harbour, inlet or creek of any Port in your Dictrict without reporting, the penalty, in the 16th Section of the Collection law will apply; otherwise, there will be no penalty for proceeding to an 'interior District'. . . ." [2]

Copy, RG 56, Letters to Collectors at Small Ports, "Set G," National Archives.
  1. Letter not found.
  2. Section 16 of "An Act to provide more effectually for the collection of the duties imposed by law on goods, wares and merchandise imported into the United States, and on the tonnage of ships or vessels" stated that the master of any vessel entering a port had to report the arrival of his vessel within twenty-four hours to the chief officer of the port (1 *Stat.* 158 [August 4, 1790]).

From John Kilty [1]

Annapolis, August 20, 1792. Asks for reimbursement for his subsistence while he was a captured officer on parole on Long Island during the American Revolution.[2]

ALS, RG 217, Miscellaneous Treasury Accounts, 1790–1894, Account No. 4216, National Archives.
  1. Kilty emigrated from England and settled in Annapolis shortly before the American Revolution. From July 1, 1778, to November 10, 1782, he was a captain in the Third Continental Dragoons. He was the father of William Kilty, compiler of the statutes of Maryland.
  2. H endorsed this letter: "Answered provisionally Aug 30 1792 reserved for consulting Comptroller." Letter not found.
  On June 28, 1793, Kilty received a warrant from the Treasury Department for $46.42 (RG 217, Miscellaneous Treasury Accounts, 1790–1894, Account No. 4216, National Archives).

From Pierre Charles L'Enfant [1]

town of paterson [New Jersey] August 21st 1792

My dear sir
  Under an Expectation of seeing you on the twenty ulterior I differed answering your last favour [2] wishing to assure you that your favorit Child will be carefully nursed and bread up to your satisfaction without Involving the parents in to Extravagant or usless Expence. My sole Embition being to deliver it worthy of its father and capable of doing honor to his Country.

The Gentleman who will hand you this—Mr Roberdeau,[3] is one of those whose assistance I much wish for as a principal overseer of the Land. I need not mention to you my attachement to him and the consideration which lead me to retain him near me. I made an offer to him in consequence of an Notority given me by the directors at their last meeting to appoint to assistant under me [4]—but the salary determined at tow dollar a day will I fear fall short from what he wish knowing as I do that he could have got at the reat of three had he accepted continuing in the work at the potomack which you will know he left from a regard for me and in consequence of his having faith fully discharged his duty.

Knowing your pour ever to persuad I should tank you to Encourag him Not to be discouraged and to join me.

To much Engaged to give you such an account as I wish of the progres making in the busines I confine assuring you I shall spare no amount to forward it.

The plan of the city & of the work I propos I shall forward to you at the first opportunity I shall hav to lay them tow.

I hav the honor to be with very great respect   Your Mos hmbl & obedient servet   P c L'Enfant

Mr secr tre

ALS, Hamilton Papers, Library of Congress.
   1. L'Enfant was the "Agent for superintending the erection of the works and buildings ordered by the Directors" of the Society for Establishing Useful Manufactures. See "Draft Minutes of a Meeting of a Committee of the Directors of the Society for Establishing Useful Manufactures," August 1, 1792.
   2. Letter not found.
   3. Isaac Roberdeau, secretary and assistant to L'Enfant, had helped L'Enfant in surveying and planning the new Federal city.
   4. The authorization which L'Enfant was given to employ an assistant is not recorded in the "Minutes of the S.U.M."

From Francis Cabot

Georgetown [*Maryland*] *August 22, 1792.* "A few days since I Shipped from this place to Alexandria a pipe of Madeira Wine belonging to my Brother Mr George Cabot[1] with the intention of having it transported to Boston as no sale could be found for it here. On its Arrival at Alexandria it was Seized by one of the

Officers of the Port for not being marked old stock agreeably to law.[2] An entire ignorance that such a law was in existance must plead my excuse. My principles of duty to the Government as well as regard to the interest of my Brother wou'd have induced the proper previous steps on my part had I have known any were Necessary. . . . I shall feel myself much indebted if you can consistently empower the Collector[3] to release upon my giving him Satisfactory evidence that there could be no intention of fraud but that it was purely the result of ignorance. . . ."

Copy, RG 56, Letters to and from the Collector at Georgetown, National Archives.
1. George Cabot was United States Senator from Massachusetts.
2. Importers of distilled spirits were required to have the stock on hand marked "old stock" during the first three days of July, 1791, under Section 27 of "An Act repealing, after the last day of June next, the duties heretofore laid upon Distilled Spirits imported from abroad, and laying others in their stead; and also upon Spirits distilled within the United States, and for appropriating the same" (1 *Stat.* 266 [March 3, 1791]).
3. Charles Lee.

To Henry Lee [1]

[*Philadelphia, August 22, 1792.* On September 10, 1792, Lee wrote to Hamilton: "I found on my return from a visit . . . your letter of the 22d. Ult." *Letter not found.*]

1. From 1792 to 1794 Lee was governor of Virginia.

From Jean Baptiste de Ternant [1]

Phile. 22 aout 1792

D'après le changement que vous avez consenti de faire à l'epoque du payement qui devoit avoir lieu le 1r. sepe. prochain,[2] j'ai à vous prier de vouloir bien faire payer au Consul de france de la forest[3] ou à son ordre, 26,088 piastres le 15 du mois prochain et 17,936 piastres le 1r. octobre suivant. Quand le montant et les epoques des besoins subséquents seront particulierement determinés j'aurai l'honeur de vous en prevenir.

LC, *Arch. des Aff. Etr., Corr. Pol., Etats-Unis,* Supplement Vol. 20.

1. Ternant presented his credentials as French Minister Plenipotentiary to the United States on August 2, 1791.

For earlier references to plans to defray the cost of supplies for the relief of Santo Domingo by using payments on the debt due to France which the United States had incurred during the American Revolution, see Ternant to H, September 21, 1791, February 21, March 8, 10, June 26, 1792; H to Ternant, September 21, 1791, February 22, March 8, 11, 12, June 23, 26, 1792; William Short to H, December 28, 1791, January 26, April 22, 25, May 14, June 28, August 6, 1792; H to Short, April 10, 1792.

2. In order to prevent the running of interest on the advance payments of the French debt, H had agreed to make payments from the Treasury at the dates when money for Santo Domingo was needed (Frederick J. Turner, ed., "Correspondence of the French Ministers to the United States, 1791–1797," *Annual Report of the American Historical Association for the Year 1903* [Washington, 1904], II, 91, 92, 157).

3. Antoine René Charles Mathurin de La Forest, who had served in the French legation in the United States during the American Revolution, was made French vice consul at Savannah in 1783. He assumed the duties of consul general in 1785 and was officially appointed to the post on March 2, 1792.

To Jean Baptiste de Ternant

Treasury Department, August 22, 1792. "I duly received your letter of this date. The arrangement proposed by you . . . is perfectly agreeable to me, and will be executed as you desire."

LS, *Arch. des Aff. Etr., Corr. Pol., Etats-Unis,* Supplement Vol. 20.

From George Washington

Mount Vernon 22d. Augt. 1792.

Sir,

This will merely inform you that your letter of the 10th. with its enclosure and that of the 11th. Inst: [1] have been duly received; and that if the Regulations of your Department, mentioned in the former, are carried strictly into execution, the most happy consequences, it is to be hoped, will result from them.

I am Sir &c.   G Washington

LC, George Washington Papers, Library of Congress.

1. Letter not found.

[*Detector No. II*] [1]

[Philadelphia, August 23, 1792]

[Philadelphia] *Dunlap's American Daily Advertiser*, August 24, 1792.

1. The first letter by "Detector" is dated July 28, 1792.

Philip Marsh has written: "A second letter by 'Detector' and in the typical style of Hamilton appeared in *The American Daily Advertiser* for August 24th, addressed 'To the MECHANICS AND MANUFACTURERS,' defending the report on manufactures" ("Hamilton's Neglected Essays, 1791–1793," *The New-York Historical Society Quarterly*, XXXII [October, 1948], 293). No conclusive evidence, however, has been found that H is the author of this letter.

To John Kean

[*Philadelphia, August 23, 1792.* Letter listed in dealer's catalogue. *Letter not found.*]

ALS, sold by Stan V. Henkels, Jr., April 21–23, 1891, Item 371.

From Joseph Nourse

Treasury Department, Register's Office, August 24, 1792. "I have carefully looked over the Journals of the late Congress and have therefrom selected their several Proceedings which relate to Indents." [1]

ALS, Hamilton Papers, Library of Congress; LC, RG 53, Register of the Treasury, Estimates and Statements for 1792, Vol. "134-T," National Archives.

1. This enclosure is entitled "References to the Journals of the Congress, in relation to Indents" (D, Hamilton Papers, Library of Congress). The dates of the entries on this list range from September 10, 1782, to August 20, 1788.

From Joseph Nourse [1]

Treasury Department
Register's Office, 24th August, 1792.

Sir,

I have the honor to enclose an abstract statement of the debt incurred by the late government, and which has been paid off from the funds of the present government, amounting to one million eight hundred and forty-five thousand two hundred and seventeen dollars forty-two cents; but this sum will be encreased, when the balance of three hundred and ninety-seven thousand twenty-four dollars fifteen cents, remaining to be appropriated in the farther purchase of the public debt, shall be applied, and which more particularly appears by the subjoined statement.

With every sentiment of the highest respect, I have the honor to be, Sir, Your most obedient, And most humble servant.

Joseph Nourse, Reg.

Honorable Alexander Hamilton, Esq.
Secretary of the Treasury.

[ENCLOSURE]

*Statement of the Balance which remains to be applied
in the further Purchases of the Public Debt.*

By the act passed 12th August, 1790, making provision for the reduction of the Public Debt, section 2d, it is enacted, that all such surplus of the product of the duties arising from impost and

[Philadelphia] *Gazette of the United States,* September 1, 1792.
1. This letter was printed as Document No. "I" and the two enclosed statements appeared as Documents No. "II" and "III." An introduction to the documents reads as follows: "The following authentic Documents respecting the Progress which has been made by the *present* Government of the United States, towards extinguishing the Debts contracted under the *former* Government, will, it is presumed, be very acceptable to the People of the United States; and it is hoped, that the different Editors of Newspapers will give the Information the general Circulation which its importance merits."
For the newspaper controversy provoked by this letter, see the two "Civis" letters, September 5, 11, 1792.

tonnage to 31st December, 1790, after satisfying the several appropriations therein specified, shall be applied to the purchase of the public debt: [2]

	Dollars.
The product of said duties were,	3,026,070 65 ⅓
The total appropriations were,	1,687,194 81
The surplus fund to 31st December, 1790,	1,338,875 84⅓
Deduct the amount paid for dollars 1,456,743 38 100 of the public debt extinguished as per abstract,	941,851 69
Leaves a balance which remains to be applied to the farther purchases of the public debt,	397,024 15⅓

[ENCLOSURE]

An abstract statement of the sum extinguished of the Public Debt, also of the payment from the funds of the present government of certain claims, which were incurred by the late government

Purchases of the Public Debt:	Dollars.
Amount thereof extinguished,	1,456.743 38
Warrants drawn by the Board of treasury under the late government, and which have been discharged in pursuance of the act of Congress of 29th Sept. 1789,[3]	157,789 94
Civil List—for various payments made upon accounts which originated under the late government,	25,768 50
War Department, being for arrearages of pay due to sundry officers of the army, and for provisions furnished,	7,308 40
Abraham Skinner, late Commissary-General of prisoners, for the board of American prisoners of war, at Long-Island; appropriated by Congress, per their act passed 12th August, 1790,[4]	38,683 13

2. 1 *Stat.* 186–87.
3. "An Act making Appropriations for the Service of the present year" (1 *Stat.* 95).
4. "An Act making certain Appropriations therein mentioned" (1 *Stat.* 185–86).

Old accounts, viz.

Representatives of Mons. Decoudray, bal. of pay	2,977 24
Do, Hon. John Lawrens, his salary on an embassy to the French Court,	6,017 31
Francis Dana, salary on an embassy to the Court of St. Petersburg,	2,410 3
Benson, Smith & Parker, their expenses attending the embarkation of the British troops at New-York,	1,000
His Most Christian Majesty, for military and ordnance stores supplied the American ships of war in the French West-Indies,	29,029 68
Oliver Pollock, for balance due him for supplies at New-Orleans, with interest thereon, in conformity with the several acts of Congress,[5]	108,605
Messrs. Gardoqui & Son, balance due for supplies furnished in Spain,	502 86
	150,542 14
Bills of exchange which had been drawn on foreign commissioners, and not paid by them,	4,185 50
Timothy Pickering, late quarter-master-general, being on account of the appropriation of 40,000 dollars, passed July 1, 1790,[6]	2,077 89

5. See Oliver Pollock to H, February 15, 1792.
6. Nourse is referring to "An Act making certain Appropriations therein mentioned" (1 *Stat.* 185–86 [August 12, 1790]).

Grants of Congress, viz.

John McCord, per act of Congress of 1st July, 1790,[7]	1,309 71	
Jehorakim McJocksin, per act of Congress of 26th March, 1790,[8]	120	
Baron de Glaubeck, per act of 29th September, 1789,[9]	140 26	
Seth Harding, per act 11th August, 1790,[10]	200	
Caleb Brewster, ditto, ditto,	348 57	
		2,118 54
Dollars,		1,845,217 42

Treasury Department,
Register's Office, August 23. 1792.

Joseph Nourse,
Register.

7. "An Act to satisfy the claims of John McCord against the United States" (6 *Stat.* 2).
8. "An Act making appropriations for the support of government for the year one thousand seven hundred and ninety" (1 *Stat.* 104–06).
9. "An Act to allow the Baron de Glaubeck the pay of a Captain in the Army of the United States" (6 *Stat.* 1).
10. "An Act for the relief of disabled soldiers and seamen lately in the service of the United States, and of certain other persons" (6 *Stat.* 3).

To Jeremiah Olney

Treasury Department, August 24, 1792. "I have to reply to your letter of the 24th Ultimo, concerning the Renewal of licenses in certain cases. I incline to the opinion that regularly *new* licenses cannot be granted (except in the cases in which licenses are required to be surrendered previous to the going on foreign voyages) until the expiration of the term of the preceding ones; even though transfers of property or alterations of the vessels should have taken place. The safest practice is for them, to run under their old licenses until the year is expired, endorsing upon them a memorandum of the casualties which have happened; and in case of change of property the former Owners must take care to indemnify themselves by counter security from the new Owners. . . ."

LS, Rhode Island Historical Society, Providence; copy, RG 56, Letters to the Collector at Providence, National Archives; copy, RG 56, Letters to Collectors at Small Ports, "Set G," National Archives.

From James Reynolds [1]

Philadelphia 24th. August. 1792.

Honored Sir.

When I Conversed with you last I mentioned that I was going to moove. Sence that I have mooved I have taken a very convenant house for a boarding house. but being disappointed in receiving Some money. put it intirely out of my power to furnish the house I have taken. I have four genteal boarders will come to live with me. as soon as I Can get the Rooms furnished. dear Sir this is my Setuvation. I am in no way of business. the Cash last len me. inable me to pay my Rent. and Some little debts I had Contracted for my Familys youse. now sir if I Can ask a favour once more of the loan of two Hundred dollars. I will give you Surity of all I process. for the payment of what I owe you. without your assistance. this time I dont know what I shall do. Mrs. Reynolds and myself has made a Calculation. and find with that much money will inable us to take in four boarders. and I am in hopes in the mean will. something will turn up in my favour. which will inable me to help myself and famy. dear Sir your Complying with the above will for ever, lay me under the greatist Obligation to you and I will. you may Rest ashured. Repay it again as soon as its in my power.

I am Honored Sir with Respect your most Obedt. and Humble Servt.   James Reynolds
                                        Vine Street No. 161 Second door
                                        from the Corner of fifth Street.
Alexr. Hamilton Esqr.

"Reynolds Pamphlet," August 31, 1797.
1. This letter is printed as document No. XXI in the appendix of the "Reynolds Pamphlet," August 31, 1797.

For background to this letter, see Reynolds to H, December 15, 17, 19, 22, 1791, January 3, 17, March 24, April 3, 7, 17, 23, May 2, June 3–22, 23, 24, 1792; H to Reynolds, December 15, 1791, April 7, June 3–22, 24, 1792; Maria Reynolds to H, December 15, 1791, January 23–March 18, March 24, June 2, 1792.

From Robert Troup [1]

[New York, August 24, 1792]

My dear friend

I have just recd. yours enclosing a note for discount.[2] I have endorsed it & enclosed it to Mr. Seton.[3] It is dated the 20th Augt. inst & will be discounted on Tuesday.

I am this moment setting off for the Dutchess Circuit & have not time to be particular although I much wish it. I have as you have learnt taken a very active part abt the wicked & abominable decision of the canvassers.[4] I think & have always thought, my good friend, this decision to be subversive of the most sacred right that can be enjoyed under any government. Quickly therefore to submit to it would argue a poverty of spirit & an indifference to the principles of freedom which would fix an indelible stigma upon our characters. I have always imagined & now see no reason for imaging otherwise that we should not obtain redress. My object has been to make a strong impression upon the public mind of the deep corruption of Clinton & his party and thus to render him odious. We have pretty well succeded in this object & I trust our sucess will be more complete. I have no apprehension that we shall endanger the political ship. It is the interest of us all that she should be kept in her present course with a fair wind &c. Be not therefore uneasy—but at the same [time] do not forget that allowances should be made for the keen anguish we suffer from the wound we have received.

God bless you   Rob Troup

24 Augt 1792 [5]

A Hamilton Esq

ALS, Hamilton Papers, Library of Congress.

1. Troup, a New York lawyer, and H had been undergraduates together at King's College before the American Revolution. When Troup wrote this letter he was serving as clerk of the Federal court for the District of New York.

2. Letter not found.   3. William Seton, cashier of the Bank of New York.
4. Troup is referring to the decision of the majority of the joint committee of canvassers appointed by the New York legislature which declared that George Clinton had been elected over John Jay in the April, 1792, New York gubernatorial election. Troup had proposed the resolutions adopted by the meeting on June 18, 1792, of those New York electors who opposed the decision of the canvassers and who referred to themselves as the "Friends of Liberty." See H to Rufus King, June 28, 1792, note 1. For other information on this election, see Philip Schuyler to H, May 9, 1792, note 4; H to John Adams, June 25, 1792, note 2; H to King, June 28, July 25, 27, 1792; King to H, July 10, 29, 1792; William Lewis to H, July 21, 1792.
5. H endorsed this letter: "filed No answer necessary."

From Wilhem and Jan Willink, Nicholaas and Jacob Van Staphorst, and Nicholas Hubbard

[*Amsterdam, August 24, 1792.* On November 5, 1792, Hamilton wrote to Willink, Van Staphorst, and Hubbard: "I have to acknowledge the receipt of your letter of the 24th. of August last." *Letter not found.*]

From Jeremiah Olney

Providence, August 25, 1792. "I have requested the District Attorney[1] to file a Libel against the Schooner Rising-Sun, burthen $23\frac{61}{95}$ Tons, Thomas Rhodes Haszard Master, from Halifax, together with her Cargo. . . ."

ADfS, Rhode Island Historical Society, Providence.
1. William Channing was United States attorney for the District of Rhode Island.

To Jeremiah Olney

Treasury Department
August 25. 1792.

Sir

I have considered the seventh Section of the Act, "concerning the Duties on Spirits distilled within the United States &c,"[1] and agree with you in the opinion, given in your letter of the 14th instant, that the abatement of two per Cent for leakage is to be made, on securing the Duty at the end of the quarter, from the whole quantity distilled during the preceding three months. The Supervisor of Rhode Island will be instructed accordingly.[2]

On the question, what steps are to be taken in cases where the quantities or proof of Spirits, notified for exportation, disagree with the certificate accompanying them, I answer that if the disagreement be such as to justify a suspicion that the Spirits are not the same, not only the drawback ought not to be allowed, but the Spirits ought to be seized. This however will require great discretion and care. Both quantities and proof are liable to vary from the *difference* of instruments and of the *accuracy* of the Persons who use them. Where there is reasonable ground to believe that all is right, the drawback [3] must be adjusted according to the Rate paid upon the quantity mentioned in the Certificate, if the Cask be full, if not full, upon the actual quantity.

I am, Sir,   Your Obed. Servant   A Hamilton

Jere. Olney Esqr.
Providence.

LS, Rhode Island Historical Society, Providence; copy RG 56, Letters to Collectors at Small Ports, "Set G," National Archives; copy, RG 56, Letters to the Collector at Providence, National Archives.

1. 1 *Stat.* 269 (May 8, 1792).

2. On August 22, 1792, Tench Coxe wrote a circular to the supervisors of the revenue stating: "A question has been incidentally brought to the Treasury concerning the allowance for leakage granted in the 7th Section of the Act concerning the Duties on Spirits distilled in the United States. It is my opinion, that, if it be the case of Spirits paying the duty by the Gallon, the allowance of two pr. Cent for leakage is absolute, and that it is to be made without subsequent examination or enquiry, whether the Cask shall have or shall not have leaked in that degree. It will be proper, that an intimation be given to the Port Inspectors to keep this allowance in view, when they shall be engaged in superintending the Exportation of domestic distilled Spirits" (LC, RG 58, Letters of Commissioner of Revenue, 1792–1793, National Archives).

3. Section 51 of "An Act repealing, after the last day of June next, the duties heretofore laid upon Distilled Spirits imported from abroad, and laying others in their stead; and also upon Spirits distilled within the United States, and for appropriating the same" provided that "if any of the said spirits (whereupon any of the duties imposed by this act shall have been paid or secured to be paid) shall . . . be exported from the United States to any foreign port or place, there shall be an allowance to the exporter or exporters thereof, by way of drawback, equal to the duties thereupon" (1 *Stat.* 210 [March 3, 1791]).

From Jonathan Dayton

Elizabeth town [New Jersey] August 26th 1792

Dear sir,

Having been absent with my family on a visit to Staten Island and to the seashore, I did not receive, so soon as I otherwise should, your letter of the 15th.[1] That Mr. Jefferson proposed to Freneau to repair to Philadelphia, and act in his department as interpreter of the French language, and that, subsequently thereto, a negotiation was had & completed between Mr. Madison and the latter to establish & conduct a newspaper there, are undeniable truths.[2] Altho' desirous of frustrating the machinations of a particular party, I cannot nevertheless consistently comply with your request in giving up to public notoriety the name of my informant. In a correspondence as confidential as ours, I have no hesitation in making it known to *you*, more especially as such communication, while it convinces you of the certainty of those transactions, will also impress you with a conviction of the impropriety of that name being again mentioned. I am indebted to Mr. Childs of New York for all that I knew and informed you relative to this matter.[3] He, you know, is one of the printers, and interested in the paper, and altho' I am well assured that he entirely disapproves the manner in which it is conducted, yet it is natural to suppose that he would not willingly be instrumental in the establishing of any fact which might operate to it's disrepute or prejudice.

With very sincere regard   Yours   Jona: Dayton

ALS, Hamilton Papers, Library of Congress.
   1. Dayton was mistaken, for the letter to which he is referring is dated August 13.
   2. See "An American," August 4, 11, 18, 1792.
   3. Before the establishment of the [Philadelphia] *National Gazette*, Philip Freneau frequently had contributed to *The* [New York] *Daily Advertiser*, published by Francis Childs. Childs agreed in 1791 to finance the publication of the *National Gazette* and to stand responsible for any loss incurred.

From George Washington

Mount Vernon Augt. 26th. 1792

My dear Sir,   (Private)

Your letter of the 18th., enclosing answers to certain objections communicated to you in my letter of the 29th. Ulto. came duly to hand; and although I have not, as yet, from a variety of causes, been able to give them the attentive reading I mean to bestow, I feel myself much obliged by the trouble you have taken to answer them; as I persuade myself, from the full manner in which you appear to have taken the matter up, that I shall receive both satisfaction and profit from the perusal.

Differences in political opinions are as unavoidable as, to a certain point, they may perhaps be necessary; but it is to be regretted, exceedingly, that subjects cannot be discussed with temper on the one hand, or decisions submitted to without having the motives which led to them, improperly implicated on the other: and this regret borders on chagrin when we find that Men of abilities—zealous patriots—having the same *general* objects in view, and the same upright intentions to prosecute them, will not exercise more charity in deciding on the opinions, & actions of one another. When matters get to such lengths, the natural inference is, that both sides have strained the cords beyond their bearing—and that a middle course would be found the best, until experience shall have pointed out the right mode—or, which is not to be expected, because it is denied to mortals—there shall be some *infallible* rule by which we could *fore* judge events.

Having premised these things, I would fain hope that liberal allowances will be made for the political opinions of one another; and instead of those wounding suspicions, and irritating charges with which some of our Gazettes are so strongly impregnated, & cannot fail if persevered in, of pushing matters to extremity, & thereby tare the Machine asunder, that there might be mutual forbearances and temporising yieldings *on all sides*. Without these I do not see how the Reins of Government are to be managed, or how the Union of the States can be much longer preserved. How unfortunate would it be, if a fabric so goodly—erected under so many Providential circumstances—and in its first stages, having acquired such respectibility, should, from diversity of Sentiments, or internal obstructions to some of the acts of Government (for I cannot prevail on myself to believe that these measures are, as yet, the deliberate acts of a determined party) should be harrowing our vitals in such a manner as to have brought us to the verge of dissolution. Melancholy thought! But one, at the same time that it shows the consequences of diversified opinions, when pushed with too much tenacity; exhibits evidence also of the necessity of accommodation; and of the propriety of adopting such healing measures as will restore harmony to the discordant members of the Union, & the governing powers of it.

I do not mean to apply this advice to measures which are passed, or to any character in particular. I have given it in the same *general* terms to other Officers of the Government.[1] My earnest wish is, that balsam may be poured into *all* the wounds which have been given, to prevent them from gangrening; & from those fatal consequences which the community may sustain if it is withheld. The friends of the Union must wish this—those who are not, but wish to see it rended, will be disappointed—and all things I hope will go well.

We have learnt through the medium of Mr. Harrison to Doctr. Craik, that you have it in contemplation to take a trip this way.[2] I felt pleasure at hearing it, and hope it is unnecessary to add that it would be considerably encreased by seeing you under this roof, for you may be assured of the sincere and affectionate regard of   Yours

Go: Washington

PS. I pray you to note down whatever may occur to you, not only in your own department but other matters also of general import that may be fit subjects for the speech at the opening of the ensuing Session.   GW.

Alexr. Hamilton Esqr.

ALS, Connecticut Historical Society, Hartford; ADfS, George Washington Papers, Library of Congress; LC, George Washington Papers, Library of Congress.

1. On August 23, 1792, Washington wrote to Thomas Jefferson about the differences of opinion among members of the cabinet and also about the newspaper attacks upon all the measures of the Government (ALS, Thomas Jefferson Papers, Library of Congress). On August 26, 1792, he wrote to Edmund Randolph on the same subjects (ALS, Historical Society of Pennsylvania, Philadelphia).

2. Richard Harrison, auditor of the Treasury Department, was the son-in-law of Dr. James Craik of Alexandria, Washington's long-time friend.

From William Ellery

Colles Offe. [Newport, Rhode Island] Augt. 27th 1792

Sir,

Last friday evening I was informed that a Sloop stripped of her sails lay in a small harbour called Slocum's harbour in Nashawina islands, which as I am told is about 15 miles from the main land, and about 7 or 8 miles from Marthas vineyard and about forty miles from this place. The circumstances of a vessel stripped at this season of the year, and the place where she lay induced a suspicion that it might be the Sloop Polly of Sandwich.[1] I communicated my information and suspicions to the Surveyor of this Port,[2] and desired him to take with him an Inspector our two boatmen & his admeasuring apparatus and proceed with our sailing boat to the place where the vessel lay as soon as wind and weather would permit. Suggesting to him, that if it were that Sloop it was probable he would find the words on her stern blacked over, and in that case a scraping or washing of the blacking carefully he might discover letters enough to determin whether it was the Sloop Polly of Sandwich or not, and admeasuring her would also tend to ascertain same point. He sailed that day and the next morning arrived at Nasshawina, found the stern of the Sloop blacked over; but on washing the blacking off he discover'd the words *Sloop Polly* plainly, and enough of other letters to satisfy him that the word which was partly erased, had been *Sandwich*. On admeasuring her, she turned out to be thirty tons which is eight tons and $^{40}\!/_{95}$ more than the tonnage expressed in the License which issued from this Port. Upon inquiring of people on the island he perceived that some of them were Suspicious that She had been employed in illicit trade, and of Mrs Slocum (her husband was absent) he found that she had arrived there about three weeks ago and was purchased by her husband of the owner of her, whose name she pretended she could not recollect. The Surveyor seized her, and would have seized her Sails; which from Mrs Slocum's conversation were concealed in their house, but there was no magistrate on or near the island to give him a search warrant, and it was not probable that they would be removed very soon. The Surveyor returned here last evening leaving the Inspector and one of the boatmen in charge of the Sloop (which lay partly on a beech with two Anchors a head) and this forenoon sailed for New Bedford to give the Collector of that District[3] information of what he had discovered and done, in order that he might cause her to be libelled and prosecuted as the Law directs.

Notwithstandg: the disagreement between the tonnage by her License, and her admeasuremt. by our Surveyor I have no doubt but that She is the identical Sloop Polly of Sandwich Samuel Bourne master from which goods were unladen at Sandwich without permit, and which was licenced here 24th. of May 1791, and at Providence the 20th. of last June. It is probable that there might be a mistake in her origl. admeasuremt: for such mistakes have happened. Upon the return of the Surveyor who will go from Bedford to Nashawina I may receive more particular information, if I should I will communicate it to you by the next Post.

I am, Sir, Yr. most obedt. servt. Wm Ellery Colle

LC, Newport Historical Society, Newport, Rhode Island.
1. See Ellery to H, August 20, 1792; H to Jeremiah Olney, July 31, 1792.
2. Daniel Lyman.   3. Edward Pope.

From Tobias Lear

Portsmouth[1] N. H. Augt. 27th: 1792

Dear Sir,

I find, on enquiry, that a suitable Character may be obtained in this part of the Country, i.e. in Massachusetts, to take charge of a private school in Philadelphia, if a proper compensation should be offered. Upon conversing with several gentlemen on this subject I have found it to be a concurrent opinion that about one thousand dollars per Annum would induce such a person to come forward in this business as would give entire satisfaction both as to respectability method, & talents.

As you appeard to be anxious on this head I have taken the liberty to give you this information, and beg the favor of you to let me know what prospect there is of making up such a school as would hold out something like the above mentioned compensation, & when it could probably be formed.

It is with pleasure I can inform you that everything in this part of the country wears the face of prosperity & contentment. The people appear to be quite happy under the present government and speak of themselves as the most fortunate people in the world. In this town, where I have had more opportunity of making observations than in any other, I find a degree of industry, enterprize & prosperity to which they have heretofore been strangers, at least since the Revolution. A sufficient circulating medium seems to have given new life to every undertaking. Not a man is unemployed, unless he chuses to lead an idle life, and so few are there of this class that they are in no repute.

Mrs. Lear desires her best wishes & affectionate regards may be presented to Mrs. Hamilton, to which you will be so good as to add my best respects. We expect to set out for Philada. about the 12th of next month.[2]

With sincere respect & attachment   I am Dear Sir   Your Most Obedt. Servt.   Tobias Lear

ALS, Hamilton Papers, Library of Congress.
    1. Lear was the son of a prosperous Portsmouth shipmaster and farmer. In 1790 he had married Mary Long of Portsmouth.
    2. On the back of this letter H wrote: "Answered Sepr 6 will promise 600 Ds for 12 and will permit more to 1000." Letter not found.
    On October 7, 1792, Lear wrote to George Washington: "I am happy to inform you that I found a person who is recommended by General [Benjamin] Lincoln & several other respectable characters as being completely qualified in every respect to take charge of and superintend the education of a small number of boys. . . . I wrote to Colo. Hamilton on the subject. . . . His answer . . . mentioned the number of twelve boys, and that six hundred dollars per annum would be given in full for all services &c. &c. This was communicated to the Gentleman who had been recommended . . . (and was accepted by him . . ." (ALS, George Washington Papers, Library of Congress).

To Benjamin Lincoln

Treasury Department, August 27, 1792. "I received your letter of the 17th Instant, enclosing an application from Mr Foster for the payment of certain drawbacks. As the case is stated, it is such an one, in which the Law is precise: & there is no discretionery power vested in me. . . ."

LS, RG 36, Collector of Customs at Boston, Letters from the Treasury, 1789–1818 (vol. unnumbered), National Archives; copy, RG 56, Letters to Collectors at Small Ports, "Set G," National Archives; copy, RG 56, Letters to the Collector at Boston, National Archives.

Treasury Department Circular
to the Collectors of the Customs

Treasury Department
August 27th, 1792.

Sir,

It would be of use in regard to the Return of exports, which is transmitted quarterly to this Office by the Collectors, if the exported articles were uniformly arranged in alphabetic order.[1]

With a view to this, I enclose you a form of such an alphabetical arrangement, and request that for the future you will have the articles of exports inserted in the said Return, agreeably to that form; expressing the different quantities of each article as therein prescribed. In all other respects the form of the Return of Exports will remain as heretofore.

I have to desire that you will furnish me with a monthly abstract of all Licenses which shall be granted to coasting and fishing vessels in your district, to be forwarded after the expiration of every month. The annexed form will shew the particulars to be inserted. It is of course not required that copies or duplicates of Licenses should be transmitted to the Treasury, as has been done in some instances.

A difference of opinion between the Collectors and Supervisors has occurred in regard to the seventh section of the Act "concerning the Duties on Spirits distilled within the United States, &c."[2] The true construction is, that the abatement of two per cent. for leakage, is to be made, on securing the Duty at the end of the quarter from the whole quantity distilled during the preceding three months —and hence it will be necessary that in cases of exportation, the

Drawbacks on distilled Spirits be adjusted with an eye to this allowance.

A doubt has arisen on the 35th, or more properly the 36th Section of the Collection Law,[3] whether molasses is to be considered as within the meaning of that Section. I am of opinion, it is, and that the allowance of two per cent. for leakage ought to be extended to that article.

With great consideration, I am, Sir, Your obedient Servant

A Hamilton

LS, to Jedediah Huntington, Federal Records Center, Boston; LS, to Jeremiah Olney, Rhode Island Historical Society, Providence; LS, Office of the Secretary, United States Treasury Department; L[S], RG 36, Collector of Customs at Boston, Letters from the Treasury, 1789–1818 (vol. unnumbered), National Archives; LS, MS Division, New York Public Library; LS, Mr. Walter N. Eastburn, East Orange, New Jersey; copy, RG 56, Circulars of the Office of the Secretary, "Set T," National Archives; copy, United States Finance Miscellany, Treasury Circulars, Library of Congress.

1. See Joseph Nourse to H, August 17, 1792.
2. See Jeremiah Olney to H, August 14, 1792; H to Olney, August 25, 1792.
3. For an explanation of the mistake in the section numbering of "An Act to provide more effectually for the collection of the duties imposed by law on goods, wares and merchandise imported into the United States, and on the tonnage of ships or vessels" (1 *Stat.* 145–78 [August 4, 1790]), see "Treasury Department Circular to the Collectors of the Customs," August 6, 1792.
Section 35 of this act reads as follows: "*And be it further enacted,* That there shall be an allowance for leakage of two per cent. on the quantity which shall appear by the gauge to be contained in any cask of liquors subject to duty by the gallon" (1 *Stat.* 166).

To George Washington

Treasury Departmt: Augt. 27. 1792.

Sir,

By the Act of the last Session entitled "An Act supplementary to the Act making provision for the Debt of the United States,"[1] authority is given to discharge the debts due to foreign Officers out of the monies which the President is authorised to borrow by the Act making provision for the Debt of the United States.[2]

The sum authorised to be borrowed by the last mentioned Act is 12.000.000. of Dollars. The whole amount of the foreign debt, exclusive of that due to foreign Officers, was 11.710.378 Dollars & 62 Cents. The difference is 289.621. Dollars & 38 cents, which is greater than the sum due to foreign Officers being about 230.000 Dollars. This debt being payable in Paris and bearing an interest of six per Cent, it is for the advantage of the United States to discharge it as soon as possible. The last loan will be a convenient fund for the purpose, and if approved by the President a part of it will be so applied.[3]

Should it appear to the President adviseable to direct this payment —a second question arises, namely, whether it shall be made in Assignats, or in a mode which shall exempt the parties from the loss which would attend the depreciation of those securities—without however occasioning loss to the United States. The last appears best to accord with the justice & reputation of the Government.

With the highest respect and the truest attachment, I have the honor to be &c.   A. Hamilton

P.S. Your Letter of the 13. instant & the Contract concerning the N. Hampshire Lighthouse were duly received.

LC, George Washington Papers, Library of Congress.
1. 1 *Stat.* 281–83 (May 8, 1792).   2. 1 *Stat.* 138–44 (August 4, 1790).
3. For a description of the 1792 Holland loan to which H is referring, see William Short to H, June 28, 1792, note 17. For background concerning the debt due to foreign officers and the payment to discharge this debt, see Short to H, August 3, 1790, note 5; H to Short, August 16, 1792.

From Joseph Willard

Harvard University in Cambridge
August 27. 1792.

Sir,

I have the honor and pleasure of acquainting you, that at our last Commencement, the degree of Doctor of Laws was conferred upon you.[1] The Corporation and Overseers of this University were happy, in having this opportunity of honoring the Society, by enrolling in their Catalogue the name of a Gentleman so highly distinguished in the literary and political world, and of publickly testifying their esteem of the Minister, to whose wisdom and unremitted exertions these United States owe so much of their present tranquility and prosperity, and the national respectability.

I shall send you a Diploma as soon as it can conveniently be engrossed. In the mean time, give me leave to subscribe,

with sentiments of the highest esteem & respect, Sir, your most humble & obedient servant   Joseph Willard Presdt.

Alexander Hamilton Esqr.

ALS, Hamilton Papers, Library of Congress.
1. A notice in the [Philadelphia] *General Advertiser* on July 31, 1792, stated that "at the late commencement at the University of CAMBRIDGE" the "degree of DOCTOR OF LAWS was conferred on his Excellency John Hancock, Esq. His Honour Samuel Adams, Esq. the Honourable Alexander Hamilton, Esq. the Hon. Francis Dana Esq. and the Hon. John Lowell, Esq."

To William Carmichael [1]

Treasury Department, Philadelphia
Augt 28 1792

Sir

It has been represented to me by the Accounting Officers of the Treasury that a regular account of all the monies which have been received by you from our Commissioners in Europe, or which have been paid by them by your direction, would be requisite in the examination and adjustment of the accounts of the said Commissioners.

I have therefore to request that you will furnish me with an account, comprising those objects, down to the 1st of November 1792. As the document called for will be considered as an essential guide in the Settlement which is contemplated, I shall make no apology for troubling you on the occasion.

With great consideration and esteem, I am, Sir, Your Obed Servant   Alexander Hamilton

William Carmichael Esqr
Charge des Affaires of the U. S.
Madrid

LS, from a typescript furnished by Mr. Frank L. Pleadwell, Honolulu, Hawaii.
1. On January 24, 1792, Carmichael, who had been United States chargé

d'affaires in Madrid since 1789, was appointed one of the commissioners to negotiate a treaty with Spain. See "Notes on Thomas Jefferson's Report of Instructions for the Commissioners to Spain," March 1–4, 1792, note 1.

From William Ellery

Colles Off: [Newport, Rhode Island] 28th Augt 1792

Sir,

In the last Proviso of the 2nd. Sec: of the Act concerning certain fisheries &c.[1] the quantity of fish when dried and cured fit for Exportation is to be ascertained according to the weight when *actually sold;* which account of the weight &c. shall in all cases be produced and sworn or affirmed to before the Collector of the District to entitle the owner, his agent or lawful representative to receive the allowance.

Out of this Proviso several questions have arisen; First whether the Fish which the owners & fisherman take to their own and for their own comsumption are to be reckoned in the Computn of twelve Qunitals for each ton. Second, Whether the Fish exported by the Owners or Fishermen, or that which is *sold* for home Consumption is to be considered in the Computation aforesaid. Of Fish imported by Vessels of more than five tons and less than twenty tons, as well as by vessels of twenty tons or upwards a part is frequently consumed by the owners or fishermen or both, or sold for domestic consumption, and a part may be exported by either of them. Third, Whether the fish to be weighed by a weigher of, and at the expence of the United States? Fourth, Who is to take the Oath before the Collector required in said Proviso?

Some fishing vessels, have already arrived in this District, their pares have been cured, and their pares distributed; and I am suspicious that some of them will fail of the promised allowance through a misunderstanding of the Law. Please to favour me with an early answer to these questions, and you'll oblige [2]

Yr. most obedt. servant   Wm Ellery Colle

A Hamilton Esqr.
Secry of T. U. States

LC, Newport Historical Society, Newport, Rhode Island.

1. Section 2 of "An Act concerning certain Fisheries of the United States, and for the regulation and government of the Fishermen employed therein" reads in part as follows: ". . . there shall also be paid to the owner of every fishing boat or vessel of more than five tons, and less than twenty tons, . . . by the collector of the district where such boat or vessel may belong, the sum of one dollar upon every ton admeasurement of such boat or vessel; which allowance shall be accounted for as part of the proceeds of the fares of said boat or vessel, and shall accordingly be so divided among all persons interested therein: . . . *And provided also,* That such boat or vessel shall have landed in the course of said preceding season, a quantity of fish not less than twelve quintals for every ton of her admeasurement; the said quantity of fish to be ascertained when dried and cured fit for exportation, and according to the weight thereof, as the same shall weigh at the time of delivery when actually sold . . ." (1 *Stat.* 230 [February 16, 1792]).

2. Ellery endorsed this letter "Answered by the Comptroller."

From Jeremiah Olney

Providence, August 28, 1792. "I have received your circular Letter of the 6th. Instant. Attention shall be paid to your directions. . . ."

ADfS, Rhode Island Historical Society, Providence.

To William Short

Treasury Department,
Philadelphia Augt 28. 1792

Sir

It has been represented to me by the accounting Officers of the Treasury that a regular account of all the monies which have been received by you from our Commissioners[1] in Europe, or which have been paid by them by your direction, would be requisite in the examination and adjustment of the accounts of the said Commissioners.

I have therefore to request that you will furnish me with an account, comprising those objects, down to the first of November 1792.

As the document called for will be considered as an essential guide in the settlement which is contemplated, I shall make no apology for troubling you on the occasion.

Your account, as Secretary to the Embassy in France, I understand has been presented at the Treasury by Mr Jefferson, terminating on the 24th of September 1789; but none has been rendered since.

With respectful consideration,   I am, Sir,   Your Obedt Servant.

Alexander Hamilton

William Short, Esquire,
Minister Resident
at the Hague.

LS, William Short Papers, Library of Congress.
1. Willink, Van Staphorst, and Hubbard.

To Wilhem and Jan Willink, Nicholaas and Jacob Van Staphorst, and Nicholas Hubbard

[*Philadelphia, August 28, 1792.* On September 19, 1792, Hamilton wrote to Willink, Van Staphorst, and Hubbard: "You will herewith receive duplicates of my letters to you under date the 28th. ultimo." *Letters not found.*]

To the President and Directors of the Bank of the United States [1]

Treasury Department
August 29 1792

Gentlemen

Samuel Meredith, Esquire,[2] having been constituted Agent to the Board of Commissioners for purchasing the debt of the United States, agreeably to a resolve of the Board of the 13th of July last,[3] I have to request that you will cause to be passed to the Credit of the said Samuel Meredith, as Agent to the Board, the amount of all the Dividends which shall appear to be due to the Commissioners named in the Act, "making Provision for the Reduction of the public debt."[4] He will receipt in the dividend book as in other cases.

I have the honor to be,   Gentlemen,   Your Obedt Servant

Alexander Hamilton
Secy of the Treasy

The President and Directors
of the Bank of the United States.

LS, Office of the Secretary, United States Treasury Department.
  1. Thomas Willing was president of the Bank of the United States.
  2. Meredith was treasurer of the United States.
  3. See "Meeting of the Commissioners of the Sinking Fund," July 13, 1792.
  4. 1 *Stat.* 186 (August 12, 1790). Under this act the Vice President, the Chief Justice, the Attorney General, the Secretary of State, and the Secretary of the Treasury were appointed commissioners of the sinking fund. The appropriation of the interest on the debt purchased by the commissioners, to which H is referring, was made by Section 6 of "An Act supplementary to the act making provision for the Debt of the United States" (1 *Stat.* 282–83 [May 8, 1792]). This second act also changed the rules governing the commissioners in purchasing the debt.

From Thomas Newton, Junior

Norfolk [*Virginia*] *August 29, 1792.* "I now inclose you a letter I have just received from Mr Jno. McCoomb respecting the Light house. The terms of payment you are so well acquainted with that there needs no comment from me on it.[1] I have to observe that Mr. McComb is deserving of every indulgence from the public for his activity in executing the work, the whole of which I expect will be finished by the time he mentions. . . ."

ALS, RG 26, Lighthouse Letters Received, Vol. "A," Pennsylvania and Southern States, National Archives.
  1. The terms of payment for the Cape Henry lighthouse are specified in the contract between John McComb, Jr., and H, which is dated March 31, 1791.

To Richard Harison [1]

Treasury Department
August 30. 1792.

Sir

On the 28th of October 1790 a contract was entered into with Theodosius Fowler for supplying the army with provisions for the year 1791.[2] Copies of which contract and of the Bond for securing the performance of it are enclosed. By an instrument, bearing date the 3d. day of January 1791, Theodosius Fowler made an assignment of this contract to William Duer, Esquire, constituting him, by the same act, his Attorney. A copy of this instrument is also enclosed.[3] On the 7th of April 1791, after notice of this assignment, I wrote a letter to the said William Duer, of which a copy is likewise herewith transmitted. All warrants which have been issued for money to William Duer describe him expressly as *Agent* to Theodosius Fowler.

On the foregoing state of facts I request your opinion whether Theodosius Fowler and his sureties do or not continue responsible to the Governmt for the fulfilment of the contract.[4]

No other transactions between the Treasury and the Parties have had place, which can at all affect the question.

For the opinion which you shall give you will please to make a charge against this Department.

With great consideration and esteem, I am, Sir, Your Obedt Servant.   Alexander Hamilton

Richard Harison, Esqr,
New York

LS, New-York Historical Society, New York City.
   1. Harison was United States attorney for the District of New York.
   2. See "Contract for Army Rations," October 28, 1790, and H to William Duer, April 7, 1791. See also Joseph Nourse to H, May 1, 1792, note 1.
   3. Copy, New-York Historical Society, New York City.
   4. Several opinions concerning this question were submitted to the committee which was considering a report of the House of Representatives of May 8, 1792, concerning the failure of the expedition against the Indians led by Major General Arthur St. Clair in the fall of 1791. The revised report, presented on February 15, 1793, states: "The Secretary of the Treasury has furnished the committee with the written opinions of the Attorney General of the United States, and several other lawyers of eminence, all of whom concur in opinion, that the securities to the bond . . . are now responsible for all damages" (*ASP, Military Affairs*, I, 42).

To John Kilty

[*Philadelphia, August 30, 1792.* On the back of the letter which Kilty wrote to Hamilton on August 20, 1792, Hamilton wrote:

"Answered provisionally Aug 30, 1792 reserved for consulting Comptroller." *Letter not found.*]

To Charles Lee

Treasury Department, August 30, 1792. "In my letter to you of the 4th Ultimo I did not mention that a boat would be to be procured for harbour service, in the room of the one which has been delivered to the Collector of Cedar Point.[1] This is however to be understood, and if it has not already been done, I request that a suitable one may be provided. . . ."

LS, RG 56, Letters to and from the Collector at Alexandria, National Archives; LS, RG 56, Letters to Collectors at Small Ports, "Set G," National Archives.

1. John Coats Jones.

From Jeremiah Olney [1]

Custom-House,
Providence 30th August 1792.

Sir.

The importation into this District, made by Mr. Cutts of Portsmouth, was on the 28th Day of May last, in the Ship Lark, Jno. Munro Master from Bordeaux. I do not recollect whether the Invoice specified the difference between Assignats and Specie; but the Duties (secured by Messrs. Clark & Nightingale,[2] owners of the Lark) were calculated on the latter amount, being 1,487 Dollars and 35½ Cents, ascertained by the best Evidence which could then be obtained; and I well remember that, at the time the purchases were made, it appeared the Assignats had depreciated 33⅓ ⅌Cent. There were no peculiar circumstances attending this Importation; nor were there any Ad Valorem Goods imported into this District from France, in April last.

I enclose my Return of Cash No. 108.

I have the Honr. to be &c.   Jereh. Olney Collr.

A. Hamilton Esquire
Secy. of the Treasury.

ADfS, Rhode Island Historical Society, Providence.
  1. For background to this letter, see H to Olney, August 18, 1792.
  2. The Providence merchant and trading firm of John Clark and Joseph Nightingale.

To William Rawle [1]

Treasury Department, August 30, 1792. Requests Rawle's opinion concerning Theodosius Fowler's contract for supplying the Army.[2]

LS, Historical Society of Pennsylvania, Philadelphia.
  1. Rawle was United States attorney for the District of Pennsylvania.
  2. With the exception of minor changes in wording, this letter is the same as the letter H sent to Richard Harison on this date.

From James Reynolds [1]

Philadelphia 30th Aug. 1792.

Honored Sir,
  you will I hope pardon me if I intrude on your goodness thinking the multiplycity of business. you have to encounter With. has been the cause of my not hereing from you. which induces me to write the Second time. flatering myself it will be in your Power to Comply with my Request.[2] which I shall make it my whole Study. to Remit it to you as soon as its in my power your Compyance dear Sir will very much
  Oblige your most Obed. and Humble Servant.   James Reynolds
                                  Vine street No. 161, one door from
                                  the Corner of Fifth Street,
Alexander Hamilton, Esq.

"Reynolds Pamphlet," August 31, 1797.
  1. This letter is printed as document No. XXII in the appendix of the "Reynolds Pamphlet," August 31, 1797.
  For background to this letter, see Reynolds to H, December 15, 17, 19, 22, 1791, January 3, 17, March 24, April 3, 7, 17, 23, May 2, June 3–22, 23, 24, August 24, 1792; H to Reynolds, December 15, 1791, April 7, June 3–22, 24, 1792; Maria Reynolds to H, December 15, 1791, January 23–March 18, March 24, June 2, 1792.
  2. See Reynolds to H, August 24, 1792.

From William Seton

New York 30 Aug. 1792

My Dear sir

Your last Letters were delivered to me just at the Moment of severe affliction.[1] I have not been able to look over them till now which I know your feeling Heart will excuse and lament with me the occasion.

The Letter for St. Vincents was forwarded by a Vessell that sailed on Sunday.[2] I could not find any Person that knew Mr. Donald.[3] My Son made particular enquirys from the Merchants here connected with that Island. The Governor is a Colonel Seton.[4] He is a distant relation of mine, but I am not personally known to him. However I would take the liberty of writing to him, if it would be doing you the least pleasure.

Agreeably to your request I enclose your Account with the Bank,—the Note for 500 Dolls was discounted & the dft of 100 paid —that there is a Balance now due you of $175\,^{31}\!/_{100}$.[5] I thank you much for the explanation of the late conduct of the Branch.[6] I must confess I was rather apprehensive it proceeded from other Motives. It is alarming to see how Banks are ⟨mu⟩ltiplying all over the States. Should any failure happen, a general discredit will fall upon all Bank Paper.

Mr. Pearce [7] the Manufacturer called upon me the other day, to shew me his Books when he had accounted for the 120 Dollars I advanced him on his arrival. I fear the repayment to me will be forgot unless the Directors of the Society are notified. I will thank you to put me on the mode of recovery.

I am with the sincerest esteem & respect   Dear sir   Your Obligd Obdt. Hue Servt   Wm Seton

Alexr. Hamilton Esqr.

ALS, Hamilton Papers, Library of Congress.

    1. Only one of the letters to which Seton is referring has been found. See H to Seton, August 17, 1792.

    On August 29, 1792, the [Philadelphia] *Gazette of the United States* printed the following notice: "Died in New-York, on Tuesday last, Mrs. Anna Maria

Seton, age 36 after a tedious illness, the much beloved comfort of William Seton, Eqr."
2. See H to Seton, August 17, 1792.   3. See H to Seton, August 17, 1792.
4. James Seton was governor of St. Vincent from 1787 to 1797.
5. See Seton to H, May 28, June 25, and August 6, 1792.
6. See H to Seton, August 17, 1792.
7. William Pearce was an employee of the Society for Establishing Useful Manufactures. See Seton to H, June 11, 25, 1792.

From William Short

The Hague Aug 30. 1792

Sir

I had the honor of writing to you on the 6th inst. previously to my going to Amsterdam to sign the contract & bonds of the last or second 4 p. cent loan.[1] Since my return here I have recd. from Mr. Pinckney [2] your letters of June 14—June 23 with its enclosures—& June 30. These letters were recieved here the 17th inst. being sent by Mr. Pinckney with the idea, that they would be forwarded to me; as he has since informed me, not supposing that I had long ago left Holland. My letters written to you & the sec. of State will have shewn how this came not to be the case.[3]

My letters also will have shewn you sir my anxiety with respect to 1. The depreciation of the Antwerp payments not being settled & my apprehension for a short time past of its not being done with the then existing government. 2. the delay of the payments from Amsterdam & consequent accumulation of monies at a dead interest in the hands of our bankers.[4] I have now the mortification to inform you that the event which I so feared has taken place, namely the expiration of the late government without the adjustment of the depreciation.[5] I will not importune you with what I have so often mentioned of the steps by which these delays have been occasioned,

ALS, letterpress copy, William Short Papers, Library of Congress.
1. The Holland loan of 1792. For a description of this loan, see Short to H, June 28, 1792, note 17.
2. Thomas Pinckney, United States Minister to Great Britain.
3. See Short to H, June 28, August 6, 1792. Short's letters of explanation to Thomas Jefferson, dated June 29 and July 20, 1792, may be found in RG 59, Despatches from United States Ministers to France, 1789–1869, January 16, 1791–August 6, 1792, National Archives.
4. See Short to H, June 28, August 6, 1792.
5. On August 10 the Jacobins had seized control of the French government and imprisoned the royal family.

& of the unavoidable passage of this business from my hands into those of M Morris. I think you will feel sir that restricted as I was from the month of Nov. last—knowing from the President's instructions to you, that it was his intention that arrangements with respect to the French debt should be made by the representative of the U.S. residing at Paris [6]—knowing that he well with respect to a permanent representative could not but be pronounced about the time—every consideration of delicacy & propriety forbad me imperiously from putting myself forward in the business & anticipating on his will where it was evident that a short delay (during which there was every reason to believe it would be pronounced) could not be prejudicial. I have repeated to you sir, these considerations even to satiety; yet my anxiety on the subject, as I apprehend more & more the interests of the U.S. will suffer from the delay, increasing daily I find it impossible to pass them over in silence, & particularly as the delay & blame might otherwise be attributed to me.

Your letter of June the 14th. recd. the 17th. inst. which tells me that the management of this matter as well as every other which may concern the reimbursement to France is to remain with me, has added beyond measure to my anxiety because I fear that this having been your intention, you will think that I ought to have understood it so & acted accordingly; in which case the disadvantages arising from delay might be imputed to me. Yet I flatter myself sir if you will have the goodness to transfer yourself for an instant to my position from the month of Nov. last to the time of recieving your last letter you will find it impossible for me not to have acted as I did until the 15th. of Jany. when I returned from Holland to Paris—from that time not to have waited until I should learn whom the President designated for Paris—& from the moment of learning the person & expecting him immediately to arrive not to await that arrival—& from that time not to consider the business as in his hands; & particularly as he seemed perfectly disposed to undertake it, as soon as he should have been properly recognized by the King. Yet I have never ceased writing & urging him on the subject & pointing out what appeared to me an inevitable means of forcing France to

6. See George Washington to H, August 28, 1790.

accelerate the arrangement desired. As this has not been done I cannot but suppose that M Morris has found it impracticable. Previously
to recieving your letter abovementioned the King was suspended &
the government of France as acknowleged by other powers overturned, & the authority usurped by men who from the nature of
things cannot hold it. This puts it out of my power or any other
person's for the present, from doing any thing in this business,
or any other with that country. It is impossible to say how long
this position of affairs will last. There will probably be several
changes before a permanent order is established—this of course will
occasion a suspension in our payments to that country which cannot
but be prejudicial to the interests of the U.S.—& the more so as the
large sums wch our bankers have on hand at Amsterdam become
every day more considerable & more embarrassing in every way.
The interest paid on it being pure loss—& there being always a
kind of risk however inconsiderable in leaving so large sums in the
hands of any house whatever. It is useless to mention these sums here.
The last acct forwarded by the bankers will have informed you how
it then stood—& at present they inform me that there remain about
1000 bonds only to be delivered.

I have frequently mentioned to you in what manner I had urged
the settling a mode with France of recieving the monies now on
hand. A few days previous to the King's suspension M. Morris
agreed with the commissaries that they should recieve ƒ1,625,000 &
wrote to America to direct that payment—the depreciation being
left unsettled; [7] settled it was nothing more than making that payment at the current rate of exchange wch might have been done as
well six months ago. His letter to me on that subject [8] was recieved
here the day after my return from Amsterdam, & at the same time
with the accts of the King's suspension. Still I gave orders to the
bankers to make the payment to the French bankers [9] mentioning

7. Gouverneur Morris wrote to Short concerning this payment on August
6, 1792 (ALS, William Short Papers, Library of Congress). He did not write
to Jefferson, however, until August 16 (ALS, RG 59, Despatches from United
States Ministers to France, 1789–1869, June 17, 1792–March 7, 1794, National
Archives).
8. Morris to Short, August 6, 9, 1792 (ALS, William Short Papers, Library
of Congress).
9. Hogguer, Grand, and Company, bankers for the French government at
Amsterdam.

in the reciept by way of precaution that this was on account of the debt due to France by the U. S. & to be held at the disposition of His Most Christian Majesty. The bankers refuse giving such a reciept—no reciept expressed in general terms, but exort that it should be expressed "qu'ils s'engagent a la *requisition* de la dit Sieur Short à ne se desaisir de cet argent qu'avec le plein & libre consentement de S. M. T. C." This wd be an express locking up of that money in their hands & of course preclusion of the U. S. from an abatement of interest thereon after the time of payment. It would be in fact nothing more than having the money in the hands of the French bankers instead of ours. I have therefore refused the condition—& still hope they will recieve it on a general rect., without any requisition on our part, but in such manner as not to leave it at the disposition of the present governing company in France, in which case the payment would be certainly contested by whatever government shall be instituted in future. I will inform you immediately on this matter being finally settled—wch. must be in a very short time. I have written to M. Morris on the subject.[10]

As there will still remain considerable sums on hand for which the payments to France may not present an outlet soon I hope you will give orders respecting them—two millions & an half will of course be kept to answer the orders you may give as announced in your letter to me of April 2d.

I shall give directions also for paying off the Spanish debt interest & principal, as stated to me formerly by you. I have no hesitation in doing this as your letter on that subject [11] shewed it wd have been agreeable to you. I have written to M. Carmichael [12] to inform him of this intention & to desire him to ascertain in what kind of money the debt is expressed—as there are different kinds of Dollars in their monetary system & of different value. I shall direct the bankers to remit bills to Madrid on the most advantageous terms, until I tell them to cease—& I shall keep within bounds until I recieve the answer from M. Carmichael.

Russia has lately opened a loan at Amsterdam at 4⅞ p. cent. It

10. Short to Morris, August 28, 1792 (ALS, Columbia University Libraries).
11. See H to Short, March 5, 1792.
12. Short to William Carmichael, Minister Resident for the United States in Spain, August 21, 28, 30, 1792 (ALS, letterpress copies, William Short Papers, Library of Congress).

would be difficult if not impossible therefore for any other power
to effect one in that market at a lower rate.

I have the honor to add assurances of the respect & attachment
with which I am, sir, your most obed't humble servt   W Short

The Honble
Alexander Hamilton Secretary of the Treasury Philadelphia

To John Wendell

Philadelphia
Augt 30 1792

Sir

I have to acknowledge your favr of the 23d of July.[1]

You are right in your conjecture that no report was made on the
case of Mr Dumon.[2]

It arose partly from my press of business & partly from a persua-
sion, that a report, if made would not have been acted upon, in the
then Session.

With regard to further evidence, I doubt how far any particular
trouble on that subject ought to be recommended. If aditional proof
respecting the burning of the house, & the reasons for it, could conveniently be obtained, it may be advisable to do it.

I learn with pleasure the family connection which subsists between
you & Mrs Hamilton [3] and should be glad to render you any good
offices in my power. You judge rightly, in the supposition, that my
present situation precludes an agency in the affair of the land in
which you are interested. Your hint respecting your son will be
borne in mind; if any thing should occur, in which his interest &
that of the public can be conciliated it will be a satisfaction to me,
to promote it.

With Esteem & Regard   I am, Sir   Yr Ob Servt
Alexander Hamilton

John Wendell Esqr
Portsmouth

LS, Massachusetts Historical Society, Boston.
    1. Letter not found.

2. On December 21, 1791, the House of Representatives recorded receipt of "A petition of Jean Baptist Dumon, son and heir of Jean Baptist Dumon, deceased, late of Canada, merchant, praying to be reimbursed certain advances made by the deceased, for the support of the American Army, and also for losses and injuries sustained, both in his person and property, by adhering to the American cause, during the late war" (*Journal of the House*, I, 479). The petition was referred to the Secretary of the Treasury, who was directed to examine it and give his opinion on it.

3. "Captain Johannes Wendell, a merchant . . . married a daughter of Dr. Abraham Staats. . . . He died in middle life, and his widow married Johannes Schuyler, the grandfather of General Philip Schuyler" (George W. Schuyler, *Colonial New York: Philip Schuyler and His Family* [New York, 1885] II, 318).

To Sebastian Bauman [1]

[*Philadelphia, August 31, 1792*. On September 3, 1792, Bauman wrote to Hamilton: "I have recieved your favour of 31st Ult." *Letter not found.*]

1. Bauman was postmaster at New York City.

To Charles Lee

Treasury Department, August 31, 1792. Encloses a copy of a letter which he has received from Francis Cabot.[1] Concludes that if Lee is "satisfied of the truth of what is alleged, and no prosecution has been commenced, it will be agreeable to me that the wine be surrendered."

LS, RG 56, Letters to and from the Collector at Alexandria, National Archives; copy, RG 56, Letters to Collectors at Small Ports, "Set G," National Archives.

1. Cabot to H, August 22, 1792.

From Nicholas Low [1]

New York August 31. 1792

Dear sir

The inclosed [2] I have this Moment recd. and have only to add that any Negociations you may make [3] in Consequence will be confirmed.

Fearing to be too late for this post—I conclude in Haste. Dr. sr.
yours sincerely &ca   Nichs. Low

ALS, Hamilton Papers, Library of Congress.
1. For background to this letter, see "Draft Minutes of a Meeting of a
Committee of the Directors of the Society for Establishing Useful Manufactures," August 1, 1792.
2. The enclosure was a letter to Low from John N. Cumming, accountant
for the Society for Establishing Useful Manufactures. Dated August 30, 1792,
it reads in part as follows: "Mr. Pierce has received a letter from his brass
Founder now in Philada informing that a quantity of Metal is expected there
in about two Weeks. None is to be had in New York as it was all purchased
up by a founder from Philada. Perhaps there may be some old brass Cannon
at West point that are useless to the United States and might be had by
applying to General Knox. Colo Hambleton would be a pro[per] person to
apply to & sepossing it most proper that application to him should come thro
you I have thought proper to trouble you thus far as a considerable quantity
of Metal will be wanting" (ALS, Hamilton Papers, Library of Congress).
3. H endorsed this letter as follows: "Answer. The object would neither be
obtainable nor adviseable." Letter not found.

From Henry Marchant

Rhode Island District
Newport Augt. 31. 1792.

In pursuance of an Act of the Congress of the United States "to
provide for the mitigating or remitting Forfeitures and Penalties
accruing under the Revenue Laws, in certain Cases therein mentioned"[1] I have recd. the Petition of Thomas Hazard Junr. of St.
Peters in the Island of St Johns owner and Master of a certain Vessell called the rising Sun[2] hereto annexed, and thereupon caused
Jeremiah Olney Collector, Ebenezer Thompson Naval Officer and
William Barton Surveyor of Providence District, the persons claim-
ing a Moiety of the said Vessell and Her Cargo now libelled before
me, if a Forfeiture should take Place, and also William Channing
Esqr. Atty. of the United States for this District to be noticed to
appear before me and shew Cause if any they have against the
Mitigation or Remission thereof who severally returning for Answer
that they conceived there was not necessity for Their Attendance,
I proceeded to examine into the Truth of the Facts set forth by the
said Petitioner in a summary Manner. The said Vessell, a Schooner,
was seised by the Collector for the Port of Providence on the twenty

fourth Day of August Currant having entered that Port the Day before from Hallifax having on Board a Cargo of Fish consisting of about one hundred Barrells of Mackerel and forty three smoaked Salmon stored in Bulk, in Said Schooner appears by the British Register to be of the Burthen of Thirty two and three Quarter Tons, but upon remeasurement Her actual Burthen is only Twenty three Tons and sixty one Ninety fifths of a Ton, The British Register bears date the twenty third Day of June AD 1787. And it appears by said Register That the sd. Petitioner and Thos. Hazard Senr. and Wm. Hazard of St Peters are sole Owners of said Schooner And that She is British built, By the Declaration of the Petitioner under Oath by me administered to him, and by other Circumstances, it appears to me that, the said Schooner was, once or twice previous to the adoption of the present Constitution by this State[3] particularly in the Year 1789, entered at the sd. Port of Providence, and paid Light Money agreably to Her Tunnage by the British Register. And the Petitioner further on solemn Oath did declare, that from that Circumstance, not himself knowing her Tunnage but from the Register, did presume it was her real Tunnage.[4] That He never was Captain of sd. Scooner, or of any other Vessell before—That unsuspicious of any Difficulty he openly entered the Port of Providence and applied to the Custom House at Providence in the usual Manner. All which I do hereby certify to the Secretary of the Treasury of the United States   Hy: Marchant

Judge of Rhode Island District

ADfS, Rhode Island Historical Society, Providence.

1. "An Act to provide for mitigating or remitting the forfeitures and penalties accruing under the revenue laws, in certain cases therein mentioned" (1 Stat. 122–23 [May 26, 1790]).

2. For an earlier reference to this case, see Jeremiah Olney to H, August 25, 1792.

3. Rhode Island adopted the Constitution on May 29, 1790.

4. For the British law concerning admeasurement, see H to James Duane, August 4, 1791, note 2. The collectors of the customs were required to measure every foreign ship subject to tonnage duties because foreign regulations uniformly resulted in a lighter tonnage. See "Treasury Department Circular to the Collectors of the Customs," December 22, 1789, September 21, 1791.

The vessel in this case was subject to forfeiture because her tonnage by American measurement was less than the thirty tons requisite to enable her to import foreign merchandise. This was a requirement of Section 70 of "An Act to provide more effectually for the collection of the duties imposed by law on goods, wares and merchandise imported into the United States, and on the tonnage of ships or vessels" (1 Stat. 177 [August 4, 1790]).

To George Nicholas [1]

Treasury Department
August 31st 1792.

Sir,

A Claim I understand is made by certain Inhabitants of Kentucky upon Messrs. Elliot & Williams [2] in their capacity of Quarter Masters to the United States for the *hire* of Horses which were killed or lost in the expedition under General Harmar; [3] the appraised value of which has already been paid to the owners.

This Claim has only lately come under my notice and my first impression was that it ought to be admitted. But having had a conversation upon the subject with the Secretary at War, I learn from him, that, he, some considerable time since, received information from very authentic sources, that it has been a constant practice in Kentucky in such Cases to receive payment for the *Value* of the Horses and to wave the *hire* that the Records and files of the public Offices of Virginia will probably shew a variety of instances in which this Rule has been the guide, and that in fine it is to be deemed *the usage of the Country*.

To this representation my first impression has of course given way, I no longer feel myself at liberty to authorise the admission of the Claim in its present extent until the fact of the usage alledged to exist has been satisfactorily ascertained either in the affirmative or negative.

I learn that a suit has been had in the District Federal Court, in which the Claim has been decided against the public.[4] But I am not apprised how far the defence was urged on the ground I have stated, nor how far the circumstances of the decision intitled it to weight. I cannot therefore take that example as a guide without further investigation.

It is consequently my wish that a second defence may be made in some other Suit, with the advantage of a Struck Jury and of full evidences as to the usage in question. If the nature of the settlements which may have been made with the State of Virginia cannot be established by testimony on the Spot, it is my desire that a Commission be taken out to examine the public Offices in that State. I shall in the mean time make inquiry there and communicate the result. Messrs. Elliot and Williams are desired to apprise you of any suit which may be brought against them, in order that you may pay the requisite attention to it.

Another Suit, if determined against the public, without apparently exceptionable circumstances, will be definitive with me. For this reason, to give it the greater authority as a Justification you will move the Court for a new Trial.

I am aware that at Common Law, in ordinary Cases, the hire is the thing recoverable, but then the loss of the Horse from any accident would be that of the Owner. It is Just that in case of a military expedition (which involves extraordinary Risk) he should be indemnified against such Loss; but if usage declares, that this is all he shall have that usage ought to prevail where no agreement to the contrary is made. The Rule ought to work both ways. The presumption must be that the Risk of loss of the hire is compensated by an increased Rate.

Nevertheless I shall be glad to receive information from you as soon as possible with regard to the course of the late trial; in particular, whether any endeavours were used to prove the usage alledged—whether the testimony was admitted or overruled—and what appeared to be the real state of the fact. If the Judge would also give a Certificate respecting the matter, it would be pleasing to me.

It is possible that these communications may supersede in my Judgment the necessity of another trial.

It is the furthest of all things from my disposition to dispute any Just demand on the public or vex the Citizens with litigious delays. But at the same time it is my duty to guard with circumspection the Interests of the nation, and to see carefully that its money is not expended for purposes, which according to established Rules are not the objects of rightful Claim.

I am Sir &c

Copy, Hamilton Papers, Library of Congress.

1. Nicholas was United States attorney for the District of Kentucky.

2. The partners in the firm of Elliot and Williams, contractors for the western posts, were Robert Elliot and Elie Williams.

3. H is referring to Brigadier General Josiah Harmar, who commanded an expedition of the United States Army and Kentucky militia against the west-

ern Indian tribes in September and October, 1791. For an account of this campaign, see "Conversation with George Beckwith and William Macomb," January 31, 1791.

4. *Philip Buckner* v *Robert Elliot and Elie Williams*, March 20, 1792 (Minutes of the Federal District Court of Kentucky, University of Kentucky, Lexington, Kentucky).

To Thomas Pinckney [1]

Treasury Department, August 31, 1792. Encloses "a letter for our Commissioners at Amsterdam,[2] one for Mr Grand banker at Paris [3] and one for Mr Carmichael" [4] and requests that Pinckney forward them.

LS, Duke University Library.
    1. Pinckney was United States Minister Plenipotentiary to Great Britain.
    2. Willink, Van Staphorst, and Hubbard. Letter not found.
    3. Ferdinand Le Grand. Letter not found.
    4. William Carmichael was the United States chargé d'affaires at Madrid. See H to Carmichael, August 28, 1792.

Treasury Department Circular to the Collectors of the Customs

Treasury Department,
August 31st, 1792.

Sir,

Agreeably to an order of the Senate of the United States, passed on the 7th of May last, a copy of which is herewith transmitted,[1] I have to request that you will furnish me, immediately after the first of October next with the particular statements required by the said order. From these a general Abstract is to be formed at the Treasury; and as Uniformity in the mode of stating the receipts and disbursements will facilitate the business, a form is hereto annexed as a guide.[2]

It is my desire that the Collectors will obtain and transmit at the same time similar documents from the Inspectors, Gaugers, Measurers and Weighers, or other persons holding under the Collectors any office or employment from which salaries, fees or emoluments are derived.

I am, with consideration,   Sir, your obedient Servant,

A Hamilton

LS, to Jeremiah Olney, Rhode Island Historical Society, Providence; LS, to
Otho H. Williams, Office of the Secretary, United States Treasury Department; LS, United States Finance Miscellany, Treasury Circulars, Library of
Congress; LS, MS Division, New York Public Library; LS, American Anti-
quarian Society, Worcester, Massachusetts; LS, sold at Sotheby & Company,
London, November 2, 1964, Lot 315.
    1. The Senate order reads as follows: "That the Secretary of the Treasury
do lay before the Senate, at the next session of Congress, a statement of the
salaries, fees, and emoluments, for one year, ending the first day of October
next, to be stated quarterly, of every person holding any civil office or employment under the United States (except the judges,) together with the
actual disbursements and expenses in the discharge of their respective offices
and employments for the same period; and that he do report the name of
every person who shall neglect or refuse to give satisfactory information
touching his office or employment, or the emoluments or disbursements
thereof" (Annals of Congress, III, 138).
    2. The enclosure consists of two columns entitled "A Statement of the
Salary, Fees and Emoluments received by the   of   during one year,
commencing on the 1st of October 1791, and ending on the 1st of October
1792" and "A Statement of the Monies actually disbursed and expended by
the   of   in the discharge of his office and employments, for the period before mentioned."

From George Washington

Mount Vernon 31st. Augt. 1792.

Sir,

The enclosed Letter was written agreeably to the date, but, by an
accident, was omitted when my other letters were sent to the post
office on Monday last; [1] since wch. 'till yesterday afternoon, I have
been absent from home.

On my return, amongst other Letters I found the enclosed from
the Inspector of the 5th. survey in the State of North Carolina.[2] The
picture drawn by him of the temper of the people in the District
entrusted to his Inspection, is a very unpleasant & disagreeable one.
It is forwarded for your consideration, & opinion of the measures
necessary to be taken in the premises; particularly whether the Governor of that State [3] ought to be written to on the subject; and in
that case, to desire that you would draft a letter proper for the
occasion.

Your Letter of the 27. instant is also before me; and my opinion
on the points therein submitted is, that part of the Loan lately ob-

tained in Holland, should be applied in discharge of the Debt due to the foreign Officers agreeably to the Authority given by the Act alluded to in your letter, & because the interest of the United States requires it to be done; and that it ought to be paid in a mode which shall exempt the parties from the loss which would attend the depreciation of Assignats, without, however, occasioning loss to the United States. The first is an act of justice due to the Officers and the latter an act of prudence becoming the Government.

I am Sir &c   G: Washington

LC, George Washington Papers, Library of Congress.
1. For the enclosure, see Washington to H, August 26, 1792.
2. The letter of Joseph McDowell, Jr., to Washington has not been found.
3. Alexander Martin.

To Tench Coxe

Treasury Department September 1st 1792

Sir
After mature reflection upon the communications handed you by the Supervisor of this District,[1] from the Inspector of Survey No 4,[2] I am of opinion, that it is adviseable for the Supervisor immediately to repair in person to that Survey.

LS, Connecticut Historical Society, Hartford.
1. George Clymer was supervisor of the revenue for the District of Pennsylvania.
Opposition to the excise tax on distilled spirits had been expressed in Pennsylvania even before the approval of "An Act repealing, after the last day of June next, the duties heretofore laid upon Distilled Spirits imported from abroad, and laying others in their stead; and also upon Spirits distilled within the United States, and for appropriating the same" (1 *Stat.* 199–214 [March 3, 1791]). It was, however, in the western survey of Pennsylvania that opponents of the act first resorted to force. On September 6, 1791, Robert Johnson, collector for Washington and Allegheny counties, was tarred and feathered near Pigeon Creek. Joseph Fox, a deputy marshal, was sent to serve process on John, Daniel, and David Hamilton because of their alleged part in the incident. Fox, instead, sent a messenger, John Conner, who was tarred and feathered (Leland D. Baldwin, *Whiskey Rebels* [Pittsburgh, 1939], 82–83).
Because of continued criticism of the excise, H suggested alterations in the act in his "Report on the Difficulties in the Execution of the Act Laying Duties on Distilled Spirits," March 5, 1792. The law was amended by "An Act concerning the Duties on Spirits distilled within the United States" (1 *Stat.* 267–71 [May 8, 1792]).
2. John Neville to Clymer, August 23, 1792 (ALS, Connecticut Historical Society, Hartford). On the cover of Neville's letter H wrote: "concerning Treatment of Faulkner & danger to himself."

The Objects of his journey will be—

I To ascertain the real state of the Survey in its several sub-divisions.

II To inquire carefully concerning the persons, who are represented to have menaced Captain Faulkner, and those who appeared in arms for the purpose of obstructing the law.[3] To obtain evidence, as precise as possible, as well to identify the persons, as to ascertain their language and conduct. To take for this purpose depositions of as many respectable characters as may be knowing to the circumstances, and to engage one or two of the best informed to come to this city. The Secretary at war will direct the commanding officer to order Captain Faulkner hither.[4] Every necessary measure with re-

3. Neville's letter to Clymer of August 23, 1792, states: "I have now to inform you that after many Sollicitations, applications and great trouble I established offices of Inspection in Washington and at Pittsbg.; the House I got at Washington for that purpose belonged to a Captn. Wm. Faulkner who commands a Rifle company in the Service of the United States; I was advised and strongly urged by my Friends respecting the danger which would attend this Measure, however conceiving the Experiment to be necessary I advertised in the Pittsburgh Gazette that I would attend two days in every week at the House of Captn. Wm. Faulkner to receive Entries of Stills &c. which I did until prevented from the Use of the House. Capt. Faulkner when in pursuit of some deserters was encountered by a Number of people in the same Neighbourhood where Mr. Johnson was abused last year, who reproached him for letting his House for such purposes. They drew a knife on him, threatened to scalp him, tar & feather him, and finally to reduce his House and property to ashes if he did not solemnly promise them to prevent the office of Inspection from being there, in consequence of which he sent me the inclosed letter and published the within Notice" (ALS, Connecticut Historical Society, Hartford).

The notice, as reprinted by the [Philadelphia] National Gazette on September 5, 1792, reads as follows: "The Pittsburgh Gazette of August 25 contains the following notification from Capt. Faulkner: 'Notice i[s] hereby given, as an inspection office has been kept by Gen. Neville, at my house in Washington, I hereby inform the public that it shall be kept there no longer. Those who are uneasy and making threats, may give themselves no further trouble.'"

The importance of this action to the collection of the revenue is described by Neville in his letter to Clymer of August 23: "I do not think it will be possible to get another House in Washington County for the purpose, of course I shall be obliged to desist from further attempts to fulfill the law. The office at Pittsburg is open but no person makes an entry, many say they would willingly comply with the Law but for the severe denunciations of fire &c. with which they are threatened in case they do" (ALS, Connecticut Historical Society, Hartford).

4. Henry Knox wrote to General Anthony Wayne concerning Faulkner on September 21, 1792, but by then it had been decided to bring the evidence before the Circuit Court for the Middle Circuit which was scheduled to be held at York, Pennsylvania, on October 11, 1792. Knox wrote: "The Secretary of the Treasury has requested, that in case the Supervisor George Clymer

gard to bearing the expence and compensating for the time of those who may come must be taken.

III To collect evidence respecting the persons, who actually composed the meeting at Pittsburg, on the 21st of August, whose proceedings are published under the signature of John Cannon Chairman, and the particulars of their behaviour.[5] Depositions on those heads will be acceptable.

---

should judge it necessary, that you will preemptorily order Capt Faulkner to repair to York Town in this State in order to give his evidence before the Circuit Court of the United States which will commence its session at that place on the 11th. of October ensuing. You will please to communicate with Mr. Clymer and order Captain Faulkner accordingly . . ." (Knopf, *Wayne*, 105).

5. The meeting to which H is referring was not the first expression of organized opposition to the excise tax in western Pennsylvania. On July 27, 1791, a public meeting at Redstone, Fayette County, had recommended meetings at the county seats of Fayette, Allegheny, Westmoreland, and Washington counties (*The* [New York] *Weekly Museum,* August 20, 1791). On August 23, 1791, the committee of Washington County passed resolutions which were later published in the *Pittsburgh Gazette.* On September 7, 1791, representatives from the four western counties met at Pittsburgh and agreed to several resolutions that were critical not only of the Excise Act but also of the general financial policies of the Secretary of the Treasury (*Pennsylvania Archives,* 2nd ser., IV, 7, 20–22).

H's earliest knowledge of the meeting of August 21–22, 1792, came from Neville's letter to Clymer of August 23, 1792, and the minutes of the meeting which Neville enclosed in his letter. Neville wrote: "About three Weeks ago a Notification appeared in our paper desiring the different districts to meet & choose committee men, the whole to meet at this place on the 21st. Inst., accordingly on that day sundry Persons assembled here, I do not believe the elections were general for you will observe they no longer call themselves a 'Committee' indeed there was not a single person present from Westmoreland County, but two from Alleghany (& those obscure Characters) but from Washington and Fayette came their leading men as you will observe from their Minutes which I inclose you; in the course of their debates they agree'd that if I would resign no other person would '*accept* the appointment:' & that it would give a '*mortal Stab to the Business*'" (ALS, Connecticut Historical Society, Hartford).

The *National Gazette* on August 4, 1792, reprinted a notice which had appeared in the *Pittsburgh Gazette* on July 21, 1792. The notice stated that, in view of the fact that Congress in its last session had not removed "the numerous evils" of which they had earlier complained, "it is hereby earnestly recommended to the inhabitants of the counties of Westmoreland, Washington, Fayette, and Alleghany, to meet at their usual places of electing members of Assembly, &c. on Tuesday the 14th day of August next, and then and there elect not more than three persons as a deputation from each of the election districts in the counties aforesaid, to meet at the house of Josiah Tannehill, in the town of Pittsburgh, on Tuesday the 21st day of the same month of August next, to deliberate on the most adviseable means of obtaining redress in the premises and other grievances" ([Philadelphia] *National Gazette,* August 4, 1792).

IV   To uphold the confidence and encourage the perseverance of the officers under the law. For this purpose, he may assure them, that vigorous measures will very speedily be taken to enforce its execution. And I further authorise him to acquaint them, on my part, that I have the fullest confidence the Government will indem-

---

The minutes of the August 21-22 meeting were issued as a broadside which reads as follows:

"At a Meeting of sundry Inhabitants of the Western Counties of Pennsylvania, held at Pittsburgh, on the 21st day of August, 1792.

"PRESENT. John Canon, William Wallace, Shesbazer Bentley, Bazel Bowel, Benjamin Parkeson, John Huey, John Badollet, John Hamilton, John M'Clel-and, Neal Gillespie, David Bradford, Thomas Gaddis, David Philips, Albert Gallatin, Matthew Jamison, James Marshel, James Robinson, James Stewart, John Smilie, Robert M'Clure, Peter Lisle, Alexander Long, Samuel Wilson, and Edward Cook.

"Colonel JOHN CANON, was placed in the Chair, and ALBERT GALLATIN appointed Clerk.

"THE Excise Law of Congress being taken under consideration and freely debated, a committee of five members was appointed to prepare a draught of Resolutions, expressing the sense of the Meeting on the subject of said Law.

"Adjourned to 10 o'clock to-morrow.

"22d. August, 1792.

"The Members of the Meeting having met according to adjournment, the Committee appointed yesterday made report, which being read twice and debated by paragraphs, was unanimously adopted as followeth, to wit.

"STRONGLY impressed with a sense of the fatal consequences that must attend an Excise, convinced that a tax upon liquors which are the common drink of a nation operates in proportion to the number and not to the wealth of the people, and of course is unjust in itself, and oppressive upon the poor; taught by the experience of other countries that internal taxes upon consumption, from their very nature, never can effectually be carried into operation, without vesting the officers appointed to collect them with powers most dangerous to the civil rights of freemen, and must in the end destroy the liberties of every country in which they are introduced; feeling that the late Excise Law of Congress, from the present circumstances of our agriculture, our want of markets, and the scarcity of a circulating medium, will bring immediate distress and ruin on the Western Country. We think it our duty to persist in our remonstrances to Congress, and in every other legal measure that may obstruct the operation of the Law, until we are able to obtain its total repeal.

"Therefore, Resolved, That David Bradford, James Marshel, Albert Gallatin, Peter Lisle, and David Philips, be appointed for the purpose of drawing a remonstrance to Congress stating our objections against the law that imposes a duty upon spirituous liquors distilled within the United States, and praying for a repeal of the same, and that the Chairman of this Meeting be directed to sign the same in the name of the Meeting, and to take proper measures to have it presented to Congress at their next sessions.

"Resolved, That in order that our measures may be carried on with regularity and concert, that William Wallace, John Hamilton, Shesbazer Bentley, Isaac Weaver, Benjamin Parkinson, David Redick, Thomas Stokely, Stephen Gapen, and Joseph Vanmetre, Andrew Rabb, Thomas Gaddis, Alexander Long, William Whiteside, John Oliphant, Robert M'Clure, and James Lang,

nify any person, whose property may suffer in consequence of his cooperation in the execution of the law, and that I engage to be personally responsible to them for such indemnity, in case of accident to the property of either of them, on account of their official situation and conduct.

V To endeavour to persuade the inhabitants of Alleghany county in particular, to come immediately and voluntarily into the

---

and Thomas B. Patterson, James Stewart, Samuel Johnson, William Plumer, and Matthew Jameson, be respective appointed committees of correspondence for the counties of Washington, Fayette and Allegheny, and that it shall be their duty to correspond together and with such committee as shall be appointed for the same purpose in the county of Westmoreland, or with any committees of a similar nature that may be appointed in other parts of the United States, and also, if found necessary, to call together either general meetings of the people in their respective counties, or conferences of the several committees.

"And whereas some men may be found amongst us, so far lost to every sense of virtue and feeling for the distresses of this country as to accept offices for the collection of the duty,

"Resolved therefore, That in future we will consider such persons as unworthy of our friendship, have no intercourse or dealings with them, withdraw from them every assistance, and withhold all the comforts of life which depend upon those duties that as men and fellow citizens we owe to each other, and upon all occasions treat them with that contempt they deserve, and that it be and it is hereby most earnestly recommended to the people at large to follow the same line of conduct towards them.

"On Motion, Resolved, That the Minutes of this meeting be signed by the Chairman, attested by the Clerk, and published in the Pittsburgh Gazette.

JOHN CANON, Chairman.

Attest. Albert Gallatin, Clerk."

(New-York Historical Society, New York City.)

The list of those who attended the meeting included four members of the Pennsylvania House of Representatives: Albert Gallatin and John Smilie of Fayette County, and David Bradford and John Cannon of Washington County. Gallatin had been clerk of the earlier meeting at Redstone on July 27, 1791, and four of those present at the August 21–22, 1792, meeting (Edward Cook, the Reverend David Phillips, Colonel James Marshal, and David Bradford) had represented their respective counties at the general meeting at Pittsburgh on September 7, 1791, Bradford, who was one of the earliest lawyers to settle in Washington County, assisted the attorney general of Pennsylvania, James Iredell, in the state courts. Marshal, who had been a county lieutenant, was appointed register for the probate of wills and recorder of deeds for Washington County on August 17, 1791. Jean Badollet, a Geneva school friend of Gallatin, had joined Gallatin on his Fayette County farm. Cook, who had been chairman of the 1791 meeting, was associate judge of the Court of Common Pleas for Fayette County. Cannon, the founder of Cannonsburg, Pennsylvania, was George Washington's land agent in western Pennsylvania. Like Cannon, Shesbazer Bentley was one of the largest landholders in Washington County. Thomas Gaddis, who had been a colonel in the American Revolution, had built Fort Gaddis before the outbreak of the Revolution.

law.[6] For this purpose, he may, in conversations with discreet men, represent the impossibility of the government remaining longer a passive spectator of such persevering and contemptuous resistance to its laws.

When there, his own judgment will suggest any other measures, which it may be proper for him to take. And having fulfilled the objects of his journey he will please to return as speedily as may be convenient to this City.

It is in my opinion absolutely necessary that a decided experiment should without delay be made of the energy of the laws, and of the ability of the government to put them in execution. The present is a preparatory step.

with great consideration & esteem   I am Sir   Your obedt Servt

Alexander Hamilton

Tench Coxe Esqr
Commissr of the Revenue

6. Neville concluded his letter to Clymer of August 23, 1792, by contrasting the situation in Washington County with that in Allegheny County:
"I have no doubt but my attendance at Washington was at the risque of my Life, I had great reason to expect abuse at the time, and last friday which was the day I had appointed to attend, but was prevented by other Business, the Road near Washington was waylaid by men in disguise, armed with Rifles, twelve or fifteen in number, and I have no doubt but I should have fallen a Sacrifice to their Violence had I have went; indeed it is the opinion of Colo. Cannon Chairman to the Meeting and a Squire [Craig] Ritchie who live in the Neighborhood who gave the information.
"When I speak of the difficulty of getting a House, and the danger of attending the Office, I confine it entirely to Washington County: in Alleghany County particularly in Pittsburg altho the law has not been comply'd with I have met with neither threat or insult, the office stands *mark'd* and unmolested, none of the Inhabitants appeared at the meeting, nor do I believe that they approve the Measures of those that did. In Westmoreland and Fayette Counties no attempts have been lately made to establish offices; indeed the Collectors are too much intimidated to undertake it, and however willing I may be, I do not see at present any chance of doing my duty in the office. I shall write the different occurrencies from time to time. . . ."
(ALS, Connecticut Historical Society, Hartford.)

From Leonard M. Cutting [1]

New York 1st: Septr 1792.

Dear Sir

The money which you directed Mr Seton to pay to me in behalf of Baron Steuben was at the time passed to my Credit at the Bank

where it has remained ever since.[2] I considered it as a trust and have
not appropriated a farthing of it even to a temporary purpose. The
money would before now have been paid to Mr De La Forest's[3]
order—But you will recollect that in a conversation had between us
three in Philadelphia it was understood that the Assigt of the judgment was to be settled *there* between you & him & of which *you was
to advise* me when it should be effected and on *such advice* I was to
pay the money. This was for *your* greater security & satisfaction.
Now some time passed after my return to N York—I received no
letter which I waited for previous to making the payment; I then
went into the Genessee Country where by sickness I was detained
longer than I expected and did not return to this place till the day
before yesterday. I have been called upon for the money & request
to know if you have any objections to my paying it over? As it is
my earnest desire that while my Client is paid, you should be secure
and satisfied.

I am with the Greatest   Esteem & Respect Your   Most Obedt:

L. M. Cutting.

ALS, Hamilton Papers, Library of Congress.
    1. Cutting was a New York City attorney who maintained a notary public
and conveyancing office.
    2. See William Seton to H, May 28, 1792.
    3. Antoine René Charles Mathurin de La Forest, French consul general in
the United States.
    One of von Steuben's creditors, Hector St. John de Crèvecœur, had given
a power of attorney to La Forest on May 28, 1790. See Seton to H, May 28,
1792, note 3.

To George Washington [1]

Treasury Departmt. 1st Septr. 1792.

Sir,

I have the honor to inclose sundry papers which have been handed
to me by the Commissioner of the Revenue, respecting the state of
the Excise Law in the Western survey of the District of Pennsylvania.

Such persevering and violent opposition to the Law gives the business a still more serious aspect than it has hitherto worn, and seems
to call for vigorous & decisive measures on the part of the Government.

I have directed that the Supervisor of the District shall repair forthwith to the Survey in question, to ascertain in person the true state of the Survey; to collect evidence respecting the violences that have been committed in order to a prosecution of the Offenders, to ascertain particulars as to the Meeting which appears to have been holden at Pittsburgh; to encourage the perseverance of the officers; giving expectations as far as it can be done with propriety, of indemnification from the Government, for any losses which they may sustain in consequence of their Offices; to endeavour to prevail upon the Inhabitants of the County of Alleghany, who appear at present the least refractory, to come into an acquiescence with the Law; representing to discreet persons the impossibility of the Governments remaining longer a passive spectator of the contempt of it's Laws.

I shall also immediately submit to the Attorney General for his opinion, whether an indictable offence has not been committed by the persons who were assembled at Pittsburgh, and of what nature, the paper which contains their proceedings; with a view, if judged expedient by you, that it may be brought under the notice of the Circuit Court, which I understand is to be holden in October at York Town.[2]

My present clear conviction is, that it is indispensable, if competent evidence can be obtained, to exert the full force of the Law against the Offenders, with every circumstance that can manifest the determination of the Government to enforce it's execution; & if the processes of the Courts are resisted, as is rather to be expected, to employ those means, which in the last resort are put in the power of the Executive. If this is not done, the spirit of disobedience will naturally extend and the authority of the Government will be prostrate. Moderation enough has been shewn—'tis time to assume a different tone. The well disposed part of the community will begin to think the Executive wanting in decision and vigour. I submit these impressions to your consideration previous to any step which will involve the necessity of ulterior proceedings; and shall hope as speedily as possible to receive your instructions.

The Secretary at War will be requested to direct Captain Faulkner's attendance at this place.[3]

With the highest respect and truest attachment   I have the honor to be &c.   Alexander Hamilton

LC, George Washington Papers, Library of Congress.
1. For background to this letter, see H to Tench Coxe, September 1, 1792.
2. The Circuit Court for the Middle Circuit met at York, Pennsylvania, on October 11, 1792. Judges Richard Peters of Pennsylvania and William Cushing of Massachusetts presided.
3. See H to Coxe, September 1, 1792, note 4.

From Sebastian Bauman

New York Septr. 3. 1792.[1]

Dear Sir,

I have recieved your favour of 31st Ult.[2] and I have to inform you that there is no letter in my Office for Gulliaum Vaillant,[3] Poste restante. If there had been, I should without delay have forwarded the same under cover to you by this days Post.

Remain with great respect Dear Sir, Your most Obd. & very humble Servt. S. Bauman

The Honble. Alexr. Hamilton

ALS, Hamilton Papers, Library of Congress.
1. This letter was postmarked "N York Sept 2."   2. Letter not found.
3. Presumably Sieur Vaillant, captain of the ship Le Coulard ("France, Consulate: United States, Register of the Chancery of the Consulate of France in the United States, at New York City," D, MS Division, New York Public Library).

From William Ellery

Collector's Office [Newport, Rhode Island]
Sept. 3d 1792

Sir,

Permit me in this letter to pursue the Story of the Sloop Polly of Sandwich.[1]

The Surveyor arrived at Bedford on the 27th of last month; and

LC, Newport Historical Society, Newport, Rhode Island.
1. See Ellery to H, August 20, 27, 1792. See also H to Jeremiah Olney, July 31, 1792; Olney to H, August 13, 1792.

upon consulting with the Colle. of New Bedford [2] was informed by
him that the Sloop was in the District of Edgartown; but as Edgartown was distant, from Nashawina, the navigation difficult, and the
prevailing winds opposed to making harbour in Martha's Vineyard,
and it was unsafe to trust the vessel in the dominions of such a rude,
turbulent character as Mr. Slocum, who owns part of Nashawina,
and hires the rest, they thought it would be most for the interest of
the United States to bring her directly across the bay to Bedford
where she might be laid up safely with little expence until a trial and
determination could be had. Accordingly after procuring sails, and
such help as was judged necessary to get the vessel off the beech,
Col. Pope was so obliging as to set off with the Surveyor for Nashawina. As soon as they arrived and Col. Pope was satisfied it was the
Sloop Polly of Sandwich, they began by bailing and throwing out
her balast to prepare for heaving her off at high water, and just as
they had completed their arrangements Mr. Slocum returned from
Nantuckett in his Ferry boat with a British flag displayed at his mast
head and under it the Flag of the United States. Finding what was
doing and intended to be done, he bounced swagger'd and threatned
like a bully, called our people plunderers & robbers forbid their
doing anything with the vessel; said that he had bought her of a
stranger who came there in distress for £70 & showed the officers
a bill of sale which had every appearance of fraud about it, and was
very irregularly drawn, which only mentioned the name—Sloop
Polly, without adding the place where she belonged; and the name
of the person who gave the bill of sale was spelt differently. Without
attendg. to Slocum's threats as soon as the tide was up our people
hauled her into the channel and would have proceeded with her to
Bedford; but the wind increasing, the sea running high, and the sails
bad they ran her ashore, and were obliged to wait untill the next
high water; when they got her afloat, and leaving her under the care
of the Collector of New Bedford, to proceed with her to Bedford as
soon as the wind should favour the Surveyor with his crew set sail
and arrived here on the 31st. of last month. Soon after their departure, the wind became favorable for the Sloop to cross over to Bedford, and without doubt she is there in safety. The substance of this
account is taken from the narrative of the Surveyor. He adds that
Mr. Slocum has ever been a great Tory, and still retains all the ran-

2. Edward Pope.

cour incidental to that character and that nothing prevented his offering violence to him, but his fear of their superior numbers. As the Elisabeth islands seem to be a good resort for smugglers, suffer me to suggest that it might be well if our Cutters were to visit them pretty frequently, and perhaps the British flagg usually worn by Mr. Slocum in his ferry boat might deserve some notice.

By the 49th. Sec of the Colln. Law [3] it is the duty of the several Officers of the Customs to make seizure of and secure any ship or vessel &c. which shall be liable to seizure by this act, as well without as within their respective Districts.

By the 66 Sec: "the Collector, within whose District the seizure shall be made, is hereby authorized and directed to cause suits for the same to be commenced and prosecuted to effect" &c. "And that all Ships or vessels &c which shall become forfeited by virtue of this act shall be seized, libelled and prosecuted as aforesaid, in the proper Court having Cognizance thereof &c.[4] I should be happy to have your opinion on this question whether an officer making seizure of a vessel without his District may not remove her from the Place where she is seized, to an adjoining District provided it can be done with convenience and safety, and either from the disposition of the inhabitants, or from the situation of the harbour, it appears that she cannot remain there in safety, and she cannot be removed without great inconvenience or hazard to any port or place in the same District: I wish also to be directed to what Collector to apply to commence a prosecution in the present case. The Collector of Edgartown [5] seems to be the person pointed out by the Law; but if it is not necessary that he should be the person, from the greater nearness of the Collector of New Bedford to Boston, where I presume this cause will be tried, than the Colle. of Edgartown, I conceive that the trial could be commenced and prosecuted to effect with more convenience and less expence by the former than the latter.

3. Ellery is referring to Section 50 of "An Act to provide more effectually for the collection of the duties imposed by law on goods, wares and merchandise imported into the United States, and on the tonnage of ships or vessels" (1 *Stat.* 170 [August 4, 1790]).

4. Ellery is referring to Section 67 of the Collection Law (1 *Stat.* 176).

5. John Pease, the collector of customs at Edgartown, on December 4, 1792, filed a libel against the sloop *Polly* in the District Court. The case dragged on until March 4, 1794, and the vessel was returned to its owners on the claim filed by Samuel Bourne. Bourne's motion for costs was denied, however, because it was held that there were "reasonable grounds for seizure" (Records of the Massachusetts District Court, Federal Records Center, Boston).

By the 68th. Sec. of the same law [6] one moiety of all penalties &c shall be divided into equal parts and paid to the Colle. Naval Offe. & Surveyor of the port wherein the same shall have been incurred; the mode of expression would seem to exclude the Colle. Navl Offe & Surveyor of the Port of Newport from any part of the moiety of the forfeiture of the Polly of Sandwich if she should be condemned. Please to favour me with your sentiments in this respect; and if it should be that they are not entitled to any part of such moiety, whether the Colle. may not avail himself of one half of such moiety as Informer.

I cannot finish this letter without mentioning that the Surveyor undertook the pursuit of the Polly of Sandwich, with great readiness and executed his duty with great activity & spirit.

I have the honour to be Sir yr. obedt. servt.   W Ellery Colle

6. Ellery is referring to Section 69 of the Collection Law (1 *Stat.* 177).

To John Jay [1]

Private   Philadelphia Sepr. 3d. 1792

My Dear Sir

The proceedings at Pittsburgh, which you will find stated in the inclosed paper and other incidents, in the Western parts of this state, announce so determined and persevering a spirit of opposition to the laws, as in my opinion to render a vigorous exertion of the powers of government indispensable. I have communicated this opinion to the President and I doubt not his impressions will accord with it. In this case, one point for consideration will be the expediency of the next Circuit Court's noticing the state of things in that quarter particularly the Meeting at Pittsburgh and its proceedings. You will observe an avowed object is to—"*obstruct* the *operation* of the law." This is attempted to be qualified by a pretence of doing it by "every legal measure." [2] But "legal measures to obstruct the operation of a law" is a contradiction in terms. I therefore entertain no doubt, that a high misdemeanour has been committed. The point however is under submission to the Attorney General for his opinion.

There is really My Dear Sir a crisis in the affairs of the Country which demands the most mature consideration of its best and wisest friends.

I beg you to apply your most serious thoughts to it, and favour me as soon as possible with the result of your reflections. Perhaps it will not be amiss for you to converse with Mr. King.[3] His judgment is sound—he has caution and energy.

Would a proclamation from the President be adviseable stating the criminality of such proceedings & warning all persons to abstain from them, as the laws will be strictly enforced against all offenders?

If the plot should thicken and the application of force should appear to be unavoidable, will it be expedient for the President to repair in person to the scene of commotion?

These are some of the questions which present themselves. The subject will doubtless open itself in all its aspects to you. With real respect and affectionate attachment I remain

Dear Sir   Your obedient servant   Alexander Hamilton

John Jay Esqr.
&c. &c.

ALS, Columbia University Libraries; copy, Hamilton Papers, Library of Congress.
  1. For background to this letter, see H to Tench Coxe, September 1, 1792; H to George Washington, September 1, 1792.
  2. H is quoting from the minutes of the August 21–22, 1792, Pittsburgh meeting. See H to Coxe, September 1, 1792, note 5.
  3. Rufus King was a United States Senator from New York and a strong supporter of Federalist policies.

To Benjamin Lincoln

Treasury Department, September 3, 1792. Informs Lincoln that "a Warrant has this day issued on the Treasurer in your favor, as Agent to John Lowell, Attorney for Jonathan Jackson, late Marshall of the District of Massachusetts, for the sum of Nine hundred & Sixty four dollars and thirty Cents." [1] Requests a receipt.

LS, RG 36, Collector of Customs at Boston, Letters from the Treasury, 1789–1818 (vol. unnumbered), National Archives; copy, RG 56, Letters to the Collector at Boston, National Archives; copy, RG 56, Letters to Collectors at Small Ports, "Set G," National Archives.

1. Warrant No. 2011 was issued to Jackson for court expenses amounting to $964.30 for the period from December 1, 1789, to July 18, 1791 (D, RG 217, Miscellaneous Treasury Accounts, 1790–1894, Account No. 1939, National Archives). Jackson ceased to be marshal when he was appointed inspector of Survey No. 2 in Massachusetts on July 18, 1792. The Senate approved the appointment on March 7, 1792.

From Tench Coxe

Treasury Department, Revenue Office, September 4, 1792. Has learned that "Thomas Davis Freeman Surveyor of the port of Plymouth [1] and Inspector of the Revenue for the same has been absent from that port since February last." Reports that Samuel Johnston, Senator from North Carolina, has recommended John Armistead to replace Freeman.[2]

LC, RG 58, Letters of Commissioner of Revenue, 1792–1793, National Archives.
1. Plymouth, North Carolina.
2. H wrote to George Washington concerning Johnson's recommendation on September 17, 1792. See also Samuel Tredwell to H, February 10, 1792.

From William Ellery

Colles Offe. [Newport, Rhode Island] Sept. 4 1792

Sir,

Since writing the long letter on the preceeding pages [1] I find a case will probably occur in this Custom house altogether new, and in which unless I am early favoured with your direction I may incurr censure embarrassment and expence. The case may be stated thus. A is indebted by bond to the United States for duties, the day of payment arrives, instead of discharging the debt he suffers a prosecution. After the commencement of the prosecution he executes a bill of sale of the cargo on board a vessel abroad to B. She arrives in this Port, the bond still unpaid. The master produces a manifest in which it is expressed that A is the owner of the Vessel, and that the Cargo is consigned to him. The Vendee appears at the Custom-house produces his bill of sale and demands an entry of the Cargo as his property, at the same time offering to give bond for the duties on said Cargo &c. Is B by his Bill of sale entitled to such entry?

But throwing the circumstances of the unpaid Bond out of the question, please to inform me, whether a bill of sale of goods abroad, entitled the Vendee to an Entry thereof on their importation, on his own account and not as agent to the Vendor, giving bond to pay the duties, and otherwise complying with the Law?

If transfers of goods abroad will give to the persons to whom they are transferred a right to the entry thereof on importation not as agents to the Vendor but on their own account, the Law which deprives Obligors of credit who do not pay their bonds in time [2] may be easily avoided by such transfers; but if bills of sale will confer the right mentioned it is conceived that it would be imprudent for a Collector to refuse an entry to a vendee on a supposition that there might be a collusion between the vendor & vendee to avoid the Law referred to; for if that should be the intention, such Collector might expect to be prosecuted, and in that case, as it is not an easy matter, where Custom Houses officers are not parties to a suit to prove collusion, he might expect to be saddled with damages and Cost. Hoping for an early answer to the foregoing questions, and your direction

I am   Sir   Yr. most obedt. servt.   Wm Ellery Colle

A Hamilton Esqre
Secry Treasy.

LC, Newport Historical Society, Newport, Rhode Island.
   1. Ellery to H, September 3, 1792.
   2. Section 41 of "An Act to provide more effectually for the collection of the duties imposed by law on goods, wares and merchandise imported into the United States, and on the tonnage of ships or vessels" concludes with the proviso that "no person whose bond for the payment of duties is due and unsatisfied, shall be allowed a future credit for duties, until such bond shall be fully paid or discharged" (1 *Stat.* 168 [August 4, 1790]).

From Jeremiah Olney

Providence, September 4, 1792. "I have received your Two Letters of the 24th and 25th of August. . . . My practice . . . shall correspond with your Opinion and construction of the Law."

ADfS, Rhode Island Historical Society, Providence.

Civis [1]

[Philadelphia, September 5, 1792]

For the National Gazette.

Certain Treasury Documents were lately published for the information of the community, without any precise designation of the purpose for which they were published. They were left to speak for themselves, with only a short introduction, denominating them

[Philadelphia] *National Gazette,* September 5, 1792.

1. H's "Civis" letter is the first of two essays. The second essay is entitled "Civis to Mercator" and is dated September 11, 1792.

"Civis" was written in reply to an article by "Mercator" which was printed in the *National Gazette* on September 1, 1792, and which was entitled "RE-MARKS *on a late authentic Document, published by the* Treasury Department, *under the signature of* Joseph Nourse, *Register.*" The "authentic document" on which "Mercator" was commenting is Nourse to H, August 24, 1792. The article by "Mercator" reads as follows:

"The object of this publication seems to be, to impress the public mind with a belief, that under the present administration of its fiscal concerns, the public debt has been actually reduced to the amount of 1,845,217 dols. and 42 cents; and that the sum of 397,024 dols. and 15 cents remains to be applied to the same object. That this is not the case, but that the public debt, instead of being diminished one farthing, has been really augmented to the amount of upwards of *one million and a half dollars;* since the present administration commenced, will I think manifestly appear by a reference to a few plain facts and documents not less authentic than the one signed by Mr. Nourse.

"The Secretary of the Treasury in a report to Congress, dated 23d January, 1792, states that the whole expenditures or demands against the government from the beginning of the year 1791, to the end of the year 1792, amounts to

	dols. 7,082,197.74
"That the amount of the nett product of the public revenues during the years 1791 & 1792 is	7,029,755.26
Leaving as a deficiency against the government	dols. 52,442.48

"It apears by Mr. Nourse's document, that the whole amount of the revenues of the United States from the time the first impost law took effect, which was the 1st of August 1789, until the 31st Dec. 1790, was — dols. 3,026,070.65

"That the total demands upon that, agreeable to the appropriations made by Congress, exclusive of any interest on the public debt, was — 1,687,194.81

Leaving a surplus in favour of the revenue, of — dols. 1,338,875.84

"It appears too, from Mr. Nourse's document, that the treasury department claims credit for having disposed of the said surplus of 1,338,875.84, so as to purchase and redeem to the amount of 1,845,217.42 of the public debt, and to have left 397,024 dollars and 15 cents to be applied to the same object. Be it so; I admit the fact in its fullest force—but what follows? That if the treasury

"Authentic documents respecting the progress which has been made by the present government of the United States, towards extinguishing the debts contracted under the former government." A writer in this Gazette of Saturday last, under the signature of Mercator, has tho't fit to come forward, and, assigning what he conceives to be the object of the publication, endeavors to shew, that the contrary of what was intended, is true.

claims credit for the use and whole amount of the revenue of the United States, from its commencement on the 1st of Aug. 1789, to the 31st of Dec. 1790, towards lessening the public credit; so it ought to be debited with the whole amount of the interest, that accrued on the public debt, during the same period, which by the treasury returns amounts to 4,036,359 dols. and 19 cents. I am aware that in objection to this it will be said, that agreeable to the act of Congress, no interest was payable on the public debt until January 1791. Granted; but what became of this interest? Has it been paid? No. Does it remain to be paid? Yes. Was it added to and made a part of the principal of the public debt, thereby encreasing that debt to the amount of 4,036,359 dols. and 19 cents, in addition to its former principal? Yes. Did not the Secretary of the Treasury himself propose that it should be so added? Yes. Is it not therefore an efficient act of his administration, and can he now claim credit with the public, upon the fallaciou[s] idea of having *bona fide* reduced the public debt upwards of two millions, when, as I have shewn above, he has produced an actual addition to the public debt of mor[e] than one million and a half of dollars?

"A simple state of the case with the Treasury department stands thus—

	DEBIT.	dols.	cts.
"For the amount of interest which accrued on the public debt between the 1st of Aug. 1789, and 31st Dec. 1790		4,036,359.19	
"For the deficiency of revenue to answer the demands of government in 1791, and 1792		52,442.4	
	Dollars	4,088,801.67	

	CREDIT.		
"By the amount of public debt redeemed and discharged out of the surplus of the revenue arising between 1st Aug. 1789, and 31st Dec. 1790		1,845,217.42	
"By balance of surplus remaining on hand of dollars 397,024.15, and which may probably redeem		500,000	
"By a deficiency against the treasury department, since its establishment, which forms an actual addition to the public debt		1,743,584.25	
	Dollars	4,088,801.67	

"That the facts and conclusions above mentioned are just, and that it is a sad and serious truth that the public debt has encreased, and is encreasing in the hands of its present administrators, is also manifest to two important classes of men in the community, I mean the MERCHANTS and FARMERS, by the present amount and encreasing weight of the duties of Impost and Excise.

MERCATOR.

Aug. 30. 1792."

What right had Mercator to suppose, that any thing more was intended, than simply to inform the public, *that besides a punctual payment of the interest on the debt, from the period, at which measures were matured to begin that payment, a considerable sum of the capital of the Debt has been extinguished, and that a fu[r]ther sum will be extinguished by a provision already made?*—leaving them to this very natural inference, which will be drawn by every candid mind, that the Government has been as attentive as circumstances would permit, at so early a period, to the extinguishment of the debt.

But admitting Mercator to be right in his suggestion of the object, it is to be presumed, that a liberal construction of all circumstances will justify this position, that the present Government has reduced the debt of the former Government to the extent expressed in the documents which have been published. This will result, if it shall appear that provision was made for the interest, as early as was reasonably practicable. To have paid the interest from that period, and to have sunk so much of the capital in addition, is in fair construction, to have reduced the debt to the extent of the capital sunk.

When Mercator undertook to suppose an object, which was not declared, he ought to have taken care to be better informed and more accurate. When he undertook to state an account with the treasury department, he ought not only to have selected just items, to have adverted to dates, times and possibilities, but he ought to have stated *the whole account.*

This he has not done; on the contrary he has both misrepresented and suppressed facts. He has shewn, in the true spirit of a certain junto (who not content with the large share of power they have in the government, are incessantly laboring to monopolize the whole of its power, and to banish from it every man who is not subservient to their preposterous and all-grasping views) that he has been far more solicitous to *arraign,* than to manifest the truth—to take away, than to afford consolation to the people of the United States.

The following particulars are proofs of his want both of accuracy and candor.

First. He charges to the treasury department arrears of interest, which accrued *prior* to its existence, that is, from the first of August 1789; whereas the department was not instituted till the 2d of September, nor organized till about the 13th, when, I am informed the Secretary of the Treasury entered upon the duties of his office.

Secondly. He takes as the standard of his calculation, the whole amount of the annual interest on the whole amount of the public debt, as it exists under the present funding system, including all the arrears of interest made principal, and the 21,500,000 dollars of assumed debt—whereas the arrears which did actually accumulate to the end of the year 1790, were only on the *principal* of the foreign and domestic debt, and fall short more than a million of dollars of the sum he states.

These simple facts prove the fallacy of his statement.

But the principle, upon which he proceeds, is not less absurd, than his calculations are fallacious.

With as much propriety might an executor be charged with increasing the debts of his testator, by suffering the arrears of interest on his bonds and notes to accumulate while he was collecting, arranging and disposing of the effects; to discharge the debts of the estate; as the present government, or if the phrase is preferred, the present treasury department, may be charged with those arrearages, which unavoidably accrued, during the preparatory measures for bringing the resources of the public estate into activity. With as much reason might it be charged with the 13,000,000 of interest, which accumulated under the imbecile system, the old confederation, to which, if not to worse,—a dissolution of the Union!—the designs of the junto evidently point, or tend.

When, proceeding upon grounds so loose and unjust, Mercator makes the extraordinary declaration, that the secretary of the treasury "has *produced* an *actual addition* to the public debt of more than one million and a half of dollars," is it not palpable, that in the most malignant spirit of party, he is endeavouring to destroy the public confidence in that officer, no matter how unfair the means, as one link in the chain of measures by which the domineering aims of his party are to be effected, or the cause of confusion promoted? Is it not clear that in the language and conceptions of *Mercator*, to *provide for* a debt, and to "*produce*" it, amount to the same thing?

To form a still better estimate of the spirit by which he is actuated, let there be a review of some leading facts.

Congress met under the present government on the first of April,

1789.[2] To put it in motion they had a vast and very arduous work before them. This was of course a primary object; a provision for the debt a secondary one. It was natural then that the first session should have been exhausted in *organizing* the government, and that a systematic provision for the debt should be postponed, as in fact it was, to the second session. A temporary and partial provision of revenue only was accordingly made, by very moderate duties of impost, far short of an adequate fund for the support of government, and the payment of the interest on the debt, to take effect on the first of August, 1789;[3] which was as early as the law could be promulgated throughout the union, and the subordinate executive arrangements made for carrying it into execution.

It has been stated, that the treasury department began to be in activity on the 13th of September. Congress adjourned on the 29th of that month, after having instructed the secretary of the treasury to report concerning the debt *at the ensuing session.* It is to be recollected that without an order of the house that officer can propose nothing.

'Tis evident then, that there was no responsibility on the side of that department, for the accumulation of interest on the debt until at earliest the second session, which began on the 7th of January, 1790.[4]

On Thursday, the 14th of January, the secretary of the treasury submitted to the House of Representatives, according to order, the plan of a provision for the public debt,[5] comprehending an additional provision of revenue for the purpose of facing the interest. But it was not till the 4th of August, that the principles of a provision for the debt were determined by law,[6] nor till the 10th of the same month, that a supplementary fund was established for paying

2. Although the opening of Congress was officially set for March 4, 1789, the House did not have a quorum until April 1, 1789, and the Senate did not have a quorum until April 6, 1789.

3. "An Act for laying a Duty on Goods, Wares and Merchandises imported into the United States" (1 *Stat.* 24–27 [July 4, 1789]).

4. Although Congress was scheduled to begin its second session on January 4, 1790, the Senate did not have a quorum until January 6 and the House did not have a quorum until January 7.

5. "Report Relative to a Provision for the Support of Public Credit," January 9, 1790.

6. "An Act making provision for the (payment of the) Debt of the United States" (1 *Stat.* 138–44).

the interest upon it;[7] and from considerations of an obvious nature, the commencement of this fund in operation was deferred to the first of January following.

Here again 'tis manifest, that there was no responsibility in the treasury department, for the accumulation of interest up to the period from which it has been punctually paid, namely, the first of January, 1791; because it was not in the power of that department to have accelerated a provision for it. Nor will any blame justly light upon Congress for the moderate delay which ensued. It was their duty to bestow much deliberation upon the subject. Much difference of opinion, much lengthy discussion, a considerable loss of time, were to be expected in relation to a subject so momentous, so perplexing, touching so differently so many chords of passion and interest.

The law providing for the debt having passed—the secretary of the treasury immediately seized the opportunity which was afforded, by an unappropriated surplus of revenue to the end of the year 1790, to make an impression on the debt. He proposed, that it should be applied to purchases of the debt, at its market prices, which was agreed to by Congress, and has been carried into execution as far as circumstances have hitherto permitted.

This was certainly the best application that could have been made of the fund. It was equally the interest of the government and of the public creditors:—Of the government, because it was a clear gain of all the difference between the sum of specie paid and the sum of debt redeemed, which is already 514,891 dollars and 69 cents, and will be more when the remaining sum appropriated comes to be applied to further purchases; because it was a clear saving to the nation of all the difference in price which was paid by foreigners in their purchases, in consequence of the competition of the government, in the market, as a purchaser. It is well known to every well informed man, that the rapid appreciation of the debt was materially owing to that circumstance, and of course the saving to the nation by it has been *very considerable*. The measure in question was equally beneficial to the public creditors—because if the fund applied to purchases had been apportioned among them in

7. "An Act making Provision for the Reduction of the Public Debt" (1 *Stat.* 186–87).

payment of interest, it would have been a mere pittance; but applied as it was, it gave a rapid spring to the whole value of their stock.

As it is therefore proved, that the treasury department is chargeable with no delay with regard to a provision for the debt, occasioning an unnecessary accumulation of interest; in a question of merit, respecting that department, which Mercator has raised, it will follow, that the department on account of the operations which have been advised by it, has an *unbalanced* claim of merit with the community.

1st. For all that has been or shall be saved by purchases of the public debt at the market prices.

2d. For all that has been saved to the nation for the more advanced prices given by foreigners in their purchases of the debt.

But there are other items of importance to be placed on the same side of the account.

1st. The saving resulting from the reduced rate on the new loans made for paying off the foreign debt.

2d. The positive gain of 1,000,000 of dollars by the institution of the Bank of the United States. The stock of the Bank being at an advance of 50 per cent, it is clear, that the government, by having become a proprietor to the extent of 2,000,000 of dollars, has by this single operation made an actual nett profit of 1,000,000 of dollars; that is, it can get three millions for what will have cost it only two.

I add nothing for any saving, which has accrued from the particular modification of the domestic debt, for two reasons; one because the subject being more complicated would require more illustration, and the other because the plan adopted by the legislature, though having the leading features of that proposed by the Treasury Department, differs from it in some material respects; a strong refutation of the idea, so industriously inculcated, that the plans of that department are implicitly followed by the legislature; and a decisive proof, that they have had no more weight than they ought to have had, that is to say than they were intitled to, from their intrinsic reasonableness in the unbiassed and independent judgment of majorities in the two houses on Congress. The result of what has been said is this— that provision was made for paying the interest of the debt as early as could reasonably have been expected—that no negligence having happened, the arrears of interest which accumulated in the interval are properly a part of the debts of the former government and consequently that the sums which appear to have been absorbed are so much of the debts of the *old* Government extinguished by the *new*. Mercator brings as a proof, that the public debt has increased and is increasing, "what he terms the present amount and *encreasing weight* of the duties of impost and excise." Let facts decide the soundness of this logic. In the last session of Congress, the only excise duty which exists, was reduced upon an average fifteen per cent.[8] The only addition which was then made to the imposts was for carrying on the Indian war,[9] and by avoiding recourse to permanent loans for that purpose, *to avoid an increase of the debt*. How then can that, which was done to avoid an increase of debt, *be a proof that it has increased?* CIVIS

8. "An Act concerning the Duties on Spirits distilled within the United States" (1 *Stat.* 267–71 [May 8, 1792]).
9. "An Act for raising a farther sum of money for the protection of the frontiers, and for other purposes therein mentioned" (1 *Stat.* 259–63 [May 2, 1792]).

To Tobias Lear

[*Philadelphia, September 6, 1792.* On the back of a letter that Lear wrote to Hamilton on August 27, 1792, Hamilton wrote: "Answered Sepr. 6." *Letter not found.*]

To James Lingan [1]

[*Treasury Department, September 6, 1792.* The catalogue description of this letter reads: "Tonnage on Ship Eliza be refunded." *Letter not found.*]

LS, sold at City Book Auction, February, 1943, Lot 80.
1. Lingan was collector of customs at Georgetown, Maryland.

To Nicholas Low

[*Philadelphia, September 6, 1792.* "I do not think the article could be procured in the quarter mentioned; and considering all that is *Said* and Sung it would not do to furnish such a handle for malicious suggestions." [1] *Letter not found.*]

ALS, sold by Bruce Gimelson, Fort Washington, Pennsylvania, Lot 22.
1. Text taken from an extract in dealer's catalogue.

From Charles Cotesworth Pinckney [1]

[*Charleston, South Carolina, September 6, 1792.* On October 10, 1792, Hamilton wrote to Pinckney: "I duly received your letter of the 6th of September." *Letter not found.*]

1. Pinckney was at this time practicing law in Charleston, South Carolina.

To William Seton [1]

Philadelphia Sepr 6. 1792

My Dear Sir

The painful cause of your short silence was easily understood and by me most sincerely sympathized in. I shall always take part in the prosperous or adverse events which attend you.

I thank you for the trouble you have so kindly taken respecting my letter and for your obliging offer of writing to the Governor of the Island. I hope the measures I have already taken will answer the end. If not I may avail myself of your friendly offer.

I find I have overdrawn my account, by a late draft for 200 Dollars —Dollars 24.67. This I will shortly remit.

The unnecessary mulplicat[ion] of Banks is an unpleasing circumstance; but I hope if the solid institutions maintain a good understanding with each other, a misfortune to any of the excrescences will be but a partial evil and perhaps a cure for the excess.

Upon the whole I think you will do well to address a line to the Directors of the Society at their next Meeting respecting your advance to Mr. Pearce,[2] mentioning that you were informed he had given Credit for it to the Society. I understand there is to be a Meeting on the 29th at which I expect to be present and will pay attention to the matter. It is very simple & can suffer no difficulty.

Believe me to be always truly and affectly   Yr friend & serv

A Hamilton

William Seton Esqr

ALS, Mr. Martin Weiner, Paterson, N. J.
1. This letter was written in reply to Seton to H, August 30, 1792.
2. William Pearce.

To Joseph Willard [1]

Philadelphia September 6th
1792

Sir

The honor, which has been done me, by the Overseers of the antient and justly celebrated institution, over which you preside, is appreciated by me, as it merits, and receives my most cordial acknowlegements. To You, Sir, I am also indebted, for the very obliging manner, in which it is communicated.

Amidst the many painful circumstances, that surround a station like mine—this flattering mark of the esteem of a body-so respectable—is a source both of satisfaction and consolation. If my past endeavours have been, in any degree, useful to the community, my future cannot but be rendered more zealous, by the approbation of the wise and good.

With real and great respect and esteem for you personally I have the honor to be   Sir

Your obedient & humble servant   Alexander Hamilton

The Reverend Mr. Joseph Willard
President of Harvard University

ALS, Harvard University Archives, Widener Library.
1. This letter was written in reply to Willard to H, August 27, 1792.

To the President and Directors
of the Bank of the United States [1]

Treasury Department
September 7th 1792

Sir

The fund appropriated for the contingent expences of this Department being exhausted, I have to request, that you will give a credit to the Register of the Treasury for fifteen hundred Dollars, to be by him applied on that account.

A temporary account will be to be opened for the purpose, which will be discharged by the Treasurer as soon as an appropriation shall be made by law.[2]

With respectful consideration, I have the honor to be, Gentlemen, Your Obedt Servant.   Alexander Hamilton

The President and Directors
Of the Bank of the United States.

LS, RG 316, Letters donated by John D. Rockefeller, Jr., August, 1955, National Archives.
    1. Thomas Willing was president of the Bank of the United States.
    2. This item is listed in Statement "B" of "Estimate of the Expenditures for the Civil List of the United States for the Year 1793," which H submitted to Congress on November 14, 1792. An appropriation for it was made by "An Act making appropriations for the support of Government for the year one thousand seven hundred and ninety-three" (1 *Stat.* 325–29 [February 28, 1793]).

Draft of a Proclamation Concerning Opposition to the Excise Law [1]

[*Philadelphia, September 7, 1792.* On September 8, 1792, Edmund Randolph wrote to Hamilton: "I have perused your draught of a proclamation . . . though I really wish that I could have more time for a critical scrutiny than has occurred between yesterday and this morning." *Draft not found.*]

    1. For background to this document, see H to Tench Coxe, September 1, 1792; H to George Washington, September 1, 1792; H to John Jay, September 3, 1792.
    After consultation with Henry Knox, H submitted his draft to Edmund Randolph and Washington. A second draft, which is in a clerk's handwriting, was submitted to Washington, who referred it to Thomas Jefferson (see the first letter H wrote to Washington on September 9, 1792). In final form, the proclamation reads as follows:
    "Whereas certain violent and unwarrantable proceedings have lately taken place tending to obstruct the operation of the laws of the United States for raising a revenue upon spirits distilled within the same, enacted pursuant to express authority delegated in the constitution of the United States; which proceedings are subversive of good order, contrary to the duty that every citizen owes to his country and to the laws, and of a nature dangerous to the very being of government:
    "And whereas such proceedings are the more unwarrantable, by reason of

the moderation which has been heretofore shewn on the part of the government, and of the disposition which has been manifested by the legislature (who alone have authority to suspend the operation of laws) to obviate causes of objection, and to render the laws as acceptable as possible: And whereas it is the particular duty of the executive 'to take care that the laws be faithfully executed;' and not only that duty, but the permanent interests and happiness of the people require, that every legal and necessary step should be pursued, as well to prevent such violent and unwarrantable proceedings, as to bring to justice the infractors of the laws and secure obedience thereto.

"Now therefore I George Washington, President of the United States, do by these presents most earnestly admonish and exhort all persons whom it may concern, to refrain and desist from all unlawful combinations and proceedings whatsoever having for object or tending to obstruct the operation of the laws aforesaid; inasmuch as all lawful ways and means will be strictly put in execution for bringing to justice the infractors thereof and securing obedience thereto.

"And I do moreover charge and require all courts, magistrates and officers whom it may concern, according to the duties of their several offices, to exert the powers in them respectively vested by law for the purposes aforesaid, hereby also enjoining and requiring all persons whomsoever, as they tender the welfare of their country, the just and due authority of government and the preservation of the public peace, to be aiding and assisting therein according to law.

"In Testimony whereof, I have caused the Seal of the United States to be affixed to these presents, and Signed the same with my Hand. Done this fifteenth day of September in the year of our Lord one thousand seven hundred and ninety two, and of the Independence of the United States the seventeenth.

GO. WASHINGTON.

"By the President.

Th: JEFFERSON."

(The Federal Gazette and Philadelphia Daily Advertiser, September 25, 1792.)

To William Ellery

[Philadelphia, September 7, 1792. On September 24, 1792, Ellery wrote to Hamilton: "I have recd. your letter of the 7th. of this month." Letter not found.]

From George Washington [1]

Mount Vernon 7th. Septr. 1792.

Sir,

The last Post brought me your letter of the first instant, with the enclosures respecting the disorderly conduct of the Inhabitants of the Western Survey of the District of Pennsylvania, in opposing the execution of what is called the Excise Law; & of the insults which have been offered by some of them to the Officers who have been appointed to collect the duties on distilled spirits agreeably thereto.

Such conduct in *any* of the Citizens of the United States, under *any* circumstances that can well be conceived, would be exceedingly reprehensible; but when it comes from a part of the community for whose protection the money arising from the Tax was principally designed, it is truly unaccountable, and the spirit of it much to be regretted.

The preliminary steps taken by you in ordering the Supervisor of the District to repair to the Survey where those disorders prevail, with a view to ascertain in person, "the true state of the Survey, to collect evidence respecting the violences that have been committed, in order to a prosecution of the Offenders; to ascertain the particulars as to the Meeting which appears to have been held at Pittsburg; to encourage the perseverance of the officers in their duty, & the well disposed inhabitants in discountenancing such violent proceedings &c. &c." [2] are prudent & proper, and I earnestly wish they may have the desired effect. But if, notwithstanding, opposition is still given to the due execution of the Law, I have no hesitation in declaring, if the evidence of it is clear & unequivocal, that I shall, however reluctantly I exercise them, exert all the legal powers with which the Executive is invested, to check so daring & unwarrantable a spirit. It is my duty to see the Laws executed—to permit them to be trampled upon with impunity would be repugnant to it; nor can the Government longer remain a passive spectator of the contempt with which they are treated. Forbearance, under a hope that the Inhabitants of that Survey would recover from the delirium & folly into which they were plunged, seems to have had no other effect than to encrease the disorder.

If it shall be the Attorney General's opinion, under a full consideration of the case (adverting, as I presume he will as well to the Laws & Constitution of Pennsylvania, as to those of the United States) that the Meeting which appears to have been held at Pittsburg was illegal, and the members of it indictable; and it shall further appear to you from such information as you may be able to obtain, & from a comparative view of all circumstances that it would be proper to bring the matter before the Circuit Court to be holden at York town in October next, you have all the sanction and authority I can give to do it.

I am Sir, &c.   G: Washington

LC, George Washington Papers, Library of Congress.
   1. For background to this letter, see H to Tench Coxe, September 1, 1792; H to Washington, September 1, 1792; H to John Jay, September 3, 1792; "Draft of a Proclamation Concerning Opposition to the Excise Law," September 7, 1792.
   2. Washington is quoting from H to Washington, September 1, 1792.

To Otho H. Williams

Treasury Department
Septr. 7. 1792.

Sir

On the 28. June 1791 the Collector of New York[1] was instructed to furnish each of the Revenue Cutters with Ten Musquets and Bayonets, Twenty Pistols, one broad axe, one Chissel of the large and one of the smallest size, and two Lanthorns.

I am informed by the Collector of Norfolk[2] that those articles were not received by him; though Mr. Lamb of New York states to me,[3] they were shipped in the Brigantine Ceres, Cornelius White, Master, who being questioned by Mr. Lamb alledged that the said articles had been delivered to the Collector of Norfolk.

I request that you will please to have enquiry made of Captain White who I understand is a resident of Baltimore, what has become of the arms and instruments before mentioned informing me of the result.

With great consideration   I am Sir   Your Obedt. servant
Alex Hamilton

P.S. Upon further examination I find it mentioned in your letter of the 16. december 1791, that Simon Deyle,[4] master of a Coasting Vessel brought you the Articles above alluded to, which he said to have received from the Collector of Norfolk for the use of the Cutter in your district. The question then will be whether you received a double set of the Articles, which appears probable; and if so I request that one parcel as above enumerated may be forwarded to the Collector of Norfolk.[5]

Otho H. Williams Esqr.
Collr. Baltimore.

LS, Columbia University Libraries.
  1. John Lamb.
  2. No letter from William Lindsay to H concerning this matter has been found.
  3. Letter not found.   4. Simon Deagle.
  5. On the back of this letter Robert Purviance wrote the following memorandum of a letter which Daniel Delozier wrote to H on October 11, 1792: "Captain Deagle says that he received, from the Collector of Norfolk, ten musquets and bayonets twenty pistols, One chizen and two lanthorns, which he delivered to Captain [David] Porter on board the Revenue Cutter Active. Communicated the above information to the Secretary of the Treasury, the 11 October 1792" (D, Columbia University Libraries). Delozier's letter to H of October 11, 1792, has not been found.

From John Jay [1]

N York 8 Septr. 1792

Dear Sir

I have conferred with Mr King on the Subject of your Letter of the 3d. Inst. We concur in opinion that neither a Proclamation nor a *particular* charge by the court to the G. Jury, would be adviseable at present. To us it appears more prudent that this Business be opened by the Presidts. Speech at the ensuing Session of congress— their address will manifest the sense of the House, & both together operate more effectually than a Proclamation.

No strong Declarations shd. be made unless there be ability & Disposition to follow them with strong measures—admitting both these Requisites, it is questionable whether such operations at this moment would not furnish the antis with materials for decieving the uninformed part of ye. Community, and in some measure render the operations of administration odious. Let all the Branches of Govt. move together, and let the chiefs be committed publickly on one or the other Side of the Question. I percieve Symptoms of the crisis you mention—if managed with Prudence and Firmness it will weaken its authors. If matters can pass on *Sub Silentio* untill the meeting of Congress, I think all will be well. The public will become informed, and the Sense of the Nation become manifest. Opposition to that Sense will be clogged with apprehensions, and strong measures if necessary will be approved & be supported.

If in the mean Time such outrages shd. be committed as to force the attention of Govt. to its Dignity, nothing will remain but to obey that necessity in a way, that will leave nothing to Hazard. Success on such occasions shd. be certain—whether this shd. be done under the President's personal Direction must I think depend on circumstances at the Time, or in other words on the Degree of Importance which those Circumstances combined may evince.

Yours affecty   John Jay

The Honb. Col. Hamilton

ALS, Hamilton Papers, Library of Congress.
    1. For background to this letter, see H to Tench Coxe, September 1, 1792; H to George Washington, September 1, 1792; H to Jay, September 3, 1792; "Draft of a Proclamation Concerning Opposition to the Excise Law," September 7, 1792; Washington to H, September 7, 1792.

From Jeremiah Olney

Custom House
District of Providence 8th Sept. 1792

Sir

At a District Court held at Newport on the 7th Ulto. Judgment was rendered against Welcome Arnold[1] Esqr. for his Bond of 478.22 Cents for duties, due on the 17th May last with Cost of Sute, and execution has Issued accordingly. By his delinquency he is by law deprived of Future Credit[2] but in order I presume to evade the law, he has Transferred his Brigantine Samuel which arrived in this District on the 6th Int. from Copenhagen, with her Cargo, to Mr. Stephen Dexter of this Town Merchant; and has or will probably Transfer to a Second Person his other Vessels and Cargoes, Soon expected to Arrive. Mr. Dexter appeared yesterday at my office, with the Master who Reported the Vessel and Cargo as the property of Said Dexter, which also appeared by an Instrument of Transfer executed by Mr. Arnold dated on the 9th Day of August last for the Consideration of Five Thousand pounds.

The Vessel has been ordered to proceed to the District of New-port, there to enter and Secure the duties on her Cargo, which will Amount, by Estimate, to Twenty Eight hundred Dollars, the Master was Furnished with a Copy of his report, an Inspector being on Board. Altho' it is more than Probable that this Transfer of Property was made with the Sole intent to effect a Further Credit in evasion of the law, yet this cannot be known to me or to the Collector of Newport,³ where Entry will be made, and as the law itself seems not to guard against an evasion of this Nature, he may, notwith-standing I have notified him of Mr. Arnolds Delinquency, be in-duced, under the present *embarassed* circumstance of the case, to admit the Duties to be Secured by Mr Dexters Bonds. On the 31st Ulto. I requested (by Letter a Copy of which is enclosed) the advise of the District Attorney ⁴ on this Point; but have not Received his Answer and as Mr. Arnold appears disposed thus to evade the law, I request Sir, your opinion and Direction for my Future Conduct with regard to Vessels and Cargoes thus circumstanced, which (not-withstanding my letter to the District Attorney) I shall invariably observe.

Yours &c.   Jereh. Olney Collr.

ADfS, Rhode Island Historical Society, Providence.
  1. Arnold was a Providence merchant.
  2. See William Ellery to H, September 4, 1792.
  3. William Ellery.   4. William Channing.

From Edmund Randolph ¹

Philadelphia September 8th. 1792.

Sir,

Persuaded as I am, that the last effort for the happiness of the United States must perish with the loss of the present Government,

Copy, Hamilton Papers, Library of Congress.
  1. For background to this letter, see H to Tench Coxe, September 1, 1792; H to George Washington, September 1, 1792; H to John Jay, September 3, 1792; "Draft of a Proclamation Concerning Opposition to the Excise Law," September 7, 1792; Washington to H, September 7, 1792; Jay to H, Septem-ber 8, 1792.

and that to be unable to execute laws because a few individuals are resolved to obstruct their operation is nothing less, than a surrender of it, I went into the consideration of the carolina and pittsburg papers [2] with a determination to spare no pains to ascertain the Law, arising from the facts which they contain.

I pass by the information from Carolina, because it offers no evidence, nor any prospect of evidence, sufficient for the objects of prosecution. That from Pittsburgh is of a more serious complexion; and yet not strong enough to warrant a judicial movement in the United States. To assemble to remonstrate, and to invite others to assemble and remonstrate to the Legislature, are among the rights of Citizens. I therefore omit special mention of the two first resolutions.[3] The last indicates a hostile temper; as it exiles from the comforts of private friendship, and intercourse, and marks for contempt the officers of Excise. Still however when we advert to the strictness, with which criminal Law is interpreted, and the latitude allowed in drawing a meaning from a libel so as to favour the accused, I must pronounce that the law will not reach the Conferees. I am aware that seditious attacks on Government will be generally covered by a measured cautious and artfull language; and it may be said that the public authority will upon my principle, be forever foiled. My answer is, that words which are calculated to withold the exercise of duties of imperfect obligation only, from men not named, but who may accept in future, will disappoint the expectation of public punishment, and thereby disgrace the United States. My maxim is to examine well; to forbear a doubtfull power, and to enforce one, clearly rightfull.

Thus, Sir, you discover my opinion to be against an attempt to a prosecution *at this moment,* when the malignant spirit has not developed itself in acts so specific, and so manifestly infringing the peace, as obviously to expose the culpable persons to the censures of the Law.

2. Presumably this is a reference to articles concerning opposition to the excise which appeared in *The Pittsburgh Gazette* and some North Carolina newspapers. Issues of the Pittsburgh paper for this period have not been found, nor have relevant issues of the *Fayetteville Gazette.* Other North and South Carolina newspapers available for this period contain no relevant information.

3. For the resolutions adopted at Pittsburgh on August 22, 1792, see H to Coxe, September 1, 1792, note 5.

Upon the first communication of this matter in your letter [4] I thought of a proclamation, as an eventual substitute, if the law should be found inadequate. It struck me that a proclamation was objectionable, because it seemed that the Executive ought to consign to the course of the law any violations of it, and not to animadvert upon acts to which no Law had prescribed a penalty, and because an improper interference of the President might excite an idea of usurpation and inlist against him even those who execrate the spirit of the Pittsburg proceedings. But after the anticipation of a part only of the consequences, which the silence of Government would produce, after recollecting that these obnoxious things have been transacted in the very state which is the temporary residence of the Administration, that they will carry with them a kind of eclat, as being done at a spot where the United States are certainly not unpopular, that the western Settlers in other States, from a Sympathy of situation, and the want of intelligence may imitate the conduct of the pennsylvania counties, unless they will be restrained by a timely admonition, that few of the serious oppositions to Government have existed, which were not capable of being blasted, if encountered before men committed themselves too deeply, and that acquiescence of the President may be imputed to a suspicion of the inconstitunality or at least gross inexpediency of the Excise Laws, I yeild to the necessity of a Proclamation. I derive the Presidents right to issue it, from the duty of seeing the laws executed, and the fitness of preventing the growth of a crime by salutary advice rather then waiting to press the infliction of punishment.

Under the influence of these sentiments I have perused your draught of a proclamation,[5] and shall without reserve suggest what I think necessary alterations; though I really wish that I could have more time for a critical scrutiny than has occurred between yesterday and this morning.

1. I should prefer, if it be practicable in the description of those proceedings which gave birth to the proclamation, that some expression be used, which may shew that it is not the *whole* of the Pittsburg resolutions which are censured.

4. Letter not found.
5. Draft not found. For the final form of the proclamation, see "Draft of a Proclamation Concerning Opposition to the Excise Law," September 7, 1792, note 1.

2. *Criminality* is too strong for a case, which the laws do not punish.

3. After the word *legislature* may it not be well to insert something to this effect "by whose authority alone the operation of the Laws can be suspended."

4. The moderation alluded to on the part of Government, must be either Legislative or Executive. If legislative be meant, the subsequent member of the sentence is explicit concerning it. If executive, I know no fact to prove that the President might have been otherwise then moderate. Perhaps then it may be better to omit words which are liable to misconstruction.

5. I have no hesitation in saying that the excise law was dictated by reasons of public necessity and policy and I presume that the President who has given his sanction to it will not scruple much on this head. But I should hope that you should remark to him in order to excite his particular attention that by such a language he exhibets himself as a peculiar Friend to the act.

6. Instead of "*maintain*," ought not the words of the constitution to be chosen?

7. Every *necessary* measure to *suppress* a *violent* proceeding would go much farther, then the executive ought, unless the measure be *legal*. The word *necessary* then might be as well changed for *legal* or qualified by saying *legal* and *necessary*. If "suppress" means something distinct from bringing the offenders to justice, I do not discover what it is. If it means the same thing, it is provided for in the second member of the Sentence. "To secure obedience thereto" is to be sure a phrase, expressive of the final object, but having some latitude it may be perverted by its connection with the other words. Might not the sentence run well enough thus "That every legal measure should be pursued not only to bring to Justice the infractors of the laws but also to prevent such violent and unwarrantable proceedings."

8. "*Seriously*" might be changed for something which could not be contrasted with what is not serious. Is not "*warn*" to nearly synonimous with "*admonish*" to be coupled with it? Suppose "*exhort*" to be substituted if two verbs necessary.

9. I think this No. stood better, before the interleniation.

10. For the reasons in No. 7 "for securing obedience thereto" would seem proper to be omitted.

11. The charge to the military would inflame the Country. Nor do I think it sufficient to let it stand upon the word *"Officers"* generally as the military have no power on the subject and where this is the case of the exciting of a suspicion to introduce them cannot be too sedulously avoided. May it not read thus "All civil Officers according to the duties of their respective Offices to exert &c."

I submit these observations; which on other occasions would appear to myself too minute; but on that of a *proclamation* are necessary.

I have the honor, Sir, to be   your Mo: obedt. servant.

Edm: Randolph

The Secretary of the Treasury.

Treasury Department Circular
to the Collectors of the Customs

Treasury Department
September 8th. 1792.

Sir

I am to request your attention to the inclosed Paper and that in the Columns opposite the described Article of Merchandise or Package (for containing them,) the rates of Freight which are paid from your Port to the Countries expressed in the Head Lines be inserted, and returned to me as early as the Inquiry will admit.

With great consideration   I am Sir   Your obedient Servt.

A Hamilton

LS, to Jeremiah Olney, Rhode Island Historical Society, Providence; L[S], to Benjamin Lincoln, RG 36, Collector of Customs at Boston, Letters from the Treasury, 1789–1807, Vol. 4, National Archives; LS, to Otho H. Williams, Columbia University Libraries; copy, RG 56, Letters to the Collector at Boston, National Archives; copy, RG 56, Letters to Collectors at Small Ports, "Set G," National Archives.

To George Washington [1]

Treasury Departmt. 8th. Septr. 1792.

Sir,

I have to acknowledge the honor of your Letter of the 31st of August.

Letters from the Supervisor of North Carolina [2] confirm the representation contained in the letter from the Inspector of the 5th. Survey to you. [3] My letter which accompanies this [4] suggests the measure which, on mature reflection, has appeared most proper to be taken upon the whole subject of the opposition to the Law. [5] If the idea is approved by you, I believe it will be adviseable to transmit a copy of the Proclamation to the Governor of each of the States of South Carolina North Carolina & Pennsylvania, calling their attention in a proper manner to the state of affairs within their respective Governments.

I am taking arrangements to cary into execution the payment of the Debt due to foreign officers, agreeably to the authorisation in the close of your Letter.

With the highest respect and the truest attachment, I have the honor to be &c.   Alex Hamilton

LC, George Washington Papers, Library of Congress.

1. For background to this letter, see H to Tench Coxe, September 1, 1792; H to Washington, September 1, 1792; H to John Jay, September 3, 1792; "Draft of a Proclamation Concerning Opposition to the Excise Law," September 7, 1792; Washington to H, September 7, 1792; Jay to H, September 8, 1792; Edmund Randolph to H, September 8, 1792.

2. Letters from William Polk to H or to Tench Coxe have not been found.

3. Joseph McDowell, Jr., was inspector of Survey No. 5 in North Carolina. On September 20, 1792, Tench Coxe wrote to Edward Carrington that McDowell had resigned because of opposition in North Carolina to the Excise Law (LC, RG 58, Letters of Commissioner of Revenue, 1792–1793, National Archives).

4. H had originally intended to accompany this letter with his official letter of September 9, 1792. He deferred sending his official letter and enclosed it in his letter to Washington of September 11, 1792. H did, however, enclose in the letter printed above his letter of September 9, 1792, in which cabinet dissensions were discussed.

5. "An Act repealing, after the last day of June next, the duties heretofore laid upon Distilled Spirits imported from abroad, and laying others in their stead; and also upon Spirits distilled within the United States, and for appro-

priating the same" (1 *Stat.* 199–217 [March 3, 1791]) was amended by "An Act concerning the Duties on Spirits distilled within the United States" (1 *Stat.* 267–71 [May 8, 1792]).

To John Adams

Philadelphia Sepr. 9. 1792 [1]

My Dear Sir

I trust you are sufficiently convinced of my respect for and attachment to you to render an apology for the liberty, I am going to take unnecessary. I learnt with pain that you may not probably be here 'till late in the session. I fear that this will give some handle to your enemies to misrepresent—and though I am persuaded you are very indifferent personally to the event of a certain election, yet I hope you are not so as it regards the cause of good Government. The difference in that view is in my conception immense between the success of Mr. Clinton [2] or yourself; and some sacrifices of feeling are to be made. But this is not the only relation, in which I deem your early presence here desireable. Permit me to say it best suits the firmness and elevation of your character to meet all events, whether auspicious or otherwise, on the ground where station & duty, call you. One would not give the ill disposed the triumph of supposing that an anticipation of want of success had kept you from your post.

You observe My Dr Sir, I speak without much *menagement*. You will ascribe it to my confidence and esteem. It is not necessary in any view to multiply words. I forbear it. But allow me to add that it is the universal wish of your friends you should be as soon as possible at Philadelphia.

I have the honor to remain very respectfully   and truly Dr Sir Yr friend & Obed servant   A Hamilton

The Vice President

ALS, Adams Family Papers, deposited in the Massachusetts Historical Society, Boston.

1. In *HCLW*, V, 28–29, this letter is dated October, 1792, and in Hamilton, *History*, V, 92–93, it is undated.

2. Governor George Clinton of New York. See H to Adams, August 16, 1792.

From Henry E. Lutterloh

[New Bern, North Carolina, September 9, 1792]

Sir,

Your favour of the 4th July a c, I had the honour to receive by the last post.[1] Tho' you did not mention, that I should sent on any Plan to a General Lottery, yet I take the Liberty to inclose one. And as in all the Old Governments, Minister raise annually a certain Revenues by Lottery; I take the Liberty to annext Two Plans, the one for 3 Classes, and the Other for one Class only.[2] The first is done to make the purchase of the Tickets easy and to give Time for Selling them. An Office, of Such an Establishment will cost Nothing, be Usefull, and produce a Surplus. People in the North like That Game.

I obtained from our General Assamble an Act[3] to raise by Way of a Lottery for 5 Years annualy, 6000 Dollr, Two years of which are now elapsed, and I have only been able to Draw last 24 of august the first Class, and which I was obliged to draw to show them the Nature of a Lottery, the most part of the Citizen here being intirely Ingnorant thereof.[4] I inclose My Grant of the Governor.[5] Mr Wm B Grove[6] informed Me That he has delivered in his Report, upon My Petition, and is fully persuated that by their next Meeting, I will obtain 740 Dollrs as allowed by the Comitty.[7] Several havy Losses, The disappointment in the drawing of My Lottery, have put Me to a great Want. All our great people here, are in Want of Cash So that I cannot get any help from Them. I would take it as an Exceeding great favour if you would assist me with a Loan in advance upon that Sum of only 3, or, 400 dollor. I would sent directly the order thereupon. I am well persuated it is quite out of the Line, in Your Station, and I do not aske it from You in Office But as an old Campain Freind, who is able to help me, in my present delemma. You See My Situation requires help, to carry The Grant of this Govermt into Execution. Therefore I beg you will take it into Consideration and Sent me a draft for it on any of your Collectors. Such an assistance will greatly help me &c. I have the honour to be with the Greatest Respect

Sir   Your Most obedient Sert   H E Lutterloh

The Honorble
Allexdr Hamilton Esqr

New Bern
Septbr 9th 1792
I am Mooved to here [8]

ALS, Hamilton Papers, Library of Congress.
    1. Letter not found.
    2. "The United States First General Lottery granted by Congress in their
        Session at Philadelphia   1792" (D, Hamilton Papers, Library of
Congress) and "*The Plan* for a Lottery of one class only" (AD, Hamilton
Papers, Library of Congress).
    3. "An Act *to authorize* Henry Emanuel Lutterloh, *to raise by way of
Lottery, a sum sufficient to enable him to bring into this state foreigners who
are artisans in various branches of business*" (D, Microfilm Collection of
Early State Records, Library of Congress). The act was approved on December 4, 1790 (Walter Clark, ed., *The State Records of North Carolina* [Golds-
boro, North Carolina, 1903], XXI, 969).
    4. A notice of the drawing for the first lottery and the scheme of the
second was published in the *Fayetteville Gazette* on September 25, 1792.
    5. The act provided that Lutterloh's scheme should be laid before the
North Carolina council of state and that a grant from the governor should be
issued. Both Lutterloh's plan of a lottery and the governor's grant of April 11,
1791, may be found in the minutes of the council under date of April 11,
1791 (DS, Microfilm Collection of Early State Records, Library of Congress).
    6. William Barry Grove represented the Fayetteville district in North Caro-
lina.
    7. Lutterloh is referring to a petition "praying to be allowed the pay and
emoluments of a Colonel, in consideration of military services rendered to
the United States during the late war," which he had sent to the House of
Representatives on April 14, 1790. The petition was rejected, but Lutterloh's
petition to the next session of Congress was received favorably. On February
6, 1793, the House of Representatives passed a "bill to reimburse Henry
Emanuel Lutterloh for expenses incurred in coming to America, to join the
Army of the United States, during the late war." The bill, however, was
rejected by the Senate (*Journal of the House,* I, 193, 220, 275, 286–87, 337,
469, 470, 604, 677, 687, 692, 704).
    8. Lutterloh had originally settled in Fayetteville, North Carolina, after the
American Revolution.
    On the back of this letter H wrote: "Mr. Lutterloh Concerning a Lottery.
Answered Sep. 26, 1792." H's letter of September 26 has not been found.

To George Washington [1]

Treasury Departmt. Septr. 9th. 1792.

Sir,

I had the honor of writing to you by the post of Monday last,[2]
and then transmitted sundry papers respecting a Meeting at Pitts-

burg on the 21st of August, and other proceedings of a disorderly nature, in opposition to the Laws laying a duty on distilled spirits; and I added my opinion, that it was adviseable for the Government to take measures for suppressing these disorders, & enforcing the laws with vigour & decision.

The result of further & mature deliberation is, that it will be expedient for the President to issue a Proclamation, adverting in general terms to the irregular proceedings, which have taken place, warning all persons to desist from similar proceedings & manifesting an intention to put the Laws in force against Offenders.

The inducements to this measure are;

1st. That it is a usual course in like cases; and seems, all circumstances considered, requisite to the justification of the Executive Department: It is now more than fourteen months since the duty in question began to operate. In the four Western Counties of Pennsylvania and in a great part of North Carolina it has never been in any degree submitted to. And the late Meeting at Pittsburg is in substance a repetition of what happened last year in the same scene.[3] The disorders in that quarter acquire additional consequence from their being acted in the State which is the immediate Seat of the Government. Hence the occasion appears to be sufficiently serious & of sufficient importance to call for such a proceedure.

II. An accommodating and temporising conduct having been hitherto pursued, a Proclamation seems to be the natural prelude to a different course of conduct.[4]

III. There is considerable danger, that before measures can be matured for making a public impression by the prosecution of offenders, the spirit of opposition may extend & break out in other quarters; and by its extension become much more difficult to be overcome. There is reason to hope that a Proclamation will arrest it, and give time for more effectual measures.

IV. It may even prevent the necessity of ulterior coertion. The character of the President will naturally induce a conclusion that he means to treat the matter seriously. The idea will be impressive on the most refractory, it will restrain the timid & wavering, and it will encourage the well disposed. The appearance of the President in the business will awaken the attention of a great number of persons of the last description to the evil tendency of the conduct reprehended, who have not yet viewed it with due seriousness. And from the cooperation of these circumstances, good may reasonably be expected.

In either view therefore, of the propriety of conduct, or the effects to be hoped for, the measure seems to be an adviseable one. I beg leave to add that, in my judgment, it is not only adviseable, but necessary.

Besides the state of things in the Western parts of North Carolina which is known to you,[5] a letter has just been received from the Supervisor of South Carolina,[6] mentioning that a spirit of discontent and opposition had been revived in two of the Counties of that State bordering on North Carolina, in which it had been before apparently suppressed. This shews the necessity of some immediate step of a general aspect, while things are preparing, if unhappily it should become necessary, to act with decision in the Western Counties of Pennsylvania, where the Government, from several obvious considerations will be left in condition to do it. Decision successfully exerted in one place will, it is presumable, be efficacious every where.

The Secretary at War and the Attorney General agree with me in opinion on the expediency of a Proclamation. The draft of one now submitted has been framed in concert with the latter; except as to one or two particulars which are noted in the margin of the *rough* draft in my hand writing, herewith also transmitted.[7] In respect to these, the objections of that Gentleman did not appear to me founded, and would, I think, unnecessarily diminish the force of the instrument.

With the highest respect and the truest attachment,   I have the honor to be &c.   Alexr. Hamilton.

LC, George Washington Papers, Library of Congress.

1. For background to this letter, see H to Tench Coxe, September 1, 1792; H to Washington, September 1, 8, 1792; H to John Jay, September 3, 1792; "Draft of a Proclamation Concerning Opposition to the Excise Law," September 7, 1792; Washington to H, September 7, 1792; Jay to H, September 8, 1792; Edmund Randolph to H, September 8, 1792.

2. H is referring to the letter which he wrote on Saturday, September 1, 1792.

3. See H to Coxe, September 1, 1792, notes 1 and 5

4. On July 11, 1792, Tench Coxe wrote to George Clymer: "In one or two late Conversations I communicated to you the Secretary's Idea; that the Inspectors of Surveys should be instructed to pursue measures for producing punctuality in the discharge of the Revenue then due. The intimations, which I presume those Gentlemen have given thro' the Collectors to the distillers, will prepare the latter for such calls as duty enjoins upon the officers, after the expiration of the Current half year. Besides the Inconveniencies to the Treasury arising from delays there is great danger that those who have

yielded due obedience to the law may change their conduct if they find no compulsion applied to their unpunctual Neighbours. You will be pleased therefore to remind the Inspectors, and Collectors within Survey No. 1 that they are to commence suits against two persons in each County, by way of Example, should payment not be duly made at the commencement of the next half year.

"It will be necessary also that suits be commenced against the several distillers in Mr. [Jacob] Humphrey's division, who have omitted or refused to comply with the directions of the law." (LC, RG 58, Letters of Commissioner of Revenue, 1792–1793, National Archives.)

On September 28, 1792, Coxe again wrote to Clymer: "As it has become necessary that suits be instituted against some two defaulting or delinquent persons in each of the Counties in the 4th. Survey, I request that the names and additions of some two persons, who are in his opinion proper to begin with, may be transmitted. It will be expedient to select such as reside within ten miles of an Office of Inspection, which has been open a competent time or which is still open. Information of the time when the Office was opened, of the time when it was suppressed, if that has been done, of the size and number of the delinquents still or Stills and of every other fact which it may be useful or necessary to establish on a suit, also the Name of the Witnesses who can or will prove those facts will require to be stated" (LC, RG 58, Letters of Commissioner of Revenue, 1792–1793, National Archives).

5. See Washington to H, August 31, 1792.

6. No letter from Daniel Stevens to H concerning renewed opposition has been found. For a reference to earlier opposition in South Carolina, see Daniel Stevens to H, May 22, 1792.

7. Neither of these drafts has been found. See "Draft of a Proclamation Concerning Opposition to the Excise Law," September 7, 1792, note 1; Edmund Randolph to H, September 8, 1792.

To George Washington

Philadelphia September 9
1792

Sir

I have the pleasure of your private letter of the 26th of August.

The feelings and views which are manifested in that letter are such as I expected would exist. And I most sincerely regret the causes of the uneasy sensations you experience. It is my most anxious wish, as far as may depend upon me, to smooth the path of your administration, and to render it prosperous and happy. And if any prospect shall open of healing or terminating the differences which exist, I shall most chearfully embrace it; though I consider myself as the deeply injured party. The recommendation of such a spirit is worthy of the moderation and wisdom which dictated it; and if

ALS, George Washington Papers, Library of Congress.

your endeavours should prove unsucessful, I do not hesitate to say that in my opinion the period is not remote when the public good will require *substitutes* for the *differing members* of your administration. The continuance of a division there must destroy the energy of Government, which will be little enough with the strictest Union. On my part there will be a most chearful acquiescence in such a result.

I trust, Sir, that the greatest frankness has always marked and will always mark every step of my conduct towards you. In this disposition, I cannot conceal from you that I have had some instrumentality of late in the retaliations which have fallen upon certain public characters and that I find myself placed in a situation not to be able to recede *for the present.*

I considered myself as compelled to this conduct by reasons public as well as personal of the most cogent nature. I *know* that I have been an object of uniform opposition from Mr. Jefferson, from the first moment of his coming to the City of New York to enter upon his present office. I *know,* from the most authentic sources, that I have been the frequent subject of the most unkind whispers and insinuating from the same quarter. I have long seen a formed party in the Legislature, under his auspices, bent upon my subversion. I cannot doubt, from the evidence I possess, that the National Gazette was instituted by him for political purposes and that one leading object of it has been to render me and all the measures connected with my department as odious as possible.

Nevertheless I can truly say, that, except explanations to confidential friends, I never directly or indirectly retaliated or countenanced retaliation till very lately. I can even assure you, that I was instrumental in preventing a very severe and systematic attack upon Mr. Jefferson, by an association of two or three individuals, in consequence of the persecution, which he brought upon the Vice President, by his indiscreet and light letter to the Printer, transmitting *Paine's* pamphlet.[1]

1. This is a reference to Thomas Jefferson's endorsement in 1791 of Thomas Paine's *The Rights of Man.* The "persecution, which he brought upon the Vice President," resulted from the fact that Jefferson's statement on *The Rights of Man* was interpreted as an attack on John Adams's *Discourses on Davila.* See "Conversation with Thomas Jefferson," August 13, 1791, note 1.

As long as I saw no danger to the Government, from the machinations which were going on, I resolved to be a silent sufferer of the injuries which were done me. I determined to avoid giving occasion to any thing which could manifest to the world dissentions among the principal characters of the government; a thing which can never happen without weakening its hands, and in some degree throwing a stigma upon it.

But when I no longer doubted, that there was a formed party deliberately bent upon the subversion of measures, which in its consequences would subvert the Government—when I saw, that the undoing of the funding system in particular (which, whatever may be the original merits of that system, would prostrate the credit and the honor of the Nation, and bring the Government into contempt with that description of Men, who are in every society the only firm supporters of government) was an avowed object of the party; and that all possible pains were taking to produce that effect by rendering it odious to the body of the people—I considered it as a duty, to endeavour to resist the torrent, and as an essential mean to this end, to draw aside the veil from the principal Actors. To this strong impulse, to this decided conviction, I have yielded. And I think events will prove that I have judged rightly.

Nevertheless I pledge my honor to you Sir, that if you shall hereafter form a plan to reunite the members of your administration, upon some steady principle of cooperation, I will faithfully concur in executing it during my continuance in office. And I will not directly or indirectly say or do a thing, that shall endanger a feud.

I have had it very much at heart to make an excursion to Mount Vernon, by way of the Fœderal City in the course of this Month—and have been more than once on the point of asking your permission for it. But I now despair of being able to effect it. I am nevertheless equally obliged by your kind invitation.[2]

The subject mentioned in the Postscript of your letter shall with great pleasure be carefully attended to. With the most faithful and affectionate attachment I have the honor to remain

Sir   Your most Obed & humble servant   A Hamilton

P.S   I had written you two letters on public business, one of which

2. See Washington to H, August 26, 1792.

will go with this; [3] but the other will be witheld, in consequence of a slight indisposition of the Attorney General, to be sent by express sometime in the course of tomorrow.[4]

The President of The U States

3. H to Washington, September 8, 1792.
4. H's other letter to Washington, dated September 9, 1792, accompanied his letter of September 11, 1792.

From William Ellery

Newport [Rhode Island] September 10, 1792. "I have received your letter of the 6th. of August.[1] The Construction of the Attorney General contained in the first paragraph, and which it is your desire should be practiced upon I think I understand; but the doubt in my mind which occasioned my stating a case, and raising a question thereon in my letter of the 30th of July last still remains. . . . I have also recd. your letter respectg. the case of Benjamin Cranston, and Nathaniel Waldron,[2] and have given them notice. . . ."

LC, Newport Historical Society, Newport, Rhode Island.
1. See "Treasury Department Circular to the Collectors of the Customs," August 6, 1792.
2. Letter not found.

From Caleb Gibbs [1]

Barre [Massachusetts] Septr. 10th: 1792.

My Dear Freind

Disagreable is the task to me to be so often interupting you by my Letters and solicitations, Yet on reflection, when I consider your repeated declarations that you truely have a warm regard for me, Still induces me to intrude upon your patience, and now and then put you in mind of your old Freind; that if anything within your power to grant, shall be reserved for him.

I wrote you On the 12th. of Decr. last [2] and am somewhat fearful wether or not a Miscarriage of the Letter has not taken place or by some means or other had been mislayed, by my not hearing from you for so long a period. The Letter was a recapitulation of the propriety of Mr. Tracy's demands against the United States,[3] and begging that I may not be totally forgotten by the President and your self.

As Congress will soon meet again My Dear freind, remember me. Certainly there will be appointments which will come from you of different kinds. Therefore Let me rest persuaded I shall not be forsaken.

Mrs. Gibbs cannot no longer content herself in this wilderness. Her seperation from her dearest connections, the great distance and extreem bad roads to Boston, and what is still more trying is the Education of her Children and an innumerable number of difficulties to incounter, has brought me to a Resolution to *Linger* out the cold Inclement winter at this place and return to Boston Early in April next if possible to get there. In the mean time let me intreat of you to drop me a line of Consolation.

Our only son Alexander Hamilton is well and a fine boy he is. May God Almighty very long continue him on the stage of Life to keep up that name to whom this *ungrateful* Country owes so much to, and live to follow the Examples and immitate the Virtues of him for whom he is named.

If a convenient opportunity offers I will thank you to mention me to the President with my warmest regards. Also to Mrs. Washington and your truely amiable Lady.

With sentiments of the sincerest regard, respect, and Esteem   I have the honor to be   My Dear friend   Your most Obedient and very humble servant   C. Gibbs.

Honble Alexander Hamilton Esqr.
&ca. &ca. &ca.
Philadelphia

ALS, Hamilton Papers, Library of Congress; ALS (duplicate), Hamilton Papers, Library of Congress. The duplicate was enclosed in Gibbs to H, February 16, 1793.

1. Gibbs, like H, had been an aide-de-camp to George Washington during the American Revolution.

2. Letter not found.

3. Nathaniel Tracy. For information on Tracy's claim, see Gibbs to H, January 16, 1791.

From Henry Lee

[Richmond, September 10, 1792]

My dear friend

I found on my return from a visit to the southwestern frontier of this state your letter of the 22d. Ult.[1] I am still depressed in my mind & continue to be the subject to unavailing woe. My son [2] on whom I cheifly counted for future comfort was suddenly deprived of life during my absence, which event on the back of what took place two years past [3] has removed me far from the happy enjoyment of life.

Yet I feel the force of old connexions & acknowledge with pleasure the truth of your recognition of my friendship for you. It is unabated & will so continue to be, altho I never did nor never can admire the funding system of which you confessedly was the father. Why cannot men differ in politics as they do in other matters and yet hold established regards?

I see no insurmountable difficulty in the way and feel its practicability.

I believe you are in some degree right in your conjecture with respect to my friends. Generally speaking those in the political line will be found arranged with you, but in the opposition are some too, loved by me & attached to me.

Why do not these virulent partys coalesce? Is there no middle ground on which a union might be formed. The public harmony as well as individual comfort would be promoted by such an event.

Whether Mr P [4] succeeds in his request for the place in the adm of the bank intended to be established here is only interesting to me from my knowledge of his worth & of my preference always to the father of a family.

The jus trium liberorum [5] I have estimated as a wise regulation, & feel the influence of the principle whenever my opinion is asked about the pretensions of competitors to office.

I could say much to you with respect to the Bank & many other congressional measures springing from the funding system, but I prefer silence to discussion when no good can result therefrom. Would to God you had never been the patron of the measure in its present shape, for I augur ill of its effect on yourself personally, as well as on the public prosperity.

The horse cost me 30 gs; but I do not think him worth so much by five;[6] I esteemed him highly as a riding horse & can replace him by one younger more costly & handsome if he does *not exactly* suit you. You gave me ten guineas, which perhaps you may have forgot. Present me to Mrs H & tell her, that I wish her all happiness.

Adieu my friend   Henry Lee
                                                   Richmond Sepr. 10th. 92

ALS, Hamilton Papers, Library of Congress.
1. Letter not found.   2. Philip Ludwell Lee.
3. This is a reference to the death of Lee's wife, Matilda Lee.
4. This may be a reference to Robert Pollard of Richmond. On July 30, 1792, Richard Henry Lee had written to Thomas Willing, president of the Bank of the United States, requesting that Pollard be appointed cashier of the Richmond branch of the Bank of the United States (Burton Alva Konkle, *Thomas Willing and the First American Financial System* [Philadelphia, 1937], 149–50).
5. In Roman law, this was a right granted to the parent of three or more children. The privileges granted under this right were exemption from guardianship, priority in holding office, and an extra proportion of corn.
6. See Lee to H, May 6, 1792.

From Gulian Verplanck [1]

Newyork Sepr 10. 1792

Dear Sir

The Legislature of the State of Newyork at their last Sessions passed an Act Authorizing the acknowledgement of Deeds before any of the Judges of the supreme Court of the U.S.[2] I shall therefore be obligd to You if You will execute the Deed for the House in Wall Street & forward it to Me as soon as it suits Your Conveniency.

If the payment of the first moiety at any time before the stipulated period, will be any accommodation to You, it will be ready whenever You please to direct the payment—on the delivery of the Deed, if You choose it, and the Bond for the Residue will be forwarded to You.

I am   with sincerest Esteem   Your Obt. Hume Sert
                                                   Gulian Verplanck
The Secretary of the Treasury

ALS, Hamilton Papers, Library of Congress.
1. Verplanck was a prominent New York merchant. As this letter states, he had purchased H's house at 58 Wall Street.
2. "An Act concerning conveyances by married women" provided in part "That all acknowledgments and proofs of deeds and conveyances of any lands tenements or hereditaments situated in this State taken or made before any judge of the supreme court of the United States shall be of like validity and force, as if the same was taken or made before a judge of the supreme court of this State" (*Laws of the State of New York*, III, 348).

Amicus

[Philadelphia, September 11, 1792]

For the National Gazette.

A writer in the Gazette of Saturday last, after several observations, with regard to certain charges, which have lately been brought forward against the Secretary of State, proceeds to make or insinuate several charges against another public character.[1]

As to the observations which are designed to exculpate the Secretary of State, I shall do nothing more than refer to the discussions which have taken place and appear to be in a train to be pursued, in the Gazette of the United States.[2]

As to the charges which have been bro't against the other public character alluded to, I shall assert generally, from a long, intimate, and confidential acquaintance with him, added to some other means of information, that the matters charged, as far as they are intelligible, are either grossly misrepresented or palpably untrue.

A part of them, is of a nature to speak itself, without comment, the malignity and turpitude of the accuser, denoting clearly the personal enemy in the garb of the political opponent.

The subject and the situation of the parties naturally impose silence—but this is not the first attempt of the kind that has been made; fruitlessly hitherto, and I doubt not equally fruitlessly in time to come. An opinion on the experience of fifteen years, the greatest part of the time, under circumstances affording the best opportunity for an accurate estimate of character, cannot be shaken by slanderous surmises. The charge of which I shall take more particular notice, is contained in the following passage—"Let him explain the public character, who, if uncontradicted fame is to be regarded, *opposed* the Constitution in the Grand Convention, because it was *too repub-lican*, and advocated the *British monarchy as the perfect standard* to be approached as nearly as the people could be *made to bear.*"

This I affirm, to be a gross misrepresentation. To prove it so, it were sufficient to appeal to a single fact, namely, that the gentleman alluded to, was the only member from the state to which he be-longed who signed the Constitution, and, it is notorious, against the prevailing weight of the official influence of the state, and against what would probably be the opinion of a large majority of his fellow-citizens, till better information should correct their first im-pressions—how then can he be believed to have opposed a thing, which he actually agreed to, and that, in so unsupported a situation, and under circumstances of such peculiar responsibility? To this I shall add two more facts; one, that the member in question, never made a single proposition to the Convention, which was not con-formable to the republican theory; [3] the other, that the highest-toned of any of the propositions made by him was actually voted for by the representations of several states, including some of the principal ones; and including individuals, who, in the estimation of those who deem themselves the only republicans, are pre-eminent for repub-lican character [4]—more than this I am not at liberty to say. It is a matter generally understood, that the deliberations of the Conven-tion which were carried on in private, were to remain undisturbed. And every prudent man must be convinced of the propriety both of the one and the other. Had the deliberations been open while going on, the clamours of faction would have prevented any satisfactory result. Had they been afterwards disclosed, much food would have been afforded to inflammatory declamation. Propositions made with-out due reflection, and perhaps abandoned by the proposers them-selves, on more mature reflection, would have been handles for a profusion of il-natured accusation.

Every infallible declaimer taking his own ideas as the perfect stand-ard, would have railed without measure or mercy at every member of the Convention who had gone a single line beyond his standard.

The present is a period fruitful in accusation. Much anonymous slander has and will be vented. No man's reputation can be safe, if charges in this form are to be lightly listened to. There are but two kinds of anonymous charges that can merit attention—where the

evidence goes along with the charge—and where reference is made to *specific facts*, the evidence of the truth or falsehood of which, is in the power or possession of the party accused, and he at liberty to make a free use of it. None of the charges brought forward in the present instance, fall within either of these rules.

AMICUS.

Sept. 11.

[Philadelphia] *National Gazette*, September 12, 1792.

1. H is referring to an unsigned article in the *National Gazette*, September 8, 1792, that was written in reply to H's attacks on Thomas Jefferson in his "An American" letters dated August 4, 11, 18, 1792. After defending Jefferson, the anonymous author concluded his article by writing:

"But as the *American* has shewn himself so unequal to the task he has undertaken, this virtuous explainer of public characters, is requested to undertake another, wherein *he* cannot be so liable to mistakes. Let him explain the public character, who, if uncontradicted fame is to be regarded, opposed the constitution in the Grand Convention, because it was too *republican*, and advocated the *British Monarchy as the perfect standard* to be approached to as nearly as the people could be made to bear, and now would impose himself on the people for a pure *republican*, and would have them distrust men who have uniformly supported the constitution on republican grounds.

"Let the explainer go on—and explain the public character who on an occasion well known to *him*, could so far divest himself of *gratitude*, and revolt from the spirit of his *station*, as to erect his little crest against the magnanimous Chief who at present is at the head of our *civil* establishment; and has on many free occasions since, spoken with levity and *depreciation* of some of the greatest qualities of that renowned character; and now gives himself out as if he were his most cordial friend and admirer, and most worthy of public confidence on that account. But all this may be explained—For, if a delicacy 'equal to that of family connections,' did not oppose, it could be proved to be the avowed policy of some, to make the most of a great name in furthering their political views, by holding up its sanction, as if extended in all cases, and by full and positive approbation, thereto.

"This explainer will be further able to throw great light on the combination attempted at the approach of peace, to establish an *efficient government*, by means *efficient* also; but very different from the *republican* and *free* plan of a Convention acting by the *authority of the people*. This piece of history is much wanted; and with the other explanations which the *American*, from his love of the *people*, *truth*, and of *liberty*, it is expected will not withhold, will be of vast utility. He will then have the merit, he now only affects, of letting the public into the true knowledge of public characters it trusts; and the satisfaction, if he is not callous to remorse, of doing full justice to the character of the Secretary of State, by placing it in contrast with some which will be so detected and brought to light." ([Philadelphia] *National Gazette*, September 8, 1792.)

2. Although H did not write any more "An American" letters, on September 15, 1792, the first of his "Catullus" letters was published in the [Philadelphia] *Gazette of the United States*. "Catullus No. I" was written in reply to a letter signed "Aristides," which appeared in the [Philadelphia] *Gazette of the United States* on September 8, 1792.

3. See "Constitutional Convention. Speech on a Plan of Government," June 18, 1787, and "Constitutional Convention. Plan of Government," June 18, 1787.

4. H may be referring to the vote on the tenure of the presidency. On July 17, 1787, the delegations from New Jersey, Pennsylvania, Delaware, and Virginia voted in favor of amending the clause to change the presidential term of office from seven years to "during good behavior" (Hunt and Scott, *Debates*, 273). Among the members of the Virginia delegation present on that date were James Madison, George Mason, and Edmund Randolph (Hunt and Scott, *Debates*, 265, 272–73).

Civis to Mercator [1]

[Philadelphia, September 11, 1792]

For the National Gazette

Civis to *Mercator*

Little other notice of the futile reply of Mercator to Civis is necessary than merely to put in a clear light the erroneousness of the standard, which he has adopted for calculating the arrears of interest to the end of the year 1790.

ADf, Hamilton Papers, Library of Congress; [Philadelphia] *National Gazette*, September 12, 1792.

1. For background to this article, see "Civis," September 5, 1792. "Civis to Mercator" was written in reply to "Mercator to Civis," which was printed in the *National Gazette*, September 8, 1792. "Mercator to Civis" reads as follows:

"When you, Civis, avow and declare the object of the Treasury Department in making the publication alluded to, I presume you speak from that intimate, accurate, and precise knowledge of *the intention* which the Secretary himself can alone possess. Would it not have been candid then, to have come forward in *propria persona*, and, under the official sanction of office, declared what the *real intention* was? To attempt a public deception through indirect means, may avoid personal impeachment, but can seldom escape detection. You say, that Mercator '*has endeavored to shew that the contrary of what was intended, is true.*' Now Mercator, has simply supposed that it was intended to impress the public mind with a belief that under the present administration of its fiscal concerns, the public debt has been *actually* reduced: This supposition then, as you declare, *was contrary to the real intention*, and, as Mercator, is not disposed to *doubt your knowledge of what the real intention was*, he rests satisfied in the admission that the public debt has *not* been diminished. But Mercator has *unluckily* suggested that the public debt, instead of being diminished one farthing, has, under *your* administration, been augmented to a considerable amount. This you regard as a deliberate act of hostility, a malicious endeavor to lessen the public confidence in you, to drive you from office, and, in the true spirit of a certain junto, to grasp all the powers of the government into their own hands. Indeed, my good Civis, you discover too much anxiety, fear, and passion—your zeal betrays you, and

He takes for his standard the *present* annual interest on the *whole amount* of the public Debt, as provided for under the funding system—that is I upon the *former principal* of the foreign and domestic debt II upon the *arrears of interest* of that principal, which on the 1st of January 1791 and *not before* became principal by the

---

in the apprehensions for the *reputation* and *continuance in office* of the Secretary of the Treasury, manifestly shews the inseparable connection between you and him. Do not, however, elevate Mercator beyond his views; give him an importance that he does not seek, or rank him with men that he does not know. Humble and moderate in his wishes, with no avidity or desire for the loaves and fishes of office, unconnected with any junto, if any there be, and disdaining the use of any power but that of truth and reason, Mercator came forward to examine a plain fact, and to assist the public investigation of it, by a reference to *other authentic documents* of the treasury department itself. Wherefore then do you impeach the purity of his motives, and accuse him of want of accuracy and candor? You have surely forgotten the scriptural admonition, 'to cast the beam from your own eye before you pluck the mote from a brother's.' Remember that an accuser should never be guilty of the thing he condemns. You accuse Mercator of charging you with the arrears of interest from the day the public revenue commenced, that is, on the 1st of August, 1789, until your department was organized on the 13th of September following, and complain that this arrearage of interest accrued prior to the existence of your department; and yet you have no scruple to avail yourself of the use of the whole public revenue from the said first day of August. I leave it to a more [plausible] sophistry than you exhibit, to reconcile this absurdity. Your next complaint is, that Mercator's standard of calculation is erroneous, because he charges you with the arrears of interest made principal, and the amount of the assumed debt. Now, as to the arrears of interest made principal, was there not allowed an interest upon it equal to that of the original principal? Did not this operate as compound interest, or interest upon interest? And have you not the *unballanced* claim of merit with the public for the proposition, which such an operation demands? In respect to the assumed debt, I ask to know at what period, prior to the assumption, the interest upon that ceased? If then, Mercator has kindly taken a lower standard of calculation than he might have done, or if instead of estimating upon the *present* rate of interest on the public debt, equal to about four and a half per cent. he had charged a full rate of six per centum upon the principal of the foreign and domestic debt, the arrears of interest and the assumed debt, thereby adding to the statement he made two or three millions more, what becomes of this charge of inaccuracy and want of candor? Mercator's design was, to expose a plain and obvious principle to the public view, without regard to nice calculation or fractional certainty: that he has been under, and not over the mark, is pretty certain, and may be easily demonstrated by figures. You can best ascertain the *precise* amount of the addition that has been made to the public debt.

"Whether the language and conceptions of Mercator justify the idea, that 'to *provide* for a debt, and to *reduce* it, amount to the same thing,' will be left to the public to determine: to whom also it is referred, how far, in the principles and practice of Civis and of the Secretary, to *reduce* the public debt and to *add* to it, are synonymous?

"The review of certain leading facts respecting the establishment of the

provisions of the funding law [2] III upon the whole amount of the assumed debt that is 21500000 Dollars.

Now the fact is, that the only arrears, which can colorably be computed, are those on the *principal* of the *foreign* and *domestic* debt, according to the terms of Interest, which they *actually bore*, up to the 1st of January 1791. I because in fact the arrears of interest on that principal did not bear interest till the 1 of Jany 1791, & consequently *no interest whatever accrued upon them*. And IIdly —because the Govert. of the United States took up the state debts as they stood, at the end of the year 1791. If arrears of interest accumulated in the mean time, 'twas the affair of the state Governmts. which were the debtors and alone responsible for a provision for it, not of the Government of the UStates, which only became responsible by virtue of the assumption from the time it took effect, that is from the 1st of January 1792; from which period the interest has been punctually paid. This is the true view of it, unless it can be shewn that the Govert of the UStates is answerable for the neglects and omissions of the state Governments. But What arrears may have really accumulated on this part of the debt is unknown, as it is understood, that there were in some states a provision for the interest.

Calculating then the arrears which did actually accrue, that is on the principal of the foreign and domestic debt, the former, according to the various rates which were stipulated upon it, and the latter at 6 ₱ Cent, the rate which it then bore, from the 1st of August 1789 to the 1st of January 1791, from which period interest has been

---

funding system, is too tedious and unimportant for the pursuit of Mercator: he has little time, and less inclination to remark upon them; like *another* elaborate report of the Secretary of the Treasury, time and truth will discover their fallacy. The boast that is made of benefit to the public, first, in the saving by purchases in the public debt at the market price; secondly, by the advanced price given by foreigners in their purchases of the public debt; thirdly, by the reduced rate of the new loans for paying off the foreign debt; and lastly, by the institution of the national bank, may be regarded as so many circumstances of little and temporary expedient, producing partial or insignificant advantage or convenience to the government, and which like all temporising expedients predicated on the sacrifice of justice and of principle, leave behind them the bitter sting of future, extensive, and permanent evil. The benefits, if any, are nearly passed away; the evil but begins to be felt and understood. What may be the issue of the public mind upon them, is left for Civis to verify.
September 5.   MERCATOR."
    2. "An Act making provision for the (payment of the) Debt of the United States" (1 *Stat.* 138–44 [August 4, 1790]).

paid—the amount is 3.003.378.47 dollars that is 1,032,980,72 Dollars less than the amount of the arrears stated for the same period by Mercator. This statement is not made from any secret sources of information but from documents long since in possession of the public. If Mercator has been inattentive to the means of information, he ought not to have come forth, the instructor of his fellow Citizens.

In a mere question of the *increase* or *decrease* of the public Debt, if the arrears of interest which accrued on the assumed debt, up to the period, from which the UStates began to pay interest upon it be placed on one side of the account—the saving or reduction, by the nature of the provision for it, ought to be placed on the other side—and the ballance will be in favour of the UStates.

Had Mercator stated an Account with the Treasury Department on his own principle candidly applied, namely that of setting off the surplus of Revenue to the end of the year 1790, against the amount of the Debt redeemed by purchases and payments—the Account would have stood thus—

Credit-side [3]

By the amount of sum which appears by the statement of the Register of the Treasury to have been redeemed & paid off

	Dolls	1,865,217.42
By sum remaining to be applied		397.024.13

Debtor side

To amount of surplus Revenue to the end of the year 1790. . . . . } 1,338,874.84

Ballance   903.366.71

being the amount of the Public Debt actually reduced, beyond the amount of the fund [4] remaining on hand at the commencement of the operation of the Funding System in virtue of antecedent provision and exclusive of reductions on the rates of Interest.

As to the concluding remarks of Mercator they depart from the question. Tis no matter, in referrence to that, whether the items which were mentioned are circumstances of temporary expedient, or results of the soundest policy. They constitute positive savings and gains to the Nation.

---

3. In the margin at this point H wrote: "Invert the Debtor first & Creditor side 2d." In the *National Gazette* the printer followed these instructions.
4. In the *National Gazette* this word is "funds."

But it was not sufficient for Mercator to assert, he ought to have shewn what sacrifice of Justice or principle was involved in them. Not having done it, tis sufficient to observe that one good effect of the measures of Finance, which have been adopted by the present Government, is at least unequivocal. *The public Credit has been effectually restored.* This may be in the eyes of Mercator of little moment. There are certain theorists who hold both private and public Credit to be pernicious.[5] But their disciples are not numerous; at least among sober and enlightened men.

The actual benefits or actual evils of the measures connected with the Treasury Department present and future would be cheerfully submitted to the *Test* of *Experience.* Happy would it be for the country, honorable for human nature, if the experiment were permitted to be fairly made.

But the pains which are taken to misrepresent the tendency of those measures, to inflame the public mind, to disturb the operations of Government are a decided proof, that those to whom they are attributable dare not trust the appeal to such a *Test.* Convinced of this, they have combined all their forces and are making one desperate effort to gain an ascendancy, in the public councils, by means of the ensuing election, in order to precipitate the laudable work of destroying what has been done.   Civis

Philadelphia Sept 11.
for Nat Gazette of Sept 12. 1792.

5. The remainder of this draft is in an unidentified handwriting.

Fact No. I [1]

[Philadelphia, September 11, 1792]

For the National Gazette.

Much declamation has been indulged against certain characters, who are charged with advocating the pernicious doctrine, that "public debts are public blessings," and with being friends to a perpetua-

[Philadelphia] *National Gazette,* September 12, 1792.
1. A second article signed "Fact" appeared in the [Philadelphia] *National Gazette,* October 17, 1792.

tion of the public debt of the country. Among these characters, if the secretary of the treasury has not been named, he has been pretty plainly alluded to. It is proper to examine what foundation there is for those charges.

That officer, it is very certain, explicitly maintained, that the *funding* of the existing debt of the United States would render it a national blessing: And a man has only to travel through the United States with his eyes open, and to observe the invigoration of industry in every branch, to be convinced that the position was well founded. But whether right or wrong, it is quite a different thing from maintaining, as a general proposition, that a public debt is a public blessing: particular and temporary circumstances might render that advantageous at one time, which at another might be hurtful.

It is known, that prior to the revolution, a great part of the circulation of the country was carried on by paper money; that in consequence of the events of the revolution that resource was in a great measure destroyed, by being discredited, and that the same events had destroyed a large proportion of the monied and mercantile capital of the country, and of personal property generally. It was natural to think, that the chasm created by these circumstances required to be supplied, and a just theory was sufficient to demonstrate, that a funded debt would answer the end.

To infer, that it would have such an effect, was no more to maintain the general doctrine of "public debts being public blessings," than the saying, that paper emissions by the authority of government, were useful in the early periods of the country, was the maintaining, that they would be useful in all the future stages of its progress.

But to put the matter out of all doubt, and to shew how destitute of candor the insinuations against the secretary of the treasury, on this head, have been, I have extracted and shall insert here some passages from three of his reports to the house of representatives; by which it will be seen, that his conduct, as well as his language, have been in uniform opposition to the doctrine charged upon him. The length of these reports, it is probable, have prevented many well disposed persons from being acquainted with their contents; the presumption of which emboldens the calumniators of public characters and measures to make assertions, of the falsehood of which, the mere perusal of official documents would convict them.

Extract from a report of the secretary of the treasury, on the subject of a provision for the public debt, presented the 14th of January, 1790.[2]

"Persuaded as the secretary is, that the proper funding of the *present debt*, will render it a national blessing; yet he is *so far* from acceding to the position, in the latitude in which it is sometimes laid down, that "public debts are public benefits," a position *inviting to prodigality*, and *liable to a dangerous abuse,*—that he ardently wishes to see it incorporated, as a *fundamental maxim* in the *system of public credit* of the United States, that the *creation of debt should always be accompanied with the means of extinguishment.* This he regards as the *true secret* for *rendering public credit immortal.* And he presumes, that it is difficult to conceive a situation, in which there may not be an adherence to the maxim. At least he feels an *unfeigned solicitude,* that this may be attempted by the United States, and that they may commence their measures for the establishment of credit with the observance of it."

Extract from a report of the secretary of the treasury on manufactures, presented the 5th of December, 1791.[3]

After using several arguments to illustrate the operation of a funded debt *as capital*—the secretary concludes thus:—"There are respectable individuals, who, from a *just aversion* to *an accumulation* of public debt are unwilling to concede to it any kind of utility, who can discover no good to alleviate the ill with which they suppose it pregnant; who cannot be persuaded, that it ought in any sense to be viewed as an increase of capital, least it should be inferred, that the more debt the more capital, the greater the burthens, the greater the blessings of the community.

"But it interests the public councils to estimate every object as it truly is; to appreciate how far the good in any measure is compensated by the ill, or the ill by the good; either of them is seldom unmixed.

"Neither *will it follow, that an accumulation of debt is desirable,* because a certain degree of it operates as capital. There may be a plethora in the political, as in the natural body; there may be *a state of things in which any such artificial capital is unnecessary.* The

2. See "Report Relative to a Provision for the Support of Public Credit," January 9, 1790.
3. See "Report on the Subject of Manufactures," December 5, 1791.

debt too may be swelled to such a size, as that the greatest part of it may cease to be useful as a capital, serving only to pamper the dissipation of idle and dissolute individuals; as that the sums required to pay the interest upon it may become oppressive, and beyond the means which a government can employ, consistently with its tranquility, to raise them; as that the resources of taxation, to face the debt, may have been strained too far to admit of extensions adequate to exigencies, which regard the public safety.

"Where this critical point is, cannot be pronounced; but it is impossible to believe, that there is not such a point.

"And as the vicissitudes of nations beget a perpetual tendency to the accumulation of debt, *there ought to be in every government a perpetual, anxious and unceasing effort to reduce that, which at any time exists, as fast as shall be practicable, consistently with integrity and good faith.*"

Extract from a report of the secretary of the treasury relative to additional supplies for carrying on the Indian war, presented the 16th of March, 1792.[4]

"The result of mature reflection is, in the mind of the secretary, a strong conviction that the last of the three expedients, which have been mentioned (that was the raising of the sum required by taxes) is to be preferred to either of the other two.

"Nothing can more interest the national credit and prosperity, than a constant and systematic attention *to husband all the means previously possessed for extinguishing the present debt, and to avoid, as much as possible, the incurring of any new debt.*

"Necessity alone, therefore, can justify the application of any of the public property, other than the annual revenues, to the current service, or the temporary and casual exigencies of the country—or the contracting of an additional debt, by loans, to provide for those exigencies.

"Great emergencies indeed might exist, in which loans would be indispensible. But the occasions, which will justify them, must be truly of that description.

"The present is not of such a nature. The sum to be provided is not of magnitude enough to furnish the plea of necessity.

4. See "Report Relative to the Additional Supplies for the Ensuing Year," March 16, 1792.

"Taxes are never welcome to a community. They seldom fail to excite uneasy sensations more or less extensive; hence a too strong propensity in the government of nations to anticipate and mortgage the resources of posterity, rather than encounter the inconveniences of a present increase of taxes.

"But *this policy, when not dictated by very peculiar circumstances, is of the worst kind.* Its obvious tendency is, by enhancing the permanent burthens of the people, to produce lasting distress, and its natural issue is in national bankruptcy.

"*It will be happy, if the councils of this country, sanctioned by the voice of an enlightened community, shall be able to pursue a different course.*"

Here is an example, added to precept; In pursuit of a doctrine, the opposite of that which is charged upon him, the secretary did not scruple to hazard the popularity of his administration with a class of citizens, who, as a class, have been among the firmest friends of the government, and the warmest approvers of the measures, which have restored public credit. The circumstance indeed has been a weapon dexterously wielded against him by his enemies; who in consequence of the increase of duties proposed have represented him as the oppressor of trade. A certain description of men are for getting out of debt; yet are against all taxes for raising money to pay it off; they are amongst the foremost for carrying on war, and yet will have neither loans nor taxes. They are alike opposed to what creates debt, and to what avoids it.

In the first case, their meaning is not difficult to be devined; in the last it would puzzle any man, not endowed with the gift of second sight, to find it out, unless it be to quarrel with and pull down every man who will not consent to walk in their leading strings; or to throw all things into confusion. FACT.

Sept. 11.

To George Washington [1]

Philadelphia Sepr. 11. 1792

Sir

Herewith is an official letter submitting the draft of a Proclamation. I reserve some observations as most proper for a private letter.

In the case of a former proclamation I observe it was under the seal of the UStates and countersigned by the Secretary of State. If the precedent was now to be formed I should express a doubt whether it was such an instrument as ought to be under the seal of the UStates; and I believe usage as well in this Country under the state Governments as in Great Britain would be found against it; but the practice having been begun, there are many reasons which in this instance recommend an adherence to it and the form of the attestation is adapted to this idea.[2]

But still if the Secretary of State should be at so great a distance or if an uncertainty of his being in the way should involve the probability of considerable delay it will be well to consider if the precident ought not to be departed from. In this case the Attestation would require to be varied so as to omit from the words "In testimony" to the words "my hand" inclusively and to substitute the word "*Given*" to "*Done*" and it may be adviseable to direct the Atty General to countersign it.

Every day's delay will render the Act less impressive & defeat a part of its object.

The propriety of issuing the proclamation depends of course upon a resolution to act in conformity to it and put in force all the *powers* and *means* with which the Executive is possessed as occasion shall require. My own mind is made up fully to this issue and on this my suggestion of the measure is founded. Your letter by the last Post, confirming former intimations, assures me that you view the matter in the same light.[3]

The words in the Proclamation "dictated by weighty reasons of public exigency and policy" are not essential to the general scope of it. They amount to an *additional commitment* of the President on the question of the merits of the law and will require to be well considered.[4]

That the Proclamation both as to *manner* and *matter* will be criticised cannot be matter of surprise, if it should happen, to any one who is aware of the lengths to which a certain party is prepared to go. It ought to be anticipated as probable.

In a step so delicate & so full of responsibility, I thought it my duty to make these observations; though I was sure they would of themselves occur.

It is satisfactory to know that a Jury in Chester County in this state convicted a person who was guilty of assaulting an Officer of Inspection. On being interrogated they answered that they had found him guilty upon the Count in the Indictment which charged him with assaulting the Officer in the execution of his duty—that the law was a constitutional act of Government and was not to be resisted by violence.[5] I have directed Mr. Coxe [6] to collect & publish the particulars.[7] The symptom is a good one.

With the most faithful & affectionate attachment. I have the honor to remain   Sir   Yr. Obed & hum serv   A Hamilton

The President of The UStates

ALS, George Washington Papers, Library of Congress; copy, Hamilton Papers, Library of Congress.

1. For background to this letter, see H to Tench Coxe, September 1, 1792; H to Washington, September 1, 8, first letter of September 9, 1792; H to John Jay, September 3, 1792; "Draft of a Proclamation Concerning Opposition to the Excise Law," September 7, 1792; Washington to H, September 7, 1792; Jay to H, September 8, 1792; Edmund Randolph to H, September 8, 1792.

2. See "Draft of a Proclamation Concerning Opposition to the Excise Law," September 7, 1792, note 1.

3. See Washington to H, September 7, 1792.

4. For Randolph's opinion on this wording, see Randolph to H, September 7, 1792.

5. Randolph had written to Washington about this case on September 10, 1792. Randolph's letter reads in part as follows: "At a late court in Chester county in this state several persons were indicted for an assault on an excise officer. Notwithstanding a strong defence, they were convicted and fined; the jury having said to the attorney-general [James Iredell of Pennsylvania], that it was not a question with them, whether the law was good, or bad; but that they would never countenance an opposition to laws in such a form. This event, which I shall endeavour to have published with all its circumstances, will increase the abhorence, which several of the very party, who are associated with [Albert] Gallatin and [John] Smilie, feel themselves compelled to express in order to avoid the imputation of a love of anarchy. The probability is, that the proceedings at Pittsburg will contribute to defeat the ticket, which has been proposed by that party" (ALS, George Washington Papers, Library of Congress).

6. Tench Coxe, commissioner of the revenue.

7. On September 26, 1792, the [Philadelphia] Gazette of the United States printed the following notice: "At the last Court of Quarter Sessions for the County of Chester, in this State, Joseph Evans and Robert Fletcher, with several others, were indicted for a riot, assault and battery on Jacob Hum-

phreys, who was in the execution of his office under what is commonly called the 'Excise Law' of the United States.

"The other defendants had not, at the time of the trial, been taken.

"The Jury convicted both the defendants, and Fletcher was fined 50 £."

From Tench Coxe

Treasury Department, Revenue Office, September 12[–18], 1792. "The particular recapitulation I had the Honor to make of the considerations which had occured on the subject of the provision for the officers of the Revenue and the expences of collecting the same, in my letter to you of the 25th July render it unnecessary to repeat them in transmitting to you the two inclosed papers relative to that Business during the first year. One of them (indorsed A) will be found to contain such items of the former Estimate as it appeared expedient to suggest to the Consideration of the President in regard to the year, which ended on the 30th of June last. . . . The paper B is a draught of an act for the purpose of submission to the President containing provisions comformable with the Estimate A, and dictated by the tenor of the Arrangement, which the President was pleased to establish on the 4th Ultimo for the Current year. . . ." [1]

LC, RG 58, Letters of Commissioner of Revenue, 1792–1793, National Archives.

1. See Coxe to H, first letter of July 25, 1792, note 18. In a postscript to the letter printed above, dated September 18, Coxe added several remarks concerning the arrangement.

To Jonathan Williams [1]

[*Treasury Department, September 12, 1792.* The catalogue description of this letter reads: "On a financial matter." *Letter not found.*]

LS, sold at Parke-Bernet Galleries, Inc., May 24, 1943, Lot 118.

1. Williams, a native of Boston and a great-nephew of Benjamin Franklin, had been prize agent and commercial agent for Congress at Nantes during the American Revolution. After the adoption of the Constitution he returned to the United States, settled in Philadelphia, and became an investor in various stock and land operations.

From Elisha Boudinot

Newark [New Jersey], 13th Sept., 1792.

My Dear Sir:

There are great exertions making to get the people to petition against the incorporation; [1] several persons are employed to go about with petitions, and the people are deceived by the most absurd falsehoods. The only mode I thought of to counteract them, was to have petitions drawn, and hire a person calculated for the purpose to go round with them, and I am in hopes it will answer the purpose effectually. We shall obtain numbers who signed the first, to sign ours, declaring they were imposed on. So much for *petitions*.

Will you sketch the substance of a law you wish with regard to apprentices [2]—or the heading of it—and I will see it carried through the Legislature? Had you not better be up a day or two previous to the first Monday in October?

The Antis are making greater exertions than you perhaps are aware of, previous to the expected general election. Our Chief Justice [3] says that a number from *Philadelphia* have been to the lower parts of West Jersey, informing the people that a strong party is forming in that city against the Secretary of the Treasury, requesting their aid, and that they will not choose a man who has supported his measures, especially Mr. Boudinot,[4] &c. &c.

My brother showed me a letter last evening, received by the post, dated Norfolk, Virginia—only a few lines—inclosing a handbill for his information, signed "James Blanchard." [5] This handbill is addressed to the Electors and Freeholders of New Jersey,[6] setting forth the dangerous consequences of the measures of the Secretary, &c., the funding system, bank, &c.; then giving extracts of speeches made by Mr. Boudinot in support of them, &c., and warning the people to take care, &c., and says that pamphlets should be distributed amongst them previous to the election.

From these things it appears as if they meant to try their strength in every State. A young gentleman of this town was lately at Philadelphia, and at his lodgings there was a gentleman from Virginia (whose name I do not at this moment recollect), very violent on the subject, and said he was going the middle and eastern States, to see what could be done with regard to displacing the Secretary of the Treasury; and, finding from the conversation of the other gentleman, that Mr. Madison was not a popular character, in Jersey at least, he asked if Mr. Morris [7] would not be agreeable, &c. If the federalists sleep whilst their enemies are awake and vigilant, some mischief may be done.

I am, in haste, dear Sir,   With respect,   Yours sincerely,

Elisha Boudinot.

JCHW, V, 525–26.

1. This is a reference to the Society for Establishing Useful Manufactures, which had been incorporated by the New Jersey legislature on November 22, 1791.

2. See H to the Directors of the Society for Establishing Useful Manufactures, October 12, 1792.

3. James Kinsey.

4. Elias Boudinot, an incumbent member of the Federal House of Representatives, was a candidate for reelection in 1792. He was Elisha Boudinot's brother.

5. Blanchard had served as quartermaster and regimental paymaster of the Third New Hampshire Regiment during the American Revolution. In 1791 and 1792 he was a persistent opponent of the funding system and an advocate of discrimination in favor of those Revolutionary War soldiers who had alienated their certificates. See Blanchard to H, February 29, 1792.

6. A broadside of August 25, 1792, addressed "To the Electors of the State of New Jersey" by "A Continental Soldier" from Norfolk, Virginia, which is similar in content to the broadside described by Boudinot, is cited in a list in the Hamilton Papers, Library of Congress, of material originally contained in that collection. A note in pencil on the last page of this list indicates that the printed broadsides in the Hamilton Papers were transferred in 1951 to the Rare Book Division, Library of Congress.

7. Possibly Robert Morris.

To Gouverneur Morris

Treasury Department
September 13th. 1792.[1]

Sir

The Legislature at their last Session having made provision for the paying off the Debt due to foreign Officers,[2] the Interest of which

LS, William Short Papers, Library of Congress; copy, Columbia University Libraries; letterpress copy, Thomas Jefferson Papers, Library of Congress.

1. The copies are incorrectly dated October 1, 1792.

2. For a description of this debt, see Short to H, August 3, 1790, note 5, and *JCC*, XXVI, 42–44, 65–66. Section 5 of "An Act supplementary to the act

is payable at the house of Mr. Grand,[3] Banker, at Paris; and the President having authorized me to carry that provision into effect,[4] I have concluded to commit such part of the business as is to be transacted at Paris to your Management; not doubting of the chearfulness with which you will render this service to the public and to my particular Department.

The object not regarding your diplomatic mission, and Mr. Jefferson being absent from the seat of Government, I open without scruple a direct communication with you on the subject.

By the tenor of the certificates which were issued the stipulation to pay at Paris is confined to the Interest. The principal is of course payable in the United States.

To enable you to make payment of this Interest Mr. Short is directed to subject to your order in the hands of our Commissioners in Holland, the sum of one hundred and five thousand Guilders.[5]

Inclosed is a list, shewing the names of the persons to be paid, and the amount of principal and interest due to each; computing interest from the 1st. day of January 1789. up to the last of the present year.

The reason of beginning at the first of January 1789. is that Congress placed a fund in the disposition of their then Minister plenipotentiary to make payments up to that time; [6] and though an account of the application of that fund has not been rendered it is understood that the payment provided for was made.

---

making provision for the Debt of the United States" (1 *Stat.* 282 [May 8, 1792]) authorized the President "to cause to be discharged the principal and interest of the said debt, out of any of the monies, which have been or shall be obtained on loan." For the negotiations on the payment of these officers, see H to Short, August 16, September 13, 1792; H to Washington, August 27, 1792; Washington to H, August 31, 1792.

3. Ferdinand Le Grand.   4. See Washington to H, August 31, 1792.
5. See H to Short, September 13, 1792. The words "one hundred and five thousand" are in the handwriting of H.
6. On August 11, 1788, the Board of Treasury made the following report to the Continental Congress:

"The Board of Treasury to whom was referred an extract of a Letter of the 6th. of August 1787, from the Honble. Mr. Jefferson,

"Beg leave to Report to Congress,

"That the critical situation in which the provision for the payment of the Dutch Interest, has been for some time placed, has hitherto prevented the Board from recommending any appropriation of the Funds in Europe for any other object; but as information has lately been received that the Loans now open in Holland will furnish timely and sufficient Funds for the above object. The Board are of opinion, that no time should be lost in making

By the list referred to you will find that the sum directed to be placed at your order is adequate to the object.

The instruction of the President to me is to cause the payment to be made in "a mode which will exempt the parties from the loss attendant on the depreciation of the assignats; and at the same time occasion no loss to the United States." [7]

The line of conduct, which has appeared to me proper to fulfill the spirit of this Instruction is to give to each Creditor his option either to receive payment in bills on Amsterdam, dollar for dollar, according to the intrinsic par of the metals at Paris and Amsterdam, or to receive an equivalent in Assignats according to the current rate of exchange between Paris and Holland, at the time.

To exemplify what is meant by an equivalent suppose the following data—

1. That 2½ Guilders are equal to a dollar according to the intrinsic par of the metals at Paris and Amsterdam.
2. That the current rate of exchange between the two places is 20 ℔. Cent. against Paris; that is, 100 Guilders at Paris, will bring only 80. at Amsterdam.
3. That the sum to be paid for principal and Interest is 100. Dollars.

The computation to ascertain the equivalent will then stand thus— If 80 be equal to 100—so will 100 be equal to *125*

125 × 2½ is = 312½ Guilders which being converted into livres, at Par, will be to be paid in Assignats at their nominal value, *livre* for *livre*.

I have made an arrangement to begin the discharge of the principal here at any time after the 15th. of October next upon demand and the production of the certificate by the party or his legal representa-

---

Provision for the Payment of the Arrears of Interest due to Foreign Officers, agreeably to the Recommendation of the Minister of the United States at the Court of France, and therefore submit to the consideration of Congress the following Resolve. Vizt.

"That so much of the Loans in Holland as shall be necessary to discharge the Interest due on Certificates issued to Foreign Officers to the 31st. December 1788, be specially appropriated for that purpose, under the direction of the Minister of the United States at the Court of France." (*JCC*, XXXIV, 409.)

Congress passed a resolution agreeing to this proposal on August 20, 1788 (*JCC*, XXXIV, 443).

7. See Washington to H, August 31, 1792.

tive or Attorney duly constituted and authorized. Notice will be given that after the last of December next, interest will cease, as to all those, who shall not have made application for their principal by that day.

I request that you will also cause some proper notification of this arrangement to be given in France.

As the Certificates will be required to be produced here; the payment of Interest at Paris must be made without the production of them. Especial care must of course be taken to ascertain that the payments are made to the identical Creditors or their certain Attornies. It will be well that duplicate or triplicate receipts be taken for such payments in order that one or more sets be transmitted with the Accounts Current.

Should there be any who may prefer receiving their whole dues, interest as well as principal here—they may have the option of doing it; but in this case, they must make known their election to you, or to some person whom you shall appoint and must obtain a certificate from you or the person appointed by you of their having made and communicated that election. Should you authorize another person for the purpose, you will please to inform me without delay who he is and send me his signature.

The payments are stipulated to be made at the house of Mr. Grand; and those which have been heretofore made have passed through his hands. The same course will be proper, unless there are good reasons to the contrary. You who are on the spot will judge how far any such reasons may have resulted from the tempests which have of late agitated the Kingdom; and you will act accordingly. No body knows better than you how important it is, to make no misteps in money concerns.

With the most respectful consideration   I have the honor to be Sir   Your obedient and humble Servant   Alexander Hamilton

P. S. Herewith you will also find the evidence of a claim which has been lodged at the Treasury on behalf of Mr Claviere [8] that

8. Etienne Clavière, French financier and politician, was made Minister of Finance under the Girondin Ministry and after August 10, 1792, was a member of the Provisional Executive Council. In 1788 Clavière had entered into an agreement with several other men to speculate in the American debt owed to France.

what is right in the matter may be done. A copy of an advertisement from the Treasurer, of the Seventeenth Instant is also inclosed.[9]

Gouverneur Morris Esqr.
Minister Plenipotentiary at the Court of France.

9. This advertisement, dated September 17, 1792, reads as follows:
"Whereas pursuant to the fifth section of the act of Congress, entitled, 'An act supplementary to the act making provision for the debt of the United States,' passed the eighth day of May last, provision has been made for discharging the debts due to certain foreign officers, on account of pay and services during the late war, the interest whereof, as expressed in the certificates granted to the said officers, by virtue of a resolution of the United States in Congress assembled, is payable at the house of Mr. Grand, Banker at Paris.

"This is therefore to give notice, that provision has been and is made for the payment of the *principal* of the said debt at the Treasury of the United States, at any time after the fifteenth day of October next, upon demand of the parties respectively to whom the said certificates were granted, or their respective lawful representatives or attornies duly constituted and authorized, and the production of the certificates in each case granted; and also for the payment of the interest which shall be due upon the said certificates, to the 31st day of December next inclusively at Paris, in conformity to the tenor of the said certificates.

"Should there be any, who prefer receiving their whole dues, interest as well as principal, at the treasury aforesaid, it shall be in their option so to do; but in this case, all such who are not within the United States at the date hereof, must make known their election to the minister plenipotentiary of the United States at the court of France, or to the person whom he shall appoint for that purpose, and must obtain from the said minister plenipotentiary, or from the person appointed by him, a certificate of his having made and communicated his election so to do.

"In consequence of the foregoing provision, interest, after the said last day of December next will cease upon all such of the said debts, for the payment whereof application shall not have been made pursuant to the tenor hereof, prior to the first day of January, one thousand seven hundred and ninety-three.

"Samuel Meredith,
"*Treasurer of the United States.*"
([Philadelphia] *Dunlap's American Daily Advertiser,* September 20, 1792.)

From Jeremiah Olney

Providence, September 13, 1792. "I have received your circular Letter of the 27th of August. The Returns & Abstract therein required shall be regularly transmitted; and due attention paid to the other Matters."

ADfS, Rhode Island Historical Society, Providence.

From Jeremiah Olney

Custom House,
District of Providence 13th Septemr. 1792.

Sir,

Since I had, on the 8th Instant, the honor of addressing you, on the Case of the Brigantine Samuel, the Brigantine Harriot, Christr. Bently Master, from Copenhagen, arrived (the Day before yesterday) in this District, being another Vessel of Welcome Arnold Esquire; and her Cargo, like the Samuel's, was, on the 10th Instant, transferred by him to Mr. Edward Dexter of this Town, Merchant, for the Consideration of Two Thousand pounds Lawful Money. The Master applied at my Office Yesterday, Reported and Entered the Vessel; and Mr. Dexter appeared, with the Instrument of Transfer, to secure the Duties. Not having heard from the District Attorney on this Subject; and the Duties on the Brigt. Samuel's Cargo having been secured at Newport by Bonds, I deemed it most advisable to adopt Mr. Ellery's [1] practice, and permit Mr. Dexter to secure thereon the Harriot's by his Bonds, amounting by Estimate, to Eleven Hundred Dollars.

This Transfer of Property, as in the case of the Saml., has been executed with the sole design to obtain a further Credit by evading the Law; and unless some effectual Check is adopted to prevent this singular mode of evasion, I apprehend it may introduce a more frequent suit of Bonds.

I have the Honor &c.   Jereh. Olney Collr.

N.B. Mr. Arnold has two other Vessels speedily expected from the West Indies.

Alexr. Hamilton Esqr.
Secy of the Treasury.

ADfS, Rhode Island Historical Society, Providence.
   1. William Ellery, collector of customs at Newport, Rhode Island. See Ellery to H, September 4, 1792.

To Jeremiah Olney [1]

Treasury Department, September 13, 1792. "I have this day decided upon the case of Thomas Hazard junr. The interest of the United States and of all others in the forfeiture is remitted to him; and he is to pay fifty Dollars to parties, other than the United States, together with costs and charges. . . ."

LS, Rhode Island Historical Society, Providence; copy, RG 56, Letters to Collectors at Small Ports, "Set G," National Archives; copy, RG 56, Letters to the Collector at Providence, National Archives.
1. For background to this letter, see Olney to H, August 25, 1792.

To William Short [1]

Treasury Department
Philadelphia Septr. 13 1792

Sir

Having been authorised by the President to take arrangements for paying off the debt due to foreign Officers,[2] the interest of which is payable at the House of Mr. Grand, Banker at Paris; and having concluded to commit to Governeur Morris Esquire being on the spot the management of the detail as to the payment of interest (that of the principal being to be made here) I am to request that you will instruct our Commissioners in Holland to pay to the order of Mr. Morris the sum of One hundred and five thousand Guilders to be applied to that purpose; and will cause him to be immediately notified of its having been done. A copy of a letter of instructions to Mr Morris is enclosed for your information.

With great consideration I have the honor to be Sir Your Obedt. servant
Alexander Hamilton

William Short Esqr
Minister Resident
at the Hague.

LS, William Short Papers, Library of Congress. A copy of this letter was enclosed in H's "Report on Foreign Loans," February 13, 1793.

1. For background to this letter, see H to Gouverneur Morris, September 13, 1792.
2. See Washington to H, August 31, 1792.

Treasury Department Circular

Treasury Department
Sept 13 1792

Sir

By an Order of the Senate of the United States, dated 7th of May past,[1] of which a copy is enclosed, it is required of the Secretary of the Treasury to lay before them at their next session a statement of the salaries, fees & emoluments, for one year ending the first of Octo next to be stated quarterly of every person holding any civil office or employment under the United States (except the Judges) and of the actual disbursements & expences in the discharge of their respective Offices & employments for the same period.

To enable me to comply with the requisition of the Senate I have to request that you will furnish me with an account embracing the objects, and stated in the manner & for the period before mentioned as it regards your office as soon after the first of Octo next as can be conveniently done.

I am Sir   With Consideration   Your Ob Servt   A Hamilton

LS, to William Rawle, Historical Society of Pennsylvania, Philadelphia; LS, to Henry Sewall, Maine Historical Society, Portland.
1. This was the same order that was enclosed in "Treasury Department Circular to the Collectors of the Customs," August 31, 1792.

From William Ellery

[*Newport, Rhode Island*] *September* [*14–21*] *1792.* "Your circular Letter of the 27th. of the last month, I received on the 14th of this month. Its contents will be duly attended to. . . . I wish to be informed whether shaken casks exported in order to be set up and filled with West India Produce for importation into the United States; and Hay, Oats or other Provender for Live Stock are to be noticed in the Returns of Exports and their value. . . ."

LC, Newport Historical Society, Newport, Rhode Island.

From Benjamin Lincoln

Boston Sept. 14th. 1792

Sir

My knowledge of your wishes to support the manufactures of your Country will apologize I hope for the trouble of this Letter on the subject of tipes. Mr. Thomas [1] of this State has it in contemplation to print the bible in two different small sizes. To do it on terms which will give him a profit among the importers he is under the [necessity] of importing tipes sufficient for the whole work before it can be compleated for they cannot do this as in other case set a part & break up the forms they must in order to save them selves set the whole & let the press stand untill the tipes are worn out. This will involve him in an expence of about ten thousand dollars the duties [2] on which is an object. He wishes to know whether all circumstances considered they can be dispensed with. He wishes to procure the tipes of american manufactures but cannot do it.

LC, Massachusetts Historical Society, Boston; copy, RG 56, Letters from the Collector at Boston, National Archives.

1. A strong supporter of the American Revolution, Isaiah Thomas of Worcester, Massachusetts, had established the *Massachusetts Spy* in 1770. His publications, more than two hundred and fifty of which were issued before the end of 1792, were well known for their typography, excellence of paper, binding, and general execution. In December, 1791, he printed the first American folio Bible and the first American royal quarto Bible in English. In 1793 he printed an octavo edition, some copies of which were printed without the Apocrypha.

2. Printer's type, a nonenumerated commodity, was subject to an import duty of seven and one-half percent ad valorem under "An Act for raising a farther sum of money for the protection of the frontiers, and for other purposes therein mentioned" (1 *Stat.* 259–63 [May 2, 1792]).

Catullus No. I [1]

[Philadelphia, September 15, 1792]

To Aristides [2]

Though there would be no great hazard of mistake, in inferring the Writer of the Paper under the signature of Aristides, from "the appropriate and prominent features" which characterise the stile of that paper; yet I forbear to imitate the example which has been

ADf, Hamilton Papers, Library of Congress; [Philadelphia] *Gazette of the United States*, September 15, 1792.
    1. This essay is the first of a series. The other essays in the series are dated September 19, 29, October 17, November 24, December 22, 1792.
    2. "Catullus No. I" was written in reply to "Aristides," whose first article, dated September 4, 1792, appeared in the *Gazette of the United States* on September 8, 1792. "Aristides" had written in reply to two articles by H, both of which are entitled "An American" and are dated August 4 and 11, 1792. The first article by "Aristides" reads as follows:
    "In your Gazettes of the 4th and 11th of last month, there appeared two publications under the signature of 'An American,' replete with the most virulent abuse of Mr. Jefferson; and containing charges against him, founded in the basest calumny and falshood. The intemperance of this writer, and his utter disregard of truth and candor, will be readily perceived by an impartial public, when they refer to one of his concluding suggestions in the first publication, to wit—that Mr. Jefferson is the patron and promoter of *national disunion, national insignificance, public disorder and discredit;*—a suggestion, made on no better foundation, than his being opposed to some of the principles of the funding system, of the national bank, and of certain other measures of the Secretary of the Treasury; an offence, which, I fear, if criminal, will involve a great majority of the independent yeomanry of our country in equal guilt. How long Mr. Jefferson has been distinguished as the Cataline of the day, or as the ambitious incendiary, who would light a torch to the ruin of his country, may be matter of useful speculation; and whether he is now, for the first time, thus distinguished, because of the manly freedom with which he declares his abhorrence of some of the leading principles of Mr. Hamilton's fiscal administration; or, that because of his known attachment to republicanism, he is feared, as the decided opponent of aristocracy, monarchy, hereditary succession, a titled order of nobility, and all the other mock-pageantry of kingly government, will be the subject of future enquiry; in which it will be considered, how far the distinguishing traits I have glanced at, form the appropriate and prominent features in the character of another political luminary, and of the measures of his administration. An enquiry like this may be useful, has been invited by the writer I refer to, and, as the invitation will not be refused, may, in the test of comparative merit, disclose facts and principles in relation to public men, which, however important for the public to know, are now concealed in the arcana of a certain convention, or remain involved in all the obscurity of political mystery and deception.

set with too little decorum, by naming or describing the supposed author. The similitude of stile or any other circumstance, merely probable, is too slight a foundation for so improper a procedure.

Peculiar circumstances, which it is not necessary to explain, uniting with the conjecture which is indulged, respecting the real *Aristides,* lead to a change of the original party to the charges. The discussion will be taken up and pursued by one, who is willing to be responsible for the allegations he shall make, and who consequently will not refuse to be known, on proper terms, to the

---

At present my sole purpose is, by a reference to certain facts, of which I have been possessed by a gentleman in this city, to exonerate Mr. Jefferson from the two principal charges made against him, and, in so doing, to prove the malignity and falshood of them. The first charge is, 'that Mr. Jefferson was opposed to the present constitution of the United States' and the other is, 'that Mr. Jefferson, when Minister to the Court of France, advised Congress to negociate a transfer of its debt due to the French nation to the hands of individuals in Holland, upon the idea, that if the United States should fail in making a provision for the debt, the discontents, to be expected from the omission, may honestly be transferred from a government able to vindicate its rights, to the breasts of individuals, who may first be encouraged to become the substitutes to the original creditors, and may afterwards be defrauded without danger.'

"In respect to the first charge, and any rational or candid inference to be derived from it, it surely could not mean that Mr. Jefferson was friendly to, and recommended the adoption of the Constitution; and yet, such is the plain and simple fact, which this writer for his own insidious purpose has tortured into an inference, that Mr. Jefferson was opposed to the constitution, and is yet an enemy to that, and to the American Union.

"Let those who regard the truth, recur to the Debates of the Virginia Convention, pages 100 and 101—where, in the speech of Mr. [Edmund] Pendleton, the President of that Convention, they will find the following sentiments:

"'I was surprised when I heard introduced the opinion of a gentleman (Mr. Jefferson) whom I highly respect. I know the great abilities of that gentleman. Providence has, for the good of mankind, accompanied those abilities with a disposition to make use of them for the good of his fellow beings; and I wish, with all my heart, that he was here to assist us on this interesting occasion. As to his letter, impressed, as I am, with the force of his authority, I think it was improper to introduce it on this occasion. The opinion of a private individual, however enlightened, ought not to influence our decision. But admitting, that this opinion ought to be conclusive with us, it strikes me in a different manner from the honorable gentleman. I have seen the letter, in which this gentleman has written his opinion upon this subject. It appears that he is possessed of that Constitution, and has in his mind the idea of amending it. He has in his mind the very question of subsequent or previous amendments, which is now under consideration. His sentiments on this subject are as follow: "I wish with all my soul, that the nine first Conventions may accept the New Constitution, because it will secure to us the good it contains, which I think *great and important.* I wish the four latest, whichever they be, may refuse to accede to it, till amendments are secured." He then enumerates the amendments, which he wishes to be secured, and adds "We

Officer concerned. It is however not meant to invite inquiry on that head. It is most adviseable, that none should be made. For any public purpose, none will be requisite. For any personal one, none will be proper. What shall be said will merely apply to public conduct, and will be supported by proof and argument.

Why then (it may be asked) the intimation of a willingness to be known, if required? The answer is—Merely to put an end to the epithets "cowardly assassin" "striking in the dark" and other tropes and figures of a similar nature. Some rhetoric may be spoiled, but the elucidation of truth will be promoted.

---

must take care, however, that neither this, nor any other objection to the form, produce a schism in our Union. That would be an incurable evil; because friends falling out, never cordially re-unite." Are these sentiments in favor of those who wish to prevent its adoption by previous amendment? He wishes the first nine States to adopt it. What are his reasons? Because it will secure to us the good it contains, which, he thinks, *great and important;* and he wishes the other four may refuse it, because he thinks it will tend to obtain necessary amendments. But he would not wish that a schism should take place in the Union, *on any consideration.* If then we are to be influenced by his opinion at all, we will ratify it, and secure thereby the good it contains.'

"The public will observe, that this part of Mr. Pendleton's speech was made in reply to another member of that Convention, who then made the same attempt to pervert Mr. Jefferson's sentiments, which the present writer has now done—and that the unexpected quotation of Mr. Jefferson's letter, with the just and judicious comment upon it, made by Mr. Pendleton, arrested the influence of the poison, in that instance, as I trust it will now do, to the satisfaction of an enlightened and impartial public, to whom, without farther animadversion, it is submitted.

"In respect to the other charge of the advice given by Mr. Jefferson to the former Congress concerning the French debt, it is worthy remark, that the accuser skulks from the charge, when, in a note subjoined to his publication, he says 'The precise terms are not now recollected, but the substance may be depended upon; the poor Hollanders were to be the victims.' Thus stabbing the reputation of an old meritorious public servant, by an unwarrantable conclusion, whilst he disavows a recollection of the facts, on which alone the conclusion could be justified. But the pitiful evasion will not avail him; he has produced a solemn charge at the tribunal of the public—a charge, which, involving no small degree of moral turpitude, will render the accused, if guilty, unworthy the confidence of his fellow citizens. It is his duty, therefore, to substantiate his charge, not by vague and unfounded inference, but by an appeal to truth, a reference to plain and simple facts, and a recital of the precise terms of the advice given by Mr. Jefferson; without a knowledge of which, the public cannot be enabled to render a just or impartial judgment. If he fails in this, the public will regard him as a base and wicked calumniator. I have no hope, however, that he will ever attempt to bring forward the proofs of this charge—satisfied with the time, manner and effect of his calumny, he will now retreat behind an anonymous signature, and vent his slanders at the reputation of any other honest man he meets, like a cowardly assassin, who strikes in the dark, and securely wounds, because he is unseen.

It occurs at once, to an observant reader, that Aristides passes over in total silence, the leading article of charge brought by the "American" against Mr. Jefferson—namely that he is the *Institutor* and *Patron* of a certain Gazette, published in this City, the object and tendency of which are to vilify and depreciate the government of the United States—to misrepresent and traduce the administration of it, except in the single department, of which that Gentleman is the head; implicating in the most virulent censure the majorities of both houses of Congress, the heads both of the Treasury and War departments; and sparing not even the Chief Magistrate himself; that in the support of this paper, thus hostile to the government, in the administration of which he holds so important a trust, he has not scrupled to apply the money of that very government; departing by this conduct from the rules of official propriety and obligation, and from the duty of a discreet and patriotic citizen.

This is the leading and main charge which has been brought by the American against Mr. Jefferson, which he supports in several ways—

1st By direct proof of an official connection between the Secretary of State and the Editor of the National Gazette, coeval with, or rather antecedent to the *first establishment* of that paper.

2 By the suggestion of his being opposed to the present Government of the UStates, while it was under the consideration of the People.

3 By the suggestion of his being opposed to the principal measures, which have been adopted in the course of its administration, particularly those relating to the Finances.

I say, he will retreat, because he well knows, notwithstanding any affected ignorance on the subject, that by an appeal to facts, the truth will appear that Mr. Jefferson gave advice to Congress expressly contrary to that which he has ascribed to him. That this was the case, and that Mr. Jefferson even pointed out a mode by which the honor and credit of the United States might be preserved, can and will be proved to the public, if the present accuser shall dare to bring forward the proof in support of his charge.

"It has been said, Mr. Fenno, that a certain head of a department is the real author or instigator of this unprovoked and unmanly attack on Mr. Jefferson —and that the time of that gentleman's departure from this city, on a visit to his home, was considered as best suited to answer the design it was intended to effect. Be that as it may, or whether the writer be of this or that state, or of this or that party, certain it is, that no man can envy the depravity of heart he possesses.

ARISTIDES."

([Philadelphia] *Gazette of the United States*, September 8, 1792.)

The object of the above recapitulation is to shew the true original state of the question; in order that it may be seen how intirely Aristides, in his defence, loses sight of the principal point—and contents himself with an indirect endeavour to involve it in uncertainty, by disputing or denying some positions, which form only the collateral evidence.

It will now remain to see how the charges of the American have been and can be supported.

As to the connection between the Secretary of State and the Editor of the National Gazette, neither of the following facts can or will be disputed—If any of them should be denied it will be proved beyond the possibility of doubt—

1 That the Editor of the National Gazette is a Clerk in the department of State for foreign languages, and as such receives a salary of [two hundred and fifty] ³ Dollars a year.

2 That he became so *antecedent* to the establishment of his Gazette; having actually received his salary from the 17th of August 1791 and not having published the first number of his paper till the [31st of October] ⁴ following.

3 That at the time he became so, there was another character, a Clerk in the same department,⁵ who understood the French language; and that the Editor of the National Gazette is a translator of that language only.

4 That the appointment was not made under any special pro-

---

3. Space left blank in MS. Material within brackets has been taken from the *Gazette of the United States*

4. Space left blank in MS. Material within brackets has been taken from the *Gazette of the United States*.

5. H is presumably referring to George Taylor, Jr., who had been promoted to chief clerk in the Department of State in the spring of 1792. On August 18, 1792, a letter addressed "To the American," and signed by "Fair Play," was published in the *Gazette of the United States*; it reads as follows:

"Being in possession of two facts which are of a nature to throw full light upon the subject you have brought into public view, I think it due to truth and to the community, to make you acquainted with them in the only manner which situation permits. One is, that the Editor of the National Gazette has received a Salary, as Clerk in the Department of State, from the 17th August 1791, near two months and an half prior to the Commencement of his paper, and prior to the Commencement of his residence in this city.

"The other, that Mr. Taylor, who long before was, and still is *a Clerk in the Department of State*, an intelligent and respectable man, has a competent knowledge of the French Language,—the only one, of which Mr. Freneau is the Translator." ([Philadelphia] *Gazette of the United States*, August 18, 1792.)

vision, marking out a particular clerkship of the kind, its duties or its emoluments; but under a general authority to appoint Clerks, and allow them salaries, not exceeding the average of 500 Dollars to each.

5 That the Editor of the National Gazette *immediately* preceding the establishment of that paper was the Superintendent or Conductor of a paper belonging to Childs and Swaine, *printed at New York.*[6]

These are the facts: The conclusion is irresistible. The secret intentions of men being in the repositories of their own breasts, it rarely happens and is therefore not to be expected, that direct and positive proof of them could be adduced. Presumptive facts and circumstances must afford the evidence; and when these are sufficiently strong, they ought to decide.

We find the head of a department taking the Editor of a Gazette into his employment, as a Clerk, with a stated salary—not for any special purpose, which could not have been accomplished otherwise; for he had, at the time, in his department, a Clerk who was capable of performing the very service required, and could without difficulty have procured others similarly qualified; nor from any particular necessity, arising from a too limited allowance, or any other cause; for he had it in his power to allow an adequate compensation to a character, who might have been regularly attached to the Department. The very existence of such a connection, then, is alone a sufficient foundation for believing, that the design of the arrangement was to secure an influence over the paper, the Editor of which was so employed. But the circumstances which attend it explain the nature of it beyond a doubt. That which has been just mentioned, namely there having been previously a clerk in the department qualified to render the service, is a weighty one. The coming of a *new* Printer, from another state to institute a *new* paper—his having been appointed a clerk in the department *prior* to his removal to this City—his having been compensated *before* he was even present, to satisfy the *appearance* of rendering service—these circumstances give a point and energy to the language of the transaction which render it unequivocal. There perhaps never was a more flimsey

6. Francis Childs and John Swaine were the publishers of *The* [New York] *Daily Advertiser.*

covering for the pensioning of a Printer. Some ostensible ground for giving him the public money was necessary to be contrived. The Clerkship of foreign languages was deemed a plausible pretext. But No man acquainted with human nature, or with the ordinary expedients of political intrigue, can be deceived by it.

The medium of negotiation between the Secretary of State and Mr. Freneau, in order to the institution of his Paper, is known. Documents are possessed, which ascertain the person. But they are at present witheld, from considerations of a particular nature. These are the more readily yielded to; because the facts, which have been stated, render it unnecessary to exhibit them.

Those facts prove to the satisfaction of every impartial mind, that Mr. Jefferson is the *Institutor* and *Patron* of the National Gazette.

As to the complexion and tendency of that Gazette, a reference to itself is sufficient. No man, who loves the Government or is a friend to the public tranquillity, but must reprobate it as an incendiary and pernicious publication, and condemn the auspices under which it is supported.

In another paper, the charges which have occasioned so much umbrage to *Aristides,* will be more correctly stated and enforced. The precise terms of the advice, which was given by Mr. Jefferson to Congress respecting the transfer of the French debt, to a company of Hollanders will be recited.[7]

This characteristic *trait,* in the political principles of that Gentleman, will be submitted to the honest feeling not only of the great body of the yeomanry, to whom such affected appeals are so often made, but of honest men of whatsoever class or condition.

7. See "An American No. I," August 4, 1792, note 10.

Treasury Department Circular

Treasury Department, September 15, 1792.

Sir,

A letter directed to William Gardner, Commissioner of Loans for New-Hampshire, containing bills of exchange to the amount of

Five Thousand Dollars, drawn by the Treasurer of the United States in favor of the said Commissioner of Loans, was put into the Post-Office at Philadelphia, on the 17th of August last.

As the letter in question however had not reached its place of destination on the 7th instant, and as from the Bills being drawn with blanks for the direction, there is a possibility in case of miscarriage (either from accident or design) that an attempt will be made to address them to persons in the receipt of public monies— I have judged it expedient to apprize you of the circumstance, that in case any draught of the abovementioned description and numbered as below [1] should be presented to you for payment, you may arrest the same, giving me immediate information thereof.

I am, with consideration,   Sir,   Your most obedient Servant,

A Hamilton

LS, to Jeremiah Olney, Rhode Island Historical Society, Providence; L[S], to Benjamin Lincoln, RG 36, Collector of Customs at Boston, Letters from the Treasury, 1789–1807, Vol. 4, National Archives; LS, to William Seton, The Andre deCoppet Collection, Princeton University Library; LS, Bureau of Customs, Philadelphia; copy, to Samuel Gerry, Essex Institute, Salem, Massachusetts; copy, to George Bush, RG 56, Letters to Collectors at Small Ports, "Set G," National Archives; copy, RG 56, Letters to Collectors at Small Ports, "Set G," National Archives; copy, RG 56, Letters to the Collector at New Bern, National Archives.

1. At the bottom of the circular there is a list containing the numbers of the drafts and the amounts for which each was drawn.

To William Ellery

[*Philadelphia, September 17, 1792.* On October 1, 1792, Ellery wrote to Hamilton: "I have also to acknowledge receipt of your letter of the 15th of last month . . . and of yours of the 17th. of the same month." *Letter of September 17 not found.*]

From Jonathan Fitch [1]

[*New Haven, Connecticut, September 17, 1792.* On September 24, 1792, Hamilton wrote to Fitch concerning the "answer to the question proposed in your letter of the 17th instant." *Letter not found.*]

1. Fitch was collector of customs at New Haven, Connecticut.

To John Jay

[*Philadelphia, September 17, 1792.* On September 27, 1792, Rufus King wrote to Hamilton: "Mr Jay . . . sent me your Letter of the 17th." *Letter not found.*]

From Rufus King

[New York] Sunday 17. Sep: 92

If the enemies of the Government are secret and united we shall lose Mr. Adams.[1] Burr is industrious in his canvass and his object is well understood by our Antis. Mr. Edwards[2] is to make interest for him in Connecticut, and Mr Dallas[3] who is here, and quite in the Circle of the Governor[4] & the Party, informs us that Mr. Burr will be supported as V. President in Pennsylvania. Should Jefferson & his friends unite in the project, the Votes for Mr. A. may be 10 reduced, that though more numerous than those for any other Person, he may decline the Office. Nothing which has heretofore happened so decisively proves the inveteracy of the Opposition. Should they succeed in degrading Mr. Adams, much would be to be apprehended in respect to the measures which have received the sanction of Government.

Yrs affectionately   R. King

Col. Hamilton

ALS, Hamilton Papers, Library of Congress.
  1. For H's earlier fears that John Adams would not be reelected, see H to Adams, August 16, September 9, 1792.
  2. Pierpont Edwards, Aaron Burr's uncle, was a New Haven lawyer and a former member of the Connecticut legislature and the Continental Congress. He was one of his state's most outspoken Antifederalists.
  3. Alexander Dallas, a Philadelphia attorney, was secretary of the Commonwealth of Pennsylvania.
  4. George Clinton was a candidate in the 1792 presidential election. The electoral college, meeting on December 5, 1792, cast one hundred and thirty-two votes for George Washington, seventy-seven for Adams, and fifty for Clinton.

From Pierre Charles L'Enfant

Paterson [New Jersey] Sept 17 1792

Dear sir

The progress of the business here has been as rapide as the time and a stady pursuit of the differents objects to pursue has permitted in the short space since 22d of last mounth that the director have agreed upon the plan which I propos for the canal.[1] The ground through which this is to be carried is already cleared of all timber and immense Rock removed from the way of operation so that I am in hope in a few weak to be enabled to make a begining of the fundation of the grand acqueduc—also to open the Rock across the ill and to make a begining Every way proportional to the number of hand as shall be collected the which daily Increase in number.

Severals of the principals streets are cut through and about clearing. Stone is Extracting from the quarry and provision of Every sort making to Enable a begining of the principals and most necessary building for the manufacture and the Employed—for whom in waiting til the building are compleated I have ordered a number of barrack to be Erected suitable to the various purposes.

Differently situated here than in a City were were a market of Every materials would have permitted an immediate provision of all necessary—we have Everything to procure from a distance store to Erect Shop for carpenter smith &c to Establish and to the very tools to work with to manufacture so that you must not be surprised if the building will not rise so rapidly as in the city of new york.

They will be pushed on as Expeditiously as possible and Everything will, you may depend be carried in concert to be all ready with the canal—the progress of which will depend greatly of the duration of good weather and tempery of the approaching season. As I have assured to you in my letter of the 21 august I shall Economise the time and the means as far as shall appear to me consistant with the Importance of the object—that of the canal is the principal and in the success of which I shall find a real gratification and nothing shall be spared to make it answerabl to the Interest of the society who will be secured a greater proportion of advantage from the Enlarged sisterne I have proposed than from any of the schemes that had been considered.[2]

Harmony prevail amongst Every one here although possibly Interest in some may differ. Pierce[3] is realy a valuable men and I believe the one upon which much confidence may be placed—time will determine who shall be the best quallified in each different branches—and I shall not here Enter into any particular which I tink usless after the observation before made to you.

A pemphflit of this day came in my hand on Contening some observation on Mr secretary A. by a Farmer,[4] which may have an effect but that it is intended to procure. I am Informed of an other production of the same kind—and of goodill of talk about at a certain quarter in the ancient dominion[5]—a little account to the publick of the progress made in tow mounth mentioning the origining of the fundation for fifty house which are now about diging—and also the number of Family collecting and work men comming from the Eastern, Would lead to paralled with the wonderfull Increase of and the progress made since one year at the grand City which at this moment may be flatering to some feeling and be of some effect for the grand sale of lots announced for october.[6]

You [will] not for this suspect me of hill wish to any—nor doubt of my real concern to the full attainement of the object I am Engaged in and shall Steadily pursue.

Assuring you I remain with respect   dear sir   Your most humble and most obedient servant   P. C. LEnfant

Alexander Amilton secretary to the treasury

ALS, Hamilton Papers, Library of Congress.
1. On August 19, 1792, L'Enfant had written to the directors of the Society for Establishing Useful Manufactures: "Having attentively considered upon the various methods how to convey the Water from above the great falls of the Passaick as might best answer the immediate exigency of the intended Cotton Manufactory as also to enable the Society the erection of other Works, I conceive that carrying a Canal across the Mountain in any of the two ways as had before been contemplated will in every respect be answerable, changing however the direction first thought of, and adopting a more safe method of execution, as will hereafter be mentioned" ("Minutes of the S.U.M.," 59–60).
2. L'Enfant had written to the directors of the society: "My object is . . . to form a large Bason or reservoir from which the Water may easily be

distributed in due quantity by different Sluices to supply the Work where may be wanted" ("Minutes of the S.U.M.," 63).

3. William Pearce.

4. In August, 1792, Eleazer Oswald published *Five Letters Addressed to the Yeomanry of the United States: Containing Some Observations on the dangerous scheme of Governor Duer and Mr. Secretary Hamilton, to establish National Manufactories. By A Farmer* (Philadelphia, 1792). This pamphlet was taken from letters written by George Logan which had appeared in Oswald's newspaper, the [Philadelphia] *Independent Gazetteer*, commencing in February, 1792 (Frederick B. Tolles, *George Logan of Philadelphia* [New York, 1953], 117–18).

5. See Elisha Boudinot to H, September 13, 1792, note 6.

6. On June 2, 1792, John McGantt, clerk of the commissioners of the Federal district, issued a notice of the sale of lots in the city of Washington to be held on October 8, 1792 ([Philadelphia] *Gazette of the United States*, July 25, 1792).

From George Washington [1]

Mount Vernon Sepr 17th: 1792 [2]

My dear Sir,   (Private)

Your private letter of the 11th, accompanying an Official one of the 9th. came safe—as did your other private letter of the 9th. I feel myself obliged by the observations contained in the first, respecting the Proclamation.

As the former Proclamations, on similar occasions, have been Countersigned by the Secretary of State, I have, for *that* reason, and for another which has some weight in my mind, thought it best not to depart, in *this* instance, from the Precedent that has been set; [3] and therefore, as it cannot (unless unforeseen delays happen) be with-held from you more than six days longer than if it had been returned by this days Post, I dispatched by Express the Proclamation to Mr Jefferson for the purpose abovementioned.

I have no doubt but that the Proclamation will undergo many strictures—and, as the effect proposed may not be answered by it; it will be necessary to look forward in time to ulterior arrangements —and here, not only the Constitution & Laws must strictly govern —but the employing of the Regular Troops avoided, if it be possible to effect order without their aid; otherwise, there would be a cry at once "The cat is let out; We now see for what purpose an Army was raised." Yet, if no other means will effectually answer, and the

Constitution & Laws will authorise these, they must be used, in the dernier resort.

If you remain in opinion that it would be advisable for the President to transmit the Proclamation to the Governors of North & South Carolina—and the Governor of Pennsylvania,[4] I pray you to draught such letters to them, to be forwarded from hence (with the Proclamations which must also be sent to me) as you may think best calculated to produce the effect proposed. I am always

Your Affectionate   Go: Washington

Alexr. Hamilton Esqr.

ALS, Connecticut Historical Society, Hartford; ADfS, George Washington Papers, Library of Congress; LC, George Washington Papers, Library of Congress.
 1. For background to this letter, see H to Tench Coxe, September 1, 1792; H to Washington, September 1, 8, first letter of September 9, September 11, 1792; H to John Jay, September 3, 1792; "Draft of a Proclamation Concerning Opposition to the Excise Law," September 7, 1792; Jay to H, September 8, 1792; Edmund Randolph to H, September 8, 1792; Washington to H, September 7, 1792.
 2. Both the draft and the letter book copy of this letter are dated September 16, 1792. The letter is dated September 16, 1792, both in *JCHW*, IV, 313–14, and in *GW*, XXXII, 152–53.
 3. See H to Washington, September 11, 1792.
 4. See H to Washington, September 8, 1792.

From George Washington [1]

Mount Vernon Septr. 17th. 1792.

Sir,

Your Letters of the 8 and 9. inst: are received. The latter came to me on Saturday morning by Express, from the Post Office in Alexandria. I gave the Proclamation my signature, and forwarded it in the afternoon of the same day, by a special Messenger, to the Secretary of State for his countersign. If no unforeseen delay happens, the return of it may be in time for Friday's Post, so as to be with you the Tuesday following.

It is much to be regretted that occurrences of a nature so repugnant to order and good Government, should not only afford the occasion, but render such an interference of the Executive indispensably necessary. When these happen, and lenient & temporizing means have been used, and serve only to increase the disorder; longer forbearance would become unjustifiable remissness, and a neglect of that duty which is enjoined on the President. I can have no hesitation therefore, under this view of the case to adopt such legal measures to check the disorderly opposition which is given to the execution of the Laws laying a duty on distilled spirits, as the Constitution has invested the Executive with; and however painful the measure would be, if the Proclamation should fail to produce the effect desired, ulterior arrangements must be made to support the Laws, & to prevent the prostration of Government.

Were it not for the peculiar circumstances of my family,[2] I would return to the Seat of Government immediately; at any rate I hope to do it in the early part of next month, or before the middle thereof.

With esteem & regard   I am &c.   G: Washington

LC, George Washington Papers, Library of Congress.

1. For background to this letter, see H to Tench Coxe, September 1, 1792; H to Washington, September 1, 8, first letter of September 9, September 11, 1792; H to John Jay, September 3, 1792; "Draft of a Proclamation Concerning Opposition to the Excise Law," September 7, 1792; Jay to H, September 8, 1792; Edmund Randolph to H, September 8, 1792; Washington to H, September 7, and the first letter of September 17, 1792.

2. Major George Augustine Washington, Washington's nephew who lived at Mount Vernon, was critically ill during the summer of 1792 and died on February 5, 1793.

To George Washington

Treasury Department, September 17, 1792. Recommends John Armistead as "Surveyor of the port of Plymouth and Inspector of the Revenue for the same" to replace Thomas Freeman, who "has been absent from That Port since February last." States that Senator William Johnston of North Carolina "represents Mr. Armistead as bred to Navigation and acquainted with business, as . . . not only as a suitable person for the offices to be filled, but the most so of any Inhabitant of Plymouth."[1]

LC, George Washington Papers, Library of Congress.

1. See Tench Coxe to H, September 4, 1792. The reference should be to Samuel Johnston rather than William Johnston.

From Henry Van Dyke [1]

New Brunswick [*New Jersey*] *September 18, 1792.* "In consequence of your very obliging favor with which I was honoured in March last [2] I have been anxiously expecting to hear from you the result of Mr Bensons [3] Application in my favor. Your long silence Alarms my fears and I am apprehensive that all the exertions of my friend have proved unsuccessful. If so, I most devoutly pray the Lord to give me more patient submission under the repeated Strokes of Adversity. . . ."

ALS, Hamilton Papers, Library of Congress.
1. Van Dyke was rector of Christ Episcopal Church in New Brunswick.
2. Letter not found.
3. Presumably Egbert Benson, a member of the House of Representatives from New York.

Catullus No. II [1]

[Philadelphia, September 19, 1792]

For the Gazette of The United States

To Aristides [2]

The *"American"* to confirm the inference resulting from the official connection between the Secretary of State and the Editor of the National Gazette, appeals to a conformity of the political principles and views of that officer, with those which are sedulously inculcated in that Gazette. If this conformity exists, it certainly affords a strong presumption, in aid of direct facts, of the operation of his influence on the complexion of that paper.

ADf, Hamilton Papers, Library of Congress; [Philadelphia] *Gazette of the United States,* September 19, 1792.
1. The other "Catullus" essays are dated September 15, 29, October 17, November 24, and December 22, 1792.
2. "Catullus No. II," like "Catullus No. I," was written in reply to an article which was signed by "Aristides" and which appeared in the September 8, 1792, issue of the [Philadelphia] *Gazette of the United States.* See "Catullus No. I," September 15, 1792, note 2, where the article by "Aristides" is printed in full. See also "An American," August 4, 11, and 18, 1792, a series of essays by H which prompted "Aristides" to write his article.

The circumstances of conformity alleged fall under two heads; one—That the Secretary of State was in the origin opposed to that constitution, which it is the evident object of the National Gazette to discredit—the other That he has been and is opposed to those measures which it is the unremitted and it may be said the avowed endeavour of that paper to censure and subvert.

In contradiction to the first suggestion, Aristides cites an authority, which the *American* appears to have relied upon in support of his assertion,—the Speech of Mr. Pendleton in the Convention of Virginia.[3] Let an analasis of this speech shew whether it supports or contradics the assertion.

Mr. Pendleton represents a certain letter of Mr. Jefferson as containing these particulars   1   a strong wish that the *first nine conventions* may accept the new constitution, because it would secure the *good* it contains, which is *great* and *important*   2   a wish that the four latest, whichever they should be, might refuse to accede to it, 'til *amendments were secured*   3   caution to take care that no objection to the form of the Government should produce a scism in the Union; which Mr. Jefferson admits to be an *incurable evil*.

From this it appears, that, though Mr. Jefferson was of opinion, that the Constitution contained "great and important good"—and was desirous, that the first nine deliberating states should consent to it, for the sake of preserving the existence of the Union; yet he had *strong objections* to the constitution—*so strong* that he was willing to risk *an ultimate dismemberment* in an *experiment* to obtain the alterations, which he deemed necessary.

If the four last deliberating States (particularly if they had happened to be states in Geographical contiguity, which was very possible) had refused to ratify the constitution, what might not have been the consequence? Who knows whether the assenting states would have been willing to have been *coerced* into the amendments which the non-assenting states might have been disposed to dictate?

---

3. The charge that Jefferson had opposed the Constitution "in some of its most important features" was advanced by H in "An American No. I," August 4, 1792. Jefferson's position was, moreover, debated at length in the Virginia Ratifying Convention. H is referring to a speech by Edmund Pendleton quoted by "Aristides" in his article. See "Catullus No. I," September 15, 1792, note 2.

Calculating the intrigues and machinations, which were to have been expected to stand in the way, who can say, if even *two thirds* of *both* houses of Congress should have been found willing to propose—that *three fourths* of the Legislature—or Conventions in *three fourths*—of the States—would have been brought to adopt—the required amendments?

Could any thing but objections to the constitution of the most *serious* kind, have justified the hazarding an eventual scism in the Union, in so great a degree, as would have attended an adherence to the advice given by Mr. Jefferson? Can there be any perversion of truth, in affirming, that the person, who entertained those objections, was *opposed* to the Constitution?

The opposition, which was experienced in every part of the UStates, acknowleged the necessity and utility of *Union;* and generally speaking, that the Constitution contained many valuable features; contending only that it wanted some essential alterations to render it upon the whole a safe and a good government.

It may be satisfactory to review what was said, in the same Convention of Virginia, by some other members, on the subject of the letter in question—

Mr. Henry (Page 109 of the Debates) [4] replies thus to Mr. Pendleton—"The Honorable Gentleman has endeavoured to *explain* the opinion of *Mr. Jefferson,* our common friend, *into* an advice to adopt this new Government. *He* wishes Nine States to adopt, and that four states may be found somewhere to reject it. Now Sir, I say, if we pursue his advice, what are we to do? To prefer form to substance? For, give me leave to ask, what is the substantial part of his counsel? It is, Sir, that four States should *reject.* They tell us, that from the most authentic accounts, New Hampshire will adopt it. Where then will four states be found to reject, if we adopt it? If we do, the counsel of this worthy and enlightened countryman of

4. *Debates and Other Proceedings of the Convention of Virginia, Convened at Richmond, on Monday the 2d day of June, 1788, for the purpose of deliberating on the Constitution recommended by the Grand Federal Convention to Which is prefixed, the Federal Constitution* (Petersburg: Printed by William Prentis, 1789), II, 109. H's quotation from these debates and Pendleton's speech which "Aristides" used in his article of September 4, 1792, may be found on pages 122 and 100–01 of the same volume. H added most of the italics for emphasis in the portions of the debates he is quoting in "Catullus No. II."

ours will be thrown away &c." Whether this Gentleman argued sincerely from his impression of the true import of the letter; or made an attempt "to *pervert* Mr. Jefferson's sentiments" as Aristides affirms, must be referred to his own consciousness, and to the candid construction of an impartial public.

Mr. Madison, in reply to Mr. Henry (Page 122 of the same debates) expresses himself thus—"The Honorable Member, in order to influence our decision, has mentioned the opinion of a Citizen, who is an ornament to this state. When the name of this distinguished character was introduced, I was much surprised. *Is it come to this then, that we are not to follow our own reason?* Is it proper to adduce the opinions of respectable men, not within these walls? If the opinion of an important character were to weigh on this occasion, could we not adduce a character equally great on our side? Are we who (in the Honorable Gentleman's opinion are not to be guided by an *erring world*) *now to submit to the opinion of a Citizen, beyond the Atlantic?* I believe, that were that Gentleman now on this floor, he would be *for* the adoption of this constitution. I wish his name had never been mentioned. I wish every thing spoken here, relative to his opinion, may be suppressed, if our debates should be published. I know that the delicacy of his feelings will be wounded, when he will see in Print what has, and may be said concerning him on this occasion. I am in some measure acquainted with his sentiments on this subject. *It is not right for me to unfold what he has informed me.* But I will venture to assert that the clause now discussed is not objected to by Mr. Jefferson. He approves of it, because it enables the Government to carry on its operations &c."

It is observable, that Mr. Madison neither advocates the accuracy of Mr. Pendletons comment, nor denies the justness of that of Mr. Henry. His solicitude appears to be to destroy the influence of what he impliedly admits to be the opinion of Mr. Jefferson, to press out of sight the authority of that opinion, and to get rid of the subject as fast as possible. He confesses a knowlege of Mr. Jeffersons sentiments, but prudently avoids disclosure; wrapping the matter in mysterious reserve; and leaving the Public to this day to conjecture what was the precise import of the sentiments communicated.

Enough however is seen to justify the conclusion that if the spirit of Mr. Jefferson's advice had prevailed with the Convention, and full credence had been given to the expected adoption by New Hampshire—Virginia, North Carolina, New York and Rhode Island would temporarily have thrown themselves out of the Union. And whether in that event, they would have been at this day reunited to it, or whether there would be now any Union at all is happily a speculation which need only be pursued to derive the pleasing reflection, that the danger was wisely avoided.

To understand more accurately what the *American* meant, in asserting that Mr. Jefferson had been opposed to the constitution, let him be compared with himself. In his first paper he expresses himself thus—"While the Constitution of the United States was depending before the People of this Country, for their consideration and decision, Mr. Jefferson being in France was *opposed* to it, *in some of its most important features*, and wrote his objections to some of his friends in Virginia. He *at first* went so far as to *discountenance its adoption;* though he *afterwards recommended* it on the ground of expediency, in certain contingencies."

From this, it is evident, that so far from denying, he has even admitted, that Mr Jefferson, at *one stage* of the business, *recommended* the adoption of the Constitution to his *fellow Citizens,* but upon a contingency. And this is literally the fact as established by the letter quoted in the debates of the Convention. The advice is to adopt, if nine states had not previously adopted; to reject if that number of states had previously adopted. This clearly is to adopt, or not, upon a contingency. Thus the authority appealed to by Aristides confirms the latter part of the *American's* assertion, without contradicting the former part of it.

Aristides has not denied, nor do I believe he will deny—that Mr. Jefferson in his early communications discountenanced the adoption of the constitution in its primitive form. I know the source of the *American's* information. It is equally authentic and friendly to Mr. Jefferson. Allowing for the bare possibility of misapprehension, it exactly accords with the statement, which has been made of it. If the fact shall be denied, the source of information will be indicated under due guards for the delicacy of the proceeding. This will serve, either to confirm, or, in case of misconception to correct.

I add, that some of Mr. Jefferson's objections to the constitution have not been removed, by the amendments, which have been proposed. Part of his objections went to the structure of particular parts of the government.

As to the second fact, with which the American corroborates the charge of Mr. Jefferson's participation in the views of the National Gazette, it is in a degree conceded by Aristides. He confesses, nay he even *boasts*, Mr. Jeffersons *abhorrence* of some of the leading principles of Mr. Hamiltons fiscal administration, that is the leading principles of those measures, which have provided for the public debt, & restored public Credit.

It would have been well, if Aristides had told us what those leading principles are, which are the objects of so much *abhorrence* to Mr. Jefferson.

The leading principles of Mr. Hamilton's fiscal administration have been—that the Public debt ought to be provided for in favour of those, who, according to the express terms of the contract, were the *true legal proprietors* of it; that it ought to be provided for in other respects, according to the terms of the contract, except so far as deviations from it should be assented to by the Creditors, upon the condition of a fair equivalent—that it ought to be *funded* on *ascertained* revenues *pledged* for the payment of interest, and the gradual redemption of principal—that the debts of the several states ought to be comprised in the provision, on the same terms with that of the United States—that to render this great operation practicable avoid the oppression of Trade and industry, and facilitate loans to the government, in cases of emergency, it was necessary to institute a National Bank—that indirect taxes were, in the actual circumstances of the country, the most eligible means of revenue, and that direct taxes ought to be avoided as much and as long as possible.

I aver, from competent opportunities of knowing Mr. Jeffersons ideas, that he has been hostile to all these positions, except, perhaps, the last; and that even in regard to that, his maxims would oblige the government, in practice, speedily to resort to direct taxes.

I aver, moreover, that Mr. Jefferson's opposition to the administration of the Government has not been confined to the measures connected with the Treasury Department; but has extended, to use the words of the American "to almost all the important measures of the Government."

The *exceptions* to the generality of both the preceding assertions,

I am content to rest on a designation by Mr. Jefferson, or by any person, who shall speak from a knowlege of his sentiments, of those principles of the Fiscal department, or of those measures of the Government of any importance which he *does approve*. I insist only, that the designation be precise and explicit, and come with such marks of authenticity, as are adapted to the nature of an anonymous discussion.

To give an idea of the accuracy with which Aristides discloses Mr. Jefferson's opinions, I shall cite one of his phrases, with a short observation. He asserts, that a suggestion against Mr. Jefferson, which he states, is "made on no better foundation than his being opposed to *some* of the principles of the funding system, of the National Bank, and of certain other measures of the Secretary of the Treasury." [5] It is matter of general notoriety and unquestionable certainty, that Mr. Jefferson has been opposed to the National Bank in *toto*, to its *constitutionality* and to its *expediency*. With what propriety, is it then said, that he has been opposed only to "*some of* the principles of that Institution"?

I proceed now, to state the exact tenor of the advice, which Mr. Jefferson gave to Congress, respecting the transfer of the debt due to France to a company of Hollanders.[6] After mentioning an offer, which had been made by such a company for the purchase of the debt, he concludes with these extraordinary expressions—"If there *is a danger* of the public payments *not being punctual*, I submit whether it may not be better, that *the discontents, which would then arise*, should be *transferred* from a *Court*, of whose *good will we have so much need*, to the *breasts* of a *private company*." [7]

The above is an extract which was made from the letter, in February 1787. The date of it was not noted, but the original, being on the files of the department of state, will ascertain that and all other particulars relating to its contents. The genuineness of the foregoing extract may be depended upon.

This letter was the subject of a Report from the Board of Treasury in February 1787.[8] That Board treated the idea of the Transfer proposed as both unjust and impolitic: *unjust*, because the Nation

5. See the article by "Aristides" quoted in "Catullus No. I," September 15, 1792, note 2.
6. See "An American No. I," August 4, 1792, note 10.
7. See "An American No. I," August 4, 1792, note 10.
8. See "An American No. I," August 4, 1792, note 10.

would contract an engagement which there was no well grounded prospect of fulfilling; *impolitic*, because a failure in the payment of interest, on the debt transferred (which was *inevitable*) would *justly blast* all hopes of credit with the citizens of the United Netherlands, in future pressing exigencies of the Union: and gave it as their opinion that it would be adviseable for Congress, *without delay*, to instruct their Minister, at the Court of France, to forbear giving his sanction to any such transfer   .[9]

Congress agreeing in the ideas of the Board caused an instruction to that effect to be sent to Mr. Jefferson *. Here then was a solemn act of Government condeming the principle, as unjust and impolitic.

If the sentiment contained in the extract, which has been recited, can be vindicated from the imputation of political *profligacy—then is it necessary to unlearn* all the ancient notions of justice, and to substitute some new fashioned scheme of morality in their stead.

Here is no complicated problem, which sophistry may entangle or obscrure—here is a plain question of *moral feeling*. A Government is encouraged, on the express condition of *not having a prospect* of making a due provision for a debt, which it owes, to concur in a transfer of that debt from a Nation well able to bear the inconveniences of failure or delay, to Individuals, whose total ruin might have been the consequence of it; and that upon the *interested* consideration of having need of the good will of the Creditor-Nation, and, with the dishonorable motive as is clearly implied, of having more to apprehend from the discontents of that Nation, than from those of disappointed and betrayed individuals. Let every honest and impartial mind, consulting its own spontaneous emotions, pronounce for itself upon the rectitude of such a suggestion. Let every sober and independent member of the community decide, whether it is likely to be a misfortune to the country, that the maxims of the

* Note at *foot*
What is here said *with regard to Congress* is from a recollection of more than 5 years standing & so far liable to error though none is apprehended to exist. The Secret Journals in the possession of the Department of State, if there is one, may correct it.[10]

9. At this point in the MS H left several lines blank.
10. The report of the Board of Treasury of February 19, 1787, and the agreement of Congress to the Board's recommendation appear in the secret journals for foreign affairs under the date of October 2, 1787 (Items 5 and 6, Papers of the Continental Congress, National Archives).

Officer at the head of its Treasury Department are materially variant from those of the Author of that suggestion.

And let Aristides prove if he can, that Mr. Jefferson gave advice "*expressly contrary* to that which has been ascribed to him." [11] Amidst the excentric ramblings of this political comet, its station, in another revolution, will not prove, that its appearance was not, at one time, at the place, which has been assigned for it.

The *American* it ought to be confessed, has, in this instance, drawn larger than the life. This he has done, by blending with the fact the sudden, though natural, comments of an honest indignation. But the original itself, in its true size and shape, without the help of the least exaggeration, is to the moral eye a deformed and hideous monster.

Say *Aristides!* did the Character, to whom you are so partial, imitate, in this case, the sublime virtue of that venerable Athenian, whose name you have assumed? Did he dissuade his countrymen from adopting a proposition, because though "nothing could be more advantageous nothing was more unjust"? Did he not rather advise them to do what was both *disadvantageous* and *unjust?* May he not, as a public man, discard all apprehension of *ostracism,* for being the *superlatively just?* [12]   *Catulus*

PS. Some additional observations are reserved for another paper.

11. See "An American No. I," August 4, 1792, note 10.
12. The details concerning the two incidents in Aristides' life to which H is referring vary in different accounts. Oliver Goldsmith's account fits H's statement. According to Goldsmith, one Athenian voted for Aristides' ostracism because he hated "to hear him praised for his justice." In rejecting a secret plan of Themistocles to assure Athenian hegemony in Greece by destroying the fleet of her ally, Sparta, Aristides is reported to have said that "nothing could be more advantageous . . . but nothing could be more unjust" (Oliver Goldsmith, *The Grecian History, from the Earliest State to the Death of Alexander the Great* [Dublin, 1774], I, 95–96, 129).

From Tench Coxe

Treasury Department
Revenue Office, Septemr. 19th. 1792

Sir,

I have the honor to inclose to you a letter of the 10th Instant this day received from the Supervisor of Virginia,[1] in answer to a letter of the 23d. Ultimo from this Office.[2] The intention of this communication is to place before you the tenor of any instructions to that officer on the subject of the 9th. Section of the Act of May 1792, concerning the duties on Spirits distilled in the United States[3] (which you will find to be conformable with the Ideas which occured in conference with you) and his intentions in consequence of the discretion which it appeared necessary to allow him.

I have the honor to be with perfect respect, Sir, your most obedt. Servt.   Tench Coxe,

Commissr. of the Revenue

The Secretary
of the Treasury.

LC, RG 58, Letters of Commissioner of Revenue, 1792–1793, National Archives.

1. Edward Carrington.

2. On August 23, 1792, Coxe wrote to Carrington: "You will perceive, on a perusal of . . . [the arrangement of compensations] that the parts of the plan of compensation contemplated in a former letter, which it was hoped might induce the Collectors to make a fair experiment of the practicability of marking have been adopted by the President. . . . It is the wish of the Secretary of the Treasury, in which (from a conviction of the importance of the certificates and a desire accurately to execute the will of the Legislature) I join him, that the business of marking may again be considered, now that you have the plan of compensation before you. It is much to be desired, that an experiment be made in the manner proposed, or in some other if one more feasible occurs. There is however so much weight in the objections suggested, that it is not desired that the matter should be precipitately or peremptorily pressed either upon the Collectors, or upon the distillers. The law certainly requires the Spirits to be marked . . . and it is possible that the non execution of the ninth Section may render it necessary to abolish the certificate System. . . . In the measures which may be *contemplated* or *attempted* . . . the refusals & resignations of worthy and capable Collectors, and the repugnance, evasion or probable resistance of the distillers must be kept in View; and indeed the possibility of those Events must govern your Conduct. Your zeal, ability and discretion in the execution of the law have been abundantly manifested, and this measure will . . . be conducted in such manner as you may . . . deem practicable and prudent" (LC, RG 58, Letters of Commissioner of Revenue, 1792–1793, National Archives).

3. This section reads as follows: "*And be it further enacted*, That every distiller of, and dealer in spirits, who may have in his or her possession, distilled spirits not marked or certified, pursuant to the act, intituled 'An act repealing after the last day of June next, the duties heretofore laid upon distilled spirits imported from abroad, and laying others in their stead, and also upon spirits distilled within the United States, and for appropriating the same,' shall, prior to the last day of September next, report the spirits in his or her possession, in writing at some office of inspection, to the end that such spirits may be marked and certified as old stock. And that from and after the said last day of September next, casks and vessels of the capacity of twenty gallons and upwards, containing distilled spirits, which shall be found in the

possession of any distiller or dealer in spirits, except at a distillery where the same were made, or in going from one place to another, without being marked according to law, or without having a certificate from some proper officer, shall be liable to seizure and forfeiture, and that it shall be the duty of the several officers of inspection, upon request of any dealer or distiller, to take measures for the marking of casks, vessels and packages containing distilled spirits, and to furnish such dealer or distiller, free from expense, with certificates to accompany the same: *Provided,* That it shall not be incumbent upon any such officer to mark or certify any cask, vessel or package which ought to have been before marked or certified according to any law of the United States" (1 *Stat.* 269–70 [May 8, 1792]).

To William Ellery

[*Philadelphia, September 19, 1792.* On October 1, 1792, Ellery wrote to Hamilton: "I have the honour to acknowledge the receipt of your letter of the 19th . . . of the last month." *Letter not found.*]

To Richard Harison

Treasury Department
September 19th. 1792

Sir,

I am to inform you, that for the purpose of discharging the bill drawn on me the 20th. of August last in favor of Robert Boyd & yourself, by John McComb Junr.[1] Contractor for erecting a Light House on Cape Henry, a Warrant has this day passed the Treasury in favor of Jonathan Burrall[2] Esquire Assignee of the said Bill, and which the Treasurer will be directed to pay in New York.

I am with Respectful Consideration Sir Your Most Obedt. Servt.

Alexander Hamilton

Richard Harison Esquire

LS, New-York Historical Society, New York.
1. See H to Harison, June 26, 1792.
2. Formerly a commissioner appointed under the Continental Congress to settle the accounts of the quartermaster and commissary departments, Burrall was cashier of the New York branch of the Bank of the United States.

To Jeremiah Olney

Treasury Department
September 19th 1792.

Sir

I have considered the case which is stated in your letter of the 8th instant concerning Welcome Arnold.[1]

If appearances of the kind continue, I am of opinion that the presumption of a design to evade the law will be sufficiently strong to justify an Officer in refusing the credit. If an action should be brought against the Officer for such refusal, means must be taken to examine all the parties upon Oath; and in the event of damages against the Officer, if he appears to have acted with due caution and upon sufficient ground of probability, it will be incumbent on the government to indemnify him.

I am Sir   Your Obedt Servant.   A Hamilton

Jere. Olney Esqr.
Collr Providence.

LS, Rhode Island Historical Society, Providence; copy, Newport Historical Society, Newport, Rhode Island.

1. See also the second letter Olney sent to H on September 13, 1792, and William Ellery to H, September 4, 1792.

From John Steele [1]

[*Salisbury, North Carolina, September 19, 1792.* On October 15, 1792, Hamilton wrote to Steele: "The letter which you did me the favour to write me of the 19th of September came to hand two days ago." *Letter not found.*]

1. Steele was a member of the House of Representatives from North Carolina.

To Wilhem and Jan Willink, Nicholaas and Jacob Van Staphorst, and Nicholas Hubbard

Treasury Department
September 19th. 1792.

Gentlemen,

You will herewith receive duplicates of my letters to you under date the 28th. ultimo.[1]

I have now to acknowledge the receipt of yours of the 1st. of June last [2] enclosing your account current with the United States to that day.

Mr. Short has been instructed [to place] with you a credit in favor of our Minister Plenipotentiary at the Court of France for one hundred five thousand Guilders.[3] The enclosed letters to Mr. Short and Mr. Morris [4] contain the instructions, and relate to the application of the said sum: which enclosures I, therefore, request you will immediately forward to their respective addresses. I do not give an immediate direction to hold that sum to the order of Mr. Morris; because it might, by possibility, interfere with some arrangement previously made by Mr. Short, in consequence of the discretion, which has been vested in him. Should Mr. Short be at Madrid, the letter to him must, of course, be forwarded thither.[5]

I am &c.   Alexander Hamilton

Messrs. Willink, Van Staphorst and Hubbard
Amsterdam.

Copy, RG 233, Reports of the Treasury Department, 1792–1793, Vol. III, National Archives. This letter was enclosed in H's "Report on Foreign Loans," February 13, 1793.

1. Letters not found.   2. Letter not found.

3. See H to William Short, September 13, 1792.

4. H to Short, September 13, 1792; H to Gouverneur Morris, September 13, 1792.

5. Short, United States Minister to The Hague, and William Carmichael, United States chargé d'affaires at Madrid, had been appointed commissioners to negotiate a treaty with Spain. See "Notes on Thomas Jefferson's Report of Instructions for the Commissioners to Spain," March 1–4, 1792, note 1.

To William Ellery

[*Philadelphia, September 20, 1792.* On October 1, 1792, Ellery wrote to Hamilton: "I have the honour to acknowledge the receipt of your letter . . . of the 20th of the last month." *Letter not found.*]

From Benjamin Lincoln

Boston September 20 1792

Sir

Our Cutter proves to be a very dull sailer, after various experiments by altering the Standing of the masts the bowsprit and altering the Sails to make her sail better, is consequently a very improper Vessel for the business assigned her. We have now an opportunity to Sell her for a Sum, with the Saving of the pay & rations for the hands, which would build one of fifty odd tons, a Size large enough for the business & much easier Sailed. If you Should think proper to sell this, another could be ready as early in the Spring, as would be proper for her to be in the Offing. By the Sale there would be a Saving of pay and rations for the Crew in the Winter. As the Season of the year is fast approaching when we expect little or no aid from the Cutter, and as her sails are pretty well worn & She too heavy for the purpose, I thought it my duty to Suggest the matter to you. An early answer will oblige the Gentleman wishing to purchase.

LC, Massachusetts Historical Society, Boston; copy, RG 56, Letters from the Collector at Boston, National Archives.

From James McHenry

[Baltimore] 20th [September] [1] 1792

My dear Hamilton.

I have been confined by a fever to my bed ⟨for⟩ 17 days. Yesterday and to-day I have sat up a little. I have just recd your letter of the

10th Ulto.² which arrived du⟨ri⟩ng the hight of my illness after having gone to Fayettville in N. Carolina and back to Philada.

I expect a visit from Bishop Carroll ³ on his return to Balt. which may be next week. I have thought if I shewed him a paragraph in your letter it might have its use; I have therefore delayed destroying it till I hear from you. The paragph is. "Your project with regard to the Presidency, in a certain event, will I believe not have an opportunity of being executed.⁴ Happily for the public tranquility the present incumbent after a serious struggle inclines, if I mistake not, to submit to another election. ⟨If it⟩ turns out otherwise I say unequivocally—I will co-operate in running the gentleman you mention as one of the two who are to fill the two great offices. Which of the two may turn up *first* or *second* must be an affair of some casualty as the constitution stands. My real respect and esteem for the character brought into view will assure him my best wishes in every event". Instruct me.

Send me Perry's letter.⁵ Adieu. If I should get to heaven before you I shall remember you. I must go to bed.

Yours affy   James McHenry

ALS, Hamilton Papers, Library of Congress.
1. McHenry mistakenly wrote "Octbr." The letter, however, is postmarked September 20.
2. Letter not found.
3. John Carroll. See McHenry to H, August 16, 1792, note 3.
4. See McHenry to H, August 16, 1792.
5. In his letter to H of August 16, 1792, McHenry had enclosed a letter from William Perry, a resident of the Eastern Shore of Maryland and a member of the Maryland Senate.

From Jeremiah Olney

Providence, September 20, 1792. "I have received your circular Letters of the 31st of August and 8th Instant; and will pay due attention to their Contents."

ADfS, Rhode Island Historical Society, Providence.

To ―――――

Philadelphia September
21. 1792

Dear Sir

I take the liberty to inclose you the copy of a letter from a very respectable friend in New York.[1] The contents surprised me—nor am I quite persuaded that the appearance of Mr. Burr on the stage is not a diversion in favour of Mr. Clinton.

Mr. Clinton's success I should think very unfortunate. I am not for trusting the Government too much in the hands of its enemies. But still Mr. C―― is a man of property, and, in private life, as far as I know of probity. I fear the other Gentleman is unprincipled both as a public and private man. When the constitution was in deliberation, his conduct was equivocal; but its enemies, who I believe best understood him considered him as with them. In fact, I take it, he is for or against nothing, but as it suits his interest or ambition. He is determined, as I conceive, to make his way to be the head of the popular party and to climb per *fas et nefas* to the highest honors of the state; and as much higher as circumstances may permit. Embarrassed, as I understand, in his circumstances, with an extravagant family—bold enterprising and intriguing, I am mistaken, if it be not his object to play the game of confusion, and I feel it a religious duty to oppose his career.

I have hitherto scrupulously refrained from interference in elections. But the occasion is in my opinion of sufficient importance to warrant in this instance a departure from that rule. I therefore commit my opinion to you without scruple; but in perfect confidence I pledge my character for discernment that it is incumbent upon every good man to resist the present design.

AL, Hamilton Papers, Library of Congress.
1. Rufus King to H, September 17, 1792.

To George Clymer

[*Philadelphia, September 21, 1792.* On September 28, 1792, Clymer wrote to Hamilton: "I was honoured with yours of the 21st." *Letter not found.*]

To William Henderson [1]

[*Philadelphia, September 21, 1792.* On September 24, 1792, Henderson wrote to Hamilton: "Your favor of the 21st. inst. I duly received." *Letter not found.*]

1. Henderson was a New York City insurance broker, a stockholder in the Society for Establishing Useful Manufactures, and a land speculator.

From Gouverneur Morris

Paris 21. September 1792.

Dear Sir

I receive this Instant a Letter from a very respectable Commercial House of Rouen Messieurs Le Couteulx and Company.[1] By the bye before I mention the business I will tell you an Anecdote of them. Louis the fourteenth desirous of encouraging Commerce and breaking down the Barriers which Prejudice had raised against it, offered to this House which was even then of great Antiquity to give the Members letters of Nobility. They refused saying that they preferred the Reputation of old Merchants to that of New Nobles and would rather be at the head of one Class than at the Tail of the other.

Messieurs Le Couteulx and Company represent to me that a Ship called the *Marie françoise* commanded by John Baptist Gossin laden on their Account at Marseilles and Cette [2] with Brandy, Wine, Liqueurs, Sulphur &c. has been seized at New York on account of fifty Cases of Brandy in Bottles which their Correspondents at Cette had persuaded them to add to their Cargo, this Brandy being very old and therefore likely to meet a good Sale, but both they and their

Correspondents being utterly Ignorant of the law of the United States which prohibits the Importation of Brandy in Bottles.[3] These Gentlemen declare to me their Innocence of all Intention to Smuggle and I am perfectly convinc'd that this Declaration is true. Indeed any such Declaration from a House of their respectability is unnecessary. They have requested me to recommend their business to the attention of our Government. And I do so warmly and without Scruple because I am certain that they are incapable of any Attempts to defraud the revenue and I am sure the United States are too just and too wise to condemn *Foreigners* for the breach of a law which they were unacquainted with.

LC, Gouverneur Morris Papers, Library of Congress.

1. The Rouen banking house of Le Couteulx de Cantaleu had been associated in 1788 and 1789 with Morris and Daniel Parker in an attempt to purchase the debt owed France by the United States. See William Short to H, November 30, 1789, note 8.

2. Sète, a French city on the Mediterranean.

3. Section 33 of "An Act repealing, after the last day of June next, the duties heretofore laid upon Distilled Spirits imported from abroad, and laying others in their stead; and also upon Spirits distilled within the United States, and for appropriating the same" provided that after June 30, 1791, "no spirituous liquors except gin or cordials in cases, jugs or bottles, shall be brought from any foreign port or place, in casks of less capacity than fifty gallons at the least, on pain of forfeiting of the said spirits, and of the ship or vessel in which they shall be brought" (1 *Stat.* 207 [March 3, 1791]).

To Arthur St. Clair [1]

[*Philadelphia, September 21, 1792.* On December 5, 1792, St. Clair wrote to Hamilton: "Your letter of the 21st. Septr. enclosing a Copy of an Order of the Senate relative to the Salaries fees and emoluments of Persons holding Offices under the united States [2] . . . came to hand a few days ago." *Letter not found.*]

1. St. Clair was governor of the Northwest Territory.

2. Although H's letter of September 21, 1792, to St. Clair has not been found, St. Clair's reply indicates that its contents were similar to "Treasury Department Circular," September 13, 1792.

To Winthrop Sargent [1]

Treasury Department, September 21, 1792. Requests information for report ordered by the Senate on May 7, 1792.[2]

LS, Western Reserve Historical Society, Cleveland.

1. Sargent, who had surveyed in the Ohio country in 1786, was elected secretary of the Ohio Company in 1787 and was active in the planting of the Ohio settlements. In 1787 Congress appointed him secretary of the Northwest Territory.

2. The contents of this letter are essentially the same as those of "Treasury Department Circular," September 13, 1792.

From George Washington [1]

Mount Vernon Septr. 21st. 1792.

Sir,

Under cover of this Letter you will receive the Proclamation which is just returned to me with the counter signature of The Secretary of State. I have erased the words "dictated by weighty reasons of public exigency," [2] & scored others with a pencil, which you are hereby authorised to take out or retain as you may think best.

As the Instrument is drawn I could do no other than fill up one of the blanks with the name of the place at wch. I *now* am; but, as it is to have a general circulation, you may decide upon the propriety of this, & alter or let it stand according to your judgment.[3]

With esteem, I am &c.   G: Washington

LC, George Washington Papers, Library of Congress.

1. For background to this letter, see H to Tench Coxe, September 1, 1792; H to Washington, September 1, 8, first letter of September 9, September 11, 1792; H to John Jay, September 3, 1792; "Draft of a Proclamation Concerning Opposition to the Excise Law," September 7, 1792; Jay to H, September 8, 1792; Edmund Randolph to H, September 8, 1792; Washington to H, September 7, and the two letters Washington sent to H on September 17, 1792.

2. Acting on Randolph's suggestion, H had called this phrase to Washington's attention (Randolph to H, September 8, 1792; H to Washington, September 11, 1792). After signing the proclamation, Thomas Jefferson returned it to Washington, together with a letter dated September 18, 1792, in which he also suggested the removal of the phrase (ALS, RG 59, Miscellaneous Letters, 1790–1799, National Archives).

3. For the proclamation as it was issued, see "Draft of a Proclamation Concerning Opposition to the Excise Law," September 7, 1792, note 1.

[Scourge] [1]

[Philadelphia, September 22, 1792]

DF, in the handwriting of William Loughton Smith, Hamilton Papers, Library of Congress; [Philadelphia] *Gazette of the United States,* September 22, 1792.

1. Philip Marsh, in discussing "Scourge," wrote: ". . . there can be no doubt as to authorship, for the manuscript, in Hamilton's hand, is in the Library of Congress, among his papers" ("Further Attributions to Hamilton's Pen," *The New-York Historical Society Quarterly*, XL [October, 1956], 355). In another place ("Randolph and Hamilton," *The Pennsylvania Magazine of History and Biography*, LXXII [July, 1948], 248) Marsh states that as "Scourge" H was "at his scarcastic best." Marsh, however, is mistaken, for an examination of the MS in question indicates beyond doubt that "Scourge" is in the handwriting of William Loughton Smith.

To George Washington [1]

Treasury Departmt. Septr. 22d. 1792.

Sir,

I have been duly honored with your Letters of the 7th and 17th instant, and perceive with much pleasure a confirmation of the expectation which your former communication had given that your view of the measures proper to be pursued respecting the proceedings therein referred to, would correspond with the impressions entertained here.

I flatter myself that the Proclamation will answer a very valuable purpose; but every thing, which the law and prudence will warrant, will be put in train, as circumstances shall indicate, for such eventual measures as may be found necessary. I do not, however, despair that with a proper countenance the ordinary course of legal coertion will be found adequate.

The enclosed copy of a letter from the Inspector of Kentuckey [2] to the Supervisor of Virginia,[3] of the 12th. of July last, and the copy of a letter from one of his Collectors to him of the 1st of June, contain interesting, and comparatively not discouraging matter respecting the state of things in that Survey.

LC, George Washington Papers, Library of Congress.
1. For background to this letter, see H to Tench Coxe, September 1, 1792; H to Washington, September 1, 8, first letter of September 9, September 11, 1792; H to John Jay, September 3, 1792; "Draft of a Proclamation Concerning Opposition to the Excise Law," September 7, 1792; Jay to H, September 8, 1792; Edmund Randolph to H, September 8, 1792; Washington to H, September 7, two letters of September 17, September 21, 1792.
2. Thomas Marshall was inspector of Survey No. 7 in Virginia, which comprised the Kentucky District.
3. Edward Carrington was supervisor of the revenue for the District of Virginia.

The Supervisor of Virginia in a letter to the Commissioner of the Revenue, of the 10th. instant, expresses himself thus—"I can truly say that the Excise is now fairly on it's legs in this District—it rests on the good-will of the greater part of the people, and our Collectors are from no cause indisposed to the service, but the apprehension of too much business for too little compensation." A letter from Mr. Hawkins (Senator) [4] to Mr. Coxe announces favorable symptoms in the part of North Carolina which is in the vicinity of his residence.[5]

On the whole, I see no cause of apprehension, but that the law will finally go into full operation with as much good will of the people as usually attends Revenue Laws.

You will be pleased also to find enclosed a letter from the Commissioner of Revenue to me dated the 12th. instant, submitting an arrangement for compensating the Officers of Inspection for the period antecedent to the commencement of the permanent arrangement which you lately established; and the plan of an Act for that purpose to be passed by the President, if approved by him; together with an Estimate of the total expence of the proposed arrangement.

The law has made provision for a restrospective increase of compensation at the discretion of The President,[6] and as the outset of the business will have been of course the most perplexing and troublesome, nothing can be more equitable than such a retrospection, except in those particulars in which the encreased compensations would either be inapplicable or liable to abuse. It will have besides, the good

4. Benjamin Hawkins lived in Halifax in Survey No. 4 in North Carolina. On September 22, 1792, the following extract of a letter dated September 12, 1792, from Halifax was printed in the [Philadelphia] *Gazette of the United States:* "A correspondent from the western part of the state observes, that the people are generally anxious to take out licences for their stills during the season; but there is no county in which there is a person authorised to grant them, owing to the difficulty of executing the former law—that they are tolerably satisfied with the present modification, as better accomodated to their rights."

5. On July 7, 1792, Tench Coxe had written to John Whitaker, inspector of the revenue for Survey No. 4 in North Carolina: "I have received this day your letter of the 13th Ultimo. . . . It is very satisfactory to learn that the beneficial Alterations in the Act are perceived by our fellow Citizens" (LC, RG 58, Letters of Commissioner of Revenue, 1792–1793, National Archives).

6. H is referring to Section 16 of "An Act concerning the Duties on Spirits distilled within the United States" (1 *Stat.* 267–71 [May 8, 1792]). For the provision made by this section, see H to Robert Ballard, May 31, 1792, note 2.

effect of stimulating the zeal of the Officers by shewing a liberal attention to their past services, hitherto defectively requited.

The Plan submitted is the result of previous consultation between the Commissioner of the Revenue and myself, and appears to me an eligible medium.

The Petition from the Keeper of the Rhode Island Lighthouse [7] has been put in a course of enquiry, and the result will be made known.

The Lighthouse in Virginia being nearly finished, a trusty keeper of it will be speedily necessary. A letter from David M. Randolph Esqr. to Governor Lee, which was transmitted by him to me, and is enclosed,[8] recommends for the purpose the name of John Waller Johnson; but I have no other information concerning him. You will probably recollect, Sir, a person who some time since was recommended by Colo. Parker [9]—a man who it seems was very active during the war and distingushed himself in some water-enterprises; [10] but who appeared much addicted to liquor, a fault peculiarly disqualifying in such a station. I regret that I forgot his name. I believe he was disabled in one of his arms. No other Candidate has been brought forward. A letter has been written to Mr. Newton,[11] mentioning Mr. Johnson to him and requesting him to communicate his opinion of him to you, and of any other character who might occur.

Pursuant to the authorisation in your letter of the 7th. instant, measures have been taken for discharging the Debts due to foreign Officers.[12] Upon a review of the tenor of the Certificates, in order to this, it appeared that the interest only was payable at Paris—the principal here. Had it been clear, that motives of accomodation

7. On October 30, 1792, Coxe wrote to William Ellery, collector of customs at Newport, Rhode Island: "It appears from a petition of Mr. William Martin, keeper of the light House in James Town under your superintendence, that he is not satisfied with the compensation he receives" (LC, RG 58, Letters of Commissioner of Revenue, 1792–1793, National Archives). Coxe requested Ellery to send further information.

8. See Henry Lee to H, June 23, 1792.

9. See Josiah Parker to H, May 11, 1792, note 1.

10. This is presumably a reference to Thomas Herbert, who had been a captain in the Virginia navy during the American Revolution. Thomas Newton, Jr., on September 28, 1792, wrote to George Washington that he "could not recommend [Herbert] as a fit person" (ALS, RG 59, Miscellaneous Letters, 1790–1799, National Archives).

11. Coxe to Thomas Newton, Jr., September 17, 1792 (LC, RG 58, Letters of Commissioner of Revenue, 1792–1793, National Archives).

12. See H to Gouverneur Morris, September 12, 1792.

would render the payment both of principal and interest there desireable, there might have been difficulty in justifying the regularity of the proceeding, and of course hazard of blame, especially if any mistake or accident in the execution had happen'd. But it is very possible that payment in the United States will be most agreeable to the greatest number. The arrangement of course embraces the payment of Interest at Paris, of principal at the Treasury; but with an option to those who choose it to receive both at the Treasury, as will be more particularly seen by the enclosed copy of an Advertisement by the Treasurer.[13]

With the highest respect and the truest attachment, I have the honor to be &c.   Alexander Hamilton

P:S. I have the pleasure to transmit herewith a letter from Mr. G: Morris [14] which was handed to me by Mr. R. Morris.[15] The Supervisor has been desired to forward to the Circuit Court at York town, such proof as he should be able to collect, addressed to the Attorney General. It will I perceive be satisfactory to that Officer to receive your direction to proceed there. His presence is of importance, as well to give weight to what it may be proper to do, as to afford security that nothing which cannot be supported will be attempted. I submit the expediency of a line from you to him.   A.H.

13. See H to Gouverneur Morris, September 13, 1792, note 10.
14. Gouverneur Morris.   15. Presumably Robert Morris.

To Charles Carroll of Carrollton

[*Philadelphia, September 23, 1792.* On October 22, 1792, Carroll wrote to Hamilton: "I received . . . your favor of the 23d. past." *Letter not found.*]

To Rufus King

[Philadelphia] Sep. 23. 1792

My Dear Sir

Though I had had a previous intimation of the possibility of such an event; yet the inteligence contained in your letter of the 17th surprised me. Even now I am to be convinced that the movement is any thing more than a diversion in favour of Mr. Clinton. Yet on my part it will not be neglected. My attention as far as shall be in any degree safe will be directed to every state South of New York. I do not go beyond it; because I presume other influences would be quite as efficacious there as mine.

A good use will be made of it in this state. I wish a letter could be written here stating the plan and Mr. Dallas's assertion respecting Pensylvania [1] which could be made use of without reserve. You will know who could write such a letter and of course to whom it might be addressed. Mr. Lewis [2] would be the most proper person to be written to. This is a matter of importance and if practicable no time should be lost.

I wrote Mr. Jay a long letter which I fear reached N York after he had set out on the Circuit; [3] informing him that I had concluded to advise a proclamation [4] and my reasons for it, which included some material facts not before communicated. I have not leisure to repeat. The Proclamation has been signed by the President & sent to Mr. Jefferson for his countersignature. I expect it here on Tuesday and have taken correspondent measures. I believe all is prudent & safe.

Yrs. truly & affy   A Hamilton

Rufus King Esq

ALS, New-York Historical Society, New York City.
    1. See King to H, September 17, 1792.
    2. Presumably William Lewis, United States judge for the District of Pennsylvania.
    3. H's letter, which was dated September 17, 1792, has not been found. See Rufus King to H, September 27, 1792, and John Jay to H, September 28, 1792.
    4. For information concerning the proclamation, see "Draft of a Proclamation Concerning Opposition to the Excise Law," September 7, 1792; Jay to H, September 8, 1792; Edmund Randolph to H, September 8, 1792; H to George Washington, September 8, first letter of September 9, September 11, 1792; Washington to H, September 7, two letters of September 17, September 21, 1792.

To James McHenry

[*Philadelphia, September 23, 1792.* On September 30, 1792, McHenry wrote to Hamilton: "I received your letter of the 23." *Letter not found.*]

Treasury Department Circular
to the Collectors of the Customs

Treasury Department.
September 23rd. 1792.

Sir:

Some very important objects in the Business of the Business of the next session of the Legislature will render the *early* transmission of the several quarterly returns and accounts that will be due the 30th inst. indispensibly necessary. The early receipt of these papers is not only requisite for some extraordinary purposes of the Department, but information drawn from them will be particularly desired by several members of the Legislature.

From the emission of returns from some of the Custom Houses when no imports or exports have taken place, and no impost or Tonnage have accrued, I find it necessary to request, that all returns may be regularly made at the periods fixed for them respectively. If no business of the kind intended to be stated in any of them, should have been done, it is nevertheless absolutely necessary that a return be made for the purpose of being filed in this office. Without the regular receipt of those papers, periodically made up no reliance can be placed on statements of this office relating to the business of the Custom House: & they should be made agreeably to the forms, transmitted by the Comptroller, including the value of exports which have been in some instances omitted.

For the convenience of filing seperately, I request that the copies of endorsements of Registers, and the returns of seizures be made in future on pieces of paper seperate from your Letters, and unconnected with any other matter.

I also wish that your papers may be folded of the breadth of the inner sheet of this letter in its folded state, and that they may be endorsed by you, according to the contents, before transmission to me.

Relying on particular attention to the several points noticed in this Letter.

I am, with respect, Sir,   Your Obt Sevt   A. Hamilton

P.S. The remarks made upon your Accounts similar to those in your past Letters to me, are hereafter to be made in the column of remarks in the accts. themselves, or at the foot of the papers, as they must go to the Auditor & Comptroller.

Copy, RG 56, Circulars of the Office of the Secretary, "Set T," National Archives; incomplete copy, Office of the Secretary, United States Treasury Department.

To George Washington

Philadelphia Sepr 23: 1792

Sir

I have the pleasure of your private letter of the 17 instant.

I continue in opinion, that it will be adviseable to address a letter with the proclamation to each of the Executives of the States mentioned, and shall prepare a draft of one to be forwarded with the requisite number of copies.[1]

A letter from Mr. King also of the 17 instant surprised me with the intelligence contained in the following extracts—"Burr is industrious in his canvass—Mr. Edwards is to make interest for him in Connecticut—and Mr. Dallas who is here, and quite in the circle of the Governor and the party, informs us, that Mr. Burr will be supported as Vice Presient in Pensylvania. Nothing which has hitherto happened so decisively proves the inveteracy of the opposition. Should they succeed much would be to be apprehended."

Mr. Burr was here about ten days since and every body wondered what was meant by it. It seems to be explained—Yet I am not certain that this is any thing more than a diversion in favour of Mr. Clinton.

I forbear any further comment on the event—But I thought it of importance enough to apprise you early of it.

With the most respectful and affectionate attachment   I have the honor to be   Sir   Your most obedient & humble servant

Alexander Hamilton

The President of The United States

ALS, Historical Society of Pennsylvania, Philadelphia,
1. See Washington to Thomas Mifflin, September 30, 1792.

From Sharp Delany

[*Philadelphia, September 24, 1792.* On September 24, 1792, Hamilton wrote to Delany: "In answer to your letter of this day." *Letter not found.*]

To Sharp Delany

Treasury Department Sept 24th 1792

Sir

In answer to your letter of this day,[1] I incline to the opinion, that the laws respecting drawbacks ought to be so construed as to admit the *entry* of goods, wares and merchandise for exportation, if made within twelve calendar months, from the time such goods, wares or merchandise were entered at the custom-house and the duties *paid* or *secured*—as equivalent to the actual exportation.[2]

In adopting this rule generally, it ought however to be understood, that the vessel in which the articles are to be exported shall be actually in port at the time, preparing for her voyage.

I am Sir   Your obedt Servt   Alexander Hamilton

Sharp Delany Esqr
Collector Philada

LS, Bureau of Customs, Philadelphia; copy, RG 56, Letters to the Collector at Philadelphia, National Archives; copy, RG 56, Letters to Collectors at Small Ports, "Set G," National Archives.
  1. Letter not found.
  2. The words "as equivalent to the actual exportation" are in H's handwriting.
  Section 3 of "An Act making further provision for the payment of the debts of the United States" provided: "That all duties which shall be paid or secured to be paid by virtue of this act, shall be returned or discharged in respect to all such goods, wares or merchandise, whereupon they shall have been so paid, or secured to be paid, as, within twelve calendar months after payment made or security given, shall be exported to any foreign port or place, except one per centum on the amount of the said duties, which shall be retained as an indemnification for whatever expense may have accrued concerning the same" (1 *Stat.* 181 [August 10, 1790]).

From William Ellery

Collector's Off: [Newport, Rhode Island]
Sept. 24 1792

Sir,

I have recd. your letter of the 7th. of this month [1] enclosing part of the margin of Certife. of Registry No. 61 and your Circular Letter of the 11th of the same month [2] enclosing an Order of the Senate of the United States, and a wrapper inclosing Letters to the Surveyors of the several ports in this District excepting the Surveyor of this Port.[3] The letters to all the Surveyors, excepting the Surveyor of Pawcatuck,[4] are already sent to them, and the letter to him will be transmitted by to-morrow's post. I have also written Letters to those Surveyors respectively requestg. them to obtain Documents from the Inspectors, Gaugers Measurers & Weighers of their several Ports similar to the Statemt. required by said Order, in season and to transmit them to me to be forwarded to you immediately after the first of Oct: next, and will furnish you with the Statemt. required of me in due time.

I wish, Sir, to provide at the public expence and with your approbation a pair of Scales & a sett of weights for this Port. The scales & part of the weights which have been hitherto used in this Port belong to the public Gauger,[5] and the unlading of vessels has been sometimes delayed for the want of another pair of scales and sett of weights. Recently a vessel has been obliged to discharge her hands on this account, which has occasioned heavy complaint and there are now three vessels in port with articles which require to be weighed, and besides the public must sustain the loss of several days pay to Inspectors when such delays take place.

Permit me here to suggest the propriety of having a public standard of weights and measures; until this is effected, and public Scalers are appointed to adjust weights and measures, an inequality will exist inconvenient to trade, and probably injurious to the Revenue.

Inclosed is one of the Receipts of the Supervisor [6] for the money I borrowed of him.

I am   Sir   Yr. most obedt. servant   Wm Ellery Colle

A Hamilton Esqe.
Secry of Treasy.

LC, Newport Historical Society, Newport, Rhode Island.
   1. Letter not found.
   2. Ellery is referring to "Treasury Department Circular to the Collectors
of the Customs," August 31, 1792.
   3. Daniel Lyman.   4. George Stillman.   5. B. Coggeshall.
   6. John S. Dexter. See Ellery to H, May 7, 1792.

To Jonathan Fitch

Treasury Department
September 24th 1792.

Sir
   In answer to the question proposed in your letter of the 17th instant,[1] I have to observe that the credit for the Duties upon distilled
spirits imported, if of the produce of the West Indies is four months;
but if of the prod⟨uce⟩ of any other foreign Country the Duties are
payable one half in six months, one quarter in nine months and the
other quarter in twelve months.[2]
   I am Sir   ⟨Your⟩ Obedt Servant

Jonathan Fitch Esqr.
Collr New Haven.

L[S], Federal Records Center, Boston; copy, RG 56, Letters to Collectors at
Small Ports, "Set G," National Archives.
   1. Letter not found.
   2. Terms of credit were specified under Section 8 of "An Act for raising
a farther sum of money for the protection of the frontiers, and for other
purposes therein mentioned" (1 *Stat.* 260–61 [May 2, 1792]). For the text of
this section, see Charles Lee to H, July 5, 1792, note 2.

From William Henderson

New York sepr. 24th. 1792

sir
   Your favor of the 21st. inst. I duly received.[1] I am sorry to inform
you that the tract of Land, of 45000 Acres for which I was in treaty

is disposed of.[2] Mr Cazenove is the purchaser and at the price which was asked for the whole.[3] I wrote to the General [4] respecting it the middle of August: and had he not been unfortunately absent on the lock navigation business, I could have easily made the bargain to his, and your satisfaction. I regret its falling into other hands, as it would have been a good purchase; for I am well assured that since the sale, 6/ per acre has been offerred for one half of it. The other tract is not yet sold, and from the description I have *lately* had of it I think it cannot by any means, be worth the money they ask for it. Had it been good Land I have no doubt Mr. C would have bought it.

The tract which is sold borders on Macomb's purchase.[5] It is therefore probable that the Land belonging to him adjoining, is nearly as valuable. He has obtained a patent for upwards of a Million of Acres, which is in the hands, and under the controul of Mr Constable [6] who went to England for the purpose of selling it. There is no advice of his having sold more than 25.000 Acres; Altho' I am informed he offerred a Million as low as *a shilling* Sterling per acre; if this information be true, Mr Church [7] may make a better purchase from him, than he can from any person here; and of such quantity as he likes. I expect to sail for England at the first Week in the next month [8] and if you think I can serve him in the Negociation I will do it with the utmost pleasure.

I take the liberty of requesting from you as soon as convenient, the Letter to Mr. Pinckney the Minister,[9] which you was so kind as to promise me, when I had last the pleasure of seeing you in Philadelphia.

I am sir with the Greatest respect   Your Humble servt.

Wm Henderson

The Honble. Alexr. Hamilton

ALS, Hamilton Papers, Library of Congress.
  1. Letter not found.
  2. The forty-five-thousand-acre tract to which Henderson is referring was in the Adgate Patent, which was located in the northern part of what is now Oneida County, New York.
  3. Théophile Cazenove had come to New York from the Netherlands in 1790 as the representative of several Dutch firms interested in speculation in American securities. The original contract gave Cazenove an option to buy two tracts of land containing one hundred and ten thousand acres at two pence less per acre than would be charged for the forty-five-thousand-acre tract alone.

4. Philip Schuyler. See Elisha Boudinot to H, August 16, 1792, note 8.

5. In 1791 the commissioners of the New York land office sold Alexander Macomb three million six hundred thousand acres of public land at eight pence an acre. Cazenove's purchase was at the southern limit of Great Tracts No. 5 and 6 of the Macomb purchase. Macomb's approved application to the commissioners of the New York land office, as well as a more modest application presented by Henderson for sixty-four thousand acres, may be found in "The Report of the Commissioners of the Land Office" (*Journal of the Assembly of the State of New-York, Fifteenth Session* [New York, 1792], 182–200).

6. William Constable.

7. John B. Church, the husband of Elizabeth Hamilton's sister, had returned to England at the conclusion of the American Revolution. H managed Church's financial affairs in America.

8. Henderson, William Denning, Jr., and Robert C. Johnson left for England on October 14, 1792, in company with Francis Childs (Vernon F. Snow, "The Grand Tour Diary of Robert C. Johnson, 1792–1793," *Proceedings of the American Philosophical Society* [Philadelphia, 1958], CII, 60–105).

9. Thomas Pinckney, United States Minister Plenipotentiary at London.

From Sarah Mumford [1]

Philadelphia, September 24, 1792. "Necessity alone has induc'd me to address you by Letter, although unknown to you in Person but having heard much of your benevolence and Humanity to the distress'd I have taken the Liberty to ask a favor of you which I hope in the end will not be prejudicial; I have for two years past taken Members of Congress to board, but from their long recess, and having been unfortunate in obtaining others and my Husband having been sick the greater part of the Summer, and at this time confin'd to his Chamber all these Circumstances have reduc'd me to a very distress'd Situation, that my Goods are at this time under Execution by my Landlord for two Quarters Rent, and he has agreed upon my making him up one Quarters Rent to wait for the other until Congress meets, the Quarters Rent is Forty Dollars, and the half of it I have already obtain from a Friend; Now Sir if you will be so obliging as to advance me the remainder it will be the means of Saving me from Ruin. . . ."

ALS, Hamilton Papers, Library of Congress.

1. Sarah Mumford, a native of New Jersey, was the wife of William Mumford, a Rhode Island state government clerk who had moved to Philadelphia in 1783. He had been unemployed since 1787 and had written to George Washington on several occasions requesting Washington's support for a Federal Government position (George Washington Papers, Library of Congress).

See also "Report on the Petitions of William Mumford, Samuel Armstrong, and the Weighers, Measurers, and Gaugers of Portland and Falmouth, Massachusetts," March 8, 1790.

To Jeremiah Olney [1]

Treasury Department Sept 24th 1792

Sir

I enclose you duplicate of my letter of the 19th instant, to which I refer you in answer to yours of the 13th.

I shall only add, that it interests the merchants as much as the Public to discountenance such a species of evasion. For could it long succeed, it would render credits for the duties inadmissible. It will be well to let this idea get into circulation among the merchants.

I am Sir   Your obedt Servt   A Hamilton

Jere. Olney Esqr
Collector Providence

LS, Rhode Island Historical Society, Providence.
   1. For background to this letter, see William Ellery to H, September 4, 1792; Olney to H, September 8, 1792.

From George Washington

Mount Vernon Septembr. 24th. 1792.

Sir,

Your Letter of the 17th. instant came to my hands by the last Post.[1] Under your statement of the conduct of Thomas Davis Freeman Surveyor of the Port of Plymouth and Inspector of the Revenue of the same, there can be no question with respect to the propriety of superceding him in Office; and from the character given of Mr. John Armistead of the place by the Collector and Inspector, and more particularly by Mr. Johnston of the Senate, there can be as little doubt of his fitness to fill it. I have no objections therefore to Mr. Armistead's doing it accordingly—of which you may inform him, and that a Commission will be sent to him for this purpose as soon as circumstances will permit.

With esteem, I am Sir &c.   G: Washington

LC, George Washington Papers, Library of Congress.
1. See also Tench Coxe to H, September 4, 1792.

From William Denning [1]

New York, September 25, 1792. "In addressing you as an old acquaintance and a Friend you will I hope consider the Occasion as a Sufficient apology. My Son William (who has always respected and very much esteemed your person and Character) will between the first and Tenth of next month embark for Europe. His object is information and useful knowledge. . . . Permit me to request the favor of you Sir to Indulge him with a Line to Such person or persons in London, Paris, Holand, Germany, Russia and any other parts of Europe as you may think proper. . . ."

ALS, Hamilton Papers, Library of Congress.
1. Denning was a New York City merchant. See William Henderson to H, September 24, 1792, note 8.

From Gouverneur Morris

Paris 25. September 1792.

Dear Sir

I transmitted on the sixteenth of last month Copies of my correspondence with the Commissaries of the Treasury to Mr. Jefferson,[1] and on the seventeenth I inform'd you thereof. I now enclose to you my Correspondence on the same Subject with Mr. Short so that you may see exactly how that Matter stands and be able to act knowingly if called on to take any steps in relation to it.[2] You will see that by an unfortunate Coincidence of Events some

LC, Gouverneur Morris Papers, Library of Congress.
1. Morris to Thomas Jefferson, August 16, 1792 (ALS, RG 59, Despatches from United States Ministers to France, 1789–1869, June 17, 1792–March 7, 1794, National Archives). On October 31, 1792, Jefferson sent this correspondence to H. Morris's correspondence with the Commissaries of the French Treasury is printed as an enclosure to Jefferson to H, October 31, 1792.
2. The enclosures are printed in chronological order following this letter. Since irrelevant sections of the letters have generally been omitted, all the enclosures have been calendared. In cases where only the pertinent sections have been extracted, this fact is noted on the source line to the enclosure.

Ground is given for question in one of the Cases which may be supposed to result from the late Overset of the Constitution.[3] Mr. Shorts zeal for the Interests of the United States led him to insist on Conditions unsuited to the State of Affairs, and as he afterwards gave up the Point it might be argued that this payment was made to a Party which he had already declared incompetent &c. &c. My answer of the twentieth to Mr. Lebruns letter of the ninth [4] (of both which Copies are enclos'd) is calculated, as you will see, to stifle that question in the Birth. I prefer sending this Correspondence directly to you, instead of passing it thro the Secretary of States Office, because the letter from Mr. LeBrun has too much the air of a Complaint against Mr. Short for me to transmit it in a Channel which may give it any publicity: and this for two reasons, first that the Obloquy to which the Servants of Government are exposed has sufficient Aliment and more than sufficient already, and next that even if Blame were due I would not be instrumental in calling it forth.

[ENCLOSURE]

William Short to Gouverneur Morris [5]

The Hague, June 18, 1792. ". . . I suppose you will before this have seen the commissaries of the Treasury, I will thank you to let

3. The constitutional changes taking place in France in the spring and summer of 1792 had complicated the negotiations of Morris and Short with the French government on the payment of the debt owed France by the United States. The Girondist Ministry under Jean Marie Roland and Charles François Dupérier Dumouriez had fallen in June, 1792, and was replaced by a series of Royalist ministries until the suspension of the King on August 10. The coalition faction then came into power, forming a provisional government until a national convention could be called to draw up a new constitution. At its first meeting on September 21, 1792, the National Convention abolished royalty. The new Jacobin Ministry which was formed after the events of August 10 was under the leadership of Pierre Henri Hélène Marie Lebrun-Tondu, Minister of Foreign Affairs, Etienne Clavière, Minister of Finance, and Gaspard Monge, Minister of Marine. Both Short and Morris were reluctant to make firm commitments to the new ministry on the American debt owed to France until they had received instructions from the United States concerning the changes in the French government.

4. Lebrun was French Minister of Foreign Affairs from August 12, 1792, to June 2, 1793. Lebrun's letter to Morris is dated September 19 rather than September 9, 1792, and is printed below as an enclosure to this letter.

5. ALS (extract), Columbia University Libraries.

me know whether you have settled with them the manner of counting the payments made from Antwerp. There will be a considerable sum at Amsterdam probably soon at the disposition of the U.S. for being applied to the French debt. I shd. suppose no time ought to be lost, & as little as possible double interest paid & I have thoughts of directing the commissioners [6] to remit it unless you have fixed on some other mode of paying it to them. I hope to hear from you on this subject daily. . . ."

[ENCLOSURE]

Gouverneur Morris to William Short [7]

Paris, June 28, 1792. "Yours of the eighteenth is just come to Hand & I have but an Instant to reply to it. The Changes of Administration and other Circumstances have prevented me from setling with the Commissaries. It will soon be done. I see in the Gazette that the Assembly has authorized the minister of the Marine to concert with me the Means of supplying their Colonies out of the Debt [8] therefore it is best to leave the funds in the Hands of the

6. Willink, Van Staphorst, and Hubbard, the bankers of the United States in Amsterdam.
7. ALS (extract), William Short Papers, Library of Congress.
8. Morris is referring to a decree passed by the Legislative Assembly on June 26, 1792. It reads as follows:
"Art. 1er. Le pouvoir exécutif est autorisé à traiter avec le ministre des Etats-Unis, afin d'en obtenir des fournitures pour Saint-Domingue, en comestibles et matières premières propres à la construction, jusqu'à la concurrence de 4 millions de livres tournois, imputables sur la dette américaine.
"Art. 2. Ce fonds de quatre millions fera partie de l'avance de six millions déjà accordés par le décret du 17 mars, à titre de secours pour la même colonie.
"Art. 3. Dans le cas où, sur les demandes des gouverneur et ordonnateur, il aurait été fait des envois des mêmes lieux et pour la même destination, lesquels ne seraient point encore acquittés, ou l'auraient été provisoirement en lettres de change sur le Trésor public, le payement sera prélevé sur ladite somme de 4 millions.
"Art. 4. Les lettres de change fournies sur le Trésor public par l'ordonnateur de Saint-Domingue, s'élevant, jusqu'au 31 décembre 1791, à la somme de 2,724,179 livres, seront acquittées par les commissaires de la Trésorerie nationale, et l'ordonnateur sera tenu d'en justifier l'emploi en dépenses publiques, dûment autorisées.
"Art. 5. Quant aux lettres de change qui auront été fournies depuis le 31 décembre, l'Assemblée nationale se réserve de statuer, d'après les bordereaux qui lui seront fournis par le ministre de la marine, si elles devront être acquittées par les commissaires de la Trésorerie nationale; et cependant ces

Bankers but write me I pray you or order them to write to me the Amount which they now have and the Sums to be receivd that I may stipulate with the Government here accordingly. . . ."

[ENCLOSURE]

William Short to Gouverneur Morris [9]

The Hague, June 28, 1792. ". . . On the 18th. inst. I write you also from this place & wait with much impatience to hear from you respecting what has been settled with the Commissaries of the treasury, as I mentioned to you in that letter there would be a considerable payment to be made them as soon as you shall have fixed the rate of the late payments & the mode in wch. the next shd. be made. I wish you to do this as soon as possible as a considerable sum is now & has been for some time accumulated in the hands of the bankers at Amsterdam. Should you not have settled the rate of the late payments from any difficulty wch. may have arisen on account of the second letter you wished to recieve from the Sec. of State [10]

---

commissaires seront tenus de mettre leur *vu* à la présentation de ces lettres, afin que le terme fixé pour leur échéance courre du jour de leur présentation.

"Art. 6. Ces fonds, avancés par la nation, à la charge de remboursement, et hypothéqués sur les impositions de cette colonie, seront payés par la Trésorerie nationale, sur les ordonnances du ministre de la marine, et le remplacement en sera fait dans la caisse du Trésor public par la caisse de l'extraordinaire." (*Archives Parlementaires*, XLV, 594-95.)

For the earlier proposals and negotiations of the French government on the plans to apply the debt owed France by the United States to the aid of Santo Domingo, see Short to H, December 28, 1791; January 26, April 22, 25, May 14, June 28, August 6, 1792.

9. ALS (extract), Columbia University Libraries.

10. Jefferson had written to Morris on April 28, 1792, entrusting him with one phase of the financial negotiations with France: "I now inclose you the correspondence between the Secretary of the Treasury and Minister of France, on the subject of the monies furnished to the distresses of their Colonies. You will perceive that the Minister chose to leave the adjustment of the terms to be settled at Paris between yourself and the King's ministers. This you will therefore be pleased to do on this principle, that we wish to avoid any loss by the mode of payment, but would not chuse to make a gain which should throw loss on them. But the letters of the Secretary of the Treasury will sufficiently explain the desire of the government, & be a sufficient guide to you" (LC, RG 59, Diplomatic and Consular Instructions of the Department of State, 1791–1801, January 23, 1791–August 16, 1793, National Archives). Morris was, however, reluctant to undertake responsibility for payments to the Commissaries of the Treasury on the French debt without specific authorization. In a letter to Jefferson of August 1, 1792, Morris ex-

—then I will thank you to see the commissaries or the minister & inform me what will be the best & most agreeable mode of making these payments. I inclose you an extract of a letter I have recd. from the sec. of the treasury respecting the fixing the rate of the late payments,[11] which will perhaps render the second letter from the sec. of State unnecessary. I inclose you also a duplicate of his letter of the 16th. of April by way of leaving nothing omitted on that subject although I do not see that the state of things in France renders any intimation of the kind necessary. I need not urge you to settle some mode or other of effectuating immediately future payments as you know that the U.S. are now paying a dead & useless interest on the sums in hand. . . ."

[E N C L O S U R E]

Gouverneur Morris to William Short [12]

Paris, July 5, 1792. "I wrote to you on the twenty eighth and have since receiv'd yours of the same Date. I call'd on the Minister the Day before yesterday and he promis'd me to come to a Settlement of the Accounts in a few Days and to adjust at the same Time the Object of the late Decree.[13] As the Affair is now left to the Responsability of the Executive I presume they will not longer delay it but I shall stimulate them to a Conclusion. . . ."

[E N C L O S U R E]

William Short to Gouverneur Morris [14]

The Hague, July 6, 1792. "I recieved yesterday your letter of the 28th. of June, & am glad to find that the settlement with the

plained his position: ". . . I am engaged at present in ⟨ex⟩amination of the Account received from the Commissioners of the Treasury. ⟨I⟩ have already mentioned to you Sir that the whole of this Account is open ⟨an⟩d I must now observe that I do not find myself particularly authoriz'd ⟨to⟩ make the final Adjustment. If it becomes necessary I will do it ⟨but I s⟩hall avoid it as long as I can. In Respect to the Payments made and ⟨m⟩aking in America I am at Ease because there I have your orders but ⟨not⟩ so in Regard to those made by Mr Short . . ." (ALS, RG 59, Despatches from United States Ministers to France, 1789–1869, June 17, 1792–March 7, 1794, National Archives).
11. See H to Short, April 2, 1792.
12. ALS (extract), William Short Papers, Library of Congress.
13. See note 8.　14. ALS (extract), Columbia University Libraries.

commissaries of the treasury will soon be made. The extract of the letter from the sec. of the Treasury, which I inclosed to you in mine of the 28th. ulto. will shew you his desire relative thereto. I am happy that the business is now in your hands & am persuaded that the U.S. will feel the benefit of it from the arrangement you will make with the commissaries. I hope the secy. of the Treasury will easily excuse my having postponed settling this business myself, from my desire to leave such operations of delicacy (as could not suffer from a short delay) to the exertions of a person enjoying a greater degree of the confidence of the government of the U.S.[15] You inform me that the assembly has authorized the minister to concert with you the means of supplying the colonies out of the American debt [16] & that therefore it will be best to leave the funds in the hands of the bankers & to inform you of the amount, that you may stipulate accordingly. You know that of the two last loans of three millions each,[17] no part has yet been applied to France, the delay from Jany. last arising from the daily prospect of the amount or a part being applied towards succours to the islands—the whole of the first loan has been recd. by the bankers & about half of the second—the other half will be recd. successively—the undertakers as you know, are not obliged to pay so soon but they have a right to do it. The whole must be paid at the end of five months from the date of the loan, & no doubt will be sooner. The payments which have been already made by the bankers on general orders, or draughts from the Secy. of the Treasury—together with the sums which he has directed me to hold at his disposition—will leave out of the two loans a surplus of near three millions of florins, to be applied to France, except only such sums as it would be found prudent to apply to the interest of the loan in Septr. in the case of new loan being opened—as it is probable will not be done before that period. The bankers have already on hand upwards of four

15. Short had assumed that the negotiations for the payment of the French debt would be taken over by Morris upon Morris's appointment as United States Minister Plenipotentiary to France. See Short to H, August 30, 1792. At the time this letter was written Short had not yet received H's letter of June 14, 1792, informing him that the negotiations would be left in his hands.

16. See note 8.

17. The Holland loan of December, 1791, and the Holland loan of 1792. For descriptions of these loans, see Short to H, December 23, 28, 1791, June 28, 1792, note 17.

millions—or thereabouts—of course my intention had been to apply immediately two or two & an half millions to France—counting on the balance in their hands & the sums to be recd. by them of the undertakers to answer the draughts already made by the secy. of the Treasury, & the amount he has directed me to hold at his future disposition, & wch. he cannot dispose of for some time to come. When you consider what large sums are on hand & how long a dead interest has been paid on a part of them, from the daily expectation held out by a former minister to you, during my absence— by you to me, & then by the succeeding ministry to me at Paris— you will no doubt feel the necessity of pressing the matter & not letting it remain longer on a meer prospect however flattering. The present unsettled state of affairs at Paris, which would tend naturally of itself to protract this business is a reason the more for our avoiding delay, as well in this matter as that relative to the late payments from Antwerp. I know not what mode you will adopt but you will I shd. imagine so contrive it that the U.S. shd. have credit immediately for the sum you engage to supply, so that they may not longer pay an useless interest on the sums in hand. It may be proper to mention to you also that the Secy. of the Treasury has informed me of his having paid to M. de Ternant or le Forest on acct. of the French debt 100,000 dollars—on the 12th. of March—& engaged to make three further payments of 100,000 dollars each, on June 1.— Sep. 1.—& Dec. 1. & also inclosed me an acct. of articles furnished on same acct. to the amount of 8962 dollars.[18] He had formerly paid two sums one of 8325 dollars & the other of 22,000 dollars. . . ."

[ENCLOSURE]

Gouverneur Morris to William Short [19]

Paris, July 6, 1792. "The above is Copy of what I wrote yesterday. After the Post was gone I receivd a Letter from the Minister of the Marine [20] praying an Interview in order to adjust the Business which he says was entamé in your Time. . . ."

18. See H to Short, April 10, 1792.
19. LC (extract), Gouverneur Morris Papers, Library of Congress.
20. Jean de Lacoste served as Minister of Marine from March 15 to July 21, 1792.

[ENCLOSURE]

Gouverneur Morris to William Short[21]

Paris, July 9, 1792. "I wrote to you a Note on the sixth mentioning the Application of the Minister of the Marine. I have not heard from him since. Probably he is collecting the Accounts for I told the Minister of foreign Affairs[22] that I must have the past Accounts settled before I could undertake any Thing new. At any Rate I shall soon get this Business done unless there be another Over Set in the Ministry. I wait impatiently to hear what Sums are now at our Disposition in Amsterdam. Mr. de Wolf has written to me several Letters respecting the Loan to be opened at Antwerp.[23] He has assured me that he will take no Engagements but such as he can punctually fulfill. He tells me that he thinks it will be much better to take only two hundred and fifty thousand Guilders per Month and to extend the Loan to three Millions. This will of Course run the Length of a Year and supposing it to begin the first of next Month I think all our Wants must be satisfied by the Time it is filled. Of Course it will be the last which he can participate in. I think there will be no Difficulty in Bargaining here for this Loan on Account of our Debt to France on such Terms as that they bear all the Expence of Negotiation and of Course we are liberated at Par which seems to be the Intention of our Government. If you approve of this Idea tell me so and I will bring forward the Proposition when I come to a Settlement. We shall gain thereby the Difference of Exchange between Antwerp and Amsterdam."[24]

21. ALS, William Short Papers, Library of Congress.
22. Stanislas Guillaume de Chambonas served as French Foreign Minister from June 17 until August 1, 1792.
23. Charles John Michael de Wolf was the Antwerp banker who had negotiated the Antwerp loan of 1791 for the United States. For a description of this loan, see Short to H, November 8, 1791, note 4, and November 12, 1791. At this time Wolf was pressing for the opening of a second loan at Antwerp. See also Short to H, June 28, 1792, and Short to Morris, July 17, 1792, printed below as enclosures.
24. A postscript to this letter reads as follows: "I think it adviseable so to manage as that our Obligations be all taken up."

[ENCLOSURE]

William Short to Gouverneur Morris [25]

The Hague, July 10, 1792. "I have this inst. recd. your letter of the 5th as you there acknowlege the rect. of mine of the 28th. of June. I have nothing further to add, to what I said in that & my last letter, than simply to mention that the decree of the assembly on wch. you count [26] seems to me not to have advanced the business at all. As far as I can understand it, it limits to four millions of livres, what the former decree passed in the time of M. de le Coste, had left at a larger sum [27]—& this restriction appears to me [to] be the result of the explanation he asked of the assembly as to enlarging the sum—& I shd. apprehend also that the sums already advanced by the U.S. in America as succours to the islands will be made to enter into it. You will be able to judge how far & how long it will be proper to wait on such an expectative. As the sums on hand at Amsterdam & those which may be soon expected at Antwerp, will however surpass the amount of four millions of livres tournois, it will be proper to take measures as to their payment. I do not write to the commissaries of the treasury, as it is much more natural that you shd. concert the business with them. I cannot help however renewing to you my anxiety at still leaving on hand such large sums on which the U.S. have been so long drawn on from day to day to pay a dead interest. I will thank you to let me know as soon as any thing is settled. I am persuaded your experience & particularly your opinion of the manner of doing business at Paris will prevent you from being drawn on to delay by probabilities or promises."

25. ALS, Columbia University Libraries.
26. See note 8.
27. On March 27, 1792, the Legislative Assembly "désirant venir au secours de la colonie de Saint-Domingue, met à la disposition du ministre de la marine une somme de 6 millions, pour y faire parvenir des subsistances, des matériaux de construction, des animaux et des instruments aratoires" (*Archives Parlementaires*, XL, 535).

[ENCLOSURE]

Gouverneur Morris to William Short [28]

Paris, July 16, 1792. ". . . I wrote to you on the ninth and it appears that while I was writing the Ministry resign'd to a Man.[29] This Measure is connected with Circumstances which are not generally known and it was entirely unexpected. I did not know it till about seven oClock in the Evening for I had been at Home till six and then went by Appointment to the Minister of the Marine who was with the King. They all hold now by Interim only. I have nevertheless urg'd the Office of foreign Affairs and Monsieur Bon Carére [30] assures me that the Commissaries of the Treasury are now making out the Account desir'd. Apropos, I wish you would direct the Bankers of the United States [31] to send me a Note of their various Remittances on this Account. You shewed me a Statement which you had and it ran in my Head that you had left it with me but I have look'd over all my Papers without finding it. You will see the Necessity of enabling me to check their Account. I have that from DeWolf. I will again apply both personally and by Letter to the Office of foreign Affairs on this Subject and if it be possible to make them do their Duty Things shall be immediately put in Train. I mention'd in a Postscript to mine of the ninth that I thought it important to take up our Obligations. If a new form of Government should take Place which may easily happen during the next three Months there might be some Cavil about the past Transactions not justifiably but unpleasantly. . . ."

28. ALS (extract), William Short Papers, Library of Congress.
29. See note 3.
30. Guillaume de Bonnecarrère, secretary of the Jacobin Society, was appointed "Directeur des Affaires étrangères" under the Girondin Ministry formed in March, 1792 (Frédéric Masson, *Le Departement des Affaires Etrangeres Pendant La Revolution, 1787–1804* [Paris, 1877], 156). Morris refers to Bonnecarrère as "confidential secretary" to Dumouriez (Morris, *Diary of the French Revolution*, II, 439). In July, 1792, Bonnecarrère was proposed for the post of Minister to the United States, but Morris's protests to the King and the Ministry prevented his appointment (Morris to Jefferson, August 16, 1792, ALS, RG 59, Despatches from United States Ministers to France, 1789–1869, June 17, 1792–March 7, 1794, National Archives).
31. Willink, Van Staphorst, and Hubbard.

[ENCLOSURE]

William Short to Gouverneur Morris [32]

The Hague, July 17, 1792. "The last post, (which brought your letter of the 9th.) arrived too late in the day for me to answer it, by the post of that day. I observe by it that you recd. a note from the minister desiring a rendezvous on the 6th. & that on the 9th. you had heard nothing further from him. He cannot have been collecting the accts. as you suppose for they were made out & stated long ago, except the payments from Antwerp, which have of course [been] regularly enregistered on the books of the commissaries of the Treasury. My two last letters of July 6. & 10. will have expressed to you my apprehensions on this subject & informed you, according to your desire of the amt. of desponible cash at Amsterdam. M. de Wolf has lately been here. He was obliged to acknowlege that he could not have fulfilled the engagement he took as to the time of completing the last loan & although he assured me as he had assured you that he would in future make no promises with which he could not comply, yet he pressed for a loan of three millions—agreeing however that instead of 600,000 florins a month which he formerly agreed for he could not now count on more than 250,000. The absurdity of so large a loan with so small sums by the month, he was at length obliged to acknowlege—still he would have had no hesitation in *promising* three millions in the course of a year & opening a loan in consequence. When I came to talk to him however about promises not sufficing, & that in future the engagement must be complete with his undertakers, &c. & that the loan must be closed at the end of six months, so as not to leave the credit of the U.S. dragging on the market, he thought it best to return & concert measures more fully with those he employs. I agreed to give him a loan of 1½ million at 250,000 a month, to which he assented—he was to write me immediately & although he has been now gone eight days, I have not heard from him. I apprehend he finds difficulty in getting the undertakers to *engage*—although he would not have had the smallest difficulty in *promising* double the sum & opening

32. ALS (extract), Columbia University Libraries.

a loan in consequence thereof. He first told you he shd. make the loan on *recepisses*—at Paris he told me it wd. be best for the first loan to have the *bonds* in the beginning—he now tells me there is no example of a loan on *recepisses* of the banker to be afterwards exchanged for *bonds* of the government, & that if I insist on it he must renounce the loan. I am therefore to supply him with the bonds successively if he can get the loan contracted for. You will thus see how that matter stands—M. Hamilton having declared his preference of loans at Amsterdam,[33] having held out himself & desired me also to hold out the hope of concentering them there on certain conditions, I should not have chosen on that acct., if there was no other reason, to have opened a loan for 12. months at Antwerp & for so large a sum—still I think it just & politic also to give de Wolf, the loan of 1¼ million. If it becomes necessary it may be represented to the bankers of Amsterdam as rather a continuation of the former than the opening a new loan—or if proper, may be employed to keep their fears alive as to our resources out of Holland. As yet it is useless for me to say any thing about your idea of contracting with the French government for the bonds at Antwerp, not knowing whether the loan will be opened. As soon as I know what Wolf does, I will give you my opinion by letter as I have formerly done viva voce—adding however, that it would be improper that my opinion should influence you. Your powers with respect to the French debt will certainly be competant thereto,[34] judging from the expressions of the general powers of the Prest. to the Sec. of the Treasury, communicated to me in the beginning of this business.[35] My own opinion of your superior knowlege on all subjects & particularly money subjects & my knowlege of your possessing a greater degree of the confidence of government would necessarily make me consider it as their wish & my duty to assent to what you shall judge most advantageous for the public interests. These considerations only prevent me from repeating the propriety & urgency of settling 1. the rate at which the payments of the Antwerp loan shd. be credited to the U.S. & adding the arguments in favor of their having a considerable profit even after allowing the real depreciation of the assignats & 2. fixing on the best mode of

33. See H to Short, April 2, 1792.　　　34. See note 15.
35. See the two letters from Washington to H, August 28, 1790.

speedily carrying to the credit of the U.S. on acct. of the French debt the large sums which have been so long on hand & at a dead interest at Amsterdam. . . ."

[ENCLOSURE]

Gouverneur Morris to William Short [36]

Paris, July 23, 1792. "I am favord with yours of the seventeenth. . . . The History you give of DeWolf proves clearly that his Hopes outrun his Judgment. You are however in a Position to see clearly and I am persuaded that however he may deceive himself he cannot deceive you. It appears to me a fortunate Thing that he cannot undertake for large Sums because his Operations will only stimulate the Exertions of the People at Amsterdam. You will be able to feel how their Pulses beat upon it and to act accordingly. You urge me much upon the Subject of the Monies lying in our Bankers Hands, but what can I do? I have already written and said to Monsieur Chambonas that unless a speedy Settlement takes Place the Money intended for them shall be otherwise disposed of. I have received a Letter from the Commissioners of the Treasury desiring to know what Bankers they are to apply to for Money which they say they learn thro different Channels is intended to pay them. I have sent them Copy of what I had written to Monsieur Chambonas. I have no Doubt but that the Payments made in Antwerp are duly registered in their Books as you mention. But how? It seems to me that they must be carried out at some Rate of Exchange and if they mean honestly and know how to act up to their meaning this Rate must be that which they have really obtained. In that Case the Rule for Settlement furnishes itself. And it is with a View to these Circumstances that I desire an Account from them. You tell me that my Powers respecting the french Debt will certainly be competent thereto but yet I do not find any particular Power or Instruction on that Subject unless by Implication under what is said respecting the Payments to be made in America.[37] Mr Hamilton has never written a Syllable to me and I shall

36. ALS (extract), William Short Papers, Library of Congress.
37. See note 10.

perhaps be told hereafter that I have meddled with Matters not confided to me. You are indeed so kind as to tell me that I possess a greater Share of the Confidence of Government but this is a Point which I much doubt of. The general Presumption is that all the Servants of Government enjoy their Confidence. If we get out of that general Position and come to particular Circumstances I should conclude the Reverse of what you advance and certainly in what regards the present Object your Mission is much more evident than mine. It is our Duty and I am sure it is our Inclination to serve the United States in the most effectual Manner which we can and perhaps it might be well to apply the Monies in Holland to the Payment of a Part of what we owe there. One of the Loans was at six per Cent Interest or more when the Premiums are calculated and if we have as you once mention'd to me the Right of paying it [38] I think it would be very well to begin there and let the Creditors know that they might either receive their money or charge their Obligations for others bearing only a common Interest of four per Cent. A similar Operation might be made afterwards on our five per Cent Loans [39] and I am thoroughly convincd that we should keep Possession of the greater Part of the Cash so as to be ready to make Payments here in due Season and yet reduce all our Holland Debt to a plain four Per Cent Interest. . . ."

[ENCLOSURE]

William Short to Gouverneur Morris [40]

The Hague, July 23[-24,] 1792. "In consequence of your letter of July 16. I have written to the bankers to desire them to furnish

38. Morris is referring to the Holland loan of 1784 for two million guilders. This loan had been negotiated by John Adams. See H to Short, September 1, 1790, note 22. Although this loan bore four percent interest, it was a lottery loan, and the bonus or premiums distributed each year brought the annual interest to more than six percent. Morris was mistaken in thinking the loan could be redeemed at will. According to the terms of the contract, the loan was to run for seventeen years, with redemption beginning in 1801. See also Short to Morris, August 4, 1792, printed below as an enclosure.

39. The Holland loans bearing five percent interest were those of 1782, 1787, 1788, 1790, March, 1791, and September, 1791. For descriptions of these loans, see Willink, Van Staphorst, and Hubbard to H, January 25, 1790; H to Willink, Van Staphorst, and Hubbard, November 29, 1790; H to Short, September 1, 1790; Short to H, February 17, August 31, 1791.

40. ALS (extract), Columbia University Libraries.

you the state of the payments they have made to France. I can inform you however in the mean time that they told me the statement made by the French treasury was just. . . . I inclose you two reciepts of the French agent at Antwerp which complete the payments made by de Wolf. I am sorry to find you have connected the settlement of these payments with the former ones, as it will necessarily occasion delay—& they are on quite a different footing —delay cannot injure the settlement of the payments from Amsterdam—they were made previously to the promise of making up depreciation. Their sum in livres tournois is fixed & the U.S. will be credited for their amount whether settled with the present or any other government of any other complexion whatsoever. As to the payments from Antwerp they are expressed you know in florins & livres tournois—as a guide—the depreciation of assignats is promised on them—& the amount which will be carried to the credit of the U.S.—depends altogether on the settlement to be made. It is urgent to ascertain the real value of the assignats with their own fathers, as they will of course be more favorable to them than any others. I do not doubt you have proper reasons for connecting the two affairs. My own opinion would have been for avoiding every thing that could possibly occasion delay in the settlement of the Antwerp payments. I do not presume to add to the various arguments which will certainly occur to you for shewing that the loss wch. the French government would have sustained in recieving & employing the assignats in France where we had a right to pay them was without comparison less than the fall in the exchange & of course will leave a considerable gain to the U.S. after having made up to France the real depreciation on assignats at home—as may be seen by a comparison of their value with the price of all articles in France during the time of these payments. The Sec. of the treasury mentions also the loss which we sustained in recieving this money by remittances from France during the time of our assignats.[41] I am exceedingly anxious that the business should be well settled & advantageously for the U.S.—of which I cannot but have the best grounded hopes since it is in your hands—& which will shew to our government the propriety of my having postponed settling it myself from the prospect of its being committed to better care. Another circumstance which I am anxious about & which I should

41. See H to Short, March 5, 1792.

suppose would aid in adjusting that already mentioned, is the sum we have now in Amsterdam. It would seem to me it would be a very expeditious operation to say to the minister—we have money to pay you—we will pay you at Amsterdam where you want it—let us therefore settle immediately at what rate the U.S. are to be credited for the payments already made at Antwerp—& at what rate you will recieve the florins at Amsterdam. This would certainly avoid all delay & put you on a ground much to be desired. It would be more desirable than waiting for the uncertain event, which has already drawn us so long, of appropriating this money to the succours of the colonies—& particularly now that we see they have voted so small a sum & with so many restrictions. I really know not how to justify myself to our government at keeping so long, so large sums on hand at a dead interest. Should the ministry be still par interim—yet I think they would not refuse the mode of settlement mentioned above—or if they should the commissaries of the treasury, who are a more permanent body, & to whom it will be ultimately referred, would not, & particularly as money is always wanted by them in Amsterdam. I have said a great deal several times on these subjects—viz. the settlement of the Antwerp payments & the mode of paying expeditiously & advantageously for the U.S. the sums on hand at Amsterdam. You will naturally concieve my anxiety, & also that if nothing definitive be soon done I shall consider myself under the necessity of directing the bankers to begin their remittances to France by bills of exchange, although the mode above mentioned being much more expeditious would be much more agreeable. . . .[42] I have just recd. your note of July 18 inclosing a letter from Carmichael.[43] I see you are no further with the minister than a *"promise to hasten the settlement of accts."* I must beg you to wait no longer on a promise—& if you cannot settle the mode of payment immediately to say so that I may direct the bankers to remit the money at our disposition. The Commissaries however wd. certainly be glad to recieve it at Amsterdam & of course willingly fix the rate at which they wd. recieve it & of course agree to the rate for the sums already pd. at Antwerp. If you wait for a settlement of the whole acct. I predict the affair will not be settled with this

42. The remainder of this letter is contained in a postscript dated July 24.
43. William Carmichael, United States chargé d'affaires at Madrid.

government—& if you confine your self to the five essential points—
it may & certainly can be done without any delay. . . ."

[ENCLOSURE]

Gouverneur Morris to William Short [44]

Paris, July 30, 1792. "My last was of the twenty third. I am now
favord with yours of the same Date. I receiv'd Yesterday the Account from the Commissioners of the Treasury and as I suppos'd
it contains a Credit for the Antwerp Payments at the Current Exchange. From the Letter which accompanies it however I observe
that the Commissrs. meant a different Thing, but the Clerks in
extracting from their Books have placed the matter on the footing
which I wish'd. I shall therefore write to them this Morning to know
whether they chuse to receive Money in Amsterdam or Paris and
if there is the least Difficulty I will direct Grand's House [45] to
draw on the Commissrs. at Amsterdam [46] and pay to the Treasury.
You will recollect that by our Contract we are to pay at Grand's
House. But I suppose we shall have no Difficulty. When I say I
will direct Grand's House to draw I know that Somewhat less will
be gain'd than by Remittances but the State of Things here is such
that Remittances on Paris are by no Means sure and Mr ⟨–⟩ whom
you know and who is careful enough of his own Concerns tells me
that he has for some Time past preferred Drafts to Remittances not
chusing to part with his Money but for valuable Consideration. Now
that which is prudent for the small Sums of an Individual is far more
so for the large Concerns of a Nation. The Commissioners have sent
me a Note of Investments made in Specie of ƒ1,350,000 at Amsterdam in July and August 1791. And of ƒ1.073.552 at Antwerp in
January 1792 So that you see they wish to bring into Consideration
the early as well as the late Payments. They state the Loss on the
latter Sum at Livres 1.368.939₶. I shall tell them that these Losses and
the Compensations if any will form a Subject for the Consideration
of our Governmt. whose orders I shall ask."

44. ALS, William Short Papers, Library of Congress.
45. The Paris banking house of Ferdinand Le Grand and Company.
46. Willink, Van Staphorst, and Hubbard.

[ENCLOSURE]

William Short to Gouverneur Morris [47]

The Hague, August 4, 1792. ". . . As to the loans at Amsterdam,
I told you we had a right to re-imburse them, at will & some have
except precisely the one of which you speak [48]—& wch. is one *sui
generis*—it is however only of 2. millions of florins I think, & was
made by Mr. Adams at an int. of 4 p. cent—with certain reimbursements & premiums by lottery wch. augment the interest to about
6.—& wch. from its nature does not admit of a reimbursement at
will—the others at 5. p. cent interest are as I mentioned to you reimbursable at will.[49] Yet as my instructions from the Sec. of the
Treasury are to hold certain sums at his dispositions & to go on
paying France with the rest,[50] I know not precisely where I shd.
find authority (not being a very bold servant, or having much
confidence in my own judgment when opposed to the orders of
government) to change the plan they have fixed in favor of a different one. Of course my own opinion would not lead me to stop
the payments in France in order to make re-imbursements in Holland. But although I have little confidence in my own judgment, I
have much in yours & therefore should you think it for the public
good, not doubting but that government will approve whatever
you shd. judge proper, I will not oppose it—but on the contrary will
direct the bankers to follow your instructions relative thereto, although I do not myself think the measure proper. I take it for
granted that government could not disapprove my giving this mark
of deference to your superior judgment. Your letter of the 30th.
informs me that under particular circumstances you shall direct the
house of M. Grand to draw. It may be proper to mention to you
from what you say as to our obligation to pay at his house—that he
sometime ago wrote to me to complain of my having these payments
made directly to the French treasury—I sent his remonstrance to the
Sec. of the Treasury, who thought it unreasonable, as I had done
myself, & directed me to continue without the intervention of an

47. ALS, Columbia University Libraries.   48. See note 38.
49. See note 39.   50. See H to Short, May 24, 1791.

useless person.[51] I shd. not suppose therefore myself that you shd. employ a third person—but on the contrary dispose of drafts immediately to the commissaries—however I barely mention these things—the reasons mentioned above will prevent my opposing your judgment—my own wd. be however fully against employing any third or useless person—the operation with the commissaries wd. be very simple & they might & would cheerfully purchase your drafts at what you shd. suppose the proper rate of exchange & it would be well I shd. suppose for you to fix with them at the same time the depreciation to be allowed them on the assignats. A much more speedy operation I shd. suppose wd. be for you to fix with them the rate at which their bankers shd. recieve these payments— as the sums might then be all pd. at once. The Sec. of the Treasury suggested my selling the commissaries my bills on Amsterdam for specie [52]—this wd. of course make up the depreciation as they wd. then give the U.S. credit for the amount only in specie. I did not adopt this plan because I thought a more advantageous arrangement might be made in estimating the real depreciation on the assignats but I always supposed that this depreciation wd. be settled by us, with the present government & not delayed to be settled with any other—as there now seems danger of. As to the depreciation on payments before the Antwerp loan, I can only refer you to my letters to M. de Lessart [53] & to the commissaries announcing the making up of depreciation—& wch. are as explicit as words can make them—as to the time of commencment. They are promised by my letters depreciation in future (viz. from the Antwerp loan forward) my promise was founded on the letter of the Secy. of the Treasury—the quantum of depreciation he left to be settled by me; [54] motives of delicacy prevented my doing it—as a short delay could do no harm—& as I knew the President intended appointing a permanent character to reside at Paris. I had no right to be sure that I shd. be the person, & in the case of its being another, considering that preference, as an unquestionable proof of his having

51. See Short to H, March 11, 1791; H to Short, June 25, 1791.
52. See H to Short, September 2, 1791.
53. Claude Antoine de Valdec de Lessart had served as French Minister of Finance from December 4, 1790, to May 18, 1791, and as Minister of Marine from September 18, 1791, to October 2, 1791.
54. See H to Short, September 2, 1791.

more the confidence of the President than I had, I thought it was best to postpone the subject to be discussed & finally settled by him. You know how much in consequence thereof I have urged you & even importuned you in this business from the time of my knowing that you enjoyed this preference."

[ENCLOSURE]

Gouverneur Morris to William Short [55]

Paris, August 6, 1792. "My last was of the thirtieth of July since which I am without advices from you. I have agreed with the Commissioners of the Treasury for the present and in Consequence I pray you will give our Bankers an order to pay to Messrs. Hoguer Grand and Company [56] the Sum of one Million six hundred and twenty five thousand florins banco and desire them at the same Time to send me a Note of the Interest paid by the United States for Money lying in their Hands that I may bring it forward in the final adjustment of Compensation. . . ."

[ENCLOSURE]

William Short to Gouverneur Morris [57]

The Hague, August 7, 1792. "I was obliged to answer with much precipitation your letter of the 30th. ulto recd. here the 4th. inst—as the post sat out from hence immediately after the arrival of yours. I hoped to have learned from you by the post of to-day what had been decided on between you & the commissaries or at least what was the answer which you expected from them at the departure of your last letter. Not having heard from you to-day I think it not amiss to mention what has been suggested to me by the last paragraph of your letter—namely that you shall tell the commissaries that the compensation if any will form a subject for the consideration of government whose orders you shall ask. As to a compensation it has been promised by our government & the footing on which

55. ALS (extract), William Short Papers, Library of Congress.
56. The partners in this Amsterdam banking house were Paul Iwan Hogguer and George Le Grand, the brother of the Paris banker Ferdinand Le Grand.
57. ALS, Columbia University Libraries.

you now put it with the commissaries seems to me to necessitate
a delay which will occasion the subject to be finally settled not with
the present government, wch. created the assignats—but with another which will have no scruple in depreciating them. It has always
seemed to me on the contrary essential to the interests of the U.S.
that this business shd. be finally settled with the present government
—and as there is probably no time to lose I think you wd. do well
to propose to the commissaries to deduct a certain per cent (from
the number of livres credited on acct. of the Antwerp payments) for
depreciation—& proportion this depreciation to the rise in the price
of commodities in France at the time of these payments, or rather
than leave it unsettled at a mean between the rise in the price of
commodities—& of gold & silver which you know was greater considerably than of commodities. This wd. be a more advantageous
arrangement than can be expected in future & if you propose this to
the commissaries coupled with an immediate payment from Amsterdam somewhat in the same way—viz. fixing the number of livres
for each florin according to the present rate of exchange & deducting therefrom for depreciation, a certain p. cent according to the
present rise of commodities in the market, I think they wd: accept
it in which case you would do well to make them credit the U.S.
on the back of each of their bonds in their possession to avoid all
questions hereafter. In that case they might immediately authorize
their bankers to recieve the florins wch. shd. be pd. them by ours at
Amsterdam."

[E N C L O S U R E]

Gouverneur Morris to William Short [58]

Paris, August 9, 1792. "I have yours of the fourth but this being
Thursday I can but barely acknowlege it. In my last of the sixth I
requested you to cause bf 1.625.000 to be paid to Messieurs Hoguer
Grand et Compagnie which I now confirm. By a strange Fatality it
happens that untill the present Hour I have not had the desired
Meeting with the Minister of the Marine.[59] Many appointments have
been made in every one of which he has fail'd. . . ."

58. ALS (extract), William Short Papers, Library of Congress.
59. The Minister of Marine from July 21 to August 10, 1792, was François
Joseph Gratet Dubouchage.

[ENCLOSURE]

William Short to Gouverneur Morris [60]

The Hague, August 17, 1792. "The post of last tuesday brought here your two letters of Aug. 6. & 9. which shews that the first had been unfortunately too late for the post of that day. I was at Amsterdam when these letters arrived here & had directed such as arrived that day not to be sent to me, as I returned here the day after (wednesday). By a mistake however they were sent & crossed me on the road & were not returned to me here till the day after (last night). It was not therefore until this evening that my letter in consequence thereof could go to Amsterdam & accordingly before giving the orders, I determined to await the arrival of this day's French post, not knowing but that the present change of Government in France, by the suspension of the King, might affect some change in your dispositions on this subject. Your letter of the 13th. is this moment recd. & seeing that you say nothing, relative thereto, I shall give the orders this evening conformably, to your letters of Aug. 6th. & 9th.—taking it for granted you have taken such precautions in having this sum carried properly to the credit of the U.S. that there can be no dispute or difficulty hereafter, with the government which may come. I am sorry you did not say in what manner you had settled with the commissaries, & what credit the U.S. are to have in livres for these florins paid. I will thank you to inform me of it by the return of post. I trust it will be an advantageous arrangement as it has been made by you & as the time & circumstances are so favorable. The subject ever gave me more uneasiness, as I fear I shall be blamed in America for having suffered so long delay, & yet I think the motives which influenced me cannot but be approved by every body & particularly the President. I should infer from your letter that the compensation for depreciation was not finally settled —& if so it must be by a future government which is what I wished above all things to be avoided, & which cannot but be injurious. I cannot express to you all the pain this circumstance gives me & the more so as it might have been avoided—there never can again be

60. ALS (extract), Columbia University Libraries.

such an opportunity of settling it advantageously for the U.S. I this morning recd. another letter from the Sec. of the Treasury urging its being settled finally & without delay.[61] I can add nothing to the urgency of my letters to you on that subject. I do not see how I could with delicacy have acted otherwise than I did in postponing this business for your zeal & abilities to take it up & as you have not done it, the proper conclusion is that it could not be done. Do let me know how it stands & what you have done with the commissaries. Arrange the matter finally before their final death if possible & yet I shd. fear what they do posterior to the King's suspension will be regarded as illegal or at least unconstitutional. When I was at Amsterdam the bankers [62] pressed much that they should be relieved from having such large sums on hand. I told them that I expected soon that you would take arrangements which wd. effect it—they observed that it wd. be proper in these arrangements to take care that they should not have so large a sum to pay all at once in bank money as that might raise the agio several p. cent to the disadvantage of the U. S. & that therefore the faculty of paying part at least in current money shd. be preserved. I told them that I was convinced you knew everything relative to such matters & that you would do everything that was requisite for the advantage of the U. S. I intended however in writing to mention to you their observations lest by chance it might possibly escape your attention. I observe however that you desire bank money to be paid. I shall therefore transmit the same order to the bankers desiring them not to make too great a sacrifice however in agio, & to insist if necessary on paying a part in current money, as I suppose this will not create difficulty with Mess Hogguer & Co. What surprizes me very much is that although your arrangement with the commissaries must have been made prior to the 6th of the month, that house had no intimation of it from them. Hogguer was with me at Amsterdam on the subject—he knew our bankers had money & pressed much to know how or when it was to be paid. I told him the matter was with the commissaries & that the delay had come from them. Had he even recd. his orders by last tuesday's post, I shd. have heard of it ere this, I

61. See H to Short, June 14, 1792.
62. Willink, Van Staphorst, and Hubbard, the bankers of the United States in Amsterdam.

imagine, as he wd. certainly have applied to our bankers. I had intended if I had not recd. from you an acct. of your taking this arrangement to have directed the Spanish debt [63] to be paid off. . . ."

[ENCLOSURE]

Gouverneur Morris to William Short [64]

Paris, August 20, 1792. "Yours of the seventh was long in coming probably mine of the 9th. was equally delayed. You will find by it that I had agreed with the Commissioners as to a pretty considerable Payment on that Day. The Events of the tenth ought not I think to make any Change in that Disposition. I think your Reasoning is good as far as it goes and if the Powers to me had been sufficient I should probably have done something very like what you mention. Nay if I could have brought the Minister of foreign Affairs [65] to treat about it I would have strain'd a Point and concluded a general Bargain for the whole of what is yet due by us to be paid by Delivery of Obligations for florins because I think with you that the Moment was favorable but the Commissioners could not settle this Matter and the Minister of foreign Affairs could not find Time to think of it so that unless I had bargaind with myself all Agreement was impossible. Add to this that in these same Money Matters I do not like to step out of the Line prescribd to me unless I can render effectual Service and compleatly for there [are] always Suspicions on such Subjects. . . ."

[ENCLOSURE]

William Short to Gouverneur Morris [66]

The Hague, August 21, 1792. "I hoped that the post of this day which has just arrived would have brought me a letter from you but it has not. I know therefore nothing further with respect to your ar-

63. For a description of this debt, see H to Short, September 1, 1790, note 19.
64. ALS (extract), William Short Papers, Library of Congress.
65. Presumably Morris is referring to Chambonas, who had served as Minister for Foreign Affairs from June 17 to August 1, 1792. See Morris to Short, July 9, 1792, printed above.
66. ALS (extract), Columbia University Libraries.

rangements with the commissaries than was contained in a simple paragraph, saying you had agreed with the commissaries for the present & desire one million &c. to be paid. Was the depreciation settled? viz. is it fixed how many livres the U.S. are to have credit for these florins? If not & I shd. fear it from an expression in your letter, the same thing might have been done six months ago—viz a payment of florins made to Mess. Hogguer & Co. I wish to know that the arrangement has been made & that it is an advantageous one for the U.S. If not I shall certainly blame myself for the delay & probably be blamed by our government. The suspension of the King seems to have made no effect on you with respect to this payment . . . (& yet it seems to me a very serious thing). I therefore did not hesitate to give the orders to our bankers. I desired them at the same time to take receipts from Hogguer, expressing that this money was paid on acct. of the debt due his Christian Majesty & to be held at his orders. I imagined that Hogguer wd. have been glad of such a clause to have saved him from the orders of the new unconstitutional ministry. He has taken time to consider of this clause as our bankers write me by a letter recd. this morning, but I don't doubt he will like it. If you had explained the nature of the agreement made by you with the commissaries I shd. have known better how to act—for instance if you have not settled the depreciation it wd. be proper to express the rect. in livres as well as florins according to the exchge of the day—as at Antwerp. . . . I do not know that Hogguer has yet recd. information from the commissaries or orders wch. is very extraordinary."

[E N C L O S U R E]

Gouverneur Morris to William Short [67]

Paris, August 23, 1792. "The last Post was gone before yours of the seventeenth reach'd me. Mine of the sixth was written the Instant I receiv'd that from the Commissioners of the Treasury which was previously necessary. It did not arrive till late and the consequent Hurry was the Cause why I omitted to mention as I intended that the Sum of Bank florins to be paid in Amsterdam was the equivalent

67. ALS (extract), William Short Papers, Library of Congress.

of six Millions of Livres. I did not stipulate for a Part in current
Money as I might have done because that would have consum'd a
Time extremely precious as Events have demonstrated and because
the Commissioners can pay at their Leizure. It occurs to me that
Hoguer's House may feel themselves embarrass'd about this Payment
and therefore may not incline to receive the Money but if they do
receive it all is strait as to us. . . ."

[ENCLOSURE]

Gouverneur Morris to William Short [68]

Paris, August 27, 1792. "I wrote to you on the twentieth and
twenty third. Yours of the twenty first is receiv'd. I mentiond to
you in one of my preceeding Letters that I had receivd the Account
of the Commissaries in which the several Payments are credited in
Livres which is unavoidable in Book-Keeping. I have also told you
that the last Payment was the Equivalent of six Millions. By the Account they sent me the Ballance due was 6.560,145₶ on the first of
July. I have made some Observations to them on that Account which
will I think reduce this Ballance but as we are paying 300000 Dollars
in America it is evident that on the broadest Basis the whole of the
Installments now due is paid. The question of Depreciation and consequent Compensation remain entire. I have written to Mr Jefferson
that I cannot consistently with my Instructions treat it untill I receive further orders unless Necessity should compel me.[69] Now as to
future questions I am quite tranquil. What was done was done by
Consent both of King and Country so that all is well done let which
ever of them get the better which Fate or Fortune may chuse. If, as
is very possible, we loose on future Payments it will be a sufficient
Reason to withhold Compensation on the past. If we do not loose
then we can come forward with a gratuitous Sum and let who will
be King or Minister those who bring Money will be well receivd
therefore I think you may rest in Peace as to that Affair. I do suppose however that you will be considerd here as an Aristocrat for
having directed the Receipt to be given in Part of a Debt *to his most
Christian Majesty and to be held subject to his orders.* I doubt

68. ALS (extract), William Short Papers, Library of Congress.
69. Morris to Jefferson, August 1, 1792. See also note 10.

whether Hoguer will give it. Had it been necessary I should certainly have desird the Receipt to be taken in florins equivalent to
livres &ca. but I had previously written to you that I would give the
Commissaries the Option to receive at Amsterdam or at Paris *and if
there was the least Difficulty* would direct Bills to be drawn &ca. Of
Course it follwd when I desird the Payment of bank florins at Amsterdam without any Mention of Exchange &c. that the Sum of
Livres was agreed on. I do not write to you in very great Minutious-
ness because I rely on your Sagacity to understand even at Half a
Word. . . ."

[ENCLOSURE]

William Short to Gouverneur Morris [70]

The Hague, August 28, 1792. "I recd. by the last post your letter
of the 20th. & this moment that of the 23d. This letter proves to me
that nothing has been done with respect to the depreciation as the
livres wch. you mention make the exchange if I do not miscalculate
32½ which I suppose was the exchange existing at the time of your
arrangement—of course the depreciation was not taken into the acct.
I need not add here what all my letters will have shewn—my mortification & uneasiness at this subject not having been settled with the
government which created the assignats. Your letter of the 20th. says
if your powers had been sufficient, you should probably have done
something like what I mention—but my dear Sir, how could this
have prevented you? I explained to you on your arrival at Paris, how
the matter stood—how my powers were sufficient—how I had deferred doing this from a distrust of my own abilities & from the
desire of its being settled by the person who shd. be named permanently at Paris—& how I wd. subscribe to whatever you shd. regulate if you would undertake it. You told me you would as soon as
you had gone through the formality of presentation & were installed
in your functions & I cd. not doubt that as soon as that was done you
wd. consider the powers sufficient. All that was essential was to fix
what you thought advantageous for the U.S wch. I begged you to
do & I wd. have signed the arrangement, my powers being sufficient

70. ALS (extract), Columbia University Libraries.

therefore. It is now too late I suppose that government being as I take it dead never to rise again. My uneasiness on this subject is much augmented thereby. The Secy. of the treasury presses me constantly to arrange the matter finally, so that it may not be brought before the government of the U. S. for future consideration, by the government of France. Another difficulty now proceeds from Hogguer—he wishes it to be stated in the rect. que le dit Sr. Short le requiert a ne se desaisir de cet argent qu'avec le plein & libre consentement de S M H wch. I don't think wd. be proper, for several considerations. The rect. shd. be so worded as to include what is right & what is our wish, without any requisition being expressed by us. I have recd. this morning only the model of the rect. he proposes, & am to give the orders this evening, the bankers think it a proper one & request the orders to pay—they say they have purchased the bank money requisite. I shall direct them however to insist on the kind of rect. formerly mentioned & as Hogguer wishes of course this money to pass through his hands, I cannot help thinking he will come into it. Had your letters been recd. here before the intelligence of the suspension there wd. have been less difficulty. As it is I really cannot help thinking there might & wd. be difficulty if this money was pd. to & expended by the present reigning powers. I hope & trust Hogguer will recieve it in the manner desired. I will inform you of it if he does not, & in the mean time I hope to hear from you relative to it. You say the business is straight as to us—but don't you think if it were paid after the known suspension of the King & expended during the *interregnum*, that there might & wd. be difficulties with respect to it? for we shd. certainly have made the payment to persons whom we are not as yet authorized to acknowlege as the government of France to whom we owe the money. Will you be so good as to let me know how our acct. stands now after the Antwerp payments of wch. the commissaries have given you an acct. According to the acct. lately transmitted to me by the Sec. of the treasury it stands thus—34,000,000ℓt. The original debt—14,000,000ℓt of this principal due Jan 1. 92. & 13,953,611ℓt—of interest from wch. deducting payts. made by M. Grand on acct. of interest *1 600,000*ℓt—leaves the balance due on acct. of interest. Jan 1. 92. 12,353,611ℓt. The payts. made from Amsterdam & Antwerp are to be deducted from the 26,353,611. of principal & interest due Jan 1. 92.—

the remaining 20,000,000₶ falling due successively to 1802—the debt to the farmers general [71] & other articles contained in the acct. of the commissaries are questionable & to be settled by our government, who think they have been already paid. . . ."

[ENCLOSURE]

William Short to Gouverneur Morris [72]

The Hague, September 4, 1792. ". . . Hogguer refuses to accept the money any other way than as has hitherto been practised, viz by giving a draught or bill on the commissaries of the treasury for the amt.—or on a reciept where it shall be expressed that at my requisition he engages himself to hold the money until the King's free consent can be obtained for its disposal. He refuses even giving a rect. in general terms—viz. so much recd. on acct. of the debt of the U.S —without the clause mentioned above—as he says it will embarass him in deciding to whom he is to pay the money—whereas if he gives a draught on the treasury as usual the embarassment does not exist. I have been waiting every day in hopes of his giving a reciept which would leave the matter so that no future government could blame us & at the same time would be a means of securing us against the payt. of interest on the sum. I was in hopes also that your letters would say something which might point out some unexceptionable way of getting out of this difficulty occasioned by the King's suspension—but you seem to have no doubt as to the propriety of the payment, insomuch as wd. make me suppose my doubts without foundation—if it were possible to shut my eyes on its being neither more or less than the case of a bond given to A. being robbed by B, or obtained by fraudulent or violent methods—now would you or could you knowing that, pay the money to B & consider yourself honestly discharged from A? This manner of viewing the subject by me, on one hand—your making no question on the other—added to its being important for us to save an interest on six millions of livres all together embarass me beyond measure & disgust me more than ever with having any thing do with matters of that kind. I should

71. For a description of this loan, see H to Short, September 1, 1790, note 26.
72. ALS (extract), Columbia University Libraries.

wait still to hear from you if the time wd. admit of it but I fear the commissaries might in that case be no more—or be removed from Paris. I shall accordingly relying on your judgment & from confidence in your knowlege of such matters & the precautions you will have taken for securing that this sum shall have been properly & inevitably carried to the credit of the U.S. direct the bankers to make the payt. to Hogguer. I cannot describe to you my anxiety on this subject but as you have made the engagement with the commissaries & as you seem to see no danger & even have no doubt on the subject I cannot but subscribe thereto. Let me beg of you however my dear Sir to have this matter so arranged that there may be no discussion hereafter. Such parts of the principal of the debt for instance as have been paid would it not be proper to withdraw the original obligations given therefore & wch. are deposited in the national treasury? I believe it is said in the original agreement that these several obligations are to be paid off a proportion of each but as we have the privilege of paying off the whole or any part I shd. imagine you might so arrange it, that the parts of principal paid shd. be applied all towards an obligation as far as necessary to annul that obligation & so on—(giving preference to the 5 p. cts.—after paying what is due on the 4 p. cts.) so that there shd. remain in the national treasury only such obligations as were still due. In calculating this the charges made in the commissaries acct. of the debt to the farmers general[73] &c shd. be left out, because we say in America that they are not due. It is only therefore the debt existing on the obligations in the public treasury, which shd be taken notice of—of course the cash pd. by 1st. Mr. Grand—2d. at Amsterdam—3d. at Antwerp—& 4thy. the present payt. of six millions shd. be applied 1st. to the payt. of the interest of the original debt of 34.000,000 wch. as I mentioned in my last was 13,953,611₶—& then all the rest to the reduction of that principal—as the compensation is to be hereafter discussed. I hope you will find means of withdrawing the original obligations now in the treasury to the amt of the sums thus applied to the reduction of that principal. I lament now most sincerely that the payments from Amsterdam have been thus deferred since the last winter without any one good end obtained by it. I never expected

73. See note 71.

that you would mention the want of power to settle the affair of depreciation: after what passed betwixt us at Paris I thought you only waited for the form of your installation, & particularly as my powers were sufficient & as I offered in consequence thereof to subscribe to whatever you should agree to. . . ."

[ENCLOSURE]

William Short to Gouverneur Morris [74]

The Hague, September 7, 1792. ". . . In my last I informed you of Hogguer's refusing to recieve the payment you had agreed for with the commissaries in any other than the mode he has hitherto practised; namely by giving a draught for the amount on the national treasury; & of my finally (after the rect. of your letter) directing our bankers to make the payment to him, not withstanding my own particular opinion was that there was danger if not impropriety in the measure. I now inclose you the second of the bill given by Messrs. Hogguer which the bankers have sent me to forward to you. They inform me also that they have by way of precaution inclosed you the first instead of sending it directly to the commissaries. I hope you will recieve them in due time & have the U. S. properly credited for the six million of livres—this I consider essential because whatever depreciation may be hereafter allowed, the interest will certainly be considered as stopped on the six million paid & so also of the prior payments in assignats. I think & trust you will have so arranged this matter that all the payments hitherto made as mentioned in my last will be deducted from the interest fallen due & then from the principal of the debt of 34 millions, & that such part of the obligations as correspond with the principal thus paid off, will have been withdrawn from the public treasury. In this manner after the resurrection every thing will stand on a clearer & better ground for the U.S. I intreat you to let me hear from you on the accomplishment of this payment of the six millions. Your agreement with the commissaries, fixing the value of the florins will of course have been in writing so that it will appear that the U.S. have a right to the credit of six millions. I hope that this disagreeable affair will end

74. ALS (extract), Columbia University Libraries.

well, though I own to you I still have uneasiness respecting it at least
I hope I shall not be obliged to trouble you with any other letter on
the subject. . . ."

[ENCLOSURE]

Gouverneur Morris to William Short [75]

Paris, September 9, 1792. "Yours of the fourth Instant arrivd yesterday afternoon and I write now that I may be in Time for the
Post of Tomorrow. I beleive the Delay of my Letter was not in this
City. As the six Millions are I suppose paid, it is not necessary to
dilate on that Subject. In Regard to the Extent of my Powers I will
explain to you my Ideas thereon. At first I suppos'd that the Management of what relates to our Debt was in some Sort a needful Appendage to this Mission. Mr Jefferson's Letter committing to me
expressly an incidental Negotiation respecting a small Part of it un-
deceiv'd me.[76] Counting however on your Concurrence in such Measures as might appear proper I should have gone on to prepare with
the Minister a Plan for the final Liquidation of this Object could I
have prevaild on him to attend to it. I have since had Occasion, when
I treated with the Commissaries of the Treasury, to examine a little
more minutely into my Powers, so far as they relate to the Debt, and
I found that the Management of it was committed entirely and of
Course exclusively to you. Whether the Knowlege they must have
acquird before the present Moment that nothing final is done . . .
will induce them to address their Orders to me I know not and you
will I trust excuse me for adding that I hope not. Of All Things I
wish to steer clear of pecuniary Transactions because they involve a
Species of Responsability which is most irksome & expose the Agent
to the Chance of being calld by every Calumniator to answer at the
Bar of public Opinion. You tell me, in the very Moment that you
express an Apprehension as to the Validity of Transactions with the
present Government, that you would be glad that I took up certain
of our Obligations &ca. &ca. On this Head I must observe to you
that the Informations you have receivd and communicated to me

75. ALS (extract), William Short Papers, Library of Congress.
76. See note 10.

respecting the State of the Account and the Objections made by the Secretary of the Treasury prove beyond a Possibility of Doubt that our Government do not mean or wish that I should meddle therein. I have not receivd a Line from the Secretary of the Treasury of any Kind. To return however to your Wish. You will doubtless see with me that our Obligations do not *constitute* but only *evidence* our Debt. To possess ourselves of them (therefore) otherwise than by due Payment would not cancel or alter the Debt. And from the Moment that you impeach the Right of the present Government to receive the Money you invalidate any Transaction respecting it which they may make. This Observation I make for your Consideration it cannot in anywise affect my Conduct because I am for the Reasons already mention'd quite unauthoriz'd and indeed *indirectly* prohibited from acting in that Behalf. . . ."

[E N C L O S U R E]

Gouverneur Morris to William Short [77]

Paris, September 12, 1792. "I have receivd yours of the seventh. I had previously sent to the Commissioners of the Treasury the Letter from the Bankers at Amsterdam. I certainly have taken no Steps in Respect to that Payment since my first Letter to you desiring that it might be made and certainly I shall not take any for the very good Reasons which will I am sure suggest themselves to you and which of Course I will not enumerate. . . ."

[E N C L O S U R E]

William Short to Gouverneur Morris [78]

The Hague, September 14, 1792. ". . . I hasten merely to observe on that part of your letter in wch: you say that the observation *cannot in any wise influence your conduct &c.*[79] Surely you do not mean after having carried the matter thus far & put it out of my reach to withdraw yourself from consummating the measure you adopted—under the idea now of being unauthorized—the measure

77. ALS (extract), William Short Papers, Library of Congress.
78. ALS (extract), Columbia University Libraries.
79. See Morris to Short, September 9, 1792, printed above.

itself never appeared to me a proper one, since the suspension of the King, & it was only what you said—the assurance in which you were —the agreement which you had made & my reliance on your judgment in such cases, which induced me to subscribe to it contrary to my own opinion. Whatever may be your opinion with respect to your authority it is impossible that you should at this moment abandon what relates to the six million payment & I cannot suppose it is your intention. The matter is now carried to that point where it is proper to make the best of it for the U.S. & I am persuaded you will do it. As to any other measure it may admit of other considerations. I suppose the present moment excludes any possibility of doing any thing with respect to future payments & also with respect to the arrangement of the depreciation. If you think any thing possible at present, say so & I will take it on myself in order that no opportunity may be lost of repairing if possible the fair chance which has been allowed to slip through our hands. With respect to what has passed you will no doubt see the propriety of the U.S. being credited as they are in livres, because this will stop the interest on the nominal sum paid & will be a saving when the depreciation comes to be made up. You say that withdrawing the original obligations wd. be of no avail since I question the validity of the payment &c. Since however the payment is made the validity will be certainly be considered as unquestionable by the U.S. & particularly by you. It was in conformity to your ideas therefore that I wished to have the obligations withdrawn. I still wish it because it will certainly facilitate matters hereafter. I hope if in settling this payment with the commissaries you can withdraw such of the original obligations as are satisfied you will do it—& shd. you have any scruples with respect to your powers I will ask you to do it for me. There will be no settlement in the case—it is simply deducting as I have formerly mentioned to you the livres tournois pd. at different times from the original of 34. millions & the interest accruing thereon of wch. I sent you a state—the other charges they make of farmers general &c. to be left out of the question & to be settled hereafter. You will have a right to ask these obligations of the commissaries at least such as are paid—the depreciation must now be of course an object of future consideration I imagine. My powers are sufficient to arrange it & if you think it possible now (though it does not appear to me so) be so good as to tell me so. . . ."

[ENCLOSURE]

William Short to Gouverneur Morris [80]

The Hague, September 18, 1792. "I answered in much haste & confusion in my last letter of the 14th. yours of the 9th. It would admit of a greater degree of developement, but it seems unnecessary in the present moment. I have recieved your letter of the 12th. in which you acknowlege the reciept of mine of the 7th & the only observation you make thereon is *that you had previously* sent to the commissioners of the treasury the letter from the bankers at Amsterdam —that you certainly have taken no step in that business since your letter desiring the payment—& that you certainly shall not take any for the very good reasons which will suggest themselves to me & which you of course do not *enumerate*. I must own to you they do not suggest themselves to me nor can I concieve on what ground you now refuse to take measures for consummating the arrangement which you begun & which must I imagine have some need yet of your ministry, unless the arrangement, was as I hope completely settled by you—for instance you gave directions for the paying 1,625,000 florins banco, in consequence of your agreement that the U.S. should be credited therefore to the amount of 6 000,000 of livres—the payment was accordingly made in florins—now certainly you have taken measures that the U.S. should be really credited for these six millions of livres & not have hereafter to ascertain the value of the florins you ordered to be paid. It is useless to go into the reasons in favor of this as they will necessarily suggest themselves to every body. Let your present ideas with respect to your powers be what they may I am sure you cannot mean to leave such an object unsettled or rather unascertained & therefore as you have taken & are decided to take no step in this business since the first letter desiring, I cannot but take it for granted that you had previously settled it so as to leave no future doubt or difficulty. This is independent of any question arising out of the late suspension of government—the payment being now made it is our business to maintain its validity & I trust the reasons which you consider as so cogent will be found proper. As to my part I shall now of course fortify them by what-

80. ALS (extract), Columbia University Libraries.

ever depends on me—not withstanding the light in which this subject presented itself to me from the beginning. So much for this
payment about which I am sorry to have been forced by my anxiety
to importune you so often. I shall cease it from hence having nothing
that it becomes essential to add with respect to it at present. The
depreciation having unfortunately not been settled before the suspension I suppose it out of the question to think of it at present. It
seems to me therefore that it will take this turn—after the payments
shall have been consummated the U.S. will give a certain sum by
way of indemnity—it is for that reason that it is to be desired that
they should be credited for the nominal sum of livres tournois at
present—it will leave a less sum unpaid of the French debt on which
the U.S. will have to pay interest. If you think with me that it is
proper for the U.S. & advantageous also by way of facilitating the
future settlement of their debt that they should withdraw from the
treasury such part of the obligations as they have extinguished—then
I repeat here my request to you to do it & lest you should have any
scruples as to your powers I will ask you at present in consideration
of its utility to be the agent in doing this at my request. I will take it
on myself & consider it as my act to which you only give the instrumentality which your geographical position puts you in the way of
& which I am persuaded you will consider a duty if you think it will
be advantageous for the U. S. as I do. It is in that hope that I repeat
what I have formerly mentioned that the debt to the farmers general [81] &c. in the commissaries acct. is to be left out of the question
& only the debt of 34. millions taken up. The parts exigible Jan 1. 92
were for interest 13.953.611₶ & principal 14,000,000₶. The several
payments made 1. by M. Grand 2. from Amsterdam & 3. Antwerp
including also the late six millions should be applied first to the
interest due & then to sink as much as possible of the principal as to
the part of the principal exigible. It gives its own rule—for such
part as is not exigible & which may be sunk we should of course
give the preference to that which is at 5. p. cent interest. This being
simply an affair of addition requiring no settlement & of course not
giving scope for scruples, I hope you will, on my responsability if
you do not chuse to act otherwise withdraw those obligations which
the commissaries cannot refuse giving up. . . ."

81. See note 71.

[ENCLOSURE]

Pierre Henri Hélène Marie Lebrun-Tondu to Gouverneur Morris [82]

Paris, September 19, 1792. "Je viens, Monsieur, de recevoir une lettre de M. Maulde, Ministre plenipotentiare de france à la haye,[83] par laquelle il m'instruit de l'insinuation perfide que M. Short a faite à M. hoguer, Banquier à Amsterdam, en l'excitant à exiger une formalité, impraticable dans la circonstance, avant de remettre à la Trésorerie Nationale un fonds des 5. ous 6. cent mille florins versés dans la caisse de ce Banquier par l'ordre des Etats-unis. J'ai L'honneur de joindre'ici, Monsieur, copie de cette lettre pour votre information particulière. Nous ne pouvons dissimuler la surprise que nous cause une telle manœuvre de la part du Ministre d'un Peuple Libre àqui nous sommes uni par la conformité des principes et par les liens de l'amitié la plus pure. Nous nous flattons qu'en soumettant au juge-

82. ALS (extract), Columbia University Libraries.
83. The letter from Maulde to Lebrun, dated September 11, 1792, reads as follows: "Voici une particularité qui vous paraitra sans doubt de quelqu'-importance.
"MM. Guillaume et Jean Williack négocians d'amsterdam se trouvaient chargés par les Etats-unis d'amérique de verser dans la Caisse de la maison hogguer grandt et Compagnie une Somme de quinze a seize cent mille florins.
"Le Jeune Ministre Américain M. Short Se rendit dernierement à amsterdam et pressa avec de vives instances le Banquier hogguer de S'engager par Sa quittance a ne payer la remise à la Tresorerie Nationale que d'apres une approbation Signée du Roi. La discussion a été aussi vive que longue, mais enfin Mr. hogguer s'est réduit aux formes ordinaires. Cette conduite du jeune Short est trés Conséquente à Son Langage comme à l'intimité de ses liaisons avec les minitres Ennemis." (Copy, Columbia University Libraries.)
On February 21, 1793, Jefferson sent to Washington extracts of letters submitted to him by Jean Baptiste de Ternant concerning the attitude of the French Ministry toward Short and Morris in September, 1792. Jefferson's translation of the extract of a letter from Lebrun to Ternant, dated September 19, 1792, reads as follows: "We complain with reason of the conduct of mr Morris. but you will see by the letter inclosed of our Minister at the Hague, that we are not less founded in reason to complain of mr Short. We charge you specially to ask satisfaction from the American ministry on a fact so much the more serious as the object of mr Short was to hinder a banking house of Amsterdam to remit to our national treasury a sum which the U.S. had deposited in the hands of the banker to be there subject to our disposal. We suppose that in submitting this maneuvre of mr Short to the judgement of his employers they will not hesitate to manifest to him their dissatisfaction at it, & to prescribe to him to be more prudent & more circumspect in future" (translation, in handwriting of Jefferson, RG 59, Miscellaneous Letters, 1790–1799, National Archives). Ternant also submitted to Jefferson a copy of the letter from Maulde to Lebrun of September 11, 1792.

ment des Etats-unis la conduite inconséquente et peu honnête de M
Short ils n'hésiteront point à l'improuver et à lui témoigner leur
mecontentement. Je passe Sous silence l'affectation marquée de M.
Short en se coalisant avec les Ministres des Cours Etrangères qui
resident à la haye, et dont la malvéillance nous est connüe. Nous
croïons que des pareilles intrigues Sont, peu dignes de notre attention: nous n'y attachons aussi aucune importance. Je n'entre avec
vous, Monsieur, dans un détail Sur cet incident que pour vous con-
vaincre d'une malvéillance la plus caracterisér de la part de M Short,
et dont il ne pourra jamais se justiffier. . . ."

[ENCLOSURE]

Gouverneur Morris to Pierre Henri Hélène Marie Lebrun-Tondu [84]

Paris, September 20, 1792. "J'ai eu l'honneur de recevoir hier votre
lettre du dix neuf.[85] J'apprends par la Copie que vous avez eu la
bonté d'y joindre de celle de Monsieur Maulde [86] qu'il s'est élevé
quelques Difficultés sur le paiement de la Somme de seize cent vingt
cinq mille florins de banque dont je suis convenu avec Messieurs les
Commissaires de la Tresorerie au Commencement D'Aout, et que je
priois Monsieur Short d'éffectuer par une lettre du Six du dit Mois
ce qu'il a fait faire le cinq du courant. Il en est resulté un delai de
quelques jours dont je suis bien faché, et d'ou j'espère cependant,
Monsieur, qu'il ne vous arrivera aucun inconvenient. Les Liaisons
des Ministres etrangérs a la Haie dont se plaint Monsieur Maulde
provienent, je crois, du locale, qui en ne leur presentant que peu de
ressources pour la Societé les force en quelque Sorte a une intimité
plus grande que celle qui subsiste ailleurs; et peutêtre aussi Monsieur
le Zele de Monsieur Maulde a t'il pu lui faire voir avec peine une
chose indifferente en elle même."

[ENCLOSURE]

Gouverneur Morris to William Short [87]

Paris, September 20, 1792. "I have receiv'd your two Letters of
the eleventh and the fourteenth. I certainly do not mean to withdraw

84. LC, Gouverneur Morris Papers, Library of Congress.
85. This letter is printed above.   86. See note 83.
87. ALS (extract), William Short Papers, Library of Congress.

myself from any Situation in which either Duty or Propriety may bid me to remain. This is a general Maxim, which will I hope govern me thro Life. I proceed now to take up again the Payment made on Account of our Debt. I did hope that there was an End of our Correspondence on that Subject; and when you reflect that Observations respecting the Legality of a Government should not be committed to Post Offices subject to it's Inspection, you will be sensible how disagreable it is to me to be forced into such Questions, and that too about an Affair which is done and which cannot be altered unless for the worse. If you will read over my Letter of the twenty third of July, you will see that my Doubt as to the Power of treating for the Debt with the Government of this Country is not new. Recollect also, that I never saw your Instructions. I proceed to state the Facts. On the thirtieth of July (having receivd on the Evening of the twenty ninth a Copy of the Account from the Treasury) I inform'd the Commissaries that the United States had Money at Amsterdam, and desired them, *in order to avoid unnecessary Delay*, to fix a Rate at which they would be willing to receive it: that if that Rate were convenient I would write in Consequence *to make the Payment to their Agent*, and if not that I would take Measures to pay them here.[88] On the same thirtieth of July, I wrote to you that I would that Day write &ca. It was Post Day and therefore the Letter to you was first written, and of Course could not contain a Copy of the other. From a similar Cause, my Letter to you of the sixth of August preceeded that of the same Date to the Commissaries.[89] I tell you '*I have agreed* with the Commissioners of the Treasury (for the present) and in Consequence I pray you will give our Bankers an Order *to pay to Messieurs Hoguer Grand and Company* the Sum of bf 1.625.000.' Immediately after, I wrote to the Commissaries 'I have given the necessary Directions for Payment of bf 1.625.000 to Messrs. H. G. & Co. which at the Exchange you have mention'd is equal to 6 000 000tt. I hope that my Letters may arrive in Season to prevent any other Appropriation, and you will of Course cause the above Sum of 6.000.000tt *to be carried to the Credit of the United States this Day*, saving always the Right of Counter Entry should the Pay-

---

88. See Morris to the Commissaries of the French Treasury, July 30, 1792, printed as an enclosure to Jefferson to H, October 31, 1792.

89. See Morris to the Commissaries of the French Treasury, August 6, 1792, printed as an enclosure to Jefferson to H, October 31, 1792.

ment not be compleated *instanter* at Amsterdam.' Here ended my
Agency. After the Solicitude which you had exprest, I could not
doubt that you would cause immediate Payment to be made. I
wrote however on the ninth as follows 'In my last of the sixth I requested you to cause bf 1.625.000 to be paid to Messieurs Hoguer
Grand and Company which I now confirm.' On the tenth a Revolution in the Government took Place. Now observe, that if in Consequence of my Letter of the sixth you had paid the Sum mention'd,
no questions could afterwards arise in the Contingency you suppose
that the present Government should be overturn'd and it's Acts
annulled. On the twenty third of August I wrote to you, 'It occurs
to me that Hoguers House may feel themselves embarrass'd about
this Payment, and therefore may not incline to receive the Money,
but if they do all is strait as to us.' This Letter was in Answer to
yours, of the seventeenth, in which you express your Fears that
what the Commissaries may do posterior to the King's Suspension
will be regarded as illegal. On the twenty first you mention to me
the Kind of Receipt which you had desird from Mr Hoguer viz that
the Money was paid *on Account of the Debt due his Christian
Majesty and to be held at his orders;* And you tell me that you suppos'd he would be glad of such a Clause, *to have saved him from
the Orders of the new unconstitutional Ministry.* In mine, of the
twenty seventh of August, I tell you that I am quite tranquil as to
future questions because that 'what was done was done by consent
both of King and Country so that all is well done.' And I express
to you my Doubt whether Hoguer would give the Receipt which
you had desird. On the twenty eighth of August you inform me
that you have still Difficulties respecting the *Receipt,* Hoguer proposing one Thing and you another, viz that which you had before
directed. On the fourth of September you inform me that you shall
direct the Payment to be made, taking *Hoguer's Bill on the Commissaries for the Amount.* This was accordingly done on the fifth
of September, One Month after my Letter of the sixth of August.
Such are the Facts. I now proceed to consider these Facts under the
Hypothesis, first that the present Government should continue; and
in that Case there is *now* no Difficulty, but if the Money had been
accepted by Hoguer on the Terms you held out, I think the Difficulty would have been great. Secondly, if the present Government

should be overturn'd: & here two possible Cases occur, first that their Acts should be deem'd valid, secondly that they should be annulled. In the first Case there is still no Difficulty. In the second Case there would (as I have already said) have been none, had the Payment been readily made; and the Questions which may hereafter arise have been created in Amsterdam. First you will observe that the *Receipt* you requir'd was as inconsistent with the late Government as it is with the present. By the Laws and Constitution, such as they existed on the ninth of August, the Debt from the United States was to the *Nation* and not to the *King* of the French, much less *to his most Christian Majesty*. Consequently it could in no wise be consider'd as the Completion of a Transaction which I had begun, but was a new & a different Transaction. And as I, acting without Authority from our Government, could only be considerd in this Behalf as the Agent of you who possess'd that Authority, it would follow *perhaps* that by your Act mine was suspended, if not annull'd. The *Receipt* which you ask'd was not given, and therefore the question above stated may not perhaps be stirred; but at length instead of a *Receipt*, or of a Payment without a Receipt and which could have been establish'd by the Books of our Bankers, you have *taken a Bill on the Commissaries*. Certainly a question may be raisd on this Ground, whether that be the Payment which I had stipulated. Thus you will see my dear Sir that while you were doubting of the Legality of the present Government, you chang'd the Form of what had been done with the former Government, and gave it the Air of a Payment to those whose Authority you denied. And then you desire me to do certain other Things, respecting this same Transaction, with those same Persons whose Authority you still deny. Now I will not enter into any Question respecting the Competency of the present Government. The Corner Stone of our own Constitution is the Right of the People to establish such Government as they think proper. In this Country Reason may perhaps say one Thing and Force another; but putting all that aside, I think it proper to adhere to the original Nature and Form of the present Payment. First because the Exchange is much more favorable than that which now rules, and secondly because (as is above hinted) there is a Difference of one Month's Interest on the Sum paid of 6.000.000₶. I must before I close this too long Letter inform you that the present Ministers of this Country complain much of your Intention to place the Sum in question out of their Reach, which Conduct they consider as evincing a hostile Disposition. . . ." [90]

[ENCLOSURE]

William Short to Gouverneur Morris [91]

The Hague, September 21, 1792. "I answered by the last post yours of the 12th. recd. that day & since that I am without hearing from you. The commissaries have acknowleged in their letter to our bankers the reciept of the draught for 1,625,000 florins, & say they will credit the U.S. therefore. I flatter myself however they mean for the value of the florins viz 6,000,000 livres & not the florins themselves—but as this value was settled by you & remains only between you & them I hope & trust you will see that it is done—for you will easily see the difference hereafter of being credited at present for the florins instead of the livres. I am anxious to learn this from you expressly—there is no time to be lost & you certainly after having carried the business to that stage cannot think of leaving it in that embarassment from any new discovery made in the nature of your powers. You must necessarily have too full a conviction of the impropriety of such a proceeding & the disadvantage which would result to the U.S. there from. It is therefore merely by way of supererogation that I write to the commissaries of the treasury this evening to require that it shd. be done if by any unaccountable circumstance, you should persist in dropping the business there as a part of your last letter might be construed to indicate. The times are now so pressing that it might be unsafe to await your answer, before writing to the commissaries, with whom you know I have ceased all correspondance, since your arrival at Paris & taking up that business which I really thought with you an appendage of your mission. I inclose you the letter open for your perusal [92] & shd. as I still flatter myself the object of it have been settled by you, then you may suppress it or return it to me as you think proper—it is written I repeat it only

90. See note 83. 91. ALS, Columbia University Libraries.
92. Short to the Commissaries of the French Treasury, September 21, 1792 (ALS, Columbia University Libraries). Since this letter is among Morris's papers, it is likely that he did not forward it to the commissaries.

by way of precaution which I flatter myself may be useless. I shall never cease lamenting the fair opportunity which has been allowed to pass—but at present it is indispensable to make the best use of the case as it stands—& which will certainly suffer if you have abruptly withdrawn your ministry, as might be apprehended from yr. late letter if it were possible to suppose you wd. leave such a business unsettled."

[E N C L O S U R E]

Gouverneur Morris to William Short [93]

Paris, September 23, 1792. "I have receivd yours of the eighteenth.[94] Mine of the twentieth [95] will have communicated to you the Reasons for leaving the Transaction to which you refer on it's Original Ground. If any Question should hereafter be raised respecting it, our Answer is that you compleated what was begun, or rather paid a Bill drawn: for, the Form differing, the substance of the Transaction was that of a Bill on the Commissioners or Bankers of the United States at Amsterdam. And the Difference of Form arose meerly from the Circumstance that (considering myself as your Agent) desird you to give an order which I was not authorizd to give. But the Sum was the Same it was paid to the same Persons and for Account of the same Persons. So much for that. The Settlement of Depreciation I consider as purely optional in us, and of Course should the Government of this Country, in whatever Hands it may be, think proper to quibble about this last Payment we have still the Staff in our own Hands. As to the Observation you make about certain Items in the Account. I had already, on receiving it, conveyed to the Commissaries my Idea that a considerable Part thereof was a double Charge and desir'd them to make an Enquiry, which they promis'd to do.[96] I wrote also to Colo. Hamilton [97] to the same Effect. As to the Charge of so much due for an Advance by the Farm,[98] I am persuaded that unless this Ballance has been discharg'd

93. ALS (extract), William Short Papers, Library of Congress.
94. See enclosure printed above.   95. See enclosure printed above.
96. See Morris to the Commissaries of the French Treasury, August 6, 1792, printed as an enclosure to Jefferson to H, October 31, 1792.
97. See Morris to H, August 17, 1793.
98. The Farmers-General.

in America, since the Organization of our new Government, it still remains due to Somebody. The questionable Articles therefore with the Interest amount to about two Millions; but as we have still certain Installments which will fall due, any Errors can be rectified at Leizure. I come now to the Idea you express of making an Adjustment with the Commissaries and *taking up our Obligations*. Since you affix so much Importance to these Evidences of our Debt, I am led to pay more Attention to them than I otherwise should do. Before any Step be taken however it may be well for you to consider the State of Facts. The Obligations are for large Sums, and therefore large Sums are needful to acquit them. Each is payable by Installments, and therefore the first Point is to pay up those Installments, and then to discharge the Ballance on one Obligation. Now a previous Point is to adjust the Value of those Payments, for you know that your Ideas differ very much from those entertained by Monsieur de Claviére. If the Commissaries attach the same Importance to the Obligations which you do, they will of Course be as tenacious as you are desirous of them; and then you must (before you can get them) come to a Settlement with the Ministry. How far it may be in your Wish to do so, you alone can determine, but before any one Step be taken, it is necessary to look forward to all the subsequent and consequent Steps, for it will not do to begin and then to stop short by reason of those Circumstances which are naturally to be expected. . . ."

[ENCLOSURE]

Gouverneur Morris to William Short [99]

Paris, September 24, 1792. "My Letter of Yesterday was written in the Idea that the Business to which it alludes is present to your Recollection but as that may not be the Case I now add in Explanation that there are three Obligations one for 18 Millions

one for 10 Millions
one for 6 Millions
together 34 Millions

99. ALS, William Short Papers, Library of Congress.

The first two are payable by Installments of which one Half are due on the thirty first of December 1791. The last is payable by Installments of which the first is due on the first of January 1797. If we admit the Articles which you object to, and here remark that an Objection by you will not alone justify the Commissaries, the Amount of the principal and Interest due the first Day of the present Year will be about 28.000.000₶

Deducting our Payments to the first of April (without allowing for Depreciations), which amount to about 24.500.000₶

There was due a Ballance of	3.500.000₶
Add six Months Interest on what remains	500.000₶
And you have for what is due the 1 July	4.000.000₶
deduct the Remittences in April May and June nearly	850.000
Remains due about	3.150.000
Add what Remains of the 4 p % Debt Principal	5.000.000
Total	8.150.000
Deduct Payment last made	6.000.000
remains . . .	2.150.000

Thus you see that without touching the Question of Depreciation, nor that of the objectionable Articles which together exceed 3,000,000₶ there is still a large Sum to be paid before you can take up the Obligation you wish, even admitting the Amount to be settled quite on your Terms. But you will remember that there are two Sides to every Question and two Parties at least to every Contract or Bargain."

From William Short

The Hague Sep. 25. 1792

Sir

All the letters which I have had the honor of writing to you for some time will I think have been uniform in shewing you my anxiety on two subjects, namely the settlement of the depreciation to

ALS, letterpress copy, William Short Papers, Library of Congress.

be allowed on the payments which I had had made to the French government since the receipt of your letter of Sep. 2. 91. relative thereto & the retardment of the sums accumulating in the hands of our bankers at Amsterdam destined for France.

I trust Sir you will have seen, that under the circumstances in which I was placed & which I have taken the liberty of so often tracing to you, it was dictated both by a sense of duty & delicacy to have pursued the line I did from the month of January last, the time of my return from Amsterdam to Paris, until Mr. Morris's [1] arrival there in May & I should perhaps be without anxiety on the subject at present if I did not find from your late letters recieved here that it is the intention that this part of the business should continue to be conducted by me [2] & therefore fear that you may think I ought to have understood it in this manner (notwithstanding the Presidents instructions [3] & other irresistible reasons) & of course place on me the blame, which I should certainly in that case deserve for having allowed to pass so favorable an opportunity of making the settlement advantageously for the U.S.

Every circumstance relative to these two subjects has been successively & repeatedly communicated to you as it occurred, with a minuteness which I was often afraid would be fastidious. I will at present therefore ask leave to take them up only from the time of Mr. Morris's arrival at Paris.[4]

I then supposed & so did he that the arrangement of the indemnity to be allowed for depreciation was within the line of his mission. I accordingly put him as fully as I could in possession of the subject—

1. Although Gouverneur Morris had been appointed United States Minister Plenipotentiary to France in January, 1792, he did not arrive in Paris until May of that year.

2. See H to Short, June 14 and July 25, 1792.

3. In his original instructions to H on the repayment of the foreign debt Washington stipulated that "if any negotiation with any Prince or State to whom any part of the said Debt may be due, should be requisite, the same shall be carried on thro' the person who in capacity of Minister, Chargé des Affaires, or otherwise, now is, or thereafter shall be charged with transacting the affairs of the United States with such Prince or State." See Washington to H, August 28, 1790. When Morris arrived in Paris to replace Short, it was assumed that he would undertake the responsibility of liquidating the French debt. For the difficulties arising out of this misunderstanding, see the correspondence between Morris and Short, enclosed in Morris to H, September 25, 1792.

4. For the correspondence discussed by Short in the following paragraphs, see the enclosures to Morris to H, September 25, 1792.

feeling however peculiarly anxious, as it had been formerly confided to me, that it should be settled advantageously for the U.S. & agreeably to the President. I urged Mr Morris to lose no time—stating to him the various reasons which occurred therefore. I mentioned to him the causes which had induced me to delay this settlement. He seemed fully disposed to enter on the business & sensible of the propriety of despatch; mentioning however two causes of short delay, that is to say his having not then been formally installed in his functions & his desire to recieve another letter from the Sec. of State explanatory of the one then in hand relative to the subject of depreciation.[5]

The settlement of the indemnity on the payments already made, being thus considered as placed in Mr. Morris's hands, by our government, necessarily gave him the direction in some measure of those to be made—because being more safe for the U.S. & more agreeable to France to recieve the florins in Amsterdam than in bills of exchange remitted to Paris, it became necessary to settle with the French government previously at what rate they would credit the U.S. in livres for these florins—which of course was fixing the depreciation or indemnity to be allowed. Accordingly when I left Paris for this place the business stood thus [6]—As to depreciation on former payments, to be settled by M. Morris, the most expeditiously possible—As to future payments I was not to order any until he should advise me of his having settled on what footing they should be recieved.

Thus the whole business was in fact placed necessarily in his hands & I became merely a passive agent. Still my desire that no time should be lost (as it became every day more sensible from the situation of affairs in France, how precarious the government which had created & lived on the assignats, was growing) made me take on myself to write from hence to M. Morris urging him with a frequency & importunity which nothing but my desire to see the business conducted advantageously for the U.S. could authorize. Every letter gave me reason to hope that the next would enable me to direct our bankers to pay the monies wch. had been so long

5. See Morris to H, September 25, 1792, note 10.
6. Short had left Paris early in June, 1792, to assume his duties as Minister Resident at The Hague.

detained were accumulating daily in their hands & augmenting my anxiety.

At length on the sixteenth of August I recieved here, after my return from Amsterdam, two letters from M. Morris of the sixth & ninth, mentioning that he had agreed with the commissaries of the treasury for a payment of 1,625,000 florins—which he accordingly desired I would direct Messrs Willinks & Van Staphorst to pay to the French bankers at Amsterdam.[7] I recieved at the same time an account of the King's suspension. It struck me that a payment under these circumstances would be improper & dangerous—but recieving a letter the day after from M Morris, of the 13th. viz. three days posterior to the suspension, in which no hint of a counter-order was given, I directed the bankers to make the payment, taking the precaution to have mentioned in the reciept that it was on account of the debt due by the U S to France & to be held at the disposition of his Most Ch. Maj.[8] I concieved that this would be rescuing us from a reproach after the resurrection of a Monarch in France & at the same time would entitle us to take credit for the payment & thereby avoid an interest on that amount to France. I did suppose also that the French bankers would be satisfied to give a reciept of that kind for various reasons. It proved otherwise & they refused recieving the money except with the stipulation as mentioned to you in my last[9] —or on giving a draught on the treasury as they had been accustomed to do.

My own opinion being that such a payment would be improper if it was to be placed at the disposition of the usurpers in France—& the refusal of the French bankers to recieve it otherwise unless locked up by my stipulation in their hands—occasioned a delay during which I recieved several letters from M. Morris. They were so uniformly positive as to the propriety of the payment that I determined to give up my opinion, which was borne down by the weight of his—by the consideration of the long delay to which these payments had been already subjected—of the sums which were

7. Hoggeur, Grand, and Company were the bankers of France at Amsterdam.

8. See Short to H, August 30, 1792. For the attitude of the French Ministry toward Short's delay in making this payment, see Morris to H, September 25, 1792, note 83.

9. Short to H, August 30, 1792.

accumulating—of the probability of the time which might elapse before such an order of things should be established in France as would authorize payments to be made them—of the advantage of stopping the interest on six millions of livres (which was the sum M. Morris afterwards informed me we were to have credit for) by a payment of 1,625,000 florins. After weighing well & with anxiety the circumstances & seeing that there was only my individual opinion in opposition to them I could not avoid yielding it—& accordingly on the 4th. of this month directed the payment to be made to the French bankers at Amsterdam & the same day gave notice of it to Mr. Morris. The determination being once taken it became urgent that it should be carried into execution without delay. The payment was made the next day—& the draught of the French bankers on the French treasury endorsed by ours to the commissaries in the usual form was remitted by them, for greater security to M. Morris. The second of the draught they sent to me to be forwarded likewise to him. This was all that could be done here. Reconverting these florins into livres & seeing that they were properly carried to the credit of the U S which was an essential part of the arrangement, lay unavoidably between M. Morris & the commissaries—no other person being privy to the arrangement, & the French bankers being of course unable to express the draught in livres, or any otherwise than in *Florins*, which indeed was the term M. Morris had desired should be used.

I mentioned that M Morris's letters posterior to the suspension had been uniform as to the propriety of this payment—mine to him had as uniformly expressed my fears & doubts. In that which I recieved from him the 4th. inst. & after which I immediately gave orders for the payment—he observes "Now as to future questions I am quite tranquil—what was done was done by consent both of King & country so that all is well done let whichever of them get the better which fate or fortune may chuse." On the 14th. I recd. from him a letter of the 9th acknowleging the reciept of mine of the 4th. (announcing to him the orders I had given for the payment) in which he says "As the six millions are I suppose paid it is not necessary to dilate on that subject" & then goes on to say that on examing his powers more minutely he had found that "the management of what relates to the debt was committed entirely & of course conclusively to you" (me). On the 18th. I recieved from him a letter of the 12th., acknowleging the receipt of mine of the 7th. inclosing him the second of the draught in which he says "I had previously sent to the commissaries of the Treasury the letter from the bankers at Amsterdam. I certainly have taken no step in respect to that payment since my first letter to you desiring that it might be made & certainly I shall not take any for the very good reasons which I am sure will suggest themselves to you & which of course I will not enumerate." I have chosen to repeat M. Morris's own expressions because being now to write to you, & having recieved no letter from him of a later date, I cannot know whether he means from thence that he should be considered as not being the author of this payment, as simply sending the draught to the commissaries without seeing that the U.S. were credited therefore in livres would seem to indicate, unless the arrangement wch. he had made with them was such as to effect this purpose previously & therefore render his interference after the reciept of the draught unnecessary. Being unacquainted with the manner in which the arrangement was made I can not know how the matter stood. I hope however & trust that he will see too clearly the importance of this step for the interest of the U.S. not to consummate the measure which he had begun & which being only between him & the commissaries could properly be effected only by him.

All my letters have been uniform on that head & since recieving his of the 9th & 12th I have urged him that whatever scruples he may have as to other measures not to neglect this which was now only within his reach—& which a short time would probably put beyond even his, as the present order of things could have but a momentary existence. Fearing that it might even be too late if I awaited to learn what he had done, I took on me to write to the commissaries of the treasury by way of supererogation [10] & inclosed my letter open in my last to him, to be used in the case he had not taken previous arrangements for having the U.S. credited for six millions of livres & persisted in not doing it. My letter to the commissaries was merely to desire they would state the account including this payment according to their agreement with M. Morris.

10. Short to the Commissaries of the French Treasury, September 21, 1792 (ALS, letterpress copy, William Short Papers, Library of Congress).

A short time will shew what has been done & I could have wished to have saved you the trouble of these details—but in its present uncertain state I could not avoid informing you of them as far as they are known to me, & shewing that nothing has been left undone by me to alter my obedience to the will of the President & my zeal for carrying into execution whatever I learn to be his wish.

I have already had the honor of mentioning to you that your letter of the 14th. of June, which shewed that it was his intention that this business should remain with me was not recieved until the 17th. of August, after the arrangement with the commissaries had been made by M. Morris, & after I had learned the King's suspension. It was evident that the only thing which could be done then, was to complete the measure begun previous to that suspension, & that no new one could be adopted until there should be a change in France.

I cannot convey to you an idea of my regret at the opportunity of settling the depreciation of the assignats with the government which created them, having been thus lost, better than by referring to the uniform contents of my past letters on the subject. The proper way of treating it seems to me at present to be this. Instead of converting the assignats into a given sum (by deducting that which might be considered as the amount of depreciation at the time of each payment & having this given sum carried to the credit of the U.S.) to have the whole *nominal* sum of assignats paid, carried to their credit & hereafter when the business shall be taken up & the debt paid, to pay over & above a given sum in lieu of depreciation. The U.S. may then come forward & offer this indemnity which will be considered at that time as a free gift—& in the mean time they stop the interest on the nominal sum paid instead of the sum reduced by deducting for depreciation at the time of payment. Although this would have been a much more fixed & proper mode of settlement & more agreeable also to the U.S. as I learn from your letters,[11] yet the other may be made to secure its advantages also—a future government will unquestionably be much less scrupulous as to the depreciation of assignats & will use various arguments that this could not, yet there will be several to oppose to them also, resulting from the manner in which the U.S. recieved the loan from them—&

11. See H to Short, June 14, July 25, 1792.

also from the delays to which they have been subjected from the situation of affairs in France, notwithstanding they have had so large sums lying dead in the hands of their bankers at Amsterdam.

In order that this subject may be brought on in the manner the least liable to question & the most advantageous for the U.S. it seems to me to be desired that the bonds or reciepts of the U.S. constituting this debt & now in the French treasury, should be with drawn as far as they have been extinguished by our payments. It is certain that interest hereafter can be claimed only on such as remain in the treasury. Suppose that to be 15. or any other number of millions, all we pay hereafter over & above that by way of indemnity will be much more within our discretion & appear a much more spontaneous generosity than if the whole number of bonds remained & were subjected to a future discussion both of interest and indemnity. I have therefore repeatedly & warmly pressed this on M. Morris. The only difficulty which occurred to me arose from a belief that it was expressed in the reciepts constituting this debt (which however were never sent to me as promised in your letter of Sep. 1. 1790.) that the payments should be in equal portions on each reciept until the whole were paid—of this however I was not sure & supposed the difficulty even if it existed might be got over. As soon as I found M. Morris determined to consider his powers as not enabling him to act I begged him to give his instrumentality to this measure in consideration of its advantage to the U.S if it appeared to him in the same light it did to me—& that if he had any scruples he might consider it as my act & under my responsibility.

For his guide I informed him that the charges made in the account of the commissaries relative to the Farmers-general &c. were not [to] be considered, some being questionable & others certainly improper—that the original debt of 34. millions alone with the interest was to be taken into view & I forwarded the statement inclosed in your letter of June 23d. shewing what interest & what part of the principal was exigible. I intreated him after applying the several payments made formerly by Mr. Grand [12] of Paris—by the bankers at Amsterdam [13]—by deWolf at Antwerp [14]—& lastly the

12. Ferdinand Le Grand, the banker of France at Paris.
13. Willink, Van Staphorst, and Hubbard.
14. Charles John Michael de Wolf, the Antwerp banker who negotiated the 1791 Antwerp loan for the United States.

six millions agreed for by him, towards extinguishing the interest &
principal due; to extend the surplus to the remaining part of the
debt at 5. p. cent & withdraw the bonds of all the principal thus
extinguished, in the manner & under the responsibility, if he chose
it, as abovementioned. Should this be done it will be putting the
subject certainly on the best vantage ground within our scope at
present—& I hope notwithstanding his last letter that this which I
have written to him since will induce him as I there mention to
give that instrumentality which his geographical position & the
present situation of France put within his reach alone.

To avoid confusion in these lengthy details I have postponed
mentioning your letter of July 25th. which I had the honor of
recieving here on the 10th. inst. You were very right Sir in supposing that no mode of applying the data there mentioned, could be
contemplated by which the U.S. were to be subjected to loss. I
rather suppose you will have misunderstood the quotation of the
exchange there mentioned. I have not the paper of that day before
me—but it must have meant that *36* was the course of the exchange
with Amsterdam—& not that the exchange was *36* p. ct below par.
The *36* which was probably the number there marked (& to which
I think the exchange had risen for a few days about that time) after
having been for a few days also as low as 26½—means that 36 half
sous of Holland were equal to three livres of France. The par is
about 54 of these half sous to the *petitecu* of three livres—of course
the gain at Amsterdam was 28 on 54.[15] The rate of depreciation
which you mention if quoted as in most of the papers did not
probably state 60. p. cent—but *100* livres in silver for *160* in assignats—which of course did not mean 60 on an hundred—but sixty
on an hundred & sixty.

I have had however formerly the honor of mentioning to you
that from the beginning of the circulation of assignats the progress
of depreciation & fall of exchange did not continue precisely the
same [16]—several causes contributed to render the advantage of the
exchange proportionally less; or in other words to raise the price
of specie on particular occasions nearer to the amount of the fall of

---

15. Short corrected this error in subtraction in his letter to H of October
9, 1792.
16. See Short to H, October 10, November 22, December 1, 30, 1791.

exchange than it had been in the beginning—a moment of considerable emigration for instance among the ignorant provincial noblesse when many chuse to carry out specie rather than depend on bills, not being accustomed to that kind of remittance & not having confidence in the bankers supposed to be deeply concerned in stock jobbing—a moment of ill humour among the people which prompted them to ill treat & in some instances, execute those concerned in selling the specie. Still I believe in adopting this rule the U.S. would find advantage—& certainly a very considerable one as explained in the beginning. After the fluctuation took place I mentioned to the commissaries that I did not think that that standard taken alone would form a really just measure of depreciation—as it would in fact be making the U.S. pay for the police of Paris not being sufficiently energetic to prevent a mob hanging a moneylender—& indeed no person can doubt that the want of efficacious protection to those concerned in that kind of commerce did raise considerably the price of that article—since they were obliged to take into the account not only the risk of the assignats but the risk of their lives.

The U.S. have in my opinion a perfect right in making up the *real depreciation of the assignats to France,* which is the term I used with them (& not the course of exchange with which they have nothing to do) to measure it by the price (in the market) of the articles of French production. This would be the most advantageous standard for the U.S. & indeed would secure to them almost the whole gain upon the exchange. It is the standard I should have proposed if the government had been in existence, at the time of learning from you the will of the President as to my ministry [17]—& fortified by that mark of his confidence I should have considered it my duty to have devoted myself to any responsibility however dangerous rather than that so favorable an opportunity for settling this business honorably & advantageously for the U.S should have been lost. On recieving your letter of Sep 2: 91. relative to this business I desired the Minister & the commissaries, as I had then the honor of informing you, to consider of some means proper for settling it on a basis that should be equally just for both parties [18]—

17. See H to Short, June 14, July 25, 1792.
18. See Short to H, November 22, 1791.

& was then obliged to leave Paris for Antwerp & Amsterdam. The price of specie would be the most advantageous standard they could have any pretext for proposing—& in fact a compromise between the two standards would be what they could not object to if the U.S. should find it proper to consent thereto, & thus give up in part the advantage arising from the standard of the price of articles of French production alone. In either case there would be a considerable gain.

The statement which I recieved from the bankers the 5th. inst. was as follows—Cash on hand & 1000 bonds to be delivered 5,730,000 florins. Interest between this & the first of March next, together with the late payment of 1,625,000 florins to France and ƒ123,750 of your draughts, they state at 2,670,000 florins—leaving a balance of 3,060,000 florins disponible. For accuracy however you may add 30,000 florins to this balance, as they by error had considered one of the 4. p. cent loans as a 5. p. cent one. The interest on the Antwerp loan of 2,050,000 florins should be deducted as I shall not open a loan there so long as matters remain in this present situation. This will give you Sir a full idea of the cash on hand.

I have also given orders to the bankers to proceed in procuring bills to pay off the debt, which your letter of March 5. 92. told me the reimbursement of would be acceptable. They have procured as many as a rise in the exchange (which they say will be momentary) has allowed them. In the mean time I am expecting an answer which will instruct me, to whom these bills should be addressed.

The letters which I have had the honor of writing to you since my arrival here (you have acknowleged the reciept of those from Paris except one short one of a line, merely to announce to you the opening of the second 4. p. cent loan) [19] have been dated June 28 Aug. 6. 30. Those which you have done me the honor to write to me, as mentioned as low down as July 25.—have been successively recieved.

I have now only to ask pardon for interrupting your more im-

19. Short announced this loan in a letter to H dated May 26, 1792. This letter has not been found. For a description of the 1792 four percent Holland loan, see Short to H, June 28, 1792, note 17.

portant occupations by so long a letter & to beg you to be assured of the sentiments of profound respect & perfect attachment with which I have the honor to be

Sir   Your most obedient &   most humble servant   W. Short

The Honble.
Alexander Hamilton Secretary of the Treasury

To ——————

Philadelphia Sept. 26.
1792

My Dear Sir

Some days since, I was surprised with the following intelligence, in a letter from Mr. King [1] (whose name I disclose to you in confidence).

"*Burr* is industrious in his Canvass and his object is well understood by our Antis. Mr. Edwards is to make interest for him in Connecticut and Mr. Dallas, who is here, and quite in the circle of the Governor and the party informs us, that Mr. Burr will be supported as Vice President in Pensylvania. Nothing which has heretofore happened so decisively proves the inveteracy of the opposition. Should they succeed much would be to be apprehended"

Though in my situation I deem it most proper to avoid interference in any matter relating to the elections for Members of the Government—Yet I feel reasons of sufficient force to induce a departure from that rule in the present instance.

Mr. Burr's integrity as an Individual is not unimpeached. As a public man he is one of the worst sort—a friend to nothing but as it suits his interest and ambition. Determined to climb to the highest honours of State, and as much higher as circumstances may permit —he cares nothing about the means of effecting his purpose. Tis evident that he aims at putting himself at the head of what he calls the "popular party" as affording the best tools for an ambitious man to work with. Secretly turning Liberty into ridicule he, knows as well as most men how to make use of the name. In a word, if we have an embryo-Cæsar in the United States 'tis Burr.

AL, Hamilton Papers, Library of Congress.
1. See Rufus King to H, September 17, 1792. See also H to ———, September 21, 1792; H to King, September 23, 1792.

To William Ellery

[*Philadelphia, September 26, 1792*. On October 9, 1792, Ellery wrote to Hamilton and referred to "your letter of the 26th of the last month." *Letter not found.*]

To Samuel Gerry

Treasury Department, September 26, 1792. "I have directed another Thermometer to be sent. . . .[1] The article being an expensive one, it is necessary that care be taken for its preservation."

LC, Essex Institute, Salem, Massachusetts.
1. See H to Gerry, August 18, 1792.

To Henry Lutterloh

[*Philadelphia, September 26, 1792*. On the back of a letter which Lutterloh wrote to Hamilton on September 9, 1792, Hamilton wrote: "Answered Sep. 26. 1792." *Letter not found.*]

To John F. Mercer [1]

Introductory Note

This letter marks the beginning of a protracted dispute between Mercer and Hamilton. In 1792 Mercer was a candidate for reelection to the

ADF, Hamilton Papers, Library of Congress.
1. Mercer, a member of a prominent Virginia family, had served during the American Revolution as an aide-de-camp to Major General Charles Lee and as a lieutenant colonel in the Virginia Militia. After the war he studied law at Fredericksburg and was elected to the Virginia House of Delegates in 1782 and again in 1785–1786. In the interim he represented Virginia in the Continental Congress. In the mid-seventeen-eighties he moved to Maryland

House of Representatives from Maryland's Second District. He was opposed by John Thomas of Susquehanna. During the campaign Mercer made a series of speeches in which he criticized Hamilton's administration of financial affairs. Mercer contended that the Secretary had paid more than the market price for stock when purchasing on behalf of the commissioners of the sinking fund; that through the agency of twenty-four Congressmen under his direct control Hamilton had usurped the fiscal prerogatives of the House of Representatives; and that in addition to aiding speculators in other ways he had exhibited his favoritism by giving the 1791 contract for supplying the western Army to William Duer in the face of equally favorable bids by other contractors.[2]

One of Mercer's leading critics in the campaign was David Ross [3] of Frederick County, Maryland. Ross had at first intended to run against Mercer for the congressional seat from the Second District but later withdrew in favor of Thomas.[4] Mercer's campaign remarks first came to Hamilton's attention with the publication on September 20, 1792, in *The* [Annapolis] *Maryland Gazette* of an address by Ross to "The Citizens of Anne-Arundel and Prince-George's county." This statement was a reply to one of Mercer's speeches at Prince George's Court House. The sections of the article which concern Hamilton and the Treasury Department read as follows:

"2. The second ground of my objection was, his impeaching the abilities of the secretary of your treasury, and the existing measure of the government, by reprobating the funding system, and asserting the six per cents were irredeemable for ever, if not redeemed within the 12 years. Here I again apprehend the colonel is very much mistaken; and, indeed, let any one read your six per cents, and he will have no doubt but that the government may pay off the whole principal, even a hundred years hence, without any breach of faith, law or contract; and so far from the irredeemable part of the funding system being faulty, that it has been one of the great means of giving the American paper a preference to the European. For what inducement could a foreigner have to sell his stock in his own country and bring his money here to buy in America, if the government could, the very next moment, reduce it to four per cent. or pay off the principal?

"But the cry of col. Mercer is, we can now borrow in Europe as much money as we please at four per cent. but the secretary's system has saddled us with six per cent. and we have not the liberty to pay either

and was a delegate from that state to the Federal Convention of 1787, where he was an outspoken Antifederalist. He was a member of the Maryland House of Delegates for the terms 1788–1789 and 1791–1792, and in 1791 he was elected to the House of Representatives to replace William Pinkney, who had resigned.

2. For a description of this controversial contract, see "Contract for Army Rations," October 28, 1790, and H to William Duer, April 7, 1791.

3. Ross had served during the American Revolution as a major in Grayson's Additional Continental Regiment. After the war he had practiced law and managed his family's extensive estates in Frederick County. From 1786 to 1788 he was a delegate to the Continental Congress from Maryland.

4. *The* [Annapolis] *Maryland Gazette,* September 20, 1792.

with four per cent. interest, or even to pay the principal, or any part of it, where the day of payment has elapsed. The gentleman does not reflect that it has been under this our secretary's prudent administration that we have acquired a national character, and enables the government to borrow these large sums he speaks of, and also that the only evidence he produces against the funding system, is this good effect, partly derived from the very system itself. Therefore I apprehend col. Mercer is not only mistaken in his ideas of the funding system, but particularly so in a very plain case, that of the six per cents not being redeemable for ever after the present times of payment have lapsed, which is additional evidence that there is a defect in his political character.

"3. The third ground is, his endeavouring to prejudice the people particularly against one of the measures of your government, that of the excise. This I apprehend is from his want of reflecting, that the reason it was formerly 'so odious to America,' is now done away by our independence. For, before the British government would have reaped the benefit at our expence, but since our independence the former objection to this kind of revenue does not exist, or at least there are no modes of taxation but what objections equally founded might be made against them. I will presume this also an error in judgment, rather than wilful intention to disgust you with your administration but, in either case, is it not an objection to his being re-elected?

"4. The fourth ground is, his publicly impeaching 24 of your members of congress, not only without naming them, but also without any kind of evidence offered to enable the audience to conclude, that it was any thing more than his assertion. Thus ungenerously confounding the innocent with the guilty, (if any there are) since the suspicions of the public must of course include the whole body, for want of opportunity of discriminating, by their names not being given by col. Mercer and thus destroying the confidence of the people in their administrators, on which their happiness so much depends; and, admitting for a moment the fact to be as he represents, yet, the very imprudence of asserting such a thing without discrimination or evidence, is proof of his unfitness to represent the prudence of liberality of our district, it being, in his own words, 'one of the most enlightened districts in the whole state.'

"5. The fifth ground is, col. Mercer's publicly impeaching the integrity of your secretary of the treasury, saying, in effect, that 'he was both buyer and seller of stock;' that 'he had purchased in such a manner as to favour a particular set of men;' that 'he gave 20s. when others were buying at 18s.' and that 'he gave 18s. when he was *offered* at 14s.' Now, Gentlemen, as I have the highest opinion of the secretary's integrity, I cannot possibly help what my own feelings suggested on this occasion, which is, that col. Mercer is at least very much mistaken; or, admitting for a moment what he says to be true, that he was yet equally imprudent in thus publicly bringing forward charges of such importance without the least degree of proof whatever being offered by him—and, Gentlemen, is not the natural presumption, if he is so imprudent to charge so boldly without offering testimony, in a case of such importance, that he will be equally so in other matters of consequence.

"6. When I represented to him the impropriety of charging the secretary without producing some proof and that it was one of the grounds of my opposition to his being re-elected, his reply was, that 'he thought himself justifiable in saying every thing he *believed* of the secretary, because he could trace the present opposition to his election up to the secretary himself.' I consider him as much mistaken here as he is in your secretary's wanting integrity, which is additional evidence of his unfitness to represent you, and you must have too high an opinion of even the strict propriety of the secretary's conduct, to believe him capable of interfering in our elections, at least till sufficient proof is brought to establish it." [5]

On September 27, 1792, in *The Maryland Gazette*, Mercer answered Ross's article. The sections concerning Hamilton and the Treasury Department read as follows:

"To curtail . . . as much as possible, I shall take in one view the Major's six per cents, which, to decypher would set at defiance the combined powers of Euclid and Newton—his excise, of which he discovers the most solemn ignorance . . . the stockjobbing—and a *private conversation* respecting the secretary's opposition to me—as they comprise what relates to that officer. . . . That I became acquainted with him at an early period of the war, before he had experienced the smiles of fortune, and when surrounding clouds had cast a dark gloom over the American cause. That I had never any difference with him; and, amidst the numerous assemblages I have addressed, I am persuaded that any real, independent, and disinterested friend of that gentleman, must have been satisfied with the delicacy of my conduct—perhaps an idle generosity led me too far in speaking of his merits.

"With respect to that in which I had opposed his measures, I stated that it was, in the first instance, in defence of my own rights, those of my constituents, the most sacred principle of our constitution, and the palladium of all free government—that the people should not be taxed but by their representatives. On a proposition in congress to refer to the secretary of the treasury to report the amount of the sums of money wanted, and the manner in which it should be raised,[6] I objected—that the right of the representatives to originate a money-bill

5. *The Maryland Gazette*, September 20, 1792.
6. Mercer is apparently referring to a resolution introduced in the House of Representatives during the debate on "An Act for making farther and more effectual Provision for the Protection of the Frontiers of the United States" (1 *Stat.* 241–43 [March 5, 1792]) which provided for three additional regiments. This resolution concerned the expenses which would be incurred by raising these regiments and reads as follows: "*Resolved*, That the Secretary of the Treasury be directed to report to the House the *Ways and Means*, by which, in his opinion, the additional sums necessary for the public service ought to be raised." The resolution was tabled but was brought up again on March 7, when it precipitated "warm and animated debate" ([Philadelphia] *Gazette of the United States*, March 10, 1792). On March 7 the resolution was passed by a vote of thirty-one to twenty-seven in the following form: "That the Secretary of the Treasury be directed to report to this House his opinion of the best mode for raising the additional supplies requisite for the ensuing year" (*Annals of Congress*, III, 437–52).

or tax, was the soul of their existence—that it was incommunicable; that we could not even make such a reference to the senate (part of the legislature.) That to give the purse-strings of our constituents into the hands of the executive, who held also the sword—who were divided from us with such caution by the constitution, and to the treasury, that part of the executive possessed of the only means of corruption, was treason against the constitution, and suicide with respect to ourselves. That, although we should still have to pass on the tax-bill which he would originate, yet reason would tell us, and experience has shewn us, that this was only nominal—for, when once the subject was referred, he might keep it until a majority was ready to receive it as he pleased—and to so late a period, that anxiety to get home would prevent all opposition, which those who have served in legislative bodies are all but too well apprized of—that when it made its appearance it would be as it had been—you must take the secretary's plan, or he will not be responsible; how can he be responsible for the good effects of a plan which he disapproves, and that he disapproves of yours is evident from his having proposed another. And, admitting that you could convince the whole house that his plan was wrong, and that you could propose another that was undeniably better, yet, as it must be committed to the execution of the secretary, who, on the rejection of his own, would feel his reputation at stake to disgrace yours, no man in his senses would risk his credit on the event—so that, in fact, all opposition would be as it had been, impossible; and we were actually more insignificant, and in a less eligible situation, than the old parliaments of Paris, called up to register the edicts of the court, for they were never blamed by the people, who knew their want of power; but here we bore all the blame of odious taxes originating with others, and rightly too, because we betrayed the trust reposed in us by the constitution—and, to illustrate this, I referred to the EXCISE—the tax devised by the secretary of the treasury. . . .[7]

"I considered that gentleman as the most improper person in the government to originate a tax; not appointed by the people, nor responsible to them, he may oppress them, and they cannot remove him; shut up in a luxurious city, surrounded by splendour, and at the fountain head, where the collected wealth of all America is poured out, he can neither know the interests, nor sympathise with the distress, of those who earn their bread by the sweat of their brow—of those distant millions, who planted throughout the American soil, must work to starve where they first drew their breath. When the first congress under the new government exercised themselves the great power conferred on them by the people—coming from all parts of the union, with the varied and diversified information of each distant district, they brought into

7. "An Act repealing, after the last day of June next, the duties heretofore laid upon Distilled Spirits imported from abroad, and laying others in their stead; and also upon Spirits distilled within the United States, and for appropriating the same" (1 *Stat.* 199–214 [March 3, 1791]). These statements paraphrase Mercer's speech in the House on January 27, 1792, on the "bill for making further and more effectual provision for the protection of the frontiers of the United States" (*Annals of Congress*, III, 349–54).

one view that combined knowledge that enabled them to form the first impost law [8]—a law that gave universal satisfaction to the continent, and brought millions into the general treasury—but when they shamefully gave up their sacred trust to the secretary, he instantly introduced the most detestable of all taxes, the excise, which has alienated the affections of the people, and as yet produced only 400,000 dollars. . . . Such then is the tax devised by a man, not elected by and not responsible to the mass of society, who has only to accommodate his measures to a monied interest and a few influential individuals. Behold also, the last impost law,[9] crammed down our throats by the tomahawk suspended over a defenceless frontier, in order to help manufacturing scrip. . . .

"The second instance in which I objected to the measures of the secretary, arose on his proposition to fund the *unsubscribed debt* of the United States, upon the principles of the former funding system, which, in my conscience, I did and do think, and can demonstrate, were equally ruinous to the country and the stockholder. . . .

"As to the stockjobbing business, giving more for stock at market than the current price, and more than it was offered at, I must refer for a full explanation of the subject to my speech in congress on that occasion, where the facts are stated and the proofs, and where the law was altered to prevent such improper conduct for the future.

"The story of the secretary's opposition to me stands thus: In private conversation with major Ross, (but it seems that the most sacred laws of society are to be violated with respect to my conversation) when I endeavoured to beg off from this news-paper controversy I gave much the information he states, and gave him my reasons, which his candour led him to suppress—that a young gentleman, whose name will not be mentioned, unless required, as his future prospects are much dependent on men in power, told Mr. Sprigg, my father-in-law,[10] that gen. Heister,[11] (whose reputation is well known) told him at Hagar's-town, that there certainly would be great opposition made against my re-election, . . . and that the secretary of the treasury was at the bottom of it. . . ." [12]

A second and more serious phase of the controversy began on October 21, 1792, when Washington wrote the following letter to Dr. David Stuart: [13]

8. "An Act for laying a Duty on Goods, Wares, and Merchandises imported into the United States" (1 *Stat.* 24–27 [July 4, 1789]).

9. "An Act for raising a farther sum of money for the protection of the frontiers, and for other purposes therein mentioned" (1 *Stat.* 259–63 [May 2, 1792]).

10. Richard Sprigg of Anne Arundel County, Maryland. In 1785 Mercer had married Sprigg's daughter Sophia.

11. Daniel Hiester had served as a colonel and brigadier general of militia during the American Revolution and as a member of the Supreme Executive Council of Pennsylvania from 1784 to 1786. In 1792 he was a member of the House of Representatives from Maryland.

12. *The Maryland Gazette*, September 27, 1792.

13. Stuart was a physician in Fairfax County, Virginia, and a friend of Washington. He was one of the commissioners to survey and superintend the development of the new Federal City.

"You informed me when I was at George Town on my way to this City, that Colo. Mercer, upon receiving, or being told of Colo. Hamiltons letter to him requesting to know if the words with which he was charged by Major Ross as having uttered in his public harangues against the conduct of the Secretary of the Treasury were true expressed, if I understood you rightly, much surprise at the application; as *he Colo. Hamilton* must be conscious of his having attempted to *bribe him Colo. Mercer* to vote for a further assumption of the State debts [14]— and that this surprize was expressed at a public *table* before many gentlemen.

"This is a charge of so serious a nature that it is incumbent on Colo. Hamilton to clear it up—or for the President of the U States to take notice of it. For this reason, before I communicate the matter to Colo. Hamilton, I beg to be informed whether I precisely understood the information you gave me, and, in that case, who were the persons that heard Colo. Mercer expresss himself to that effect.

"It was my intention to have asked this at the time you mentioned the matter but I was diverted from it by something that occurred at the moment, and the variety of things which have been thrown in my way since I came to this place have prevented it till now." [15]

Stuart replied on November 5 as follows: "I recieved your letter of the 21st ulmo a few days ago, but deferred answering it, 'till I could again see Mr. [William] Bayly, & Mr [Daniel] Carroll of Duddington, my informants respecting Col'l Mercer's speech. Inclosed, I send you Mr. Bayly's certificate of what passed.[16] Mr. Carroll tho' he agrees with Mr Bayly, that Coll. Mercer expressed himself as stated, has I know not for what reasons declined sending me his certificate, as he promised. The conversation happened at dinner at Marlborough, in the presence of many and I have heard it spoke of by many since, and with but little variation. Mr. Samuel Hanson among others, informed me as I passed through Alexa., that his Brother Coll. Thomas Hanson, who heard Coll.

14. This incident apparently took place in the spring of 1792 during the debates on "An Act supplementary to the act making provision for the Debt of the United States" (1 *Stat.* 281–83 [May 8, 1792]).

15. ADfS, RG 59, Miscellaneous Letters, 1790–1799, National Archives.

16. The statement of William Bayly, a Montgomery County planter, reads as follows: "On Tuesday the second day of the Election, at upper Marlbro, after I got there, I heard that Colo Mercer had said that Mr Hamilton the Secretary had offered him money if he would vote for the assumption. I asked Colo. Mercer if he had said so. He answered yes, by God he had. Mr. W[alter] Bowie who was sitting by Colo. Mercer, said it was in a jocular way. I then asked Colo. Mercer if he thought Mr. Hamilton was serious or jesting. He answered that he had a right to take it either way. I repeated the same question to which he made the same answer. But said he would tell me how it was. He then said He had been down at Mr. Hamiltons office in order to settle some accounts, or to receive some money that was due him from the U States, but that Mr Hamiltons Clerks or understrapers would not pay it. And on Colo. Mercers return from the office he met Mr Hamilton who observed to him, if he would vote for the assumption He (Mr Hamilton) would pay the money" (copy, Hamilton Papers, Library of Congress).

This copy of Bayly's certificate was enclosed in Uriah Forrest to H, November 7, 1792.

Mercer, at the same time with Mr. Bayly, had given him the same idea of Coll. Hamilton's having offered Coll. Mercer a bribe, as is certified by Mr. Bayly. From my acquaintance with Mr. Bayly, and his general character, I think him as much to be depended on, as any man in the State of Maryland and, if it is thought proper to investigate the charge, I am satisfied Mr. Bayly's certificate can never be done away." [17]

Mercer's statement on his remarks on the alleged bribe is contained in an undated letter to Walter Bowie and Richard Sprigg, presumably written as a result of Washington's inquiries into the matter. This letter reads as follows:

"On the second day of the late election for the second District, Mr. Mercer being informed at upper Marlbro', that Mr. Hamilton had written a letter to Major Ross, and another to himself,[18] copies of which were soon procur'd. On Mr. Mercer's reading them he observed his expressions were entirely perverted by Mr. Hamilton, and that he had said nothing in public or private that could warrant the turn given to them by Mr. Hamilton, & added that the taking a part of what he had said seemed to be a favorite mode with his adversaries, & that his private conversations had been brought forward against him in the same manner, & only such mutilated parts repeated as would suit sinister purposes. . . .[19] That this was a dangerous mode of proceedure, and entirely subversive of private confidence between man & man, & that if Mr. Mercer cou'd have prevailed on himself to adopt similar arts, he could on the same principles have taken much more serious advantages of Colo. Hamilton, Mr. Gale & several others who had become his adversaries; as for instance, he could with perfect truth say, that Mr. Hamilton had offered him a sum of money to vote for the assumption, but that it was proper that the whole story should be related—it had arose in this manner. On the limitation being removed by Congress,[20] Mr. Mercer had produced a charge, duly authenticated, among other charges, for

17. ALS, Hamilton Papers, Library of Congress.

18. H to Mercer, September 26, 1792, and H to Ross, September 26, 1792.

19. Presumably these "conversations" occasioned the rumors which reached Washington in October, 1792, that statements were being circulated by Mercer and his supporters that Mercer's election to Congress was favored by Washington. See *The Maryland Gazette*, October 4, 1792. These claims were brought to Washington's attention by George Gale, supervisor of the revenue for Maryland (Gale to Washington, September 23, 1792, ALS, George Washington Papers, Library of Congress). For the President's reaction, see *GW*, XXXII, 147, 155, 165–66.

20. "An Act providing for the settlement of the Claims of Persons under particular circumstances barred by the limitations heretofore established" provided that the acts of limitation passed by the Continental Congress during the Confederation "so far as they have barred, or may be construed to bar the claims of any officer, soldier, artificer, sailor or marine of the late army or navy of the United States, for personal services rendered to the United States, in the military or naval department, shall from and after the passing of this act, be suspended, for and during the term of two years. And that every such officer, soldier, artificer, sailor and marine having claims for services rendered to the United States, in the military or naval departments, who shall exhibit the same, for liquidation, at the treasury of the United States, at any time during the said term of two years, shall be entitled to an adjustment,

an horse wch. was killed under him by the Enemy in the action of Green Spring, for which he had given 45 Guineas not three hours before—that the Comptroller refused it; upon which Mr Mercer told him that he believed that he would not have refused any other man on the Continent such a claim. On quitting him & going down Stairs he met Colo. Hamilton at the door, to whom he observed that he had had a very just claim rejected & stated what it was. Colo. Hamilton remark'd in a jocular manner that the limitation had been removed only with respect to personal services, & that unless he, Colo. Mercer, could prove that he & his Horse were one person, it could not pass. Mr. Mercer observed that the charge arose from rendering such personal services as required indispensably an Horse, & therefore he imagined it must be included by the Act, Mr. Hamilton replied that to cut the matter short he had only to vote for the assumption & he would pay the Account out of his own pocket. Mr Mercer was then asked whether he thought Colo. Hamilton in earnest. He replied instantly—certainly he could not have taken him in earnest, or he must have knocked him down if he was able. At Dinner, several hours afterwards, Mr. Bailly asked Mr. Mercer whether he had said that Mr. Hamilton had offered him money to vote for the assumption. Mr. Mercer replied yes, but that it was necessary to relate the whole story, which he immediately did as nearly as possible to the above; but reflecting that some such use might be made of it as had been of whatever he had said, he desired Mr. Bailly to bring him pen, ink & paper, & that he could commit to writing what he had said, that no mistakes cou'd then arise & that he might make any use of it that he pleased. This Mr. Bailly declined saying it was only for his own satisfaction. . . ." [21]

The details of the dispute between Hamilton and Mercer are contained in the following documents: H to Mercer, September 26, November 3, December 6, December, 1792, March 1, 14, 1793; Mercer to H, October 16–28, December, 1792, January 31, March 5, 26, 1793; H to Ross, September 26, November 3, 1792; Ross to H, October 5–10, November 23, 1792, March 13, April 8, 25, July 23, August 30, 1793; Uriah Forrest to H, November 7, 1792; "Statement on Remarks by John F. Mercer," April, 1793.

Philadelphia September 26th
1792

Sir

In a publication signed "David Ross" in the Maryland Gazette of the 20th instant,[22] stating certain grounds of objection to your re-

---

and allowance thereof on the same principles, as if the same had been exhibited, within the term prescribed by the aforesaid resolutions of Congress: *Provided,* That nothing herein shall be construed to extend to claims for rations or subsistence money" (1 *Stat.* 245 [March 27, 1792]).

21. Copy, Hamilton Papers, Library of Congress.

22. At this point H wrote and crossed out "I find it is stated, among other things, that you asserted in some public discourse."

election, I find the following passage—"The fifth ground is Col Mercer's publickly impeaching the integrity of your Secretary of the Treasury saying in effect 'that he was both buyer and seller of Stock' that 'he had purchased in such a manner as to favour a particular set of men' that 'he gave 20/ when others were buying at 18/' and that 'he gave 18/ when he was *offered* at 14/.' "

As assertions of this kind impeaching the rectitude of my conduct both as a public officer and as a man call upon me to pursue means for a full and effectual[23] investigation and vindication, I am to request as a preliminary measure, that you will inform me, as speedily as possible,[24] how far Mr. Ross's statement is accurate or otherwise—in other words what you did really say, upon the occasion alluded to.

I take it for granted, that you cannot have publicly alleged any thing which you will not be willing explicitly to avow.

I trust also, that you will not only state with precision what you may have asserted, but the grounds of it, with as much particularity of time place and circumstance, as the nature of the case will admit.

I am Sir   Your humble servant

Mercer Esqr

23. H substituted "effectual" for "complete."
24. At this point H substituted "as speedily as possible" for "with precision and explicitness."

To David Ross [1]

Philadelphia September
26. 1792

Sir

I have this day seen a publication in the Maryland Gazette of the 20th instant, signed by you, in which among other things, you state Mr Mercers having brought a charge of a very serious nature against me. I allude to the fifth ground of objection, stated by you, to his reelection.

I have written to Mr Mercer a letter of which a copy is inclosed.[2] Allow me at the same time to ask of you to revise your recollection of what was said by him, in relation to me, and to favour me with the result, stating as accurately as possible his precise expressions, and giving as much particularity as you can to the whole matter.

I feel myself indebted to you for the favourable sentiments you have so openly expressed of my character and principles; and I pledge myself to you and to every friend of mine that the strictnest scrutiny into every part of my conduct, whether as a private citizen or as a public officer, can only serve to establish the perfect purity of it, and to prove incontestibly that it has never deviated from the most exact line of the most scrupulous probity. Arraigned, as I appear to have been, I feel myself justifiable in making this strong declaration in my own favour.

According to the statement you have made of Mr. Mercers assertions, they amount to a gross and wicked slander; as a thorough investigation shall evince.

I have not only never bought nor sold, nor been concerned directly or indirectly in the buying or selling of Stock or Certificates since I have been in my present office (except as will be presently explained) but I do not now recollect, that I ever sold a certificate, in my life, or was ever interested in any sold by any other person; and all the buying of Certificates (except as hereafter mentioned) in which I now recollect to have ever had any interest or concern was for the purpose of paying for a share in two several tracts of land, in the purchase of which I became interested. This too was a considerable time prior to adoption of the present constitution.

The exceptions above made relate wholly to *purchases* of the public Debt, on account of the United States, by the Commissioners of the sinking fund. As one of that board, I have had an official concern in directing those purchases, the immediate agents of which, by *appointment of the board,* have been Samuel Meredith Treasurer of the United States, William Seton Cashier of the Bank of New York, Benjamin Lincoln Collector of Boston, and William Heth Collector of Bermuda Hundred all men of exemplary reputation for integrity. As Secretary of the Treasury, it fell to my lot to instruct those Agents in the details of their purchases, in conformity to law; but the actual execution of the business was with them.

I add, though it is extraordinary and disgustful, that any occasion should have called for such a declaration on my part, that I never had directly or indirectly, any species of interest in any stock or

Certificate, which has been purchased by either of those Agents, or in any manner, by the authority of the abovementioned Commissioners; and that what Mr Mercer is stated to have said in reference to it is gross misrepresentation.

You are at liberty to make any use of this letter you may think proper, not including its insertion in a News Paper; which I should not think compatible with the decorum of my situation.

With real esteem & regard I have the honor to be Sir Your obed serv

P S To avoid Cavil, I think it well to add that while in practice as a lawyer, long before my appointment to my present office I received a small payment in Indents on account of a fee for one of my Clerks which completes the whole of my certificate transactions.[3]

ADf, Hamilton Papers, Library of Congress; broadside, Rare Book Room, Library of Congress.
  1. For background to this letter, see the introductory note to H to John F. Mercer, September 26, 1792.
  2. See H to Mercer, September 26, 1792.
  3. On the left-hand margin of the draft H mistakenly designated the addressee of this letter as "Col Mercer." At the end of the broadside copy the following sentence appears: "Be so good as to forward the enclosed immediately to colonel Mercer."

To George Washington [1]

Treasury Departmt. Septr. 26th. 1792.

Sir,

The Post of yesterday brought me your letter of the 21st instant, with the Proclamation enclosed, which was immediately published through the Secretary of State's Office in Brown's Federal Gazette; [2] and means will be taken to accelerate a general circulation of it.

I have the honor to be with the highest respect & truest attachment.

Sir, Your most Obedient and humble servant

Alexander Hamilton

LC, George Washington Papers, Library of Congress.
  1. For background to this letter, see H to Tench Coxe, September 1, 1792;

H to Washington, September 1, 8, first letter of September 9, September 11, 22, 1792; H to John Jay, September 3, 1792; "Draft of a Proclamation Concerning Opposition to the Excise Law," September 7, 1792; Jay to H, September 8, 1792; Edmund Randolph to H, September 8, 1792; Washington to H, September 7, two letters of September 17, September 21, 1792.

2. The proclamation appeared in the September 25, 1792, issue of *The* [Philadelphia] *Federal Gazette and Philadelphia Daily Advertiser,* published by Andrew Brown.

From Rufus King

[New York] 27 Sep. 1792

Care has been taken to put our friends at the eastward on their guard.[1] Measures have been pursued to ascertain opinions in different quarters, and on this as on a former occasion,[2] the object may be silently abandoned should it appear absolutely desperate. If Clinton should be supported this will be the case; if not the Party must resort to some other *northern* character, hence the Hopes of this gentleman.

The conversation with Mr. Dallas,[3] passed between him & me, and it would not be well that I should be publickly quoted—as he was almost all his Time with the Party here. I dont find that I can obtain such a Letter as you propose.[4]

Mr. Jay who returned yesterday, unwell, sent me your Letter of the 17th.[5] I wish that the Proclamation[6] may produce the Effects you promise yourself. If the Country will support the judiciary all will be well. My apprehensions on this point led me to wish the Effort to be made under circumstances the most favorable to its success. I like as little as you possibly can do, the omission of the Executive to exercise its power on a plain and important occasion— still allowances must be made for the actual condition in which we find ourselves. You cannot stop with the Proclamation unless the opposition subsides. The Executive must proceed, & if requisite force must be employed to carry the Law into Effect.

One good point will be secured by the Proclamation, which possibly would have been precarious without it. There might have been a disinclination to enforce the Law, had its violation been submitted to legislative consideration previous to any step on the part of the Executive to carry it into execution. This cannot be the case now.

The good from inclination, & others from a less worthy motive will support the executive and enforce the Law.

Yrs &c	R King

ALS, Hamilton Papers, Library of Congress.

1. King is referring to the possibility that Aaron Burr would be a presidential candidate. See H to ———, September 21, 27, 1792; King to H, September 17, 1792; H to King, September 23, 1792.

2. King is referring to Burr's candidacy for governor of New York in the April, 1792, election against the incumbent, George Clinton. On March 15, 1792, a month before the election, Burr had indicated that he would not run (The [New York] Daily Advertiser, March 24, 1792).

3. Alexander Dallas was secretary of the Commonwealth of Pennsylvania and a leading Republican of Pennsylvania.

4. See H to King, September 23, 1792.

5. Letter not found.

6. For background concerning the proclamation, see H to Tench Coxe, September 1, 1792; H to George Washington, September 1, 8, first letter of September 9, September 11, 22, 26, 1792; H to John Jay, September 3, 1792; "Draft of a Proclamation Concerning Opposition to the Excise Law," September 7, 1792; Jay to H, September 8, 1792; Edmund Randolph to H, September 8, 1792; Washington to H, September 7, two letters of September 17, September 21, 1792.

To James McHenry

[Philadelphia, September 27, 1792. On September 30, 1792, McHenry wrote to Hamilton: "I received . . . yours of the 27th." Letter not found.]

Treasury Department Circular to the Commissioners of Loans

Treasury Department
September 27th. 1792

Sir,

The Comptroller of the Treasury [1] being absent, I have found it necessary to avoid an interruption of the public business, to direct Mr Henry Kuhl his principal Clerk to countersign the warrants of transfer until his return; you will therefore regard his signature (a specimen of which is here enclosed) as authentic and enter the warrants thus countersigned on your Books as in the other case. The Comptroller on his return will announce it to you which will terminate the object of this instruction.

I am Sir, with consideration   Your obedt Servant

Alexander Hamilton

LS, to Thomas Smith, from the original in the New York State Library, Albany; LS, dated September 29, 1792, The Huntington Library, San Marino, California.
1. Oliver Wolcott, Jr.

From George Clymer [1]

[Pittsburgh, September 28, 1792]

Sir

The last article in the order of my instructions [2] was as I conceived to be the first on my arrival here—for as my reception should be so might be my success in every of my objects. I therefore obtained a meeting with several of the principal characters, and the better to gain their confidence made a full disclosure to them of my whole business. They all of them gave assurances that the town of Pittsburgh had no representation whatever in the committee which sat there on the 21 August, nor as they believed the County of Allegany at large, and that the town had not been at all in sentiment with the committee.[3] I observed that as the proceedings of the committee stood published to the world it appeared otherwise, and as Pittsburgh was well known through the Union as the capital of the western Country the more effect it gave to those proceedings; but as the town took in reality no part therein a publick disavowal of them would be honourable to it and well thought of by government. They replied that as individuals such declaration would not well become them, but that they would take measures to assemble the inhabitants on the occasion—And there is a call for them accordingly for to-morrow evening. I have recommended to some of the Gentlemen that if the attempt at something beyond it has a chance of provoking an opposition the end of which might not be foreseen, to confine themselves simply to a disavowal of the proceedings in question on the score of having had no part therein.

Understanding that Mr Cannon, their chairman [4] was not a man of the strongest mind I requested General Wayne [5] to send for him under pretence of consulting him about supplies &c—and by this means obtained a private interview with him. I represented to him his particular predicament as the chairman in a light so strong as thoroughly to frighten him. He asked my advice. I then hinted that a publick declaration that having now had time to reflect on the business of the Committee he disapproved of it, and of the part he had had in it, engaging my honour in that case to represent him favourably to government, which having its choice of objects might pass him by in a prosecution. He promised to give the matter a very serious consideration and if he does not soon fall into bad hands some fruit may be expected from it. A desertion in one set up as a leader would I conceive go further to break the measures of this seditious confederacy than even the most successful prosecution. Why I make any present mention of this Affair is that if it should be thought well of, any process with respect to him might be suspended for a little while until the part he takes shall be known.

Captain Faulkener's deposition is just finished and comes under cover [6]—as will that of some others. It being represented to me on all hands that I cannot venture to shew my self in Washington I have written to the judge of the district (state) Court [7] to take depositions —and have named the persons to him who may be examined.

I had written this length for the post when I was honoured with yours of the 21st.[8] This in some measures confines my measures to the Washington transactions and gives a new designation to the witnesses who are now to proceed to York instead of Philadelphia. These additional instructions I shall pay due regard to. In my passage upwards through the different Counties I had the most satisfactory assurances of a pretty general acquiescence in the Excise—the people of the Country having had time to compare its lightness with the heaviness of a tax in any other form. I believe that some examples being made to justice that but little difficulty will attend its execution. I should however make some exceptions here—several gentlemen friends to the government having told me that the scarcity of specie in this Country will always make a natural difficulty in the collection even when opposition ceases—the distillations being very extensive indeed.

I have the honour to be   Sir   Your most obedt servt

Geo Clymer

Pittsburgh Sept. 28. 1792.

Secretary of the Treasury.   I shall now either bring the depositions with me or send them on to York instead of transmitting them to Philadela.

ALS, Connecticut Historical Society, Hartford.

1. For background to this letter, see H to Tench Coxe, September 1, 1792; H to George Washington, September 1, 8, first letter of September 9, September 11, 22, 26, 1792; H to John Jay, September 3, 1792; "Draft of a Proclamation Concerning Opposition to the Excise Law," September 7, 1792; Jay to H, September 8, 1792; Edmund Randolph to H, September 8, 1792; Washington to H, September 7, two letters of September 17, September 21, 1792; Rufus King to H, September 27, 1792.

2. Clymer's instructions concerning his journey to western Pennsylvania are listed in numerical order in H to Coxe, September 1, 1792. On September 6, 1792, Coxe wrote to Clymer: "You will find in this inclosure a copy of a letter to me from the Secretary of the Treasury, which I mentioned to you in our last conversation" (LC, RG 58, Letters of Commissioner of Revenue, 1792–1793, National Archives).

3. For a description of this meeting, see H to Coxe, September 1, 1792, note 5.

4. John Cannon was chairman of the August 21–22, 1792, meeting at Pittsburgh. See H to Coxe, September 1, 1792, note 5.

5. Major General Anthony Wayne had been appointed to replace Brigadier General Arthur St. Clair, who had resigned from the Army.

6. William Faulkner's deposition is dated September 28, 1792 (DS, Pennsylvania Miscellany, Whiskey Rebellion, Vol. 1, Library of Congress).

7. Clymer's letter to Alexander Addison, dated September 28, 1792, has not been found. Addison was presiding judge of the County Court of the western district of Pennsylvania.

8. Letter not found.

From John Jay

New York 28th. Sepbr. 1792

Dr. Sir,

On Monday the 17th. inst. I set out for Sussex in New Jersey with design after dispatching some private business I had there to proceed from thence on my Circuit. On the 19th. I found myself with a slight inflamation on one eye & some flying Rheumatic pains, to which not suspecting any thing serious I paid little attention. By the 25th. my Eyes were so much inflamed that it was with difficulty I read your letter which I received that morning.[1] Throughout the course of the day those symptoms attended with a little fever increased & convinced me that I was not to be well in a few days. Under these circumstances it appeared to me best if possible to return home. I set out the next day, the weather was favorable, & I arrived with much pain the day before yesterday. Not withstanding

bleeding & physick, both inflamation & Rheumatism continue obstinate. As my eyes would not permit me to answer your letter I've sent it to Mr. King.[2] Judge Cushing [3] does not appear yet. It wd. be a sad thing if he also shd. be laid up. Respecting the duration of my confinement I can as yet form no conjectures. The moment I regain sufficient health for the purpose I shall again proceed on my circuit.
    Yours sincerely

AL, Columbia University Libraries.
    1. H's letter, which was dated September 17, 1792, has not been found.
    2. See Rufus King to H, September 27, 1792.
    3. William Cushing of Massachusetts was an associate justice of the Supreme Court. Cushing and Jay were to preside at the session of the Middle Circuit Court to be held at Trenton, New Jersey, on October 2, 1792. Cushing presided over the session alone (RG 21, Minutes of the District Court of New Jersey, 1790–1879, National Archives).

From Thomas Smith

Philadelphia, September 28, 1792. States "The amount of Stock remaining on the Books of this Office subject to Interest for the Quarter ending the 30th Septr Inst is . . . twenty seven thousand Six hundred & ninety eight dollars Nine Cents."

LC, RG 53, Pennsylvania State Loan Office, Letter Book, 1790–1794, Vol. "615-P," National Archives.

Catullus No. III [1]

[Philadelphia, September 29, 1792] [2]

FOR THE GAZETTE OF THE UNITED STATES.

ARISTIDES complains that the AMERICAN has charged Mr. Jefferson with being the patron and promoter of *national disunion, national*

[Philadelphia] *Gazette of the United States,* September 29, 1792.
    1. For background to this article, see "Catullus No. I," September 15, 1792, and "Catullus No. II," September 19, 1792. The other "Catullus" essays are dated October 17, November 24, December 22, 1792.
    2. This essay was written before September 26, 1792. On that date John Fenno, editor of the *Gazette of the United States,* noted that he had deferred publication of "Catullus No. III" in order to provide space for the first portion of the "Vindication of Mr. Jefferson" (*Gazette of the United States,* September 26, 1792).

insignificance, public disorder and discredit.[3] The American however, has only affirmed, that "the real or pretended political tenets of that gentleman *tend*" to those points.[4]

The facts which have been established clearly demonstrate, that in the form in which it is made, the charge is well founded.

If Mr. Jefferson's opposition to the funding system, to the bank, and to the other measures which are connected with the administration of the national finances had ceased, when those measures had received the sanction of law; nothing more could have been said, than, that he had transgressed the rules of official decorum, in entering the lists against the head of another department (between whom and himself, there was a reciprocal duty to cultivate harmony) that he had been culpable in pursuing a line of conduct, which was calculated to sow the seeds of discord in the executive branch of the government, in the infancy of its existence.

But when his opposition extended beyond that point; when it was apparent, that he wished to *render odious,* and of course to *subvert* (for in a popular government these are convertible terms) all those deliberate and solemn acts of the legislature, which had become the pillars of the public credit, his conduct deserved to be regarded with a still severer eye.

Whatever differences of opinion may have preceded those acts—however exceptionable particular features in them may have appeared to certain characters, there is no enlightened nor discreet citizen but must agree, that they ought *now* to remain *undisturbed.* To set afloat the funding system, after the faith of the nation had been so deliberately and solemnly pledged to it—after such numerous and extensive alienations of property for full value have been made under its sanction—with adequate revenues, little burthensome to the people—in a time of profound peace *—with not even the shadow of any public necessity—on no better ground than that of theoretical and paradoxical dogmas—would be one of the most wanton and flagitious acts, that ever stained the annals of a civilized nation.

* *The partial Indian hostilities which exist, can hardly be deemed an interruption of the general peace.*

3. For this statement by "Aristides," see "Catullus No. I," September 15, 1792, note 2.

4. H had made this charge in "An American No. I," August 4, 1792.

Yet positions tending to that disgraceful result have been maintained in public discourses, by individuals known to be devoted to the Secretary of State; [5] and have been privately smiled upon as profound discoveries in political science.

Yet the less discreet, though not least important partizans of that officer, talk familiarly of undoing the funding system as a meritorious work: Yet his Gazette (which may fairly be regarded as the mirror of his views) after having labored for months to make it an object of popular detestation, has at length told us in plain and triumphant terms, that "the funding system has had its day;" [6] and very clearly, if not expressly, that it is the object of the party to overthrow it.

The American, then, has justly, and from sufficient data, inferred, that Mr. Jefferson's politics, whatever may be the motives of them *tend* to national disunion, insignificance, disorder and discredit. That the subversion of the funding system would produce national discredit, proves itself. Loss of credit, the reason being the same, must attend nations, as well as individuals who voluntarily and without necessity, violate their formal and positive engagements.

Insignificance and disorder, as applied to communities, equally with individuals, are the natural offspring of a loss of credit, premeditatedly and voluntarily incurred.

Disunion would not long lag behind. Sober-minded and virtuous men in every State would lose all confidence in, and all respect for a government, which had betrayed so much levity and inconsistency, so profligate a disregard to the *rights of property*, and to the obligations of good faith. Their support would of course be so far withdrawn or relaxed, as to leave it an easy prey to its enemies. These comprize the advocates for separate confederacies; the jealous partizans of unlimited sovereignty, in the State governments—the never to be satiated lovers of innovation and change—the tribe of pretended philosophers, but real fabricators of chimeras and paradoxes—the Catalines and the Cæsars of the community (a description of men to be found in every republic) who leading the dance to the tune of liberty without law, endeavor to intoxicate the people with delicious but poisonous draughts to render them the easier

5. See H to Edward Carrington, May 25, 1792.
6. This statement appeared in an article signed "L" ([Philadelphia] *National Gazette*, August 8, 1792).

victims of their rapacious ambition; the vicious and the fanatical of every class who are ever found the willing or the deluded followers of those seducing and treacherous leaders.

But this is not all—the invasion of sixty millions of property could not be perpetrated without violent concussions. The States, whose citizens, both as *original* creditors and *purchasers* own the largest portions of the debt (and several such there are) would not remain long bound in the trammels of a party which had so grossly violated their rights. The consequences in experiment would quickly awaken to a sense of injured right, and interest such of them, whose representatives may have wickedly embarked, or been ignorantly betrayed into the atrocious and destructive project.

Where would all this end but in disunion and anarchy? in national disgrace and humiliation?

ARISTIDES insinuates that the AMERICAN has distinguished Mr. Jefferson as "the CATALINE of the day—the ambitious incendiary." [7] Those epithets are not to be found in either of the papers, under that signature. But the American has said, that Mr. Jefferson "has been the prompter, open or secret, of unwarrantable aspersions on men, who as long as actions, not merely professions, shall be the true test of patriotism and integrity need never decline a comparison with him of their titles to the public esteem," [8] and he is supported in the assertion by facts.

Not to cite or trace those foul and pestilent whispers, which clandestinely circulating through the country, have, as far as was practicable, contaminated some of its fairest and worthiest characters, an appeal to known circumstances will justify the charge.

Some time since, there appeared in print certain speculations, which have been construed into an advocation of hereditary distinctions in government.[9] These (whether with, or without foundation, is to this moment matter of conjecture) were ascribed to a particular character—pre-eminent for his early, intrepid, faithful, presevering

7. For this statement by "Aristides," see "Catullus No. I," September 15, 1792, note 2.
8. H is quoting the closing paragraph of "An American No. II," August 11, 1792.
9. This is a reference to a series of essays by John Adams entitled *Discourses on Davila*, which had appeared in the *Gazette of the United States*, in 1791.

and comprehensively useful services to his country—a man pure and unspotted in private life, a citizen having a high and solid title to the esteem, the gratitude and the confidence of his fellow-citizens.

The first volume of the "Rights of man"[10] makes its appearance— The opportunity is eagerly seized, to answer the double purpose of wounding a competitor and of laying in an additional stock of popularity; by associating and circulating the name of Thomas Jefferson, with a popular production of a favorite writer, on a favorite subject.

For this purpose the Secretary of State sits down and pens an epistle to a printer in the city of Philadelphia, transmitting the work for republication, and expressing his approbation of it in a way, which we learn, from the preface of that printer to his edition of the work, was calculated not only to do justice to the writings of Mr. Paine, but to do honor to Mr. Jefferson; *by directing the mind* to a contemplation of that *republican firmness* and *democratic simplicity*, which ought to *endear him* to every friend to the "Rights of Man."[11]

The letter, as we learn from the same preface, contained the following passages: "I am extremely pleased to find it will be reprinted here, and that something is at length to be publicly said against the *political heresies*, which have sprung up among us. I have no doubt

10. Part I of Thomas Paine's *Rights of Man* was published in London early in 1791. In May of the same year the first American edition was printed by Samuel Harrison Smith at Philadelphia.

11. The statement in the preface to the Smith edition of Paine's *Rights of Man* reads as follows: "The following Extract from a note accompanying a copy of this Pamphlet for republication, is so respectable a testimony of its value, that the Printer hopes the distinguished writer will excuse its present appearance. It proceeds from a character, equally eminent in the councils of America, and conversant in the affairs of France, from a long and recent residence at the Court of Versailles, in the Diplomatic department; and, at the same time that it does justice to the writings of Mr. Paine, it reflects honour on the source from which it flows, by directing the mind to a contemplation of that Republican firmness and Democratic simplicity which endear their possessor to every friend of the 'Rights of Man.'

"After some prefatory remarks, the Secretary of State observes:

" 'I am extremely pleased to find it will be reprinted here, and that some thing is at length to be publicly said against the political heresies which have sprung up among us.'

" 'I have no doubt our citizens will *rally* a second time round the *standard* of Common Sense.' " (*Rights of Man: Being an Answer to Mr. Burke's Attack on the French Revolution. By Thomas Paine, Secretary for Foreign Affairs to Congress in the American War, and Author of the Work Intitled Common Sense. Second Edition* [Philadelphia: Re-Printed by Samuel Harrison Smith, 1791].)

our citizens will *rally* a second time round the *standard* of common sense."

There was not a man in the United States, acquainted with the insinuations, which had been propagated, who did not instantly apply the remark—and the signal was so well understood by the partizans of the writer, that a general attack immediately commenced. The newspapers in different States resounded with invective and scurrility against the patriot, who was marked out as the object of persecution, and if possible of degradation.

Under certain circumstances general expressions designate a person or an object as clearly as an indication of it by name. So it happened in the present case. The Javelin went directly to its destination.

But it was quickly perceived, that discerning and respectable men disapproved the step. It was of consequence to endeavor to maintain their good opinion. Protestations, and excuses as frivolous as awkward were multiplied to veil the real design.

"The gentleman alluded to, never once entered into the mind! It was never imagined, that the printer would be so incautious as to publish the letter or any part of it—nothing more was in view than to turn a handsome period, and to avoid the *baldness* of a note that did nothing but present the compliments of the writer!"

Thus a solemn invocation to the people of America, on the most serious and important subject, dwindled at once into a brilliant conceit, that tickled the imagination too much to be resisted. The imputation of levity was preferred to that of malice.

But when the people of America presented themselves to the disturbed patriotic fancy, as a routed host, scattered and dispersed by political sorcerers; how was it possible to resist the heroic, the chivalrous desire, of erecting for them some magic standard of orthodoxy, and endeavoring to *rally* them round it, for mutual protection and safety.

In so glorious a cause, the considerations—that a citizen of the United States had written in a foreign country a book containing strictures on the government of that country, which would be regarded by it, as libellous and seditious [12]—that he had *dedicated* this

---

12. It was generally understood that Paine's *Rights of Man* was one of the publications against which the royal proclamation of May 25, 1792, concerning seditious writings was directed. The work was suppressed in England, and Paine himself was outlawed.

book to the chief magistrate of the union—that a republication of it under the auspices of the Secretary of State, would wear the appearance of its having been promoted, at least of its being patronized by the government of this country—were considerations too light and un-important to occasion a moment's hesitation or pause.

Those who, after an attentive review of circumstances, can be deceived by the artifices, which have been employed to varnish over this very exceptionable proceeding must understand little of human nature—must be little read in the history of those arts, which in all countries, and at all times have served to disguise the machinations of factious and intriguing men.

The remaining circumstance of public notoriety, which fixes upon Mr. Jefferson the imputation of being the prompter, or instigator of detraction, exists in his patronage of the National Gazette.

Can any attentive reader of that Gazette doubt, for a moment, that it has been systematically devoted to the calumniating and blackening of public characters? Can it be a question, that a main object of the paper is to destroy the public confidence in a particular public character, who it seems is to be *hunted down* at all events, for the unpardonable sin of having been the steady, invariable and decided friend of broad national principles of government? Can it be a question, that the persecution of the officer alluded to, is agreeable to the views of the institutor of the paper?

Does all this proceed from motives purely disinterested and patriotic? Can none of a different complexion be imagined, that may at least have operated to give a *stimulous* to *patriotic* zeal?

No. Mr. Jefferson has hitherto been distinguished as the quiet modest, retiring philosopher—as the plain simple unambitious republican. He shall not now for the first time be regarded as the intriguing incendiary—the aspiring turbulent competitor.

How long it is since that gentleman's real character may have *divined*, or whether this is only the *first time* that the *secret* has been disclosed, I am not sufficiently acquainted with the history of his political life to determine; But there is always "a *first time*," when characters studious of artful disguises are unveiled; When the vizor of stoicism is plucked from the brow of the Epicurean; when the plain garb of Quaker simplicity is stripped from the concealed voluptuary; when Cæsar *coyley refusing* the proffered diadem, is seen to be Cæsar *rejecting* the trappings, but tenaciously grasping the substance of imperial domination.

It is not unusual to defend one post, by attacking another. Aristides has shewn a disposition to imitate this policy. He by clear implication tells us, and doubtless means it as a justification of the person whom he defends—that attachment to *aristocracy, monarchy, hereditary succession,* a *titled order of nobility* and all the *mock pageantry* of Kingly government form the *appropriate* and *prominent* features in the character to which he boasts Mr Jefferson's opposition,[13] and which it seems to be a principal part of the business of his Gazette to depreciate. This is no more than what has been long matter for malevolent insinuation; I mistake however the man, to whom it is applied, if he fears the strictest scrutiny into his political principles and conduct; if he does not wish there "were windows in the breast," and that assembled America might witness the inmost springs of his public actions. I mistake him, however a turn of mind less addicted to *dogmatising* than *reasoning,* less fond of *hypotheses* than *experience,* may have led to speculative doubts concerning the probable success of the republican theory—if he has not uniformly and ardently, since the experiment of it began in the United States, *wished* it success—if he is not sincerely desirous that the sublime idea of a perfect equality of rights among citizens, exclusive of hereditary distinctions, may be practically justified and realized— and if, among the sources of the regret, which his language and conduct have testified, at the overdriven maxims and doctrines that too long withstood the establishment of firm government in the United States, and now embarrass the execution of the government which has been established, a *principal one* has not been their tendency to counteract a *fair trial* of the theory, to which he is represented to be adverse. I mistake him if his measures, proceeding upon the ground of a liberal and efficient exercise of the powers of the national government have had any other object than to give to it stability and duration; *the only solid and rational expedient for preserving republican government in the United States.*

It has been pertinently remarked by a judicious writer, that *Cæsar,* who *overturned* the republic, was the WHIG, *Cato,* who

13. See "Catullus No. I," September 15, 1792, note 2.

died for it, the TORY of Rome; such at least was the common cant
of political harangues; the insidious tale of hypocritical demagogues.

CATULLUS.

To George Clymer

[*Philadelphia, September 29, 1792.* On October 1, 1792, Clymer
wrote to Hamilton: "I am favoured with yours of the 29 Sept."
Letter not found.]

To Benjamin Lincoln

Treasury Department
Septr 29th. 1792

Sir

I have concluded upon consideration of the circumstances represented in your letter of the 20th. instant to authorize the sale of the
Revenue Cutter as you propose.

In the building of a new one, I must recommend care to be
taken, that the vessel be of a proper size; and that her cost be
within the limits mentioned in your letter.[1]

I am with great consideration   Sir   Your obedt Servant

Alexander Hamilton

Benjn Lincoln Esqr
Collector Boston

LS, RG 36, Collector of Customs at Boston, Letters from the Treasury and
Others, 1790–1817, Vol. 10, National Archives; copy, RG 56, Letters to the
Collector at Boston, National Archives.

1. The words "mentioned in your letter" are in H's handwriting.

To Benjamin Lincoln

Treasury Department, September 29, 1792. "I have duly received
your letter of the 14th Instant, purporting a request from Mr
Thomas . . . : however grateful it might be to me, to promote the
plan undertaken by Mr Thomas, I cannot dispense with the law to
do it."

LS, RG 36, Collector of Customs at Boston, Letters from the Treasury, 1789–1807, Vol. 4, National Archives; copy, RG 56, Letters to the Collector at Boston, National Archives; copy, RG 56, Letters to Collectors at Small Ports, "Set G," National Archives.

To Jeremiah Olney

Treasury Department
September 29th 1792

Sir,

I am to acknowledge the receipt of your letter of the 18th of August last, relative to seven Puncheons of Foreign Spirits entered at the Custom House in Providence by Arnold Rhodes, Master of the Sloop Bacon from Washington in North Carolina.

I have therefore to request, that you will concur with the Supervisor of Rhode Island (who has been instructed for that purpose by the Commissioner of the Revenue) [1] in making an immediate examination into the matter in question, and if it shall appear to your mutual satisfaction, that there are no other unfavorable circumstances than a deficiency of particular certificates; you are hereby authorized to release the Spirits, transmitting however to this Office, a joint opinion on the Subject, respectively subscribed by yourself and the said Supervisor.

I am with consideration   Sir   Your most Obedient Servant
Alexander Hamilton

Jeremiah Olney Esquire
Collector of Providence

LS, Rhode Island Historical Society, Providence; copy, RG 56, Letters to Collectors at Small Ports, "Set G," National Archives; copy, RG 56, Letters to the Collector at Providence, National Archives.

1. Tench Coxe wrote to John S. Dexter concerning this matter on September 27, 1792 (LC, RG 58, Letters of Commissioner of Revenue, 1792–1793, National Archives)

To Jeremiah Olney

Treasury Department
September 29th 1792.

Sir

The Attorney for the District of Massachusetts [1] will prosecute in the case of the Sloop Polly of Sandwich,[2] which, as I learn from your letter of the 18th Ultimo, was licensed at your Office.

It is probable he will have occasion for the license bond, which I request you will forward to him upon his application.

I am, Sir,   Your Obedt Servant.   Alexander Hamilton

Jeremiah Olney Esqr.
Collr Providence.

LS, Rhode Island Historical Society, Providence; copy, RG 56, Letters to Collectors at Small Ports, "Set G," National Archives; copy, RG 56, Letters to the Collector at Providence, National Archives.
  1. Christopher Gore.
  2. For background to this case, see H to Olney, July 31, 1792, and Olney to H, August 13, 18, 1792.

George Washington to Thomas Mifflin [1]

United States, Septr. 29th. 1792.[2]

Sir

Inclosed you will find the copy of a Proclamation, which I have thought proper to issue, in consequence of certain irregular and refractory proceedings, which have taken place in particular parts of some of the states, contravening the law therein mentioned.

I feel an entire confidence, that the weight and influence of the Executive of (Pensylvania) will be chearfully exerted, in every proper way, to further the object of this measure, and to promote, on every occasion, a due obedience to the constitutional laws of the Union.[3]

With respect, I am, Sir   Your Excellency's Obedt servt

Excellency
Thomas Mifflin Esqr
Governor of the Common~ of Pensyla

Df, in the handwriting of H, RG 59, Miscellaneous Letters, 1790–1799, National Archives; LC, George Washington Papers, Library of Congress.
  1. For background to this letter, see H to Tench Coxe, September 1, 1792; H to Washington, September 1, 8, first letter of September 9, September 11, 22, 26, 1792; H to John Jay, September 3, 1792; "Draft of a Proclamation

Concerning Opposition to the Excise Law," September 7, 1792; Jay to H, September 8, 1792; Edmund Randolph to H, September 8, 1792; Washington to H, September 7, two letters of September 17, September 21, 1792; George Clymer to H, September 28, 1792; Rufus King to H, September 27, 1792.

2. The dateline is in Washington's handwriting.

3. On the back of this letter Washington wrote: "The Governors of Pennsylvania No Carolina & So Carolina 29th. Septr. 1792." Washington sent the same letter on the same date to Alexander Martin of North Carolina and Charles Pinckney of South Carolina.

From William Samuel Johnson [1]

New York, September 30, 1792. ". . . My Son Robert Charles Johnson . . . has now taken his Passage on Board a Ship bound to Bristol which proposes to Sail on Sunday next. His sole Object ⟨i⟩s Instruction & Improvement, & as I wish him to Travel as ad⟨v⟩antageously as may be, & am persuaded no Name in this Country can be a more valuable recommendation to him than yours, I beg the favour of Letters of Introduction for him. . . ."

ALS, Hamilton Papers, Library of Congress.

1. Johnson was president of Columbia College from 1787 to 1800. He had been a delegate from Connecticut to the Constitutional Convention and was one of the first two Senators elected from Connecticut. He resigned from the Senate in 1791, when the Federal Government moved from New York City to Philadelphia, in order to continue his duties as president of Columbia.

For a reference to Robert C. Johnson's trip to Europe, see William Henderson to H, September 24, 1792, note 7. See also William Denning to H, September 25, 1792, note 1.

From James McHenry

[Baltimore] Sunday 30th Septr. 1792

My dear Hamilton.

I received your letter of the 23 in the order of the mail, and yesterday yours of the 27th.[1] With respect to the former I have made no use of the quoted paragraph and hesitate between shewing it to the Bishop [2] or the principal himself.[3] Altho I think I may trust the Bishop, and am certain that it would be communicated yet if I shew it to the latter it may be in less danger of getting abroad and produce the same effect. I shall as far as in my power resist the

New York project.[4] I think it full of danger to the public. Is Adams to be supported?

I wish your letter of the 27th had arrived on Thursday.[5] The notification could then have appeared in Goddards paper [6] of last friday and would have had time to have circulated in Anne Arundel & Prince George's Counties, (Mercers district). Now it cannot appear till tuesday next, and the election begins to-morrow and ends on thursday, so that it will scarcely be heard of till after the election. I have greatly retarded my recovery by the part I have taken in this business. The first Valerius I wrote a little before I was taken ill and that published in last fridays paper [7] under a depression of spirits and great debility. I have also employed Major Hopkins of Anne Arundel County,[8] who is under considerable pecuniary obligations to me to circulate hand bills which contains popular charges against Mercer and fixes upon him some falsehoods. But after all I only don't despair of his being defeated. I am not able yet to go abroad, except walking a little in my garden.

An express arrived yesterday from Hagers Town that Gen William's [9] life was dispaired of. Should he die I must intreat you to remember Mr. Purviance [10] who is naval officer and of course the natural heir to his office. You know or may have heard that he was one of the first merchnts in this Town, is qualified to discharge its duties, has never shrunk from the right cause and has a very numerous & young family to maintain. These circumstances make me desirous that he should in the event of the generals death succeed him: and then you would have an opportunity to serve me by Mr. Salmons [11] taking Mr. Purviances place. It is impossible to get a man better qualified than Mr. Salmon for either office. He is popular, a man of *honor* and a respected judge in our criminal and orphans courts. If neither can be appointed I request that I may hear from you before you determine upon a successor. The office nets perhaps better than £2000 ℔ annum—possesses vast influence, and ought not to be given away *lightly* or without due consideration of character.

By Fenno's Gazette [12] of the 26 it appears to me that the writer in Dunlap's paper [13] or the Attorney General quotes a letter written to him subsequent [to] the adoption of the constitution by Virginia and nine States. I think so because it seems a reply to the arguments

used in that body in support of the constitution in the form it issued from the convention. The letter in question quoted by Judge
Pendleton and pushed out of view by Mr Maddison that writer has
withheld.[14] That is the evidence upon which the charge rests. Explanations of Mr. Jefferson likes or dislikes when the thing was out
of his reach does not do away the advice offered in his concealed
letter.

I flatter myself that Maryland will at least elect five or six federal
representatives out of her eight.

Yours most sincerely & affetionately   James McHenry

Since writing the above I learned from the printer that Mr Ross
was in Town and sent to him to come out. He has not received
your letter,[15] and is here to get a reply published for the polls in
answer to a justification of Mercers which appeared in Greene's last
paper.[16] I have seen neither; but Ross tells me the charge against
you is not denied. You will have Greene no doubt on Tuesday. I
wish Ross had as much ability as he has honesty and good intentions. Mercer circulated that the President wished that he should be
elected. This has been traced, the President has denied it and of
course the lie has lodged where it ought.[17]

Farewel, God bless my dear Hamilton.

Yours affectionately   James McHenry

ALS, Hamilton Papers, Library of Congress.
    1. Neither letter has been found.   2. Bishop John Carroll.
    3. Presumably Charles Carroll of Carrollton. See McHenry to H, August
16, 1792.
    4. See H to ———, September 21, 26, 1792.
    5. H's letter of September 27, 1792, undoubtedly described the charges
against H by John F. Mercer of Maryland. See the introductory note to H
to Mercer, September 26, 1792; H to David Ross, September 26, 1792.
    6. The [Baltimore] *Maryland Journal and the Baltimore Advertiser* was
published by William Goddard and his brother-in-law, James Angell. Goddard, who founded the paper in 1773, had announced that he was transferring
his share in the paper to Angell ([Philadelphia] *Gazette of the United States,*
August 25, 1792).
    7. The first "Valerius" article, dated August 27, 1792, appeared in *The
Maryland Journal and the Baltimore Advertiser* on August 31, 1792. The
second "Valerius" article appeared in the September 28, 1792, issue of the
same newspaper.
    8. Presumably David Hopkins.
    9. Otho H. Williams was collector of customs at Baltimore.
    10. Robert Purviance.   11. George Salmon.
    12. The *Gazette of the United States* was published by John Fenno.

13. The "Vindication of Mr. Jefferson" first appeared on September 22, 1792, in [Philadelphia] *Dunlap's American Daily Advertiser*, which was published by John Dunlap. See "Catullus No. IV," October 17, 1792, note 4.

McHenry first wrote "Aristides" and then crossed it out. He then wrote "the writer in Dunlaps paper" above "Aristides." For background concerning "Aristides," see "Catullus No. I," September 15, 1792, note 2.

14. This is a reference to H's charge that Thomas Jefferson had recommended early in 1788 that four states withhold their assent to the Constitution. See "An American No. II," August 11, 1792. See also "Catullus No. IV," October 17, 1792, note 3.

15. See H to Ross, September 26, 1792.

16. The [Annapolis] *Maryland Gazette* was published by Frederick and Samuel Green.

17. See H to Mercer, September 26, 1792, note 19.

To John Daves

Treasury Department, October 1, 1792. "I enclose you a letter for Captn Cooke.[1] . . . I have . . . concluded to alter the station of the Revenue Cutter from New Bern to Wilmington. The Collector of that port [2] will of course have to perform the duties which were heretofore committed to you relative to the Said Cutter."

Copy, RG 56, Letters to the Collector at New Bern, National Archives; LC, RG 26, Revenue Cutter Service Letters Sent, Vol. "O," National Archives.

1. William Cooke was commander of the *Diligence*, the revenue cutter for North Carolina.

2. James Read was collector of customs at Wilmington, North Carolina.

From William Ellery

Collector's Office Port of Newport [Rhode Island]
Oct. 1st 1792

Sir,

I have the honour to acknowledge the receipt of your letter of the 19th and of the 20th of the last month,[1] the first in answer to mine of the 4th. respectg. the Sale of property on board vessels abroad, the 2nd in answer to mine of the 10th of the same month respectg. the credit on salt &c; and hope to be favoured, as soon as you can make it convenient, with answers to my letter of the 20th. August last respectg. drawbacks on Spirits distilled in the United States, and touching the bond & license of the Sloop Polly, to my letter of the 28th. of the same month on the proviso to the 2nd. Sect: of the Act concerng. certain fisheries &c., and to my letter of the 3d. of Sept. last respecting the Sloop Polly &c. I have also to acknowledge the receipt of your letter of the 15th of last month [2] apprizing me of the circumstances of certain bills of exchange &c and of yours of the 17th. of the same month [3] with part of the margin of Certife. of Registry No. 21. I have not time to write my Sentiments on your Letter of the 19th by this Post, but propose to do it by the next.

I have the honour to be   Sir, Yr. most obedt. servant

Wm Ellery Colle

A Hamilton Esqr
Secry Treasury

LC, Newport Historical Society, Newport, Rhode Island
    1. Neither letter has been found.
    2. See "Treasury Department Circular to the Collectors of the Customs," September 15, 1792.
    3. Letter not found.

From Meletiah Jordan

[*Frenchman's Bay, District of Maine, October 1, 1792.* On November 17, 1792, Hamilton wrote to Benjamin Lincoln: "The Collector of Frenchmans Bay in his letter to me dated October the 1st." *Letter not found.*]

To William Short

Newark, N.J. Oct. 1.[–15] 1792

Sir,

On my arrival here, upon an excursion of a few days, I find the intelligence of a suspension of the King of France, and of a new revolution in that country. I take it for granted, that after such an event, no further payments will have been made to France.[1] It is now impossible to calculate anything concerning the affairs of that country, and of course the validity, as well as the utility to itself of future reimbursements would be questionable. This letter serves for the present barely to convey this idea.

With much consideration & esteem, I am, &c.   A.H.[2]

Copy, Massachusetts Historical Society, Boston.

1. For a discussion of the problems involved in the payment of the American debt to France after the suspension of the King on August 10, 1792, see Gouverneur Morris to H, September 25, 1792, and Short to H, September 25, 1792.

2. At the bottom of this letter the following notation appears: "Addition to the Triplicate of the foregoing letter, sent Oct. 15th. "P. S. The President confirms the object of the above letter, & has directed a similar communication to Mr Morris."

Morris was informed of the suspension of payments on the French debt in a letter from Jefferson dated October 15, 1792. Jefferson wrote: "We are informed by the public papers that the late Constitution of France, formally *notified to us,* is suspended, and a new Convention called. During the time of this suspension, and while no legitimate government exists, we apprehend we cannot continue the payments of our debt to France because there is no person authorized to receive it, and to give us an unobjectionable acquital. You are therefore desired to consider the payment as suspended until further orders. Should circumstances oblige you to mention this (which it is better to avoid if you can) do it with such solid reasons as will occur to yourself, and accompany it with the most friendly declarations that the suspension does not proceed from any wish in us to delay the payment, the contrary being our wish, nor from any desire to embarrass or oppose the settlement of their government in that way in which their nation shall desire it: but from our anxiety to pay this debt justly and honorably, and to the persons really authorized by the nation (to whom we owe it) to receive it for their use, nor shall this suspension be continued one moment after we can see our way clear out of the difficulty into which their situation has thrown us" (LC, RG 59, Diplomatic and Consular Instructions of the Department of State, 1791–1801, January 23, 1791–August 16, 1793, National Archives).

From George Washington

Mount Vernon Octobr. 1st. 1792.

Sir,

Your letter of the 22d. ulto., with it's enclosures, came duly to hand.

Lest any *material* disadvantage should result from delay, I have signed the Act which has been drawn by the Commissioner of the Revenue & approved by you, for arranging allowances to the Supervisors &c. and now forward it; but I would rather, if this is not likely to be the case, have it retained in your hands until my arrival in Philadelphia, as I wish for some explanations, which I have not the means of obtaining from the want of the former Act of the 4th. of August;[1] a copy of which I requested might be returned to me, but from a misconception of my meaning, a copy of my letter was sent in lieu thereof.[2] I now request a copy of the Act of the 4th. of Augt. & of the present one also.

Before any nomination, or appointment of a Keeper of the Lighthouse on Cape Henry takes place,[3] it would be proper to examine the List of Applicants (& I think there are several) who have applied to me for this Office, & is to be found among my papers by Mr. Lear.[4] If the person recommended by Colo. Parker is intemperate in drinking, it is immaterial whether you can recollect his name or not; for, with me, this would be an insuperable objection, let his pretensions & promises of reformation be what they may. I have been once taken in by the fair promises of Major Call[5] to refrain, & the strong assurances of his friends that he would do it; but will not, knowingly, trust again to the like from any one.

I have, by this Post, directed the Attorney General to attend the Circuit Court in York Town, & see that the Indictments are legally presented & properly supported.[6]

I am &c   G: Washington

LC, George Washington Papers, Library of Congress.
    1. For the "former Act," which concerned the arrangement for compensation of revenue officers for the year ending June 30, 1793, see the first letter Tench Coxe wrote to H on July 25, 1792. For the arrangement of retroactive compensation for these officers, see Coxe to H, first letter of July 25, 1792, note 18, September 12, 1792; H to Washington, September 22, 1792.
    2. See Washington to H, August 5, 1792; H to Washington, August 10, 1792.
    3. See H to Washington, September 22, 1792.
    4. Tobias Lear, Washington's secretary.
    5. On March 3, 1791, Washington had appointed Richard Call a major in the First Regiment. On August 19, 1792, Washington wrote to Henry Knox: "There can be no doubt of the propriety of bringing Major Call before a Genl. Court Martial for his intemperate conduct, for authorizing the raising of three troops of Horse at the expence of the Union . . . and for leaving a party of Soldiers on the So. Westn. frontier without an Officer, even a sergeant to comd. and provide for them" (GW, XXXII, 123).
    6. Washington to Edmund Randolph, October 1, 1792 (ADfS, RG 59, Miscellaneous Letters, 1790–1799, National Archives).
    For background concerning these indictments, see H to Tench Coxe, September 1, 1792; H to Washington, September 1, 8, first letter of September 9, September 11, 22, 26, 1792; H to John Jay, September 3, 1792; "Draft of a Proclamation Concerning Opposition to the Excise Law," September 7, 1792; Jay to H, September 8, 1792; Edmund Randolph to H, September 8, 1792; Washington to H, September 7, two letters of September 17, September 21,

1792; George Clymer to H, September 28, 1792; Rufus King to H, September 27, 1792; Washington to Thomas Mifflin, September 29, 1792.

From Thomas Marshall and William Pearce [1]

Paterson [New Jersey] Octr. 3d: 1792

Sir

Having taken into Consideration your kind request of this Morning, we respectfully Submit the following to your Approbation, but first we beg to be Understood that we entertain bothe Esteem and Friendship for Major L'Enfant [2] and Col: Cummings [3] whose behaviour since their Appointment has every way Satisfied and pleased us, and nothing herein is meant in the most distant manner to glance at them.

In An Undertaking like this the Masterly Completion of the Machinery depends very much upon a Judicious Selection of Tools and Materials, which Nought but a Knowledge of the Purposes to which they are meant to be apply'd can enable the Purchaser to give Satisfaction to the Workmen or do Justice to the Society; peculiar Applications require peculiar properties, for that Tool or Material which may be prime in the *first* Stage, becomes, (very often) totally useless in the *Second*.

The Training up youth in the Different Branches of the Manufactory we consider Politic and Reqisite; in many of the Different Stages of our respective Businesses a Stout Boy, by a Twelvemoths Instruction wou'd be able to Stand in the Shoes of an Adult person, and in a Country like this where Wages are so exceedingly high, a Material Saving wou'd Eventually acere to the Society if Apprentices were taken under certain Regulations.

As the Payment of Wages carries an Amazing Influence with it over the minds of the people employ'd, we respectfully Submit to you, to permit us to send our Account Book, to Col Cummings, *every* Saturday Morning, for his Examination, and Scrutity, and if the Account shou'd appear to him right and Just, that he may send us the *precise* Sum of *that* Weeks Wages to be by us paid to our respective Tradesmen.

Mahogany, Iron, Wire, Scantling &c of peculiar properties being now wanted, some of which we shall one of us be obliged to go to

Mount Hope, Andover, and Pompton for, likewise to York, our Salaries will not admit of Journeys being taken without our Actual Reimbursement of our unavoidable Expences, a Standard to go by is what we wish and of whom we are to draw Stipulated Sums for those Outgoings, the Iron is now wanted, and the Men Cannot work in the Morning as they ought to do for want of Stoves, these regulations we respectfully Submit to your Determination, and are Sir

Your Most Obedt. Humble Servts.   Thomas Marshall
                  and Wm. Pearce

Honble.
Alexander Hamilton Esqr.

LS, in the handwriting of Thomas Marshall, Hamilton Papers, Library of Congress.

1. Marshall and Pearce were employees of the Society for Establishing Useful Manufactures.

2. Pierre Charles L'Enfant had been appointed "Agent for superintending the erection of the Works and buildings ordered by the Directors" of the Society for Establishing Useful Manufactures. See "Draft Minutes of a Meeting of a Committee of the Directors of the Society for Establishing Useful Manufactures," August 1, 1792.

3. In August, 1792, John N. Cumming had been appointed "Agent for procuring such workmen and materials, and at such periods as" L'Enfant might need, "to pay the expences accruing thereon, keeping regular accounts of the same, and also to procure such materials for Machinery as shall be required in their respective branches by William Hall, Thomas Marshall and William Pearce" ("Minutes of the S.U.M.," 57).

From George Clymer [1]

[Pittsburgh, October 4, 1792]

Sir

Not one of the expectations mine by last post might have raised has been realised.[2] Cannon undoubtedly fell into bad hands for 'tho

ALS, Connecticut Historical Society, Hartford.

1. For background to this letter, see H to Tench Coxe, September 1, 1792; H to George Washington, September 1, 8, first letter of September 9, September 11, 22, 26, 1792; H to John Jay, September 3, 1792; "Draft of a Proclamation Concerning Opposition to the Excise Law," September 7, 1792; Jay to H, September 8, 1792; Edmund Randolph to H, September 8, 1792; Washington to H, September 7, two letters of September 17, September 21, October 1, 1792; George Clymer to H, September 28, 1792; Rufus King to H, September 27, 1792; Washington to Thomas Mifflin, September 29, 1792.

2. See Clymer to H, September 28, 1792.

he still avows to me his disapprobation of the Proceedings of the
21 August [3] into which he was as he says unwarily drawn, no publick recantation has come from him. Neither has any thing favourable turned up here. The people I mentioned were content with
calling a Town-meeting at which many of themselves appeared, and
nothing was proposed. They then made a new promise, and talked
of signing a disavowal individually which they said would have a
better effect. A postponement succeded on hearing of a new meeting intended here of the Countey Committee. And all the satisfaction I have is to find them out—that they greatly want sincerity or
spirit or both, still professing friendship to the federal government.
This new assembling of the Committees was it seems projected on
the first rumour of my being here and runners dispatched to bring
together a numerous band of the chieftains of opposition from all
quarters. Their deliberations, if I can call them so, were open, for
nothing was done but the repeated readings of a petition to Congress—agreed to without dissent. I have not had a sight of this
piece, but I am told it contains a declaration of their readiness to
contribute their share to the public exigencies, a complaint of the
peculiar hardship of the Excise, prays for an abolition of it and the
substitution of a direct tax. This they know will be refused, and is
only a device to keep up the mad temper of the people.

Mr Addison [4] the circuit judge has affected to mistake the nature
of my application—this together with his constitutional objection
to take any part in the business have disappointed me in that quarter.[5] Or rather I would say has not disappointed me for my ex-

3. For the proceedings of August 20-21, 1792, see H to Coxe, September 1,
1792, note 5.
4. Alexander Addison was presiding judge of the County Court of the
western district of Pennsylvania.
5. Addison's letter to Clymer of September 29, 1792, reads as follows:
"Your letter of yesterday from Pittsburgh states to me that among other
objects of your journey to this country one is to take Depositions respecting
the persons who in various ways have obstructed the revenue laws of the
united states, and have those depositions and some of the best informed witnesses sent to York before the 11th Octr. when the Circuit federal court will
begin its session, that you have been induced to fear it is much too hazardous
for you to attend to this business in person; and therefore request that I will
execute this part of your commission and transmit the Depositions to you
at Pittsburgh.
"I am convinced Sir, that your information or suspicions of personal danger
in the execution of this commission at this place have no real foundation. For

pectations from any Washington magistrate could not be great, 'tho of necessity obliged to resort to him. Indeed had he been willing to the business little could have been done. The few well disposed people there being all afraid to say more than that they saw an un-

---

your coming here is not to set up an office of Inspection in this county and fix on the distillers the penalties of the Revenue Law; and it is against this that the passions of the people are directed. If however my opinion should fail to give you confidence, several Gentlemen of this town and county, who, having been members of the Pittsburgh Committee, may be supposed to have influence with the opponents of the duty, will be in Pittsburgh in a few days; in whose company, you will not doubt, you may come safely, and who, I am confident, will pledge their word for your security.

"If after all this you should believe there is danger in the business, you must believe it owing to some very deep rooted resentment in the minds of the people, and that the object of this resentment is not the person but the thing. Do you believe that your person can be liable to danger from any inhabitant of this county except in so far as your presence here opposes their interests, or opinions? Or do you believe that any respectability of person or character will save a man from dislike, if his office or employment obstruct the interests or opinions of those among whom he is? Ask General [John] Nevill. If therefore it be true (and you cannot doubt it) that it is the measure, and not the man, that the people hate, is it proper for you who have accepted this commission from the President of the united States to devolve the execution of it on one in whom no confidence is placed by it? Or is it proper, if the measure be odious in this corner of the country to require the exercise of it from an inhabitant of this corner, every day exposed to the passions of the people in it, and who, from the nature of another office with which he is honoured, ought, if possible, to possess the affection, the esteem, and the confidence of those among whom he is? And is it not more reasonable, if this measure be necessary that it should be effected by a man not resident here, in whom the confidence of this people is not necessary, and to whom their opinions of him is of no immediate concern? I am persuaded, Sir, you did not see these things in the light in which I do.

"But I have more important reasons for declining this commission. It is my fixed opinion that the judicial system of the United States is impracticable, unless it is intended to sacrifice to it the essential principles of the liberty of the citizens, and the just authority of the state courts. As a citizen and as a judicial officer, it is my duty to preserve both. As you state therefore that the object of this enquiry is to found a prosecution in the federal courts, if even you had authority to delegate your power (of which I doubt) and it were my duty to execute this delegated authority (which is not hinted) I should do it with reluctance, because I should be serving a cause, which I think unfavourable to liberty and the just authority of the state Courts. As it is, I shall certainly not be a volunteer in this affair. I consider the Laws of Congress as the rules of judgement in the state Courts and the citizens as punishable in the state courts for their infraction, as much as the respective state laws. I have taken and shall continue to take all such measures as appear to me proper to bring to justice in the proper Courts of Pennsylvania those persons of whose violence it is the object of your mission to enquire. But this is all that is to be expected of me untill I am convinced that it is my duty to do more. . . ." (ALS, Connecticut Historical Society, Hartford.)

distinguished mob at Falkener's house.[6] One person supposed to be as well informed as any there I sent Captain Falkener for but he could testify to nothing more, and I have sent him back. So that the whole amount of the testimony collected after the daily and hourly pains taken by General Nevil[7] and my self—is that of Falkener who declares to the threats uttered against him by two of the County Magistrates[8] some time previous to the riot—and that of one Peter Myers[9] now one of Falkener's Soldiers but who at the time of the riot was in the charge of his house at Washington—his deposition identifies two of the mob, one of them of sufficient consideration to be prosecuted.[10] Falkener and Myers have the Commander in chiefs order to proceed tomorrow for York,[11] which I am fearful they cannot reach before the 10th—Falkener having spent a much longer time at Washington in search of evidence than I expected or intended. I shall inclose their depositions to the judge of the circuit Court at York[12] together with some others 'tho they mean little. Falkener's deposition also identifies the persons of the

6. Faulkner kept a tavern at Washington. Addison's charge to the Grand Jury at the September session of the County Court describes the incident as follows: ". . . in Washington, in the evening of the 24th of August last . . . About thirty men, armed and blacked, rode through the streets; surrounded, entered, and searched, the house of William Faulkner, with a design to seize and punish the Inspector of Excise, who had advertised an Inspection office at that house" (Alexander Addison, *Charges to Grand Juries of the Counties of the Fifth Circuit, in the State of Pennsylvania* [Washington: Printed by John Colerick, 1800], 50).

7. John Neville was inspector of the revenue for Survey No. 4 in the District of Pennsylvania.

8. DS, Pennsylvania Miscellany, Whiskey Rebellion, Vol. 1, Library of Congress.

Seven individuals are mentioned in Faulkner's deposition as having threatened him directly. David Hamilton, one of the seven, was justice of the peace for Nottingham township in Washington County (*Pennsylvania Archives*, 9th ser., I, 331).

9. The deposition of Peter Myers is dated September 29, 1792 (D, Pennsylvania Miscellany, Whiskey Rebellion, Vol. 1, Library of Congress). Meyers's mark was subscribed to before John Gibson, one of the judges of the Court of Common Pleas for Allegheny County.

10. Alexander Berr and William Kerr, cited in Meyers's deposition, were the two men against whom proceedings were instituted in the Middle Circuit Court which met at York, Pennsylvania, on October 11, 1792.

11. See Clymer to H, September 28, 1792, note 10.

12. William Cushing, Associate Justice of the Supreme Court, and Richard Peters, judge of the District Court of Pennsylvania, presided over the meeting of the Circuit Court at York, Pennsylvania, on October 11, 1792.

Committee of 21 Augt. as well as one Mr. Tannehils' [13] which I send with it. Perhaps these latter testimonies may be still useful there, for I can hardly persuade my self that the laws have left the Commonwealth defenceless in a part where she may be attacked as successfully as by force of arms. If so, great will be my chagrin in losing my first and principal object.

You have under cover Addison's letter to me,[14] and I have taken the liberty to accompany it with a copy of my reply to him.[15]

13. Josiah Tannehill's deposition has not been found. The meeting of August 20–21, 1792, was held at his tavern. See H to Coxe, September 1, 1792, note 5.

14. See note 8.

15. Clymer's letter to Addison, of October 1, 1792, reads as follows:

"I am favoured with yours of the 29 Sept. and am sorry to observe in it several grounds of objection to a compliance with the request made in mine of the 28th.

"I did not mean you should act under a delegated powers having no powers myself but to point out to the magistrate certain witnesses who might be examined by him: this Sir I presumed might have been done by me as well at a distance of twenty miles as in your immediate presence—that presence nevertheless I should have sought but for an opinion of personal danger founded on the general apprehension here, and which you will pardon me in saying your letter is by no means fitted to remove—for if in the performance of a judicial duty not voluntarily engaged in but properly called to, you who stand so well with your people could not hope to escape the popular odium, what ought the prompter himself, and one too in my predicament, to expect? something beyond the passiveness of hatred. Neither to avoid this hazard would I so much affront my character as a publick agent to accept the protection which you say may be had, of any of those persons composing the Assembly at Pittsburgh, who in putting the officers of the revenue under the ban of society, by which they must necessarily cease to act and a law to operate, have in fact undertaken to annul the law itself, for the law exists but through its Officers and in its execution—thus beginning the measures of opposition where the most decided enemies of government would have ended, in a bold and open hostility to its authority. . . .

"I am not so competent to examine the constitutional reason assigned for declining my request—a doubt entertained of the judicial rights of a federal court in this business: 'tho I can discover in it another battery raised against the United states—but it must seem plain to the plainest understanding that it must be an indispensable of any government to have the cognizance of crimes committed against itself, and not to be obliged to devolve upon any other the case either of its honour or of its defence. Neither do I well comprehend why an offence against the Union can be an Offence only as it may happen to disturb the peace or order of any of its component members, for on this ground can the pretensions of the States individually to such exclusive jurisdiction only rest.

"But Sir were my personal apprehensions got over to what purpose does your invitation tend, for proposing to act only through you as the most reputable magistrate how could the shortening any distance between us change

Two of General Nevil's collectors have been with me. They complained of having led a dog's life among their neighbours, proposed to resign, but Nevil fearing the very bad effects of that step I have been obliged to offer them at the rate each of one hundred dollars for such time as they may continue during the current year, beyond what they may in possibility get of the ordinary emoluments of office.

In coming here I left the escort of horse behind me at Bedford but this new stirring of the waters of bitterness yesterday, has it is supposed encreased the personal risque of the revenue Officers and General Wayne [16] has without any application of mine ordered a party to attend me in the morning.

I have the honour to be   Sir   Your most obedt hum st

Geo Clymer

Pittsburgh Oct. 4.

1792.

Secretary of the Treasury

---

any of the circumstances which have disinclined you to serve me." (ALS, marked "copy" by Clymer, Connecticut Historical Society, Hartford.)

16. On September 11, 1792, Knox wrote to Major General Anthony Wayne requesting that he provide any necessary protection to Clymer on his return and that "in doing this, you will be careful to keep yourself within the limits of the law; and will doubtless act with all due caution and circumspection" (Knopf, *Wayne*, 92).

From Sharp Delany

[*Philadelphia*] *October 4, 1792.* "Mr Thomas Lea of this City Merchant has informed me of his address to you respecting a quantity of Rum shipped by him for Dublin, and there refused by the Consignee and the whole returned without his knowledge and greatly to his damage. I informed Mr Lea of the necessity of having your opinion & instructions on this subject. . . . I inclose Mr Lea's state of the Case [1] and have taken every proof on Oath from him & the Captain." [2]

ALS, RG 217, Philadelphia, Revenue Collectors, 1789–1803, National Archives.

1. Lea's statement, which is dated October, 1792, summarizes the case and concludes by asking H "to direct that the bonds entered into on the Shipment

of the said Rum at this Port of Philadelphia may be Cancelled" (DS, RG 217, Philadelphia, Revenue Collectors, 1789–1803, National Archives).

2. On the back of this letter H wrote: "Collector of Pensylvania concerning certain Rum of Mr. Lea. The only mode in which relief can be afforded is by application through the district Judge which it is adviseable should be made without further delay."

Also on the back of this letter there is a notation in an unknown handwriting which reads: "27 December Answered." Letter not found.

From Jeremiah Olney

Providence, October 4, 1792. "I have been Honor'd with your favours of the 19th. and 24th. Ulto. in Reply to my Letters of the 8 & 13th Ulto. . . . I beg leave respectfully to answer, that as you have not been Sufficiently explicit with respect to a Refusal of Credit in Similar cases, I shall not think myself safe in doing it untill the Law is amended or I may Receive your further and particular instructions on this point. . . . If an action for damages should be commenced against me and it should be possible, that, upon Tryal I could not make it appear to the Satisfaction of the court that the Transfer was made with Intent to evade the law, Heavy damages might be Recovered, and I should Remain without Remedy. . . ."

ADfS, Rhode Island Historical Society, Providence.

From William Heth

Private   Berm[ud]a Hundred [Virginia] 5. Oct. 1792

Here am I, my dear Sir, at 8. OC. at night barrd & bolted up, in one end of a dreary Lumber House—after a fatiguing days work—with a smart fever upon me, and not a being on earth, to whom I can speak. And in case necessity Should oblige me to open the door, it is at all times, at the risque of being stab'd or shot, for sake of the cursed dross, contained in the Iron chest.

Really, my present situation is deplorable—and if I did not possess more than a common share of spirits—I should certainly *run away from myself*. On my return from Phila. I found one of my Clerks gone home sick, & the other, my Deputy, complaining; who, immediately made preparations to go up the country, & left me a few days after—I believe to be marryd, & not to return.

The extreme anxiety of my mind, & great fatigue which I experienced in coming from Phila—for on my arrival at Pet[ersbur]g I found I had beaten the stage which left Phila. the day I did, two Hours—brought on a bilious fever, which attacked me the 9th day after my return, & Just as the fall arrivals commenced. At that time, I was lucky enough to get Mr. J. Stewart [1] to assist me, & the pressure of business being far beyond any thing ever before experienced here, I endeavord to bear up against the fever, til I fairly sunk under it, & was obligd to be carryd home. Mr Stewart having assisted some days last fall, he was well acquainted with the business of estimating of Duties, but totally ignorant of the other duties of the Office; my uneasiness therefore to return, brought me from home last Thursday, a few days sooner than I ought to have come out. The Consequence was a severe Cold, & hectic Cough, under which I now labor, with a fever every evening: and Mr Stewart, being obligd to leave me on Friday last in order to prepare to attend upon the assembly as one of the Clerks, I am now alone, & with well founded apprehensions of a relapse, and without being able to get any person qualified to do the business of this Office, to come to so miserable, & so unhealthy a place. Ever since my return, to get a person qualified for a deputy hath been my object, but to no purpose. Should I again sink under my indisposition, God knows what will be the consequence.[2] The Goods already enterd & the Cargo's expected, are beyond all conception. Duties to amount of 100,000 Dollars & upwards are already secured (but at Norfolk, I am told they are not so great as last fall—most of the vessels with large Cargos having come here).

One object of this long private address, is to prepare you for a petition wch. I expect will be presented to Congress to remove the Office [3] to Petersburg—and which I suspect I must not only acquiesce in, but use my Interest with the Richmond Merchants to agree to. (It will be a measure much against my private inclinations & Interest). For the risque of keeping money here, is too great, & there is no getting a Man of respectability & Capacity to reside here. I offerd, in my late distress, nearly one half the emoluments of my Office to J Stewart—and as to moving here myself, it is *impossible*—

because there is not a hut of any kind to be rented, or purchased, at, or near the place—so that, I must either continue to be a slave, banished from my family—ruin my Constitution entirely, & sink under the labors of a public office, or consent to its being removed.

The second Object, is to inform you that my quarterly accounts will not be rendered as heretofore, within a few days after the expiration of a quarter. There is not a single Manifest or entry recorded since the first of July last—every book is behind—& business strong. Yet from a mode of doing the business, which from what I have seen is peculiar to myself, I shall be able after one or two entries on gross estimates are adjusted, to inform you of the Amt of Duties on Impost and Tonnage to the 30th sept last and also of the Gross Value of Exports, sufficiently accurate for you to form estimates upon.

A late Hour, & great indisposition calls upon your friendship to excuse this scrawl. I know the sensibility of your feelings and am sure you will sympathise with

Dear sir   Your real & afft friend   W Heth

Col A Hamilton

ALS, Hamilton Papers, Library of Congress.
   1. John Stewart.
   2. Heth had written to H concerning the problems of clerk hire and the unhealthy neighborhood of the collector's office more than a year before he wrote the letter printed above. See Heth to H, July 2, 1791.
   3. See Heth to H, February 27, 1792.

From David Ross [1]

[Bladensburgh, Maryland, October 5–10, 1792]

Dear Sir

I did not return to Bladensburgh after an absence of 8 or 10 days 'till Monday the 1st. of October, the day of our Election when I found yours to me enclosing a letter to Colo. Mercer.[2] Expecting to find him at Marlborough where the election is held for this part of the District I took his letter with me and not finding him there, I proceeded on to Annapolis, which place he had left for Marlborough, and we missed each other, by taking different roads. But he received it the next day as a young Gentleman carried the letter for me who was particular at my request in seeing it delivered—and Colo Mercer had before received Copies of yours to him & myself, which I had left for him in case we should so miss each other.

In answer to yours to me—I refer you to Colo Mercers and my own Publications and you will judge for yourself from these and the answer Colo Mercer may write you how far he admits or denies his having impeached your Integrity, and charged you with interfering in our Election. I can only assure you I have not wilfully misrepresented any thing altho' I admit I may have been mistaken as to the precise words he may have made use of, except that "he gave 18/ when he was offered 14/." as I took them down instantly this being at Bladensburgh—but having no intention of any thing of the kind, when he spoke at Marlborough I cannot be so positive as to the other words, as they rested only on my memory for some days but I took the precaution before I published to show it to several Gentlemen with a request that they would rectify any thing I had in their apprehension, misunderstood. And when I heard him at Bladensburgh I had not the most distant impression that I had misapprehended him at Marlborough. And the following is additional evidence given to me in writing and signed by one whose character for veracity you may rely on with liberty to make use of his name if necessary.[3] At Marlborough after Colo Mercer had received Copies of your letter to him and of yours to me instead of immediately and publickly denying that he had impeached or meant to impeach your Integrity, and informing those present (who or at least some of them also knew the contents of the letters) that I had misapprehended him he said—

"That since private conversation had been divulged respecting himself he now declared that Mr Hamilton had offerred him money if he would vote for the Assumption." After walking across the room for a minute or two (Some of the Company astonished at the charge) he added as nearly as I can recollect in the following words—"I had a claim against the United States for two or three hundred dollars which by the act of Limitation[4] I was prevented receiving payment for. However last session of Congress we opened the door for claims in that situation[5] and I accordingly produced my claim, and at one time was told it would be paid and at another time was told it would not—at length going to the Office respecting it I met with Mr Hamilton and told him I was much surprised my account was not admitted and paid, for every article in it was just, and if it belonged to any man in the United States but myself it would be admitted and paid. Mr Hamilton made some objections to the account, and then in a jocular manner said if you will vote for the Assumption I will pay you your account out of my own Pocket. Colo Mercer also added if he thought Mr Hamilton had been serious at the time he would have knocked him down."

As I did not receive yours till the day of the Election I took the liberty to have some

AL (incomplete), Hamilton Papers, Library of Congress.
1. For background to this letter, see the introductory note to H to John F. Mercer, September 26, 1792. See also H to Ross, September 26, 1792.
2. See H to Ross, September 26, 1792.
3. This quotation is taken from a statement dated October 5, 1792, written by Thomas Cramphin, a Montgomery County planter who had served in the Maryland legislature. The statement was among the documents forwarded to H by Ross on November 23, 1792.
4. JCC, XXIX, 866; XXXIII, 392. For these acts, see "Report on Sundry Petitions," April 16, 1792, note 2.
5. See H to Mercer, September 26, 1792, note 20.

To William Irvine and John Kean [1]

[Philadelphia, October 6, 1792. On October 11, 1792, Irvine and Kean acknowledged the receipt of Hamilton's letter of October 6, 1792. Letter not found.][2]

1. Irvine and Kean were commissioners for settling the accounts between the United States and the individual states.
2. Although this letter has not been found, the answer to it indicates that its contents were similar to those of "Treasury Department Circular," September 13, 1792.

To Thomas Jefferson

Treasury Department, October 6, 1792. Requests information for report ordered by the Senate on May 7, 1792.[1]

LS, partly in the handwriting of H, Thomas Jefferson Papers, Library of Congress.

1. The contents of this letter are essentially the same as those of "Treasury Department Circular," September 13, 1792.

To Samuel A. Otis [1]

Treasury Department, October 6, 1792. Requests information for report ordered by the Senate on May 7, 1792.[2]

LS, RG 46, Second Congress, 1791–1793, Reports of the Secretary of the Treasury (2A-F2), National Archives.
1. Otis, who was secretary of the Senate, was the younger brother of James Otis and the father of Harrison Gray Otis.
2. The contents of this letter are essentially the same as those of "Treasury Department Circular," September 13, 1792.

From William Polk [1]

[*October 6, 1792.* On November 3, 1792, Tench Coxe wrote to Polk: "The Secretary of the Treasury has just sent to this office your letter to him of the 6th of October." [2] *Letter not found.*]

1. Polk was supervisor of the revenue for the District of North Carolina.
2. LC, RG 58, Letters of Commissioner of Revenue, 1792–1793, National Archives.

To Edmund Randolph

[*Philadelphia, October 6, 1792.* On October 17, 1792, Randolph wrote to Hamilton: "On my return home, I found your letter of the 6th instant." *Letter not found.*][1]

1. Although this letter has not been found, the answer to it indicates that its contents were similar to those of "Treasury Department Circular," September 13, 1792.

From Jean Baptiste de Ternant

Philade. 8 d'octobre 1792
l'an 4e. de la liberté francoise

Par suite de ma lettre du 22 aout dernier je vous prie de vouloir faire payer au Consul general de la forest [1] ou a son ordre la somme

de 24,660 piastres au 15 du present mois, et celle de 19,961 au le.
Nove. suivant.

LC, *Arch. des Aff. Etr., Corr. Pol., Etats-Unis,* Supplement Vol. 20.
1. Antoine René Charles Mathurin de La Forest.

From William Ellery [1]
Collector's Off: Port of Newport [Rhode Island]
Oct. 9th 1792

Sir,
  In answer to your letter of the 19th and that part of your letter
of the 26th of the last month [2] which respects fictitious sales &c
permit me to observe, that I had been seasonably informed by the
Colle. of Providence District of the delinquencies of Mr. Arnold
respectg. a certain bond, that I had reason to suspect that he intended to transfer his property in the Samuel to Stephen Dexter,
and that Dexter would apply for an entry at the Custom House in
Newport. This and the advice of the District Atty. [3] occasioned the
Statements in my letter of the 4th. of last month. It was his opinion
that it would not be safe for me to refuse a credit to Mr. Dexter if
he should ask for an entry, producing a regular bill of sale, offering to give bond and otherwise to comply with the Law, notwithstanding the sale might appear to be fictitious. Before I received
your letter, the Samuel arrived in this Port, Mr. Dexter applied for
an entry, produced a regular bill of sale of vessel and cargo & I
entered them. Your opinion expressed in the letter of the 19th is
"that if appearances of this kind continue the presumption of design
to evade the law will be sufficy. strong to justify an Offe. in refusing the credit." "If an action be brought against the Offe for
such refusal, means must be taken to examine all the parties upon
Oath, and in the event of damages against the Offe. if he appears
to have acted with due caution, and upon sufficient ground of probability, it will be incumbent on the Government to indemnify him."
Such circumstances as would justify a refusal should I conceive in-
sure an indemnification, but this is not needed I expect that it would
be insured by your letter of the 19th. Your Letter of the 26th.
would give greater encouragement to expectation, were it not for

the clause which concludes its last sentence, "as I have already mentioned in my former letter" which reference connects what is expressed in this with your former letter. Considered in this view, let me ask what means could be legally used to compell the Plt. in a prosecution agst an Offe. for refusing credit to sustain an examination under Oath before a State Court? and I know not of any Law of the United States which restricts actions against Officers in such cases to federal Courts. Our State Courts never exercise such a power.

Due caution and *sufficient ground of probability* are general expressions which admit of great latitude of Construction, and I have remarked that when persons have not succeded in an undertaking, their want of success has been attributed to incautiousness, or to their not having proceded on probable ground. Good or ill success stamp applause or censure on conduct.

I did not conceive when I wrote my letter of the 4th that you was authorized by law to promise an indemnification to an Officer who on probable ground of collusion should refuse a credit, and in consequence thereof should be sued, and suffer damage; but to intimate that until a Law should be enacted which would assure to an officer indemnification in the event of damages against him, it ought not to be expected that he should refuse a credit; and thereby expose himself to injury, and that damages and probably heavy damages would in that case be recovered against him, I was then and am now, upon mature consideration, satisfied would be the event of such a prosecution. An Act of Congress insuring indemnification to Officers who acting by your advice or by the advice of the District attorney when there would not be sufficient time to obtain your advice, should any case be prosecuted and damages be recovered against them would free Officers from embarrassment, and would not I believe be disadvantageous to the Public. An Act of Congress if such an act could be framed which would prevent a delinquent obligor from availing himself of a fictitious sale, to obtain credit would put a stop to such unjustifiable conduct in future, and it appears to me that a Law confining suits against Officers of the United States to a federal Court might not be improper.

It is probable that an application may again be made to me for credit, by a vendee of Mr. Arnold; other wise I should not have troubled you with this letter.

I have expressed my sentiments perhaps with too great freedom. I trust they will be received with candour. In this confidence and with perfect consideration

I am   Sir   Yr. most obedt. servt.   Wm Ellery Co

A Hamilton Esqr
Secry Treasy.

LC, Newport Historical Society, Newport, Rhode Island.
    1. For information concerning Welcome Arnold and the *Samuel*, see Jeremiah Olney to H, September 8, second letter of September 13, 1792. See also H to Olney, September 19, 24, October 4, 1792.
    2. Neither of these letters has been found.   3. William Channing.

From Joseph Nourse

Treasury Dept. Registers Office
9 Octr: 1792.

Sir,
    I have the Honor to enclose certifyd Copies from the Treasury Books of an Acct. depending betwixt His Mo: Catholic Majesty and the United States, for Monies recd. on Loan. I cannot find that this Loan has been recognized on the Journals of Congress in a like Manner with the french and Dutch Loans. It is founded on a settlemt made by the late Comr. for settling the foreign Accts. entitled Loans from the Court of Spain.[1] This money was paid to the Hon: James Gardoqui[2] and has been regularly accounted for by him, having been expended in the purchasing of Cloathing and in the payt. of Bills of Exn. drawn by order of Congress. The principal

	Cts.
sum recd. was	Drs. 174.011
To which add Interest thereon to the 31	
Dec: 1792	99.007:89
Total Amt. of Principal & Int. as 曾 Statement [3]	273.018.89

    Altho' there is no Recognition of this Debt on the Journals of Congress, by a Copy of the Original Contract or otherwise, yet in all the Estimates made by the late Government the annual Appropriations have been made for the payment of its Int. and in the various Reports from Committees of Congress it has been noticed as an Existing Claim due from the united states.

There is an Acct. opened in the Treasury Books under the Title of Don Carlos Dildephonso Rico Hombre D'Espagne a Copy of which I inclose.[4] This I have understood from Mr. Lee [5] is to be viewed as a Gratuity and not as a Loan.

I have the Honor to be sir with Real Respect   Your mo: ob: & Mo: hb: Serv.   J. N.

LC, Register of the Treasury, Estimates and Statements for 1792, Vol. "134-T," National Archives; LC, RG 39, Letter Book, 1789-1795, National Archives.

1. The statement of the Spanish loan appears on Folio 198 of the first of two ledger volumes which Thomas Barclay used in his settlement of the European accounts of the Continental Congress (D, RG 39, Foreign Ledgers, Public Agents in Europe, 1776-1787, National Archives).

2. In accounting for these subsidies Don Diego de Gardoqui, who was a minor official in the Spanish Ministry of Finance, signed himself James Gardoqui, and the accounts of the purchases made for the United States which he transmitted to Arthur Lee are headed James Gardoqui and Company, Bilboa. Subsequent United States purchases were made through the firm of Joseph Gardoqui and Company, which had been established at Bilboa before the American Revolution by Don Diego's father.

James Gardoqui's account may be found on Folio 195 of Thomas Barclay's ledgers (D, RG 39, Foreign Ledgers, Public Agents in Europe, 1776-1787, National Archives).

3. See enclosure.

4. "Don Carlos Dildephonso Rico Hombre D'Espagne" was an alias used by the Spanish government in placing credit in Amsterdam at the disposal of the American agents at Paris. Fearful of a British declaration of war against Spain, the Spanish authorities also drew the bills in favor of Arthur Lee rather than directly in favor of the United States. The money, contributed in two equal installments commencing in May, 1777, was used to purchase supplies in Spain for the American Army (Lee's account, ADS, Papers of the Continental Congress, National Archives). The "Don Carlos" account debited with Lee's expenditures may be found in RG 217, "Ledger B, 1776-1789, Register's Office," National Archives.

5. Lee's reports to the Continental Congress concerning the subsidy he obtained from Spain may be found in the Papers of the Continental Congress, National Archives.

Dr: His mo: Catholic Majesty in A/c with the united states   Cr:

By Int. on 17,892 dollars from 1 January 1781 to 31 dec. 1792 is 12 years @ 5 p.c.
1781 January 1. for so much recd. of the Court .... 17.892.
    Feb: 28 & March 6.   do .... 32.000.
    April 28 .... do .... 9.036.
    May 9 .... do .... 14.000.
    June 22 .... do .... 12.000.
    Aug. 18 .... do .... 12.000.
    Dec: 23 .... do .... 51.083.
1782 March 21 .... do .... 26.000.

174.011.

By Int. on 17,892 dollars from 1 January 1781 to 31 dec. 1792 is 12 years @ 5 p.c. 10.735.20
do .. on 32,000 do.   from 28 Feby. 1781 to do .... is 11.10.3 @do .. 18.946.67
do .. on 9,036 do.   from 28 April 1781 to do .... is 11. 8.3 " .. 5.274.76
do .. on 14,000 do.   from 9 May 1781 to do .... is 11. 7.22 ..... 8.151. 9
do .. on 12,000 do.   from 22 June 1781 to do .... is 11. 6. 9 ..... 6.915.
do .. on 12,000 do.   from 18 August 1781 to do .... is 11. 4.13 ..... 6.821.66
do .. on 51,083 do.   from 23 decr. 1781 to do .... is 11. 0. 8 ..... 28.152.40
do .. on 26,000 do.   from 21 March 1782 to do .... is 10. 9.10 ..... 14.011.11

99.007.89
Dolls 273.018.89

99.007.89

Treasury Dept.
Registers Office 9th. Octo: 1792

6. LC, Register of the Treasury, Estimates and Statements for 1792, Vol. "134-T," National Archives.

From William Short

The Hague Oct: 9. 1792

Sir

I must premise this letter by begging you a thousand pardons for the error committed in my last[1] in stating from an oversight in subtraction that 36 taken from 54 left *28*—instead of *18*.

According to that quotation therefore which you mention the depreciation that day was more than the fall of exchange & if adopted as the rule of indemnity would occasion a loss to the U.S. which is not the intention of any party. You will have observed in my letter of Dec. 30. 1791. (of which you have acknowleged the rect.) I mentioned having previously informed you "*that the* depreciation of assignats & fall of exchange in France though clearly connected with each other were not uniform in their progression. In the late unprecedented fluctuation the assignats were even lower than the *exchange &c.*"

This was about the time of the payments being commenced from Antwerp[2] & which was one of the reasons that made me so desirous that they should be made to an agent there on the spot instead of being remitted by bills on Paris. But long before that letter I considered the depreciation as having too nearly gained on the fall of exchange, to be the proper criterion for fixing of itself the indemnity & accordingly I had the honor of mentioning to you in my letter of Nov. 22. (of which also you have acknowleged the rect.) that I did not propose to the commissaries to sell them my bills for specie, as you had mentioned, because their laws &c. had increased intrinsically the value of gold & silver & I add that the difference between assignats & specie has gone on much more rapidly than the difference of exchange. In my letters of Dec 1. from Antwerp, & Dec. 15, from Amsterdam (of which you have never acknowleged the receipt expressly, but which I hope were recieved as they were enumerated to you in my letter of Jan. 26 & their miscarriage not

ALS, letterpress copy, William Short Papers, Library of Congress.

1. See Short to H, September 25, 1792.

2. The loan negotiated by Short at Antwerp commenced on December 1, 1791. For a description of this loan, see Short to H, November 8, 1791, note 4, and November 12, 1791.

mentioned by you) I repeat the subject & mention, why the course of exchange & depreciation are not the just measure of indemnity for the U.S. but the data on which it should be found. My letters since that time have resumed the same subject & added the reasons for my deferring to fix finally this measure & leaving it until the President should have named the person who was to represent the U.S. permanently at Paris.

You may have observed from my several letters (written before & after receiving yours of Sep. 2. 91. announcing the intention of the President as to the indemnity) that the progress of these duties has been as follows. In the beginning of the assignats the fall in the exchange was much more considerable than the rise of specie. This continued for some time. Several causes then beginning to operate, which it is useless to enumerate—specie went on faster in its rise than the exchange in its fall, still however so as not to overtake it for some time. About the month of Dec. last it overtook & passed it in some of its violent fluctuations, as I then mentioned to you.[3] After this again the exchange fell more than the specie rose, & had gone as low I think as 26½ in Amsterdam, when the Jacobin ministry came in & M. de Claviere,[4] famous for his skill in *agiotage,* among them. It was thought he employed artificial means for raising the exchange, in order to confirm the popularity of the ministry —certain it is that an immediate & astonishing rise did take place, I believe as high as 36. for a few days. During this momentary rise in the exchange, assignats probably appreciated also, but I recollect it was not as rapid (the emigrations probably keeping the price of specie nearly the same). Of course if one of those few days were fixed on the standard would be much against the U.S. But even if the price of specie were taken as the measure of indemnity (which I long ago mentioned to you had ceased to be a just.[5] 2) there could be no reason for fixing on the epoch which was the most unfavorable—& which was of short duration—for the exchange soon after fell down again as low as (& perhaps lower than) 30—the assignats I believe remaining about the same. A mean term taken

3. See Short to H, December 30, 1791.
4. Etienne Clavière served as French Minister of Finances from March 23 to June 13, 1792, and resumed this post on August 10, 1792, under the new Jacobin Ministry.
5. See Short to H, November 22, December 1, 1791.

of the fall of exchange & the rise of specie, would shew the former
to be more considerable & of course present a gain for the U.S.
—though less than I think they are entitled to.

The repetition which I have here given you of the progress of
the exchange & of depreciation, & their alternate & irregular fluctuations, will of itself shew that they cannot be considered as the
measure of indemnity, independent of what I have formerly mentioned to you. They must be taken however as the data for finding
out this measure & it is in that light I have presented them to you.
These data being fixed, I considered a short delay in applying
them, as attended with no inconvenience, always supposing however
that that delay would not be extended beyond the existence of the
government which created the assignats.

The manner of applying these data was simple—the exchange
gave the value of the florins paid, in livres tournois. Had gold &
silver continued objects of free commerce & had their place been
fully supplied by the circulating medium substituted to them, so
as that they should have been subjected to no artificial rise of price,
then there would have been nothing to do but to subtract from
the livres tournois paid the difference between specie & assignats.
But as it was; the want of freedom in the commerce of those
articles & the want of assignats of small denomination for ordinary
purposes & other causes, dependent on the national assembly & not
on the U.S. are known to have increased the price of Specie. Of
course this artificial rise becomes an article of consideration, if the
price of specie is to be taken. Various considerations will suggest
themselves. I will mention only one, in addition to what I said on
the subject in my last letter—for some time the assignats were of so
large a denomination, that specie was indispensable for current uses
& this want manifested itself so pressingly that there was a considerably higher value annexed to assignats of a smaller denomination, those of five livres for instance, cost for some time from seven
to ten p. cent when purchased with those of a large denomination.
This shews that the assignats suffered two kinds of depreciation
of which one was owing to their being of such a denomination as
was inconvenient, & which depended on the decree of the assembly.
This part of the depreciation should not certainly regard the U.S.
I will exemplify my idea. Had a decree of the assembly abolished
the circulating coin as existing in Louis, crowns &c. converted them

into bars of the same alloy of 1000 & 2000 livres (as was the case for some time with the assignats) these bars, having lost the advantage of convenience, would probably have had a small decrease in value or the same number of florins wd. have paid a larger quantity of this matter in bars—still the U.S. would certainly have had a perfect right to have taken the advantage & France would have had no right to have asked an indemnity.

I mention these things merely as arguments which will occur in fixing the indemnity, asking leave to refer you to what was said in my last of Sep. 25th. on the subject. I repeat what I then said also —that had I recieved your letter of June 14. before the abolition of the late government in France, I should have considered it my duty not to have let pass that opportunity, & have acted in compliance with the President's will. As matters stand at present & which shew that nothing can possibly be done for some time, so that you may give further instructions, I cannot help repeating how much more agreeable it would be to me if I were associated with some other person in this business—the fixing the indemnity becomes a pecuniary operation of so much importance that it involves a kind of responsibility the most painful & disagreeable of all others, & particularly when confined to an individual. This operation might be without inconveniences concerted with the minister at Paris or London, or both—& if there should be no objection, it would add much to my satisfaction if it were authorized. The interests of the U.S. would also be consulted with more advantage by their ministry being employed, as, no doubt, many considerations would occur to them which escape me.

No post has arrived here since my last to you (supposed to be occasioned by the Austrian army) & I therefore can add no information to what I then said respecting the late payment to France; a circumstance which has much prolonged my uncertainty & consequent anxiety. Spain has lately opened a loan of six million of florins at Amsterdam at 4½ p. cent. The bankers are going on procuring bills to pay that debt. The late loans at 4½ p. cent added to an article printed here in a Dutch gazette, under the head of New York; which gives an idea of a system of anarchy being begun there has much depreciated the American *obligations*. The bankers however suppose the fall will be momentary. I have had the honor of recieving your letters of Aug. 4. & Aug. 16. My late letters will have shewn you that the debt to the foreign officers will take but a small part of what remains on hand.[6] I inclose you a valuable work, worthy of confidence. It was written by M. Pitt's secretary & corrected by Ld. Auckland.[7] Your obedt. servt.   W Short

The Honble
Alexander Hamilton Secretary of the Treasury.

6. See Short to H, August 3, 1790, July 19, August 8, 23, October 10, 1791, and H to Short, August 16, September 13, 1792.
7. Short may be referring to the draft of an Anglo-Dutch treaty which was drawn up by William Wyndham, Lord Grenville, and corrected by William Eden, Lord Auckland, British Ambassador to The Hague.

To James Watson [1]

Philadelphia October 9
1792

My Dear Sir

I was very glad to find your name on the list of Directors of The Manufacturing Society.[2] I trust it will be in your power to give a portion of your time and attention to it; from which I am persuaded it will profit.

When I was last at New Ark,[3] I thought I perceived something like an intention to bring forward Mr. Samuel Ogden [4] as Superintendant of the Manufactory. To you I do not scruple to say that in my judgment it would be fatal to the Society.

I   Mr. Ogden is without exception one of the most opiniated men I ever knew. On this particular subject he seems to think there is nobody, but himself, who has a single rational Idea. In one week, he would drive L'Enfant [5] off the ground. Already he has affirmed that L'Enfant knows nothing of *Water works*, when it is well known that he was regularly bred to this, as a part of his profession. He is *by Trade* what is called in France a *civil Engineer* that is an Artist acquainted with Mechanics generally; particularly in reference to Architecture *Aqueducts Canals* &c &c including necessarily a knowlege of Hydraulicks. This is the mans profession, & from my knowlege of him I *rely* that he will undertake nothing which he is not able to execute solidly and well. I should therefore deem it a misfortune that any thing should happen to deprive the Society of his Services.

2 Mr. Ogden is generally what may be called a Projector & of course not a man of sound views.

3 He has a multiplicity of other affairs and s[c]hemes on hand and would not be a *totus homo* to the Institution.

4 He is extremely disliked by all the persons who are to be at the head of the particular branches of the Manufactory which has proceeded from his overbearing and excessive pretensions.

5 He is a man too much addicted to hospitality and conviviality, and does not possess those habits of minute attention regular disapline & strict œcononomy which are essential to such an undertaking. He is particularly deficient in the talent of making the most of the labour of a number of hands. On this last point I speak from the most *authentic information* founded *on experience*. This in especial confidence.

You are however at liberty to make known my opinion & the reasons of it substantially to Walker, Clarkson, Le Roy—& with somewhat more of caution to *Rickets.*[6]

Yours with sincere esteem & regard   A Hamilton

James Watson Esqr

ALS, National Society, Daughters of the American Revolution, Washington, D.C.

1. Watson, a New York City merchant and bank director, was a stockholder in the Society for Establishing Useful Manufactures.

2. Watson had been elected a director of the Society for Establishing Useful Manufactures on October 3, 1792. The election was recorded in the society's minutes for October 12, 1792 ("Minutes of the S.U.M.," 52–53, 72).

3. H had been in Newark, New Jersey, in early October.

4. Ogden, who was the brother-in-law of Gouverneur Morris and the founder of Ogdensburg, New York, was a New Jersey iron manufacturer and land speculator. From 1789 to 1791 Ogden was the manager of Robert Morris's manufacturing establishment on the Delaware River near Morrisville, Pennsylvania. On July 6, 1792, Robert Morris noted that he had agreed to buy Ogden's share in the "Delaware Works" since the enterprise had proved unsuccessful under Ogden's management. A part of the payment for Ogden's share was arranged when Morris assumed full responsibility for a loan made by the Bank of North America in 1789, which had been "borrowed at Mr. Ogdens request for the use of the said Delaware Works, under his most solemn promise that no part thereof should be applied to any other use" (D, partly in the handwriting of Robert Morris, Wastebook, 1792–1796, Historical Society of Pennsylvania, Philadelphia).

5. Pierre Charles L'Enfant had been appointed to superintend the erection of the works of the Society for Establishing Useful Manufactures.

6. Benjamin Walker, Matthew Clarkson, Herman Le Roy, and James Rick-
etts were directors of the Society for Establishing Useful Manufactures.

To the President and Directors
of the Bank of the United States

[*Philadelphia, October 10, 1792.* On January 2, 1793, Hamilton
wrote to the president and directors of the Bank of the United
States and referred to "my letter to you of the 10th of October
last." *Letter not found.*]

From George Clymer [1]

[Pittsburgh, October 10, 1792]

Sir

It remains, to compleat the several objects [2] which I stand instructed on, that I state to you the condition of the westermost
Survey of my district.

The Survey includes in it five Counties—Washington, Fayette,
Westmoreland, Allegany and Bedford. The temper and disposition
of the first four of these Counties with respect to the Excise may be
understood generally from what I have already wrote, but there are
shades of difference between them to be remarked, proceeding
from the character and views of individuals who have obtained
influence among the people.

Washington—This county is the most repugnant to the law and
furnishes the most examples of violence. Bradford a lawyer who
prosecutes in the state courts under the attorney general, and
Marshal, once county lieutenant now register, are the great leaders.[3]
The justices of the peace and clergy also are among the most outrageous.

Fayette—Scarce more moderate than the former 'tho occasion has
not ministered to as many acts of violence. Smilee and Gallatin [4]
both members of the state assembly are the professed leaders.

Westmoreland—Engaged in the general opposition, 'tho the father
of all the disturbances of the Western Country [5] has to save his own
character given it in this County a particular direction. He has

accordingly kept his people of Westmoreland out of Combinations and Committees, thinking it more adviseable to hand a petition around the county to be signed individually. An Officer however has no better treatment here than in other counties.

Allegany—has taken no decided part—it has proceeded to no violences yet afraid to run counter to the general spirit. I do not know any professed leader of opposition nor yet any one of sufficient Courage to advocate the Law. Consequently, 'tho an officer should have nothing to fear from combination, yet he would not be protected from individual insult.

It may seem strange that among so numerous a people as inhabit these Counties, none are to be found willing to support the government of the United states—in Truth, the whole mass, under Finley and Smiley, being once thoroughly corrupted and disaffected to it would now at best, the Excise out of the question, be but perfectly indifferent to it. Individuals there are, undoubtedly, who think rightly, but all their men of distinction are either sordid shopkeepers, crafty lawyers or candidates for office, not inclined to make personal sacrifices to truth or honour. There is besides no small reason to suspect an infusion of state jealousy. It may be said too, in general, that the duties of Citizenship are but poorly understood, or regarded where the moral sense is so greatly depraved as it is in this Country, by the intemperate use of the favourite drink. He must be inattentive indeed who does not make this observation.

Bedford—the last in the Survey—the duty here has not been yet collected, not so much from any opposing spirit as from some other causes, for under the influence of Mr. George Woods,[6] and Mr. Espy [7] and some of their friends of the town of Bedford, this County is well attached to the federal government. But the County, 'tho of great extent, is very thinly inhabited and poor, 'tho Collector has not found security, and General Nevil [8] would perhaps have as much to fear from the ferocious spirit of the people of Washington for pretending to execute the law in Bedford as in that County, and Bedford interposing a great barrier has kept the contagion from travelling easterly. Particular attention must however be immediately paid to Bedford, as it is in the passes of that County we must expect to stop the contraband liquors of the other four Counties.

In estimating the demandable revenue of the four Counties, General Nevil goes upon the Supposition of fifteen hundred Stills yielding annually five hundred gallons each. And Marshall, in the last Committee, spoke of twelve hundred as the number of the Stills, and forty three thousand dollars as the Sum of the duties; there is however no certainty in this matter, for the law not being executed there are of course no authentic documents.

I am Sir With the greatest consideration and respect Your most obed st   Geo Clymer

October 10. 1792
Secretary of the Treasury.

ALS, Connecticut Historical Society, Hartford.

1. For background to this letter, see H to Tench Coxe, September 1, 1792; H to George Washington, September 1, 8, first letter of September 9, September 11, 22, 26, 1792; H to John Jay, September 3, 1792; "Draft of a Proclamation Concerning Opposition to the Excise Law," September 7, 1792; Jay to H, September 8, 1792; Edmund Randolph to H, September 8, 1792; Washington to H, September 7, two letters of September 17, September 21, October 1, 1792; Clymer to H, September 28, October 4, 1792; Rufus King to H, September 27, 1792; Washington to Thomas Mifflin, September 29, 1792.

2. See H to Coxe, September 1, 1792; see also Clymer to H, September 28, 1792, note 2.

3. David Bradford and James Marshal had attended the August 21–22, 1792, meeting at Pittsburgh. See H to Coxe, September 1, 1792, note 5.

4. John Smilie and Albert Gallatin also had attended the August 21–22, 1792, meeting. See H to Coxe, September 1, 1792, note 5.

5. William Findlay, who had emigrated from Ireland to America before the American Revolution, had served in the Pennsylvania legislature during the Confederation period. A "constitutionalist" in state politics and an Antifederalist in national politics, he followed the political views most prevalent in western Pennsylvania. Findlay had been an outspoken opponent of the Excise Act and was reputed at this time to be the author of the articles signed "Sidney," which were among the strongest attacks on H's financial policies to appear in the Philadelphia newspapers.

6. Woods was an associate judge of the Court of Common Pleas of Bedford County.

7. David Espy was prothonotary of the Court of Common Pleas of Bedford County.

8. John Neville was inspector of the revenue for the four western counties in Pennsylvania.

To Sharp Delany

Treasury Department October 10th 1792

Sir

If a vessel bound to a foreign port, is by distress of weather, compelled to put into any port of the united States, where upon *due examination* such vessel is found to be unfit to proceed on her voyage, so as to render the transferring of her cargo to another vessel necessary, I am of opinion, that the Tonnage duty is not to be demanded. But an entry must be made of the cargo and the duties paid or secured, and the proceedings for drawing back the duties must be as in other cases of reexportation.

I am Sir   Your obedt Servant   Alexander Hamilton

Sharp Delany Esqr
Collector Philadelphia

LS, Bureau of Customs, Philadelphia; copy, RG 56, Letters to Collectors at Small Ports, "Set G," National Archives; copy, RG 56, Letters to the Collector at Philadelphia, National Archives.

To Charles Cotesworth Pinckney

Philadelphia October 10th
1792

My Dear Sir
    I duly received your letter of the 6th of September;[1] and have sent an extract of it to Mr Church[2] for the explanation which is necessary.

    I feel myself truly obliged by your friendly allusion to my unpleasant situation, and for the consolation you are so kind as to offer me. The esteem of the discerning and virtuous must always support a mind properly formed under the pressure of malevolence and envy. I will not pretend that I am insensible to the persecution which I experience; but it may be relied upon, that I shall desert no post, which I ought to endeavour to maintain, so long as my own reputation or the public good may render perseverance necessary or proper. When it is not requisite either to the one or the other my friends will excuse me, if I recollect that I have a growing and hitherto too much neglected family.

    It is to be lamented that so strong a spirit of faction and innovation prevails at the present moment in a great part of this Country. The thing is alarming enough to call for the attention of every friend to Government.

Let me not be thought to travel out of my sphere if I observe that a particular attention to the election for the next Congress is dictated by the vigorous and general effort which is making by factious men to introduce every where and in every department persons unfriendly to the measures, if not the constitution, of the National Government.

Either Governor Clinton or Mr. Burr of New York, both decidedly of the description of persons, I have mentioned, is to be run in this quarter as Vice President in opposition to Mr. Adams.[3] The former has been invariably the enemy of National Principles. The latter has no other principle than to *mount at all events* to the first honors of the State & to as much more as circumstances will permit—a man in private life not unblemished. It will be a real misfortune to the Government if either of them should prevail. Tis suspected by some that the plan is only to divide the votes of the N & Middle States to let in Mr. Jefferson by the votes of the South. I will not scruple to say to you in confidence that this also would be a serious misfortune to the Government. That Gentleman whom I once very much esteemed, but who does not permit me to retain that sentiment for him, is certainly a man of sublimated and paradoxical imagination—entertaining & propagating notions inconsistent with dignified and orderly Government. Mr. Adams whatever objections may be against some of his theoretic opinions is a firm honest independent politician.

Some valuable characters are about to be lost to the House of Representatives of their own choice. I feared once that this would be the case with Mr. Smith of your state;[4] but I believe his present intention is rather to continue to serve. I trust there can be no doubt of his success and I wish means to be used to determine his acquiescence. He is truly an excellent member—a ready clear speaker of a sound analytic head and the justest views—I know no man whose loss from the House would be more severely felt by the good cause.

The delicacy of these observations from me will of course occur to you. I make them without reserve confiding equally in your friendship & prudence. Accept the assurances of the cordial esteem & regard with which I have the honor to remain

D Sir   Yr. Obedient servant   Alex Hamilton

Charles Cotesworth Pinckney Esqr.

ALS, Charleston Library Society, Charleston, South Carolina.
1. Letter not found. See, however, H to Pinckney, June 25, 1792.
2. John B. Church.
3. For the possible candidacy of George Clinton and Aaron Burr, see H to John Adams, June 25, August 16, September 9, 1792; Rufus King to H, September 17, 27, 1792; H to ———, September 21, 26, 1792; H to King, September 23, 1792; H to George Washington, September 23, 1792.
4. William Loughton Smith was a Federalist Congressman from South Carolina and a frequent spokesman for H in the House of Representatives.

From Jean Marie Roland

Paris, le 10 Octobre 1792, l'an 1.er de la Republique Françoise.

J'ai l'honneur de vous adresser ci-joint, Monsieur, un imprimé revêtu du sceau de l'Etat, de la Loi du 26 Août dernier, qui confère le titre de Citoyens François à plusieurs Etrangers.[1] Vous y lirez, que la Nation vous a placé au nombre des amis de l'humanité & de la société, auxquels Elle a déféré ce titre.

L'Assemblée Nationale, par un Décret du 9 Septembre, a chargé le Pouvoir exécutif de vous adresser cette Loi;[2] j'y obéis, en vous priant d'être convaincu de la satisfaction que j'éprouve d'être, dans cette circonstance, le Ministre de la Nation, & de pouvoir joindre mes sentimens particuliers à ceux que vous témoigne un grand Peuple dans l'enthousiasme des premiers jours de sa liberté.

Je vous prie de m'accuser la réception de ma Lettre, afin que la Nation soit assurée que la Loi vous est parvenue, & que vous comptez également les François parmi vos Frères.

Le Ministre De L'Intérieur
de la République Françoise.
Roland

M. Jean Hamilton, dans les Etats-unis de l'Amerique

LS, Hamilton Papers, Library of Congress.
1. This letter was addressed to "M. Jean Hamilton." On the back of the letter H wrote: "Letter from Government of French Republic transmitting me a Diploma of Citizenship mistaking the *Christian* name."
2. The enclosure is entitled "LOI. Qui confère le titre de Citoyen François à plusieurs Etrangers. Du 26 Août 1792, l'an quatrième de la Liberté." This is a printed document and it is in the Hamilton Papers, Library of Congress. It reads as follows:
"L'Assemblée Nationale, considérant que les hommes qui, par leurs écrits & par leur courage, ont servi la cause de la liberté, & préparé l'affranchissement des peuples, ne peuvent être regardés comme étrangers par une Nation que ses lumières & son courage ont rendue libre.

"Considérant que, si cinq ans de domicile en France, suffisent pour obtenir à un étranger le titre de citoyen François, ce titre est bien plus justement dû à ceux qui, quelque soit le sol qu'ils habitent, ont consacré leurs bras & leurs veilles à défendre la cause des peuples contre le despotisme des rois, à bannir les préjugés de la terre, & à reculer les bornes des connoissances humaines.

"Considérant que, s'il n'est pas permis d'espérer que les hommes ne forment un jour devant la loi, comme devant la nature, qu'une seule famille, une seule association, les amis de la liberté, de la fraternité universelle, n'en doivent pas être moins chers à une Nation qui a proclamé sa renonciation à toutes conquêtes, & son desir de fraterniser avec tous les peuples.

"Considérant enfin qu'au moment on une convention nationale va fixer les destinées de la France & préparer peut être celle du genre humain, il appartient à un peuple généreaux & libre, d'appeler toutes les lumières & de déférer le droit de concourir à ce grand acte de raison, à des hommes qui par leurs sentimens, leurs écrits & leur courage s'en sont montrés si éminemment dignes.

"Déclare déférer le titre de citoyen François au docteur Joseph Priestley, à Thomas Payne, à Jérémie Bentham; à William Wilberforce, à Thomas Clarkson, à Jacques Mackintosh, à David Williams, à N. Gorani, à Anacharsis Cloots, à Corneille Pauw, à Joachim-Henry Campe, à N. Pestalozzi, à Georges Washington, à Jean Hamilton, à N. Maddisson, à H. Klopstock, & à Thadée Kosinsko."

From Daniel Delozier

[*Baltimore, October 11, 1792.* On October 16, 1792, Hamilton wrote to Otho H. Williams: "Mr Delozier mentions in his letter of the 11th instant." [1] *Letter not found.*]

1. For background concerning this letter, see Williams to H, December 16, 1791; H to Williams, September 7, 1792.

From William Irvine and John Kean

[*Philadelphia*] *October 11, 1792.* "Conformably to the order of the Senate of the United States to you of the 7th of May last,[1] and to your request in your letter of the 6th. instant[2] we herewith inclose the account required."

LS, RG 46, Second Congress, 1791–1793, Reports of the Secretary of the Treasury (2A-F2), National Archives.
1. For this order, see "Treasury Department Circular to the Collectors of the Customs," August 31, 1792, note 1.
2. Letter not found.

To Thomas Jefferson

Treasury Department
October 11th 1792.

sir

I have it in contemplation to make arrangements for the payment of the debt, which appears on the Books of the Treasury, to be due to His Most Catholic Majesty, being for advances made on account of the United States during the late War with G Britain.[1]

I make this communication, in order that if any reasons against the payment exist in the knowlege of the Department of State they may be made known.

I have the honor to be   Very Respectfully   sir Your Obedt Servt
Alexander Hamilton

The Secretary of State

LS, Thomas Jefferson Papers, Library of Congress.
1. See Joseph Nourse to H, October 9, 1792.

To Jeremiah Olney [1]

Treasury Department
October 12th 1792.

Sir

In answer to your letter of the 4th instant I cannot but express my regret and disappointment, that you should have considered my letter of the 19th Ultimo as not sufficiently explicit to induce you [2] to receive entries in case of collusive transfer. I have revised my letter, and to me it appears very explicit and very decisive.

What more could I do, than give my opinion, that the appearances stated by you afforded the presumption of a design to evade the law sufficiently strong to *justify* an Officer in refusing the credit; and that if an action should be brought against an Officer for such refusal, in the event of damages against him, if he should appear to have acted with due caution, and upon sufficient ground of probability, it would be incumbent on the Government to indemnify him?

Suppose a law were to be passed prohibiting such collusive transfers, under penalties, and authorising the Officers to refuse entries, when there appeared probable cause of their having been made, would it not still be necessary, in order to his justification and indemnity, that he should appear to have acted with due caution and upon sufficient ground of probability? Ought he not, so far, to act at his own peril, as a guard against capricious and causeless obstructions to the Merchant?

In the event therefore of the law you mention, the same necessity of due caution would be a condition of your indemnification, as is made such by my letter.

In similar cases, an Officer is bound to act with circumspection, and acting with prudence, it is proper he should confide in the justice of the Government.

It was foreseen that after due caution, from the difficulty of adducing proof inherent in similar trans-actions, it might happen that the decision would be against the Officer and he subjected to damages; in which case the expectation of indemnity is given.

I trust that should fresh instances occur of similar collusive transfers warranted by circumstances equally probable with those which have attended Mr Arnold's case, that you will refuse to receive the entries. The practice which appears to have been introduced by him is of the most pernicious tendency, contrary equally to the interest of the Merchant and of Government; for should it become prevalent, it would inevitably put a stop to the allowance of Credit. It is consequently in my view essential, that it should be withstood in its infancy.

With consideration,   I am, Sir,   Your Obedt Serva⟨nt⟩

A Hamilton

Jere. Olney Esqr.
Collr Providence

LS, Rhode Island Historical Society, Providence; copy, Newport Historical Society, Newport, Rhode Island.

1. For background concerning Welcome Arnold's "collusive" transfers, see William Ellery to H, September 4, October 9, 1792; Olney to H, September 8, second letter of September 13, October 4, 1792; H to Olney, September 19, 24, 1792.

2. A note at this point in the copy states: "The word *not* appears to have been omitted here in the letter."

To the Directors of the Society for Establishing Useful Manufactures [1]

[Philadelphia, October 12, 1792]

Minute of Matters which appear to require the attention of the Directors of the Society for establishing useful Manufactures.

I The appointment of a Superintendant, if an unexceptionable person should present; but if none such should occur it may be still most adviseable to defer till the buildings shall be erected and the works in operation.[2]

II An Application to the Legislature to remove all doubts concerning the power of forfeiting the interest of those who do not pay up. This appears indispensable to the successful prosecution of the business.

III Application to the Legislature to make the Indentures of Minors of equal force with the Contracts of full Aged persons. Perhaps it will be well to authorise at once the taking of apprentices.[3]

IV The authorising the sale of a certain number of Lots to persons (other than Mechanics) who may incline to build and settle. In this case the price of a lot ought to be set high (say not less than 150 Dollars for *one* consisting of a quarter of an acre) and a condition ought to be annexed to oblige the erecting upon it within a year a building of a certain value to be defined. Perhaps Twenty lots will suffice for this purpose. Tis desireable to accelerate some establishments besides those of the Society.[4]

V A person in the character of Store keeper is much wanting. He ought to keep a book and make regular entries in it of all articles *received* and *issued* specifying from and to whom, that a strict accountability may be established. An exact inventory of tools & implements in the possession of each person ought to be taken, when any is broken the *parts* returned when a new one is demanded—when lost a report to be made to the store keeper & noted in some proper column. Here is much opportunity for abuse and waste. It will be well that all articles purchased and sent to the Manufactory should be accompanied with something in nature of a bill of lading or cocquet to be delivered to the Storekeeper so that his books may shew as well by whom & how articles are sent as the particulars of the articles.[5]

A board yard well regulated to be under the care of the Storekeeper or some person under him seems much wanted.[6]

VI   Some reductions of persons or wages may be found practicable but in this it will not be well to dismiss persons who though not immediately essential will be proper to be retained to be prepared for the works when ready. Such persons however will probably be content with half wages till the Manufactory goes into operation.

VII   The Machines ordered were not going forward for want of some materials.[7] It is interesting that all impediment should be removed. It will perhaps be most advantageous to contract for them by the piece but in this case a proper allowance would be to be made to the Society for the use of Shops tools &c.

VIII   *Piece-work* in every branch has been found preferable to working upon wages. Somebody ought to be charged in time with preparing for the Society a scale of allowances *or rates*. The *highest allowances* in England would seem to be the proper standard; which considering collateral advantages will probably suffice.[8] *Young* in his annals gives the rates of wages & compensations in England.[9]

AD, Passaic County Historical Society, Lambert Castle, Paterson, New Jersey.

1. This document is endorsed "October 12th: from Colo. Hamilton respecting objects of immediate use & consequence." Most of the proposals in this document were considered at a meeting of the directors of the Society for Establishing Useful Manufactures at Paterson on October 13, 1792.

2. On October 13, 1792, the directors of the society appointed a committee of four "to Treat with such Person as they may deem proper to be appointed as Superintendant, and make Report to this Board at their next meeting" ("Minutes of the S.U.M.," 73).

3. In the margin opposite the preceding paragraph the word "agreed" is written. Opposite this paragraph "Do." appears.

On October 13, 1792, the directors passed a resolution which incorporated both suggestions in this paragraph ("Minutes of the S.U.M.," 74). On November 16, 1792, Elisha Lawrence of Monmouth County, vice president of the New Jersey Council, presented a petition from the society and brought in a bill concerning the petition which was amended and passed (*Journal of the Proceedings of the Legislative-Council of the State of New-Jersey, Convened in General Assembly at Trenton, on Tuesday the 23d Day of October 1792. Being the first Sitting of the seventeenth Session* [Trenton: Printed by Isaac

Collins, 1793], 20–21). The act as it was passed contains no reference to apprentices ("A Supplement to the Act, intitled, 'An Act to incorporate the Contributors to the Society for establishing useful Manufactures,' " *Acts of the Seventeenth General Assembly of the State of New-Jersey. At a Session begun at
Trenton the 23d Day of October 1792, and continued by Adjournments. Being
the First Sitting* [Trenton, 1792], 804–05).

4. In the margin opposite this paragraph the word "deferred" is written.

5. In the margin opposite this paragraph is written "to be executed by Mr.
Griffiths." On August 20, 1792, James Griffiths had been appointed "Ac-
comptant" of the society ("Minutes of the S.U.M.," 67).

6. In the margin opposite this paragraph is written "to be executed by
Mr. Griffiths."

7. See Thomas Marshall and William Pearce to H, October 3, 1792.

8. Below this suggestion is written: "Committee Mr. [Herman] Le Roy
Mr. [Matthew] Clarkson & Mr. [Cornelius] Ray." The directors' resolution
appointing this committee may be found in "Minutes of the S.U.M.," 74.

9. *Annals of Agriculture, and Other Useful Arts. Collected and Published
by Arthur Young, Esq., F.R.S.* (London, 1784–1815).

Treasury Department Circular
to the Collectors of the Customs

Treasury Department, October 12, 1792.

Sir,

I request that henceforth immediately at the close of every quarter, you will furnish me with a summary of the amount of all Duties,
which shall have accrued in your Office, during such quarter. It will
at the same time be requisite to state the Drawbacks (if any) and
the payments to Inspectors and other charges by computation, where
the true amount cannot immediately be ascertained, in order to know
the net proceeds of the Duties as nearly as may be practicable. In
all cases where the returns for any past quarter have not yet been
transmitted to the Treasury, it will be necessary that the summary
statement be forwarded without delay. It is matter of much moment
that early information of the product of the Duties should be received by the Treasury; which renders a careful attention to this
instruction particularly necessary.

It has occurred that vessels bound to foreign ports have by distress
of weather been compelled to put into ports of the United States,
where upon proper examination such vessels were found to be unfit
to proceed on their voyages, so as to render the transferring of their
cargoes to other vessels necessary, and a question has arisen, whether
such vessels are liable to the Tonnage duty.

I am of opinion that under those circumstances no Tonnage duty is to be demanded. But regular entries must be made of the cargoes, the Duties paid or secured, and the proceedings for drawing back the Duties must be as in other cases of re-exportation.[1]

With great consideration,   I am, Sir, Your obedient Servant,
Alexander Hamilton

LS, to Jedediah Huntington, MS Division, New York Public Library; L[S], to Benjamin Lincoln, RG 36, Collector of Customs at Boston, Letters from the Treasury, 1789–1807, Vol. 4, National Archives; LS to Jeremiah Olney, Rhode Island Historical Society, Providence; LC, to Samuel Gerry, Essex Institute, Salem, Massachusetts; copy, to James Seagrove, Circulars of the Office of the Secretary, "Set T," National Archives; LS, Federal Records Center, Boston; LS, Office of the Secretary, United States Treasury Department.
   1. See H to Sharp Delany, October 10, 1792.

From Thomas Jefferson

Philadelphia Oct. 13. 1792.

Sir

In pursuance of powers which mr Short had confided to me, and urged by the circumstances of the moment, I thought it expedient to desire on the 19th. of April last that no transfer might be permitted of any stock standing in his own name or in the name of any other for his use.[1] The circumstances no longer existing which dictated that caution I desire that the caveat may be considered as withdrawn. I have the honor to be with great respect

Sir   Your most obedt. humble servt   Th: Jefferson

The Secretary of the Treasury

ALS, letterpress copy, Thomas Jefferson Papers, Library of Congress.
   1. See Jefferson to H, April 19, 1792.

From Tobias Lear

United States 13 Octo. 1792

By the President's command T. Lear has the honor to inform the Secretary of the Treasury that the President has appointed William

Lewis to be keeper of the Light-house on Cape Henry,[1] with a salary of four hundred Dollars per annum. The president does not conceive that the circumstance of mr Cormicks[2] being employed to oversee the building of the Lighthouse, tho' in his favor, as sufficiently strong to recommend him as the most proper person to be Keeper of it. Tobias Lear. S. P. US.

T. Lear has mentioned to the president the Auditor's[3] wish to go to Virginia, & he has no objection to his going.

LC, George Washington Papers, Library of Congress.
 1. See H to George Washington, September 22, 1792; Washington to H, October 1, 1792.
 Lewis had been surveyor of the port and inspector of the revenue for the port of Fredericksburg, Virginia.
 2. Lemuel Cornick's contract with Thomas Newton, Jr., which had been made at H's request, is dated August 22, 1791 (copy, RG 26, Lighthouse Letters Received, "Segregated" Lighthouse Records, National Archives).
 3. Richard Harrison.

From Otho H. Williams

Baltimore, October 13, 1792. "Agreeable to your request, of the 8th of last month,[1] I now enclose to you a list of the average freight usually paid from this port.[2] The several rates of the respective articles usually exported from hence, have been ascertained by the Merchants who compose the insurance company, and whose information I deem the most to be relied on. . . ."

Df, RG 53, "Old Correspondence," Baltimore Collector, National Archives.
 1. See "Treasury Department Circular to the Collectors of the Customs," September 8, 1792.
 2. The list is called "Average rates of the Freight of Merchandize exported from the United States to foreign Countries in a time of peace" and is broken down under the following headings: "Description of Mdze or packages for containing them"; "To foreign America East & North of the United States"; "To foreign America So. of the U. States & the West Indies"; "To Europe & its Islands and africa on this side of Cape of G Hope"; "To the East Indies & North West Coast of America" (AD, RG 53, "Old Correspondence," Baltimore Collector, National Archives).

From William Heth

B[ermuda] Hundred [Virginia] 14th. Oct. 1792

Dear Sir

Private

The Distressing dilemma in wch I felt myself when I last addressd you in this way,[1] induced me to turn to the 8th Sect. of the Collection Law.[2] The Surveyor of *this Port*,[3] was, & still is, laid up himself, unable to come out of his room. But, if he was ever so hearty, he is, as totally incapable of performing any one part of the duties of my Office, as *your* French valet. He is seldom here, and knows nothing of the business. The next alternative was, to inform the Surveyor of Petersburg[4] of my situation, & to request *his* attendance immediately, in order to receive such instruction as I might be able to give while up, in case I should be obliged again to leave the office. He attended on Monday and Tuesday last—but having got clear of my fevers for two days, and finding myself recruiting in spite of close confinement, and laboring from sun rise, till 8. OC at night—and that, as he writes so bad a hand, he could be of little use to me, he returned. And tho' I have only the assistance of neighbour, who, as yet, can only Copy—yet, as I trust I am geting Strong, I am not afraid of the reputation of my Office Suffering, respecting current business—for the throng in that way, will be presently over when, like the bears, I may suck my paws all winter. All that mortifies me is that I shall not be able to render my accounts with my usual dispatch.

ALS, Hamilton Papers, Library of Congress.
  1. See Heth to H, October 5, 1792.
  2. Section 8 of "An Act to provide more effectually for the collection of the duties imposed by law on goods, wares and merchandise imported into the United States, and on the tonnage of ships or vessels" provided that "in case of the disability or death of a collector, the duties and authorities vested in him shall devolve on his deputy, . . . in defect of a deputy, the said authorities and duties shall devolve upon the naval officer of the same district . . . ; and if there be no naval officer, upon the surveyor of the port . . . ; and if none, upon the surveyor of the port nearest thereto" (1 *Stat.* 155 [August 4, 1790]).
  3. Christopher Roan.   4. James Gibbon.

From the little tryal which I have had of Major Gibbon's capacity for business, I find that, he is not so well versed in figures as I expected, and that, it would be some time before he could conduct the business of this Office—so, *as to save it from Protest:* Yet, as he is in every respect greatly superior to Roane—is better acquainted with the revenue laws—understands better what he reads, is a man of superior understanding, and a more respectible character, he ought really to be the Surveyor of this Port—for his pride and Ambition would induce him to be active, prying, and inquisitive, and to make himself, at least so well acquainted with the Duties of this Office, as to be able to supply my place, in case of dire necessity; and I think he would be more attentive to orders than Roane—because, he has more sense. 'Tis now four days, since I have seen the boat or hands, or have heard any thing from Roane, notwithstanding the busy season, & my repeated orders to let me have an opportunity of communicating with him every day that the weather will permit. He not only pretends to be disgusted with his Office, & speaks of it with contempt (tho' he receives more than double what he had as Searcher under the State Government, for performing less Services—As his emoluments now, by the late *Salary*, & *Sinecure* fees for measuring the Same Vessel over & over again, are greatly more than adequate to the services which he performs) but is really engaged in making money so many other ways, by hiring his Negros to Load Vessels— a boat to land Ballast—hiring horses—and he will presently have a coasting vessel afloat—as to give me reason frequently to wish, notwithstanding my esteem for him as a blunt honest man, that he would either resign his Office, as he Sometimes talks of, or devote his whole attention to the discharge of the duties of it—i.e. the Surveyors Office, for he is so unequal to what is now imposed upon him, considering him as *Inspector of the Revenue* also, that if he did not employ one of the Inspectors of the Customs and they Share certain emoluments it seems—he would not be able to render a single account required. He is a single man, & Rich. Gibbon, has a family, and wants more than he receives. If their appointments could be changed, I am persuaded the public would be better served: for if Roane should decline going to Petersburg, an Inspector of the Customs on Salary, as mentioned to you in Phila. would be all the Officer necessary *there*, & which, as a *Port of delivery*, ought to be annihilated; and the few Coasters which are able, and do go there, ought to be enterd & cleard at City Point. The Salary, now given to the Surveyor there—130 Dlls—would, I should suppose, be sufficient for the Inspector. This change, is an Idea of my own altogether, and which, has only struck me within this day or two—for I pledge you my honor, that it was never suggested, or thought of by me, while Gibbon was here, nor do I know whether he would approve of it, for he has Just rented for five years the Seat of the late Jermon Baker decd—opposite Petersburg. But has proceeded altogether, from my not receiving that aid & communication from Mr Roane, wch I have a right to expect, and which, the laws have contemplated; and from a full conviction, that he has not the capacity of the other. My personal esteem, & friendship for them, I do assure you, is equal. Nor would I, if in my power, make the change immediately—nor without apprizing Roane that such a thing might take place, unless he paid more application, & made himself better acquainted with business—if in his power—for which subject, I mean to have some serious conversation with him—for I disdain the very Idea, of ever attempting to bring about any Scheme, by underhanded work. But, if this Office Should be removed to Petersburg on the Petition of the Merchants,[5] Roane, I am afraid, will be totally inadequate to certain duties, which must, in consequence of the removal, be imposed upon the Surveyor here. He is a good officer, as far as he has capacity—but the Office of *Searcher*, which he held under the State Government (at about £80 ℀ Annum I believe) was fully commensurate with his abilities.

The construction of the law, which produced your *Schedule of Duties*,[6] hath drawn forth against you, a good deal of abuse. This, can not but irritate me, while I hold your principles, and views, in as high estimation, as I long have done, however wide we may differ in opinion, on certain questions.[7] Some say, it is proof of your attachment to the British Interest, and others, that it proceeds from your fondness to make things complex, and difficult to understand, like the ⅔ds *of* ⅔ds *&c* and that, it is a forced, and unwarrantable

5. See Heth to H, October 5, 1792.
6. See "Treasury Department Circular to the Collectors of the Customs," June 25, 1792. See also H to Charles Lee, August 3, 1792.
7. See Heth to H, June 16, November 20, 1791; H to Heth, June 23, 1791.

construction. And tho I agree with the general voice, that the construction cannot possibly be consistent with the *intention* of Congress, if we are to Judge from every preceding act on the subject of duties—Yet, when I have shewn that the Attorney General gave the opinion,[8] you have still borne the blame, and *he* has been calld a time server, and the *supple creature of the Minister.* The Merchants, rather than lose the time which it takes to cull an Invoice, & estimate Duties ℔ a British Bottom, & be detained at so wretched a place as this, have begd to be charged as if an American Bottom, and then add ten ℔ Ct. as heretofore.[9] The difference in time which it takes is very great, to say nothing of the difficulty and perplexity which it occasions to many to calculate fractions of a ℔ Cent. You have enclosed a copy of an endorsation Just made on an entry ℔ a British Bottom—with what it *would have* been, on an american. You will find eight estimations in one, and only four in the other and the difference only *6¾* ℔ Ct in favor of the american, instead of *Ten,* which was the Intention of Congress, say every member, with whom I have conversed, since I had the pleasure of seeing you. However *Just* the construction which you have given of the Law, *may be,* Yet it produces too many absurdities, for any man of *common understanding* to believe that, it is consistent, with the spirit, letter, or intention of the act. For instance, Iron—*cast slit* & rolld—is at 10¾ —but *Manufactures of Iron* is 10½ ℔ a Foreign Bottom—and *all* ten ℔ Ct ℔ an American bottom—again—Glauber salts is at 200 Cts ℔ Cwt and ¾ ℔ Ct. ad. Val—in two or three instances—this ad. Val-duty has amounted to matter of *two Cents.* Now is not this too ridiculous & contemptible, for any man to suppose it was ever contemplated by Congress. (The same thing may be said of Porter &c. ℔ dozen). And do you not think that the trouble wch. it occasions, will induce many of the Collectors to overlook a few pounds of Salts when found mixd with other medecines?—for there is seldom an hundred wt imported by one Man—and Why Should Epsom & Rochele salts be more favord? In Short Sir, to enumerate all the

8. In his circular of June 25, 1792, H had stated that the Attorney General concurred in H's opinion regarding duties under "An Act for raising a farther sum of money for the protection of the frontiers, and for other purposes therein mentioned" (1 *Stat.* 259–63 [May 2, 1792]).

9. See "Treasury Department Circular to the Collectors of the Customs," June 25, 1792.

absurdities and inconsistencies which are daily discoverd, would take up too much of your time, and I am persuaded you must long since have been convinced, that the Law ought to be amended so as to place the business upon the former footing after the first of January next.

I am Dear Sir, with most sincere affection   Yr friend & Hbe St

W Heth

Colo. A Hamilton

[*Americanus*] [1]

[Philadelphia, October 15, 1792]

[Philadelphia] *Gazette of the United States,* October 20, 1792.
   1. Although Philip Marsh has stated that " 'Americanus' . . . sounds very like Hamilton" ("Hamilton's Neglected Essays, 1791–1793," *The New-York Historical Society Quarterly,* XXXII [October, 1948], 295), there is no conclusive evidence that H was the author of this essay.

Draft of George Washington's
Fourth Annual Address to Congress [1]

[Philadelphia, October 15–31, 1792]

It is an abatement of the satisfaction, with which I meet you, on the present occasion, that in felicitating you on a continuance of the

ADf, Hamilton Papers, Library of Congress.
   1. On August 26, 1792, Washington wrote to H requesting suggestions on "matters . . . of general import that may be fit subjects for the speech at the opening of the ensuing Session" of Congress. He sent similar requests to Henry Knox, Edmund Randolph, and Thomas Jefferson (Washington to Knox, September 3, 1792, LC, George Washington Papers, Library of Congress; Randolph to Washington, October 28, 1792, ALS, George Washington Papers, Library of Congress; Washington to Jefferson, August 23, 1792, LC, George Washington Papers, Library of Congress).
   Knox sent his proposals to Washington on October 14, 1792, and on the following day Jefferson submitted two paragraphs to Washington which H used in his draft of the President's message (Knox to Washington, ALS, George Washington Papers, Library of Congress; Jefferson to Washington, AD, letterpress copy, Thomas Jefferson Papers, Library of Congress).
   The President's message, which was delivered to Congress on November 6, 1792, was derived essentially from H's draft, although it contained a few changes and additions, some of which had been suggested by Knox and

national prosperity, generally, I am not able to add to it information, that the Indian hostilities, which have for some time distressed our N Western frontier, have terminated.

You will doubtless learn, with as much concern as I communicate it, that reiterated endeavours to effect a pacifaction have hitherto issued only in new and outrageous proofs of persevering hostility on the part of the tribes, with whom we are in contest. An earnest desire to procure tranquillity to the frontier, to stop the further effusion of blood, to arrest the progress of expence, to promote the prevalent wish of the Country for peace, have led to strenuous efforts, through various channels, to effect that desireable end; in which neither my own calculations of the event, nor any scruples which may have occurred concerning the dignity of government have been permitted to outweigh the important considerations that have been mentioned.

A detail of the measures, which have been adopted, will be laid before you, from which I persuade myself it will appear to you, that means as proper and as efficacious, as could have been devised have been employed. The issue indeed of some of them is yet depending; but while a favourable one is not to be despaired of, every antecedent and collateral circumstance, discourages an expectation of it.

In the course of these attempts, some valuable citizens have fallen victims to their zeal for the public service. A sanction hitherto commonly respected even among savages has not been sufficient to protect from slaughter the messengers of peace.

It will I presume be duly considered whether the occasion does not call for an exercise of liberality towards the families of the deceased.

It must add to your concern to know that, in addition to the continuation of hostile appearances among the tribes, North of the Ohio, some threatening symptoms have lately been revived among some of those South of it. According to the last accounts, an attack upon the settlements within the Territory of the US[2]

Jefferson subsequent to H's draft (Knox to Washington, October 27, 1792, LC, George Washington Papers, Library of Congress; Jefferson to Washington, November 1, 1792, AD, letterpress copy, Thomas Jefferson Papers, Library of Congress; AL, George Washington Papers, Library of Congress). In *HCLW*, VIII, 102–09, this document is dated November 6, 1793.

2. At this point H left several lines blank in his draft and in the middle of the blank space wrote: "were meditated on the part of."

Further evidence however is necessary to ascertain the reality and extent of the evil; and in the mean time defensive precautions only have been permitted.

It is not understood that any breach of Treaty or aggression, on the part of the UStates or their Citizens is even alleged, as a pretext for the spirit of hostility in this quarter. Other causes for it are indicated which it would be premature to particularise.

I have reason to believe that every practicable exertion has been made to be prepared for the alternative of a continuance of the War in pursuance of the provision made by law.[3] A large proportion of the troops authorised to be raised have been recruited—but the number is still incomplete. A particular statement from the proper department, on this subject, and in relation to some other points, which have been suggested, will afford more precise information as a guide to the Legislative consulations; and among other things will enable Congress to judge whether some additional stimulous to the recruiting service may not be adviseable.

In looking forward to the future expences of the operations which may be necessary, I derive consolation from the information, I receive, that as far as the product of the revenues for the present year is known at the Treasury, there is a strong prospect that no additional burthens on the community will be requisite for the supplies of the ensuing year. This however will be better ascertained, in the course of the present session; and it is proper to add, that the information proceeds upon the supposition of no material extension of the spirit of hostility.[4]

I cannot dismiss the subject of Indian affairs, without recalling to your attention, the necessity of more adequate provision, for giving energy to the laws throughout our Interior Frontier, so as effectually

On October 27, 1792, Knox wrote to Washington: "The statement relatively to the Cherokees will be made tomorrow, or next day at the furthest. The intelligence received this afternoon from Governor [William] Blount [of the Southwest Territory] renders alterations necessary" (LC, George Washington Papers, Library of Congress). In the address delivered by Washington two paragraphs concerning Indian depredations were inserted at this point (*GW*, XXXII, 206–07).

3. H is referring to "An Act for making farther and more effectual Provision for the Protection of the Frontiers of the United States" (1 *Stat.* 241–43 [March 5, 1792]).

4. In MS, "hostilility."

to restrain depredations upon the Indians, without which every pacific system must prove abortive; and also for enabling the employment of qualified persons to reside as Agents among the Indians; an expedient of material importance in the sucessful management of Indian affairs. If some efficacious plan could be devised for carrying on Trade with the Indians upon a scale adequate to their wants and under regulations calculated to protect them from extortion and imposition, it would prove hereafter a powerful mean of preserving peace and a good understanding with them.

The prosperous state of our Revenue has been intimated. This would be still more the case, were it not for the impediments which in some places continue to embarrass the collection of the duties on home made spirits. These impediments have lessened and are lessening, as to local extent, and as applied to the community at large the spirit of acquiescence in the law [5] appears to be progressive.

But symptoms of an increased opposition having recently manifested themselves in certain quarters, particularly in one where the enjoyment of immediate benefits from the common contributions of the country was to have been expected to fortify the general sense of respect and duty towards the government and its laws and the disposition to share in the public burthens—I thought a special interposition, on my part had become proper and adviseable; and under this impression I have issued a proclamation [6]

Measures have also been begun for the prosecution of offenders: and Congress may be assured that nothing within constitutional and legal limits which may depend on me shall be wanting to assert and maintain the just authority of the laws. In fulfilling this trust, I shall

5. The excise was collected under "An Act repealing, after the last day of June next, the duties heretofore laid upon Distilled Spirits imported from abroad, and laying others in their stead, and also upon Spirits distilled within the United States, and for appropriating the same" (1 *Stat.* 199–214 [March 3, 1791]) as amended by "An Act concerning the Duties on Spirits distilled within the United States" (1 *Stat.* 267–71 [May 8, 1792]).

6. See "Draft of a Proclamation Concerning Opposition to the Excise Law," September 7, 1792.

At this point in the MS H left several lines blank. In the address as delivered by Washington this sentence was completed as follows: ". . . warning against all unlawful combinations and proceedings, having for their object or tending to obstruct the operation of the law in question, and announcing that all lawful ways and means would be strictly put in execution for bringing to justice the infractors thereof, and securing obedience thereto" (*GW*, XXXII, 208–09).

count intirely upon the full cooperation of the other departments of Government and upon the zealous support of all good citizens.

I cannot forbear to bring again into the view of the Legislature the expediency of a Revision of the Judiciary system. A representation from the Judges of the Supreme Court,[7] which will be laid before you points out some of the inconveniences that are experienced. In the course of the administration of the laws, considerations arise out of the structure of that system, which tend to impede their execution. As connected with this subject, some provisions respecting the taking of bail upon processes out of the Courts of the United States, and a supplementary definition of offences against the constitution and laws, and of the punishments for such offences are presumed to merit particular attention.[8]

The interests of a nation when well understood will be found to

7. On November 7, 1792, Washington submitted to Congress the representations of the judges of the Supreme Court and of the Circuit Court of North Carolina (LC, George Washington Papers, Library of Congress; printed in *ASP, Miscellaneous,* I, 51–53).

8. On October 28, 1792, Randolph replied to Washington's request for information for his message to Congress as follows:

"On revolving the subjects, with which I am officially connected, I discover none, deserving the notice of congress, except those, which are comprehended in the necessity of reforming our judicial system. The detail of them would be almost infinite; and certainly too minute for a communication from the executive: Nor can the congress forget the admonitions, which they have already received on this head. And yet I am so deeply impressed with the dangers to which the government is exposed from this quarter, that it would be a happy circumstance, if they could be stimulated to the discussion.

"Were I to indulge myself in a general review of our political situation, I should probably repeat without use topics, which have presented themselves to your own mind, or which have been suggested more accurately by others, to whose departments they belong: I confess indeed, that I feel at the present crisis these strong solicitudes: that the public be assured of stability in the *existing* fiscal arrangements; that the redemption of the public debt be commenced at no distant day; that the land office, if the hostility of the Indians will permit, be employed, as one of the instruments of redemption; that the state-governments be prohibited from intermeddling with the Indian tribes, to the utmost limit of the constitution; that some temporary mode be provided for the relief of many crippled soldiers, who must beg or starve, until the schism between the legislative and judiciary shall be adjusted; and that the violence of the sanguine states, which may be disappointed on the final settlement of their accounts with the United States may in some manner or other be softened.

"I cannot undertake to say, that these hints are capable of being carried into practice, or are intitled to your attention. But I submit them, according to your instructions, without a comment; as you will know how to appreciate them." (ALS, George Washington Papers, Library of Congress.)

coincide with their moral duties. Among these, it is an important one to cultivate peace and friendship with our neighbours. To do this we should make provision for rendering the justice we must sometimes require from them. I recommend therefore to your consideration whether the laws of the Union should not be extended to restrain our citizens from committing acts of violence within the territories of other nations, which would be punished were they committed within our own. And in general the maintenance of a friendly intercourse with foreign Nations will be presented to your attention, by the expiration of the law [9] for that purpose, which takes place, if not renewed at the close of the present session.

In execution of the authority given by the Legislature measures have been taken for engaging some artists from abroad to aid in the establishment of our Mint; [10] others have been employed at home. Provision has been made of the requisite buildings, and these are now putting into proper condition for the purposes of the establishment. There has been also a small beginning in the coinage of half dismes and cents; the want of small coins in circulation calling the first attention to them.[11]

9. Section 2 of "An Act providing the means of intercourse between the United States and foreign nations" provided that the "act shall continue and be in force for the space of two years, and from thence until the end of the next session of Congress thereafter" (1 *Stat.* 129 [July 1, 1790]).

10. Section 2 of "An Act establishing a Mint, and regulating the Coins of the United States" provided that the director of the mint should employ necessary workmen subject to the approbation of the President (1 *Stat.* 246 [April 2, 1792]).

11. The two preceding paragraphs were written by Jefferson and sent to Washington on October 15, 1792 (see note 1). On November 1, 1792, Jefferson submitted the following alterations which Washington incorporated in his speech to Congress:

"Instead of the paragraph 'The interests of a nation &c.—within our own,' formerly proposed, the following substitute is thought better.

"All observations are unnecessary on the value of peace with other nations. It would be wise however, by timely provisions, to guard against those acts of our own citizens, which might tend to disturb it, and to put ourselves in a condition to give that satisfaction to foreign nations, which we may sometimes have occasion to require from them. I particularly recommend to your consideration the means of preventing those aggressions by our citizens on the territory of other nations, and other infractions of the law of Nations, which, furnishing just subject of complaint, might endanger our peace with them. And in general the maintenance &c." (AD, letterpress copy, Thomas Jefferson Papers, Library of Congress.) On November 1, 1792, Jefferson wrote a second letter to Washington in which he suggested minor changes to his first letter (AL, George Washington Papers, Library of Congress).

The regulation of foreign coins in correspondency with the principles of our national coinage will I doubt not be resumed and completed, being a matter essential to the due operation of the system and to order in our pecuniary concerns.

It is represented that the regulations contained in the law which establishes the Post Office operate in experiment against the transmission of News Papers to distant parts of the Country.[12] Should this, upon due inquiry, be found to be the fact, the Legislative wisdom will doubtless apply a remedy; under a full conviction of the great importance of facilitating the circulation of political intelligence and information.

Information has been received of the adoption of a Constitution for the State of Kentuke.[13] An event so interesting to the happiness of the part of the nation to which it relates, cannot but make a correspondent impression. The Communications concerning it will be laid before you.

It is proper likewise to inform you, that since my last communication on the subject, in further execution of the Acts severally making provision for the public Debt and for the Reduction thereof [14] three new loans have been effected one for 3000000 of florins at Antwerp at 4½ ℔ Ct and   [15] ℔ Ct charges and two others each for 3000000 of florins at Amsterdam at 4 ℔ Ct &   [16] ℔ Ct. charges.[17]

12. Section 22 of "An Act to establish the Post-Office and Post Roads within the United States" stated the rates to be charged upon newspapers (1 *Stat.* 238 [February 20, 1792]).
13. Kentucky adopted a constitution on April 19, 1792, at a convention held at Danville, Kentucky. On October 20, 1792, Washington acknowledged a letter from Samuel McDowel which enclosed a copy of the constitution (ALS, RG 59, Miscellaneous Letters, 1793–1799, National Archives).
14. "An Act making provision for the (payment of the) Debt of the United States" (1 *Stat.* 138–44 [August 4, 1790]) and "An Act making Provision for the Reduction of the Public Debt" (1 *Stat.* 186–87 [August 12, 1790]).
15. Space left blank in MS.   16. Space left blank in MS.
17. In the President's speech the description of the foreign loans reads as follows: ". . . three new loans have been effected, each for three millions of Florins. One at Antwerp, at the annual interest of four and one half per Cent, with an Allowance of four per Cent in lieu of all charges; and the other two at Amsterdam, at the annual interest of four per Cent, with an allowance of five and one half per Cent in one case, and of five per Cent in the other in lieu of all charges. The rates of these loans, and the circumstances under which they have been made, are confirmations of the high state of our Credit abroad" (*GW*, XXXII, 211).
On November 3, 1792, Washington wrote to Jefferson in reply to Jefferson's

Among the objects to which these funds have been directed to be applied, the payment of the debts due to certain foreign officers according to the provision made for that purpose during the last session [18] is included.

H of R.[19]

I entertain a strong hope that the state of the National Finances is now sufficiently matured to enable you to enter upon systematic and effectual arrangements for the regular redemption and discharge of the public debt, according to the right, which has been reserved to the Government. No measure can be regarded as more desireable whether viewed with an eye to its intrinsic importance or to the general sentiment and wish of the Nation.

Provision likewise is requisite for the reimbursement of the loan which has been made of the Bank of the UStates pursuant to [20] Section of the Act by which it is incorporated. In fulfilling the public stipulation, in this particular, a valuable saving may it is expected be made.

Appropriations for the service of the ensuing year and for such

---

second letter of November 1, 1792 (see note 11): "The erasures from the Speech—as you advise⟨d⟩—are made, except exchange the word 'high' for 'just.' If facts will justify the former (as I think they indubitably do) policy, I conceive, is much in its favor. For while so many unpleasant things are announced as the Speech contains, it cannot be amiss to accompany them with communications of a more agreeable nature" (ALS, Thomas Jefferson Papers, Library of Congress).

18. "An Act supplementary to the act making provision for the Debt of the United States" (1 *Stat.* 281–83 [May 8, 1792]).

19. In the margin opposite this abbreviation H wrote: "Qr as to Regulation of Compensations." No reference to compensations was made in Washington's speech to Congress.

20. Space left blank in MS. Section 11 of "An Act to incorporate the subscribers to the Bank of the United States" reads as follows: "*And be it further enacted,* That it shall be lawful for the President of the United States, at any time or times, within eighteen months after the first day of April next, to cause a subscription to be made to the stock of the said corporation, as part of the aforesaid capital stock of ten millions of dollars, on behalf of the United States, to an amount not exceeding two millions of dollars; to be paid out of the monies which shall be borrowed by virtue of either of the acts, the one entitled 'An act making provision for the debt of the United States,' and the other entitled 'An act making provision for the reduction of the public debt,' borrowing of the bank an equal sum, to be applied to the purposes, for which the said monies shall have been procured; reimbursable in ten years, by equal annual instalments; or at any time sooner, or in any greater proportions, that the government may think fit" (1 *Stat.* 196 [February 25, 1791]).

extraordinaries as may have occurred will demand and I doubt not will engage your early attention.

Senate & H of Repres

I content myself with recalling your attention generally to such objects suggested in my former communications as have not yet been finally acted upon and as are not previously particularised.

The results of your joint deliberations, hitherto, will, I trust, be productive of solid and durable advantages to our constituents; which by conciliating more and more their approbation may tend to strengthen and confirm their attachment to that Constitution of Government upon which depend under Divine Providence, union safety and prosperity.

Still further to secure these inestimable ends, there is nothing, which can have so powerful a tendency as the careful cultivation of harmony combined with a due regard to stability in the public councils.

From William Ellery

Colles Office [Newport, Rhode Island] Oct. 15 1792

Sir,

This letter will be accompanied by a Statement of fees &c recd. and expenditures made by me from Oct. 1, 1791 to Oct. 1792. and by similar Statements from the Inspector &c &c in this District;[1] by the quarterly return required exceptg a Return of distilled Spirits exported, and a return of Exports, and their value which will be transmitted by the next Post. I have not received the expected Letter from the Comptroller, and therefore have put on an account only of the expenditures on the Light House for the last quarter.[2]

I am, Sir, Yr. most obedt. servt.   W Ellery Colle

A Hamilton Esqr
Secry Treasury

LC, Newport Historical Society, Newport, Rhode Island.
    1. See "Treasury Department Circular to the Collectors of the Customs," August 31, 1792, and Ellery to H, September 24, 1792.
    2. See Ellery to H, July 16, August 20, 1792.

From Thomas Randall [1]

New York, October 15, 1792. "Please to pay to Tench Coxe Esqr. Three Hundred and Eighty Dollars 77/100 for Oil bought . . . for the Light house at Cape Henry Virginia."

ALS, RG 26, Lighthouse Letters Received, Lighthouse Expenses, National Archives.
1. Randall was superintendent of the lighthouse at Sandy Hook, New Jersey.

To John Steele

Philadelphia October
15. 1792

My Dear Sir

The letter which you did me the favour to write me of the 19th of September came to hand two days ago.[1]

The late symptoms of acquiescence in the duty on distilled spirits, which you announce in your quarter are particularly satisfactory. If the people will but make trial of the thing, their good will towards it will increase. This has hitherto happened every where, where the law has gone into operation. There certainly can be no tax more eligible or less burthensome.

Though I impose on myself great circumspection on the subject of elections for the Fœderal Government, yet in relation to the characters you mention, I feel myself more at liberty, and my intire confidence in you will not permit me to affect reserve.[2] I take it for granted that in all the Northern and Middle states, the present President will have an unanimous vote. I trust it will be so in the South also. A want of unanimity would be a blot in our political hemisphere and would wound the mind of that excellent character, to whom this Country is so much indebted.

For Vice President, Mr Adams will have a nearly unanimous vote in the Eastern States. The same thing would happen in New York, if the Electors were to be chosen by the People; but as they will be chosen by the Legislature, and as a majority of the existing assembly are Clintonians, the electors will I fear be of the same complexion. In Jersey Mr. Adams will have a unanimous vote and according to present appearances in Pensylvania likewise. The parties have had a trial of their strength here for representatives, and though the issue is not finally ascertained, there is a moral certainty from the returns received that the Ticket supported by the Fœderal Interest will prevail by a large majority. The electors *nominated* by the same interest will all or nearly all favour Mr Adams. I believe the weight of Delaware will be thrown into the same scale. And I think it probable there will be votes for Mr. Adams in Maryland. I presume none in Virginia or Georgia. Of North Carolina you can best Judge. In South Carolina, he will have votes but I am at a loss to judge of the proportion.

This statement will inform you, that Mr. Adams is the man, who will be supported in the Northern & Middle States by the friends of the Government. They reason thus—"Mr. Adams like other men has his faults and his foibles. Some of the opinions he is supposed to entertain, we do not approve—but we believe him to be honest firm faithful and independent—a sincere lover of his country—a real friend to genuine liberty; but combining his attachment to that with the love of order and stable government. No man's private character can be fairer than his. No man has given stronger proofs than him of disinterested & intrepid patriotism. We will therefore support him as far preferable to any one, who is likely to be opposed to him."

Who will be seriously opposed to him I am yet at a loss to decide. One while Governor Clinton appeared to be the man. Of late there have been symptoms of Col Burr's canvassing for it. Some say, one or both of these will be played off as a diversion in favour of Mr. Jefferson.

I do not scruple to say to you, that my preference of Mr. Adams to either of these characters is decided. As to Mr. Clinton he is a man of narrow and perverse politics, and as well under the former as under the present Government, he has been steadily since the termination of the war with Great Britain opposed to national principles. My opinion of Mr. Burr is yet to form—but according to the present state of it, he is a man whose only political principle is, to *mount at all events* to the highest legal honours of the Nation and as much further as circumstances will carry him. Imputations not favourable to his integrity as a man rest upon him; but I do not vouch for their authenticity.

There was a time when I should have ballanced between Mr. Jefferson & Mr. Adams; but I now view the former as a man of sublimated & paradoxical imagination—cherishing notions incompatible with regular and firm government.

Thus have I opened myself to you with frankness. I doubt not that I am perfectly safe in doing it.

You give me pain by telling me that you have declined serving in the house of Representatives after the 3d. of March next [3] and that it is doubtful whether you will attend the next session.

I anxiously hope that you will find it convenient to attend and that you will change your resolution as to not serving in a future house. The ensuing session will be an interesting one, and the next Congress will either anchor the Government in safety or set it afloat. My apprehension is excited when I see so many valuable members dropping off. Mr. Laurance & Mr. Benson [4] will not serve again. Mr. Barnewell [5] also declines. The house will I fear lose more of its talents than it can spare.

With the truest esteem and regard   I remain Dr Sir   Your obedient servant   Alexander Hamilton

John Steele Esqr

ALS, Southern Historical Collection, University of North Carolina Library.
    1. Letter not found.
    2. For the possible candidacy of George Clinton, Aaron Burr, and Thomas Jefferson, see H to John Adams, June 25, August 16, September 9, 1792; Rufus King to H, September 17, 27, 1792; H to ———, September 21, 26, 1792; H to King, September 23, 1792; H to George Washington, September 23, 1792; H to Charles Cotesworth Pinckney, October 10, 1792.
    3. The October 17, 1792, issue of the [Philadelphia] *Gazette of the United States* contained a letter from Steele dated September 22, 1792, to the grand jury of the Salisbury district. In this letter Steele stated officially that he would not run for reelection. Although Steele apparently expected to obtain a seat in the United States Senate (H. M. Wagstaff, ed., *The Papers of John Steele* [Raleigh, 1924], I, 100), Alexander Martin, who had been governor of North Carolina for five terms, was elected to the Senate seat in question in 1792.
    4. John Laurance and Egbert Benson of New York.
    5. Robert Barnwell had represented the Beaufort, South Carolina, district in 1792.

Fact No. II [1]

[Philadelphia, October 16, 1792]

For the National Gazette.

Genuine Truth never deviates into misrepresentation. That an impostor has assumed its name in the National Gazette of the 10th inst. is sufficiently evinced by the following circumstance. The writer, who appears under that signature, after endeavouring to torture certain expressions of the Secretary of the Treasury, into a meaning which, construed with candour, and in connection with their context, never could be put upon them—proceeds thus, "If these opinions seem to be contradicted in any manner or degree by the other observations of this officer, namely, that 'the creation of debt should always be accompanied with the means of extinguishment,' and 'that there should be a constant effort to reduce the present and avoid new debts as far as may be,' it is most fairly to be explained by allowing for a more cautious language *latterly produced by the public alarm taken at such doctrines,*" *Etc.* Now, it happens, unfortunately for this uncandid interpretation, that the first of the above quoted positions (to wit) that "the creation of debt should always be accompanied with the means of extinguishment," is contained in the *very first* communication, or report, which the Secretary of the Treasury ever made on the subject of the public debt; [2] in that *very report* which contains the expressions tortured into an advocation of the doctrine that public debts are public blessings; in immediate connection with the *very expressions* upon which that construction has been put.

Again: The phrase "critical point," quoted from a report of the Secretary of the Treasury on Manufactures,[3] is made to refer to that *point* at which public debts cease to be public blessings; whereas in the true sense in which the phrase is used, it refers really to that point, at which "A public debt may be swelled to such a size, as that the greater part of it may cease to be *useful as capital,* serving only to pamper the dissipation of idle and dissolute individuals, as that the sums required to pay the interest of it may become *oppressive &* *beyond* the means which a government can employ *consistently with its tranquility,* to raise them; as that the *resources of taxation* to face the debt may have been strained too far, to *admit of extension adequate to exigencies which regard the public safety;*" (see page 25 of the report of the Secretary of the Treasury on Manufactures). It is this *"critical point,"* including a complication of circumstances of which the Secretary speaks, and concerning which he observes, that *"where it is* cannot be pronounced; tho' it is impossible to believe that there is not such a point:" this is a further sample of the disposition to mistake and misrepresent. In fine, the just and obvious construction of what the Secretary has said is simply this—that while it cannot be admitted as a general proposition, that public debts are public blessings, with which latitude the doctrine is sometimes laid down, yet there may be *particular situations* of a country, in which a portion of a public debt, funded on right principles, may be advantageous *by supplying a deficiency of actual capital*—and that such was the situation of the United States, at the time the question concerning a provision for the public debt was depending, that the proper funding of the existing debt would render it a public advantage—and hitherto at least the position is verified by experience.

Gloomy predictions of the future, it is true, are thrown out, by factious, or hypochondriac politicians; but these being mere predictions, must be referred for their fulfilment or refutation to *Time.*

In any event, the doctrine charged upon the Secretary of the Treasury, which he emphatically terms *"a doctrine inviting to prodigality, and liable to dangerous abuse,"* is not attributable to any thing he has said, still less to any thing he has done. If conduct is allowed to be a test of sincerity, the course he took in the last session, in regard to the war with the Indians, is a pregnant and energetic proof of his *aversion* to an accumulation of debt.[4] Whatever may be the good or ill qualities of that officer, much flexibility of character is not of the number. He is not therefore liable to the suspicion of having disavowed any principle which he really entertains, because it may have excited a degree of clamour.   FACT.

Philad. Oct 16

[Philadelphia] *National Gazette,* October 17, 1792.
    1. "Fact No. II" was written in reply to an article dated October 8, 1792, and signed "Truth" which appeared in the *National Gazette* on October 10, 1792. "Truth" was writing in reply to H's "Fact No. I," September 11, 1792. The article by "Truth" reads as follows:
    "I have read with sedulous attention all the late discussions about the political

doctrines of the Secretary of the Treasury, (the political opinions of public men being of public importance to every citizen) and have carefully gone over his reports, so far as relating to or declaratory of his particular opinions; as well as repeatedly perused the various published extracts therefrom with the comments; and, upon the whole, I think it *impossible* for *candour* to deny, or for *prudence* to attempt to *explain away*, the following positions, or the deductions flowing therefrom. From *his own shewing*, it is clearly his opinion,

"That, tho' he cannot accede to the position 'in *the latitude*, in which it is *sometimes* laid down, that *public debts* are *public blessings*,' tho' 'there may be a *plethora* in the body politic,' in this respect, 'as in the natural body'; tho' 'there *may be* a state of things in which every such artificial capital is unnecessary.'

"Yet that in *a certain latitude*, short of what is *sometimes* contended for, 'at *a critical point*,' which it is impossible to doubt the existence of; and in the *ordinary* state of things, *public debts* are *public blessings;* and particularly, that 'the proper funding of the *present* debt (amounting to above *seventy millions*) will render it (not the funding, paying or *providing for*, but said *debt itself*) a *national blessing*.'

"If these opinions seem to be contradicted in any manner or degree, by the other observations of this officer, namely that 'the creation of debt should always be accompanied with the means of extinguishment,' and 'that there should be a constant effort to reduce the present and avoid new debts, as far as may be,' it is most fairly to be explained, by allowing for a more cautious language latterly, produced by the public alarm taken at such doctrines; and also by the expectation, that there will be no fear of having enough of this *national blessing*, 'as the vicissitudes of nations beget a *perpetual* tendency to the *accumulation* of debt'; and 'as there is *too strong a propensity* in the government of nations, to anticipate and *mortgage* the resources of *posterity*, rather than encounter the inconveniencies of a present increase of taxes.

TRUTH."

([Philadelphia] *National Gazette*, October 10, 1792.)
2. "Report Relative to a Provision for the Support of Public Credit," January 9, 1790.
3. "Report on the Subject of Manufactures," December 5, 1791.
4. For information on the "course" which H "took in the last session, with regard to the war with the Indians," see "Fact No. I," September 11, 1792. See also "Report Relative to the Additional Supplies for the Ensuing Year," March 16, 1792.

From John F. Mercer [1]

Annapolis Octr. 16th. [-28] 1792 [2]

Sir

You must attribute the delay of my answer to yours of the 26th. of September to the extreme indisposition of my family. In replying

LS, Hamilton Papers, Library of Congress.
1. For background to this letter, see the introductory note to H to Mercer, September 26, 1792. See also H to David Ross, September 26, 1792; Ross to H, October 5–10, 1792.
2. Although this letter is clearly dated and endorsed "October 16," it could

now I cannot avoid noticing the Letter which you address'd to Major Ross at the same time and on the same subject[3] and which that Gentleman consider'd himself as authoriz'd to circulate in an hand-Bill whilst my Election was depending.

Altho we naturally enter with warmth into the feelings of any Gentleman, who even fancies that his integrity has been publickly questioned—yet a mind divested of the impulse of passion must condemn the hastiness of your adopting the vague statements of an avow'd Partizan—nor can it admit that decorum of situation was in the least regarded, in committing your name, with the harsh expressions you have used in regard to me, to be publickly handed about and pasted upon Sign Posts to influence the weak and uninform'd during a contested Election.

So far as your name or conduct has been involv'd in public discussion during the late contest in this District you may render thanks to your Worthy and respectable Friends. It has been involuntary on my part. You have in fact been lugg'd into this business by those who thro' weakness or wickedness or perhaps both have been already real Enemies to your reputation and may eventually prove more so.

Prompted by a delicacy which your absence imposed I cautiously confin'd my justification against the charges leveled at my conduct, (as far as they related to you and as far as circumstances wou'd permit) to what I had asserted uncontradicted on the floor of Congress[4]—and I am at a loss to conceive how even an hurried impression from the groundless publication to which you refer coud have led you into the Error that I had in any manner represented you as a Stock Jobber or Dealer in Certificates on your own Account—for altho' in general it may be imagin'd by minds unsophisticated by financial refinement that a Man entrusted with the public Money wou'd lay it out to the same advantage as his own—Yet even pursuing the statement of Major Ross, it must have been no slight infatuation that cou'd lead an intelligent being seriously to suppose that I

---

not have been sent on that date. The enclosures which accompany this letter (see notes 6 and 7) are all dated after October 16, the latest bearing the date of October 26. Either Mercer misdated the letter or he retained it until the enclosures had been assembled.

3. See H to Ross, September 26, 1792.
4. See Mercer's speech of January 27, 1792, in the House of Representatives (*Annals of Congress*, III, 349–54).

had accused you of giving 18/. of your own Money for Stock when offered it at 14/.

I stated that in my judgment you had unjustifiably sacrificed the other Interests of the United States to a particular and by no means a meritorious Class—and even the great bulk of that Interest together with the rest of the Community to a few unworthy Individuals, who from their immediate situation on the spot—their connections and information (however acquired) of the intended purchases of Stock on public Account, coud make a certain profitt of the measures of Government by your *giving* or *directing* to be given on Account of the United States 20/. for 6 pr Cents when the current price averaged from 17/6. to 18/6 and 12/. for 3 pr Cents when others bought @ 10/. and 10/6 for these were statements that I had before made on the floor of Congress and produc'd in their support the public papers of Philadelphia and New York and after repeated public enquiry, did not understand that they wou'd be denied. And that when you receiv'd Stock, under Sealed proposals for the Sale—where three different parcels were offered at three different prices, instead of taking the whole of the lowest offer, you took equal proportions of each, by which means for elucidation, I stated that you had given 18/. when offered at 14/. and altho' that these were exactly the prices, is what I cannot precisely affirm, yet that the statement was substantially and effectively true, is what I apprehend, will not be denied. At least if denied, I shall hold myself bound to prove it—nor will it I suppose be urged that any immediate Agent in this business has acted otherwise than in conformity to your orders or those of the Board of which you are a Member.[5] Or that a Majority of this Board have not regularly determin'd in strict unison with your sentiments and views, altho' more than one may have differ'd with you on the propriety and justice of these principles of promoting public Credit.

But that you were privately interested in any of these, or any similar transactions, directly or indirectly, is what I never conceiv'd myself nor hinted a suspicion of to others. And that I never impeach'd your integrity as an Individual or public Officer (farther than that in the pursuit of public objects) without any other private

5. See H to Ross, September 26, 1792.

view than that of encreasing your own influence and attaching to your administration a Monied Interest as an Engine of Government, your political principles differed from my own, may be so construed, in either a public address or private conversation the Certificates enclosed will I hope fully and effectually establish. With respect to my public address they are from Gentlemen, who having been present at the time alluded to by Major Ross and having divided in sentiment on the Election, have maintain'd thro' life such a Moderation of Character and propriety of conduct, that their impressions from the Statements and sentiments I delivered can in no wise be attributed to a political biass.[6] With respect to my private conversation, they are from Characters whose veracity and direct views being above all suspicion, are those with whom I have been in the habits of the utmost confidence and to whom I have unbosom'd myself without reserve on my Objections to your Administration.[7] These Certificates are taken with a view to justify

6. Mercer had addressed the following letter, dated October 18, 1792, to Clement Hill, David Craufurd, Henry Rozier, and Notley Young:

"In reply to a Letter of the Secretary of the Treasury to me and one to Major Ross on the same subject (a printed Copy of which is enclosed) I have written the answer herewith transmitted.

"It has become necessary for me Gentlemen to Sollicit seperate answer from each of you to the following Queries—

"1st. Did you in my address to the People at Prince George's Court, conceive that I either express'd or hinted a charge or suspicion that the Secretary of the Treasury was a Buyer or Seller of Stock on his private account directly or indirectly. 2nd. Did you conceive that I in any manner impeach'd his integrity as a private Individual or public Officer. I wou'd also be much Obliged to you to add your own Impressions how far the mention I made of this Gentleman in my address was honorable or dishonorable to him.

"I have directed this Letter to you Gentlemen for the reasons stated in my letter to the Secretary and from a confidence that your love of truth and justice will lead you to rectify any erroneous impressions made thro' mistake or for sinister purposes." (Copy, Hamilton Papers, Library of Congress.)

Mercer enclosed the following replies which he had received to his letter: Hill to Mercer, October 21, 1792; Craufurd to Mercer, October 22, 1792; Young to Mercer, October 23, 1792. Most of these letters testify in Mercer's behalf (copies, Hamilton Papers, Library of Congress).

7. Mercer addressed another letter, dated October 18, 1792, to Samuel Chase, William Paca, Jeremiah Chase, and Walter Bowie, requesting them to state whether he had ever in private conversation made defamatory remarks about H's integrity (copy, Hamilton Papers, Library of Congress). The replies to this letter are the following: Samuel Chase to Mercer, October 19, 1792; Paca to Mercer, October 26, 1792; Jeremiah Chase to Mercer, October 19, 1792; Bowie to Mercer, October 22, 1792 (copies, Hamilton Papers, Library of Congress). At the bottom of the letter from Paca Mercer wrote: "No answer has yet been received from Mr. Henry Rozier."

myself to the World and to prove that I am incapable of taking any advantage of the absence of any Individual to impeach his integrity. They are not intended as a justification to you—the terms of your address to Major Ross, the manner and purposes for which it has been used, forbid this. I refine a publication under the Signature of the Secretary of the Treasury of the United States (an Officer of distinguish'd merit during a great Revolution) stuck up throughout this District [8] among the dirty and infamous libels of a desperate Banditti (copies of some of which I have enclosed) compells me tho' reluctantly to a reply in terms more explicit and much harsher than I have ever either publickly or privately used before with regard to you.[9]

    I am Sir   With due respect &ca   Yr. Ob sr   John F. Mercer

Colonel Alexander Hamilton
Secretary of the Treasury
of the United States

8. H to Ross, September 26, 1792, had been printed and circulated as a broad-side.

9. On a page following the enclosures sent with this letter, Mercer wrote the following: "Postscript—I do not find from enquiry, that I ever represented Mr. Hamiltons views to any Persons in public or private as having a tendency to increase his personal Influence with the Monied Interest—but as that impression has been on my own Mind—I thought it probable that I had mentioned & have stated it in this Letter. John F. Mercer."

To William Short

Treasury Department
Philadelphia October 16th 1792

Sir

    There being a Vessel in port ready to sail for Amsterdam, I take the opportunity to enclose you triplicates of my letters of the 13th Ultimo and 1st instant, and to note to you that I have directed the Treasurer to draw upon our Commissioners [1] at Amsterdam for one hundred thousand guilders, in addition to the sums mentioned in my letter of the 25th of July.

    This I have done in consequence of a persuasion that the late events in France will have interrupted payments to that Country.[2]

I shall however forbear further draughts 'till I receive further advices.

I also enclose a letter to our Minister in France which I request you to forward to him.[3]

With great consideration and esteem, I have the honor to be, Sir, Your Obedt Servant   Alexander Hamilton

William Short Esqr
Minister Resident of the United States at the Hague

LS, William Short Papers, Library of Congress. A copy of this letter was enclosed in H's "Report on Foreign Loans," February 13, 1793.
1. Willink, Van Staphorst, and Hubbard.
2. For the difficulties involved in the payments on the American debt to France after the suspension of the King on August 10, 1792, see Gouverneur Morris to H, September 25, 1792; Short to H, September 25, 1792.
3. Letter not found.

To Otho H. Williams [1]

Treasury Department
October 16th 1792.

Sir

I request that you will have enquiry made *on board the Cutter Active*, whether she is in possession of a double set of arms muskets, pistols, &ca. The Collector of New York [2] was directed to furnish each Cutter with ten muskets and bayonets, twenty pistols, two chissels, one broad axe and two lanthorns. These articles, it appears, have been shipped by Mr Lamb for each of the Cutters—but none have been received at Norfolk.

In my letter to you of the 7th Ultimo I requested this examination to be made, and if it should be found that the Maryland Cutter had received the quantity of arms and instruments above mentioned twice, I desired that one parcel might be forwarded to the Collector of Norfolk.[3] Mr Delozier mentions in his letter of the 11th instant [4] that Simon Deagle delivered one set of the said articles to David Porter, but the real state of the business is not ascertained.

With great consideration, I am, Sir, your Obedt Servant
Alex Hamilton

Otho H Williams Esqr.
Collr Baltimore

LS, Columbia University Libraries.
    1. For background to this letter, see Williams to H, December 16, 1791; H
to Williams, September 7, 1792.
    2. John Lamb.   3. William Lindsay.   4. Letter not found.

To Wilhem and Jan Willink, Nicholaas and Jacob Van Staphorst, and Nicholas Hubbard

Treasury Department
October 16th 1792.

Gentlemen,
    I enclose you the triplicate of my letter of the 19th ultimo—and
have by this opportunity barely to inform you that I have directed
the Treasurer to draw upon you for one hundred thousand guilders
in addition to the sum mentioned in my letter of the 26th of July
last.
    I am &c.   Alexander Hamilton.

Messrs. Willink, Van Staphorst, & Hubbard,
Amsterdam.

Copy, RG 233, Reports of the Treasury Department, 1792–1793, Vol. III, National Archives. This letter was enclosed in H's "Report on Foreign Loans," February 13, 1793.

Catullus No. IV [1]

[Philadelphia, October 17, 1792]

    Attempts in different shapes have been made to repel the charges
which have been brought against the Secretary of State. The defence
of him however in the quarter in which he has been principally
assailed, has hitherto gone no further than a mere shew of defending
him. I speak as to his improper connection with the Editor of the

ADF, Hamilton Papers, Library of Congress; [Philadelphia] *Gazette of the United States*, October 17, 1792.
    1. For background to this document, see "Catullus No. I," September 15, 1792. The other "Catullus" essays are dated September 19, 29, November 24, and December 22, 1792. See also "An American No. I," August 4, 1792, and "An American No. II," August 11, 1792.

National Gazette.[2] But a more serious and more plausible effort has been made to obviate the impression, which arises from his having been originally an objector to the present Constitution of the United States.[3]

For this purpose several letters said to have been written, by Mr. Jefferson, while in Europe, have been communicated.[4] How far they are genuine letters or mere fabrications—how far they may have been altered or mutilated is liable from the manner of their appearance to question and doubt. It is observable, also, that the extract of a letter of the 6 of July [5] contained in the American

2. Philip Freneau.

3. At this point H wrote and crossed out the following paragraph: "For this purpose, several letters said to have been written by Mr. Jefferson while in Europe have been communicated. The first observation, which strikes us concerning them, is that they do not include that letter, which was the subject of animadversion in the Convention of Virginia, the existence of which was admitted by both sides of the Convention, and which is relied upon by the 'American' as supporting one part of his allegation." See James McHenry to H, September 30, 1792.

4. These letters from Jefferson were included in a series of six unsigned articles which were first printed in [Philadelphia] *Dunlap's American Daily Advertiser,* September 22, October 10, 20, 30, November 8, December 3, 31, 1792.

As originally published these articles appeared without a title. When the first of them was reprinted in the [Philadelphia] *National Gazette* on September 29, 1792, it appeared under the heading: "DEFENCE of Mr. Jefferson's political Character, in reply to several Pieces which have appeared against it in the Gazette of the United States." When these articles were reprinted in the [Philadelphia] *Gazette of the United States,* the first three were given no title, but the remaining ones were called "Vindication of Mr. Jefferson."

The first two articles in the "Vindication of Mr. Jefferson" contain extracts of letters which Jefferson wrote from Paris. Jefferson's letters, most of which concern the Constitution, are dated December 20, 1787; February 6 (misdated July 6 in "Vindication of Mr. Jefferson"), May 3, July 31, November 18, 1788; March 15, August 28, 1789. All these letters were addressed to James Madison, and all are printed in full in Boyd, *Papers of Thomas Jefferson,* XII, 438–43, 568–70; XIII, 129–33, 440–44; XIV, 187–90, 659–63; XV, 364–69.

5. In the second article of the "Vindication of Mr. Jefferson" (*Dunlap's American Daily Advertiser,* October 10, 1792) this letter is incorrectly dated July 6, 1788. Its correct date is February 6, 1788. The extract of this letter printed in the "Vindication of Mr. Jefferson" reads as follows: "I am glad to hear that the new constitution is received with favour. I sincerely wish that the nine first conventions may receive and the four last reject it. The former will secure it finally, while the latter will oblige them to offer a declaration of rights in order to compleat the union. We shall thus have all its good, and cure its principal defect. You will of course be so good as to continue to mark to me its progress. I will thank you, also, for as exact a state as you can procure of the impression made on the sum of our domestic debt, by the sale of lands and by federate and state exertions in any other manner."

Dayly Advertiser of the 10th instant though it seems to be intended as part of the one, which is mentioned in the debates of the Virginia Convention, does not answer to the description given of it by Mr. Pendleton, who professes to have seen it. For Mr. Pendleton expressly states with regard to that letter that Mr. Jefferson, after having declared his wish, respecting the issue of the deliberations upon the constitution, proceeds to *enumerate the amendments which he wishes to be secured.*[6] The extract, which is published, speaks only of *a bill of rights,* as the essential amendment to be obtained by the rejection of four states; which by no means satisfies the latitude of Mr. Pendleton's expressions.

Such nevertheless, as it is, it affords an additional confirmation of that part of the American's statement, which represents Mr. Jefferson as having advised the people of Virginia to adopt or not *upon a contingency.*

It happens likewise that the letters, which have been communicated ⟨tend⟩[7] to confirm the only parts of the American's statement of the sentiments and conduct of Mr. Jefferson in relation to the Constitution, which remained to be supported; namely "that he was opposed to it *in some of its most important features,* and at first went so far as to discountenance its adoption." By this I understand, without previous amendments.

From the first of those letters dated "Paris the 20th of December 1787" it appears, that Mr. Jefferson among other topics of objection "disliked and *greatly* disliked the abandonment of the principle of *rotation* in office and *most particularly* in the case of the President": From which, the inference is clear, that he would have wished the principle of rotation to have extended not only to the executive, but to other branches of the Government—to the Senate at least, as is explained by a subsequent letter. This objection goes to the structure of the government in a very important article, and while it justifies the assertion, that Mr. Jefferson was opposed to the Con-

6. For Edmund Pendleton's remarks as quoted in "Aristides," see "Catullus No. I," September 15, 1792, note 2. See also "Catullus No. II," September 19, 1792, note 4. The letter to which Pendleton referred is Thomas Jefferson to Alexander Donald, February 7, 1788 (Boyd, *Papers of Thomas Jefferson,* XII, 570–72).

7. The words within broken brackets in this document have been taken from the *Gazette of the United States,* October 17, 1792.

stitution, *in some of its most important features*, it is a specimen of the visionary system of politics of its Author. Had it been confined to the office of Chief Magistrate, it might have pretended not only to plausibility but to a degree of weight and respecta[bility.[8] By being extended to other branches of the government, it assumes a different character, and evinces a mind prone to projects, which are incompatible with the principles of stable and systematic government; disposed to multiply the outworks, and leave the citadel weak and tottering.

But the *fact* not the *merit* of the objection is the material point. In this particular, it comes fully up to the suggestion which has been made.

It now only remains to see how far it is proved; that Mr. Jefferson at first *discountenanced* the adoption of the constitution in its primitive form.

Of this a person acquainted with the manner of that gentleman, and with the force of terms, will find sufficient evidence in the following passage: "*I do not pretend to decide*, what would be the best method of procuring the establishment of the manifold good things in the constitution, and of *getting rid of the bad*: whether by adopting it *in hopes* of future amendment; or after it has been duly weighed and canvassed by the people; after seeing the parts they generally dislike, and those they generally approve to say to them; 'we see now what you wish—send together your deputies again— let them frame a constitution for you; omitting what you have condemned, and establishing the powers you approve.' " [9]

Mr. Jefferson did not explicitly decide which of these two modes was best; and while *it is clear*, that he had not *determined in favor* of an adoption without previous amendments, it is not difficult to infer from the terms of expression employed, that he preferred the last of the two modes; a recurrence to a second convention. The faintness of the phrase "*in hopes* of future amendment," and the emphatical method of displaying the alternative are sufficient indications of the preference he entertained.

8. A portion of the draft is missing at this point. The material within brackets has been taken from the *Gazette of the United States*, October 17, 1792.

9. This quotation is from the extract of Jefferson's letter of December 20, 1787, which was printed in the first article in "Vindication of Mr. Jefferson" (*Dunlap's American Daily Advertiser*, September 22, 1792).

The pains which he takes in the same letter to remove the alarm naturally inspired by the insurrection which had happened in Massachusetts, are an additional illustration of the same bias. It is not easy to understand what other object his comments on that circumstance] could have, but to obviate the anxiety, which it was calculated to inspire, for an adoption of the constitution, without a previous experiment to amend it.

It is not possible to avoid remarking by the way, that these comments afford a curious and characteristic sample of logic and calculation. "One Rebellion in *thirteen* states, in the course of *eleven* years is but one for each state in a Century and a half": While *France*, it seems, had had three insurrections in three years. In the latter instance the subdivisions of the intire nation are confounded in one mass. In the former, they are the ground of calculation. And thus a miserable sophism is gravely made a basis of political consolation and conduct. For according to the data stated, it was as true that the *U States* had had one rebellion in eleven years, endangering their common safety and welfare, as that *France* had had three insurrections in three years.

Thus it appears from the very documents produced in exculpation of Mr. Jefferson—that he in fact discountenanced in the first instance the adoption of the Constitution; favouring the idea of an attempt at previous amendments by a second Convention; which is the only part of the allegations of the American that remained to be established.

As to those letters of Mr. Jefferson which are subsequent to his knowlege of the ratification of the Constitution by the requisite number of states, they prove nothing, but that Mr Jefferson was willing to play the politician.[10] They can at best only be viewed as acts of submission to the opinion of a Majority, which he professes to believe infallible—resigning to it, with all possible humility, not only his *conduct* but his *judgment*.

It will be remarked, that there appears to have been no want of versatility in his opinions. They kept pace tolerably well with the progress of the business; and were quite as accommodating as circumstances seemed to require. On the 31st of July 1788, when the

10. The letters by Jefferson to which H is referring are dated July 31, November 18, 1788; March 15, August 28, 1789. See note 4.

adoption of the Constitution was known, the various and weighty objections of March 1787 had resolved themselves into the single want of a bill of rights. In November following, on the strength of the authority of three states (overruling in this instance the maxim of implicit deference for the opinion of a majority) that lately solitary defect acquires a companion, in a revival of the objection to the perpetual reeligibility of the President. And another Convention, which appeared no very alarming expedient while the intire constitution was in jeopardy, became an object *to be deprecated*, when partial amendments to an already established constitution were alone in question.

From the fluctuations ⟨of sentiment⟩ which appear in the letters that have ⟨been published,⟩ it is natural to infer, that had the whole of Mr Jefferson'[s] correspondence on the subject been given to the public much greater diversities would have been discovered.

In the preface to the publication of the letters under consideration, this question is put—"Wherein was the merit or offence of a favourable or unfavourable opinion of the constitution and to whom rendered?" [11]

It is a sufficient answer to this question—as it relates to the present discussion, to say, that the intimation which was given of Mr. Jeffersons dislike of the Constitution, in the first instance, was evidently not intended as the imputation of a positive crime, but as one link in a chain of evidence tending to prove that the National Gazette was conducted under his auspices, and in conformity to his views. After shewing that the Editor of that paper was in his pay, and had been taken into it some short time previous to the commencement of the publication, the inference resulting, from this circumstance, of that paper being a political engine, in his hands, is endeavoured to be corroborated, first by the suggestion, that Mr Jefferson had originally serious objections to the Constitution, secondly by the further suggestion, that he has disapproved of most of the important measures adopted in the course of the administration of the Government.

In this light and with this special reference were these suggestions made. And certainly as far as they are founded in fact the argu-

---

11. The quotation is from the first article in the "Vindication of Mr. Jefferson" (*Dunlap's American Daily Advertiser*, September 22, 1792).

ment they afford is fair and forcible. A correspondency of the principles and opinions of Mr. Jefferson with the complexion of a paper, the conductor of which is in the regular pay of his department—is surely a strong confirmation of the conclusion—that the paper is conducted under his influence and agreeably to his views.

Nothing but a known opposition of sentiment on the part of Mr. Jefferson to the doctrines inculcated in the National Gazette could obviate the inference deducible from his ascertained and very extraordinary connection with it. A coincidence of sentiments is a direct and irresistible confirmation of that inference.

An effort scarcely plausible has been made by *another* Aristides,* [12]

---

* The total dissimilarity of stile and manner leaves no doubt that the writer of the first piece signed Aristides is a different person from the Writer of the last. The forces are well marshalled.

12. The first article by "Aristides" had appeared in the *Gazette of the United States* on September 8, 1792. It is quoted in full in "Catullus No. I," September 15, 1792, note 2. The second and final article by "Aristides" was printed in the *National Gazette* on September 26, 1792. This article reads in part as follows: "The last charge, respecting the French debt, and the advice thereupon: which it is asserted Mr. Jefferson gave to Congress, requires more particular notice. In order to support this charge, recourse has been had, as in the other charges, to direct falsehood and the most palpable evasion. A suppression of the truth it is well known is equal to a suggestion of falsehood; and in this instance not only an important part of Mr. Jefferson's letter has been suppressed, but all the circumstances which relate to the extract given, and which would satisfactorily explain it to the public are withheld, altho' those circumstances form part of the letter from which the extract is taken. It may be sufficient perhaps briefly to inform the public that the mutilated paragraph of Mr. Jefferson's letter, quoted by *Catulus*, refers to an offer made by a speculating Dutch company to the French court to purchase the American debt due to that nation at a discount of six or eight million, of livres, to which offer, when communicated by the French minister to Mr. Jefferson for his approbation, he replied that he had no power to approve or disapprove; that Mr. Jefferson made the same answer to the agent of the Dutch company, and in his letter to Congress on the subject, in which he presumes that the same agent would make application to that body, he simply suggests to Congress to consider, if they apprehend any future danger of the punctuality of payment, how far it might be advisable to transfer the discontents, arising from that source, from the French court, whose friendship we ought to cultivate, to the breasts of a private company of adventuring speculators, who foreseeing the possible delays of payment, had calculated the probable loss, and were willing to encounter the hazard. At the same time Mr. Jefferson adds in the next paragraph, what Aristides glances at in his former publication, and what Catulus and his associates have purposely suppressed, to wit—'that in his opinion the honor and credit of the United States may be preserved inviolate.' and then he proceeds 'to suggest the mode and give the advice, by which the French debt may be discharged without discount or loss to that nation, and the stipulations of the United States be complied with to all its creditors' " (*National Gazette,* September 26, 1792).

to explain away the turpitude of the advice, which was given respecting the French Debt. It is represented that a Company of adventuring Speculators had offered to purchase the debt at a discount, foreseeing the delay of payment, calculating the probable loss, and willing to encounter the hazard. The terms employed by Mr. Jefferson refute this species of apology. His words are "If there is a *danger* of the public payments *not being punctual,* I submit whether it may not be better, that *the discontents which would then arise,* should be *transferred* from a *Court,* of whose *good will we have so much need,* to the *breasts* of a *private Company."* [13]

He plainly takes it for granted that *discontents would arise* from the want of an adequate provision and proposes that they should be *transferred* to the breasts of Individuals. This he could not have taken for granted, if in his conception, the purchasers had calculated on delay and loss.

The true construction then is that the Company expected to purchase, at an under value, from the probability, that the Court of France might be willing to raise a sum of money on this fund at a sacrifice—supposing that the U. States counting on her friendly indulgence might be less inclined to press the reimbursement; not that they calculated on material delay or neglect, when the transfer should be made to them. They probably made a very different calculation (to wit) that as it would be ruinous to the credit of the U. States abroad to neglect any part of its debt, which was contracted there with *Individuals,* from the impossibility of one part being distinguishable from another in the public apprehension; this consideration would stimulate to exertions to provide for it. And so it is evident from his own words that Mr. Jefferson understood it.

But the persons, who offered to purchase, were *speculators.* The cry of Speculation as usual is raised; and this with some people is the *panacea,* the *universal cure* for fraud and breach of faith.

It is true, as alleged, that Mr. Jefferson mentioned an alternative, the obtaining of the money by new loans to reimburse the Court of France; but this is not mentioned in any way that derogates from or waves the advice given in the first instance. He merely presents an alternative, in case the first idea should be disapproved.

13. This quotation is in an unknown handwriting.

It may be added, that the advice respecting the transfer of the Debt was little more honorable to the U.States, as it regarded the Court of France, than as it respected the Dutch Company. What a blemish on our National character that a debt of so sacred a nature should have been transferred at so considerable a loss to so meritorious a Creditor!

A still less plausible effort has been made to vindicate the National Gazette, from the charge of being a paper devoted to the calumniating and depreciating the Government of the UStates. No original performance, in defence of the Government, or its measures, has, it is said, been refused by the Editor of that paper.[14] A few publications of this tendency have appeared in it—principally if not wholly since the public detection of the situation of its conductor.

What a wretched apology! Because the partiality has not been so daring and unprecedented, as to extend to a refusal of original publications in defence of the Government, a paper which industriously copies every inflammatory publication against it, that appears in any part of the United States, and carefully avoids every answer which is given to them, even when specially handed to the Editor for the purpose is not to be accounted a malicious and pernicious engine of detraction and calumny towards the Government!!!

But happily here no proof nor argument is necessary. The true character and tendency of the paper may be left to the evidence of every Reader's senses and feelings. And Aristides as often as he looks over that paper must blush, if he can blush, at the assertion "that it has *abounded*, since its commencemt. with publications in ⟨favor⟩ of the measures of the Government." [15]

Deception, however artfully vieled, seldom fails to betray some unsound part. Aristides assures us—that Mr. Jefferson "*has actually refused* in any instance to mark a single paragraph, which appeared in the foreign prints for republication in the National Gazette." [16]

---

14. "Aristides" had written: ". . . the editor of the National Gazette has never refused, in a single instance, to publish an original piece in favor of the measures of government that has been sent to him for publication" (*National Gazette*, September 26, 1792).

15. This is a quotation from the article by "Aristides" in the *National Gazette*, September 26, 1792.

16. This is a quotation from the article by "Aristides" in the *National Gazette*, September 26, 1792.

On what ground was such an application to Mr. Jefferson made, if he was not considered as the Patron of the Paper? What Printer would make a similar application to the head of any other department? I verily believe none. And I consider the circumstance stated as a confirmation of the Relation of *Patron* and *Client*, between the Secretary of State and the Editor of the National Gazette.

The refusal, if it happened, is one of those little under plots, with which the most intriguing man in the United States is at no loss, to keep out of sight the main design of the Drama.

Catullus

From Tench Coxe

Treasury Department, Revenue Office, October 17, 1792. "I have the honor to inclose you a copy of an original Certificate transmitted to me by Thomas Newton Junr.[1] Esquire, and signed by Lemuel Cornick[2] the person employed by him to oversee the building of the Chesapeak light House. It appears from this Document that Mr. John McComb Junr. had completed the execution of his contract on the 2nd Instant.[3] The three Beacon Boats for the three shoals near the entrance of the Bay of Chesapeak having been contracted for in Norfolk for the sum of six hundred and thirty three dollars and two thirds, it has become necessary that provision be made for the payment of that sum into the hands of Thomas Newton Junr. Esqr. to enable him to comply with the public engagement made thro' him. If your direction be given to the Collector of Norfolk,[4] Mr. Newton who seems disposed to superintend the building will receive it from him as there may be occasion. . . . I have the Honor to enclose a copy of the Presidents Act of the 4th August relative to the Business of the Revenue. . . ."[5]

LC, RG 58, Letters of Commissioner of Revenue, 1792–1793, National Archives.
1. Newton was inspector of the revenue for Survey No. 4 in Virginia.
2. See Tobias Lear to H, October 13, 1792.
3. See Newton to H, August 29, 1792.   4. William Lindsay.
5. See Coxe to H, July 25, 1792; H to George Washington, July 30, 1792; Washington to H, August 5, October 1, 1792.

From Edmund Randolph

Philadelphia Octr. 17. 1792.

Sir

On my return home, I found your letter of the 6th. instant.[1] My answer is short; being no more, than this, that there is not a single fee or emolument incident to my office; that I have paid the expences without taking any account, as I expected no retribution; and that my salary is 1900 dollars per annum.[2]

I have the honor, sir, to be with respect Yr. mo. ob. serv.

Edm. Randolph

The Secretary of the Treasury

ALS, RG 46, Second Congress, 1791–1793, Reports of the Secretary of the Treasury (2A-F2), National Archives.
1. Letter not found.
2. Randolph is referring to a Senate order of May 7, 1792. See "Treasury Department Circular to the Collectors of the Customs," August 31, 1792.

From Joseph Whipple

Collectors Office Portsmouth [New Hampshire] Octr. 17. 1792

Sir

Conformably to the order of the Senate of the United States passed the 7th. of May last and with your directions dated the 31st. of August,[1] I have the honor to transmit you herewith, a Statement of my emoluments for one year ending the 1st. of October instant —And also those of the Several Officers who have been appointed by me.

It is with much reluctance that I am led on this Occasion to renew a Subject which must be uninteresting whether viewed in an official light or otherwise. It is respecting my emoluments as Collector of Portsmo: The favourable opinion which I had entertained of the approaching happiness of my country, & the peculiar Satisfaction with which I anticipated the effects of the Federal Government (and which has been amply verified in the administration of the department under which I act) induced me not only to accept but to Seek an Occasion of contributing in some degree towards the execution of it. This ultimately threw me into the office which I now hold, and although the emoluments was not the first object, I entertained an Idea that they would in due time, and when it should be known how to form an opinion of the value of the Services be advanced to an equitable compensation. At the last Session of Congress an addition was made to my emoluments of 100 dollars pr. year & ½ ⅌ Ct. Comm~.[2] This Scarcely yet begins to operate—when it does fully it will yield Several hundred dollars Short of a reasonable reward for the Services, & there will be no kind of consideration for the deficiencies in the three past years, the emoluments of which were

for the first	net 225.92
the second	295. 8
the third	546.88

An unwillingness to relinquish an office that I am not averse to, hath induced me again to mintion this matter to you,[3] and to request that you will be pleased to inform me whether there is a probability of such augmentations being made as will enable me independently of other resources to continue in the execution of it—and whether any further application on my part would be necessary to that end. If the returns now made have any relation to that Object the noticing of the emoluments for the two first years is not I apprehend improper, especially if compensations or grants for deficiencies are admissible.

I think it cannot be conceived that the Services incident to my Several functions as agent for the Cutter superintendent of the Light house & Collector can be executed for less or be worth less than one thousand dollars Net pr. Year, the two former give nothing but are attended with considerable care.

I am with Sentiments of respect & esteem   Sir Your Most Obt. & hume Servt.

The Hon. Alx Hamilton Secy of the Treasy.

LC, RG 36, Collector of Customs at Portsmouth, Letters Sent, 1792–1793, National Archives; copy, RG 56, Letters from the Collector at Portsmouth, National Archives.

1. See "Treasury Department Circular to the Collectors of the Customs," August 31, 1792.
2. The increase in salary and commission was granted by Section 1 of "An Act relative to the compensations to certain officers employed in the collection of the duties of impost and tonnage" (1 *Stat.* 274 [May 8, 1792]).
3. See Whipple to H, June 9, 1791.

From Stephen Cross

Newburyport [Massachusetts] October 18, 1792. "In my letter of May 25th [1] I mentioned that I should make some Observations respecting my being removed from Office. . . . Had not the under officers a right to give the other Officers their whole pay or any part of it if they pleased, and what danger of abuse would arise there from if they did. The money represented to be passed by me. . . . was voluntary left in my hands without any agreement made or suggested by me or by my proposal. . . . What could be the reason of an enquiery whetter some of the under officers were not my near connections, was there any Impropriety in appointing them, or was it not A disgust some persons took on discovering my sons privately watching A Vessell where I suspected A Fraudelant design which I always ordered when I suspected such design it is a satisfaction howeve[r] to me that those People do not Pretend any neglect or Improper conduct in either of them. . . ."

Copy, RG 59, Miscellaneous Letters, 1790–1799, National Archives.
   1. Letter not found.

To Tobias Lear

[Philadelphia] 18th. October 1792.

Dr. Sir,

Before a final step is taken respecting a Keeper of the Virginia Lighthouse,[1] I wish it to be known to The President (what I did not advert to yesterday) that Mr. Cornick [2] was appointed by Colo. Newton [3] to oversee the building of a Lighthouse, for which he will receive a *quantum meruit.* This is a circumstance in his favour tho' a very slight one, and such as may be overruled by any other consideration. Propriety, however, requires that it should be brought into the President's view. If I hear nothing to the contrary to day, the letter to Mr. Lewis will go.[4]

Yrs.   A: Hamilton

LC, George Washington Papers, Library of Congress.
1. See Lear to H, October 13, 1792.
2. Lemuel Cornick. See Tench Coxe to H, October 17, 1792.
3. Thomas Newton, Jr.
4. William Lewis. See Lear to H, October 13, 1792.

To Benjamin Lincoln

Treasury Department
October 18th 1792.

Sir

I have received the petition of John Mackay, Master of the Ship Charlotte, praying for a mitigation or remission of the damages found against him by the Jury, together with a statement of facts on the same subject from the District Judge of Massachusetts.[1]

As the fine was in the discretion of the Jury the imposition of one so considerable as two hundred and fifty Dollars furnishes a presumption that there may have been something more than mere unintentional neglect.[2] I request that you will give me any information that may throw light on the subject.

Is it probable that a remission of the *interest of the United States* only in the penalty imposed could have any disagreeable effect on the minds of the Jurymen, or tend to throw a damp upon the zeal of future Juries?

The present decision at all events does credit to the disposition of the Jury, shewing a firm intention to carry the laws into effectual execution.

I am, Sir, with great consideration,   Your Obedt Servt

A Hamilton

Benjamin Lincoln Esqr.
Collr Boston.

LS, RG 36, Collector of Customs at Boston, Letters from the Treasury, 1789–1807, Vol. 4, National Archives; copy, RG 56, Letters to Collectors at Small Ports, "Set G," National Archives; copy, RG 56, Letters to the Collector at Boston, National Archives.

1. John Lowell.
2. Under the date of June, 1793, the minutes for the District Court of Massachusetts state that H did not remit this penalty (Records of the Massachusetts District Court, Federal Records Center, Boston).

From Tench Coxe

Treasury Department
Revenue Office, October 19th 1792.

Sir,

In pursuance of your desire I have the honor to make to you the following Report of the present Situation of the Revenue on Spirits distilled in the United States in Regard to the acquiescence in and opposition to the laws relative thereto.

In the district of New-Hampshire,

No appearance of opposition has occured: but since the promulgation of the Act of the   [1] May last a sense of the benefits resulting to the distillers from its provisions has been communicated from thence.

In the district of Massachusetts,

also there is no appearance of opposition, and altho' the distillers have from the beginning manufactured more than those of all the other districts wherein the law has been executed, the revenue in the last returned quarter was considerably more than in any of the preceeding. When the defalcation of Molasses, the difficulty of procuring it, and the high price of that raw material are considered, this increase will evince a judicious estimation of the advantages to the Manufacturers resulting from the whole of the laws relative to foreign and domestic Spirits, a satisfaction under the same and an increased confidence in the present establishment of the distilling branch of Business; [2] while it countenances a presumption that the

LC, RG 58, Letters of Commissioner of Revenue, 1792–1793, National Archives.
1. Space left blank in MS. Coxe is referring to "An Act concerning the Duties on Spirits distilled within the United States" (1 Stat. 267–71 [May 8, 1792]).
2. The slave revolution in Santo Domingo, which had commenced in August, 1791, had laid waste the sugar plantations. As a result the price of available molasses rose to exorbitant levels. New England distillers had begun to convert stills previously used to produce rum to the production of other spirits. On

revenue sustains no material injury from Evasion, in that quarter.

In the district of Rhode Island and Providence
there is ground for observations similar to those, which have been made in regard to Massachusetts. It appears that the distilling business in proportion to population is nearly twice as great in this District as in any other, and that the process is so well understood as to warrant an expectation, that the proof and flavor of its grain and molasses Spirits will be rendered in a short time, so like those of foreign Spirits, as to defy discrimination by a great majority of the Consumers.[3] This desireable effect appears to have been commenced thus early in consequence of the difference in favor of the domestic manufacture, created by the laws relative to distilled Spirits.

In the district of Connecticut
this revenue appears to have some degree [of] actual popularity, which indeed seems to be the Case throughout the Eastern States. It is manifest there is no uneasiness concerning it, nor any disposition to embarrass or oppose it.

In the district of Vermont
No unfavorable symptoms have appeared.

In the district of New-York
No discontents exist upon the subject.

In the district of New-Jersey,
the business of distillation from domestic materials is increasing. A few inconsiderable distillers have talked of impeding the execution of the law, but it does not appear that any attempts of that Nature were seriously meditated or have been made. Some complaints have been communicated informally from a respectable quarter in that district, representing the hardship of executing a Revenue law in the greater part of the Union, which is not enforced in all, and suggesting that it might occasion impediments in New Jersey, which are not in the intentions of the people of that district at this time.

June 1, 1792, Coxe had written to Nathaniel Gorham, supervisor of the revenue for Massachusetts: "I am very glad to find the symptoms of the grain and fruit distillery on Connecticut River are such as to have attracted your serious Attention. I have a Confidence that it will become a capital object in the United States" (LC, RG 58, Letters of Commissioner of Revenue, 1792–1793, National Archives).

3. For an attempt to sell Rhode Island rum as produce of the West Indies, see Jeremiah Olney to H, May 31, 1792; Robert Purviance to H, June 14, 1792.

These remarks were produced by the Deportment of the distillers in the Western survey of Pennsylvaa.[4]

In the district of Pennsylvania this revenue is variously treated. No opposition has been made in the City and Liberties of Philadelphia. Objections and Prejudices existed there both on the score of business and government. Among the distillers these have so far given way to reflexion that there is no probability of opposition. Indeed I have no doubt that a repeal of all the laws relative to foreign and domestic Spirits would give great dissatisfaction to them. In the Vicinity of German Town which lies in the County of Philadelphia some efforts have been made against the tax. So far as respects actions, these have been confined to a few guarded & covert ones. Declamation and declamatory writing has been freely used, but it is not understood that the Collector for the division comprehending the County of Philadelphia has met any opposition. In the western part of the County of Chester a voilent attempt was made upon the Collector [5] after the destruction of the Collectors sign at German-Town [6] and some of the disorders in the western Survey, which was probably excited by those examples. But from the firmness of the Officer, the decided conduct and good management of one of the Judges of the state common pleas,[7] some of the persons were taken and thro' the judicious exertions of the Attorney general of the State [8] and of the assistant council retained by the Collector they were duly convicted,[9] and from the Circumstances which occured before and

4. See H to Coxe, September 1, 1792, note 1.   5. Jacob Humphreys.

6. On May 31, 1792, the following "Extract of a letter from Germantown, May 29" was printed in the [Philadelphia] *National Gazette:* "An Excise officer in this place, some short time since, put over his door a sign, notifying that, *there* was THE OFFICE OF INSPECTION. A number of citizens took the liberty however, next day, to pull down the Inspector's sign. Three or four days afterwards, the four quarters of a carrion were hung up in the place of the board that contained the notification."

See also H to John Adams, June 25, 1792, note 3.

7. Walter Finney was an associate judge of the Court of Common Pleas for Chester County. On June 22, 1792, Joseph Evans had been committed to jail "by Judge Finney on a charge of having together with several other persons all in Disguise violently assaulted Beat and Abused Major Jacob Humphreys an Excise Inspector with Guns Clubs &c" (D, Records of the Court of Quarter Sessions, Chester County, Pennsylvania).

8. Jared Ingersoll.

9. See H to George Washington, September 11, 1792, note 7.

during the trial and appearances since there is no present reason to expect any fresh Difficulty in that Quarter. In the county of Northampton which lies up the Delaware, there are at this Moment some delays and impediments not apparently of a very serious complexion, and which have been owing principally to an aversion to pay a tax which the distillers see is successfully refused in other Quarters. This has been and is the state of the Revenue business on the Eastern side of the Susquehanna, which part of the district contains about three fifths of its whole population. To this may be added the County of York the lowest on the western side of that River and the most populous in the State, and the County of Franklin next westward of it which distill largely and in which no difficulties have been stated to exist. These comprehend above two thirds of the Population of Pennsylvania. In Cumberland the Collector when abroad on duty was compelled to give up the Minutes of his Business by some of the distillers. The supreme Court of the State being then in Session at Carlisle, the Judges took up the matter with decision on the application of the Collector, and the offenders were apprehended and held to bail to abide the legal issue, which there is no reason to believe, will be inconsistent with justice and the laws. There has recently appeared a disposition in a vicinity a little North of Cumberland to avoid the payment of the duty. A particular distiller had taken pains to induce his Neighbours to refuse to pay the Monies, which were soon to become due from them. He was successful but they have since given way and paid the duty. The Instigator continues refractory and legal measures have been instituted.[10] This situation is remote wherefore it is possible the

10. On October 4, 1792, Coxe had written to James Collins, inspector of the revenue of Survey No. 2 in Pennsylvania: "Some little delay has arisen in the institution of legal measures . . . in order that the best mode of proceeding under various circumstances might be deliberately settled. . . . The Attorney for the District of Pennsylvania [William Rawle] has had instructions to institute process, and no doubt has fulfilled them. Your letter to the Supervisor [George Clymer] . . . [was] put in his hands for the purpose" (LC, RG 58, Letters of Commissioner of Revenue, 1792–1793, National Archives).

On October 17, 1792, Coxe wrote to Collins: "I have your letter of the 3d. inst. and as the intention of the Government is not to occasion any Inconvenience or Expence to those . . . who cease to delay the public business, . . . the suits against two of the persons mentioned will be discontinued. The Attorney . . . has proceeded in the case of Mr. [John] Baty" (LC, RG 58, Letters of Commissioner of Revenue, 1792–1793, National Archives).

example of the Western Survey may occasion him to receive encouragement and Support from a Vicinity composed in a great degree of the same description of persons. The residue of the District on this side of the Allegany mountain has not shewn any disposition to oppose the law. As the situation of the Revenue in Pennsylvania requires its temper to be accurately stated, it is proper to observe that the above mentioned Dispositions to oppose, which are all that have appeared on this side the Allegany Mountain, relate to a tract of Country comprizing about six sevenths of the population of the State, the Seat of its foreign trade, its principal scenes of manufactures and a very large proportion probably nineteen twentieths of its property. It is however to be observed further that prejudices against this kind of tax exist in the minds of many in different parts of the state, who, being too much influenced by the Name do not advert to the difference between our excise laws and those of Great Britain & Ireland, and who erroneously suppose that the exceptionable parts of those foreign Systems, which have been carefully avoided by Congress have been actually adopted. These Prejudices however are abating.

In the four Western Counties of Pennsylvania [11] the prejudices and opposition are such as almost entirely to defeat the execution of the revenue laws, to render the situation of the complying distillers universally uncomfortable and almost every where dangerous, and to hazard the peace and safety of the persons and property of the Officers of Inspection, and of the civil officers, witnesses and others who may be required to perform legal services or to obey the summons of the judicial-courts.

In the district of Delaware.

some disposition to oppose appeared in one County, but the Resolution of the persons being put to the trial by the firmness of the

11. For information concerning the opposition to the Excise Law in Westmoreland, Fayette, Washington, and Allegheny counties in Pennsylvania, see H to Coxe, September 1, 1792; H to Washington, September 1, 8, first letter of September 9, September 11, 22, 26, 1792; H to John Jay, September 3, 1792; "Draft of a Proclamation Concerning Opposition to the Excise Law," September 7, 1792; Jay to H, September 8, 1792; Edmund Randolph to H, September 8, 1792; Washington to H, September 7, two letters of September 17, September 21, October 1, 1792; George Clymer to H, September 28, October 4, 10, 1792; Rufus King to H, September 27, 1792; Washington to Thomas Mifflin, September 29, 1792.

Collector, the due execution of the law ensued. It is remarked by the Supervisor, that the people of that Vicinity had not paid their State Taxes for a series of years.[12]

In the district of Maryland,

some unfavorable dispositions, rather of discontentment than opposition appeared in the two lowest Counties on the Eastern Shore [13] on the promulgation of the first law.[14] But those were evident misconceptions on the subject, which have been removed, and this being followed by the improvements of the system in the last act [15] the Supervisor is of opinion that, there is no ground of apprehension on that side of Chessapeak. There was for a long time no appearance of discontent on the Western Shore of Maryland but some murmers at the non-execution of the laws in the Western Survey of Pennsylvania and slight symptoms of discontentment, excited by the irregularities in that Survey, have appeared,[16] tho not recently. The revenue seems to have a degree of popularity among the principal planters.

In the district of Virginia

exclusive of Kentucke, the law may be considered as completely in operation so far as it is capable of execution, except in the four North West Counties, where however there has been no opposition. The obstruction has been merely the difficulty of procuring Col-

12. On January 11, 1793, Coxe wrote to Andrew Barrett, supervisor of the revenue for the District of Delaware, stating that he had spoken to "Mr. Pollock, Collector of the Revenue . . . in Sussex [county] and find from him . . . a different scene from what had been heretofore known. . . . I wish to know the names and places of residence of the men of property in Sussex County, who, you suppose have never paid a State tax, their reasons for refusing, and the reasons of the forebearance of the State and of the tax Collectors, as particularly as possible" (LC, RG 58, Letters of Commissioner of Revenue, 1792–1793, National Archives).

13. Worcester and Somerset counties.

14. "An Act repealing, after the last day of June next, the duties heretofore laid upon Distilled Spirits imported from abroad, and laying others in their stead; and also upon Spirits distilled within the United States, and for appropriating the same" (1 Stat. 199–214 [March 3, 1791]).

15. "An Act concerning the Duties on Spirits distilled within the United States" (1 Stat. 267–71 [May 8, 1792]).

16. On October 29, 1792, Coxe wrote to George Gale, supervisor of the revenue for the District of Maryland: "The example set by the distiller in Frederic County is a wise one. . . . If this conduct were to be observed by a few firm and independent citizens, distillers or others in each County around the scenes of opposition it would be of infinite service" (LC, RG 58, Letters of Commissioner of Revenue, 1792–1793, National Archives).

lectors for the original compensations. These being meliorated, by the last Acts of the President on that subject,[17] the Inspector of the North West Survey [18] is now engaged in the appointment of Collectors. There were some early appearances of dispositions to obstruct the first law in the lower parts of Virginia, but they have been completely checked by the exertions of the Supervisor.[19] More serious dispositions of the same kind appeared in the County of Augusta,[20] but this was eradicated by the voluntary proceedings of the grand Jury of a State Court held at Stanton, which presented certain persons who had associated against the law. The associaters to avoid the legal Consequences, signed a declaration of error and recantation.

In the district of Kentucke,

there was for some time considerable discontentment, and some opposition.[21] The law is but partially in operation there, tho' it is now in much better train than it has been in that district. There does not appear any reason to doubt, that Kentucke may acquiesce, without any very unpleasant Circumstances in the execution of the law, if external circumstances have not too strong an effect upon the Inhabitants. They complain of the inconvenience to them from the non execution of the law in the Country above them on the Western Waters.[22]

17. See the enclosure to the first letter Coxe wrote to H on July 25, 1792.

18. James Brackenridge was inspector of Survey No. 6 in Virginia.

19. Edward Carrington was supervisor of the revenue for the District of Virginia.

20. On June 2, 1792, Coxe wrote to Carrington requesting "a brief account of the Movements in Augusta, against the revenue law, their origin and their suppression," and added: "If copies of the Association and the presentment of the Grand Jury are attainable you will much oblidge me by transmitting them" (LC, RG 58, Letters of Commissioner of Revenue, 1792–1793, National Archives).

Zechariah Johnston, Augusta County delegate in the Virginia House of Delegates from 1778 to 1791 and a Federalist member of the Virginia Ratifying Convention, had signed the association, later described by Johnston as "an improper ill-worded remonstrance, which has in the last these words: Until we can Petition for redress or repel by force." Johnston's son and a neighbor, both captains in the Virginia Militia, also signed the association, and the allegiance of the signers to the Government was questioned (William P. Palmer and Sherwin McRae, eds., Calendar of Virginia State Papers [Richmond, 1885], V, 481; Howard McKnight Wilson, The Tinkling Spring Headwater of Freedom [Fishersville, Virginia, 1954], 197, 227, 235).

21. See H to Washington, February 14, 1792.

22. On September 7, 1792, Thomas Marshall, inspector of the revenue for Survey No. 7 in Virginia, had written to Coxe: "I have not yet had it in my

In the district of North Carolina,

On the Sea-borde no opposition has been made but it is lately represented by the Supervisor, that he is apprehensive the law is laxly executed in a great part of the Country towards the Coast.[23] In the fourth Survey (around Halifax) the first law was not carried into execution for want of Collectors, and from pretty strong dis-

---

power to establish the necessary offices of Inspection in this Survey; and I am fearfull I shall experience much difficulty in accomplishing this object. Mr. Cameal one of the collectors goes in a few days on the South Side of the Kentuke river where I expect all the opposition for that express purpose. No inconvenience has yet accrued from the delay of this business as the season has prevented the distillers from doing any thing.

"The People of Monongehala have latterly sent down large Quantities of Spirits to Kentuke and the North-west side of the Ohio; this circumstance has given rise to much Complaint among the distillers of this Survey, the importers of that liquor have Sold it as low as one quarter of a Dollar ℔ Gallon, which is much lower than it can be afforded, provided the excise is paid. The prevailing opinion is, that the Whisky is Smugled off leaving the duty unpaid, and there is no provision in the law enabling the officers here to require a Certificate 'that the duty has been paid or secured to be paid.' This evil might I think be remidied by an Amendment to the law, making such Certificate necessary empowering the officer to Sieze Spirits removed from another State & unaccompanied with Such Certificate, and appointing an officer on the North West Side of the river Ohio or annexing that Teritory to this Survey: without Such an amendatory law it is my opinion that the people of Monongehala may for a Considerable time evade the payment of the duties by sending their whiskey down the river to the contractors or to this country and by underselling our distillers (who I doubt not will comply with the law) defeat this Source of revenue not only in their own Country but also in Kentuke." (ALS, RG 58, General Records, 1791–1803, National Archives.)

23. On August 1, 1792, Coxe wrote to Thomas Benbury, inspector of the revenue of Survey No. 3, the most northerly of the seacoast surveys in North Carolina: "There are some appearances of discontentment among regular and punctual distillers in Virginia because the distillers in North Carolina near to them do not (as is alleged) pay duty, and have no measures taken to oblige them to do so. . . . The information does not point to the survey or division in which the facts occur, and therefore I only mention it to you generally, with a request that you will communicate to me the State of your survey. . . . I wish to know the reason why none of the Inhabitants will undertake the Collection in the Counties, which you meant to comprize in one division" (LC, RG 58, Letters of Commissioner of Revenue, 1792–1793, National Archives).

On November 10, 1792, Coxe wrote to William Polk, supervisor of the revenue for the District of North Carolina: "The arrangement of your three Sea Coast Surveys and indeed of your whole district will be reconsidered immediately on advice from you as already required. In the mean time I have written to them [the inspectors] to make a report of all matters relating to their Surveys, which I presume will occasion them to state their transactions and their omissions with the reasons. Matters will no longer be left as they have been in those quarters" (LC, RG 58, Letters of Commissioner of Revenue, 1792–1793, National Archives).

contents.[24] But that Survey has assumed a different appearance since the favorable provisions of the second law were promulgated, and the Presidents Act of the 4th of August was communicated to the Inspector.[25] In the 5th. or Western Survey of North Carolina menaces of the property of the Officers and strong dispositions to Violence have appeared. The irregularities in that Survey are not particularly stated by the Inspector who resigned [26] nor yet by the Supervisor, but it is generally mentioned by the former that he has been unable to execute the laws, and by the latter that the discontents and dispositions to opposition which existed before, had suddenly become very voilent. I consider that Survey as the most opposed of any in the United States except No. 4 in Pennsylvania. The Supervisor who appears to have great firmness & considerable weight and popularity does not seem to have any despondency in regard to the final establishment of the law.

In the district of South-Carolina

the appearances of opposition had subsided and it was understood that some respectable disapprovers of the tax, had recommended an acquiescence in it.[27] But latterly obstructions to the execution of the law have again occured, which have been carried so far as menaces so violent and serious as to occasion the Collector to refrain from the execution of his Duty.[28] This was in the quarter adjacent

---

The October 9, 1792, issue of the *Fayetteville Gazette* carried a notice signed by Polk stating that he had appointed Duncan McCrea as a collector in Survey No. 1 in North Carolina, but that four other counties in James Read's Survey No. 1 were still not provided with collectors.

24. See H to Washington, September 22, 1792, notes 4 and 5.

25. Polk's discussion of the new provisions contained in the May 8, 1792, Excise Act revision, as well as John Neville's address concerning the excise, was printed in the September 25, 1792, issue of the *Fayetteville Gazette*.

26. Joseph McDowell, Jr., had resigned his position as inspector of Survey No. 5 in North Carolina because of the difficulty in implementing the Excise Act in his survey. See Washington to H, August 31, 1792; H to Washington, September 8, 1792, note 3. On October 27, 1792, Coxe wrote to Polk requesting information on "the Causes of the sudden change of feelings and opinions in the 5th. Survey and . . . the real causes internal or external and the particular acts of their objections and oppositions" (LC, RG 58, Letters of Commissioner of Revenue, 1792–1793, National Archives).

27. See Daniel Stevens to H, May 22, 1792.

28. On October 28, 1792, Coxe wrote to Stevens: "I beg the favor of being informed with as much expedition and accuracy as possible whether the *complainants* against the law in South Carolina—also whether the abusers of the officers and the fomenters of that abuse are *natives* of the United States

to the Western Survey of North Carolina, and the Supervisor of South Carolina[29] ascribes these new obstructions to the influence of the Western Survey of the Northern District. The opposition in the Western part of South Carolina is very similar to that in North Carolina, as might be expected where similarity of Character exists among people not separated by any substantial Boundaries.

In the district of Georgia, the Supervisor represents that the alterations made by the Act of May last, seem to afford general satisfaction to the Community and particularly to the distillers, and that nearly the whole duty of the first year, which however is small, had been collected without legal compulsion.[30]

It may be useful to state, Sir, that there has been a great increase of distilleries from domestic materials and of course that the very great difference in favor of domestic Spirits, co-operating with the defalcation and dearness of melasses, has rendered the excise-system really beneficial to the landed interest, of which there is a growing sense among the substantial farmers and planters. It is also true that the greater part of the Town distillers and of the principal distillers in most of the well populated Conties, consider the system as favorable to their Business. Refinements in regard to the danger of what they denominate *insensible* taxes, prejudices against the Name of excise derived from foreign laws of that kind of a very different nature and really dangerous at least as examples, erroneous opinions that excises are of a more growing nature than other taxes, the want of perception that the Consumer and not the Distiller finally bears the tax, and the objections which every part of Mankind have to taxes of which they are the payers, the aversion of some to this and of others to all government, and the influence of the example, the reproaches & the menaces of the violent few even where the many are really well disposed, are in my opinion the principal, and almost all the Causes of the degree and discontentment and opposition which prevails.

---

or foreigners by birth and of what Nation or Country and what you suppose to be their real objections, what their ostensible objections to the Revenue" (LC, RG 58, Letters of Commissioner of Revenue, 1792–1793, National Archives).

29. Daniel Stevens.   30. See John Mathews to H, May 1, 1792.

I have the honor to be with the most respectful Attatchment,   Sir,
your most Obedient Servant   Tench Coxe,
                                              Commisr. of the Revenue.
The honble.
The Secretary of the Treasury.

To Thomas Jefferson

[Philadelphia, October 19, 1792]

The Secretary of the Treasury presents his respects to The Secretary of State requests him to name some hour tomorrow forenoon when it will be convenient to him to receive at his house the Secry of the Treasury & Attorney General on the subject of the sinking fund.[1]

October 19. 1792

AL, Thomas Jefferson Papers, Library of Congress.
    1. At the bottom of this letter Jefferson wrote: "This was to dispose of 50,000 Doll. in the purchase of paper. It was agreed to repeat the order of July 13. 92. to wit to advertise for offers at the lowest price, to be delivered sealed, and on this day sennight to meet again. Note not a single offer had been made in consequence of the order of July 13."
    See "Meeting of the Commissioners of the Sinking Fund," July 13, 1792.

From James McHenry

[Annapolis, October 19–23, 1792]

My dear Hamilton.

Knowing that I was apt to lose letters out of my pocket, and recollecting that you are a little subject to lose them by not putting them into yours, I thought it best that we should burn them. I can therefore answer to your inquiry [1] (reced. last night) only from memory. I think I, as mere intelligence, mentioned to you the names of some of our candidates for Congress and subjoined some sketch of their respective characters.[2] I mentioned among others Mercer [3] with some epithet of disapprobation which I think you responded: but I do not remember that more passed respecting that gentlemen than the epithet of disapprobation against his political principles. In a letter which spoke of a certain philosopher helping a brother philosopher I beleive you said that the *capitol* was in danger and that it behoved good men not to slumber when the enemies of all order were so busy.[4] On the whole, the little I did against Mercer was not the consequence of any thing you said about him. I had read his speeches in Congress and in all companies where the opportunity offered had expressed their fallacy and consequences and mischievous nature of his politics. I can safely acquit you of having either led my mind to give him opposition, or to have excited in it any ideas which were not in it before.

A little piece in Goddards last tuesdays paper [5] has drawn an answer respecting Mr. Adams signed a consistent federalist, which will serve to give the alarm to our friends. As it was necessary to allow it time to travel from Annapolis it does not appear till next tuesday.[6] I shall write to the Eastern shore and take such other steps as may be proper in such a conjuncture.

I am getting more strength. Yours affectionately James McHenry

One of your letters respecting candidates in a certain event is not burn't. It is in my trunk. But, that concerns not the present business.

ALS, Hamilton Papers, Library of Congress.
  1. Letter not found.
  2. See McHenry to H, August 16, 1792.
  3. John F. Mercer. See H to Mercer, September 26, 1792, and H to David Ross, September 26, 1792.
  4. Letter not found.
  5. William Goddard was publisher of *The* [Baltimore] *Maryland Journal and Baltimore Advertiser.* McHenry is referring to an article printed in that newspaper on October 16, 1792, signed by "A citizen." This article advocated substituting Charles Carroll of Carrollton for John Adams as a Federalist candidate in the 1792 presidential election.
  6. The reply, which was dated October 19, 1792, and signed by "A Consistent Federalist," appeared in Goddard's paper on October 23, 1792. The article ridiculed "A citizen" for perpetrating an Antifederalist plot to take votes away from Adams and aid the cause of an Antifederalist candidate.
The article concluded: "To these observations I think I may venture to subjoin, that it is not to disgrace a worthy and patriotic citizen that will draw Mr. Carroll into the lists of competition; and to predict, that if he ever becomes a candidate for continental favour, his merit and high qualifications will raise him to a more dignified station. But who can look forward to that moment, when we shall stand in need of all his merits and all our courage; when the United States will be convulsed to their centre by embrio Cæsars, struggling for empire, and scarcely saved by the friends of order and virtue? Who, I say, can anticipate that solemn crisis, of which this is only the prelude, without devoutly wishing to the present beloved Incumbent the years of the Patriarchs

who lived before the flood?" (*The* [Baltimore] *Maryland Journal and Baltimore Advertiser*, October 23, 1792.)

To George Washington

[*Philadelphia*] *October 19, 1792.* "The Secretary of the Treasury . . . has the honor to observe that the absence of the Auditor [1] renders it requisite for the President to designate the person who shall execute the duty of Auditor in his absence. . . . The first Clerk [2] naturally presents himself to consideration; and will, it is believed, be adequate to all necessary business."

LC, George Washington Papers, Library of Congress.
1. Richard Harrison. See Tobias Lear to H, October 13, 1792.
2. William Simmons.

From Tench Coxe [1]

Treasury Department, Revenue Office, October 20, 1792. "I have the Honor to transmit to you certified copies of the Acts of the President of the United States of the 4th of August and of the 29th September [2] relative to the Revenue on distilled Spirits. . . ."

LC, RG 58, Letters of Commissioner of Revenue, 1792–1793, National Archives.
1. For background to this letter, see George Washington to H, August 5, October 1, 1792; Coxe to H, first letter of July 25, September 12–18, 1792; H to Washington, September 22, 1792.
2. After the word "September" there is an asterisk which refers to a marginal note that reads as follows: "The dates of this Act was afterwards altered to the 29th of October 1792. by the President of the United States."

Meeting of the Commissioners of the Sinking Fund

Philadelphia, October 20th, 1792.

At a meeting of the trustees of the sinking fund,

Present: The Secretary of State, the Secretary of the Treasury, and the Attorney General of the United States

It appeared to the Board, from the information of the Secretary of the Treasury, that there were certain moneys on hand, belonging to the fund, constituted by the 7th section of the act, entitled "An act supplementary to the act making provision for the debt of the United States." [1]

Resolved, That the interest received on account of the sinking fund up to the 30th of September, 1792, and all other moneys remaining on hand, belonging to the said fund, and unexpended, be applied to the purchase of stock, in the same manner as is prescribed by a resolution of this Board, of the 13th of July last; that Samuel Meredith be the agent, and Philadelphia be the place of purchase. [2]

ASP, Finance, I, 237.
1. For Section 7 of this act, see "Meeting of the Commissioners of the Sinking Fund," July 13, 1792.
2. See H to Thomas Jefferson, October 19, 1792.

From Thomas Jefferson

[*Philadelphia, October 21, 1792. Letter not found.*] [1]

1. Letter listed in Jefferson's "Summary Journal of Letters," Thomas Jefferson Papers, Library of Congress.

From Thomas Jefferson

[*Philadelphia, October 21, 1792. Letter not found.*] [1]

1. Letter listed in Jefferson's "Summary Journal of Letters," Thomas Jefferson Papers, Library of Congress. This is the second of two letters that Jefferson wrote to H that is listed for this date.

To Benjamin Bourne, William Channing, John S. Dexter, and Jeremiah Olney

Treasury Department
October 22. 1792

Gentlemen

A report has reached this place, through a channel so respectable as to claim notice, that the affairs of the Bank of Providence are in considerable disorder. On this occasion I take the liberty to commit to your care the interests of the United States and to request your aid.

It is probably known to all of you that the Bank of Providence has been made a place of deposit for all the public monies arising within the State of Rhode Island. At the date of the last return, there was a sum of about 25000 Dollars in Bank on account of the United States; for 10000 Dollars of which the Treasurer has been Directed to Draw. But further accessions have probably accrued since, by payments from the respective officers.

Aware that a sudden order to withold the public deposits and withdraw the public money might contribute to render any partial derangement, which may exist, a total one, to the great prejudice of all concerned, I forbear to take such a step.

I prefer to rest a discretionary power in persons who will combine a regard to the public interest with a disposition friendly to the Bank and to the Trade, to act as upon examination circumstances may appear to render prudent and adviseable; in which view, I ask your particular and immediate attention to the matter.

I request you therefore to inquire carefully into the facts represented; and for this purpose, to use this letter as a commission from me to the Directors, and either to continue things in their present state or to withdraw the public monies if practicable and stop further deposits; for which last purpose, your instructions are hereby made obligatory upon the Supervisor of the Revenue & the Collectors of the respective districts.

Perhaps affairs may be so circumstanced as to render it most adviseable to observe a medium between the two modes of proceeding. Or perhaps it may be found expedient and practicable to obtain security from persons of competent responsibility in the direction of the Bank, to indemnify the Government for a limited period, on the condition of a continuance of its countenance and support for such period.

These you will consider as merely hints. Your own judgments on the state of things before you must guide.

I wish nothing to be precipitated, and yet a due caution to be observed.[1]

With much esteem & consideration I have the honor to be
Gentlemen Your Obedient Servant Alex Hamilton

The Honorable Mr. Bourne Representative
The Attorney of the District
The Supervisor of the Revenue
The Collector of Providence

ALS, Rhode Island Historical Society, Providence; copy, RG 56, Letters to the
Collector at Providence, National Archives; copy, RG 56, Letters to Collectors at Small Ports, "Set G," National Archives.

1. Moses Brown's biographer describes this incident as follows:
"The bank was scarcely a year old when a crisis developed in its affairs that
demonstrated the need for a watchdog. In October 1792 the Secretary of the
Treasury heard a rumor, whether maliciously circulated or not, that the public
funds in the Providence Bank were not secure. Hamilton immediately ordered
the customs officers to investigate and to remove the customs receipts, if the
rumor were true. The federal officers . . . came to Providence and requested
permission from John Brown to examine the bank's books. Since they would
not permit him to read Hamilton's order, however, he indignantly refused,
and wrote to Moses for advice. The request, he added, 'of course gave me a
little alarm.'

"John was more than a 'little' alarmed. His refusal to give the customs
officers any satisfaction and the tone of his letter to Moses suggests that the
bank's books could not stand examination. If that had been the case the examiners would probably have recommended that the customs receipts be withdrawn, thereby creating public distrust of the bank's soundness. The consequences of such action were not pleasant to contemplate. Fortunately, after
prolonged argument, Hamilton's examiners told John that they would be content to deal with Moses, in whose impartiality and honesty they apparently
had the utmost confidence—he was the only member of the Board to whom
they would show Hamilton's letter ordering the examination. What passed
between Moses and the customs officers is not known but he apparently convinced them that the bank was sound, for later Hamilton wrote to Providence
saying that he had been misinformed about the bank's condition." (Mack
Thompson, *Moses Brown, Reluctant Reformer* [Chapel Hill, 1962], 253–54.)
For H's letter stating that he had been misinformed about the bank's condition, see H to Bourne, Channing, Dexter, and Olney, October 25, 1792.

From Charles Carroll of Carrollton [1]

Annapolis 22d. Oct 1792

Dear Sir
I received on the 7th. instant your favor of the 23d. past.[2] I have
delayed thus long answering it with a hope that I might discover
whether the antifederal party in this State had in view the person [3]

referred to in your letter. I suspect a communication of Sentiments is maintained by the leaders of this party throughout the United States; however I have not heard his name even whispered; his character I could not well see thro' during the time we were together. I noticed a disposition to perplex & puzzle, which left an unfavorable impression on my mind; he appeared to me not to want talents, but Judgt. & Steadiness, and I suspect he possesses of ambition a quantum sufficet for any man.

I hope the friends of stability and order, in other words, the *real* friends of liberty & their country will unite to counter-act the schemes of men, who have uniformly manifested a hostile temper to ye. present Government, the adoption of which has rescued these States from that debility & confusion and those horrors, which unhappy France has experienced of late, and may still labour under. I beg respects to Mrs. Hamilton and remain with Sentiments of respect and regard

    Dear Sir   Yr. most hume. Servant   Charles Carroll of Carrollton

ALS, Hamilton Papers, Library of Congress.
    1. For background concerning this letter, see Rufus King to H, September 17, 27, 1792; H to ———, September 21, 26, 1792; H to King, September 23, 1792; H to George Washington, September 23, 1792; H to Charles Cotesworth Pinckney, October 10, 1792; H to John Steele, October 15, 1792.
    2. Letter not found.   3. Presumably Aaron Burr.

Contract with George Dannacker and William Young

Philadelphia, October 22, 1792. A contract for "the several articles of Clothing specified" for United States troops for the year 1793 was concluded on this date.

Copy, Historical Society of Pennsylvania, Philadelphia; copy, RG 233, Papers of the Select Committee Appointed to Examine the Treasury Department, Third Congress, National Archives.

From Gaspard Joseph Amand Ducher [1]

Paris Le 22 8bre 1792.
L'an 1er. dela République

Je joins ici, Monssieur, plusieurs pièces authentiques pour vous faire connoitre La verité sur Les grands évenements qui ont eu Lieu en france dépuis Le 10 aout der. La Liberté française triomphe de tous ses ennemies en europe, et trouvera, j'espere, d'intimes alliés dans Le Nouveau Monde. Les vrais américains applaudissent Sans doute au courage dont ils nous ont donné L'exemple.

Peut-etre partirai-je bientot pour me rendre au près de vous.[2] Conservez moi votre amitié. *Publius,* ou Le federaliste vient d'etre traduit et de paroitre en deux forts volumes.[3] Cet ouvrage obtient ici Les succès que je vous avais annonceé il ya trois ans.[4]

J'ai reçu votre Lettre du 22. juin der [5] mais jen'ai pas encore reçues Les Lettres de change que vous vous proposiez alors de M'envoyer.

Je vous embrasse de tout mon Coeur et fais des voeux pour vous et votre famille.   Ducher

ALS, Hamilton Papers, Library of Congress.
  1. Ducher was appointed vice consul *ad interim* at Portsmouth, New Hampshire, in 1786, and in 1788 was transferred to Wilmington, North Carolina. He returned to Paris in 1790, and for the next three years he sought to induce the French government to adopt a policy of encouragement to trade and navigation similar to that embodied in the English navigation laws (Nussbaum, *Commercial Policy in the French Revolution,* 14, 17, 35, 271–304).
  2. There is some evidence that Ducher hoped at this time to be named to a diplomatic post in the United States (Nussbaum, *Commercial Policy in the French Revolution,* 227).
  3. The second edition of *The Federalist* was published in two volumes in Paris in 1792 under the following title: *Le Fédéraliste, ou Collection de quelques Écrits en faveur de la Constitution proposés aux États-Unis de l'Amérique, par la Convention convoquée en 1787; Publiés dans les États-Unis de l'Amérique par MM. Hamilton, Madisson et Gay, Citoyens de l'État de New-York* (A Paris: Chez Buisson, Libraire, rue Hautefeuille, No. 20, 1792).
  4. See Ducher to H, November 1, 1789.   5. Letter not found.

From Henry Hill [1]

[Philadelphia] Octo. 22d. 1792

Sir

Wishing the Secretary to waste no time in the pursuit of such Will's o' the wisp I wou'd take upon me the publication mention'd & leave my name with the Printer.

The last paragraph if approv'd of might read thus—"Printers willing to administer an antedote to similar poisons will give a place in their respective papers to this sample of the rumours continually propagated to destroy the Confidence of their fellow Citizens in public Characters." [2]

I am Sir with all regard—Your most Obedt. Servt. &c.

Henry Hill

P.S. Be pleas'd to return the inclos'd if you allow me to proceed.

ALS, Hamilton Papers, Library of Congress.

1. Hill, one of the founders of the Bank of North America and a member of the Pennsylvania legislature during the American Revolution, was a Philadelphia merchant.

2. An article which closed with this paragraph appeared in the [Philadelphia] *Gazette of the United States* on October 31, 1792. It reads as follows:

"About a fortnight since, at Christiana, in the State of Delaware, five or six gentlemen being together in conversation on public subjects and public characters,—one of the company, a Mr. M'Kennon, told a story of the Secretary of the Treasury, and as he supposed upon undoubted authority, nearly in the following words:

"'Colonel Hamilton, said he, applied to Governor Mifflin; and represented the propriety of restricting the democratic ascendency in the national government, which might be effected by the introduction of aristocrats; adding, that if he (Governor Mifflin) would co-operate in the formation of this counterpoise, the Secretary would pledge himself to get him elected Vice-President of the United States.

"'The Governor declined these overtures, alledging that he had never discovered to any one, and should maintain his reserve, whether he was attached to this or the other principle, in government; but he knew full well the unalterable bias of those who supported him. And, as to the Vice-Presidency, he did not hesitate to declare, that he was more ambitious of remaining at the head of Pennsylvania.'

"A gentleman of the State of Delaware, to whom this conversation was communicated, in order to an investigation of the truth of the story, called upon Governor Mifflin, who in unequivocal term, declared, that,

"'*No such conversation ever happened, nor could he recollect any circumstance that could give birth to so ridiculous a tale.*'

"Printers willing to administer an antidote to similar poisons, will give a place in their respective papers to this sample of the unfounded rumours continually propagated to destroy the confidence of their fellow-citizens in public characters." ([Philadelphia] *Gazette of the United States*, October 31, 1792.)

To Thomas Jefferson [1]

[Philadelphia, October 22, 1792]

Mr. Hamilton presents his Compliments to Mr. Jefferson, requests to be informed, if there are any circumstances within his knowlege, more than are mentioned in the inclosed papers, which throw light upon the subject of them; particularly whether the *discharge* of the Vessels was communicated to The Baron De Steuben at the time it

took place or at any time antecedent to the date of the Baron's last
letter to Capt Lewis.[2]

Monday October 22. 1792

AL, Thomas Jefferson Papers, Library of Congress.
1. For background to this letter, see "Report on the Petition of Joseph
Ball and Isaac Ledyard," November 21, 1792.
2. William Lewis.

From Thomas Jefferson [1]

[Philadelphia, October 22, 1792]

Th: Jefferson presents his compliments to the Secretary of the
Treasury & is sorry he is unable to give him any information relative
to the Ship Renown, having no recollection of the details of the
armament of which she made a part. The expedition against Portsmouth was, as he thinks, by order of the Commander in chief, desiring the aid of the state to the Continental commander. Should it be
decided that the vessel & cargo are to be paid for, it should be attended to that tobacco, during the greater part of the war, was not
worth more than five or six shillings real money the hundred in
Virginia, that probably it was at it's honest value about the time of
this expedition, and that a valuation in tobacco would be made according to it's price at the moment.

Oct. 22. 1792.

AL, letterpress copy, Thomas Jefferson Papers, Library of Congress.
1. See H to Jefferson, October 22, 1792; "Report on the Petition of Joseph
Ball and Isaac Ledyard," November 21, 1792.

From Thomas Jefferson [1]

[Philadelphia, October 22, 1792]

Th Jefferson presents his compliments to the Secretary of the
Treasury and incloses him a statement of the salaries & disbursements
of his office here, and as perfect a one as he has materials to furnish

of the foreign establishments according to the order of the Senate of May 7. 1792.[2]

Oct. 22. 1792.

AL, letterpress copy, Thomas Jefferson Papers, Library of Congress.
1. This letter was written in reply to H to Jefferson, October 6, 1792.
2. See "Treasury Department Circular to the Collectors of the Customs," August 31, 1792.

To William Seton

[Philadelphia, October 22, 1792]

My Dear Sir

I will thank you to forward me, as soon as convenient, copies of all the letters you have received from me, respecting the purchase of public Debt.[1] In the hurry of dispatching some of them, no copy was kept. And some incidents of late require, that I should carefully review the ground.

I regretted to have been obliged to draw lately a portion of my intended deposits from your Bank; but I hope to replace & keep it up.

William Seton Esqr

AL[S], Bank of New York, New York City.
1. Seton had been appointed one of the agents for purchasing the public debt under the direction of the commissioners of the sinking fund.

From Jeremiah Olney

Providence, October 23, 1792. Encloses "Account of Emoluments &c. . . . from Octr. 1791 to Septr. 1792, inclusive; together with similar Accounts from all the Officers appointed by, and acting under me, as Collr. of the Customs for this District." [1] States that the "average Rates of freight shall be forwarded as soon as it can be obtained from the Merchants." [2]

ADfS, Rhode Island Historical Society, Providence.
 1. See "Treasury Department Circular to the Collectors of the Customs,"
August 31, 1792.
 2. See "Treasury Department Circular to the Collectors of the Customs,"
September 8, 1792.

From Jeremiah Olney

Providence, October 23, 1792. "The Act laying a Duty of 10 ℔.
Cent Ad Valorem on *Sail-Cloth*,[1] admits of different constructions:
I have considered Sail-Cloth and Duck as synonimous, and accordingly charged that rate of Duty on *Ravens* Duck. Some Importers of
this Article here contend that my construction is erroneous, and that
Ravens Duck is not, by the Act, chargeable with a higher Duty
than 7½ ℔ Cent, the same as paid on Ticklingburgh, which is
often used for light Sails. I wish Sir, for your Opinion on this
Point. . . ."

ADfS, Rhode Island Historical Society, Providence.
 1. Sailcloth is listed among the commodities taxed at ten percent in "An
Act for raising a farther sum of money for the protection of the frontiers, and
for other purposes therein mentioned" (1 *Stat.* 260 [May 2, 1792]).

Metellus

[Philadelphia, October 24, 1792]

FOR THE GAZETTE OF THE UNITED STATES.

The votaries of Mr. Jefferson, whose devotion for their idol kin-
dles at every form, in which he deigns to present himself, have de-
duced matter of panegyric from his opposition to the measures of
the government. 'Tis according to them the sublimest pitch of virtue
in him, not only to have extra-officially embarrassed plans, originating with his colleagues, in the course of their progress, but to have
continued his opposition to them, after they had been considered
and enacted by the legislature, with such modifications as appeared
to them proper, and had been approved by the chief magistrate.

[Philadelphia] *Gazette of the United States,* October 24, 1792.

Such conduct, it seems, marks "a firm and virtuous independence of character."[1] If any proof were wanting of that strange inversion of the ideas of decorum, propriety and order, which characterizes a certain party, this making a theme of encomium of what is truly a demonstration of a caballing, self-sufficient and refractory temper, would afford it.

In order to shew that the epithets have been misapplied, I shall endeavor to state what course a firm and virtuous independence of character, guided by a just and necessary sense of decorum, would dictate to a man in the station of Mr. Jefferson.

This has been rendered more particularly requisite, by the formal discussion of the point, which appears to be the object of a continuation of a defence of that gentleman, in the American Daily Advertiser of the 10th inst.[2]

The position must be reprobated that a man who had accepted an office in the executive department, should be held to throw the weight of his character into the scale, to support a measure, which in his *conscience he disapproved*, and *in his station had opposed*—Or that the members of the administration should form together *a close and secret combination, into whose measures the profane eye of the public should in no instance pry*.[3] But there is a very obvious medium between *aiding* or *countenancing*, and *intriguing* and *machinating* against a measure; between opposing it in the discharge of an official duty, or volunteering an opposition to it in the discharge of no duty; between entering into a close and secret combination with the other members of an administration, and being the active leader of an opposition to its measures.

The true line of propriety appears to me to be the following: A member of the administration, in one department, ought only to *aid* those measures of another, which he approves—where he disapproves, if called upon to *act officially*, he ought to manifest his disapprobation, and avow his opposition; but out of an official line he

---

1. This quotation is from the second of the six articles entitled the "Vindication of Mr. Jefferson" ([Philadelphia] *Dunlap's American Daily Advertiser*, October 10, 1792). See "Catullus No. IV," October 17, 1792, note 4.

2. See note 1.

3. Most of this paragraph was written in response to a series of rhetorical questions in the second article in the "Vindication of Mr. Jefferson" (*Dunlap's American Daily Advertiser*, October 10, 1792).

ought not to interfere, *as long as he thinks fit to continue a part of the administration.* When the measure in question has become a law of the land, especially with a direct sanction of the chief magistrate, it it is peculiarly his duty to acquiesce. A contrary conduct is inconsistent with his relations as an officer of the government, and with a due respect as such, for the decisions of the legislature, and of the head of the executive department. The line here delineated, is drawn from obvious and very important considerations. The success of every government—its capacity to combine the exertion of public strength with the preservation of personal right and private security, qualities which define the perfection of a government, must always naturally depend on the energy of the executive department. This energy, again, must materially depend on the union and mutual deference, which subsist between the members of that department, and the conformity of their conduct with the views of the executive chief.

Difference of opinion between men engaged in any common pursuit, is a natural appendage of human nature. When only exerted *in the discharge of a duty,* with delicacy and temper, among liberal and sensible men, it can create no animosity; but when it produces officious interferences, dictated by no call of duty—when it volunteers a display of itself in a quarter, where there is no responsibility, to the obstruction and embarrassment of one who is charged with an immediate and direct responsibility—it must necessarily beget ill humour and discord between the parties.

Applied to the members of the executive administration of any government, it must necessarily tend to occasion, more or less, distracted councils, to foster factions in the community, and practically to weaken the government.

Moreover the heads of the several executive departments are justly to be viewed as auxiliaries to the executive chief. Opposition to any measure of his, by either of those heads of departments, except in the shape of frank, firm, and independent advice to himself, is evidently contrary to the relations which subsist between the parties. And it cannot well be controverted that a measure becomes his, so as to involve the duty of acquiescence on the part of the members of his administration, as well by its having received his sanction in the form of a law, as by its having previously received his approbation.

In the theory of our government, the chief magistrate is himself responsible for the exercise of every power vested in him by the constitution. One of the powers entrusted to him, is that of objecting to bills which have passed the two houses of Congress. This supposes the duty of objecting, when he is of opinion, that the object of any bill is either *unconstitutional* or *pernicious*. The approbation of a bill implies, that he does not think it either the one or the other. And it makes him responsible to the community for this opinion. The measure becomes his by adoption. Nor could he escape a portion of the blame, which should finally attach itself to a bad measure, to which he had given his consent.

I am prepared for some declamation against the principles which have been laid down. Some plausible flourishes have already been indulged. And it is to be expected, that the public ear will be still further assailed with the commonplace topics, that so readily present themselves, and are so dexterously retailed by the traffickers in popular prejudice. But it need never be feared to submit a solid truth to the deliberate and final opinion of an enlightened and sober people.

What! (it will probably be asked) is a man to sacrifice his conscience and his judgement to an office? Is he to be a dumb spectator of measures which he deems subversive of the rights or interests of his fellow-citizens? Is he to postpone to the frivolous rules of a false complaisance, or the arbitrary dictates of a tyrannical decorum, the higher duty, which he owes to the community?

I answer, No! he is to do none of these things. If he cannot coalesce with those, with whom he is associated, as far as the rules of official decorum, propriety & obligation may require, without abandoning what he conceives to be the true interest of the community, let him place himself in a situation in which he will experience no collision of opposite duties. Let him not cling to the honor or emolument of an office whichever it may be that attracts him, and content himself with defending the injured rights of the people by obscure or indirect means. Let him renounce a situation which is a clog upon his patriotism; tell the people that he could no longer continue in it without forfeiting his duty to them, and that he had quitted it to be more at liberty to afford them his best services.

Such is the course which would be indicated by a firm and virtuous independence of character. Such the course that would be pursued by a man attentive to unite the sense of delicacy with the sense of duty—in earnest about the pernicious tendency of public measures, and more solicitous to act the disinterested friend of the people, than the interested ambitious and intriguing head of a party.

METULLUS.

From Gouverneur Morris

Paris 24 October 1792

My Dear Sir

I have receiv'd yours of the twenty second of June & am in the hourly Hope to hear farther from you. I need not tell you that it will give me Pleasure. Enclosd you will find the Copy of a Letter which I wrote to Mr. Jefferson the seventh of November 1791.[1] This with some other Communications at the same Epoch he never acknowledged, I know not why, but I think the Paper enclosd in that Letter will be agreable to you tho not very amusing. It would seem that your Friend Scipio[2] is not much attach'd to Paulus[3] at least if I may judge from some things which I see. However there is a great Chasm in my News Papers which breaks the Thread of my Conjectures as well as of my Information for I have little I might almost say none of the latter but from the Gazettes: of Course I know what passes about two Months after every Body else. Tell me I pray you how Scavola[4] stands affected between the Parties just nam'd. I think he never had a very high opinion of the first mentioned but he was attach'd to Tarquin[5] unmeasurably and that with some local Circumstances may have form'd a stronger Chain that I should otherwise suppose.

You will have seen that the late Constitution of this Country has overset a natural Accident to a Thing which was all Sail and no Ballast. I desire much very much to know the State of Opinions with us on that Subject. Some Gentlemen who considered it as the Achmé of human Wisdom must I suppose find out Causes which Persons on the Spot never dreamt of. But in seeking or inventing these Causes what will be their Opinion of present Powers what the Conduct they wish to pursue. These are to me important Questions. Brutus[6] will doubtless triumph but I wish to feel the Pulse of Opinion with you or rather to know before Hand how it is like to beat. There are pros and cons whose Action I cannot estimate. The Flight of Monsieur de la fayette [7] the Murder of the Duc de la Rochefoucaule [8] and others with many similar Circumstances have I know affected the Ideas of some. But what will be the republican Sense as to the new Republic? Will it be taken for granted that Louis the sixteenth was guilty of all possible Crimes and particularly of the enormous one of not suffering his throat to be cut which was certainly a nefarious Plot against the People and a manifest Violation of the Bill of Rights. Paulus who is no Enemy to Kings will not believe that they are all Tygers but I am not certain that if he were here he would not consider them as Monkeys. However we are done with them in France at least for the present. There are two Parties here. The one consists of about half a dozen and the other of fifteen or twenty who are at Dagger's Drawing. Each Claims the Merit of having begotten the young Republic upon the Body of the Jacobine Club and notwithstanding the Dispute is very loud and open the People is as fond of the Child as if it were its own. But this has a Relation to antient Manners for there has been a Practice here from Time whereof there is no Memory of Man to the contrary viz that one Sett of Men were employd in getting Children for another Sett. My public Letters and the Gazettes will bring you acquainted with Things here as fully as I can in any Way communicate them. It is not worth while to detail the Characters of those now on the Stage because they must soon give Place to others.

LC, Gouverneur Morris Papers, Library of Congress.

1. Morris's letter to Thomas Jefferson of November 7, 1791, enclosed "some Hints relative to Coins Currency Weights and Measures," which Morris had compiled (LC, Gouverneur Morris Papers, Library of Congress).

2. In his letter to Morris of June 22, 1792, H suggested that he and Morris "settle some appellations for certain official characters." The pseudonyms used by Morris in this letter are those suggested by H in his letter of June 22. "Scipio" was Thomas Jefferson.

3. Alexander Hamilton.   4. George Washington.   5. James Madison.
6. John Adams.

7. After Lafayette failed in his attempt to use the National Guard to save the royal family, he fled from France and was formally declared a traitor by the French Assembly on August 19, 1792 (*Archives Parlementaires*, XLVIII, 387–88). On August 20, 1792, he was captured by the Austrians and imprisoned at Olmütz. He remained a prisoner for the next five years.

8. Louis Alexandre, Duc de La Rochefoucauld, had been murdered by a mob at Gizors early in September, 1792.

To Thomas Willing

[*Philadelphia, October 24, 1792.* Letter listed in dealer's catalogue. *Letter not found.*]

LS, sold at Merwin-Clayton Sales Company, November 12, 1906, Lot 1100.

From Oliver Wolcott, Junior

Treasury Department, Comptroller's Office, October 24, 1792.
"Some time since a claim was presented for settlement by Mr. Samuel Young of this City in favour of William Lewiss late a Soldier of the Virginia Regiment of the Army, which . . . has been certified by the Register of the Treasury. The delivery of the Certificate was however suspended. . . . The claim is now renewed by Mr. George Stout who has applied for & obtained Letters of Administration. . . . It has been conceeded by Stout & is proved by the documents herewith transmitted, that he had no claim upon the property of William Lewiss, than what could accrue to him by virtue of an assignment of the power of Attorney. . . . Under these circumstances I have judged it to be my duty not to admit Stout to receive the Certificate in favour of William Lewiss. . . . I take the liberty to request that the . . . documents may be submitted to the Attorney General of the United States for his opinion."

ADf, Connecticut Historical Society, Hartford.

To Benjamin Bourne, William Channing, John S. Dexter, and Jeremiah Olney

Treasury Department
Oct 25. 1792

Gentlemen
Since mine to you of the 22d. I have reason to believe that the information which gave occasion to that letter was a misapprehension

of the party from whom I received it; but whose general accuracy left me no suspicion of such a possibility at the time. I hasten to give this intimation, that no inconveniences may ensue from my first communication.

With perfect esteem I have the honor to be   Gentlemen   Your obed servant   A Hamilton

The Honorable Mr. Bourne
The Attorney of the District
The Supervisor of the Revenue
The Collector of Providence

ALS, Rhode Island Historical Society, Providence; copy, RG 56, Letters to Collectors at Small Ports, "Set G," National Archives; copy, RG 56, Letters to the Collector at Providence, National Archives.

From Jeremiah Olney

Providence, October 25, 1792. "I have received your Letter of the 12th inst. which removed the apprehensions I before had; and should similar Instances of colusive Transfers [1] occur, I shall refuse credit for the Duties, agreeable to your expectations."

ADfS, Rhode Island Historical Society, Providence.
    1. For background concerning the question of "collusive" transfers, see William Ellery to H, September 4, October 9, 1792; Olney to H, September 8, second letter of September 13, October 4, 1792; H to Olney, September 19, 24, October 12, 1792.

Treasury Department Circular
to the Collectors of the Customs

Treasury Department, October 25, 1792.

Sir,
    Pursuant to the discretion vested in me by the sixth section of the act, entitled, "An Act making alterations in the Treasury and War Departments," [1] I have concluded to commit the immediate superintendance of the Collection of the duties of impost and tonnage to the Comptroller of the Treasury.

You will therefore henceforth correspond with that officer, relatively to all matters arising out of the laws, which respect the laying or collecting of those duties; and you will consider his communications and instructions, in regard to such matters, as of the same force and validity, which they would have, if coming from me.

This however is not to be understood to comprehend the disposition and payment of the monies accruing from those duties; which as heretofore will be under my immediate direction.[2]

Accordingly all the returns and documents which you have been accustomed to transmit to the Secretary of the Treasury, are hereafter to be transmitted to the Comptroller; except the following, 1, weekly return of monies received and paid. 2, monthly schedule of bonds. 3, monthly abstract of bonds unpaid. 4, paid draughts, and receipts for monies paid to Banks and otherwise under special directions from me.

I request to be furnished as early as possible with an estimate from the best materials that can be procured, of what is likely to be the amount of the bounties payable within each District on fishing vessels (where they exist) pursuant to the act, entitled, "An Act concerning certain fisheries of the United States, and for the regulation and government of the fishermen employed therein," [3] and to be informed at the same time, how far the monies likely to be in hand by the period of payment, which is the last of December, will suffice for, or fall short, of the sum necessary.

Those Collectors who shall have any of the before mentioned bounties to pay, and who have instructions to make their remittances to any of the Banks, are herewith authorised to retain in their hands, out of the monies which they have, and shall receive, a sum sufficient to answer the purpose.

With great consideration,　I am, Sir,　Your obedient Servant,

A Hamilton

LS, to Jeremiah Olney, Rhode Island Historical Society, Providence; L[S], to Benjamin Lincoln, RG 36, Collector of Customs at Boston, Letters from the Treasury, 1789–1807, Vol. 4, National Archives; LS, to William Webb, United States Finance Miscellany, Treasury Circulars, Library of Congress; LS, Office of the Secretary, United States Treasury Department; LS, MS Division, New York Public Library; LC, Essex Institute, Salem, Massachusetts; copy, RG 56, Circulars of the Office of the Secretary, "Set T," National Archives; copy, United States Finance Miscellany, Treasury Circulars, Library of Congress.

1. Section 6 of this act provided "That the Secretary of the Treasury shall direct the superintendence of the collection of the duties on impost and tonnage as he shall judge best" (1 *Stat.* 280 [May 8, 1792]).
2. See Tench Coxe to H, May 6, 1792.
3. 1 *Stat.* 229–32 (February 16, 1792).

From William Seton

New York 26 October 1792

Dear sir

Agreably to your desire [1] I now enclose Copies of all the Letters I received from you respecting the purchase of Public Debt. I hope no disagreable event has occurred to cause a review of what was so eminently beneficial to the Community at large.

The present high rate of Exchange & the over great Importations from Europe, I fear will soon begin to drain the Banks of Specie— unless the price of Stocks falls to that point at which the foreigners will purchase.

I am with the sincerest respect & esteem   Dear sir   Your obliged Obed Humb Servt   Wm Seton

A. Hamilton Esqr.

ALS, Hamilton Papers, Library of Congress.
    1. See H to Seton, October 22, 1792.

To George Washington

[Philadelphia, October 26, 1792]

The Secretary of the Treasury presents his respects to the President, and encloses him a letter received yesterday from the Supervisor of New York.[1] The Secretary will have the honor of reminding the President of the subject when he has that of waiting upon him next.

26. October 1792

LC, George Washington Papers, Library of Congress.
    1. The letter from Richard Morris to H has not been found. See, however, Morris to H, November 10, 1792.

From Joseph Nourse

Treasury Department
Register's Office 27. October 1792

Sir,

In the returns from the Treasury Dept. which will be laid before you in pursuance of your Directions founded on the order of the Senate of the United States of May 7. 1792 [1] there will be wanting an Account of the Contingent Expences of the Treasury Department, for Wood, rent and other payment, which have not been considered as forming a Part of the Expence of any particular Office, but which will apply generally to all the Offices of the Treasury Department. Under an Idea that such Expences come within the Intention of the Senate, I have had the said General Account of Expenditures stated, and which I now beg Leave to Enclose,[2] marked

A. Amounting to . . . . Dollars 478.62.
B.   " 416.48⅔
C.   " 322.84
D.   "   . . . .   696.53.

Amounting to Dollars 1914.47.⅔

I have the Honor to be sir   with the greatest Respect   Your most obedt: hb: Servt.   J:N:

The Hon: Alexr. Hamilton Esqr.
Secy. of the Treasury

LC, RG 53, Register of the Treasury, Estimates and Statements for 1792, Vol. "134-T," National Archives.
   1. See "Treasury Department Circular to the Collectors of the Customs," August 31, 1792.
   2. The four enclosures to this letter, which are marked A, B, C, and D, are documents signed by Nourse. They may be found in RG 53, Register of the Treasury, Estimates and Statements for 1792, Vol. "134-T," National Archives. Each document lists the contingent expenses for one of the quarters of the year ending June 30, 1792.

From William Short

The Hague Oct 27. 1792

Sir

The French post arrived here the day before yesterday & brought some of the mails which have been so long detained on the frontiers. I received thereby several letters from M. Morris, from whom I mentioned to you in my last[1] I was waiting with impatience to hear. It does not appear that he has seen the commissaries as I wished in order to satisfy himself that they had given credit to the U.S. for 6,000,000₶ according to his agreement for the 1,625,000 florins.[2]

He does not seem to apprehend there will be any difficulty at present—but that there would have been if the French bankers had given the kind of reciept I desired viz. *on account of the debt due to France & to be held at the disposition of His Most Christian Majesty.*[3] This would indicate an opinion of the duration of the French commonwealth which certainly wd. not have existed at the time of my asking this rect. And indeed this reciept was nothing more than a certificate that the money was paid by the U.S. to & put at the disposition of that Agent or representative of the French nation who alone could be known to or was acknowleged by foreign nations. I still think this was the only mode of making the payment so as to entitle to the U.S. to credit for the six millions of livres & at the same time exempt them from reproach with whatever government should be in future established. Without entering into the question of national sovereignty & the right to change govern-

ALS, letterpress copy, William Short Papers, Library of Congress.

1. See Short to H, October 9, 1792.
2. For the correspondence between Short and Gouverneur Morris concerning the payment of the installment of the French debt due in July, 1792, see the enclosures to Morris to H, September 25, 1792. See also Short to H, September 25, 1792. Morris's correspondence with the Commissaries of the French Treasury is enclosed in Jefferson to H, October 31, 1792. See also Short to H, August 30, 1792.
3. For the negotiations with Hoggeur, Grand, and Company, the bankers of France in Amsterdam, concerning this receipt, see Short to Morris, August 21, September 4, 1792, and Morris to Short, August 27, September 20, 1792. These letters are printed as enclosures to Morris to H, September 25, 1792.

ments with which I had certainly nothing to do, I did not suppose I had a right to treat with or make the payment to any other than the authority acknowleged by the U.S. In ordinary times the person would have been understood but after what has happened as the person might be doubtful it seemed to me proper that he should be expressed. I made use of the term of His M.C. Majesty which M. Morris objects to, but it sufficiently designated the person meant & the rest would have been a mere dispute about words which no government would have raised. I repeat it again let what will be the issue of the control in France I cannot concieve that I had any right to consider the present ministry as the agents of the French nation, until they were acknowleged by the U.S. nor of course more right to pay them the money than to pay it to any other collection of individuals in France. I have already mentioned how, being singular in my opinion, I had yielded it to that of M. Morris & also for what reasons.[4]

M. Morris seems very desirous to prove that if any question should hereafter arise as to this payment, it can proceed only from there having been a delay, & from our bankers [5] having taken a bill instead of a reciept. As to the delay which was from the 17th. of Aug. the day on which my first order was given to the bankers,[6] until the 4th. of Sep.—it proceeded in the first instance from the French bankers asking time to consider of the reciept they would give. As to the bill instead of the reciept, it was the usual practice as our bankers inform me when payments had been ordered to the French bankers. All that I did in any case was simply to order the payment, supposing the bankers would know at least as well as I did how to make it. Had there been no suspension of the King & of course no delay in the payment it would have been made in the same manner. M. Morris simply desired me to direct our bankers to make the payment to the French bankers of 1,625,000 florins. I should simply have repeated the same thing—& the payment of course would have been made as usual & as it was made at last viz. by the French bankers giving a draught for the amount on the French treasury, which was indorsed to the commissaries. Of course

4. See Short to H, September 25, October 9, 1792.
5. Willink, Van Staphorst, and Hubbard.
6. See Short to H, August 30, 1792.

there can be no more question at present as to this payment being the same agreed for by Morris than there would have been if there had been no suspension. But to prevent all doubts & questions I have sollicited M. Morris again & again merely to consummate the arrangement he began with the commissaries in seeing that the U.S. were credited for the six millions he agreed for; which is all that is necessary & would remove all doubts, as it is not to be expected that they would credit them for both the six millions of livres & the 1,625m florins. Why he does not do it I cannot say, but suppose of course he considers it unnecessary.

As to what I had proposed to him about withdrawing such of the obligations or reciepts of the U.S. constituting their debt (as already mentioned to you) [7] as were paid off; he informs me that the whole debt consists in three obligations only [8] & of course neither of them is totally extinguished. I had thought that the obligations had been divided into much smaller parcels & particularly, that the debt of 18,000,000 had been in twelve reciepts. M. Morris says I was mistaken & therefore all I had said on that subject I consider as nul.

I hope you recieved my last of the 9th. inst soon after that of the 25th. of Sep. as I apologized for the error in subtraction committed & which made me consider *28* as the difference between *36* & *54*.

I flatter myself I shall recieve your orders with respect to the large sums which still remain in our bankers hands & which were destined for France. I am waiting to recieve those you announce with respect to the mode of discharging the total of the debt due to foreign officers,[9] which however together with the debt to Spain will only absorb a small part.[10] The loans lately made by Russia & Spain at 4½. pr. cent & the present state of Europe render it impossible for the U.S. to borrow at the moment at 4. p. cent. I think it a fortunate circumstance therefore to be able to remain so long without coming in the market, as it appears to me the U.S. should for serious reasons make a point of not raising their late rate of

---

7. See Short to H, September 25, 1792.
8. Morris to Short, September 24, 1792 (LC, Gouverneur Morris Papers, Library of Congress).
9. See H to Short, September 13, October 1–15, 1792.
10. See Short to H, August 30, 1792.

interest. This once established in people's minds would produce hereafter good effects & particularly with respect to the reduction of the interest on the debt already existing abroad. Besides if as I learned from M. Sterett,[11] the bank were willing to lend government at 5. p. cent interest without charges & the right to re-imburse at will, I should consider this more advantageous on the whole than making foreign loans at any higher rate than 4. p. cent.

The interruption of the post has prevented my learning from M. Carmichael[12] to whom the bills should be remitted on account of the Spanish debt. His last letter informed me he had written both to Count d'Aranda[13] & M. Gardoqui[14] on the subject, & was expecting their answer daily. In the mean time the bankers here are procuring the bills & as some of them are drawing to their term they have thought of remitting them to the Minister of finance as the most proper person.

I have already taken the liberty sir of mentioning to you my desire not to be employed alone in the business of settling the indemnity to be allowed to France.[15] It is a pecuniary operation of so much importance & of course an object of so much delicacy that it is impossible not to wish to be allowed to concert the measure with such persons as possess the confidence of government. It might be done with the Minister at Paris or London or both without inconvenience & with advantage for the U.S. The situation of France rendering it impossible that any thing should be done there for the present emboldens me to re-iterate my request as it will not be the cause of the delay.

My late letters to you have been dated June 28. Aug. 6, 30. Sep. 25. Oct. 9.—those which you have done me the honor to address me have been regularly recieved as low down at that of Aug. 16. already acknowleged.

11. Samuel Sterett of Baltimore, Maryland. See Uriah Forrest to H, November 7, 1792.

12. William Carmichael was United States chargé d'affaires at the Spanish Court. In January, 1792, he and Short had been appointed commissioners for settling the outstanding differences of the United States with Spain.

13. Pedro Pablo Abarca de Bolea, Conde de Aranda, was a member of the Spanish Council of State.

14. Diego de Gardoqui had served as Spanish Minister to the United States from 1785 to 1789. In 1792 he was Spanish Minister of Finance and was placed in charge of the negotiations with Carmichael and Short.

15. See Short to H, October 9, 1792.

I have the honor to be with sentiments of the most perfect respect & attachment

sir, your most obedient & most humble servant   W: Short

The Honble
Alexander Hamilton Secretary of the Treasury

To Stephen Cross

Treasury Department, October 29, 1792. "I duly received your letter of the 18th instant, to which I shall reply at the first moment of sufficient leisure. . . ."

Copy, RG 59, Miscellaneous Letters, 1790–1799, National Archives.

To Henry Knox

Treasury Department
October 29. 1792

Sir

Herewith you will find a Warrant for Thirty five thousand dollars for the use of the Quarter Master generals department.[1] I request that you will direct it to be received in Bank post Notes, which for greater security had better be made out in the Name of the Quarter Master General. Experience shews that these Notes answer as well as specie, and Considerations of the Moment induce me to wish that there may be no transportation of Specie at this time from the seat of Government.

I have the honor to be very respectfully, Sir Yr. Obedient servant   Alexander Hamilton

The Secretary at War.

Copy, RG 94, Hodgdon and Pickering Papers, National Archives.
1. This warrant was issued to James O'Hara, the quartermaster general, and was the largest issued to him during the second half of 1792 for various expenditures for the Indian Department and the Department of War (copy, RG 217, Miscellaneous Treasury Accounts, 1790–1894, Account No. 4461, National Archives).

From Otho H. Williams

Baltimore 29th October 1792

Sir

I took occasion to mention to you while I was absent from my Office, that a necessary attention to my health required my leaving Baltimore for a time.[1]

My stay in the Country was attended with so many indications of returning health that I thought the time well spent; and was returning home full of confidence that business would again be a pleasure to me when a very unexpected and violent attack on my breast banished all my sanguine expectations, and reduced me almost to the last extremity.

An Hemorrhage from the lungs, which continued several days, attended by the most alarming symptoms, made it requisite, in the opinion of my Physicians, to make among other applications repeated and liberal use of the launcet which, in addition to the loss of blood from the lungs and a fever, which attended me for about two weeks, weakened me extremely.

I have happily recovered much apparent health and strength, but my lungs remain very sore and irritable: and my Physicians recommend a Voyage to some of the West India Islands for the Winter as the best means of restoring my health perfectly.

Although I am sensible, in all situations, of my responsibility for the execution of the duties of my office I would not willingly leave the continent without the consent of the President. It is, Sir, with a view to obtain from you the favor of asking permission of the President that I give you the trouble of these particulars. I trust you will pardon the liberty.

The unanimous opinion of my Physicians and the universal solicitations of my friends press my speedy departure, an early answer to this letter will therefore much oblige

Sir, Your Most Obedient and Most Humble Servant

O. H. Williams

A Hamilton Esqr.

ADfS, Maryland Historical Society, Baltimore.
1. See Williams to H, June 28, 1792.

To Otho H. Williams

Treasury Department
October 29th 1792.

Sir

I herewith transmit you the copy of a letter written by the Collector of Salem to the Attorney for the District of Massachusetts respecting certain Persons, who, it is stated, have left that State and gone to Baltimore, being indebted to the United States for duties bonded, without leaving sufficient property to secure the debt.[1]

I have to request that you will take such measures as you shall be legally advised to pursue, for securing the United States concerning the bonds in question. In doing this I must call your attention to the 44th or strictly the 45th Section of the Collection law, which, in certain cases, gives a priority to the United States.[2]

With great consideration,   I am, Sir, your Obedt Servt.

Alexander Hamilton

Otho H Williams Esqr
Baltimore

LS, Columbia University Libraries.
 1. Joseph Hiller's letter to Christopher Gore is dated October 17, 1792, and refers to two bonds payable in January and June, 1793. In this letter Hiller pointed out that creditors were about to secure their debts by attaching the property of merchants who had left Massachusetts and gone to Baltimore. Hiller, therefore, asked Gore to take action in this matter before the bonds fell due so that the property would not be sold to satisfy creditors other than the United States (copy, Columbia University Libraries).
 2. Section 45 of "An Act to provide more effectually for the collection of the duties imposed by law on goods, wares and merchandise imported into the United States, and on the tonnage of ships or vessels" reads as follows: "*And be it further enacted,* That where any bond for the payment of duties shall not be satisfied on the day it became due, the collector shall forthwith cause a prosecution to be commenced for the recovery of the money thereon, by action or suit at law, in the proper court having cognizance thereof; and in all cases of insolvency, or where any estate in the hands of executors or administrators shall be insufficient to pay all the debts due from the deceased, the debt due to the United States, on any such bond, shall be first satisfied" (1 *Stat.* 169 [August 4, 1790]).
 For the confusion in numbering the sections of this act, see "Treasury Department Circular to the Collectors of the Customs," August 6, 1792.

From William Ellery

Colls Offe. [Newport, Rhode Island] Oct. 30 1792

Sir,

My bondsmen as Commr of the Loan-Office [1] have applied to me to know whether my bond had been cancelled. It was not in my power to give them positive information. If my accounts as Commr of the Loan-Office have been adjusted and found to be right as I presume they have, I wish that bond may be transmitted to me; unless it is cancelled, or it should be contrary to usage to deliver up bonds under such circumstances. If the latter I should be happy to be made acquainted with the reasons on which such usage is founded. If my accts. have not been adjusted I wish it may be done as soon as possible.[2]

I am, with great consideration   Sir, Yr. most obedt. servant

Wm Ellery

A Hamilton Esqr.
Secry Treasy

LC, Newport Historical Society, Newport, Rhode Island.

1. Ellery had been elected commissioner of the Continental loan office of Rhode Island on April 18, 1786. His accounts as loan officer were settled at the Treasury on October 21, 1791 (copy, RG 217, Miscellaneous Treasury Accounts, 1790–1894, Account No. 1677, National Archives).

2. On November 29, 1792, Oliver Wolcott, comptroller of the Treasury, under H's direction answered Ellery's letter as follows: ". . . it has not been the usage of the Treasury to deliver up, on the settlement of accounts, the bonds which have been taken to secure the fidelity of public Officers.

"As reasons in support of this practice, it may be observed that it is a supposeable case, that what was intended as a final settlement & acquittance, may have been made on a partial or erroneous representation of the manner in which the trust was executed, in which case it is clear that the bond would not be discharged. It may also be necessary that the Office of the Treasury should be able to produce bonds, which have been discharged in vindication of their own conduct, if it should be called in question.

"The nature of your office, as well as the manner in which it was executed, will however fully exempt you or your sureties, from any inconvenience from the practice which has obtained, & to which in some cases it is obviously necessary to adhere.

"I have for your satisfaction & for that of your sureties enclosed triplicate Certificates from the Registrar, as evidence that all your accounts as Loan Officer are closed in the books of the Treasury by a final settlement." (ADf, Connecticut Historical Society, Hartford.)

From Charles Lee

Collectors Office Alexandria [Virginia] 30th. Octr. 1792

Sir!

A considerable sum in cut silver is now in my Office, which has been accumulating for some time past, as in no case except now and then it has been in my power to pay any part, in discharge of a Treasury Draft. An offer to pay this kind of money to a holder of a warrant upon this Office, gives dissatisfaction, and supposing this kind of money might be useful at the mint, I have thought it my duty to communicate the matter to you.

I am Sir! very respectfully   Your most Obedt. Servant

Charles Lee
Collector at Alexandria.

Copy, RG 56, Letters to and from the Collector at Alexandria, National Archives.

From Jeremiah Olney

Providence, October 30, 1792. "In conformity to your circular Letter of the 4th of June last, I enclose a copy of the rough Estimate of Duties on the Cargo of Brigantine George William, from Bordeaux, which contains an Abstract of the Invoices exhibited, and the computations made toward ascertaining the Duties, previous to taking the Bonds. A note at the bottom of the Abstract, will show how nearly the Two first Criterions correspond with each other; but I am not possessed of the requisite information to discover how nearly the *Third* agrees with the other Two. . . ."

ADfS, Rhode Island Historical Society, Providence.

A Plain Honest Man

[Philadelphia, October 30–November 17, 1792]

For the Gazette of The UStates [1]

In consequence of the intimation contained in the first Number of the Vindication of Mr. Jefferson which originated in the American Dayly Advertiser that "if any doubt should be suggested of the authenticity of the extracts published they should be immediately made accessible to others" [2] a person called upon Mr. Dunlap [3] to obtain an inspection of those originals. He replied, that they had not been left with him; neither [was he possessed of the necessary information where to direct an enquirer;] [4] but that if desired he would by advertisement notify to him the application for a perusal of the letters. A statement of this answer, as extraordinary as it was unexpected, was prepared to be inserted in this Gazette and was communicated to Mr. Dunlap with a view to verifying its accuracy. The Evening before that destined for its appearance Mr. Dunlap called upon the person and informed him that the Originals [were now to be seen &] would be communicated to any person who might incline to see them—observing at the same time that [it appeared to him] it could not be necessary to publish the statement which has been mentioned, as intended. This was accordingly foreborne.[5]

On the   [6] [a] Note appeared in Mr. Dunlaps paper of that day which after commenting on the disingeniousness of some doubts hinted in one of the papers under the signature of Catullus gives "notice, that any Gentleman of *known honor* and *delicacy,* who shall be *named* to the Editor, of the American Dayly Advertiser shall have an opportunity of examining not only the passages extracted but the intire contents of the original letters."

What Gentleman of real *delicacy* would be willing to present himself under the professed character of a "Gentleman of *known honor* and *delicacy*" at the hazard of being affronted by a rejection, to obtain the proffered access? Is not an offer so clogged a *felo de se?* What is the natural inference?

If I am not Mr Printer a "Gentleman of known honor and delicacy" I hope you will not think the worse of me for being only

A plain Honest Man

ADf, Hamilton, Papers, Library of Congress.

1. Although this article was written for publication in the [Philadelphia] *Gazette of the United States,* it has not been found in that paper.

2. For the "Vindication of Mr. Jefferson," see "Catullus No. IV," October 17, 1792, note 4. The first number of this series appeared in [Philadelphia] *Dunlap's American Daily Advertiser,* September 22, 1792.

3. John Dunlap, editor of *Dunlap's American Daily Advertiser.*

4. The material within brackets in this article is in the handwriting of John Fenno, editor of the *Gazette of the United States.*

5. Fenno returned this draft to H with a note in the margin which reads as follows: "On the 17 Nov. Mr. Dunlap was again applied to and again proposed an advertisement—but afterwds., hinted as a preliminary condition of the Letter's being seen, that the person in whose possession the Letters were should be made acquainted with the name of the person who applied for that purpose. Mr. D. afterwds. sd. he would apply again for the Letters, & have them in his own possession, to shew them agreeable to the Declaration published —but after this being again applied to, ansd. as before that the applicant must be previously known."

6. Space left blank in MS. H is referring to October 30, 1792, which is the date on which the "Note" that H is quoting in this paragraph appeared in *Dunlap's American Daily Advertiser.*

From Otho H. Williams

Baltimore 30th October 1792

Sir

I have too much reason to expect that a decree in the Court of Chancery for this state will very soon make it necessary for me to provide for the payment of a considerable sum of Money, for which I became security, but which I cannot do, in due time, without disposing of the inconsiderable share I have in the public funds.

To my astonishment I have been told that I cannot dispose of my *own* funded Certificates (and it will be found upon a comparison of the books that I funded almost none but my own) without incurring a penalty under a certain act of Congress.[1] Certainly this opinion is not correct. If it is am I not deprived of the use of property rendered sacred by the repeated voluntary obligations of Government; and may I not in effect, be eventually deprived of my liberty by the operation of such a law? For the want of that same property may expose me to a state Execution by which I may be legally locked in a Goal. If it is law it is not justice. But just or unjust I would not intentionally violate a law of Congress, if I could help it.

In the present case I am without an alternative, unless the Treasurer of the United States will take my Stock at *"the lowest"* market price which will afford me the plea of having received a debt. Surely it would not pertinaciously be called dealing in stock. Mr. Christopher Richmond my agent will call upon you and if the treasury does not purchase at present I will acknowledge it as a singular favor if you will instruct him how to conduct the business, if it be possible, so as to avoid a malicious prosecution

I have the honor to be Sir,

ADf, Maryland Historical Society, Baltimore.
1. "An Act making alterations in the Treasury and War Departments" forbade "all officers of the United States concerned in the collection or disbursement of the revenues thereof" from dealing in the funds or debts of the United States or of any state (1 *Stat.* 281 [May 8, 1792]). For the opinion of the Attorney General on the interpretation of this law, see Edmund Randolph to H, June 26, 1792.

From Tench Coxe [1]

Treasury Department,
Revenue Office, October 31st. 1792.

Sir,

I have the Honor to inform you that it appears by a letter this day received from Capt. William Lewis of Fredericksburg that he has undertaken the duty of Keeper of the light House on Cape Henry. This alteration in his situation will render it necessary that the pleasure of the President be known in regard to some other person to fill the offices he held in the internal and external Revenues.

I have the honor to be with most respectful Attatchment, sir, your most Obt. Servt.   Tench Coxe,
Commissioner of the Revenue

The honble the
Secretary of the Treasury.

LC, RG 58, Letters of Commissioner of Revenue, 1792–1793, National Archives.
    1. For background to this letter, see Tobias Lear to H, October 13, 1792; H to Lear, October 18, 1792.

From Thomas Jefferson

Philadelphia Oct. 31. 1792.

Sir

I have the honor to inclose you sundry communications [1] from the Minister of the U.S. at Paris,[2] which relating to the Treasury department I can only offer myself for the conveyance of any instructions or authorities which it may be expedient to send him.

I am with great respect Sir   Your most obedt. humble servt.

Th: Jefferson

The Secretary of the Treasury

[ENCLOSURE]

Gouverneur Morris to William Carmichael [3]

Paris 3rd. July 1792.

Two Days ago I saw Mr. Le Couteulx,[4] who told me that his friend had made application to the Spanish Court to obtain an assignment on the Debt from the United States in discharge of a Debt due to him; and that Mr. Gardoqui [5] said the United States owed Spain above a Million of Dollars, being in part for advances made in America.[6] This assertion struck me, and as I had formerly some knowledge of the state of our Finances, I ruminated on the Subject and have thereby brought back to my recollection, the objects which I suppose he contemplated. They are twofold, first advances for the United States, and secondly for the State of Virginia. These advances have

ALS, letterpress copy, Thomas Jefferson Papers, Library of Congress; LC, RG 59, Domestic Letters of the Department of State, Vol. IV, National Archives.
    1. See enclosures.   2. Gouverneur Morris.
    3. Extract, letterpress copy, Thomas Jefferson Papers, Library of Congress.
    4. See Morris to H, September 21, 1792.
    5. Diego de Gardoqui. See William Short to H, October 27, 1792, note 14.
    6. For a description of the Spanish debt, see H to Short, September 1, 1790, note 19.

been regularly charged against the State and the United States by the Persons to whom they were made, and to these persons I believe full payment, but I am pretty sure that at least partial payments have been made. It seems therefore, most advisable to leave the settlement of the American Account to be made in america. As to the advances made to us by the Court in Europe, I suppose it will be right to adjust them in Europe.

[ENCLOSURE]

Gouverneur Morris to the Commissaries of the French Treasury [7]

Paris 30th. July 1792

Gentlemen,

I did not receive until yesterday yours of the twenty eighth instant. I will proceed to the examination of the account [8] enclosed in it immediately. We have money at Amsterdam; if you chuse to receive it there, be so kind as to inform me, and of the person to whom it is to be paid. It will be necessary in that case to fix a rate of exchange, and in order to avoid unnecessary delay, I pray you to state the rate at which you are willing to receive it. If the same is convenient, I will write in consequence to make the payments to your agents if not, I will take measures to pay you here.

I observe the note you transmit of losses on the purchase of specie. The United States desire to discharge their debt honorably. We are now actually paying specie in America for supplies to St. Domingo,[9] and I shall agree to liberal terms for the sums which may be appropriated in that manner, notwithstanding the loss which we sustain thereby. I will write also my idea of the compensation to be made for such injury as you may sustain by the depreciation of

7. Letterpress copy, Thomas Jefferson Papers, Library of Congress. For a description of the difficulties encountered by Morris and Short in making the payment due to France in the summer of 1792, see Morris to H, September 25, 1792.

8. A letterpress copy of this account entitled "Etat des Sommes dues Par les Etats Unis de l'Amerique Septentrionale pour cause des prêts qui leur ont été faites par la France au 1er. Juillet 1792 L'An 4e de la Liberté" may be found in the Thomas Jefferson Papers, Library of Congress. Jefferson enclosed a copy of this account in his October 31 letter to H.

9. For a description of the attempts to apply the United States debt to France for the relief of Santo Domingo, see Morris to H, November 2, 1792, note 4.

your assignats, and doubt not that I shall be authoriz'd to act liberal-
ly. These objects will require time, and come properly into notice
at a future day. That which more immediately presses, is to supply
the treasury in the present moment, and with the smallest possible
delay, in which you may rely on my utmost exertions.

Gouverneur Morris

Messrs. les Commissionaires⎫
de la Tresorie Nationale   ⎬ Paris
                            ⎭

[ENCLOSURE]

Gouverneur Morris to Thomas Jefferson [10]

Paris 1. August 1792.

My last was of the tenth of July. Mr: Livingston, who is on his
way to America, presents an opportunity of writing, which must
not be neglected, altho' I am engaged at present in Examination of
the account received from the Commissioners of the Treasury. I
have already mentioned to you, Sir, that the whole of this account
is open, and I must now observe that I do not find myself particularly authorized to make the final adjustment.[11] If it becomes necessary, I will do it, but I shall avoid it as long as I can. In respect to
the Payments made and making in america, I am at ease, because
there I have your orders, but not so in regard to those made by
Mr. Short. I shall hope, however, to be favored with your instructions in consequence of his communications. I shall write particularly
respecting the account, when I have gone thro' it.

[ENCLOSURE]

The Commissaries of the French Treasury to Gouverneur Morris [12]

Paris le 2 Aout 1792. l'an 4e de la liberté

Trèsorerie Nationale,

Nous avons reçu, Monsieur, votre lettre du 30 juillet. Nous ferons

10. Extract, letterpress copy, Thomas Jefferson Papers, Library of Congress.
11. See Morris to H, September 25, 1792, note 15.
12. Letterpress copy, Thomas Jefferson Papers, Library of Congress.

volontiers recevoir à Amsterdam les ommes que les Etats unis sont dans l'intention de rembourser à la nation française à compte de leur dette, et nous en chargerons M M. Hoggeur Grand et Compe. les memes banquiers qui ont jusqu'à present suivi toutes les operations relatives à cet remboursement.[13]

A l'égard du taux du change auquel devra se faire le nouveau remboursement et que vous nous invitez à fixer, nous aurons l'honneur de vous observer que, lorsque M. Short nous eut fait connoitre la resolution qu'avoient prise les Etats unis de ne point profiter, dans les remboursements qu'ils pourroient nous faire, de la défaveur ou se trouvoient les changes à l'égard de la France; nous lui proposames, à cet effet, d'autoriser les banquiers des Etats unis à recevoir nos récépisses pour la valeur en Florins de Banque, qui devoient nous etre comptés à Amsterdam, de manière à pouvoir régler en définitif le change, non pas d'après les cours, tels qu'ils existent depuis longtems, mais d'après le pair du change connu entre Paris et Amsterdam. Mais cette somme qui avoit paru alors simple et juste ne peut en ce moment etre proposée, puisque les pertes que peut éprouver la France dans ces remboursemens paroissent devoir etre seulement comprensèes, en vertu d'une transaction postérieure aux remboursemens et pour la quelle vous avez besoin d'autorisation spéciale. E'n conséquence, Monsieur, et attendu qu'il est très important pour la tresorèrie de se procurer le plutot possible le numéraire qui doit nous revenir par l'effet du nouveau remboursement, nous proposons, ainsi que vous le désirez, que le change auquel nous serons fait les nouveaux paiemens à Amsterdam soit fixé, suivant le cours actuel à vue qui doit etre porté au moins à 32½.

Si vous agreès cette proposition, Monsieur, nous vous prions de nous en informer et de nous instruire egalement du moment où vous aurez donné ordre à vos Banquiers d'Amsterdam d'effectuer les premiers paiements.

Les Commissaires de la Tresorie Nationale.

M. Morris, Mtre. des Etats unis de l'Amerique.

13. For the negotiations concerning this payment, see the correspondence between Morris and Short, printed as enclosures to Morris to H September 25, 1792.

[ENCLOSURE]

Gouverneur Morris to the Commissaries of the French Treasury [14]

Paris 6. August 1792.

Gentlemen,

Your letter of the second instant did not reach me until yesterday afternoon. I am afraid that the delay may be attended with some ill consequence, however I have given the necessary directions for payment of one million, six hundred and twenty five thousand bank florins to Messrs. Hoguer Grand and company, which at the exchange you have mentioned, is equal to six million of livres. I hope that my letters may arrive in season to prevent any other appropriation, and you will of course cause the above sum of 6,000,000₶ to be carried to the credit of the United States ⟨th⟩is day, saving always the right of counterentry should the payment not be compleated *instanter* at Amsterdam.

As the account which you did me the honor to transmit [15] I observe a charge of 196,481₶.15.3, for gunpowder, a charge of 1,052,345₶.11.6, for arms, and a charge of £134.065.17.6 for cloathing. These three articles amounting together to £1,382.892₶.14.3 are I believe erroneous and it is not impossible that there may have been some malversation in this respect which ought to be enquired into. I send you therefore an account of loans and subsidies from the Court of France to the United States of America in the years 1778. 1779. 1780. and 1781, by which it will appear that Monsieur Grand [16] their banker received from the Court on the fourth day of December 1781, the sum of 146000₶. over and above those loans and subsidies. I have also the honor to send you an account of the loan of 5,000,000, florins made for account of the United States in Holland,[17] and afterwards taken to account of the King, you will observe Gentlemen that in this account credit is given for the above mentioned balance of 146,000₶. and that the last payments on this account, in the month of December 1782, compleated only one half of the sum. The other half was reserved for reimbursement of

---

14. Letterpress copy, Thomas Jefferson Papers, Library of Congress.
15. See note 8.   16. Ferdinand Le Grand.
17. For a description of this loan, see Willink, Van Staphorst, and Hubbard to H, January 25, 1790, note 3.

cloathing, arms and ammunition. I am therefore to request that you would cause an examination to be made of the sums applied for those purposes. The United States are fully satisfied, that a just application had been made of the full amount, but they did not imagine that there was any further claim against them for such supplies.

I hope to be favord Gentlemen with your answer as speedily as circumstances may permit, in order that I may make a full communication on the subject, to the Ministers of the United States.

Gouverneur Morris

Messrs: les Commissionaries ⎱
de la Tresorie Nationale. ⎰ Paris

[ENCLOSURE]

The Commissaries of the French Treasury to Gouverneur Morris [18]

Paris le 9. Aout 1792 An 4. de la Liberté

Notre lettre du 2. de ce mois, Monsieur, ayant tardé à vous parvenir par des causes que nous ignorons, nous aurons attention pour que cet inconvenient ne se réprésente plus de vous faire porter celles que nous aurons l'honneur de vous ècrire.

Les erreurs que vous croyez qui existent dans le compte que nous vous avons remis, donnent lieu à des recherches qui sont être faites; elles exigeront un peu de tems, mais aussitot que nous aurons tous les renseignemens necessaires nous nous haterons de vous les communiquer.

Votre observation, Monsieur, sur la remise que vous vous proposer de faire faire à M. M. Hoguer Grand, &. Cie, nous fait craindre de ne nous être pas assez clairment expliquér par notre lettre du 2 de ce mois.

En y exprimant que le *change auquel seroient faits les nouveaux paiemens à Amsterdam seroit fixé suivant le cours actuel à vue, qui devroit être porté* au moins à 32.½. nous n'avons point entendu admettre la perte résultante du cours de ce change sur l'opération, mais seulement que le dit cours serviroit uniquement à indiquer

18. Letterpress copy, Thomas Jefferson Papers, Library of Congress.

une base pour regler dans la suite la perte que pourra éprouver la France, abstraction faite de celle qui a lieu aujourdhui sur les assignats, et seulement d'aprés le pair du change connu entre Paris et Amsterdam. C'est ce que nous avons prévu en vous marquant que la compensation seroit reglée, par une transaction posterieure lorsque vous auriez reçu l'autorisation speciale que, vous attendez pour prendre un parti definitif.

En effet, Monsieur, lorsque Monsieur Short nous proposa de la part du Congrès des indemnités pour les payemens précédens relativement aux revolutions. Survenues dans le cours des changes, nous lui observames que nous ne pouvions décider cette question, dont la solution concernoit le Ministre des affaires etrangeres, mais que pour l'avenir le moyen qu'il n'y eût aucune difficulté à cet égard seroit que les remises que le Congrès feroit faire servient effectués en florins, et que jusqu'au compte définitif on laisseroit toute entiere la question de l'evaluation des chànges, dont one se borneroit à prendre une note à la date des payemens.

C'est dont Monsieur, sans alterer le fond de cette mesure, déterminée par l'intention que nous a été manifestèe de la part du Congrès, mais en adoptant simplement la forme qui paraissoit vous convenir le plus, que nous avons indiqué le change à 32½ sur la remise que vous comptrez faire faire a M. M. Hoguer, Grand & Cie.

Nous sommes persuadés, Monsieur, que les développemens que nous venons de faire sont conformes à vos vues, et ne peuvent apporter aucun changement à vos dispositions, dont nous vous prions d'agreer tous nos remercimens.

                    Les Commissaires de la Trésorerie nationale.

M. Morris. Ministre Plenipre. des Etats unis. Rue de la Blanche à Paris

[ENCLOSURE]

Gouverneur Morris to Thomas Jefferson[19]

                                        Paris 16. August 1792.

I shall send herewith a Packet containing my Correspondence with the Commissioners of the Treasury, relative to our Debt, and

19. Extract, letterpress copy, Thomas Jefferson Papers, Library of Congress.

in the same packet you will find a Letter from Mr. Cathalan [20] to you relative to a Riot at Marsielles &c.

I have already had occasion to mention to you, Sir, that I did not find myself authorized to go into the Settlement of the account *finally* with the Commissioners of the Treasury. This observation I must again in this place repeat and add that notwithstanding my utmost Efforts, I have not been able to bring the minister of foreign affairs [21] to consider for a moment the Question referred to me respecting the Sums paid and paying in america. What is still more surprising is, that the minister of the marine, altho' authorized to treat with me for supplies to the colony of St. Domingo, has done nothing in that affair. Two ministers have occupied that place since the Decree.[22] Each has given me various rendezvous, but neither has appeared at the time and place because circumstances of the moment have obliged them to attend to something else.[23] Indeed the Executive of the late Constitution has been at the last agony for this three months, and of course has thought more of saving it's life than of doing it's Business. The present Executive is just born and may perhaps be stifled in the Cradle. If a general arrangement could have been made with the late Government for paying the whole of our Debt at some fixed Exchange so as to do Justice and fulfil the honorable intentions of the United States, I should have been well pleased, and altho' not exactly authorized, should probably have taken on me to make the needful Engagements and in so doing I should have made a grave Sacrifice to the Public because I wish of all things to be free from any pecuniary Transactions, for I know by experience that the utmost possible Purity will not prevent malicious insinuations which, however unfounded, will always find some believers. It appears, however, a probable Event that before our Debt be paid we may experience some considerable losses on exchange not to mention the dead charges which are considerable too. It has therefore appeared to me most advisable to make one general statement and settlement of the whole, and if it shall ap-

20. Stephen Cathalan, United States vice consul at Marseilles.
21. Pierre Henri Helene Marie Lebrun-Tondu.
22. The Minister of Marine was Gaspard Monge, who had replaced François Joseph Gratet Dubouchage on August 12, 1792. For the decree of June 26, 1792, authorizing the Minister of Marine to open negotiations with the United States Minister on aid to Santo Domingo, see Morris to H, September 25, 1792, note 8.
23. See Morris to H, November 2, 1792, note 4.

pear that we have gained and that they have lost by the modes of Payment, then to give a good round sum as a compensation and, as it were, gratuitously, because by that means we have the Reputation of the good we do, and the sacrifice we make, and because otherwise the agents of this Government might attribute to their address an advantage gained instead of giving Credit to our generosity for a Compensation granted. And it seems important to establish the latter Idea because it cannot fail to extend our credit throughout the world and consequently to facilitate all pecuniary operations which hereafter we may have occasion to make.

[ENCLOSURE]

Gouverneur Morris to Thomas Jefferson[24]

Paris 17. August 1792.

Dear Sir,

If I have not hitherto mentioned the Application made to me by the foreign Officers who have certificates whereof the interest is payable in this City, it has not been for want of sufficient cause, but because I did daily hope to have received some news on that subject.[25] Many have spoken to me, written to me, and called upon me. I have given to all the general assurances that justice would be done, that I would transmit their claims and the like. I now enclose a letter from the polish Envoy relative to the claims of Brigadier General Koskiusko,[26] and I have told the Count d'Oraczewski that I daily expect dispatches from you on this subject. I did this because General du Portail[27] told me that he has information from Colonel

24. Extract, letterpress copy, Thomas Jefferson Papers, Library of Congress.
25. For H's instructions to Morris on the payment of foreign officers who had served in the American Revolution, see H to Morris, September 13, 1792.
26. This letter, signed by "L. Anc. D'Oraczewski, Ambassador and Minister Plenipotentiary of Poland," was dated August 15, 1792, and stated that "General Kosciusko, a native of Poland, who has served in America, to whom you yourself have rendered the justice of saying that he is a man of distinguished talents, has a promise from the treasury of the United States for a sum of £66,314 18s. 9d. which is equal to $12,280 49⁄90 of the current money in America" (*ASP, Foreign Relations*, I, 335). Thaddeus Kosciuszko had come to the United States from Poland during the American Revolution and had served as a lieutenant colonel with Pulaski's Legion.
27. During the American Revolution, Louis Le Bèque Du Portail had commanded a corps of engineers. He had been made a major general in 1781.

Ternant [28] that these claims are all honorably provided for. In the uncertainty as to what may have been done, I feel it my Duty to bring the matter to your recollection, persuaded that you will do every thing which may be proper on the occasion.

28. Jean Baptiste de Ternant, the French Minister to the United States, had served as a lieutenant colonel with Pulaski's Legion during the American Revolution.

Meeting of the Commissioners of the Sinking Fund

[Philadelphia, October 31, 1792]

At a meeting of the trustees of the sinking fund, on the 31st day of October, 1792,

Present: The Secretary of State, the Secretary of the Treasury, and the Attorney General of the United States.

Resolved, That the resolutions of this Board, by which Samuel Meredith, Esquire, the agent for the sinking fund in the city of Philadelphia, hath been restricted to sealed proposals of sale,[1] be rescinded; and that he be at liberty to purchase stock, according to the prices, limited in his last instructions, either openly, and without sealed proposals, or with sealed proposals, as to him shall seem expedient.

ASP, Finance, I, 237.
1. See "Meeting of the Commissioners of the Sinking Fund," July 13, October 20, 1792. See also H to Thomas Jefferson, October 19, 1792.

To George Washington

[Philadelphia, October 31, 1792]

The Secretary of the Treasury presents his respects to the president of the U: States, encloses the arrangement for retrospective compensations to officers of the Revenue, which, agreeably to the intimation of the president, has been retained.[1] Mr. Hamilton will wait on the President between 12 & one to give the explanations desired.

Wednesday Morning 31. Octr. 1792.

LC, George Washington Papers, Library of Congress.
1. The "arrangement" was dated October 29, 1792. See Washington to H, October 1, 1792; H to Washington, September 22, 1792; Tench Coxe to H, first letter of July 25, September 12–18, October 20, 1792.

To George Washington

Treasury Departmt. Octr. 31. 1792.

The Secretary of the Treasury has the honor respectfully to communicate to the President an authenticated copy of the Contract for the last Loan made in Holland, for three millions of florins,[1] bearing date the 9th. of August 1792, at a rate of four per cent interest, of which Contract a ratification of the President as heretofore, is required. Alexander Hamilton

Secy. of the Treasury.

LC, George Washington Papers, Library of Congress.
1. This is a reference to the Holland loan of 1792. For a description of this loan, see William Short to H, June 28, 1792, note 17.

INDEX

COMPILED BY JEAN G. COOKE

Adams, Thomas Boylston: and John
Adams's salary, 208-10; *letter to* John
Adams, 209
Addison, Alexander: *letters to* George
Clymer, 518-19, 521-22; and Whis-
key Insurrection, 496-97, 518-19, 521-
22
Adgate Patent, 422
Albany, N.Y.: and disputed New York
gubernatorial election (1792), 20-21
The Albany Gazette, 212
Alexandria, Va.: boat for, 290; collec-
tor of customs at, *see* Lee, Charles;
and proposed branch of Bank of the
U.S., 84
Allegheny County, Pa.: and Whiskey
Insurrection, 305, 307, 309-10, 312,
495, 520, 540-41, 596
Allibone, William: and contracts as
superintendent of establishments on
the Delaware River, 14-15, 22, 23;
payment to, for building pier, 225
"An American," 356, 382, 383, 393, 394,
397, 398, 399, 401, 498-99, 500, 501, 580
"An American No. I," 152-64
"An American No. II," 188-93
"An American No. III," 224
American Revolution, 547; assistant
quartermaster general, 26; and public
debt, 229
"Americanus," 558
"Amicus," 354-57
Amsterdam: French bankers in, *see*
Hogguer, Grand, and Co.; U.S.
bankers in, *see* Willink, Van Staphorst, and Hubbard. *See also* Loans
in Holland
Andress, Jonathan: Army contract,
183
Angell, James: and *The Maryland
Journal and the Baltimore Adver-
tiser*, 511
Anne Arundel County, Md., 94; court
of, 213; and John F. Mercer's elec-
tion, 510
"Anti-Defamer," 259-60
Antifederalists: and election of 1792,
369-70, 387, 480; and public debt, 258
Antwerp: proposed new loan, 171;
U.S. loan at, 103, 105-6, 178-80, 220-
21, 432, 479, 534, 564, contract for,
171, and French debt, 176-77, 425-
69, 469-80
*An Appendix to the Impartial State-
ment of the Controversy Respecting*
*the Decision of the Late Committee
of Canvassers:* and disputed New
York gubernatorial election (1792),
66
Appleton, Nathaniel: *letter to,* 210
Aranda, Pedro Pablo Abarca de Bolea,
Conde de: and Spanish debt, 627
"Aristedes," 393, 394, 395, 397, 399,
401, 498-99, 501, 505, 580, 584, 586
Armistead, John: appointment of, 424-
25; recommendation of, 318, 392
Armstrong, Samuel: petition of, 424
Arnold, Welcome: and collusive transfers of ships, 12, 335-36, 375, 404,
529-30, 547-48
Assignats: depreciation of, 103-4, 283,
290, and payment of French debt,
172-77, 293-97, 425-69, 469-80, 532-
37, 637-44, and payment of U.S. debt
to foreign officers, 305, 370-74
Assumption of state debts, 112, 113,
117, 212; attacked, 398; defended,
323, 357-61; James Madison's comments on, 238-39; in Massachusetts,
238; and Mercer-Hamilton dispute,
487-90, 526-27; objections to, and
Hamilton's defense of, 230-32, 235-
36, 238-39, 254-58; in Pennsylvania,
142-46; in South Carolina, 238
Attorney General, 510-11; and "Coasting Act," 69-77; compensation and
expenses of, 588; and questions of
law, 69-77. *See also* Randolph, Edmund
Auckland, Lord: and Anglo-Dutch
Treaty, 538
Auditor of the Treasury Department,
see Harrison, Richard; Wolcott,
Oliver, Jr.
Augusta County, Va.: and opposition
to "Excise Act," 598

Bacon, 226, 507
Bailey, Francis: and *The [Philadel-
phia] Freeman's Journal*, 158
Baker, Jermon: estate of, 556
Ballard, Robert: and Otho H. Williams, 119-22, 204-6
Baltimore, Md.: archbishop of, 213;
city council, 214; collector of customs at, *see* Williams, Otho H.; deputy collector of customs at, 121-22;
dispute between revenue and customs officers at, 46-56, 119-22; in-

phorst, and Hubbard, bills on, 42, 118, 576, 578
"Metellus," 613-17
Meyer, John, 106, 107
Mifflin, Thomas, 610; *letter from* George Washington, 508-9; and Pennsylvania debt, 113, 142-46
Mint: cut silver for, 632; Dutch paper on, 220; expenses of, 22; report on progress of, 563
Mississippi River: navigation of, 1-3, 178
Monarchy: Antifederalists on, 131-32; Hamilton's comments on, 251-54, 355-56
Monge, Gaspard, 426, 643
Montgomery County, Md., 94
Moore, John: petition of, 206-7
Morris, David: and New York revenue cutter, 117-18
Morris, Gouverneur, 415; and Antwerp loan, 171, 220-22; appointment of, 173; comments on loans in Amsterdam, 221; and depreciation of French assignats, 103-4, 173-78, 425-69, 469-80; on French Revolution, 465; and Thomas Jefferson, 103-4, 220-21; *letters from*, 220-22, 409-10, 425-69, 438-41, 446-48, 617-18; *letters from* Commissaries of French Treasury, 638-39, 641-42; *letters from* Thomas Jefferson, 428, 514; *letters from* William Short, 426-27, 428-29, 429-31, 433, 435-37, 442-44, 444-45, 448-49, 451-53, 453-55, 455-56, 457-58, 459-60, 466-67; *letter to*, 370-74; *letter to* William Carmichael, 636-37; *letters to* the Commissaries of the French Treasury, 637-38, 640-41; *letters to* Thomas Jefferson, 428-29, 638, 642-43, 644-45; *letters to* Pierre Henri Hélène Marie Lebrun-Tondu, 461-62, 462; *letters to* William Short, 427-28, 429, 431, 432, 434, 437-38, 441, 444, 445, 448, 449-50, 450-51, 456-57, 457, 462-66, 467-68, 468-69; and Samuel Ogden, 539; and William Short, 294-97; Jean Baptiste de Ternant's comments on, 461; and U.S. debt to foreign officers, 376, 405; and U.S. debt to France, 105, instructions on, 220-22, 428-29, 430, 436, 437-38, 450, 451-52, 454-55, 456-57, 457-58, 459, 460,

465, 470-71, 473-74, 476, payment of, 173-78, 293-97, 425-69, 469-80, 577, 624-26, stoppage of, 514; and Charles John Michael de Wolf, 179
Morris, Richard, 3, 89, 95, 622
Morris, Robert, 370, 415; "Delaware Works," 539; and Jerome Trenet, 216
Mort, Joseph: and Society for Establishing Useful Manufactures, 13, 211
Mount Vernon, Va., 42
Mud Island, Del.: pier for, 225
Mumford, Sarah (Mrs. William): *letter from*, 423-24
Mumford, William: petition of, 423-24
Munro, John: and the *Lark*, 290
Myers, Peter: and Whiskey Insurrection, 520

Nails: duty on, 60-61
Nantes: U.S. prize agent at, 368
Naval officers: and coasting fees, 201; for the port of Baltimore, Md., *see* Purviance, Robert; of Providence, R.I., *see* Thompson, Ebenezer
Nesbit, Archibald: and canals, 211-12
Neville, John: *letters to* George Clymer, 306, 307, 310; and Whiskey Insurrection, 305, 519, 520, 522, 541-42, 600
Newark, N.J.: and Society for Establishing Useful Manufactures, 10, 11-12, 14, 41, 134, 211, 216-17
New Bedford, Mass.: collector of customs at, 279
New Bern, N.C.: collector of customs at, 207; revenue cutter for, 512
New Brunswick, N.J., 393
New Castle, Del.: boat for, 3
New Castle, N.H.: lighthouse at, 98
New England: attitude toward general government, 209; distilleries, and Santo Domingo slave revolts, 592-93
New Hampshire: collectors of revenue, compensation of, 96; commissioner of loans for, *see* Gardner, William; execution of "Excise Act" in, 592; legislature, 4; lighthouse in, 156-57, 199, 283; ratification of Constitution (U.S.), 395; revenue cutter, 117, 167; state superior court, 4; supervisor of revenue for the District of, *see* Wentworth, Joshua;